COLOR AND COGNITION IN MESOAMERICA

ROBERT E. MACLAURY

COLOR AND COGNITION IN MESOAMERICA

Constructing Categories as Vantages

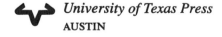
University of Texas Press
AUSTIN

First edition, 1997

Requests for permission to reproduce material from this work should be sent to Permissions, University of Texas Press, Box 7819, Austin, TX 78713-7819.

⊚ The paper used in this publication meets the minimum requirements of American National Standard for Information Sciences—Permanence of Paper for Printed Library Materials, ANSI Z39.48-1984.

LIBRARY OF CONGRESS CATALOGING-IN-PUBLICATION DATA

MacLaury, Robert E., 1944–

   Color and cognition in Mesoamerica : constructing categories as vantages / Robert E. MacLaury. — 1st ed.

     p.   cm.

   Includes bibliographical references (p.   ) and index.

   ISBN 978-0-292-72955-1

   1. Indians—Psychology.   2. Indian philosophy—Latin America.   3. Colors, Words for.   4. Color—Latin America—Terminology.   5. Color vision—Latin America.   6. Visual perception.   7. Culture and cognition—Latin America.   8. Language and culture—Latin America.   9. Indians—Languages—Semantics.

I. Title.

E59.P87M33   1997

152.14'5'08997072—dc20   96-10072

TO MY PARENTS

RICHARD J. MACLAURY
and
MARGARET C. MACLAURY

It is not clear what is to be understood here by "position" and "space." I stand at the window of a railway carriage which is travelling uniformly, and drop a stone on the embankment, without throwing it. Then, disregarding the influence of the air resistance, I see the stone descend in a straight line. A pedestrian who observes the misdeed from the footpath notices that the stone falls to earth in a parabolic curve. I now ask: Do the "positions" traversed by the stone lie "in reality" on a straight line or on a parabola? Moreover, what is meant here by motion "in space"? . . . In the first place we entirely shun the vague word "space," of which, we must honestly acknowledge, we cannot form the slightest conception, and we replace it by "motion relative to a practically rigid body of reference." . . . If instead of "body of reference" we insert "system of co-ordinates," which is a useful idea for mathematical description, we are in a position to say: The stone traverses a straight line relative to a system of co-ordinates rigidly attached to the carriage, but relative to a system of co-ordinates rigidly attached to the ground (embankment) it describes a parabola. With the aid of this example it is clearly seen that there is no such thing as an independently existing trajectory (lit. "path-curve"), but only a trajectory relative to a particular body of reference.

In order to have a *complete* description of the motion, we must specify how the body alters its position *with time,* i.e., for every point of the trajectory it must be stated at what time the body is situated there.

ALBERT EINSTEIN
Relativity: The Special and General Theory

CONTENTS

FOREWORD

You are shown a small card, approximately 3 × 2 cm, on which is mounted a monochrome chip, about 1.5 × 1 cm. You are asked to name the color of the chip. You proffer a term from your native language.

What determines your behavior on this task? What cognitive processes intervene between the neural response to the chip in your retina and your naming of its color?

These are the questions that MacLaury addresses in this book. He frames his answer in terms of a new, and radical, theory of categorization—Vantage Theory.

It is appropriate that Vantage Theory should emerge from color research. Color has long been a privileged domain for the study of categorization, and research on color has not infrequently had major implications outside the domain of color itself. The language specificity of color categories was, for the structuralists, the textbook example of the arbitrariness of the linguistic sign. Color was a favored testing ground for the Whorfian hypothesis that language categories influence the way a person perceives and cognizes the world. Then came Berlin and Kay's discovery of the focal colors, and their hypothesis that languages expand color vocabulary in a predictable sequence. Their work not only encouraged strong claims that linguistic categories may reflect universal aspects of perception, it was also the germ for the development of prototype theories of categorization. These, as is well known, have enjoyed a considerable fortune beyond the domain of color.

MacLaury's work builds on, and extends, this long tradition of color research. In presenting this book to potential readers, I would like to draw attention to three aspects: data elicitation techniques; some aspects of the data so elicited; and the theory that was developed in order to explain the data.

Whereas previous researchers had tended to rely on a variety of ad hoc techniques for the collection of color data, MacLaury employed a simple yet robust procedure for the systematic elicitation of data in the field. A crucial aspect of the procedure is its combination of the onomasiological (the subject *names* a random sequence of Munsell color chips) and the semasiological (the subject *maps* each of his color terms onto an array of Munsell chips).

The elicitation procedure was applied in hundreds of interviews in the course of an areal survey of Mesoamerican languages. The protocols show, in the first place, that subjects rarely divided up the color space into a set of discrete, static categories. They also show that speakers of the "same" language can differ radically in their performance on the naming and mapping tasks. (Everybody knows that the "homogeneous speech community" is a fiction; MacLaury's data constitute perhaps the most explicit rebuttal to date of the fiction.) More importantly, the protocols bear witness to the dynamics of category evolution, with color categories overlapping and intersecting in a variety of ways. One kind of relation between color categories deserves special mention. It is a relation which, to my knowledge, has not been previously recognized; indeed, its discovery was only possible thanks to the systematic combination of the onomasiological and the semasiological. This is the relation of *coextension*.

Coextension is characterized, first, by the fact that some segment of the color space is named, in apparently random fashion, by each of two terms (occasionally, more than two). From the onomasiological perspective, the two terms would be considered synonyms in free variation. Yet, from the semasiological perspective, the two terms are definitely not synonyms. In the first place, they are focused (i.e., their "best examples" are located) in different places. Typically, one of these terms (the "dominant" and, in certain cases, older and better established term in the language) is focused towards the center of the category. This term is readily mapped over the whole of the category. The other ("recessive") term is focused on the periphery and is initially mapped onto only a small portion of the larger category. (From the semasiological perspective, therefore, the relation is one of hyponymy, or inclusion.) If pressed, however, subjects may be prepared to extend their mapping, in several steps, so that eventually the recessive term, too, can cover almost the entire range of the dominant term.

Careful documentation of coextension must count as a major achievement of this book. MacLaury, however, has gone further and has proposed a new and ambitious theory of categorization, within whose scope the facts of coextension find a natural and compelling explanation.

The basic premise of Vantage Theory is that people actively construct their categories by differential emphasis on similarity and distinctiveness with respect to cognitive reference points (mostly, in the case of color categories, the neurophysiologically determined "elemental hues"). A category is therefore a "point of view," or "vantage," that a person adopts by the selection and manipulation of coordinates. Categorization is a process of "placing" a stimulus with respect to these (variable) coordinates. (It is therefore not fortuitous that people, Western and non-Western, discuss categorization in spatial terms!) Increased emphasis on distinctiveness can create a new vantage and so presage the emergence of a new category. The relation of coextension is symptomatic of just this process, with the recessive term indicative of a new distinctiveness vantage. As regards the factors that trigger increased attention to distinctiveness in the first place, MacLaury suggests that the crucial factor may be the rate of change in a person's psychological environment. Not only individuals in technologically advanced societies, but also individuals confronted with extreme hardship in eking out their daily existence, are likely to emphasize distinctiveness at the expense of similarity.

Vantage Theory is not only a theory of *how* people categorize, it addresses a number of more basic issues, and proposes solutions. To this extent, therefore, Vantage Theory goes beyond prototype theories—theories which, as already noted, also originated in color research. What, actually, *is* a category? And having constructed a category, how does a person maintain its stability over time? What prompts a person to create a new category, e.g., by splitting a pre-established category? What are the dynamics of category creation? What constrains the categories that a person constructs? Above all: What mental capacities underlie all these activities?

Vantage Theory squarely construes categorization as a cognitive phenomenon, with a human being as active agent. Like all good theories, it not only unifies a wide range of apparently disparate observations, it offers solutions to a number of long-standing problems and also raises new ones. (The major implications are summarized in §6.4.) Within the domain of color research itself, the theory explains (and refines) the evolutionary sequence hypothesized by Berlin and Kay; the theory is also applied to such specific issues as the Russian blues, the Hungarian reds, migrating foci, and the structure of green-blue categories. Amongst the phenomena that are brought under the scope of the theory is the seemingly puzzling observation that peripheral members of a category are judged "closer" to central members than central members are to peripheral ones. New issues that the theory raises concern the frame within which judgments of similarity and distinctiveness are made, how a person counterbalances these judgments to stabilize a category, and how selected segments of a category can themselves become the object of attention.

Although primarily an areal study of color categories in Mesoamerican languages, this book is also about much else: the nature of categories; their origin and internal structure; the relations between categories; the dynamic processes by which categories come into existence, change their internal organization and size, and eventually split; the relation of private cognition to the environment, and of cognition to the neurophysiology of perception; the extent to which an individual has free license to categorize, or whether categorization is determined by the norms of the linguistic community; questions of development and phylogeny; and, importantly, the cognitive processes which underlie categorization behavior. As such, the book will be essential reading for cognitively oriented linguists, psychologists, and anthropologists alike. Above all, it presents its readers with a challenge. This is to explore the possibility that MacLaury's findings in the color domain, and the theory he developed in order to account for them, may have general significance beyond the original site of research.

JOHN R. TAYLOR
UNIVERSITY OF OTAGO

PREFACE

More than one hundred indigenous languages are spoken in widely scattered areas over Mexico and northern Central America. Most have occupied their current localities since pre-Columbian times. Each language partitions the color spectrum with words and categories according to a pattern that is unique in one way or another. But every local system of color categories also shares characteristics with the systems of other Mesoamerican languages and of languages elsewhere in the world. This report addresses the results of the Mesoamerican Color Survey, which I conducted principally in Mexico and Guatemala with the help of collaborators during 1978–81. We interviewed 900 speakers of 116 languages and dialects by means of replicable techniques based on Munsell color samples. Our objective was to compile an overview on the organization and semantics of color categorization throughout the region.

The results serve three areas of scholarship. First, the cross-cultural data are of potential value to Mesoamericanists of any persuasion. Second, the data pertain directly to (a) issues of vision research, (b) notions of linguistic relativity, and, especially, (c) the development of Berlin and Kay's universalist hypothesis. The findings based upon these data extend a tradition of research on color categorization that has fomented one controversy upon another since Gladstone (1858:488) observed of Homer "a system in lieu of colour, founded upon light and darkness." Third, the Mesoamerican data call for a revised concept of categorization. The model proposed herein pertains to a body of theory regarding the organization of categories that is unfolding from the cognitive branches of psychology, linguistics, and anthropology. The model incorporates spatial analogy, viewpoint, dynamics of change, and the active role of the categorizer. As color is an attribute whose structure resides in our light sense, whatever cognition we impose upon it is, in the vast number of cases, independent of the objects that reflect light. In the domain of color, questions of cognition may be explored with uncommon detachment from a number of material variables. My scheme, then, is to link the academic interests in Mesoamerica, color, and categorization in a way that, I hope, will make them maximally attractive.

Many Mesoamerican languages categorize two or three pure colors under a single name, such as green-with-blue, red-with-yellow, or black-with-green-with-blue. The broad groupings involve diverse internal compositions, semantic relations, and phases of change, some of which are heretofore unreported. This analysis will focus on processes within these broad categories while I defer for another book a discussion of categories that pertain only to white, black, single hues, blends of hues, and desaturated color.

Chapters fall into four parts. Part One: Preliminaries presents the theoretical and technical background prerequisite to exploring a compilation on color categorization. Most preliminaries have accrued during 138 years of scholarship in color ethnography and vision science; I add a few ground rules of my own, which I call "axioms." Chapter 1 sketches the milieu at the University of California at Berkeley, 1981–85, that prompted my analysis; it describes the all-important Munsell stimulus materials by which the data were collected, and it recounts the history of efforts to replicably describe color categories. Chapter 2 reviews other research concerning color categorization in particular; it provides a worldwide overview of color categorization with diagrams of selected color-naming systems from outside Mesoamerica. Chapter 3 demonstrates how data are collected, analyzed, and displayed in black-and-white. Chapter 4 presents newly synthesized information on the physiology of color vision and integrates the physiology with the perceptual and cognitive axioms that form the basis of explanation in succeeding chapters; it exemplifies with a case-study use of the axioms to explain data.

Part Two: Viewpoint and Category Change presents the central thesis that a color category is constructed as an analogy to a point of view in physical space and time; people accomplish change in category organization and its semantics by the same method through which they adjust a spatiotemporal vantage. Chapters 5, 6, and 7, respectively, emphasize data pertaining to the early, middle, and late ends of a continuous process of category change. Chapter 6 is devoted equally to data and theory; it introduces the vantage model, which steps up the analysis to a level that is sustained throughout the rest of the book. The specific objective of Chapter 6 is to account for the internal patterns of the "coextensive semantic relation" and to bring out what it implies about categorization. Cognitive anthropologists, linguists, and crosscultural psychologists have not heretofore recognized that this semantic relation is of a unique type and, thus, have not appreciated the problems of cognitive theory that it poses. Chapter 7 further contrasts conventional versus reformulated notions of what categories are and how they are related.

Part Three: Further Dynamics, Reflectivity, and Complex Categorization analyzes six additional categorization processes. It relates each process to the way categories are constructed as points of view. All data derive from the widely reported "cool" category, which includes both green and blue. Chapter 8 addresses organizational change and division in the simplest and most common kind of cool category, that which is named with one term by people who pick out hue as its most important referent. Chapter 9 compares the ways people respond to interview procedures; their diverse treatments of the cool category suggest that people in distinct communities categorize at different degrees of engagement and removal. Chapter 10 introduces a rare and distinctly complex kind of cool category. Its qualities are such as to suggest that the people who construct it place more importance on the relation between hues than on hues as individuated perceptions. Chapter 11 compares color categorization in Mesoamerica to that reported elsewhere in an attempt to separate universals from results of diffusion.

Part Four: Conclusion, Chapter 12, encapsulates this study on three levels: it lists all observations; it reviews how vantage theory ties them together under a unified account; and it recapitulates what the theory implies about categorization.

Entirely in retrospect, it seems to me that the approach I have taken to interdisciplinary problems is uniquely suited to linguistic anthropology. I hope this study represents one of the ways in which those who practice my field contribute to other fields. In particular, I ask philosophers, psychologists, and linguists to consider what this analysis may offer them that they have not encountered before, momentarily setting aside at least some of the differences of approach that serve each discipline. (I have in mind exchanges with colleagues at the 1992 interdisciplinary conference Color Categories in Thought and Language [for proceedings, see Hardin and Maffi, eds., in press], wherein one asserted that the Munsell chips are an inadequate standard, another was appalled that I do not measure ambient light with a meter during interviews, while a third advocated CRT technology in a darkroom—enough new procedures and paraphernalia to require a staff and helicopter on my next field trip!)

I conceived of the central thesis regarding viewpoint and category change after much of the data had been collected and their analysis was under way. The original goal was to reconstruct color categorization in Mesoamerican proto-languages, such as Proto-Otomanguean, Proto-Mayan, and Proto-Mixe-Zoquean, and to trace the descent of the proto-systems to contemporary forms. I surmised that prolonged contact between preColumbian cultures had occasioned color categories to evolve in almost the same manner throughout Mesoamerica such that reconstruction would shed more light on Berlin and Kay's hypothesis of universal color-category evolution. I projected that the undertaking might yield insight into the ways that areal diffusion influenced the evolution. Since the literature reported that most Mesoamerican languages name five native color categories—white, black, red, yellow, and green-with-blue—I sought to identify the linguistic group that originated this system. First, I planned to assemble lexical data from published sources, manuscripts, card files, and archives. Second, I made arrangements with missionary linguists and academics to conduct forty original investigations of genetically diverse languages throughout Mesoamerica. The field studies were to illuminate points that completed works might have overlooked. Another seventeen investigations of Mesoamerican languages were scheduled under the World Color Survey, a distinct but complementary project.

But the field studies, once in progress, revealed that the effects of areal diffusion were inconspicuous and the published sources had given no clue of the actual situation. Some Mesoamerican languages did not partition the color domain into the expected five categories, but only into three or four. Yet the categories, their internal compositions, and the words used to name them bore relationships of unanticipated variety and complexity. So the historical and areal concerns were replaced with a focus on color-category composition, relations, and semantics. I expanded the project to eighty field studies. In Appendix I, the total corpus of data—the Mesoamerican sample—is inventoried, attributed to collaborators, and plotted on the map. Appendix II relates the languages genetically.

Since 1975, two other surveys of color categorization have been conducted with the same issue of Munsell chips. The methodological benefit of the three surveys is that they enable analysts to decide what is universal and what is unique about color data from any particular language. The World Color Survey (WCS) was conducted by members of the Summer Institute of Linguistics in the Americas, Asia, Africa, Australia, the Philippines, and New Guinea under an NSF Grant to Brent Berlin, Paul Kay, and William Merrifield. It produced interviews of 2,513 individuals in 111 languages. The Mesoamerican Color Survey (MCS) is an area-specific counterpart of the WCS. Together they provide an overview of color categorization from global and regional perspectives. After completing the MCS,

I began a survey of color categorization in the Pacific Northwest, mainly among Salishan languages of British Columbia. The systems there differ greatly from those of Mesoamerica. They proffer a perspective from yet another linguistic area. In 1991, I built additional perspective by interviewing speakers of Zulu and other South African languages. In 1992, I interviewed Karuk speakers on the Klamath River of Northern California.

The overview on color categorization that has accrued from these and other efforts now calls for an assessment of what the new information may contribute to concerns that are wider than color ethnography itself, especially questions pertaining to the nature and production of categories. I hope to show in greater depth than has previously been possible how this specialized field feeds into a much larger course of events in cognitive science. To reach the broadest spectrum of readers, I have tried to use accessible language while defining terms with a glossary. All of my efforts will be very well invested if even a few readers use the contents of this book or enlarge upon my findings in their own ways.

R.E.M.

ACKNOWLEDGMENTS

I owe profound gratitude to the many people and institutions who made the Mesoamerican Color Survey possible. They are all whose names appear in Appendix I (table I.1), the U.S. Office of Education that awarded me a Fulbright-Hays fellowship for fieldwork in 1979, the Wenner-Gren Foundation for Anthropological Research that conferred the Carley Hunt Memorial Postdoctoral Fellowship supporting manuscript development in 1991, Nick Hale of Hale Color Consultants, Inc., who produced the attached colored copy of the Munsell array, and Brent Berlin, Paul Kay, and William R. Merrifield of the World Color Survey, who placed data at my disposal, lent equipment, and extended major tactical support. Such support also came from Prof. Leonardo Manrique C. on behalf of the Instituto Nacional de Antropología e Historia de México, Dr. Gordon Alsop on behalf of the Summer Institute of Linguistics of Mexico, Steven Echerd in Guatemala on behalf of the Summer Institute of Linguistics of Central America, Dr. Tim Knab, and architect Luís Marcial Corzo. I thank the 898 speakers of Mesoamerican languages and the speakers of other languages who undertook the interview. I am equally thankful for contributions outside the major surveys: Tzeltal foci from Brent Berlin and interview results in Western Apache, Hungarian, and Russian from, respectively, Philip J. Greenfeld, Zoltán Kövecses, John R. Taylor, and Henrietta Mondry. Stephen Zegura sent me the quotation from Darwin when he noticed its relevance to my work. Bernd Heine assisted me with his quotation regarding Chamus. Marjorie L. Crouch, Donald Stewart, and Doris Bartholomew, all of the Summer Institute of Linguistics, kindly answered my letters with details on, respectively, Vagla, Mazahua, and Otomian. Carole Biggam provided extensive information on Old English textual reference to color and evaluated my use of sources. Heinrich Zollinger, Andrés Lionnet, James M. Stanlaw, Andrea Brugmann, Eleanor Irwin, Keiko Matsuki, Tania Kuteva, and Ian Davies assisted me with bibliographical information, and

Dr. Lionnet included lists of Eudeve and Ópata color terms from sources beyond general access. In 1982, Terence Kaufman wrote me a letter about sound change among Mayan color terms, which I have often used and use now. Dr. Mondry and Joanne Kelly advised on Russian orthography. Three anonymous reviewers devoted their time and offered useful comments. Manuscript editor Jane H. Chamberlain contributed immeasurably.

My color survey of the Pacific Northwest was funded at the University of California, Berkeley, by the Ronald Leroy Olson Fund, Department of Anthropology, 1985, and by the Survey of California and Other Indian Languages, Department of Linguistics, 1987. It was supported by the Jacobs Fund of the Whatcom Museum Society, Bellingham, 1988 and 1990. I enjoyed the tactical sponsorship of Vincent Sarich, Leanne Hinton, Allen and Mariah Meyers, M. Dale Kinkade, Phyllis Chelsey, and Lawrence Andrews, the collaboration of Brent Galloway, Jan Van Eijk, and Ronald Beaumont, and the cooperation of the Makah, Shuswap (Alkali Lake), Halkomelem, Lillooet (Mt. Currie), and Sechelt bands. My interviews in South Africa were funded by the Human Science Research Council, Pretoria, under a grant requested on my behalf by John R. Taylor, then of the University of the Witwatersrand. One of the most fortunate meetings of my career has been with Dr. Taylor, who became my colleague and friend, who undertook color interviews himself, and who has been so generous as to write the foreword. My interviews in Northern California were supported by the Jacobs Fund for Karuk and by the Phillips Fund of the American Philosophical Society for Hupa and Yurok. In 1992, Dr. Clyde L. Hardin organized and gained NSF support for Color Categories in Thought and Language, a conference bringing together vision psychologists, psychophysicists, and linguistic anthropologists at Asilomar, California. Since then, Dr. Hardin and Dr. David Miller, one of the participants in that conference, have contributed technical information and advice on theory. Nick Hale equally clarified technical points. I assume sole responsibility for the representation of their input. I thank each of my supporters for helping me to improve this book.

For all her backing in the past and to the moment, I thank my wife, María I. MacLaury.

R.E.M.

PERMISSIONS

Permission to use copyrighted work has been granted by the following: The American Anthropological Association to reprint my own work from the *American Anthropologist* 89:2 as figures 1.2–3 and §4.1.1.1–2 revised and from the *Journal of Linguistic Anthropology* 1:1 as figure 2.33 revised; the Linguistic Society of America to reprint my own work from *Language* 67:1 and my own work as figures 4.3–9 and sundry passages revised; the University of Chicago Press to use my own work from *Current Anthropology* 33:2 as figures 2.32*a*, 8.9, 8.21, and 8.33*b* and passages in §6.1, © 1992 by The Wenner-Gren Foundation for Anthropological Research (All rights reserved); the Chicago Linguistic Society to reprint my own work as figures 6.1–4 and 6.20, 6.31*a*, 7.2, and 7.16*a* from *Papers from the 23rd Annual Regional Meeting of the Chicago Linguistics Society;* The University of California Press, quotations (Berlin and Kay 1969: 13, 35–36, and 141); Academic Press, Inc., of Harcourt Brace Jovanovich, Inc., quotation (Kay 1977:24); Cambridge University Press, two redrawn figures (Kay 1975: figs. 2–3); Harper Collins Publishers, one quotation (Klineberg 1935:144); Walter de Gruyter of Mouton de Gruyter, one quotation (McNeill 1972:513); the American Psychological Association, Inc., for one quotation (Medin, Goldstone, and Gentner 1993:254); Elsevier Science B. V., one quotation (Moss et al. 1990:314); the British Psychological Society, two quotations (Geddes 1946:35; Rivers 1905:321–22); Karl G. Heider, one quotation from his *The Dani of West Irian* (1972:4); Smith College, courtesy of Dr. Nancy Shumate, chair of the Department of Classics (Wallace 1927:29); The University of Chicago Press, one quotation (Hollenbach 1969:263).

Material from "Aguaruna Color Categories," by Brent Berlin and Elois Ann Berlin, reproduced by permission of the American Anthropological Association from *American Ethnologist* 2:1, February 1975. Not for further reproduction.

CONVENTIONS

In these discussions of color, stylistic differences in text distinguish a color, its category, its name, and its gloss. The color itself is in simple roman text—red; to indicate the category, either the word *category* is appended to the color name—the red category—or the context clearly implies this usage; the name of a color is italicized—*red*, Tzeltal *¢ah;* and its gloss is set in single quotes when it immediately follows its name—*¢ah* 'red'. Meanings appear in double quotes when cited in text apart from their names—the Mayan "red" term. In the legends of figures that display data, females are "f," males "m," and the number following these designations is the age of the subject: for example, "f 35" means "female, age 35." Many figures include parts *a, b, c,* etc. Often these parts display data from different individuals, whose data and figure-part will be referenced in text, for example, as "In *a* . . ." or "Part *a* . . ." or "Speaker *a* . . .". Different speakers of the same language may be distinguished as "speaker 1," "speaker 2," and so forth, when their data appear in separate figures that are discussed conjointly. Figure and table numbers identify the chapter or appendix before a decimal; for example, "figure 6.10" means "tenth figure of Chapter 6," and "table VIII.2" means "second table of Appendix VIII." Arabic numbers and Roman numerals distinguish chapters and appendices. Acronyms are WCS for World Color Survey, MCS for Mesoamerican Color Survey, OSA for Optical Society of America, NCS for (Swedish) Natural Color System, LGN for "lateral geniculate nucleus," JND for "just noticeable difference," and CRT for "cathode-ray tube." Abbreviations are S for similarity and D for distinctiveness; W, BK, R, Y, GN, BU, BN, PL, PK, O, and GY stand for, respectively, white, black, red, yellow, green, blue, brown, purple, pink, orange, and grey. Symbols in formulae are defined in table VIII.1. An asterisk before a term or clause, such as *greenish red, means the term is grammatically or logically unacceptable. An asterisk before an italicized term, such as *bhleu,* means that it is a reconstruction of an ancient term, thus hypothetical. An original place-name occurs by itself, while the namesake is qualified, as "Cambridge" and "Cambridge, Mass." distinguish the English and North American cities. The glossary defines terminology.

PART ONE

PRELIMINARIES

Color ethnography is a 138-year tradition of fieldwork and theory in which scholars and scientists representing the spectrum of disciplines have confronted one issue upon another with hardly a pause. Although this subfield has never been practiced by more than a cadre of devotees at any of its phases, it has earned the hallmark of fomenting contention and shattering doctrine—always for the better—but more than once by replacing an old creed with a new one. Why does such a tiny field repeatedly raise a stir? I suspect the honor owes to its measuring devices, which render data so stark and undeniable that they force the observer to take a stand on exactly how people think. The present investigation offers further findings on just this point. In the best of worlds, these claims will keep the dust in the air. The Mesoamerican analysis hinges on particular understandings of perception and cognition, and assumptions about their interaction, herein called "axioms." Part One takes up each of these topics in turn.

CHAPTER 1

CONCEPTUAL AND
MATERIAL EQUIPMENT

Two resources are vital to this project. First are concepts that I have used to make sense of the data. These include the theories of categorization that were available when the project began, those proposed by other researchers afterward, and those that I developed as it became clear that none of the circulating models could do their job. Second are the Munsell stimulus materials or "color chips" that provided the replicable standard of measurement. Since it will be impossible to read even Chapter 2 without knowing of the Munsell system, I shall describe it here, although its introduction would otherwise appear in Chapter 3 where its use is explained. Both the Munsell metric and the improved interviews based upon it are responsible for the quality of data the MCS produced, on which, in turn, the theoretical advances depend entirely. As has happened many times before, a conceptual formulation owes all to the improvement of a measuring device and a means of generating observations.

1.1. Influential Concepts

The interviewing techniques we developed during the survey produced at least three classes of data from each individual. The data were of a quantifiable and fine-grained sort that could be matched and verified between the classes. These descriptions characterized not only individual categories but categories within whole domains, where they overlapped, assumed various other relations, and exerted pressures on each other. Our results show that categorization is a dynamic process and that categories constantly change.

The two theories of categorization that I took to the field were structural in nature and, therefore, provided no "mechanism" to deal with the kinetic quality of categories. Yet both had gone a long distance toward replacing abiding misconceptions and thus provided me with enough background to venture an explanation of my own. I am indebted to Berlin and Kay's theory of universal color-category evolution and to Eleanor Rosch's prototype concept. As a graduate student and prior to my fieldwork, 1974–1978, I studied directly under Brent Berlin and Paul Kay at the Language Behavior Research Laboratory (LBRL) of the Anthropology Department, University of California (UC), Berkeley. I absorbed Rosch's thinking as it spread from cognitive psychology to linguistics (Fillmore 1975; Coleman 1975) and to linguistic anthropology, the subfield to which the LBRL was solely devoted in 1975.

Berlin and Kay (1969) proposed the concept of "basic color terms," which number from two to eleven in any language, whose predictable meanings imply a universal evolutionary order, and whose best examples or "focal colors" are shared across languages. These claims set the stage for a critique of the belief in linguistic relativity that, throughout the 1950s and 1960s, had been elevated to an ideology within linguistics and anthropology (Lucy 1992). Berlin and Kay were asserting that people everywhere perceived color in the same way and differed only in the number of terms with which they named it; color perception predominated sufficiently to determine the order in which any people anywhere would add basic color terms to their language—white versus black first, red second, green third, and so on—and it determined the color that people would pick as a best example or "focus" of any basic category. Berlin and Kay's claim of universal foci was the direct predecessor of Rosch's category prototype. Their book reached her while she was in the field among the Dani of Irian Jaya searching for a dissertation topic. Then Eleanor Heider, she was the student of Roger Brown, who had collaborated in a renowned experiment (Brown and Lenneberg 1954) that correlated codability and memorability of Munsell color chips. Codability is a correspondence between shortness of expression, brevity of response latency, and consistency of use between trials and between subjects. Memorability is the success with which a subject recalls a chip from an array after having viewed the chip in isolation and then having lost sight of it. Brown and Lenneberg assumed the correlation showed that an aspect of language is related to an aspect of cognition, and they stated—seemingly without justification—that codability determines memorability.

Heider found that the Dani named color with only two basic terms, representing Berlin and Kay's earliest evolutionary stage. One term covered light and warm colors while the other covered dark and cool. This meant that language would not bias the Dani during psychological experiments that probed their underlying perceptions of color differences within the broad ranges. Heider did this by teaching Dani speakers to use terms that she extracted from their social organization to name small sets of Munsell color chips in three kinds of arrangement, each on a card. One arrangement included a Berlin-and-Kay focal color in its center, another included a focal chip on its edge, and a third included no focal chip. Learning speed matched this order. Heider concluded that the Dani shared universal focal colors, which aided their memories independently of language. That is, universal focality simultaneously determines both codability and memory; language and thought are both determined by this universal perception while neither determines the other. Brown and Lenneberg's acclaimed experiment had not made a case for linguistic relativity. Heider conducted similar procedures with shape and facial expression before concluding fieldwork (1971, 1972a–b; Heider and Oliver 1972).

At UC Berkeley, Rosch (1973a–b, 1974, 1975b) distinguished "perceptual categories," as of color, shape, or facial expression, from "semantic categories," as of bird, toy, or science. She noted that both kinds were structured around a core of better members. Then, from this she extracted the "prototype" construct (1973a: 113 first usage). A color category is a perception in which a point of unique hue or other strong color is a natural prototype; nonprototypical members belong to the category to the extent that they resemble the prototype. As this principle of cohesion works on a single attribute of one hue, it pertains within a color category, say, of red, differently than it does within the organization of nonperceptual semantic categories—say, of toy—that are based on cognizance of multiple attributes. In general, any semantic category is composed by a principle of *family resemblances:* members share attributes with a prototype that, in turn and by circular reasoning, is the member or the image of a member that shares most attributes with its category and least with prototypes of contrasting categories (Rosch and Mervis 1975). Members may share different attributes with the prototype and few or none with each other, which allows a category to include members of diverse appearance or function. Since members have different numbers of attributes and since attributes are of unequal value, membership in a category is a matter of degree, and category structure is graded. The motive for categorizing is functionally defined as reducing limitless variation to manageable types. It follows from this that category structure matches "the correlational structure of the environment" (p. 575), which breaks the circularity.

Rosch et al. (1976) worked further with prototypes in taxonomic hierarchies, showing that a "basic level" of categorization is the highest on which a prototype can be mentally envisioned or imaged; for example, one can imagine a typical or representative chair but not an item central to furniture. The basic level is relative, moving toward greater detail and specificity with development of cultural interest or expertise. Rosch et al. also explored the relative contributions to category cohesion of attributes, motor movement, shape, and expectation based on prior experience. Rosch (1975a) extended the prototype concept by equating it and other canons— such as multiples of 10 and planes at right angles—with the reference points of spatial reasoning. This work included experiments with asymmetry judgments between members of a category: that is, judging a prototype and a nonprototypical member to be "closer" when using the former as a fixed reference but "more distant" when comparing in the other way. (Rosch [1975a] especially prefigures vantage theory.) Mervis and Rosch (1981) summarize this research, which, because of its many facets, cannot be minimized as mere observation that category membership is graded.

Rosch (1978) ultimately denied that natural prototypes and family resemblances comprise a theory of categorization. She offered that, although such a theory must incorporate "the known facts about prototypes," it must also address cultural values and contrast within systems. The evidence of gradation was heralded as an alternative to the set-theoretic "2,000-year-old classical" view of categories—hastily blamed on Aristotle! (but see Lansing 1995)—that categories are like all-or-none containers that fit or do not fit an observer-independent world and that are applied by logic correctly or incorrectly. Rosch's work on category structure inspired extensive research programs in psychology (Smith and Medin 1981). Prototype effects were welcomed by linguists as an antidote to distinctive features, truth conditions, and autonomous syntax (Lakoff 1987; Taylor 1989; MacLaury 1991c).

The year 1974–1975 was also active for Berlin and Kay, whose work I review in §2.4 (Berlin and Berlin 1975; Kay 1975; Kay and McDaniel 1975; Dougherty 1975; Kuschel and Monberg 1974; Heinrich 1974; Hage and Hawkes 1975). After receiving a half-dozen reports of broad color categories, such as Heider's description of Dani light-warm and dark-cool, Berlin and Kay revised their evolutionary sequence from the naming of focal colors one after the other to the progressive partitioning of categories that, at any stage, will encompass all colors. Nevertheless, at any stage but the earliest, the categories will be focused predictably. In an apparent attempt to preserve the notion that categories are logical operations, Kay and McDaniel (1975) formalized Berlin and Kay's revised scheme as fuzzy sets, which I address in §2.4.2. By this time, McDaniel (1972) and Zollinger (1972) had found that since the nineteenth century theoreticians had offered physiological models of focal colors. Vision psychologists had begun to explore analogues of the projected human system in the optical nerve of primates while producing promising initial results (De Valois, Abramov, and Jacobs 1966).

In sum, when I began fieldwork in Mesoamerica, color categories were thought of as graded in structure and organized around prototypes that were determined by universal physiology. Although no one voiced this prospect, both Rosch's model and Berlin and Kay's model predicted that real people would select best examples of color categories at precisely the focal colors while all deviant selections would fall out randomly. But the main problem was the inability of either formulation to account for the change that constituted Berlin and Kay's evolutionary sequence—either their first of 1969 or their revision of 1975—or to address any kind of trajectory whatsoever. If, in Rosch's words, color categories mirror "the correlational structure of the environment," why, in some languages, does the cool category divide into separate basic categories of green versus blue when year after year the grass and leaves become no greener and when the sky retains its eternal azure?

The present work will address these questions in depth (§§4.5 through 7.4); but to relate my efforts with additional traditions in psychology and linguistics, I adumbrate that discussion with a thumbnail enumeration. First—and recognizing that this is not original—I determined that, with shifts in outlook, colors (or, for that matter, virtually any collection of entities) can be regarded in terms of their similarities to each other or in terms of their differences. Either judgment can be emphasized at the expense of the other. Any category would require that both judgments contribute to its composition: emphasis on similarity would hold its members together as a class while an emphasis on distinctiveness would delimit the class at some finite border. Further, the judgments need not be of the same strength, nor should their strengths, whatever they be, remain the same indefinitely, say, over years. A shift of balance in favor of differences would cause the margins of a category to contract toward its middle, leaving some of its former members outside its range. In effect, a piece of an old category could break off and become eligible material for inclusion within a new category. In this way, categories may multiply, as they do in the color domain when, say, the original cool category divides into separate basic categories of green versus blue. Judgments of similarity and difference are a well-studied aspect of categorization, as reviewed by Medin, Goldstone, and Gentner (1993), even though the exact way they contribute to a category remains controversial and ill defined.

Second, I attempted to account for more than mere change. Many

Mesoamerican color categories are named with two terms, both of which cover the category but which are focused on opposite sides. Further, one is always named on a few more color chips than the other, while its focus is closer to the category center. To account for this pattern, I regarded the opposite semantic ranges to be names of different points of view, and I took the judgments of similarity and difference and the stable Berlin-and-Kay focal colors to be the coordinates. In reference to these, a category is constructed by analogy to physical experience as though it were one or more points of view on a spatial terrain. A category is an analogous vantage that can be contracted or expanded in accord with (1) the emphasis that is assigned to coordinates and (2) how the coordinates are arranged in relation to each other. A person maintains the category by participating in this construction, at very least, whenever the category is needed.

The foregoing sketch will help explain why certain additional theoretical developments became relevant to the Mesoamerican analysis. When I left for the field in 1978, those lines of thought were only beginning to come together under the rubric of "lexical semantics"; but when I returned to Berkeley in 1981, the thinking had coalesced into "cognitive semantics." I mention this movement for two reasons. First, as I formulated my model of Mesoamerican color categories, the continuing advances of cognitive semantics informed me that I was not the only one who thought that such processes as analogy, viewpoint, and personal involvement were critical to categorization. This knowledge was reassuring, because the alternatives to these processes—set theory and correlational structure—were venerated by prominent linguists and psychologists and appeared to me, at least, to constitute prevailing doctrine. Second, cognitive semantics itself offered no model of commonplace categorization, even though many were proposing models of "radial categories" held together by polysemous linkages of various kinds, such as image transformations, metonymies, and mythic beliefs (Brugman 1989, Lakoff 1987, Smith 1991; Rudzka-Ostyn 1985; Janda 1986). Most of these polysemous categories pertain to grammatical classes, such as prepositions or prefixes, or they are patently exotic, such as Djirbal numeral classifiers (Dixon 1982). Wittgenstein (1953) had shown a similar "complexity" regarding the notion of "game," and probably this principle could be found in some of the categories Rosch had experimented with, such as "toy" and "sport." But ordinary categories, such as those pertaining to colors, shapes, birds, or cars, are of seemingly less imaginative origin. Color in particular is an attribute domain that is named by all reported languages. Although color may be categorized in ways foreign to us (as we shall see in §2.6 and beyond), any color category pertains mainly to sensations such as hue, brightness, or saturation. Since Rosch intended to account for categories of this ilk, we need a model that pursues her objective but supersedes the direct reflection of physical form. Rosch herself called for such (1978).

Reviewing even a little of what has been accomplished in cognitive semantics over the past five years would fill another book as long as Lakoff (1987). Here I only highlight events that inspired me to build a model of color categorization. Lakoff and Johnson's (1980) treatment of metaphor underscored how pervasive in human thinking is the strategy of organizing an abstract or conceptual domain in terms of the organization of a concrete or physical domain. I invoke analogy instead of metaphor to model color categorization: people employ this strategy when they construct a color category as though it were a viewpoint of space-time. Metaphor is a selective equation between parts of two structures or scenarios; for example, AN ARGUMENT IS A BUILDING (and, therefore, an argument needs a foundation and a framework) or AN ARGUMENT IS A WAR (and, therefore, arguments are fought, won, lost, or blown to bits). Analogy is an equation between two systems of relations; for example, AN ATOM WORKS LIKE THE SOLAR SYSTEM. In my formulation of color categorization, an analogy pertains between the coordinates of spatiotemporal reckoning and mental points of reference that compose a category.

Johnson's (1987) notion of embodiment characterizes the involvement that a person maintains with a category. Embodiment means that people construct a concept by means of metaphor or analogy to an experience they regularly undergo by virtue of being inside their bodies, not merely between impersonal domains such as arguments and wars or atoms and solar systems. Johnson draws examples from Rosch's basic-level categorization, the mental imagery of Talmy's (1985) force dynamics, and Sweetser's (1984, 1990) joining of metaphor and force dynamics to analyze the semantics of modal auxiliaries. When I include within my model of color categorization an analogy with the coordinate system by which people keep their balance or maintain awareness of their position in terrain, I am applying Johnson's concept to ordinary categorization. Langacker (1990b) and his disciple Casad (1982; Casad and Langacker 1985) use constructs of "point of view" and "vantagepoint." The psychologists Barsalou and Sewell (1984) built viewpoint into an account of variable category organization and included a literature review, but they have not sent their work to press.

My own proposal of viewpoint differs from these others in the sense that viewpoint in color categorization is constructed specifically in reference to coordinates and on the level of coordinates. The others do not venture such specification, although I think they demonstrate the need to do so.

Langacker's (1985, 1990a) essay on "subjectification" (and objectification) prompted me to add a version of these concepts to my model of categorization as viewpoint (§§9.4–5), although I am uncertain that I have done justice to Langacker or even understood him. Notions that, at least, parallel his two concepts will be essential to account for categorization at more than one level of abstraction. People treat their own categories at varying degrees of removal from themselves, which I show to be the case with certain Mesoamerican color categories under special conditions.

1.2. Stimulus Materials

Data were elicited during interviews in response to the Munsell color standards, 1976 issue. The full Munsell system consists of 1,600 "chips" that radiate in 40 directions on 9 levels of brightness from a neutral vertical shaft such that they represent equal psychological intervals throughout a three-dimensional "solid" of hue, value, and chroma. Hue (dominant wavelength) is the horizontal circumference of prismatic colors such as red, yellow, green, blue, and purple. Value or "brightness" is the vertical dimension of light-to-dark or white-grey-black, depending on degree of saturation. In figure 1.1a, chroma or "saturation" (purity of wavelength) is the horizontal in-to-out distance of a color from the white-grey-black axis, its vividness; white-grey-black are of zero saturation or desaturated. At maximum saturation, some hues, such as red, green, yellow, blue, purple, pink, and orange, are distant from the axis; others, such as brown, lavender, and beige, are closer. In b, an exterior depiction of the Munsell color solid shows that yellow is perceptually closer in brightness to the white pole than is blue, whereas blue is closer to the grey axis than is yellow. (For

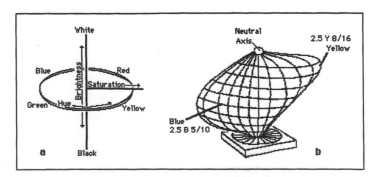

FIGURE 1.1. (a) The three dimensions of (b) the Munsell color solid.

	1	2	3	4	5	6	7	8	9	10	11	12	13	14	15	16	17	18	19	20	21	22	23	24	25	26	27	28	29	30	31	32	33	34	35	36	37	38	39	40	
0 A																																									9.5
0 B	2	2	2	2	2	2	2	4	6	6	6	6	2	2	2	2	2	2	2	2	2	2	2	2	2	2	2	2	2	2	2	2	2	2	2	2	2	2	2	2	9.0
0 C	6	6	6	6	6	6	6	8	14	16	14	12	12	12	4	10	8	8	6	6	6	6	4	4	4	4	4	4	6	6	4	4	4	4	6	6	6	6	6	6	8.0
0 D	8	8	10	10	10	14	14	14	12	12	12	12	12	6	10	10	10	8	8	8	8	8	8	6	6	6	6	6	8	8	8	6	6	6	6	8	8	10	10	8	7.0
0 E	12	12	12	14	16	12	14	12	10	10	10	10	10	8	12	12	10	10	10	10	8	8	8	8	8	8	8	8	10	10	10	8	8	8	8	10	10	10	12	12	6.0
0 F	14	14	14	16	14	12	10	10	8	8	8	8	8	8	10	10	12	12	10	10	10	10	8	8	8	8	8	8	10	12	12	10	10	10	10	12	12	12	14	14	5.0
0 G	14	14	14	14	10	8	8	6	6	6	6	6	6	2	8	8	10	10	10	10	8	8	8	6	6	8	8	10	10	12	12	10	10	10	10	12	12	12	12	14	4.0
0 H	10	10	12	10	8	6	6	6	4	4	4	4	4	4	10	6	6	8	8	8	8	8	6	6	6	6	6	6	8	10	10	12	10	10	10	10	10	10	10	10	3.0
0 I	8	8	8	6	4	4	4	2	2	2	2	2	2	4	4	4	4	6	6	6	4	4	4	4	4	4	6	6	6	8	10	8	8	8	6	6	8	8	8	8	2.0
0 J	2.5	5	7.5	10		5		10		5		10		5		10		5		10		5		10		5		10		5		10		5		10		5		10	0.5
	R				YR				Y				GY				G				BG				B				BP				P				RP				

FIGURE 1.2. Minimally (/0) and maximally (/2–16) saturated Munsell colors used as stimulus materials during the World Color Survey and Mesoamerican Color Survey.

overviews of the Munsell system, see Birren 1969 or D'Andrade and Egan 1974; see *Color* in any major unabridged English dictionary or encyclopedia of quality.)

Stimulus materials used by the WCS and MCS comprised 10 desaturated and 320 saturated chips of the axis and surface; the very dark level 1 of the full Munsell system is not used. Figure 1.2 schematizes the 330 chips in two dimensions. Each graph cell represents a different color. White, 8 greys, and black are depicted at left, the hues in columns 1–40; rows represent levels of brightness. The number in each cell indicates the saturation of its respective color, 0–16; heavy lines divide 8–16 from 2–6. The figure relates two notations: (1) row-letters and column-numbers on the left and top; (2) internationally recognized Munsell codes on the right and bottom. In the discussion of Mesoamerican data, only row-letters and column-numbers will be used. For example, chip C9 (a vivid yellow) is of chroma or saturation /16. Using the expression "C9" is simpler than referring to the color by Munsell symbols as "2.5 Y 8/16," which means 2.5 Y hue, 8/ brightness, and /16 chroma. The two-dimensional representation of the color-solid surface involves the same distortion as a Mercator projection of the world map in which longitudes diverge as they approach the poles. Thus, there is progressively less psychological distance between columns as they become lighter or darker. In rows A and J, the white and black poles are represented by one graph cell because one color would extend through each row.[1]

In figure 1.3, *a* relates the Munsell scheme to the eleven basic color terms of American English. These were elicited from a single individual who named the color chips one-by-one during an interview. The subject also chose a best example or "focus" of each term. The figure provides English-

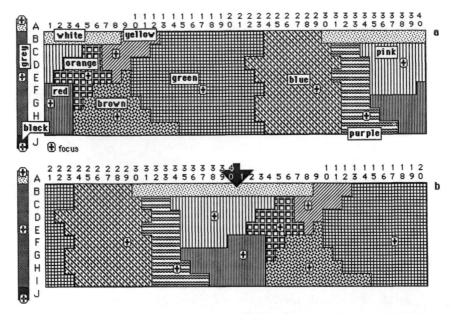

FIGURE 1.3. (*a*) Obverse display of color terms and foci elicited from a speaker of American English, m 35, 1980; (*b*) reverse display.

speakers with a reference against which to compare Mesoamerican color categories. In the figure, *b* is a "reverse" display of the same English speaker's data. Columns 1–20 and 21–40 are reversed as 21–40,1–20, which breaks the array through bluish green to display red continuously. Any break is artificial. The left column of white-grey-black keeps its position throughout *a* and *b*.

1.2.1. A Short History of Standards

In the finest tradition of nineteenth-century empiricism, the first color ethnographers paid meticulous attention to descriptive method. Then, as now, the primary concern was to collect data by systematic procedures and in reference to reproducible standards. Magnus (1878, 1880, 1883; cf. Allen 1879) conducted the first world survey by mailing instructions and stimuli to missionaries and colonial officials; his materials consisted of Holmgren's wools, which the Swedish physiologist (Holmgren 1877, 1878) had developed for testing the color vision of Laplanders. Rivers (1901*a*) used the same yarn test, although he mainly interviewed Torres Straits islanders with Lovibond's Tintometer (Gibson and Harris 1927). Bartlett (1928) surveyed color categorization in Javanese and Batak languages with watercolored papers identified by pigment name. Ray (1952, 1953) used a darkroom and the light from a spectroscope as his replicable standard. Meanwhile, the Munsell colors had been developed (Munsell 1905; Newhall, Nickerson, and Judd 1943). Lenneberg and Roberts (1956) introduced them to ethnography by arranging 320 saturated hues as an array to elicit data from Zuni. They eliminated one row from the eleven of the Munsell system, although they do not specify which row. Their method consisted of (1) preparing in advance a list of Zuni color terms and (2) after covering the array with acetate, asking individuals to outline with a grease pencil (*a*) the range of each term and (*b*) its "most typical example" or focus.

Berlin and Kay (1969) adopted this 320-chip Munsell array as well as the acetate-mapping method with steps *a* and *b*. They rephrased *b*, requesting the "best example." They precluded Munsell row 1.0/ at its maximum saturation, and they modified the array by adding a left column of 9 chips of white-grey-black; they bordered the 40 columns of hues along their lightest and darkest ends with rows of 40 white (9.5/N) and 40 black (1.0/N) chips, which facilitated interviews. Later they expanded and revised the achromatic column to include white 9.5/N, black 0.5/N, and the eight greys 2.0–9.0/N that match the eight brightness levels 2.0–9.0/ of the hue columns (Berlin and Berlin 1975). That study, Dougherty (1975), and Saunders (1992*a*:143–51) exhibit Berlin and Kay's technique exactly, while others experiment with variations (Heider 1972*a;* Harkness 1973; Heinrich 1974; Kuschel and Monberg 1974; Hage and Hawkes 1975).

Collier (1973; Collier et al. 1976) miniaturized the Munsell array by cutting 1/4-in. discoidal chips with a paper punch. These are mounted in the familiar rows and columns on a neutral matte but with a small space separating each from its neighbors. The miniaturization does not hinder performance, and the result is a reduced expenditure of the costly Munsell materials, an array that is easier to transport, and a visual effect that helps interviewees to separately consider each chip as they map categories.

The World Color Survey and the Mesoamerican Color Survey combined Collier's miniaturization with Berlin and Kay's design. The WCS replaced acetate mapping with a separate naming of each of the 330 Munsell colors in a fixed random order followed by identification of a focus for each name volunteered. The MCS added to this method a direct mapping procedure and recording of qualifiers. The MCS enhanced the Collier-Berlin-Kay design with an obverse-reverse pair of arrays (formatted as is fig. 1.3) to allow focusing and mapping of any category without distortion caused by the artificial break. Both surveys derandomized data on a grid representing the array, the WCS by computer and the MCS by hand.

Uchikawa, Uchikawa and Boynton (1989) elicited responses with 424 chips formulated and spaced by the Optical Society of America (OSA) so as to represent points at equal distances throughout the solid, but our attempt to translate between OSA and Munsell elicitations achieved imperfect results (Boynton, MacLaury, and Uchikawa 1989; cf. Smith, Whitefield, and Wiltshire 1990a). Sivik (1974; Sivik and Taft 1994) elicited Swedish color categories with the Natural Color System (NCS). Tornay (1973) used *Letracolor* pigments to conduct interviews in Sudan, and he sponsored their use elsewhere (1978a). Birren (1979) reviews some forty different color standards. Computer programs projecting luminant stimuli on a monitor (CRT) will provide extensive possibilities (French 1992). Any system will enjoy some advantages while forfeiting others until the translation problem is solved (Chang and Carroll 1980), perhaps by a program that estimates how data collected by any particular physical system would look if they had been collected by the material embodiment (which need exist only as a concept) of a theoretical system intermediate to all (cf. Smith, Whitefiled, and Wiltshire 1990b).

1.3. Summary

The Mesoamerican Color Survey began its progress on a foundation established by others. Berlin and Kay tightened a nineteenth-century hypothesis of color-category evolution, added stipulations on structure and universals, and developed a set of Munsell materials suitable for investigating further. Their findings stimulated Rosch's work on prototypes which, in turn, provided impetus for subsequent developments in lexical and cognitive semantics. During the MCS survey, revised use of the Munsell measurement generated observations of a quality that overtaxed the explanatory capacities of available cognitive theories, but these data also suggested directions for building on the earlier concepts. Berlin, Kay, and Merrifield's World Color Survey provided additional Mesoamerican data as well as a worldwide overview. The latter will prove invaluable as a means to distinguish areal specifics from universals in the Mesoamerican sample. Most important, the WCS provides the means to test the global import of hypotheses derived locally by the MCS or by other regional studies.

CHAPTER 2

ISSUES IN COLOR ETHNOGRAPHY

Since 1858, more than 3,000 manuscripts, articles, dissertations, and books have addressed color terms as a dominant theme. This bibliography includes most of the anthropological linguistic sources. Berlin and Kay (1991) list 200 references that postdate 1969. (See also the bibliographies of Biggam 1993, Brenner 1982, Chandler and Barnhart 1938, Conklin 1972, Godlove 1956, Grossman 1988, Maerz and Paul 1930:15–22, Saunders 1992a, and Skard 1946.) Color ethnography is entering its fifth resurgence following four waves of earlier foment separated by troughs of reduced activity (§§2.1–5). A different question inspired each rise. My Mesoamerican results contribute to the recent consolidation of interest under which all issues, long-standing and recent, are on the table anew. This chapter merely outlines pivotal developments; its scope permits little more than a mention or classification of each project, some in notes only. Highlights of WCS data are diagrammed so as to illustrate the kinds of systems that many of the earlier accounts reported verbally. These examples allow me to introduce the subsequent analysis of Mesoamerican data against a backdrop of color categories that are notably non-Mesoamerican.

2.1. Language versus Vision: An Evolutionary Debate

The classicist Gladstone (1858:458–499) reported that Homeric Greek color terms emphasized brightness, asserting that the ancients were disinclined to name "colour proper" and had no term for blue. He took this to mean that the human color sense had recently evolved to its present acuity. A debate ensued (Allen 1878, 1879; Andree 1878; Bacmeister 1874; Fäger 1877; Gatschet 1879a–b; Geiger 1869, 1871:45–60, 1872:243–289; Gladstone 1877; Kirchhoff 1879; Krause 1877, 1880; Magnus 1877a–b, 1878, 1879; Marty 1879; Rabl-Rückhard 1880; Virchow 1878, 1879) in which Geiger, a philologist analyzing ancient texts, posed that comparative study of color terms showed that the latter-day light sense had evolved through a particular sequence, but the biologist Allen countered that differences in color naming must be purely linguistic because evolution of color perception would have required vast time. To test Allen's hypothesis among contemporary primitives, Magnus sent Holmgren's wools with instructions to missionaries and colonial officials across four continents, the first worldwide color survey. Meanwhile, Virchow administered the wool test to Nubians visiting Germany.[1] Although they named blue and black with the same term, they discriminated these and other colors accurately, which supported the linguistic argument. Andree mined fifty-seven reports, vocabularies, and grammars, some of them centuries old, for data on the diverse ways that ethnic peoples named color; his catalogue of types supported the linguistic aspect of Geiger's scheme. After Magnus's (1880, 1883) results trickled in, he drew the same conclusions as Virchow and Andree and concurred with Geiger to the extent that longer wavelengths were named first in evolutionary order. But his survey was received as anticlimactic (Rivers 1901c:46). Improvement of laboratory anthropometry (Galton 1885) and psychological testing (Wundt 1900) were superseding the yarn-matching method, whose faults became an issue (Rivers 1901b:246).[2]

2.2. Crosscultural Perception

Color ethnography peaked a second time under the energies of W. H. R. Rivers (1901a–d, 1903, 1905a–b; Seligman 1901; Franklin 1901), who visited five island peoples in Torres Straits, Arab peasants on the Upper Nile, the Greenland Eskimo (in London), and the Uráli, Shologa, and Toda of Tamil Nadu. He combined Holmgren's wools with Nagel's cards (Nagel 1900) and Lovibond's Tintometer (Lovibond 1887), instruments invented after Magnus had stopped contributing. Rivers, a medical doctor and the first editor of *The British Journal of Psychology,* was foremost in establishing anthropology as a science and as an institutional career. His work on color vision and color naming served his aspiration to lodge psychological testing at the root of anthopological method (Mandelbaum 1980). The Cambridge Expedition to the Torres Straits, including four scientists directed by A. C. Haddon, was devoted to measuring native senses and testing mental acuity in several capacities of vision, touch, hearing, smell, and taste, the color sense among them. Rivers thought that Virchow and Magnus had failed to resolve the recurrent reports of weak blue-black discrimination among pigmented peoples. So he examined numerous subjects with the Tintometer to determine the degree of red, yellow, and blue that they would verbally identify, comparing natives and Englishmen. While he found the former to be keener at detecting red, the latter excelled in identifying blue, a difference which he attributed to variable pigmentation in the macula lutea (Rivers 1901c:52; cf. 1901a:95, 1903:6). Yet he devised an evolutionary sequence of color naming among the different groups he visited, which he matched to their performances on the acuity tests, such as distance discrimination and susceptibility to optical illusions. While Rivers eschewed Gladstone and Geiger's notion of sensory evolution, he tried to account for color-naming differences with a mixture of perceptual, mental, aesthetic, and even environmental traits, too much of a medley to explain anything. However, his refinement of psychological method in Egypt and India seemed able to provide a basis for testing whether there is a correlation between stages of color naming and various aptitudes that people apply generally (Rivers 1901b:245, 1905a:396), a topic to be resumed in §§4.3 and 9.4–5.

In attendance at the 1904 St. Louis (World) Fair were some 300 individuals representing Ainus, Eskimos, Filipino Negritos and Igorots, Patagonians, Africans, and scores of other vaguely identified but widespread ethnic groups. Various perceptual psychologists, in the tradition of the emerging behaviorist school, seized this opportunity to pointedly follow up on the findings of the Torres Straits team. Woodworth (1910a–b, cf. 1906) reviewed numerous "tests," genuine and fanciful, which suggested that on the mean people everywhere discriminate their senses with equal acumen, including their color sense. But at the fair, at least in regard to color, his subjects only paired light and dark shades of tinted paper, each pair varying within a single hue.

> We were able, at St. Louis, to try on representatives of a number of
> races a difficult color matching test, so different indeed from that of
> Rivers that our results can not be used as a direct check on his; with
> the result that all other races were inferior to whites in their general
> success in color matching, but that no special deficiency appeared
> in the blues. We could also find no correlation between ill success
> in this test and the degree of pigmentation. On the whole, the color
> sense is probably very much the same all over the world. (Woodworth
> 1910a:179)

The matching test excelled methodologically over Rivers's use of the Tintometer because the investigator did not mention color terms during the procedure. Mainly, however, the preponderance of facts, none of which was definitive by itself, had accumulated to an extent that social scientists were predisposed to accept Woodward's sole experiment as the marker of a turning point and his conclusion as the new common wisdom. Doubtless, his voice was amplified by his preeminence (Frontispiece 1900). Forthwith, Rivers (1911) tempered his evolutionary stance, making it consistent with the mounting outlook of the times. The chain of events brought anthropology to a state in which neither racial differences nor any scalar arrangement of mental capacities could provide a plausible hypothesis of ethnic diversity. Woodworth, in 1904, was on the faculty at Columbia University with Franz Boas and acknowledged Boas's communication in this work (Woodworth 1910*b*:note 5).[3]

2.3. Relativism

Boas swiftly combined the behaviorist formulation with his objection to the comparative method of anthropology (1896), his interest in classification (1911*a*:14, 24–43), and his field experience with color naming:

> Differences of principles of classification are found in the domain of sensations. For instance: it has been observed that colors are classified in quite distinct groups according to their similarities, without any accompanying difference in the ability to distinguish shades of color. What we call green and blue is often combined under a term like "gall-color," or yellow and green are combined into one concept . . . The importance of the fact that in speech and thought the word calls forth a different picture, according to the classification of green and yellow or green and blue as one group can hardly be exaggerated (Boas 1911*b*:190).

This statement is among Boas's earliest on linguistic relativity (if not absolutely his earliest); it antedates any like locution issued by his student, Edward Sapir, or by Sapir's disciple, Benjamin Whorf, who are commonly accredited, respectively, with the weak and strong versions of that view. Lucy (1992), while pursuing missions of his own, compiles copious quotations revealing that all three men enunciated the gamut of unsystematic pronouncements from mild to radical on this doctrine. The following assertion by Boas, issued nine years after his first statement and at the acme of his titanic influence on the formation of American anthropology, is forceful enough to suggest that the so-called Whorf-Sapir hypothesis should really be called the Boasian protocol: ". . . the categories of language compel us to see the world arranged in certain definite conceptual groups which, on account of our lack of knowledge of linguistic processes, are taken as objective thoughts" (Boas 1920:320).

Although Maass (1912) and Bartlett (1928) conducted descriptive surveys of color terms in Malaysian languages, during Boas's era and for the three decades thereafter, studies of color categorization featured cultural relativity (Cuervo Marquez 1924; Gómez 1933; Dal 1938; Beaglehole and Beaglehole 1938:356; Beaglehole 1939; Kallay 1939; O'Neale and Dolores 1943; Jettmar 1953; White 1943; Geddes 1946; Zahan 1951; Gutia 1952; Ohman 1953:133; Pritsak 1954; Conklin 1955; Holmer 1956; Gerschel 1966; Hollander 1966; Swadesh 1971:202–205): "The Fijian is as capable of discerning the hue as we are of discerning the intensity. The difference is merely one of emphasis upon one or the other of the two qualities" (Geddes 1946:35); "We have made our classification entirely on the basis of hue, with no regard for intensity or saturation. Other groups have chosen to make their classification differently" (Klineberg 1935:144).

Geddes and Klineberg discussed emphasis or choice among what all peoples see, but Ray (1952:258) took the deterministic stance: "There is no such thing as a 'natural' division of the spectrum. Each culture has taken the spectral continuum and has divided it into units on a quite arbitrary basis." He states that perception is unstructured and implies that people impose order by categorizing the visual flow; beyond this primary end, categorization is arbitrary; linguistic categories mold thought just as stimuli condition behavior.

Ray's data consist of spectroscopic measurements at middle brightness of single speakers' responses in ten languages (1953:fig 1), which is like partitioning only row F of the Munsell array.[4] But, aligned side by side, the ten displays make a stark case for unfettered relativity. Gleason (1961:2–5) fashioned like diagrams of English, Shona, and Bassa color terms for the opening lesson in his widely used textbook of introductory linguistics. Bloomfield (1933:140, 280) and Hjelmslev (1953:33) made appeals in kind with their seminal treatments of the science (quotations of other notables appear in Berlin and Kay 1969:159–160). Cognitive psychologists Brown and Lenneberg (1954) of, respectively, Harvard and M.I.T. used Munsell chips in procedures that seemingly showed that "memorability," an aspect of thought, correlates with "codeability," an aspect of language; they argued language determines thought, gratuitously so it seems (§1.1).[5] Yet many regarded their study to be the imprimatur of cognitive anthropology (e.g., Kay 1966:22), whose proponents adopted linguistic relativity as their ideological cornerstone (Tyler, ed. 1969:3). Lenneberg and Roberts (1956) extended their claims to Zuni color naming as they introduced the Munsell array to anthropological fieldwork. The relativity of language had become a crusade with color as its banner.

2.4. Universalism à la Berlin and Kay

It seemed to Berlin and Kay (1969; Berlin 1970) that color terms could easily be translated because people everywhere saw and named the same colors. Chomsky (1965) had provided a bold new impetus by stressing the universality of language on a formally expressible underlying level; he further encouraged a union between cognitive psychology and linguistics. In this atmosphere, Berlin and Kay tested the relativist assertions by interviewing speakers of twenty languages with the Munsell array and acetate method, and they analyzed seventy-eight color-term lexicons from dictionaries, reports, and correspondence. Their original hypothesis was this:

1. Among the color terms of any language, "basic color terms" can be distinguished. They are taxonomically superordinate (nonhyponymous), easily remembered and frequently used (salient), usually short and morphologically simplex (monolexemic), and not confined to a limited class of referents (non–context specific). Basic color terms are widely shared, usually designate only color, and are seldom recently borrowed. A basic color term names a "basic color category."

2. The speakers of any language will focus basic color categories on the same colors, a specific 30% of the Munsell array. Foci will vary as much within a language as between languages. There are eleven universal "focal colors."

3. Some languages name only two focal colors, some name all eleven, and others an intermediate number. A language will employ from two to eleven basic color terms.

4. The number of basic color terms in a language predicts the focal colors that it names, which implies a seven-stage sequence through which basic color terms evolve in any language that elaborates them, figure 2.1. Grey may be encoded "prematurely."

5. The stage of basic color-term evolution manifested by a particular language correlates loosely with the societal complexity of its speakers.

6. The invariability of eleven focal colors suggests a physiological determinant, and the evolutionary sequence suggests the same.

7. The range of a basic color term "extends" beyond its focus; for example, at Stage I "white" extends to high brightness, "black" to low bright-

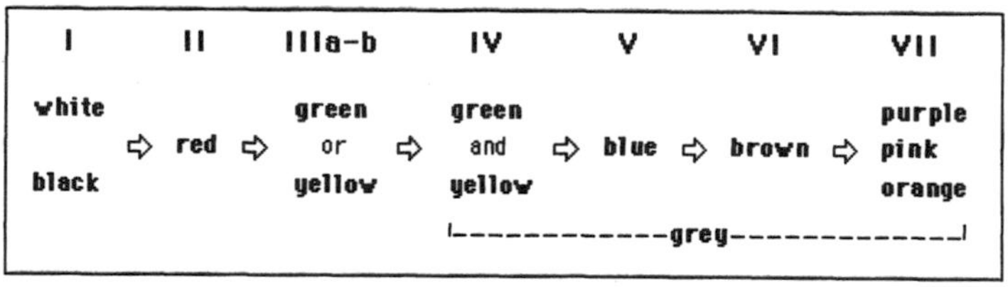

I	II	IIIa–b	IV	V	VI	VII
white		green	green			purple
⇨ red ⇨		or ⇨	and ⇨	blue ⇨	brown ⇨	pink
black		yellow	yellow			orange
			⌐――――――――grey――――――――⌐			

FIGURE 2.1. Berlin and Kay's 1969 sequence of basic color-term evolution.

ness. However, "in marked contrast to the foci, category boundaries proved to be so unreliable, even for an individual informant, that they have been accorded a relatively minor place in the analysis. *Consequently, whenever we speak of color categories, we refer to the foci of categories, rather than to their boundaries or total area,* except when specifically stating otherwise" (1969:13, emphasis original).

8. An illusion of cross-linguistic relativity is created by the different numbers of basic color terms in distinct languages; it is reinforced by differences among boundaries. The illusion is further enhanced by language-specific proliferation of nonbasic terms.

9. A color category is the application of a color term to a focal percept that is neurally determined. Basic color terms are universal because neurology determines that there is no other way to see. "In sum, our two major findings indicate that the referents for the basic color terms of all languages appear to be drawn from a set of eleven universal perceptual categories, and these categories become encoded in the history of a given language in a partially fixed order" (1969:5).

10. Color-category evolution is movement toward full linguistic expression of panhuman categories that exist in perception prior to naming. Evolution is purposively directed at this predetermined goal. The change is evolutionary because as society becomes complex lexical elaboration is functionally useful, if not indispensable, to the individual and to the society.[6]

Berlin and Kay phrase their propositions in diametric opposition to relativism as a genre, but without distinguishing the views represented by Ray from the kind reflected by Geddes and Klineberg (quoted §2.3). By dismissing boundaries as "unreliable," Berlin and Kay avoid having to account for the difference between systems that emphasize brightness and those that emphasize hue. In Conklin's (1973:937) words, "In the key New Guinea case cited by Berlin and Kay (pp. 23–25), it is noteworthy that lower-level 'reds' are 'black' in Jalé, but 'white' in Danian (cf. Heider

1972*a*)." Berlin and Kay's "Stage III*b*" (1969:30, fig. 13*c*, 67–73) is a residual class harboring yellow-focused categories of every range—yellow, yellow-with-green, and yellow-green-blue: they found too much difference between languages to justify lumping all such cases into one type. Their depiction of Stage III*b* (1969: fig. 13*c*), represented by Ibo, leaves blank unique green and blue at middle brightness. (See fig. 2.31 of Tifal and note 28 herein.)

Berlin and Kay (1969) received sixteen book reviews and data-oriented discussions prior to 1974, apart from stimulating eight tests in the field (listed in Maffi 1991; e.g., Gartell 1971; Mitsunobu 1972; Panoff-Eliet 1971). Skeptics criticized the sample (Hickerson 1971; Durbin 1972) and the lack of explanation (Newcomer and Faris 1971; Conklin 1973), which, respectively, the WCS and MCS have since attempted to address. The aforementioned Hickerson and Conklin, along with McNeill (1972), queried Berlin and Kay's data from Pukapuka and Arunta, which name all of yellow, green, and blue with one term, and from Daza, whose terms for these colors differ by a phonological feature. Hickerson (1971) insisted that her report of yellow-green-blue in Lokono was reliable (1953); Bright (1952:56) described the same range in Karuk of Northern California, but it was seemingly centered in blue (1957:390 [item 1469.4 "blue, green, yellow, 'like bile'"], 408, 449). McNeill (1972:30) cited Chiri's (1953) report of Ainu "blue-yellow" (that Hattori [1964:283] confirms as 'blue-green-yellow' in four dialects) and added Indo-European historical cases:

> . . . in Russian, *plovyj* refers to both *blue* and *yellow* (Vasmer 1955: 395). The same meaning is also shared by *plowy* in Polish (Brückner 1957:422) and *plavy* in Czech (Machek 1957:372). Miklosich lists a Proto-Slavic term *polvu* meaning both 'blue' and 'yellow.' . . .
> In Latin, *flavus*, meaning 'yellow' and 'blond' corresponds to *blao* 'blue' in Old High German, *bla* 'yellow' in Medieval German and *blau* 'blue' in Modern German (André 1949; Walde and Hofmann 1938:513).

There were reports of green-with-yellow categories (Gatschet 1879*b*: 482; see Saunders's [1992*a*:154] reference to Dawson 1887).[7] According to Rivers (1901*c*:46), "In an Australian tribe, from the district of Seven Rivers, on the eastern shore of the Gulf of Carpentaria, several natives only used three color epithets; red, purple and orange were called by the same name, 'oti'; white, yellow and green were called 'yopa', while black, blue, indigo and violet were all called 'manara'. Other natives from an adjoining

tribe used the names 'owang', 'wapok' and 'unma' in the same sense . . ."
Almqvist (1883:47) found the Siberian Chukchi to name 'yellow-green-blue' at different emphases and levels of brightness with *utera, tschäaro, tau-*, and *dlilil* 'galle (bile)'. Zahan (1972:366, from a draft of Caprile 1974) translates, "we find that among the M'bay of Moïssala in the Republic of Tchad the following colours are classified as red: pink, light pink, mauve, yellowish green, bright green, yellow, orange and warm brown; white includes: light grey, light green, light beige; and under black we find: grey, dark grey, very dark red, dark green, medium blue, dark blue, and dark brown." Rather than accept some reports while rejecting others, Berlin and Kay in 1975 joined with their positive critic Merrifield (1971) to propose the World Color Survey, the object of which was to improve the sample by verifying with Munsell interviews a variety of current color-naming systems.[8]

2.4.1. The 1975 Hue Sequence

Meanwhile, investigators followed up with Munsell interviews in eight languages, confirming each of the seven stages but not reporting yellow-with-green, yellow-green-blue, or any other unpredicted system: Stage I, Dani of Irian Jaya (Heider 1972*a*); Stage II, Bellonese of Polynesia (Kuschel and Monberg 1974); Stage III*a*, Aguaruna of Amazonian Peru (Berlin and Berlin 1975);[9] Stage III*b*, Binumarien of Papua New Guinea (Hage and Hawkes 1975); Stages III*a* – VII, Futunese of Polynesia (Dougherty 1975); Stages IV – V, Eskimo of Canada (Heinrich 1974); Stages IV – VII, Aguacatec of Guatemala (Harkness 1973). These supplement Berlin's (MS-1) interviews of forty Tzeltal, reported as Stage IV (1970; Berlin and Kay 1969).

First, these studies showed that speakers of a single language could represent different stages of Berlin and Kay's sequence; variation presages evolutionary change (Kay 1975; Dougherty 1977). Second, each of these languages, whatever its stage(s), could name all 330 Munsell colors with its basic color terms. Evolution, therefore, consists of lexically partitioning categories rather than applying basic terms to focal colors that previously were not named or were named fortuitously or indefinitely.

Berlin and Kay revised the sequence as shown in figure 2.2. At early stages some terms cover three or two focal colors, but it is predictable which colors will be combined as a category: Stage I *light-warm* (including white, red, yellow), *dark-cool* (black, green, blue); Stage II *white, warm* (red, yellow), *dark-cool;* Stage III*a white, warm, black, cool* (green, blue) or Stage III*b white, red, yellow, dark-cool;* Stage IV *white, red, yellow, black,*

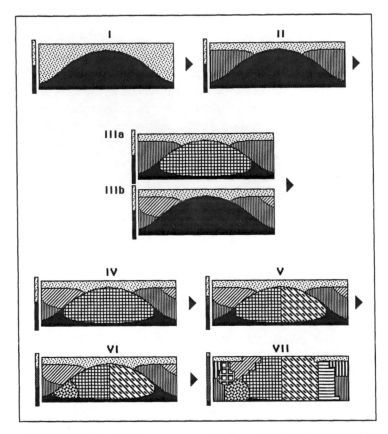

FIGURE 2.2. The 1975 hue sequence (Berlin and Berlin 1975; Kay 1975).

cool; Stage V *white, red, yellow, black, green, blue;* Stage VI adds *brown;*
Stage VII adds *purple, pink,* and *orange. Grey* remains wild.

Finally, these new data may now allow us to restate the evolutionary
progression of the linguistic recognition of the eleven universal perceptual color foci in a way which expresses the relationship of foci
to one another assuming an original dichotomy of light-warm versus
dark-cool: (1) At Stage I, the warm-light category, encompassing the
universal foci of *white, red, yellow, brown, orange, purple,* and *pink,*
is lexically opposed to a category comprised of the cool-dark foci,
black, green, and *blue.* High brightness *greys* are included in the
warm-light category, low brightness *greys* in dark-cool. Foci for both
of these two primordial categories are fluid and unstable, though we
may now speculate that *red* tends to dominate WARM-LIGHT and that

black tends to dominate COOL-DARK. This position would be in keeping with Heider's results for the Dugum Dani. (2) At Stage II, WARM-LIGHT begins to separate into two linguistically distinct categories. The original term for WARM-LIGHT becomes more restricted to high-brightness chromatic hues with *white* becoming focal. A new term emerges and becomes firmly established in focal *red* with extensions into the chromatic warm hues. *Black* continues to become focal for COOL-DARK, though it is still floating at this time. (3) At Stage III, two possible developments may occur: The COOL-DARK category may divide (Stage IIIa), leading to the emergencc of GRUE. The ancient unity of *black, blue,* and *green* may still be recognized, however, by the extension of black into these cool chromatic hues. Focal GRUE may be either *blue* or *green.*

The WARM-LIGHT chromatic category dominated by focal *red* may divide (Stage IIIb) leading to the emergence of *yellow.* The cool-dark category in Stage IIIb systems remains essentially unchanged from that of Stage II. (4) At Stage IV, Stage IIIa systems will encode focal *yellow* while Stage IIIb systems will encode GRUE, the latter finding a focus, as before, in either *blue* or *green.* (5) At Stage V, undifferentiated GRUE will divide. The new category may encode either *blue* (if *green* was focal in the GRUE period) or *green* (if *blue* was focal in GRUE). (6) At Stage VI, focal *brown* will emerge from the WARM-LIGHT category. (7) At Stage VII, focal *purple, pink, orange,* and *grey* will become encoded in no particular order (Berlin and Berlin 1975:84–85).

Specific recognitions include (1) "floating" foci in categories of "warm-light" and "cool-dark," (2) "the ancient unity of the cool-dark category" persisting after "grue" (or cool) emerges, and (3) a "grue" focus in either green or blue. But the major change is to resolve category boundaries in favor of hue and at the expense of discounting the contribution that brightness makes to the meaning of some color terms. By ignoring brightness, they make the hypothesis fully consistent with "eleven universal perceptual categories" that are linguistically recognized one by one as the evolution of color terms proceeds. The 1975 sequence excludes reports that are not collected with Munsell chips, for example, "The Fitzroy River aborigines studied by Rivers (1901a) have four terms, *bura* 'white', *guru* 'black, blue, indigo', *kiran* 'red, purple', and *kalmur* 'yellow, green, orange, blue-green'," which Berlin and Kay (1969:30) had classed as Stage IIIb.

Kay (1975:258–259, figs. 2–3) consolidates this position with a diagram that excludes the Stage I Jalé system and features the Dani type as the

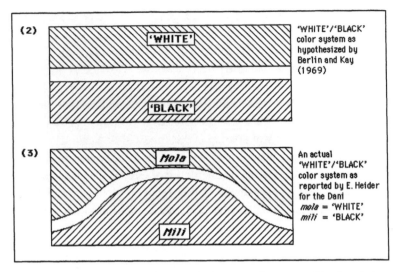

FIGURE 2.3. Paul Kay's revision: "the boundary between *mili* and *mola* is roughly that shown in (3) rather than that hypothesized in Berlin and Kay (1969:17) and reproduced as (2)." A redrawn facsimile of Kay 1975:figs. 2–3.

only Stage I, figure 2.3 (cf. Conklin 1973:937, quoted in §2.4). The diagram commits to boundaries that skirt specific triads of pure hues and pure black or white and that are determined by these perceptions. Dougherty (1975: 14–17, 136–138) and Branstetter (1977: fig. 2), while they trained under Berlin and Kay, diagrammed the sequence of boundary divisions as they appear in figure 2.2; Kay and McDaniel (1978:616, fig. 3) republished Kay's figures 2–3.[10]

2.4.2. Fuzzy Sets and Neural Response Categories

The 1975 revision required a formal model of categorization that would do more than specify that universal perceptual foci are named in a constrained order. The model had to unite foci and boundaries by one expression, a need that Berlin and Kay (1969:13) had anticipated.

First, it is possible that the brain's primary storage procedure for the physical reference of color categories is concerned with points (or very small volumes) of the color solid rather than extended volumes. Secondary processes, of lower salience and intersubjective homogeneity, would then account for the extensions of reference to points in the color solid not equivalent to (or included in) the focus. Current formal theories of lexical definition are not able to deal naturally with such phenomena. If empirical results of this kind accumulate, simple Boolean function theories of lexical definition will have to be revised in favor of more powerful formalisms.

Kay and McDaniel (1975, 1978) applied to color categories Zadeh's (1965) fuzzy-set calculus, building upon four prior developments. First, Lakoff (1973) had paved the way by experimenting with the formalism in linguistic semantics (cf. Hersh and Caramazza 1976; Kempton 1978); gradation of meaning was a venerable issue (Bolinger 1961; Labov 1973; Sapir 1958). Second, Rosch (1973a–b, 1975b) had developed evidence that categories of color, as of many objects and concepts, were graded in structure (§1.1). Third, McDaniel (1972) and Zollinger (1972) had related Hering's (1920 [1878]; Hurvich and Jameson 1957) nineteenth-century model of opponent post-retinal neural processes to Berlin and Kay's proposals of color-category universals; the vision researchers De Valois and Abramov (1966; cf. De Valois and De Valois 1975) had revised Hering's model on the basis of an analogue they had monitored in the optical nerve of macaque monkeys. Fourth, the psychologists Sternheim and Boynton (1966) had confirmed a parallel to the model of macaque vision in color-naming experiments with humans.

In the simple 1975 version of opponent-process theory, one nonopponent and two opponent neuron classes convey signals from the retina to the cortex, where they are sensed as brightness or hue. The nonopponent class conveys sensations ranging from black to white with slow to fast rates of neuronal firing; intermediate rates result in perceptions of middle lightness. Each opponent class fires at a basal rate when not conveying signals. One of them conveys signals resulting in red sensation when firing faster than the basal rate, but it signals green when firing slower. The other class alternates signals resulting in yellow or blue. When the first class is not conveying information and the second class is firing fast, the observer senses pure yellow, because no input from the first channel contributes a percept of red to make the yellow orangish or a sense of green to give the yellow a lime tinge. The pure sensation is "unique yellow." The opponency likewise produces sensations of unique red, green, or blue. For these reasons, humans identify as unitary colors only white, black, and the four unique hues; we see other colors as blends of the elemental six.[11]

The opponency model seems to explain why none of the hue categories in Berlin and Kay's revised 1975 sequence contains red-with-green or yellow-with-blue: since these pairs cannot be seen at the same place and

time, they contrast or otherwise appear maximally distinct. The model explains why we can say "greenish blue" or "yellowish red" but never *"yellowish blue" or *"greenish red." Most important, it explains why we see
pure black and white and unique red, yellow, green, and blue as irreducible,
but we can analyze orange, chartreuse, turquoise, purple, pink, brown, or
grey as deriving, respectively, from blends of at least red-yellow, yellow-
green, green-blue, blue-red, red-white, yellow-black, or white-black. The
opponent-process model seems to account partially for Berlin and Kay's
neurally determined "focal colors," which are perceptually prior to linguistic expression in any language; to their thinking, a focus should at least be
a unique hue, pure white or black, or one of the perfectly balanced blends.
I say "partially" because unique hues have wider ranges than elemental
hues; Berlin and Kay refer only to the latter as "focal colors" in four of the
six major cases.

Sternheim and Boynton (1966) demonstrated unique hues by asking
subjects to name color with limited vocabularies; when deprived of "orange," they could name this color "red-yellow" or "yellow-red" but when
deprived of "red" or "yellow" they could not name pure red or yellow with
a compound containing "orange." Orange is perceived as a mixture, red or
yellow as irreducible.[12]

With support of the foregoing vision research, Kay and McDaniel
(1978) proposed that any color category is a smoothly graded fuzzy set in
which values of membership match inversely the degree to which any of
the six neurally determined "focal colors" intergrades with a neighboring
member of the six. In keeping with Berlin and Kay's notion that focal colors are perceptually prior to linguistic categorization, Kay and McDaniel
renamed these six the "neural response categories."[13]

Figure 2.4 illustrates how different kinds of color categories are composed by applying fuzzy-set logical operations to neural responses. Thick
lines represent operations, thin lines neural responses. The operations are
fuzzy-set union, fuzzy-set identity, and fuzzy-set intersection, which, respectively, apply to three or two, one, and zero neural response categories.
A "composite basic color category" is a union of three or two neural responses; a "primary basic color category" is an identity of one neural response; a "derived basic color category" is an intersection of two neural
responses that excludes both unique hues (or black or white in lieu of one
of them). The membership of any color in a category ranges from a maximum of 1.0 to a minimum of 0. In figure 2.4, for example, *a* represents a
primary basic color category that is formed by applying identity to the
neural response of unique green. Unique yellow and unique blue mark the
margins of the green category; unique green is its focus at a maximum

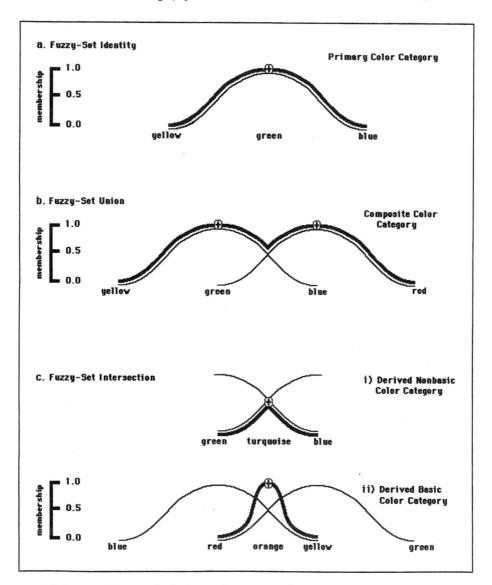

FIGURE 2.4. Fuzzy-set logical operations on neural response to wavelength.

membership of 1.0; and both yellowish green and bluish green are of medium membership at 0.5. In *b,* a composite basic color category is formed by applying union to the neural response of green or blue. Membership has dual maxima at *either* unique green *or* unique blue and dips to intermediate value both between these unique hues and between each of them and the zero-value margin at unique yellow or unique red. In *c,* a nonbasic derived color category of turquoise is formed by applying intersection to green and blue; its focus is found at the point where *both* unique green *and* unique blue contribute to an equal extent, although—with troubling disparity—both unique hues are precluded from the operation. Kay and McDaniel (1978: fig. 13) re-express the 1975 hue sequence as composite categories that initially divide into primary categories, subsequently joined by derived categories that emerge between them; derived categories of grey and brown may emerge "prematurely" before "green-or-blue" divides.[14]

The fuzzy-set model of color categorization induces eight problems:

1. How can intersection apply to unique hues when they are not included in the intersection? (How can the intersection of A and B not include A and B?) Should we suppose that a derived category is negatively composed in contrast to entities outside of it? To compose a category as intersecting hues while not including them means that a person must, nevertheless, keep them in mind. The model of categorization as intersection demands more theory than Kay and McDaniel offer.

2. Fuzzy-set logic does not provide the embedded frames of reference that would account for relative scales. The psychologists Mervis and Roth (1981) find that subjects rate specific colors at higher value of membership within a secondary category than within the basic category that includes it; for example, a certain greenish blue will be rated at 0.8 in turquoise but only 0.3 in blue.

3. Fuzzy-set logic cannot address shrinkage of color categories, which causes a two-pronged problem. First, Kay and McDaniel had to supersede Zadeh's formalism to model derived basic color categories, such as (*d*) the orange category in figure 2.4. They doubled the value of the red *and* yellow intersection because people feel that the orange focus has a value of membership in the orange category that is as high as the value of unique red or unique yellow in those categories. A fuzzy-set intersection is capable of representing the maximum of a derived category at only half the value attained by the primary categories from which it is derived, as the figure represents the maximum of nonbasic turquoise in *c*. Second, in English and in other languages that name orange and purple with basic terms, the primary basic red category is not strictly a fuzzy-set identity; violet colors between maximum purple and elemental blue cannot be called *red* or categorized as red, even though they are perceived to contain red; nor can saffron colors between maximum orange and elemental yellow, even though they too contain perceivable red. This assertion does not contradict the findings of Sternheim and Boynton (1966), because their subjects named orange only with the compounds "yellow-red" or "red-yellow." Chaucer groped in his

Middle English to innovate a term for colors that had been left without a name after the margins of Old English *geolo* and *reed* had retracted from orange.

> When Chaucer wishes to describe the colour of a fox, evidently find-
> ing *red* alone inadequate, he resorts to paraphrase: "His colour was
> bitwixe yelow and reed" (CT. VII. 2932). Similarly, the eyes of the
> gryphon-like Lyagurge in The Knight's Tale are conceived as the or-
> ange pupils of a bird of prey:
>
> > The cercles of his eyen in his head,
> > They gloweden bitwixen yelow and reed.
> > (CT. I. 2132)
>
> From usages of this kind, it appears that Chaucer is endeavoring
> to indicate a colour perception for which his language lacked a suit-
> able single term. There seems to have been a lexical gap which was
> later filled by the BCT *orange . . . Orange,* although used to denote
> the fruit, is not yet a part of the English colour lexicon (Burnley
> 1976:43–44)

4. As Kay and McDaniel (1978:630) regard the data, placement of foci in either green or blue or in both green and blue evidences the bimodal membership of the fuzzy-set union.

> In the experimental studies that have been conducted subsequent to
> B & K's work, it has been frequently observed (as B & K found for
> Tzeltal) that early-stage categories, including grue, are often multiply-
> focused. In these studies, focal grue selections have often proved to be
> bimodal, being chosen from both the focal blue and focal green re-
> gion. But grue has never been found to be focused in the intermediate
> blue-green region. The absence of focal choices from this intermedi-
> ate region is strong evidence that these colors have lower grue mem-
> bership values, and that grue has the membership structure stipulated
> by the fuzzy union analysis.

This argument glosses over differences between languages. In some, all speakers choose only blue foci, in others only green foci; in some, many speakers disjunctively choose both a green focus and a blue focus, and in others each speaker chooses only one focus, which may be either green or blue. Figures 2.5 and 2.7–9 display data that Kay and McDaniel had on hand; figure 2.6 adds fuller representation.

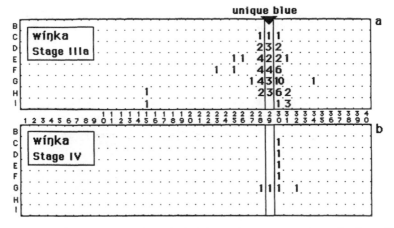

FIGURE 2.5. Aguaruna Jívaro foci of the cool category, *wíŋka*, at Berlin and Kay's Stages IIIa and IV, San Loreto, Peru, 1974, from Berlin and Berlin (1975: figs. 9 and 16); column 17 represents unique green, column 29 unique blue.

Figure 2.5 shows foci from 39 Aguaruna speakers, 34 at Stage IIIa and 5 at Stage IV (see fig. 1.3a for format). The number in each cell tallies the individuals who chose that color as a focus. The sum is 89 because individuals broadened foci over adjacent colors. None selected dual foci on nonadjacent colors. Almost all focused in blue.

Figure 2.6 shows that 16 Huastec Mayan speakers focused the cool category in green, one in blue. The Huastec foci were not available to Kay and McDaniel, although Harkness's (1973: figs. 5–6) normalizations of Mam Mayan cool-category foci are green.

Of forty Tzeltal speakers, ". . . thirty-one located the center of *yaš* in the green area and nine in the blue area . . ." (Berlin and Kay 1969:11–12). No Tzeltal focused the cool category in column 23 between green and blue (fig. 8.34a). None chose dual foci.

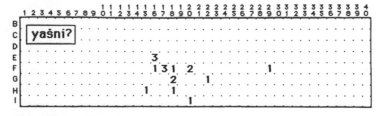

FIGURE 2.6. Huastec foci of the cool category, *yašni?*, Tantoyuca, Veracruz, Mexico, 1978, WCS.

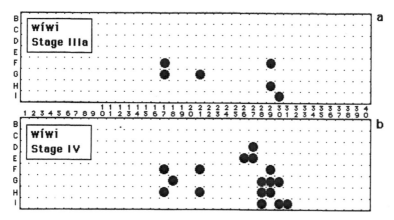

FIGURE 2.7. Futunese foci of the cool category, *wíwi,* at Stages IIIa and IV, West Futuna, Polynesia, from Dougherty (1975:figs. 2.11 and 2.18).

Figure 2.7 shows foci that Dougherty collected from Futunese speakers. She symbolized with dots the colors chosen as foci without indicating the number of individuals who chose each color. Doubtless more than one consultant chose the same chip, as there are fewer dots than subjects in her sample. Some dots represent dual foci, although the dual foci cannot be distinguished from others. Five Futunese speakers represent Stage IIIa: "two informants . . . placed the focus of *wíwi* in blue. Two others . . . placed the focus of *wíwi* in green. One informant . . . placed the focus of *wíwi* in both blue and green" (Dougherty 1975:47–48). Nineteen speakers represent Stage IV: "Four individuals . . . focus *wíwi* disjunctively in both green and blue, twelve . . . restrict the focus to blue and three . . . restrict the focus to green" (p. 56).

Figure 2.8 shows foci of (*a–b*) the Binumarien dark-cool category, which encompasses (*c*) a cool category. The Binumarien name the dark-cool category with two terms, *rundua* and *difeefee,* which are focused, respectively, in black and blue for the most part. It seems the Binumarien name the category differently when they regard it with emphases on black or blue. They focus the cool category in green.

> In this scheme, if two categories have the same range but differ in focus they are regarded as the same category. Thus if focal GREEN covers GREEN and BLUE and focal BLUE covers BLUE and GREEN, they are both BLUE-GREEN or in Berlin's term GRUE . . . Similarly, if focal BLUE covers BLUE, GREEN and BLACK, and focal BLACK covers BLACK, GREEN, and BLUE they are both BLACK or the "dark-cool" category . . . (Hage and Hawkes 1975:297)

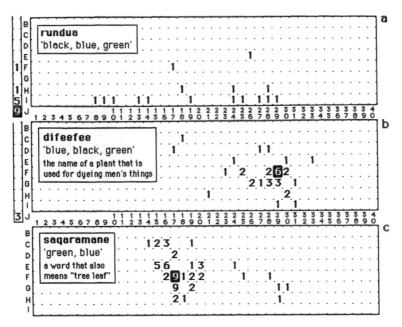

FIGURE 2.8. Binumarien foci of the dark-cool category, *rundua* and *difeefee,* and the cool category, *saqaramane,* East Central Highlands, Papua New Guinea, from Hage and Hawkes (1975:tables 2 and 3); darkened cells mark elemental colors: JØ, F17, F29.

Figure 2.9 shows the foci that Rosch's 40 Dani subjects volunteered for (*a*) light-warm and (*b*) dark-cool. Berlin and Berlin (1975:84–85 quoted in §2.4.1) call them "floating" foci, because only 5 of 80 choices match an elemental color point (G2). But the two focus aggregates show

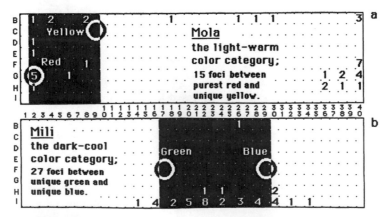

FIGURE 2.9. Dani foci of the (*a*) light-warm and (*b*) dark-cool categories, *mola* and *mili,* Grand Valley, Irian Jaya, Indonesia, 1969, from Heider (1972*a*:table 2).

a significant difference in pattern: 15 of the 40 light-warm foci fall between unique red and unique yellow; 27 of the 40 dark-cool foci fall between unique green and unique blue, clustering in the category center (15:25 versus 27:13 p<.01 chi square). Rosch elicited data with a half set of Munsell chips, omitting those of odd-numbered columns.

The fuzzy-set model fails to account for conspicuous language-specific differences between preferences for single foci in blue, single foci in green, single foci in either green or blue, and disjunctive dual foci. The model is at a loss to explain the "semantic emphases" that characterize Binumarien color terms of a shared range. Dani foci do not "float" but show different patterns between light-warm and dark-cool. Dani speakers focus the dark-cool category between unique hues, which fuzzy-set logic disallows. Such patterns deviate nonrandomly from neural response, even though the fuzzy-set theory perforce predicts that deviation of foci from "unique hue points" will be random.

5. While the fuzzy-set model does not explain or even describe the data in hand, it permits categories that would contravene the 1975 hue sequence if they were attested: "white-or-green," "yellow-or-green-or-white," "black-or-red," "yellow-or-red-or-black."

6. The fuzzy-set model does not impose a ceiling on the number of basic hue categories that people may tolerate, although psychologists and anthropologists have acknowledged cognitive limits in general (Miller 1956; Simon 1974; Wallace 1961).

"If no language investigated so far has more than eleven basic color terms, with the possible exception of Russian (see B & K, 35–36), this is more an accident of the present moment in world history than a theoretical inevitability. Russian goluboy 'light blue' (white + blue) is a potential instance of a twelfth basic color term; it is surely a basic term for some Russian speakers, though probably not for all. . . . it is possible that several now non-basic color terms in English . . . will become basic in the future, e.g. aqua/turquoise (green + blue), maroon/burgundy (black + red), and chartreuse/lime (yellow + green). . . . The process that characterizes derived category formation has not been logically exhausted by any known language; so there is no apparent reason to believe that the process will not continue, extending basic color-term lexicons beyond their present eleven terms (Kay and McDaniel 1978:640–641).

No close study of an advanced system substantiates more than eleven basic terms (al-Jehani 1990; Benhar and Zollinger 1974; Bolton 1978*a;*

Charencey 1899; Corbett and Morgan 1988; Frish 1972; Ikegami 1978; Johansen 1992; Mills 1984; Spense 1989; Stanlaw 1987; Uchikawa and Boynton 1987; van der Hoogt 1975; Wattenwyl and Zollinger 1981; Zarruk 1978).[15]

7. Neither traditional logic nor any of its derivatives, including fuzzy-set theory, incorporates a mover of category change, evolutionary or other. Burgess, Kempton, and MacLaury (1983, 1985) made the sole attempt to model as fuzzy sets color categories described ethnographically. Distributions of Tarahumara qualifiers and mappings separately substantiate graded structure in composite and primary categories. But all of the categories are skewed, which requires us to express lopsidedly the unimodal and the bimodal fuzzy-set curves. Skewing increases in correlation with independent evidence of advancing category division, such as innovation of a secondary term for colors of lowest membership value. In the cool category, the process of change first depresses and finally eliminates one half of the bimodal value curve, which seems to disregard the purported relation of neurally determined perception to membership contour. Although we did not link category skewing and division to specific cognitive dynamics, the Tarahumara data indicate the need to identify processes other than logical operations.

8. Neither classical logic nor its fuzzy-set offshoot specifies a relation between categories and the people who actively construct, maintain, and change them. The logics are represented as detached systems to be impassively applied to an observer-independent world.

Fuzzy-set calculus is under continuous development for use in engineering and artificial intelligence (McNeill and Freiberger 1993). It is the major articulate alternative to the model that I apply to Mesoamerican color categories. Apart from our venture with Tarahumara, only Zimmer (1982: figs. 2–12) used fuzzy sets to model color categories and, then, only to express introspection. Most 1970–1985 publications on color categorization address Berlin and Kay's 1969 hypothesis; a few take note of its 1975 revision.[16]

2.4.3. Semiotic Models

The color field has spawned models of categorization other than those set forth by Berlin, Kay, McDaniel, and Rosch. Whereas Berlin and Kay (1969) propose that people name universal perceptions directly, Kay and McDaniel (1978) add only that fuzzy logic mediates between neural response and naming. Rosch (see §1.1) similarly believes that category structure matches the correlational structure of the environment while family resemblances to a prototype derive directly from computation of shared attributes. The other models, including the one that I develop in Chapters 4–9, attribute categorization to processes that exceed the naming of unedited senses. Sahlins (1976) indicates that people must accomplish the meanings of color terms regardless of the universality of the perceptions that are named, whereas Turton (1981), Wierzbicka (1990, 1993), and Stanlaw (1987) take Sahlin's proposal a step further to specify how color categories—hence, the meanings of terms that name them—are constructed. But regardless of our shared mission, these models differ widely.

Sahlins notes that Berlin and Kay's claim of universal, predetermined color categories appears to challenge the autonomy of culture as well as the arbitrariness of the semiotic sign à la Ferdinand de Saussure. They reduce culture to nature, sign to signal, concept to percept, and cognition to recognition. But in Sahlin's view, perception supplies only the raw material that people variously invest with meaning; for example, Stage IIIa engages equipollent sensations of hue (e.g., warm versus cool) while Stage IIIb features a privative contrast of bright and projecting categories (red, yellow, white) against an ensemble of dark and receding sensations (dark-cool). Each arrangement is a culturally imposed structure making use of natural systems that otherwise would be insignificant. People formulate effective symbolism by incorporating the independent facts of their biology, as semiotic theory indeed demands.[17]

Turton (1980) bases his proposal on Lienhardt's (1961:12–13) notion of central themes in symbolism and Lévi-Strauss's (1963:77) structuralism: "It is not the resemblances but the differences that resemble each other." People may construct a system of categories by equating it with contrasts in another part of the environment that is exceptionally valued. The Mursi value their cattle, which they classify with compound lexemes that pair any one of seven basic color terms with any among various names of patterns. The color terms that name the distinct and limited colors of cows—white, black, reddish brown, yellowish brown, flesh, brown, and grey—also name decontextualized colors, respectively, white, black, red, yellow, pink, brown, and cool. (Many languages include grey in the cool category, as cited in note 5 of §8.3.) The cattle equation diverts Mursi basic color terms from Berlin and Kay's prediction that cool will divide before either brown or pink are named with basic terms; while cow hair offers brown and pinkish beige, it evinces nothing equivalent to the contrast of green versus blue. Yet, in accord with the structuralist formulation, the Mursi focus their abstract color categories on the pure and intense sensations stipulated by Berlin and Kay, not on the subdued shades that typify their herds. Turton suggests that his model may apply to the homologies that McNeill (1972), under a different premise, ascribes to environmental determinism (see note 19). Turton observes that other cultures may not constitute basic color categories by asserting a structural parity.

Wierzbicka (1990) offers a general account of color-term semantics. Meaning is what people "have in mind"—perhaps "in the depths" of their minds—when they use a word. A definition must characterize mental process in a way that specifies both centers and boundaries of color-term meanings, as well as their relations. First, one considers the image of a color, say BLUE, which some things are like. Next, one considers the fact that other things are not like this, such as things like GREEN. Finally, one makes an association between the image and a typical physical referent, such as the sky, which one may think of when seeing blue. One may make finer associations, such as the experience of having an impeded or unimpeded view, as do speakers of Polish or Russian when they name two categories of blue on an axis of dark to light. Overall, and "roughly speaking," color concepts are anchored in universal associations, such as day and night, fire, the sun, vegetation, the sky, and the ground.

On the positive side, Wierzbicka's hypothesis is clearly expressed and testable. On the negative, and to speculate prior to such tests, they may reveal diverse associations in some languages and none in others apart from an image of a color alone. Certainly, when color-term etymologies are transparent, they suggest, at least, that associations with distinctive colored parts of nature occurred when the word was adopted to abstract color-naming. The Karuk language derives all of its color terms by postpounding "-like" to a nature term that is otherwise unaltered (MacLaury 1992b). True to Wierzbicka, Karuk black is "night-like," brown is "soil-like," and green is "plant-like." But then red is "blood-like," yellow is "porcupine quill-like," white is "foam-like," blue is "smoke-like," and all of yellow, green, and blue is "bile-like." (This broad association of bile is recurrent in color terminology, e.g., Rivers 1901d: 148; Nichols 1980: 267). Hickerson (1972, 1975), who analyzes Rivers's (1901a) Murray Island color terms, finds that many are reduplications of otherwise unaltered nature terms: for example, black-with-blue from "cuttlefish," white from "lime," two reds from "blood" and "red ochre," two yellows from "turmeric" and "yellow ochre," green from "bile," and blue as *bulubulu*, which is not the "sky" term, has no reported association and is, perhaps, an English loanword. Wierzbicka (1993) repeats her program of identifying simple semantic elements of color terms but now adds emphasis to a difference between "point of reference" and "exemplar," an association versus a pure color image.

Points of reference can be multiple for terms of broad range, so English "blue" now has associations of both sky and water. Accordingly, she expands her 1990 universal association of fire to blood, night to charcoal. She expresses hope of showing that such "semantic elements" are primitives.

The problems are (1) to statistically differentiate widespread associations from local ones across a world sample, (2) to show that a significant number of basic color terms within the cross-linguistic sample harbor the hypothesized pervasive associations, and (3) to model formally how the associations interact with pure color images to account for the structure and ranges of particular color categories. (Why do some languages entertain such associations while others apparently do not?) Positive findings would not conflict with the model of color categories that I will advance in these pages, nor would negative findings.

Stanlaw (1987) puts forth an "extended features" model of color-category meaning which departs from the minimal contrasts and markerese that crippled classical feature theory (Katz and Fodor 1963). He amends Hinds's (1974) finding that each Japanese color term has a loan-word counterpart adopted from English to a native meaning. Some of the loans are lighter in range, many are restricted to manufactured or even foreign referents, a few are seldom used, and all are "stylish" in the sense of linking the user to prestige. Stanlaw extensively interviewed native speakers who plotted ranges and foci of the color-term pairs on the Munsell array, and he identified their emotive associations by means of Osgood, Suci, and Tannenbaum's (1957) semantic differential test. To take the Japanese purple category as an example, its native name includes features of dark and "traditional," as when one specifies the thread of a kimono, while the loan-word includes features of light and "modern," as when one refers to the label on a can of grape drink. The loan seems clever to men but women think it is silly.

In my model, I submit that people form color categories by adopting such features, associations, and images as the mental coordinates for points of view that they construct by analogy to the physical coordinates, fixed and mobile, with which they comprehend their positions in real terrain. Some of the coordinates are indispensable to any category, such as the emphases on similarity and difference; others are obligatory choices among universal options, such as elemental hue points, levels of brightness, or degrees of saturation; still others are entirely subject to cultural prescription, such as Stanlaw's features of traditional versus modern, Wierzbicka's associations with natural events, or Turton's contrasting cattle types. However, the main thrust of my vantage model is to specify how a color category is constituted, maintained, and altered, processes that transpire regardless of which perceptions, emphases, and ideas the category may incorporate. For this reason, I fully concur with those who propose that constructs from beyond the light sense contribute to color categories.

2.4.4. Surveys and Reformulation

During the 1980s at U.C. Berkeley, results came in from the World Color Survey, Mesoamerican Color Survey, and Pacific Northwest fieldwork. The mass of data would require reformulation of thinking. I began such a project with a cognitive account of Mesoamerican data (MacLaury 1986a), while Stanlaw (1987) independently conducted his interviews and psychological tests regarding emotive values and contextualization of Japanese color terms. Stanlaw, who trained under Dougherty, builds on the latter's universalist work while simultaneously addressing intricacies that relativists had faulted the Berlin-Kay model for ignoring (Kuschel and Monberg 1974; Turton 1978; Whiteley 1973). Both dissertations unite the interests of universalists and relativists.

Berlin, Kay, and Merrifield (1985) reported the new data at conferences (Kay, Berlin and Merrifield 1991a [1989]). Some of their graduate students and postdoctoral collaborators published all their work on color (Branstetter 1977; Dougherty 1975, 1977, 1978a–b, 1980; McDaniel 1972; Kay and McDaniel 1978; Kay and Kempton 1984; Boster 1986; Snow and Molgaard 1978). MacLaury and Stewart (1984) delivered a conference paper showing that in Mesoamerica basic binary categories can evolve before composite cool divides; a few can evolve before warm divides. I reported the Pacific Northwest yellow-with-green category and, after consulting with R. and K. De Valois, suggested additions to the physiological model that might explain why "cool" is universally last to divide and why yellow-with-green is rare (MacLaury 1987a; reviewed in §4.1.1). The other Northwest Pacific data, mostly from Salishan, are accessible (MacLaury 1986b, 1987a, 1988b, 1990; MacLaury and Galloway 1988; Galloway 1993). Kinkade (1988) reconstructed a Proto-Salishan yellow-green-blue category as the origin of contemporary yellow-with-green. Greenfeld (1986), after participating in the MCS, compared his Apache data with Dougherty's (1975) Futunese data to analyze the composition of "desaturation categories," which are often focused in grey but pertain throughout the color-solid core to emerge on the least saturated areas of its surface, such as brown, lavender, and beige. Maffi compiled a literature review (1989 ms), Berlin and Kay's (1991) bibliography, and two articles (1984, 1990).[18]

The concept of color categories as analogous points of view first appeared in limited circulation (MacLaury 1987*b*). Later, I published an article on color-category dynamics, minus the critical construct of viewpoint (MacLaury 1991*a*). A few years earlier, Saunders and Van Brakel (1988*a*–*b*, 1989*a*–*b*, 1991; also Saunders 1992*a*–*b* and Van Brakel 1991, 1992, 1993) had launched their postmodernist critique of universalist premises, emphasizing the role of multiple perspectives while questioning the evidence of unique hues. In their eyes, people lack fixed points of reference and can be molded to any thinking: widespread regularities of color categorization are conditioned by western influence.[19] Kay, Berlin and Merrifield (1991*b*) completed the World Color Survey and derandomized the data. It was time for someone in the universalist camp to issue an articulate account of all that had accrued from the WCS, MCS, and my work in the Pacific Northwest.

Kay, Berlin and Merrifield (1991*a:* fig. 3), in a "preliminary report," published a radical departure from the 1975 hue sequence, reproduced herein as figure 2.10. They proposed creating multilineal avenues of color-category evolution by expanding the sequence with the categories of yellow-with-green and yellow-green-blue; yet they omitted others, such as red-yellow-green-blue, white-with-black, and systems that combine yellow-with-green with any assortment of the composite categories acknowledged in 1975. Although they departed from their earlier model, they neither distinguished categories of brightness from categories of hue nor suggested how the two kinds might differ in the ways they evolve. Their uniform treatment of hue categories and yellow-green-blue appeared to call into question the Hering opponent-process model, which stipulates that yellow and blue are antagonistic and, thus, maximally distinct. Categorization of yellow and blue under one name would transgress the fundamental purpose of a category, which is generally understood to be the grouping of percepts that are similar. Thus, in the notable absence of qualification, evidence of yellow-green-blue categories would suggest that either the opponent-process model is a fable or the purpose of a category has been widely misunderstood. Kay, Berlin, and Merrifield's preliminary statement leaves the universalist approach in an indefensible position. Finally, the cluttered multilineal arrangement eclipses the legitimate finding of a single hue sequence, which the 1975 model expresses clearly (fig. 2.2 herein.), thus purveying a misimpression that the hue sequence has been supplanted.

There is a more elegant way of modeling the data: color category evolution begins with an emphasis on either brightness or hue but must always end with an emphasis on hue; brightness categories, such as yellow-green-

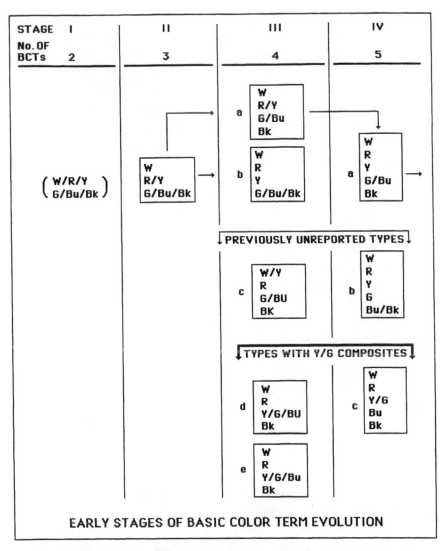

EARLY STAGES OF BASIC COLOR TERM EVOLUTION

FIGURE 2.10. Paul Kay's multilineal evolutionary classification, 1991. Redrawn facsimile from Kay, Berlin, and Merrifield (1991*a*: fig. 3).

blue, merge into the hue sequence, although change in the reverse direction has not been observed (MacLaury 1992*a:* fig. 19). People who categorize on the basis of brightness do not place enough emphasis on hue to enable its constraints to influence their category boundaries. Neural opponency can only determine the color categories of people who intend to categorize the hues. Under specific conditions, people can opt to categorize in reference either to brightness or to hue; under other conditions, hue categories will always predominate. Unlike the reviewers of Berlin and Kay's 1969 model, some who commented on my 1992 account asked how a progressive development of color categories could be called evolution (Toren 1992; Wescott 1992).

2.5. A Dynamic Model

To locate the Mesoamerican data in a worldwide design, I elaborate my (1992*a*) evolutionary sequence, explain why it is evolutionary, and support it with data from the World Color Survey (Kay, Berlin, and Merrifield 1991*b*) and other data, §2.6. The mainspring of my scheme is a shift of selective emphasis from similarity to distinctiveness. People progressively emphasize distinctiveness as their sociophysical environments become richer and more complex through time, which provokes proliferation of vocabulary throughout many domains, including that of color terms.

> The right basis for comparison is to insist on the unity of human experience and at the same time to insist on its variety, on the differences that make comparison worthwhile. The only way to do this is to recognize the nature of historical progress and the nature of primitive and of modern society. Progress means differentiation. Thus primitive means undifferentiated; modern means differentiated. Advance in technology involves differentiation in every sphere, in techniques and materials, in productive and political roles (Douglas 1966:77).
>
> World and classical languages thus provide richer resources for communicative subtlety than do local languages in that the former frequently offer a larger variety of names for a given thing, depending on the level of abstraction at which the speaker wishes to place his description and the features of the denotatum or denotata to which he wishes to draw attention (Kay 1977:24).

Malkiel (1941) considers the link between worldly process and lexical proliferation in a particular time and society:

> In the memory of man, there are few turnovers as radical as the one experienced by the Spanish from the end of the fifteenth century onward, for one or two hundred years. Inebriating discoveries and conquests in remote continents, peaceful and warlike intercourse of equal intensity with the rest of Europe, transmuted a hitherto inconspicuous country into the very focal point of the world. . . . Bright colors, shrill sounds, pungent flavors, exotic fragrances, fascinating merchandise,

accounts of dreamlike adventures must have excited the nerves and stimulated the sensual susceptibility of the average Spaniard. This tumultuous throng of fresh impressions immediately provoked the desire for an equivalent variety of expressions (p. 284).

Duncan (1975), with specific reference to color terms, shows that the lexical explosion of the Spanish Age of Discovery began its rise in the prior century, likely in response to the very reformulated thought that engendered the era: "The fourteenth century shows us also writers of *belles lettres* whose use of color terms is much greater than their predecessors" (p. 58). Ducatez and Ducatez (1980), in a study of the Arabian Classical Age, show that adjectives in general and color terms in particular became abstract "as new forms of urban sociability were coming into being" (p. 78).

Increasing attention to distinctiveness enables an individual to more effectively sort out novel experience and, in this sense, it is adaptive to environmental demand, social or physical. The mental change is evolutionary because it helps individuals and their society to cope with diverse circumstances. The expansion of vocabulary as a consequence of mental change is simultaneously adaptive, because it encodes and fosters the more differentiating and analytical worldview.[20]

Incremental growth of novel experience has been accelerating since the advent of the handax, but for untold millennia the increment was imperceptible during any person's lifetime. Over the past few thousand years, however, the pace has redoubled many-fold to become the astronomical rate of change experienced today (Clark 1992). Now the influx of novelty is felt almost everywhere. Peoples of formerly remote cultures are beginning to adapt mentally by shifting toward the analytical view, as others have done before them in what since have become worldly societies.

Wherever the shift progresses, people who primarily use brightness categories reconfigure them into hue categories, usually those of Berlin and Kay's Stage II, III or IV. As the shift advances, hue categories evolve through the 1975 sequence until basic units number eleven. With further change, speakers name abundant secondary hue categories by object metonymy (e.g., *mustard*) or linguistic borrowing (e.g., *écru*) (Casson 1994).

People who attend strongly to similarity may be inclined to categorize brightness, whereas those who attend strongly to distinctiveness mainly categorize hue. Thus, brightness categories will tend to precede hue categories in evolutionary order. The physiological basis may be that neural channels conveying luminance respond faster than those conveying hue sensations; thus brightness is the first impression when experiencing color. It takes greater acuity to sort out the second impression of hue.[21]

Although speed of luminance channels is integral to opponent processes, models of color categorization have not exploited channel speed; this physiology assists explanation only when combined with selective emphases on similarity and on distinctiveness—the cognitive aspects of categorization.

Finally, as will be elaborated in §4.1, some unique hues, such as red and yellow, are perceived to differ more from each other than hues of other pairs, such as green and blue. As people increasingly emphasize difference, they first separately categorize the former pair and last separate the latter; the warm category universally divides before the cool category. Again, this dynamic makes sense only if it includes the shift of selective attention.

The universal consequence of this color-category evolution is sketched

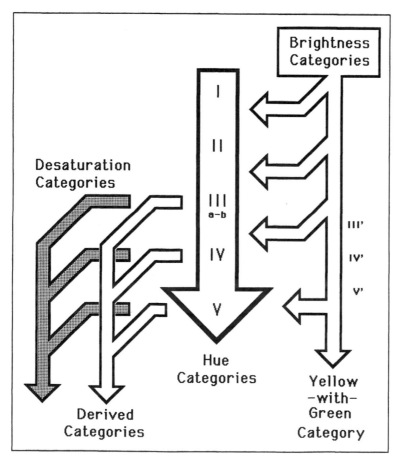

FIGURE 2.11. Basic color-category evolution depicted schematically in two dimensions.

abstractly in figure 2.11 and representationally in figure 2.12; examples follow in figures 2.13–33. The figures and examples underrepresent the worldwide variety of brightness categories and desaturation categories, which assume many combinations and types. Binary categories occur in any combination of 2, 3, 4 or 5, and they co-occur with desaturation categories. However, the hue sequence is least complicated; its Stage I through V are of the 1975 order, which preserves the heart of Berlin and Kay's earlier and long-standing proposal.

Figure 2.11 schematizes the universal development of color categorization as four trends. First, the five composite-to-elemental hue stages are as Berlin and Kay described them in 1975; abundant data show that they constitute the contemporary core of universal color-category evolution. Providing that people have decided that hue is what they will categorize, the configuration of categories represented by Stage I through V shows less difference between languages than do configurations among other kinds of color categories. We recently collected data from Lani (fig. 2.13), a language related to Dani, in which Heider (1972a) reported Stage I. Lani usage of Stage I hue categories corroborates Heider's description. If these Danian systems evolve, they may undergo Stage I through V.

Second, broad categories of brightness merge with the hue sequence at any of Stages I through V. The formal account (MacLaury 1992a: figs. 8–10) plots this process closely in terms of four kinds of categories: types D, C, B, and A. (These uppercase letters differ from the lower case *a*, *b*, *c*, and *d* that distinguish figures.). A category of type D pertains only to brightness; type C pertains mainly to brightness but somewhat to hue; type B pertains mainly to hue but somewhat to brightness, and type A pertains only to hue. Full explanation of this sequence requires other information and theory (see Appendix VIII or MacLaury 1992a). Its critical points are: (1) Any brightness category becomes a hue category by evolving through the typology toward type A; (2) As a single system transforms emphasis from brightness to hue, different color categories will represent different types such that the typology applies to individual categories rather than to the complete system; (3) Therefore, a transitional system can include all of category types A, B, C, and D, although a fully transformed system will include only type A; and (4) It appears impossible to predict the specific stage of the hue sequence at which a brightness system will complete its merger into a system of hue with all of its categories becoming type A (the unpredictability is addressed in §12.1.2.1). Casson and Gardner (1992) document the intracategorical transitions in Old English and in Paliyan; both systems include several category types at once.

Third, in some languages and linguistic areas, a brightness category of yellow-green-blue becomes a type A yellow-with-green category, which is not among the stages of the widely recurrent hue sequence. Salish languages of the Pacific Northwest offer a classic example (fig. 2.33). Figure 2.11 treats the yellow-with-green hue category as an exception to Berlin and Kay's 1975 evolutionary order; the figure allows that yellow-with-green can co-occur in a system with a warm, a dark-cool, and/or a cool category, or it can remain as the only composite. These combinations constitute exceptional Stages IIIa', IIIb', IV$'$, and V$'$.

Fourth, binary categories tend to become basic seldom at Stages IIIa or IIIb, frequently at Stage IV, and so commonly thereafter that systems of only the six elemental basic categories are rare, at least in Mesoamerica. Usually, binary categories emerge to encompass colors that are left uncategorized at the margins of composite or elemental categories as they contract (Burnley 1976, quoted §2.4.2; cf. Krieg 1979:431); increased attention to distinctiveness encourages this shrinkage and the subsequent innovation that fills the gaps. Desaturated categories, described by Dougherty (1975) and Greenfeld (1986) as naming a broad core of desaturated and blended color, do not appear in all languages. When they emerge, however, they begin to show up at Stage IIIa or IIIb, often reach full development at Stage IV, and may diminish or become redefined as evolution progresses.

In overview, figure 2.11 suggests that early stages of the hue sequence and brightness categories are disappearing throughout the world, while later stages, binary categories, and desaturated categories are proliferating. The WCS did not find any language at Stage I. This part of the evolution would be first to disappear anywhere, and at this early phase people would be most likely to disregard hue while categorizing brightness, thus never forming Stage I hue categories. But the WCS did not locate a Stage I brightness system either.

Figure 2.12 expresses the evolution with simulations. Its "brightness sequence" fails to represent the vast variety of possibilities documented by the WCS. Five brightness systems are diagrammed in MacLaury (1992a: figs. 11–18) and another nine appear in figures 2.16a and 2.25–32. Individual variation abounds within each; diagonal arrows represent the merger of brightness categories with hue categories, which each become type A from a starting point of type D, C, or B. Letters over each system express this trend among categories as an abstract average, even though different categories in one system will be of distinct types. At the top of the brightness sequence, under type D, the ranges of two terms are liberally intermixed. Next, in the first of three depictions of type C, a third term names a band of middle brightness with concentration in red. In the second type C system, the third term expands over warm colors while a fourth term domi-

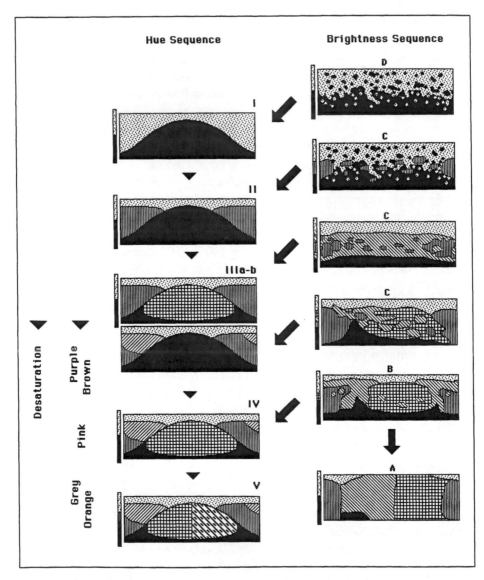

FIGURE 2.12. Basic color-category evolution represented by simulated systems.

nates the middle band. In the last type C system, the third term names a warm hue category while the fourth term and a fifth name a category of yellow-green-blue with distinct concentrations in yellow and cool. Next, under type B, only the fourth term maintains a slight emphasis on brightness. At bottom, under type A, the system has reconfigured into a hue system with a Salishan-style yellow-with-green category (fig. 2.33). At any phase, all categories of brightness can merge with the hue sequence. At left, binary categories are represented in the order of purple, brown, pink, grey, and orange, which MacLaury and Stewart (1984) found to be the most common implicational order; however, unlike the hue sequence, the order of binary categories is only a tendency. A desaturation category is also represented.

The proposal of figures 2.11–12 situates the 1975 hue sequence in the greater scheme of variation. This formulation does not isolate the 1975 model but shows how systems that depart from it are, nevertheless, related to it. Overall, I hope to defuse the consuming controversy over whether the hue sequence is valid. Indeed it is, even though other ways of categorizing color abound! With this understanding in the background, each of the other systems may be studied in its own right without the obligation to dominate every analysis of color categorization with pro-or-con reference to an evolutionary hue sequence.

2.6. World Overview

The figures that follow exemplify common stages of the hue sequence, binary categories and desaturation categories, different configurations of brightness categories, transitional categories, Salishan yellow-with-green, and another apparent exception to the hue sequence (fig. 2.26).

Figure 2.13 represents the only data in this book that were not elicited with Munsell chips. Those in *a* were elicited with Berlin and Kay's (1969) paper chart and those in *b–d* with Nick Hale's (1989) chart, which is enclosed herein and, until it fades, will provide the reader with exactly the stimuli used in the interviews of Lani speakers. Apart from Heider's aggregated foci of figure 2.9, these are the only stimuli-array elicitations on record of Stage I systems that are shared by most speakers of a language. Jones and Meehan (1978:27) describe in cultural context the Anbarra use of *-gungaltja* 'brilliant' and *-gungundja* 'dull'. In *a,* their figure 2 is redrawn, showing the result of their sole formal interview.

Tests on the Munsell a-chromatic scale showed that *-gungaltja* referred to only rows C, B, A bright levels (fig. 2). On the other hand *-gungundja* extended from row J (black) through to row E, thus including all of the 'greys' (fig. 2). Further confirmation that the *-gungundja* / *-gungaltja* dichotomy occurs high up on the brightness scale came when we asked our informants to indicate the deployment of the two terms of the chromatic chart. At first, Gurmanamana said that there were no *-gungaltja* colours there at all and pointed from the chart to a piece of reflective foil used for cooking, lying on a bench in the tent. Conklin's comments that the Berlin and Kay's test colours are all in the 'surface mode' are relevant here (1973:933). The true -*gungaltja* colours require a touch of brilliance or 'animation' as well as a high degree of brightness. Having made his protest, Gurmanamana then proceeded to outline the approximate boundary of the -*gungaltja* colours as shown on fig. 2. It can be seen that only about 10% of the colour chips are included in this category, the main bulk of the chart belonging to the -*gungundja* class.

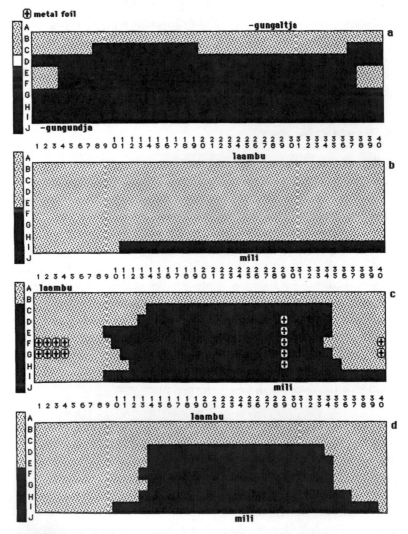

FIGURE 2.13. (*a*) Anbarra Gidjingali, Blyth River, Arnhem Land coast, Australia, 1972, male, late middle age, adapted from Jones and Meehan (1978:fig. 2), stimulus: Berlin and Kay's 1969 paper chart; (*b*–*d*) Danian Lani, Grand Valley, Irian Jaya, 1992, m 15, m 50, m 45 (collected by Wesley Dale), stimulus: Nick Hale's 1989 paper chart, herein.

The authors' numerical Munsell notation of 8, 9, 10, 1, and 6 for color-array rows is replaced with "row" plus capital letters, C, B, A, then J and E, which make their notation consistent with that used throughout this book and, thus, easier to comprehend. My redrawing squares the sweeping curves of their depiction of word boundaries. They imply that the Anbarra name color as spectral light rather than as surface reflectance (see Appendix III), which would be more effectively investigated with another instrument than Munsell chips or its paper copy. Yet, after expressing his preference, the consultant adapted his color naming to the reflective stimuli. His system comes close to fitting the simulation of type D that appears in the upper right of figure 2.12, although, unlike the simulation, his data show little chip-by-chip interspersion of responses; he mapped over a whole array and did not name chips one at a time.[22]

Wesley Dale elicited the Lani data with the Hale array after Munsell chips failed to reach him by mail. He cut a chip-size rectangle in a neutral card and passed this aperture over the array while each of his ten consultants named the chips in horizontal sequence one at a time. From some he elicited foci, while others could not decide on any. By a third procedure (§3.1), he collected mappings of *laambu* and *mili* from two consultants, which matched faithfully the Stage I hue naming of *c* and *d*. But three of his helpers named the chips as in *b*, covering at least 90% of the array with *laambu* and applying *mili* to only black and grey or, as in *b*, to dark as well. But one of the three mapped the two terms as a Stage I hue contrast of light-warm versus dark-cool, the configuration in which chips are named in *c* and *d*. Four others named the chips with five or six terms and one named them with twelve. Speakers *b* and *d* declined to focus *laambu* and *mili*, while speaker *c* focused them broadly (and differently than Dani foci on single chips, figure 2.9). These intriguing data suggest that, at a particular level of concentration, the Lani name luminous color as simulated by type D at the upper left of figure 2.12. But on another level, they name reflective samples as hue, showing Berlin and Kay's Stage I (figs. 2.12, 2.2 and 2.3 bottom). On their most differentiating level, they show variation similar to that among the Australian Martu Wangka, who apply *yakuri yakuri* to green-with-yellow, green, or green-with-blue (fig. 2.26). The multiterm Lani data are not diagrammed, however, as they are only responses to the paper chart.

Limited information is available about Stage I and its type D counterpart. The provider of Berlin and Kay's (1969: fig. 11, 47) Jalé two-term brightness system is deceased. Sloane's (1989:205) source for her Igbo (Ibo) two-term report was a visiting Nigerian musicologist at Yale University who is no longer there; although his personal communication to Sloane differs from reports of Igbo color as Stage IIIb (Berlin and Kay 1969:71; Wescott 1970: chart I), Igbo color terms may apply differently at distinct levels, as do the Lani terms. Also, Igbo may involve dialectical variation. Dixon's (1982:4) citation of Welmers's analysis of Igbo (1973; Welmers and Welmers 1969) corroborates Sloane. Dixon presents Alambak of Sepik district, New Guinea, as having only "black" and "white" (p. 41). Stapleton's (1903:255) report of Ngombe color, justifiably typed by Berlin and Kay (1969:48) as Stage I, describes five transparent color terms of restricted range. Hulstaert (1969) reports that Mongo, a Bantu language, uses two basic terms to name a Stage I hue-brightness system, optionally names "rouge vif" with a third term, and names other restricted hue ranges with reduplicated, compounded, and transparent terms. Color terms on Vaitupu of the Ellice Islands principally contrast light and dark but also include nature terms that name contextualized experiences of middle brightness, iridescence, and sheen (Kennedy 1931:102–103). Berlin and Kay's (1969: 48–51) treatment of Paliyan as Stage I is a misclassification of a five-term system of both luminance and brightness categories (Gardner 1966; Casson and Gardner 1992: figs. 1–3). Wierzbicka (1990:115) identifies Australian Luritja as a light-dark Stage I language, thanking Ian Green for the information. These data, together with Heider's account (1972a; fig. 2.9) and Bromley's (1967:305–06) Danian lexicostatistic tables, tender all that we in academia know about Stage I and its type D counterpart. This is pathetically little in comparison to what such early systems suggest of the options that people select as they categorize their impressions of color and light.[23]

Figure 2.14 displays Ejagam Stage II hue systems, whose contours skirt the elemental colors in the predicted manner in spite of minor variation between speakers. Speaker (d) names yellow with secondary ogok and awawa, suggesting evolution toward Stage IIIb. Stages IIIa and IIIb are straightforwardly represented in the WCS by individuals, as in figures 2.16b and 2.32c, but not by a majority in any language—at least not in an uncomplicated way (see fig. 2.24)—even though Berlin and Berlin (1975) and Hage and Hawkes (1975) described Stages IIIa and IIIb, respectively. Figure 2.15 shows Colorado Stage IV systems, which give the misimpression of simplicity; other Colorado speakers name a desaturation category, lopoban, with characteristic variation, including continuous applications through brown and purple as well as a readaptation of the category to blue.

Figure 2.16 exhibits a standard development of the desaturation category in Tucano, borojaro. Speaker (b) at Stage IIIa shows its incipient development in grey (EØ) and lavender (E31) with a grey focus (FØ).

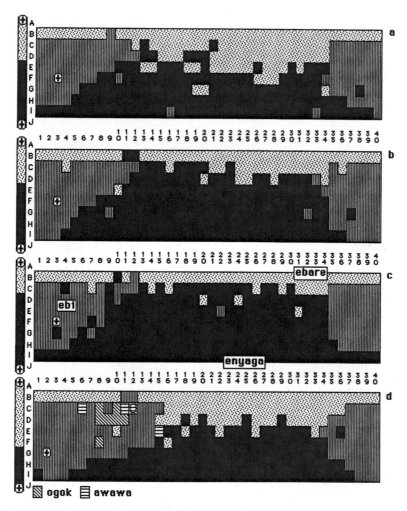

FIGURE 2.14. Ejagam, Kembong, Cameroon, 1976: (*a*) f 65, (*b*) f 50, (*c*) f 80, (*d*) m 80 (WCS 11, 10, 13, 2).

Speaker (*c*) at Stage IV shows its full development in grey (FØ), brown (G9), lavender (D33), and beige (C5), with a brown focus (I9). Speaker (*d*), also Stage IV, shows exceptionally strong development focused in light blue (C28) and extending throughout white, grey, and black. The erratic appearance of the desaturated category stems from its varying widths and its variable linkage with different levels of brightness, which give rise to individual foci that are widely separated at rows F, I, and C. A desaturation category is like a brightness category in the sense that neither is con-

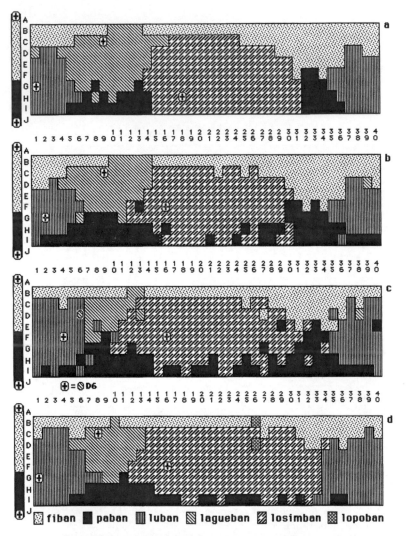

FIGURE 2.15. Colorado, Santo Domingo, Ecuador, 1979: (*a*) m 47, (*b*) m 40, (*c*) f 45, (*d*) m 37 (WCS 7, 19, 8, 25).

strained by universal hue perception of fixed elemental points; thus both kinds of categories vary extensively. Yet each can be a basic color category, even though it fluctuates more than does a category of hue.

Figure 2.17 displays an individual Quiché system in which all five binary categories coexist with an undivided cool category; four of them were shown to be basic by independent mapping procedures (MacLaury and Stewart 1984). Usually, fewer than five binary categories coexist with

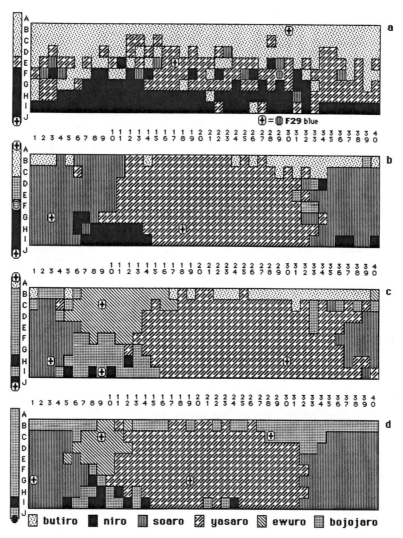

FIGURE 2.16. Tucano, Acaricaura, Vaupes, Colombia, 1977: (*a*) m 32, (*b*) f 17, (*c*) m 34, (*d*) m 23 (WCS 16, 1, 17, 13).

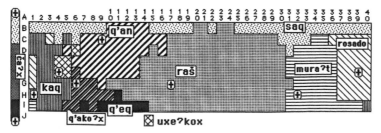

FIGURE 2.17. Quiché, Santa Catalina Ixtahuacán, Guatemala, 1980, m 69.

composite hue categories (Davies et al. 1992:1190–94; Turton 1980:308, 314–16).

In figure 2.18, four Western Apache speakers demonstrate the linkage of a desaturation category, *-baah* (often inflected as *li-baah*), with brightness. Speakers *a* and *c* focus *-baah* at CØ and DØ, lighter than the divide at middle lightness between rows E and F; they collectively apply the term 56 times on the light side versus 12 times on the dark side. Speakers *b* and *d*

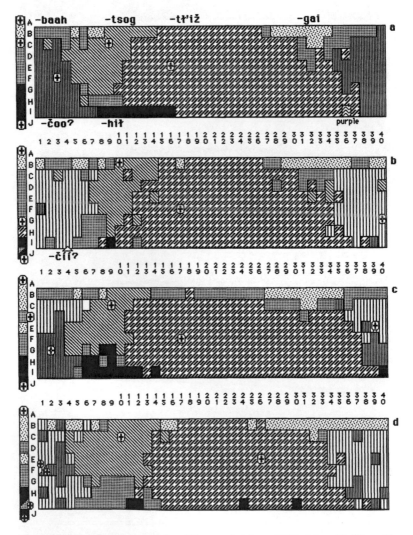

FIGURE 2.18. Western Apache, Cibecue, Arizona, 1980: (*a*) m 42, (*b*) m 66, (*c*) f 50, (*d*) m 55 (collected by Philip J. Greenfeld).

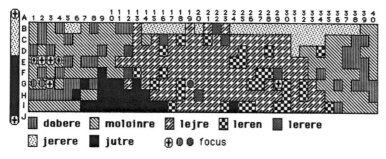

FIGURE 2.19. Buglere, Rio Luís, Veraguas, Panama, 1978, f 30 (WCS 5).

focus -*baah* at GØ and IØ on the dark side; together they apply the term 23 times to light chips versus 29 to dark chips (cf. Greenfeld 1986).

Figures 2.19 and 2.20 show, respectively, cases from Buglere and Menye. The Buglere speaker names the warm category with one commingled set of terms, *dabere* and *moloinre,* the cool category with another commingled set, *lejre* and *leren.* The Menye speaker likewise names the warm category *hängecäqä* and *yaicäqä* and the black category *hiawiqä* and *henguaningä.* Despite the coextensive terms, neither system has evolved beyond Stage IIIa; the Menye "black" might be the dark-cool of a Stage II system in the lingering sense that Berlin and Berlin (1975, quoted in §2.4.1.) observed of Aguaruna *bukúsea.*

Figure 2.21 shows Zulu type B categories in a late phase of transition from brightness to hue; the system combines (a) a binary basic hue category, *k^ωebezana* 'purple', with categories of brightness, of desaturation, and of hue. The speaker (b) extends *mpɔfu* throughout light colors, elemental yellow (C9), and elemental blue (F29); she (c) extends green-focused *łaza* to yellow (C10) and to similar light colors; she (d) names a desaturated

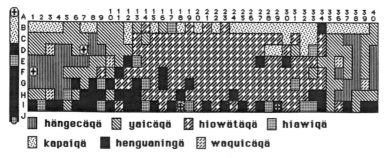

FIGURE 2.20. Menye, Morobe, Akwanja, Papua New Guinea, 1978, f 50 (WCS 13).

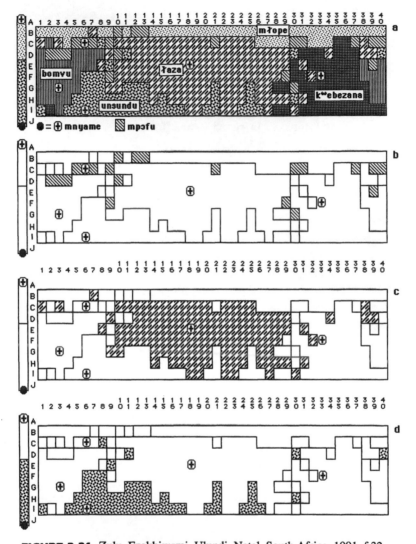

FIGURE 2.21. Zulu, Ezakhiwemi, Ulundi, Natal, South Africa, 1991, f 32.

category *unsundu,* giving it a dark focus (I7) and extending it to black (JØ). Red, *bomvu,* is a hue category. Among the 25 Zulu speakers interviewed at Ezakhiwemi (MacLaury MS-2), many used *mpɔfu, łaza,* and *unsundu* to name type A hue categories of yellow, cool, and brown; they named black *mnyame.*

Figure 2.22 shows type B categories of Konkomba that approximate Stages IIIa and IV; however, the transitional brightness categories show subtle differences from categories of hue. Speaker *a* names a standard

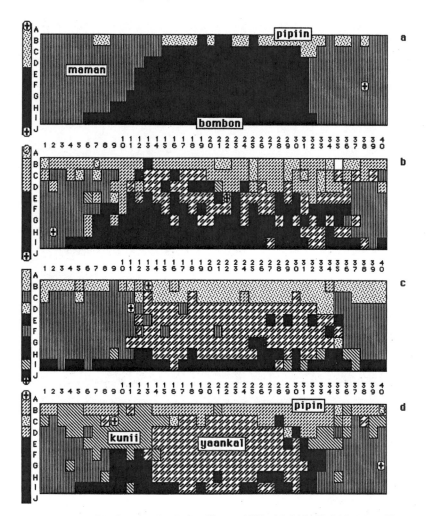

FIGURE 2.22. Konkomba, Buakuln, Ghana, 1978: (*a*) f 15, (*b*) f 15, (*c*) m 32, (*d*) m 15 (WCS 1, 2, 23, 15).

Stage II system, while speaker *b,* although also at Stage II, names a brightness category focused in light green, *yaankal* (E22). Speaker *c* adopts this brightness category to a cool range but focuses it in olive (F12). Although to others *maman* means 'warm', he focuses this term in lime yellow, D11, and extends it to green, F15 and F21; and he applies *kunii* to low brightness in rows H and I. Speaker *d* applies *kunii* to yellow and other shades of high brightness while extending *yaankal* to yellow, C8 and B11. The slight attention to brightness gives this emerging Stage IV system a distribution different from the Stage IV type A hue categories of figure 2.15.

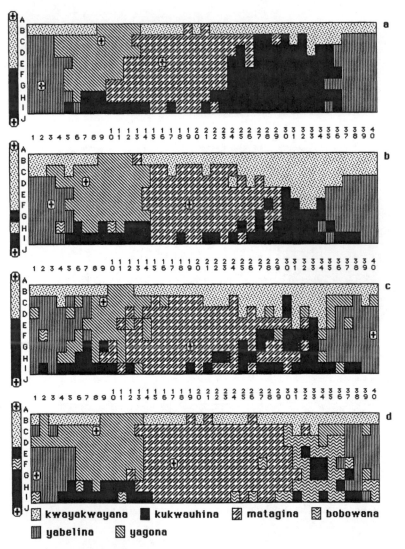

FIGURE 2.23. Iduna, Wakonai, Papua New Guinea, 1986: (*a*) f 23, (*b*) f 41, (*c*) f 63, (*d*) m 49 (WCS 3, 5, 10, 22).

Figures 2.23 and 2.24 demonstrate how borderline data may entice analysts to overburden typology. Kay, Berlin, and Merrifield (1991*a*: fig. 3) add categories of blue-with-black (Bu/Bk) and white-with-yellow (W/Y) to their revised evolutionary sequence, figure 2.10. However, such categories represent extremes in a range of variation by which a cool naming range is weakly applied to blue, or a white naming range is extended to the

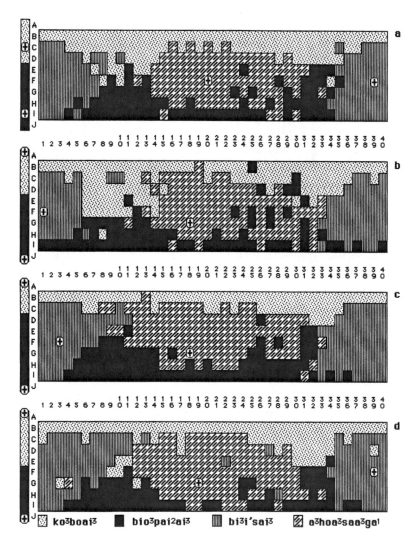

FIGURE 2.24. Múra Pirahá, Rio Maici, Brazil, 1977: (*a*) m 29, (*b*) f 45, (*c*) f 43, (*d*) f 30 (WCS 16, 7, 12, 2).

yellow part of the warm category. Probably they represent transitions between the recognized stages rather than "previously unreported types."

Figure 2.23 shows variation among Iduna speakers. In *a, kukwauhina,* focused in black, names all of blue. In *b,* the cool term, *matagina,* names elemental blue at F29 even though some of blue and all of blue-purple is called *kukwauhina.* In *c,* terms are mixed as they are in *b* but with *matagina* naming purple in column 32. In *d, matagina* assumes an ordinary cool range while *kukwauhina* and a secondary term, *yagona,* contend for purple. The WCS shows no stronger evidence of a blue-with-black type of system. Figure 2.24 shows a like range of variation among cool categories, minus an extreme example such as that of *a* in figure 2.23. Rivers (1901*c*:48) proposed a separate category of black-with-blue: "The languages which have this characteristic fall into two main classes; those which, as in Kiwai, have the same word for blue and black, and those which have the same word for blue and green. The former class includes the languages of Hovas and Bushman, as well as of many Australian and Melanesian tribes. The second group comprises a very large number of languages, including one so near home as Welsh . . ."

Perhaps Rivers failed to detect variation of the cool range when he gauged it with Lovibond's Tintometer. Bornstein (1973*a*:263), citing Berlin and Kay (1969 [probably their p. 32]), took it from them that Tzeltal has a category of black-with-blue, but Tzeltal names color with five salient terms, including a cool term, that have underlying relationships ranging through Stages II, III*a*, and IV, as shown in figures 4.2–9 herein. Bartlett (1928) notes similar ambivalence, for example, "Blue, as usual, is generally confused with green, or, if not with green, with black" (p. 37). The latter kind of system may include a "green" hyponym within a basic dark-cool category, being at Stage III*b* while evolving toward Stage IV. A secondary hyponym need not conform to any proposed order of basic color terms and can name only green at Stage III*b* or earlier.

Figure 2.24 shows the Stage III*a* system of Múra Pirahá in which some categories, perhaps of type B, show slight attention to brightness. Speaker *a* focuses a "white" category on CØ, not AØ, and applies its name, *ko³boai³*, to yellow. Speaker *b* uses *ko³boai³* in the same way but also applies *bi³i'sai³* to yellow at C9–10, which she focused in red (F1). Speaker *c* names yellow with *bi³i'sai³* and with the cool term, *a³hoa³saa³ga¹*, which gives the latter a yellow-green-blue meaning and suggests slight attention to brightness. Speaker *d* shows almost a Stage III*a* configuration of hue categories, except for "stray" uses of *ko³boai³*, *bi³i'sai³*, and *a³hoa³saa³ga¹* that are consistent with the final transition from a brightness system. Probably the putative and variable white-with-yellow category accompanies the assimilation of a prior brightness system to Stage III*a*. It is easier to regard it in this way than to revise the evolutionary hue sequence to include yet another "unreported type."

Figures 2.25–32 feature brightness categories of types D and C. An isolated Tucano example appears in *a* of figure 2.16, but the data from Tucano yielded no transitional systems linking this with the hue systems of *b*–*d*.

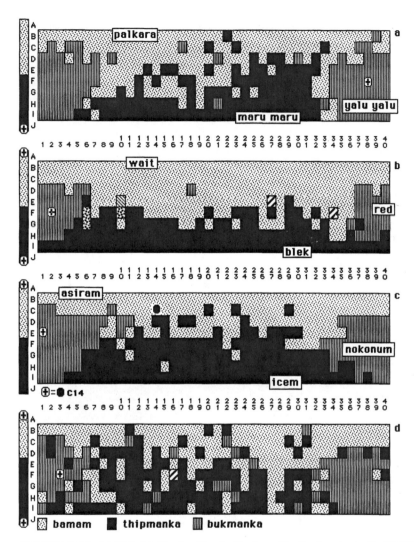

FIGURE 2.25. (*a*) Walpiri, Hooker Creek, Northern Territories, Australia (NTA), m 70; (*b*) Kriol, Ngukurr, NTA, f 20; (*c*) Kwerba, Aurimi Baru, Irian Jaya, Indonesia, f 30; (*d*) Murinbata, Fort Keats, NTA, f 52; 1978 (WCS 23, 9, 7, 8).

Figure 2.25 represents individual speakers of four languages who manifest categories of light versus dark, type D. They inspired the simulation at upper right in figure 2.12, although these systems include a hue category focused in red. They appear to emphasize brightness more than do the Stage II Ejagam systems of figure 2.14, even though these four and Ejagam show similar three-term formats. No focus was recorded for Walpiri *palkara,* but another speaker (WCS 22) focused *palkara* on DØ and *maru*

maru on EØ. The Kriol speaker used terms from English with aboriginal meanings; other Kriol speakers represent Stage V. The Kwerba speaker focused dark-cool or "dark" *icem* at C14, which is consistent with the widely shared tendency to intersperse the ranges of light and dark categories (see fig. 2.13). The Murinbata speaker applied "red" *bukmanka* 11 times to colors between columns 11 and 31, suggesting that this term names a type C brightness category coexisting with type D dark and light.

In figure 2.26, only one Martu Wangka speaker among eight conforms

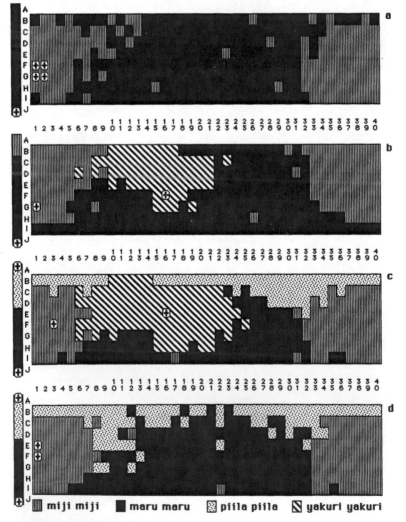

miji miji   maru maru   piila piila   yakuri yakuri

FIGURE 2.26. Martu Wangka, Jigalong, W. Australia, 1978: (*a*) f 60, (*b*) m 19, (*c*) m 60, (*d*) f 65, (*e*) f 58, (*f*) f 50, (*g*) f 60, (*h*) f 40 (WCS 6, 10, 17, 14, 4, 11, 18, 15).

to any of the configurations that Berlin and Kay or I have placed in a sequence (figs. 2.1, 2.2, 2.10, 2.11, 2.12). In *a,* a two-term hue system would represent Stage I; however, *maru maru,* which is focused in black at JØ, names all but the warm category, even white. As the pattern is strong, it is probably what the speaker intended. It may be another extreme variant of naming most colors with one term, as shown in figure 2.13 by (*a*) the Anbarra "dark" term, *-gungundja,* and (*b*) the Lani term, *laambu,* that speakers either refuse to focus or focus in red. Such pairs of ranges are repre-

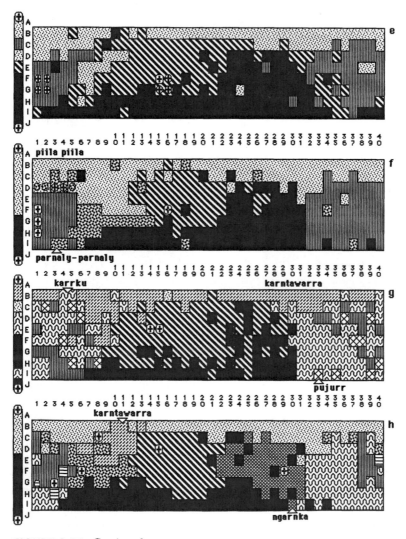

FIGURE 2.26. *Continued*

sented at the upper left of figure 2.12, which allows either to expand at the other's expense.[24] The expanded ranges likely are of type D. In *a*, Martu Wangka *miji miji* names warm color with signs of type B brightness categorization, as at H15, E23, and D29. This unusual relation between naming ranges may result from the wide disparity between types D and B, which, nevertheless, may develop during the transition of a system from brightness to hue. Speaker *d* names a stock Stage II system with signs of type B brightness. Speaker *b* almost names a perfect Stage I system; however, he names a yellow-with-green hue category, *yakuri yakuri*, focused in yellowish green (F16), one column left of unique green. Speaker *c* does the same, but with a broader range, within what otherwise would be an ordinary Stage II hue system. In this way, both *b* and *c* sharply depart from any system in the hue sequence. I could call them Stages I′ and II′, predecessors of the yellow-with-green Stage III′ of figure 2.11, but such naming would ignore systems *e* and *g*. In *e*, a speaker also focuses *yakuri yakuri* in yellowish green but names a range that sweeps from yellow C8 through green F17 to purple F33, with the truncated indications of type B brightness. Speaker *g* applies *yakuri yakuri* to cool hue while retaining its yellowish green focus (E14–15). Speakers *f* and *h* show degrees of confining *yakuri yakuri* to only green, while both steadfastly retain the yellowish green focus. Only speaker *h* adds a blue term, *ngarnka*, although she may preserve the dark cool range of *maru maru*, which places her system outside of proposed sequences in yet another way. Speakers *d–f* name yellow *piila piila*, which is focused in white AØ; speaker *g* mainly assigns the same duty to *karntawarra*, while speaker *h* confines *karntawarra* to yellow and *piila piila* to white. The Martu Wangka hue system resists classification, to say the least. The fluctuating range of *yakuri yakuri* with its consistently yellowish green focus is the most unique of its many uncommon traits. Data from Homeric Greek (Maxwell-Stuart 1981) and latter-day Hanunóo (Conklin 1955) suggest similar yellowish green-focused anomalies, although the three are not alike. We shall return to the problem of accounting for the flip-flopping range of *yakuri yakuri*, but only in §12.1.2.4 after theory has been developed.

In figure 2.27*a*, a Kuku Yalanji speaker shows the only two-term system described by the WCS other than that of figure 2.26*a*. But this Kuku Yalinji speaker intermixes the terms so thoroughly that they do not reveal discrete categories, at least not from an outsider's point of view.[25] Speakers *b*, *c*, and *d* confine *ngala ngala* to red and *kambal kambal* to dark-cool; they add *bingaji*, 'white' or 'light', and they elaborate a fourth category of brightness. Speaker *b* calls it *burrkul*, applies the name sparely to yellow and light

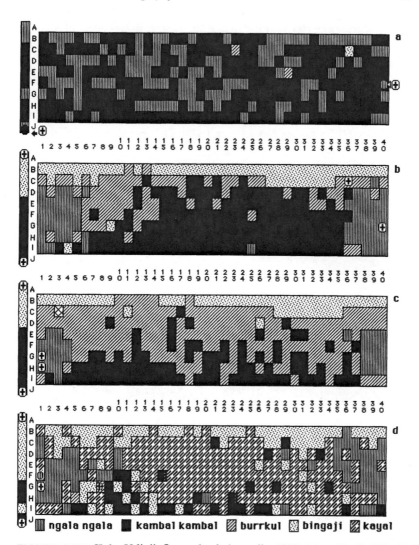

FIGURE 2.27. Kuku Yalinji, Queensland, Australia, 1978: (a) m 55, (b) f 50, (c) f 60, (d) f 65 (WCS 18, 7, 9, 11).

colors, and focuses it at C36. Speaker c also calls it *burrkul* but applies it throughout a broad band of middle brightness encompassing red, yellow, green, and blue (focus unrecorded). Speaker d applies *kayal* to a broader swath of middle brightness (focus unrecorded). These data may show how a broad middle-brightness category emerges in a rudimentary system. Hargrave (1982) provides a preliminary report detailing additional data on the five Australian systems represented in figures 2.25–2.27.

Figure 2.28 suggests another route by which a category of middle brightness may spread through a three-term system, (if, in this case, it is not contracting or merely varying). Gunu speaker *a* names a Stage II system with type B brightness. Speaker *b* adds a term that he confines to blue, *buluma* (a loanword?). Speaker *c* applies the term to purple, green, and yellow at D7. Speaker *d* expands the range of the brightness term to name 200 of the 330 colors, including black, dark red, blue, green, and all of yellow.

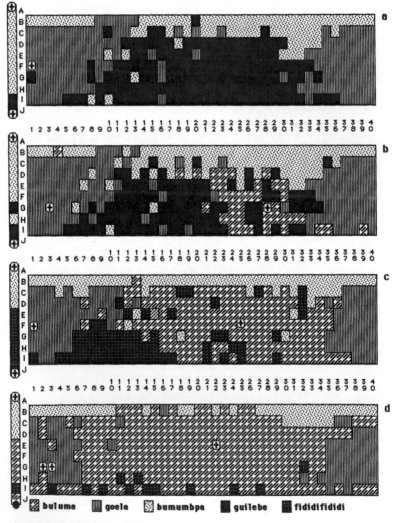

FIGURE 2.28. Gunu, Ombessa, Cameroon, 1978: (*a*) m 45, (*b*) m 65, (*c*) m 39, (*d*) f 18 (WCS 18, 25, 15, 1).

In figure 2.29, Cayapa speaker *a* names an immense category of middle brightness with coextensive terms; *laĭ-* is focused on unique yellow (C9) and unique blue (E29), while *luš-* has a darker focus (H30) but the same semantic range. Speaker *b* curtails the shared range slightly, focusing *laĭ-* in light yellow (B12) and red (F40) and *luš-* in green (G21) and blue (F28). Speaker *c* has concentrated these ranges to form modified brightness categories, perhaps type B (as in fig. 2.12), which simulate the outlines of a

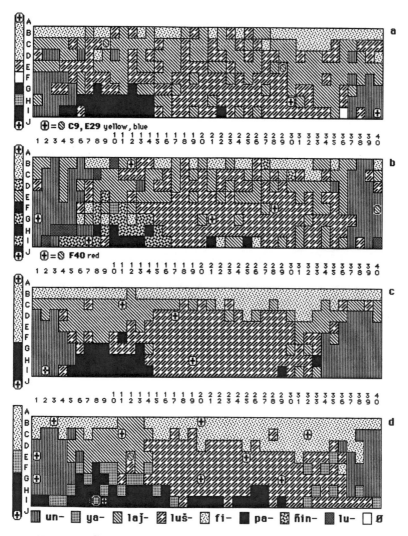

FIGURE 2.29. Cayapa, Esmeraldas, Ecuador, 1978: (*a*) f 28, (*b*) f 35, (*c*) f 30, (*d*) f 28 (WCS 6, 8, 7, 5).

Stage IV hue system. Speaker *d* shows a fully formulated Stage IV system with the cool category elongated, a desaturation category (focus I8), and multiple foci. The elongation and multiple foci suggest that some emphasis on brightness may remain.[26]

In figure 2.30, three generations of Slave speakers show: (*a–a'*), a co-extensively named brightness category, *a* being an extraction from *a'*, the full system; (*b*) a Stage IV hue system with pink (focus F38), a desatura-

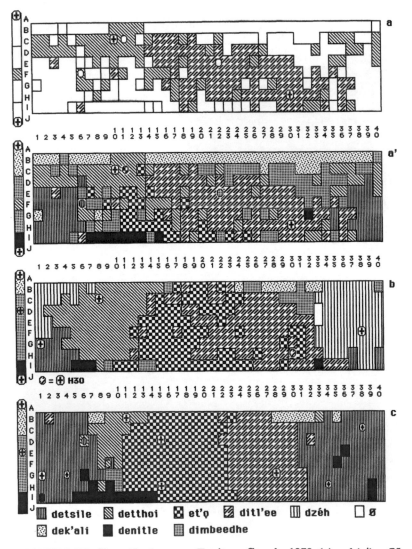

FIGURE 2.30. Slave, Northwestern Territory, Canada, 1978: (*a*) and (*a'*) m 75, (*b*) m 40, (*c*) m 22 (WCS 25, 13, 7).

tion category (focus DØ), and a coextensively named cool category; (c) a Stage V hue system with the desaturation category (focus EØ). In both comparisons, *a* to *b* and *b* to *c,* terms that are coextensive in the older system name separate hue categories in the younger system.[27]

In figure 2.31, Tifal speakers show: (a) substantial commingling of 'light' and 'dark' terms in combination with a broad yellow-focused brightness range, *titak;* (b) a reduced range of *titak* that applies throughout yel-

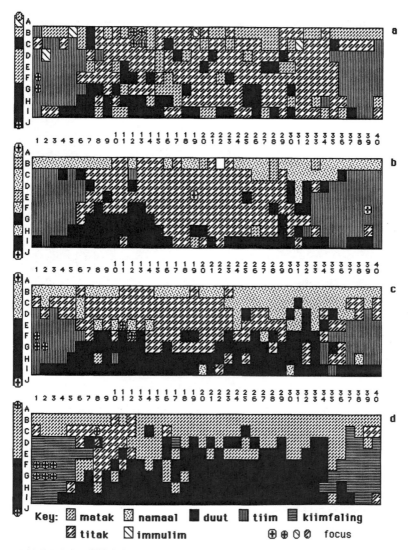

Key: ▨ matak ▨ namaal ■ duut ▥ tiim ▤ kiimfaling
▨ titak ◩ immulim ⊕ ⊕ ◐ Ø focus

FIGURE 2.31. Tifal, Papua New Guinea, 1979: (a) f 25, (b) m 34, (c) f 28, (d) f 48 (WCS 4, 23, 7, 12).

low, green, and blue; (*c*) *titak* further reduced; (*d*) *titak* confined to yellow within a configuration approaching Stage III*b*. *Titak* could be expanding or shrinking or merely varying, like Gunu *buluma* in figure 2.28.[28]

Figure 2.32 probably represents change, with Agta speakers *a, b,* and *c* suggesting a progression in steps toward the truncated system of speaker *d*. Speaker *a* names a band of brightness covering red, yellow, green, and blue (MacLaury 1992*a*: fig. 2 bottom). Speaker *b* focuses a loanword (< Sp. *azul*

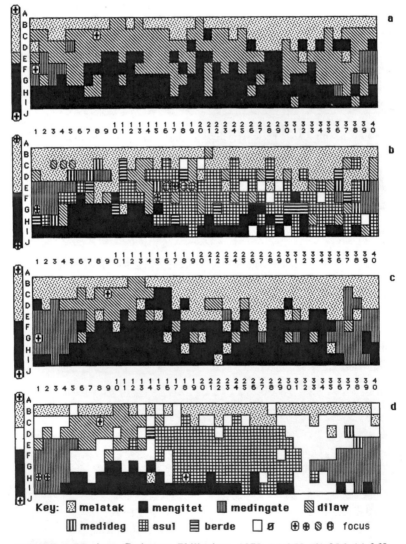

Key: ▨ melatak ■ mengitet ▥ medingate ▨ dilaw
   ▥ medideg ▦ asul ▤ berde ☐ ∅ ⊕⊕⊗⊖ focus

FIGURE 2.32. Agta, Casiguran, Philippines, 1978: (*a*) f 59, (*b*) f 26, (*c*) f 62, (*d*) f 52 (WCS 11, 2, 14, 10).

'blue') in green (E15–19) and applies it coextensively with the native term, *dilaw* (< "turmeric") to middle brightness. Speaker *c* reduces the brightness category to a thin band, verging on Stage III*b,* which exposes categories of 'light' and 'dark', *melatak* and *mengitet.* Speaker *d* represents Stage IV, but with loss of traditional naming facility among the colors that some languages categorize as desaturated (figs. 2.16*c,* 2.18, 7.22*a*).

Figure 2.33 compares Stage V′ Salishan systems of the Pacific North-

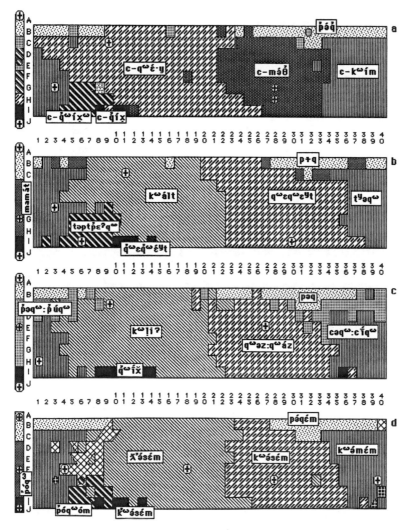

FIGURE 2.33. Salishan, British Columbia, Canada, 1985–1990: (*a*) Halkomelem f 60, (*b*) Shuswap f 45, (*c*) Lillooet f 73, (*d*) Sechelt f 63. Adapted from MacLaury (1991*b*:fig. 1).

west that name yellow-with-green: (*a*) Central Salish Halkomelem, (*b–c*) Interior Salish Shuswap and Lillooet, (*d*) Central Salish Sechelt. Halkomelem names yellow-with-green with the cognate of terms with which the other languages name blue and purple. This and other patterns prompted Kinkade (1988) to reconstruct a Proto-Salishan yellow-green-blue category of high brightness. No one has explained why languages throughout this region have evolved to Stage V′ instead of merging with the more common stages of hue categories, as did, for example, Athapascan Slave to the north of Salish (fig. 2.30). Some Salish speakers retain both a yellow-with-green category and a cool category, which overlap throughout green (MacLaury 1987*a*: fig. 3; 1991*b*: fig. 10), but many have retracted the former cool category to only blue. This event overrides the neurally determined perception that yellow and green are more distinct than green and blue (§4.1.1). In *a*, the Halkomelem usage of *c-mə́θ* at F18 green suggests a vestige of a cool category; *c-mə́θ* is cognate with Shuswap *mamát*, a desaturation term focused in grey (GØ). In *b* and *c*, the Interior Salish yellow-with-green terms, *kʷált* and *kʷḷiʔ*, are cognates (Kinkade). Possibly Proto–Interior Salish (PIS) named yellow-green-blue coextensively, as do Cayapa (fig. 2.29*a*) and elder Slave (fig. 2.30*a*); the PIS ranges would have anteceded those that presently overlap throughout green (MacLaury 1987*a*: fig. 3; 1991*b*: fig. 10). The Stage V′ Salish systems include desaturation categories and binary categories, as do the Stage IV systems of figures 2.17–18. The derivation of desaturated and binary categories applies to the hue Stages IV and V′ (theoretically to IV′) on both sides of figure 2.11 (whose relation could be effectively diagrammed as a wraparound depiction).[29]

The foregoing examples (figs. 2.13–33) illustrate how the sequence of figures 2.11–12 accommodates diverse data on color categorization and how it helps to identify exceptional systems. The sequence incorporates Berlin and Kay's 1975 proposal (fig. 2.2.) while integrating it with subsequent observations. The examples lend background and perspective to the study of Mesoamerican color categories, almost all of which pertain to hue or desaturation at Stage II or later.[30]

2.7. Summary

Color ethnography is founded on a 138-year tradition of investigating issues at the nexus of anthropology, linguistics, and psychology. These queries have included the role of race versus language in determining categorization, methods of exploring crossculturally the relation between analytical predisposition and ways of categorizing, linguistic relativity, and universal perceptual constraints on word meaning and category structure. Completion of the World Color Survey stimulated further modeling in an attempt to incorporate heretofore underacknowledged categories of brightness and yellow-with-green. Kay, Berlin, and Merrifield's model amalgamates all types of categories into a multilineal scheme, while my scheme portrays brightness categories merging with Berlin and Kay's 1975 hue sequence. The proposal of brightness-to-hue attributes specific dynamics to the constitution of color categories, including reciprocal emphases on similarity and difference. Samples from the WCS and elsewhere substantiate many kinds of color-category systems. Although most of these systems support the current models of change, some present surprises. The profusion of systems affords a backdrop of comparison for the analysis of Mesoamerican color categories, which represent only a slice of the variety found in language.

CHAPTER 3

DESCRIPTIVE METHOD

Color naming within any particular community was investigated by interviewing members one by one, then comparing or aggregating the separate analyses. Methods include (1) equipment, (2) elicitation, (3) data organization, (4) analysis of individual cognition, (5) comparison, and (6) display. This chapter treats (1), (2), (4), and (6), and Chapters 4 through 11 treat (5). Methods of data organization (3) are summarized in Appendix VI. See §1.2 for specification of stimulus materials and history of equipment design.[1]

3.1. Equipment

The design includes loose swatches of 10 minimally saturated and 320 maximally saturated Munsell colors and obverse and reverse arrays of the same (fig. 1.3).[2] The loose "chips" are numbered in fixed random order, aligned in a box, and accompanied by the arrays and a film canister containing rice grains. Numbered sheets, graphs in Munsell format, carbon paper, clamps, and colored pencils enable an investigator to organize data in the field while consultants are accessible for further questions. Organizing data takes three times as long as collecting them; the field may provide the ideal opportunity to devote the required hours. Equipment design and organization procedures are purposely "low tech" and light-weight to avoid dependency on major funding, electricity, a laboratory, or a vehicle.

3.2. Elicitation

Before starting an interview, the consultant was invited to use any word for as many colors as seemed appropriate and to decline to designate colors that were difficult to name. The consultant was also told, "Everyone names color differently and there are no wrong answers. We agree on a fee of (X-amount), which you can earn in about two hours if you move along without trying too hard." Onlookers were asked not to help. Most interviews were conducted in the native language by a fluent speaker or with aid of an interpreter; a few were conducted with prepared phrases. The interview required minimum dialogue. Conversation in Spanish was avoided whenever possible, as it could influence word choice.

1. *Naming.* The consultant named the 330 loose chips one by one in the random order, which yielded color-term head lexemes and their qualifiers, as well as hesitations, alternatives, afterthoughts, reportatives, and null responses. All were recorded on numbered sheets (fig. VI.1).

2. *Focus Selection.* The consultant was shown the arrays and asked to pinpoint the "best example" of each head lexeme volunteered while naming chips. This resulted in a focus for each term. The obverse array was used to elicit categories of dark and cool colors, the reverse array for categories of light and warm colors (fig. VI.2).

3. *Mapping.* For each head lexeme volunteered, the consultant was asked to place a grain of rice on every color of the array that the term could name. After stopping as if finished, the consultant was asked to "put rice on more colors that you can call X-name." Some mappings proceeded through several steps until the consultant insisted that the term applied to no other colors. Each step was recorded as row letters and column numbers. The objective was to elicit a complete mapping, not to encourage steps; but the tendency of individuals to pause and then respond to a further request led to mapping steps as additional data. The rice was swept aside before the next mapping commenced. Adjacent categories were widely segregated in the mapping sequence. Mapping directives did not contain qualifiers, such as "light" or "dark," and the interviewer never pointed to the array (figs. VI.3–4).

Data were organized by encoding them on graphs of the format shown in *a* of figure 1.3 (figs. VI.5–10 detail procedures). The independent results could be checked for accuracy or otherwise interpreted against each other. The most reliable interpretation addressed correspondences between results, not any one of them. The 330 color chips contributed critical quantification, which made the full set indispensable.[3]

3.3. Display of Individual Data

Results from an interview of a Guarijío speaker exemplify how data are displayed.

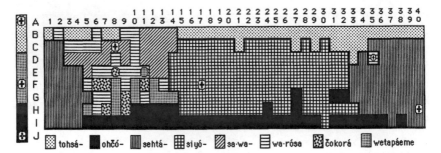

FIGURE 3.1. Guarijío, Alamos, Sonora, Mexico, m 35, 1979: naming ranges of head lexemes and foci.

3.3.1. Naming Ranges and Qualifier Distributions

Naming data include any of the words or reactions an individual volunteers in response to the 330 loose chips, mainly head lexemes and their qualifiers. Head lexemes from each interviewee are derandomized into their spectral relationship by encoding them on 330-cell graphs corresponding to the Munsell array. Each term is symbolized by a distinct letter, which is written into every graph-cell that represents the chip named by the term. The distribution of the letter on the graph plots the "naming range" of the term. The naming range of each lexeme is outlined in ink. Qualifiers are derandomized and encoded on a separate graph, which displays their distributions. Naming-range outlines can be superimposed on qualifier distributions with carbon paper. The relationship of each qualifier to naming ranges can be isolated by passing the outlines and only the symbol of that qualifier to yet another graph, again with carbon paper. With this technique, any part of the data or any relationship can be displayed by itself (see Appendix VI).

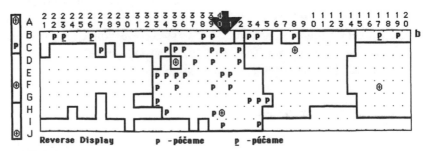

FIGURE 3.2. A Guarijío speaker's every use of two qualifier suffixes in relation to naming-range outlines of head lexemes.

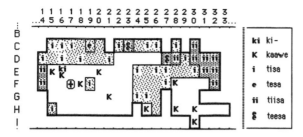

FIGURE 3.3. Uses of one prefix and five preposed qualifiers within the naming range of Guarijío *siyó-* (cf. fig. 3.1).

In the graphics, letter-symbols of head lexemes are converted to hatchings that fill each naming-range outline. Qualifiers are still represented by letter-symbols. Figure 3.1 displays the head lexemes and foci of the Guarijío speaker. (Figures 3.1 and 1.3 may be compared.) Figure 3.2 exhibits the distribution of two of his qualifiers. They modify only white-focused *tohsá-* and red-focused *sehtá-*.

Figure 3.3 displays only one category. Distributions of qualifiers with short vowels versus those with long vowels are contrasted. The symbols of a third group are displayed against an unshaded background. The thin lines will facilitate comparison of the qualifier distributions with mapping steps in figure 3.9.

3.3.2. Foci

The same foci appear in different diagrams. In figure 3.1, ⊕ represents a focus that matches its naming range: the chip that was chosen as the focus of a term was also named with this term (e.g., H40, C8, F17, D35, FØ, AØ, and JØ). Since focusing and naming are independent, data need not coincide. When data mismatch, the focus is marked as an oval filled with the hatching ⊗ ⊞ (e.g., E8 and E11) that elsewhere represents the naming range of the focused term. The Guarijío speaker focused one term, *wetapáeme,* on two colors, FØ ⊕ and E11 ⊞. One focus matches the naming range while the other does not. The symbol Ø, as in "FØ," refers to the achromatic (left) column of the array, which is not numbered in figures.

3.3.3. Mappings

In figure 3.4, *a* represents with herringbone lines the mapping of *siyó-name.* The lines intersect the graph-cells corresponding to color chips on which the consultant placed rice grains. Each line is framed and segmented with numbers marking the steps by which the category was mapped and in-

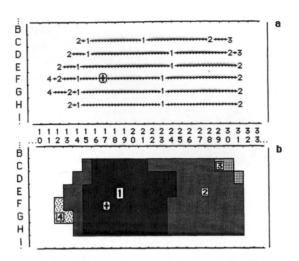

FIGURE 3.4. (*a*) A four-step mapping of Guarijío *siyóname;* (*b*) the mapping steps depicted with shading.

dicating the order in which the steps were volunteered. Since single steps were mapped on more than one row and on discontinuous segments within a row, the same step numbers appear on different rows and frame discontinuous segments. The earliest step on a row is bracketed at both edges, later steps at the outer edge. In *b*, the same mapping appears in a different style, which is easiest to see. But the style of *a* allows different mappings to overlap in one diagram.

Figure 3.5 demonstrates the overcrowded result of displaying the mappings of five categories. Subsequent figures combine fewer mappings. In spite of its busy appearance, the figure shows (1) one individual's full system of basic color categories and (2) his overlapping ranges. The later steps of certain mappings correspond to overlaps, for example, mapping steps 2, 3, and 4 of *siyóname.*

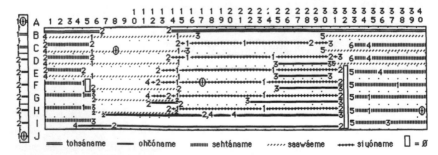

FIGURE 3.5. A Guarijío speaker's mappings of basic color categories.

The Guarijío speaker did not map the colors whose graph cells are enclosed by a rectangle (e.g., F5, E–I 32). His range of yellow-focused *saawáeme* (C8) extends throughout the yellow and brown colors of columns 5–14, which were named by four terms: *saawáeme, waarósa* (< Sp. *barrosa* 'muddy'), *čokorá* (< Sp. *chocolate*), and *wetapáeme* (fig. 3.1). The basic color term is *saawáeme;* its mapping encompasses the colors mapped for the other three, which are not diagrammed.

3.4. Analysis of Individual Data

Correspondences between different kinds of data support a hypothesis of how an individual cognitively organizes the color domain. This example concentrates on green-focused *siyóname,* black-focused *ohčóname,* and their overlap in blue.

3.4.1. Naming Ranges and Mappings

Figure 3.6 exhibits correspondence between the naming range and mapping of *siyóname.* The naming range is represented by its outline.

The figure shows that the first mapping step and the naming range fail to match only at C21, whereas the second step and naming range mismatch at H24, C27, G–H27, and G31. If column 23 is taken to represent the universal divide between perceptions of green and blue,[4] the green-focused category was named 50 times on the green side of the column and 47 times on

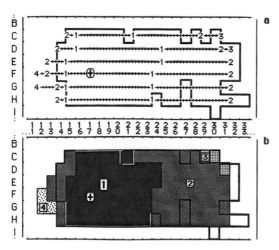

FIGURE 3.6. Correspondence between the naming and mapping of *siyóname* depicted in two styles, (*a*) and (*b*).

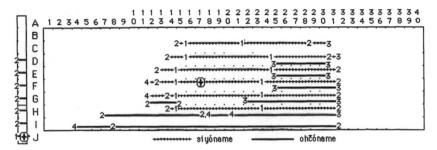

FIGURE 3.7. One individual's mappings of *siyóname* and *ohčóname*.

the blue side; the category was mapped throughout 58 color chips on its green side and 47 on its blue side. The quantitative biases in naming and mapping correspond with each other and with placement of the focus and the first mapping step on green. The correspondences support the hypothesis that this Guarijío speaker organizes *siyóname* by favoring green over blue.

3.4.2. Correspondence among Mappings

Figure 3.7 displays the relation between mappings of *siyóname* and *ohčóname*. Throughout blue, the second mapping step of *siyóname* corresponds with the third step of *ohčóname;* these categories overlap in their areas of low membership but not in areas of high membership. Blue colors are categorized from *two perspectives,* one that is green-focused and another that is black-focused.

The mappings also suggest that blue has higher membership in *siyóname* than in *ohčóname,* which is corroborated by abundant application of *siyóname* to blue colors while *ohčóname* names few blues, figures 3.1 and 3.8.

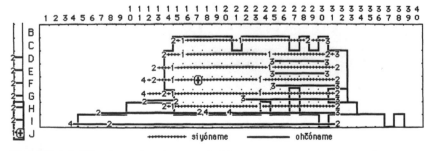

FIGURE 3.8. Mappings of *siyóname* and *ohčóname* superimposed on naming-range outlines.

3.4.3. Qualifiers and Mappings

Figure 3.9 combines figures 3.3–4*a* to show correspondence among preposed qualifiers of the root *siyó-* and the mapping of *siyóname*.

In figure 3.9*a*, diminutive qualifiers meaning "little" are shaded and augmentative qualifiers meaning "very good" are unshaded. In *b*, the mapping appears by itself. In *c*, the diminutives tend to correspond to second and third mapping steps and to the edges of the mapping; the augmentatives correspond to the green focal region of the first mapping step and to the bluest colors of the second step.

However, an equal number of augmentative qualifiers occur on the green and the blue sides (see note 4), which does not concur with the attested low membership of blue. The noncorrespondence indicates the need to test further by eliciting a mapping of *kaawe siyóname*. The one prefixation of *ki-* to an augmentative qualifier in green might intensify its augmentative value, but this minuscule datum was not investigated during fieldwork.

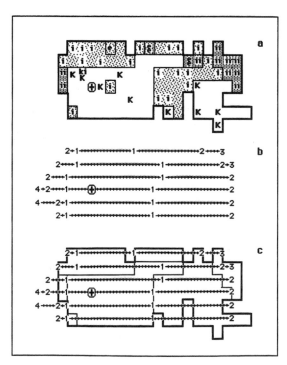

FIGURE 3.9. The category *siyóname:* (*a*) outlines of its preposed qualifiers and (*b*) its mapping are (*c*) superimposed.

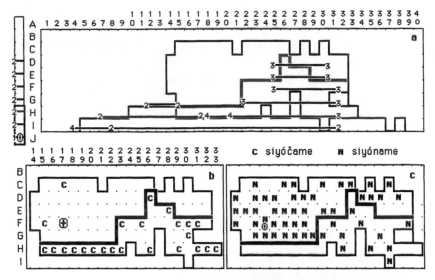

FIGURE 3.10. Correspondence of the mapping of *ohčóname* with the naming of (*a*) *siyóčame* and distributions of the qualifications (*b*) *siyóčame* and (*c*) *siyóname* within the naming range of *siyó-*.

Figure 3.10 shows correspondence between a suffixed qualifier, *-čame,* of the root *siyó-* and the overlap of green-focused and black-focused category mappings. In *a–b,* the Guarijío speaker used the suffixed qualifier, *-čame,* to specify colors of the green-focused category that either were peripheral (F15, C17) or shared with the black-focused category. He not only mapped the overlap of two categories with late steps but named it as he did peripheral colors, *siyóčame.*

3.4.4. Complementation of Qualifiers

In figure 3.10, *b* and *c* display complementary distributions of qualifiers. Whereas *-čame* designates the area of overlap and low membership, *-name* predominantly designates the green colors of highest membership; however, *-name* less frequently but regularly names colors of lower membership throughout margins and blue. This distribution of *-name* is consistent with its meaning as the general designation of the whole category, properly called *siyóname.* The consultant was most inclined to apply the name of the whole category to colors about its focus; he tended to associate the whole with its most typical part.[5]

3.5. Summary

Correspondences among independently elicited data suggest that the Guarijío speaker cognitively organizes green-focused and black-focused categories with unequal values of membership in each. Highest values occur about category foci; lowest occur at margins and in blue where the categories overlap. Blue is categorized from the two perspectives of green and black foci.

The analysis calls up further questions. It would have helped to elicit mappings of *kaawe siyóname, siyóčame,* and *siyomúrame,* and to establish the meaning of *ki-*.

Since elicitation and data organization require only color chips, paper, and sunlight, analyses can proceed in the field while consultants are on hand for following up. Most data of the Mesoamerican Color Survey were extracted from single interviews and analyzed away from the field, although approximately 100 individuals were reconsulted and a few were interviewed by both the MCS and the WCS. Almost every analysis stood by itself without further fieldwork.

CHAPTER 4

AXIOMS

Color categorization is both perceptual and cognitive. Observations of color categories will be most effectively explained and united by hypotheses that are built upon a combination of perceptual and cognitive axioms. Only four axioms suffice to thoroughly address all the regularities observed among composite hue categories of the Mesoamerican kind. The axioms are elaborated in §§4.1–4 while §4.5 demonstrates their use in explaining data. Categories of brightness, desaturation, and hue blends would require a few more axioms pertaining to such events as neural channel speed, categorization by default, and filling of voids, but they are beyond the present scope.

Let us begin by summarizing the four axioms: (1) people perceive six elemental colors, fifteen potential pairs; (2) the colors of each pair are to an extent similar and to an extent distinct; (3) each pair differs in these extents; (4) an individual attends simultaneously to similarity and to distinctiveness and can reciprocally shift the emphases.

The first three statements describe perception; they are not axioms in the strict sense because they are supported by findings in visual physiology. The fourth describes selective emphasis, and it is purely a postulate; it is supported only by its success in providing a coherent account of 100 disparate cross-linguistic observations whose interrelation otherwise would not be apparent (Appendix VII). It is possible to build into axioms the distinction between perception and cognition because the physiology of color perception is somewhat understood. Color may be exceptional in that sense. This distinction is indispensable to accounting for individual variation, change, and cross-cultural differences while acknowledging universals.

The origin of color perception in precortical physiology determines that its sensory input will be constant and, therefore, directly controllable only by other peripheral physiology, such as dilation or constriction of the pupil.

Its quantitative control in the cerebral cortex must be achieved cognitively by accentuating or ignoring what is perceived. In this sense, color perception and its cognition are conceptually separable for purposes of a theoretical discussion. In practice, perception and selective emphasis are inseparable, because any point in the range of attention from none to an intense amount is, nevertheless, a degree of attention. Even attention in a semi-waking state or default mode constitutes a baseline of cognitive interest.

4.1. Perceptual Axioms

Color perception consists of sensation that is produced when the visual cortex responds to processes that have originated in the retina and optic nerve. Although other notions of perception include phenomenal interplay of sensation, cognitive structuring, and memory, perception is defined here as elemental sensory reflexes in the cortex in response to precortical events.[1] The physiology of color perception is shared throughout the human species. Consequently, the axioms pertain identically to all normal observers, allowing for a small range of nonanomalous variation (Neitz and Neitz 1995). The sameness imposes strong constraints on color categorization in every language and in every individual system. We infer such constraints from their manifestation in behavior, and we call them "universals" when they consistently govern the ways subjects respond to color chips during independent interviews or experiments.[2]

4.1.1. Evidence[3]

Axiom 1 (of six elemental sensations) is consistent with the opponent neural processes discussed in §2.4.2. Axiom 2 (each pair similar and distinct to an extent) follows from axiom 3 (of distinct perceptual distances), while axiom 3 is supported by two sources. The weakest evidence concerns the measurement of "discrimination distance" between pure colors, and the strongest concerns the contributions of retinal photopigments to response of LGN cell types. The latter bears specifically on weak discrimination between green and blue, affording a modified but very specific version of axiom 3: green and blue appear more similar to each other than do red and yellow, yellow and green, or red and blue. This is sufficient for the present analysis, because most Mesoamerican composite categories are cool or warm.

Rivers (1901c:56; cf. 1901a:95; Bartlett 1928:46) stated, "there is a closer resemblance between blue and black and between green and black than between red and black and this difference in the degree of similarity . . . may account in some measure for the . . . nomenclature." And so it would seem. But research has yielded nothing concerning the relative perceptual distances among the other twelve of the fifteen possible pairs of elemental colors, notably those including black, white, or both. To include in the analysis the Mesoamerican dark-cool categories, I must assume that Rivers and Bartlett are right.[4] Mesoamerican light-warm categories are so rare and dubious that they are not at issue. Major categories based on brightness likewise are nil in Mesoamerica.

4.1.1.1. Discrimination Distance

There is a way to measure relative similarity among pairs of colors, although it might be unreliable for colors as different as elemental hues. Wyszecki and Stiles (1967:450–501, table 6.3) construe color difference as a combination of differences in brightness and in "chromaticness," hue and saturation at one brightness, which they express as "just noticeable differences." A JND is the smallest difference one can detect between nearly identical colors. There are various scales and formulae for counting JNDs between distinct points of color. Wyszecki and Stiles (460–461 [6.3.7.]) recommend the "1964 CIE-(U*V*W*) system," which Kempton programmed.[5] I used it to obtain distances between red (G2), yellow (C9), green (F17), and blue (F29) of Munsell chips from the MCS (MacLaury 1987a):[6] green/blue = 83.63; red/yellow = 222.92; yellow/green = 234.58, yellow/blue = 280.87. But two distances were unpredictably close: red/green = 156.21 and red/blue = 123.62 (the red Munsell chip is yellowish). Why base calculation on the Munsell solid as opposed to the theoretical solid? Why base it on any particular level of saturation? Why on geodesic distance? Sun (1983) used a different formula to calculate euclidian distances between unique hues saturated to theoretical maxima, finding greater distance between green and blue than red and yellow.

4.1.1.2. The Disadvantage of Short-Wavelength Cones

Different cone types make distinct contributions to discrimination among paired colors. Discrimination of green and blue relies mainly on change in the output of short-wavelength cones. Yet this cone type, in comparison to others, is slow to respond to stimuli, peripherally distributed on the retina, and sparse. The condition foreordains a paucity of neurologically conveyed information, which may weaken the ability to discriminate if that ability depends on the amount of information received.

There are three types of cones, each containing a different kind of photopigment. Although each is sensitive to all wavelengths, each is maximally sensitive to a different wavelength. The pigment of S cones most readily absorbs short-wavelength photons, M cones medium-wave, and L cones long-wave.

De Valois and De Valois (1975) note that any sensation, regardless of its modality, requires a neural response to a comparison of at least two inputs; a sensation never involves a direct, lineal connection between an external stimulus via one neuron to a cortical reflex. The comparison of inputs is fundamental to sensory physiology, because it enables the distinction of quality from quantity.[7] For example, one red-green (RG) cell in the lateral geniculate nuclei (LGN) is excited by a ratio of inputs from at least two different cone types; it is the *ratio* itself that stimulates the LGN cell, not the amount of input. Since the ratio remains constant under normal variation of ambient daylight, an observer will sense the same red color regardless of the quantity of photons absorbed by the cones.

RG and YB channels each are of two kinds. As described in §2.4.2, one kind of RG fires fast to stimulate red and slow to stimulate green, $+R-G$; however, the other kind fires slow for red, fast for green, $-R+G$. Likewise YB consists of both $+Y-B$ and $-Y+B$.

De Valois and De Valois (1975:132, fig. 5) offer a model of how the three cone types activate the six LGN channels: $+L-M \rightarrow +R-G$, $+M-L \rightarrow +G-R$, $+L-S \rightarrow +Y-B$, $+S-L \rightarrow +B-Y$, $+L+M \rightarrow +W-Bk$, $-L-M \rightarrow +Bk-W$. For example, $+L-M \rightarrow +R-G$ means that the L cones feed in an excitatory manner $(+L)$ and the M cones in an inhibitory manner $(-M)$ into a $+R-G$ cell. When the L- and M-cone inputs differ such that the L-cone input is greatest, the cell excites $(+R)$. Its excitation stimulates a sensation of red in the visual cortex. When the ratio differs such that the M-cone input is greatest, the cell inhibits $(-G)$. Its inhibition stimulates a green sensation. The inputs of $+M-L \rightarrow +G-R$ work in the opposite fashion.[8]

Ratliff (1976:321–325) related retinal structure to the late evolution of a "blue term" in Berlin and Kay's original sequence of 1969. Unlike L and M cones, S cones do not occur in the *fovea centralis* where cones are concentrated and they are late to interact with other cone types. Thus, "the blue end of the spectrum might exert weaker influence on the responses of the . . . opponent cells" (322). Ratliff's argument does not address the relative discriminability of green and blue versus that of red and yellow or of yellow and green, which would be required to explain the 1975 sequence. Why might normal observers have greater difficulty differentiating green and blue if green itself is not subject to the same disadvantage as blue?

Evidence concerning the lesser discriminability of green and blue involves the "confusion lines" of color-deficient individuals that transect the 1931 CIE chromaticity chart (fig. 4.2, but see Appendix III for a caveat). Confusion lines connect colors within the chart that cannot be distinguished by individuals who suffer partial "color blindness." These individuals are called "dichromats," because they lack one or another of the three photopigments while retaining the other two. Individuals with normal color vision are "trichromats," which will be relevant below.

There are three kinds of dichromats, each of which lacks a different pigment: protanopes lack the L pigment, deuteranopes lack the M pigment, and tritanopes lack the S pigment. Accordingly, each is deprived of the ability to make a different set of color discriminations. Thus, the confusion lines of each kind of dichromat crosscut the CIE chromaticity chart from a different point of origin. In figure 4.1, parts a–c show the crosscutting of the chart by protanopic, deuteranopic, and tritanopic confusion lines.

As an aside, it must be stressed that the chart represents wavelength of stimuli, not color appearance. The latter is sensed in the brain after ratios of wavelength, such as those represented in the chart, trigger photochemical and neural responses in the retina, ganglia, and optical nerve. Figure 4.2 gives nontechnical readers a sketch of how wavelength might translate, circumstances permitting. Here, rudimentary designations provide an idea of the colors that would be sensed in the brain after corresponding ratios of wavelength on the chart trigger the physiological processes, at least under many normal conditions although certainly not under all. (See Appendix III for discussion.)

Each confusion line represents not only the discriminations that one of three kinds of dichromats is incapable of making, but also the degree of input from one or another cone type that would contribute to a successful discrimination by a trichromat. In a normal individual, the input from a cone type is strongest at the wavelengths that would be closest to the origin of a dichromat's confusion line, and the input weakens in proportion to the distance from the origin. Thus, for example, in figure 4.1a, protanopic confusion lines suggest that the inputs of L cones in a trichromat are stronger for responses leading to red sensation than for responses leading to green or blue sensations. In b, deuteranopic confusion lines suggest that for trichromats the inputs of M cones are also strongest for responses leading to red, although they are almost as strong for responses leading to blue; and in

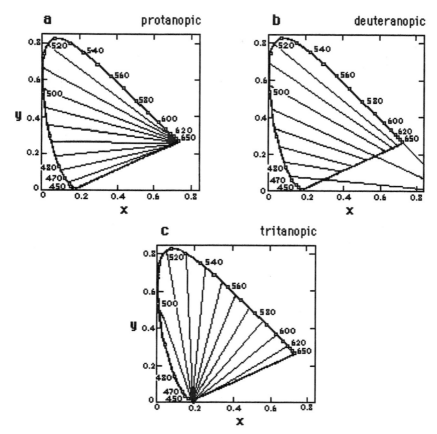

FIGURE 4.1. Color-vision deficiencies exhibited by the chromaticity confusions within the 1931 CIE chromaticity chart of the three kinds of dichromat: (*a*) protanope, (*b*) deuteranope, (*c*) tritanope. Adapted from Hurvich (1981:294, fig. 13).

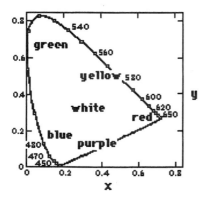

FIGURE 4.2. A rough approximation of color appearances that under specific conditions may be sensed in the cortex in response to the stimuli so labeled on the chromaticity chart (independent of other authors).

c the tritanopic confusion lines suggest that for trichromats the inputs of S cones are stronger for responses leading to blue than for responses leading to green or to red. Furthermore, the protanopic and deuteranopic confusion lines suggest that the strength of inputs from L cones and M cones is almost constant across wavelengths that trigger processes stimulating green and blue; but the tritanopic confusion lines suggest that, for people with normal vision, strength of input from the S cones differs greatly between responses that result ultimately in green and blue sensations.

Thus, the three sets of confusion lines derived from color-blind people evidence a critical principle for normal color vision: discrimination between blue and green depends mainly on change in excitation of S cones. Blue-versus-green discrimination depends little on changes in the excitation of M cones or L cones, because there is almost a constant ratio of M-cone and L-cone inputs over the range of wavelength that initiates the stimulation of blue-to-green color senses.

This evidence combines with Ratliff's point about retinal structure: since S cones are sparse, slow to interact with LGN cells, and peripherally distributed in the retina, the S cones are at a disadvantage as a mechanism that produces information to be used in the visual cortex for discriminating colors. Discrimination that depends on S-cone output, such as that between blue and green, would be less acute than that depending on L-cone and M-cone outputs, such as that between red and yellow, yellow and green, or red and blue.

4.1.1.3. Other Evidence

Boynton and Olson (1987 : fig. 5) diagram relative geometric distances between centroids of "linked" basic color terms within the Optical Society of America (OSA) solid; linked terms optionally name colors between centroids, as, for example, either "green" or "blue" may name turquoise. The solid specifies that green and blue centroids are closer together than green and yellow, which, in turn, are closer than yellow and red; red and blue are farthest apart. Blue, grey, and green form a compact triad of exceptionally short distances; white and black are excluded. Ekman (1954) used "similarity analysis" to determine subjects' ratings of distances between blue, green, yellow, and red at different wavelengths, closer colors receiving higher scores. At some wavelengths, group data almost match Boynton and Olson's figure 5; for example, with B 472nm, G 504nm, Y 584nm, and R 651nm, Ekman's table 1 shows B−G .25, G−Y .14, Y−R .20, B−R .04, B−Y .02, and G−R .02. But slightly different wavelength combinations change the relative scale. De Valois and De Valois (1975 : fig. 4) find that $+G-R$ cells fire above the basal rate in response to "blue" wavelengths as short as 430nm with smooth but steep increase to 480nm where the curve begins to flatten as it approaches the "green" peak at 520nm. In sum, wavelengths that predominantly initiate blue sensations stimulate the neural response associated with green! Pickford (1951; cf. Hardin 1988:163) found that naive English-speaking subjects performed with least accuracy on matching tests with green-blue colors, showing less sensitivity to the green-blue distinction than to distinctions between other hues. Halsey and Chapanis (1951:1057) and Houston and Washburn (1907:523) found greatest discriminatory error among green and blue. Boster (1986) asked naive English speakers to sort into progressively smaller groups Munsell chips of Berlin and Kay's eleven "focal colors" while imagining that they spoke primitive languages whose color terms numbered only 2, 3, 4, and so forth. A significant number duplicated the 1975 hue sequence (fig. 2.2), dividing green/blue as the last composite category.

4.2. Cognitive Axioms

Cognition consists of the ways in which people modify their perceptions by means of selective emphasis. There are at least three such modifications of color perception: (*a*) an individual simultaneously attends to the perceived similarity and the perceived distinctiveness between any pair of pure color sensations; (*b*) the two emphases are mutable, that is, each can be strengthened or weakened; (*c*) their strengths are reciprocally related; weakening of one will always correspond to strengthening of the other, that is, both emphases will never be strengthened or weakened at the same time. Axiom 4 collapses these propositions: an individual attends simultaneously to similarity and to distinctiveness and can reciprocally shift the strengths of emphasis.[9]

Axiom 4 is the mainspring of internal change and division among, at least, categories that are composed in reference to one or more of the elemental colors. Its engagement with perceptual axioms 1, 2 and 3 is discussed under §4.4.

4.3. Motivation

The reciprocal shift in emphases on similarity and distinctiveness will not occur without motivation. People must have a reason to perpetrate the cognitive change. None of the available proposals of motivation covers all observations.

Berlin and Kay (1969) proposed that stages of basic color-term evolution roughly correlate with increments of societal complexity. Bartlett (1928:3), Berlin and Berlin (1975:83), and Dougherty (1975:187–191, 222–223) noted that color categories divide under the influence of culture contact; although loan words can be used to name new categories, they are innovated in the predicted order of evolution (Dougherty, p. 219). Berlin and Kay observe that the languages of some simple societies use more basic color categories than would be expected and the languages of some complex societies use fewer than expected. For example, Eskimo of the Arctic Circle and Bushman of the Kalahari Desert both name five salient color categories; but most of the languages of state-level societies in ancient Mesoamerica also named five. Mesoamerican languages in remote, impoverished regions name more basic color categories than do languages of large towns that occupy fertile farmland within a hour's bus ride to a state capital, for example, Zapotec of San Juan Mixtepec versus Zapotec of Santiago Apóstol (figs. 10.17 and 5.11–13) or Cakchiquel of Santa María de Jesús (fig. IV.2)—a marginal town without on-site water—versus Cakchiquel of Patzún (figs. 8.32–33).

It is feasible that color-category evolution is motivated by exposure to novelty rather than by societal complexity or culture contact per se, although complexity or contact would induce novelty. Novelty is motivational because it forces individuals to attend more to distinctiveness as a general strategy of sorting out and comprehending a world that differs from one day to the next. A society need not be complex in order to experience novelty as a daily event. Hardships and economic disadvantage can expose the members of a simple society to uncertainties that demand close attention to detail and frequent innovation. The analytical strategy they choose will provoke lexical differentiation across innumerable domains, including the naming of colors. Marginal peoples who must shift for a livelihood and/or migrate outside their territory will use many salient color categories, even though their society is small, monolingual, and culturally cohesive. Conversely, people whose daily lives are seldom imperiled will use fewer color categories, even though they might live within the orbit of a metropolitan center. The Dani, for example, who name only *light-warm* and *dark-cool* (Heider 1972*a*), live under circumstances that might not compel them to elaborate domains that are not of economic interest or culturally inspired focus.

> Each Dani is at once a farmer, a warrior, and a swineherd. If he is not
> killed by an enemy, he will live out his life in a casual manner. Much
> of his time will be spent sitting around a fire smoking cigarettes,

weaving or knitting, and just gossiping with his fellows. There is
no lack of land, no over population, and little serious disease in the
Dani's land; many Dani live to old age, and none go hungry. Even his
malevolent ghosts and the deadly warfare do not seem to cause fear
or anxiety. Finally, and perhaps related to the casual life of the Dani,
they have little elaboration of art, or music, or even oral literature
(K. Heider 1972*a*:4).

The Labrador Eskimo exploit many ecological niches during the season of sunlight. Rivers recorded these observations:

My previous experience of very defective colour nomenclature has
been derived from races inhabiting the tropics and it seemed somewhat unnatural to find a far more highly developed language for
colours in the inhabitants of a subarctic country such as Labrador.
    The Eskimo, however, told me that in the autumn they could see
all the colours that I had shown them in the hills and it is possible that
when colour is only a transient occurrence in the year's experience, it
may excite more attention and therefore receive more definite nomenclature than in those parts of the world where luxuriance of colour is
so familiar that it receives little notice.
    So far as I can gather from reading accounts of Eskimo life, colour
does not appear to be largely used in the dress or decorations of these
people. . . . those whom I examined were working with beads of various
colours . . . (Rivers 1901*d*:149).[10]

Environmental diversity and extreme climate would seem to explain
Eskimo color categorization more convincingly than does Rivers's theory of
transience, because the former would apply globally to people in harsh surroundings. The Kalahari habitat may impose the same cognitive incentive
on the Bushman, to whom Berlin and Kay attribute Stage IV color terms.

There is a vast sweep of dry bush desert lying in South-West Africa. . . .
in the long drought of the year the sun bakes the desert to powdery dry
leaves and dust. There are no surface waters at all, no clouds for cool-
ness, no tall trees for shade, but only low bushes and grass tuffs. . . . The
Kalahari would be very barren, very devoid of landmarks, if it were
not for the baobab tree, and even these grow far from each other . . .
When there is no wind . . . the temperature rises to 120° Fahrenheit
and more. . . . June and July are the months of winter . . . the icy wind,

pouring steadily across the continent from the Antarctic. (Thomas 1959:3–6).[11]

Baines (1986:238) observes that Egyptians used the same four basic color terms and only those from the third millennium B.C. to the Middle Ages, even though the society was complex and its changes were vast over the 3,500 years. This stability of basic color terms is startling, even if the system had reconfigured categories from brightness to hue, as in Tucano, Cayapa, or Slave (figs. 2.15 and 2.28–29). Probably the amount of novelty that impinged on any individual in ancient Egypt over the course of a lifetime was slight in comparison to that which pervades contemporary Mesoamerica.[12]

This hypothesis holds, further, that stronger attention to distinctiveness as a general adaptation to novelty would encourage lexical elaboration of many domains, not only of basic color terms. This point has been elaborated in §2.5 with support of the quotations by Douglas, Kay, Malkiel, and Duncan.

4.4. Engagement of Axioms

The four axioms of perception and cognition engage with each other in a manner that can explain change that progresses within universal constraints. Providing that people intend to categorize hue rather than levels of brightness, they will not categorize under one name opponent pairs of red/ green or yellow/blue. Then it will be predictable that a category of relatively distinct hues, such as red and yellow, will always divide before a category of more similar hues, such as green and blue. The distinct degrees of similarity and of difference that pertain between separate hue perceptions would have no bearing on evolutionary change unless a person picked them out for selective attention from among the assorted perceptions pertaining to color (§2.4.3., Sahlins [1976] on semiotics). Although, under specific conditions, people may choose between brightness and hue (MacLaury 1992a), it appears that people always balance this choice against emphases on similarity and distinctiveness when categorizing color.[13]

4.5. Using the Axioms

A case-study of color categorization in Tenejapa Tzeltal demonstrates how shift in attention from similarity to distinctiveness can explain co-occurring events. Further, the case exemplifies method beyond analysis of individual cognition: numerical comparison of Tzeltal systems substantiates the change that characterizes this sample. Finally, the model of change suggests how Berlin and Kay's "basic color category" and Rosch's "basic level of categorization" are related, a question unanswered until now. Thus, this case shows how the axioms are of use to theory.[14]

4.5.1. Tzeltal Hue Categories

Data were collected from nine speakers of Tenejapa Tzeltal, eight of whom reside at Paraje Nabil, a rural district located on the north side of a towering escarpment that borders Tenejapa center like a wall. The ninth speaker moved as an adult to San Cristóbal de las Casas; she represents the most advanced system of this sample, Stage IV, and is the only Tzeltal-Spanish bilingual. Another of the nine produced aberrant data (fig. 6.32), analyzed in §6.3.6. Speakers are identified as 3 through 10 to coincide with figures 4.3 through 4.10. Speakers 6 and 8 are the parents of speaker 10.

Figure 4.3 shows that ($b-c$) mappings are broader than (a) naming ranges, even though the naming of each category is salient. The broad mappings imply that there may be fewer basic categories than salient color terms and that the terms assume different kinds of semantic relations. In b, a relation of complementation obtains between the mappings of *ʔihk'* and *sak,* which are focused in pure black and pure white, respectively: neither mapping covers the focus of the opposite term, even though they overlap; the mapping of *sak* covers all of white, yellow, and red in the configuration of a light-warm category. In a, an outlying use of *sak* at G1 on elemental red corresponds to the mapping. The mapping of *ʔihk'* indicates a dark-cool category of black, green, and blue. In c, superordinate *ʔihk'* includes subordinate *yaš:* the mapping of *ʔihk'* covers the mapping and the focus of *yaš,* but the mapping of *yaš* covers neither the focus of *ʔihk'* nor its first mapping step. In d, the mappings of *¢ah* and *k'an* both cover all of the warm colors and almost the same colors, even though the terms are focused widely apart. In a, the ranges of *¢ah* and *k'an* are concentrated around their respective foci. Yet there are a few isolated uses of each name, such as *¢ah* at E10 and B12 or *k'an* at H3 or F34, that match the far reaches of each broad mapping (d). The mappings and outlying uses of *¢ah* and *k'an* are not mistakes; rather they independently reveal the range and organization of the Tzeltal warm category in a way that could not be inferred from naming data alone. The particular kind of semantic relation that pertains between *¢ah* and *k'an* will be introduced as "coextension" in Chapter 5. Here the important point is that coextension differs from other kinds of semantic re-

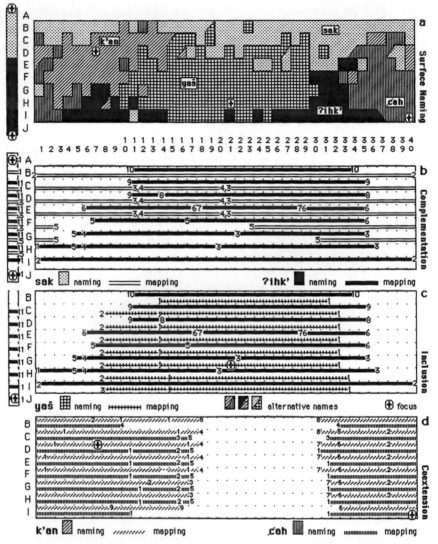

FIGURE 4.3. Tzeltal, San Ildefonso Tenejapa, Chiapas, Mexico, f 60, 1980: (*a*) naming ranges, (*a–d*) foci, and (*b–d*) mappings that show three types of semantic relations.

lations, such as inclusion and complementation. For example, the mappings of *¢ah* and *k'an* cover each other's foci.

How can we relate this individual system to Berlin and Kay's evolutionary stages of basic color terms? The mappings allow us to take into account the ranges and relations among categories in addition to the salient uses of terms. The light-warm range of *sak* is, perhaps, a vestige of an earlier system; this speaker is the only one in the Tenejapa sample who plotted its range over warm color. We might expect that a basic color category would be shared by a few speakers. The cool category *yaš* is not basic in spite of its salient naming range; because it is completely encompassed by the range of *ʔihk'*, it fails to meet Berlin and Kay's criterion of nonhyponymy (§2.4). This Tzeltal speaker seems to represent Berlin and Kay's Stage II, having three basic color categories of white (with a vestigial light-warm range), dark-cool (of uneven naming salience), and coextensively named warm. The system is in transition to Stage IIIa, as evidenced by its salient "cool" category.

So far, two observations are possible:

1. The system of color categories is in transition such that it retains a remnant of its past while forecasting its future. An identification of its current basic color categories requires a choice of one interpretation among options. This choice lies between the conservative and progressive extremes.

2. Different kinds of semantic relations pertain within, between, or both within and between categories; they correspond to the different extents to which categories have divided. The dark-cool and vestigial light-warm categories show a relation of complementation, which typifies basic categories that have always been separate or have separated completely. Division of the light-warm category would convert a Stage I system to Stage II. The dark-cool category exhibits a relation of inclusion which foretells of its immanent division into two basic categories of black and cool. A division of the dark-cool category would convert Stage II to Stage IIIa. The basic warm category is named with two terms whose coextensive ranges are focused widely apart; they appear to presage an eventual division of warm into categories of red and yellow, which nevertheless is not substantially underway. A division of the warm category would convert Stage IIIa to Stage IV. The cool category is named with a single term; the category is nonbasic, and it shows no evidence of splitting into distinct green and blue categories other than a slight skewing toward green in its naming range and focus. A division of the cool category would convert Stage IV to Stage V. Thus, a relation of complementation, a relation of inclusion, a coextensive relation, and a single term together indicate four phases of division that parallel or foreshadow the Berlin-and-Kay order (fig. 2.2). Ongoing division pervades all categories but advances to a different degree in each.

Further analysis will be confined to the changing relation between *ʔihk'* and *yaš*. Four of the eight interviewees retain the dark-cool range of *ʔihk'* and four do not; they will be called, respectively, "group 1" and "group 2." The four in group 1 represent Stage II. Three in group 2 represent Stage IIIa while one represents Stage IV. Each individual reflects a different degree of progress within a stage; no two are alike.

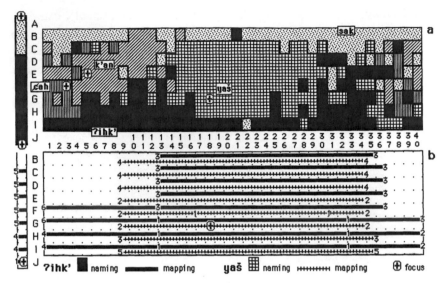

FIGURE 4.4. Tzeltal, Tenejapa, Mexico, m 65+, 1980: (*a*) naming ranges, (*a–b*) foci, and (*b*) mappings.

The systems of group 1 appear in figures 4.3–6, respectively, speakers 3–6. Speakers 4–6 have intermixed their naming ranges of *?ihk'* and *yaš* more than has speaker 3, although all mapped *?ihk'* as a dark-cool cate-

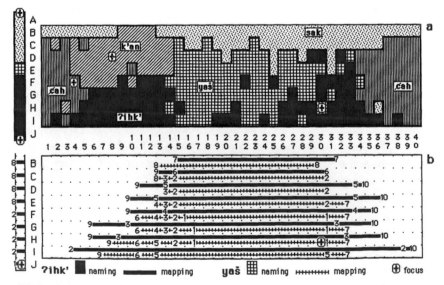

FIGURE 4.5. Tzeltal, Tenejapa, Mexico; f 60, 1980: (*a*) naming ranges, (*a–b*) foci, and (*b*) mappings.

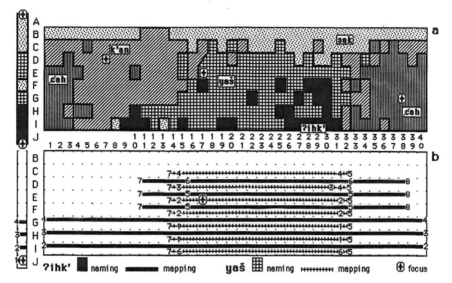

FIGURE 4.6. Tzeltal, Tenejapa, Mexico; m 90, 1980: (*a*) naming ranges, (*a–b*) foci, and (*b*) mappings.

gory. Speakers 3–5 mapped *ʔihk'* broadly and to row B, but speaker 6 mapped *ʔihk'* with a range that omits rows B and C, which suggests he has begun to separate the categories *ʔihk'* and *yaš* by retracting the range of *ʔihk'* toward its black focus. Speakers 3–6 used *yaš* to name, respectively, 102, 80, 101 and 86 color chips, an average of 92. They intermixed terms in ways that could give a misimpression of sloppiness when their naming ranges are compared with the cleanly bounded manner in which speakers of group 2 named color.

Figures 4.7–10 display data from group 2, speakers 7–10. The mappings show all have retracted the category *ʔihk'* to a range of only black and dark colors while *yaš* has emerged as basic. The categories *yaš* and *ʔihk'* are in complementation. Speakers 7–10 name the cool category 124, 152, 119, and 160 times, averaging 139. This count includes only *yaš* for speakers 7–8, but it includes coextensive *selestre* and *asul* for speaker 9 and secondary *elemoneš* and *k'abuhš* for speaker 10, because mapping data show that these secondary terms name parts of the cool category. Speaker 7 shares with group 1 the use of *only* the five terms common to all. Speakers 8–10 use additional terms. Only speaker 9 has adopted other terms to a coextensive relation with *yaš*. Figure 7.3 shows that speaker 10 divides the warm category and represents Berlin and Kay's Stage IV; she names an emerging orange category, *aʔlčaš*, between yellow *k'an* and red *ȼah*.

Observations (1) and (2) above can be joined by another four:

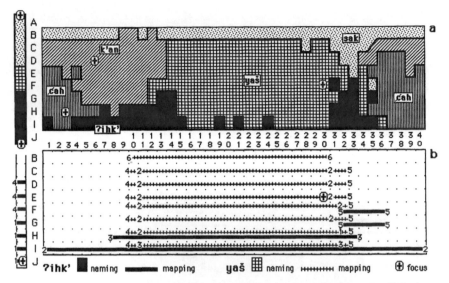

FIGURE 4.7. Tzeltal, Tenejapa, Mexico; m 55, 1980: (*a*) naming ranges, (*a–b*) foci, and (*b*) mappings.

3. Speakers of a language do not bed down for the night at one evolutionary stage to awaken on the morning at the next stage. Evolution progresses continuously. Speaker 6 represents the most advanced case of Stage II, while speaker 7 represents the most conservative version of Stage III*a*. The

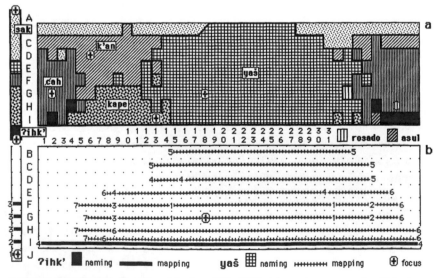

FIGURE 4.8. Tzeltal, Tenejapa, Mexico; f 70, 1980: (*a*) naming ranges, (*a–b*) foci, and (*b*) mappings.

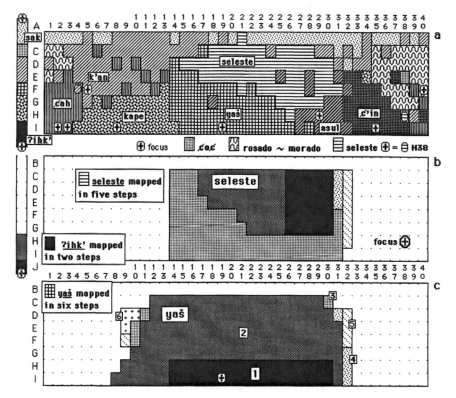

FIGURE 4.9. Tzeltal, Tenejapa, Mexico; f 37, 1980: (*a*) naming ranges, (*a–c*) foci, and (*b–c*) mappings.

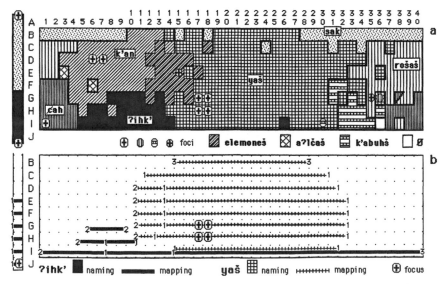

FIGURE 4.10. Tzeltal, Tenejapa, Mexico; f 34, 1980: (*a*) naming ranges, (*a–b*) foci, and (*b*) mappings.

gradual change consists of rearranging cognitive relations among pre-existing terms and pre-existing categories (see Hage and Hawkes 1975: 288–289, quoted in note 6 of §5.2).

4. As a color category becomes basic, its naming range expands; group 1 names an average of 92 chips as a secondary cool category, whereas group 2 names an average of 139 chips as a basic cool category.

5. As evolution progresses through Stages II, IIIa, and IV, terms are added to the system that assume a relation of coextension or inclusion with one or another of the five terms that are shared by all speakers.

6. As evolution progresses, the naming ranges of the five shared terms exhibit less intermixture and project sharper boundaries.

In sum, color-category evolution is accompanied by quantifiable trends, observations 1–6. How do axioms 1–4 tie them into a single account?

4.5.2. A Model of Variation in Tzeltal Color Categorization

Perceptual axioms 1–3 account for the general outline of Stages II–IV. For example, in Stage IV, the cool category remains as the last composite category, because elemental green and elemental blue appear more similar to each other than do the elemental colors of any other pair. Accordingly, *yaš* is the only composite category named with just one term throughout the stages; in Stage II the dark-cool category is named with basic *ʔihk'* and secondary *yaš,* and in Stages II and IIIa the warm category is named co-extensively with both *¢ah* and *k'an.* Since contrasts of red/yellow and black/cool appear more distinct than green/blue, the dark-cool and the warm categories divide before the cool category while inviting complex semantics.

Cognitive axiom 4 provides the dynamics of change. As individuals attend less to similarity and more to distinctiveness, they become less at ease with thinking in terms of very broad categories and more comfortable using narrow categories. Thus, they retract the range of dark-cool *ʔihk'* toward its black focus while increasing their preference for applying *yaš* to green and blue. The revision induces a broader naming range of *yaš.* The increase in emphasis on distinctiveness simultaneously encourages individuals to name subsections of basic color categories with loan words and natural-object terms, thus bringing about the innovation of secondary color vocabulary.

All of the eight Tzeltal speakers named color chips with the same conscientious care for exactitude; all seemed lucid, thoughtful, and at ease during the interview. In spite of this, the intermixed naming ranges of group 1 appear "sloppy" in comparison to the "neat" naming ranges of group 2. However, a judgment of sloppiness would presuppose an objective standard that one could either meet or fail. Axiom 4 might offer insight: greater attention to distinctiveness would enhance an individual's preconception of precision such that an accurate performance in the eyes of a speaker at Stage II would appear inaccurate to speakers at Stages IIIa and IV or, for that matter, to an English speaker at Stage VII. The concept of accuracy sharpens in accord with the other changes.

The variable degrees of evolutionary advance correspond to age, but perhaps insignificantly: the mean ages of groups 1 and 2 are, respectively, 69 and 55 years. But speaker 6, age 90, is the most advanced member of group 1. If we entertain the hypothesis of motivation—that distinct exposures to novelty provoke unequal degrees of differentiation—then we should expect that separate members of one small community will have encountered new experience to variable extents. That in itself seems safe to assume. But it is also likely that some individuals will recognize novelty more than others, and some will try to ignore it. The hypothesis of differing exposure to novelty is consistent with the range of variation in Tenejapa Tzeltal color categorization and with its weak correlation with age.

The incremental change is governed by the reciprocity of emphases on similarity and distinctiveness. Although recognition of distinctiveness becomes stronger, it is counterbalanced by the awareness of similarity. The tension between the emphases prevents change from surging forward in a quantum leap from a traditional system to a radically altered relation among categories. A continuum of intermediate phases will characterize any sample of data taken from several individuals at one time and place, providing that they have not suffered some trauma.

4.5.3. Issues of Theory

Application of the four axioms to Tzeltal data appears to answer two long-standing questions of theory concerning color categorization.

First, What is the relation between Rosch's "basic level of categorization" and Berlin and Kay's "basic color categories"? (See §§1.1 and 2.4.) On one account (Berlin and Kay 1969:2), the basic level of color categorization is represented by a fully developed Stage VII system, such as that of English. These eleven basic categories correspond to the major perceptual divisions that speakers of every language are tempted to duplicate linguistically (cf. Wattenwyl and Zollinger 1978, 1979). Speakers of some languages have achieved the complete match of basic color terms with the basic level; speakers of other languages have not. This view ignores the relation of categorization to cognition.

On another view, Rosch's basic level of categorization coincides with whatever color categories are basic in the system of an individual. In her words (Mervis and Rosch 1981:93), "Dougherty and Rosch et al. both provide examples of the relativity of the basic level" (cf. Dougherty 1978c, Rosch et al. 1976:432). In the present framework of axioms, the basic level can move from broader to narrower concentration as attention to distinctiveness increases. In Tzeltal, some speakers place the basic level at or near the breadth of a dark-cool category; others place it at greater specificity to establish the foremost cut between cool and black categories. In other Mesoamerican languages, such as Pame or Southern Cakchiquel (figs. IV.1–2), all speakers have established the basic level at even closer differentiation, so that green, blue, and black are separate basic color categories, as they are in English.

The basic level of categorization is, perhaps, more mobile among color categories than in many other domains. Color is a domain of attributes rather than of entities, as is, for example, a biological taxonomy (see §12.1.2). Nothing intrinsic to the morphology of objects can impede the mobility of basic color categorization, even though color perception and universal cognitive abilities may work together to impose a ceiling and a floor (as argued in Appendix IV). It is unlikely that speakers of a language will envelop all color within a single basic category or that categories equivalent to those we call "periwinkle" and "heliotrope" will become basic in some language; rather, the basic level will vary through the gamut between upper and lower limits (Rosch et al. 1976:432). Rosch's basic-level mobility is consistent with the cognitive axiom of reciprocal emphases on similarity and distinctiveness.

Second, Are Berlin and Kay's criteria of a basic color category subject to internal contradiction? They offer as criteria both maximum inclusiveness (nonhyponymy) and salience (see item 1 of §2.4). Yet Tzeltal speakers 3–6 of Stage II encompass a highly salient cool category within a dark-cool category whose naming range, in turn, is nonsalient among cool colors. Would this imply that one of the criteria should be ranked over the other to enable a clean decision as to whether the cool category is basic?

The mobility of the basic level of categorization dispels this dilemma. Since the basic level moves without an abrupt jump from a relation of inclusion to a relation of complementation between *ʔihk'* and *yaš*, then, during the transition, the basic level may obtain between the superordinate and subordinate categories. Part of the superordinate category will wane in its status as the subordinate category becomes basic. At that point, Berlin and Kay's criteria will be split between the categories, nonhyponomy pertaining to *ʔihk'* but salience to *yaš*. It would be inconsistent with the gradual nature of cognitive change to force the criteria into an all-or-none application. Revising them or assigning priorities among them will not improve our insights.

4.6. Summary

Four axioms help to explain diverse observations of data on color categorization that result from the three-part interview. Three axioms describe perception and one specifies cognition. They distinguish perception from cognition as a prerequisite of modeling color categorization within universal constraints.

Data from eight Tzeltal speakers demonstrate the capacity of the axioms to provide a unified account of six observations, including individual variation and incremental change. An individual system of color categories retains a part of its past, projects its future, and maintains a constellation of basic categories in the present. The basic level of categorization is mobile: its defining criteria can pertain exclusively to the superordinate category in a relation of inclusion between two categories, or the criteria can extend to the subordinate category one at a time as change progresses.

PART TWO

VIEWPOINT AND CATEGORY CHANGE:
A Continuous Typology of Relations

Detailed data support the hypothesis that any color category is a point of view fashioned by analogy to space-motion coordinates. A person may change the size and shape of a category by shifting emphases among coordinates. Some people construct one category from two views by rearranging the coordinates; they separately name, focus, and map each vantage, coextending the ranges over almost the same colors. The alternative arrangements entail different emphases that, in turn, predict quantitative differences in size and shape within each configuration of data, an outcome called the "dominant-recessive pattern." Categories of two or more vantages provide the vital test of vantage theory.

The dominant-recessive pattern of coextension is critical to theories of categorization because a category named throughout with two terms is, nevertheless, shaped differently under each, even though one individual applies them to the same stimuli during a short interview under singular conditions of lighting and environment. Because all variables are constant except the thoughts of the interviewee, the source of this patterned difference between ranges must reside solely within the individual. It is impossible to assert that such categorization is objective.

The dominant-recessive pattern is a synchronic segment of a diachronic trajectory of semantic relations which pertain between the ranges of terms that name one category. As the category divides, the difference in size and shape of ranges increases. Near synonymy, coextension, inclusion, and complementation follow one upon another. This path of ideal types, too, is predictable.

The chapters of Part Two describe and formally model the types of semantic relations and their variants. While Chapter 5 introduces the type called "coextension," Chapter 6 develops its theoretical implications for categorization and related issues of cognition. Chapter 7 addresses the advanced end of the continuum wherein broad categories split into separately named complementary halves. None of the data along its length fit expectations of conventional logicians, fuzzy-set theorists, or friends of the prototype model. The latter have isolated engaging problems—such as asymmetry judgments or the roles of similarity and difference in categorization—that the vantage model may accommodate.

CHAPTER 5

COEXTENSIVE SEMANTIC RANGES

Early in the Mesoamerican survey, as we refined interviewing methods with the help of Uspantec speakers (MacLaury, McMillen, and McMillen 1979), a semantic relation emerged in the data that did not fit our preconception of synonymy, near synonymy, inclusion, or complementation. A seventy-four year-old man named numerous red and yellow chips either *kʸaq* or *q'en* and focused *kʸaq* near elemental red and *q'en* near elemental yellow; he mapped *kʸaq* throughout red and yellow and mapped other categories after that. Finally, we asked him to map *q'en*, but he protested that he had already mapped the term. We told him that he had mapped *kʸaq*, but now we would like to see him map *q'en*. He replied to the effect of "If you say so," and he mapped *q'en* throughout yellow and red. For the most part, his mappings of *kʸaq* and *q'en* covered the same warm colors, but he laid down the rice in opposite directions: for *kʸaq*, he mapped red and later yellow; whereas he mapped *q'en* in the reverse order. The first mapping step of each term matched its respective focus, which was placed at maximum distance from the focus of the other.

It appeared that both terms named the warm category but with distinct stresses. The differences between foci and directions of mapping seemed too great to be identified as "near synonymy." Yet, since each range covered almost the same colors, "inclusion" also failed to describe the relation. I took note of the peculiar data and puzzled over them. Later, as the survey moved to other languages, at least 100 examples of the same semantic relation were attested by the three-part method; they were recorded by different investigators when I was not present, and the relation pertained to names of various categories, for example, cool, dark-cool, green, brown, purple, and desaturated color. I called the relation "coextensive semantic ranges" or "coextension." After the survey, the data on coextension prompted me to hypothesize that color categorization is based on a space-time analogy, as outlined in §6.2.

My objective here is to introduce semantic coextension by describing its attributes. The description shows that coextension is sufficiently distinctive to constitute a type of its own which has heretofore escaped a pointed recognition. Other investigators have described coextension in passing, as Hage and Hawks (1975) report differently focused Binumarien terms for the dark-cool category (quoted in §2.4.2., see fig. 2.8; see also Rivers 1901a:57, 60; Maass 1912:142–143; Bartlett 1928:8, 17, 24, 27; Berlin and Berlin 1975:figs. 5–7; Beek 1977:15–16; Baxter 1983:11–12). Merrifield (1971: 264), in sketching Amuzgo color terms, notes that "the two terms for green have different foci but the same range." However, few researchers have addressed the relation as a subject in itself, and none has pursued its potential contribution to a theory of categorization.[1]

Coextension involves more than just an unexplored semantic relation: (1) it is characterized differently in distinct perceptual environments, and (2) it is linked to other semantic relations in specific ways and for particular reasons. A minimal but nonreductionist introduction requires a description of both qualities.

1. Coextension typifies the warm category of Mesoamerican languages, but in the cool category it occurs less often. Coextension exhibits more dichotomous characteristics in the warm category than in the cool category. The differences corroborate the evidence from visual physiology that red and yellow appear more distinct than green and blue.[2] The same engagement of perceptual and cognitive axioms that explains why the warm category divides before the cool category in universal evolutionary order also explains the differences shown by coextension in the two environments.

2. Near synonymy, coextension, and inclusion are segments of a continuum, not discrete kinds of relation. At one extreme, strong attention to similarity produces near synonymy; at the other, strong attention to distinctiveness produces inclusion. Midway on the continuum, closer equilibrium of the two emphases produces coextension. Off the end of this scale, very strong attention to distinctiveness produces complementation. It will be shown why complementation stands apart (§6.4). The same interaction of perception and cognition that causes the continuous evolution of basic color categories also causes evolution along a continuum from one semantic type to another within a particular category as it divides.

The semantic side of coextension is featured throughout this introduction, while its critical cognitive characteristic is treated in Chapter 6. Semantic coextension is inexplicable solely in terms of perceptual axioms, because different organizations of the same colored stimuli by a single individual during one short interview do not inhere in neural response to wavelength. It is the observer who assumes opposite slants on the same sensations and names them differently from each angle. Explanation of the latter requires a cognitive ingredient. This argument is of the same force as that regarding the inability of invariant perception to account for the division of an attribute category. Both coextension and category division constitute strong but separate reasons for incorporating cognition into a theory of categorization.

5.1. Characteristics of Coextension

Semantic coextension is manifested distinctly in the warm category and the cool category. The differences appear to be physiologically conditioned. They agree with the evidence that red and yellow are perceived to be farther apart than green and blue, axiom 3.

5.1.1. Coextension in the Warm Category

Figure 5.1 displays the naming ranges and mappings by which the Uspantec elder originally showed us coextension. Richer examples appear in figures 6.1–4. The data exemplify four attributes of coextensive semantic ranges within the warm category: (1) one category is named with two terms; (2) each term is focused in reference to a different elemental hue; (3) the mapping of each term encompasses the focus of the opposite term; and (4) the mappings substantially overlap throughout the category; in *b–c*, they overlap on 121 colors, or 79% of the 153 colors covered by both. These attributes vary across individual systems, as will be shown.

Three other attributes (5–7) vary even more, although they too are quite common: (5) mappings that progress in opposite directions; (6) intermixture of terms; and (7) polarized foci. Figure 5.1 shows mappings that progress in opposite directions: in *b*, the first mapping step includes yellow and red, and subsequent steps cover brown and purple; in *c*, the first step includes red, orange, and purple, the second covers elemental yellow, and subsequent steps cover yellowish green, brown, and light pink. The converse mappings further demonstrate the strong relation of each coextensive range to an opposite elemental hue. Attribute 5 varies in that one of the two ranges may be mapped with a first step that covers both elemental hues, as in *b;* figures 5.4 and 6.3 strikingly exemplify converse mappings. Coexten-

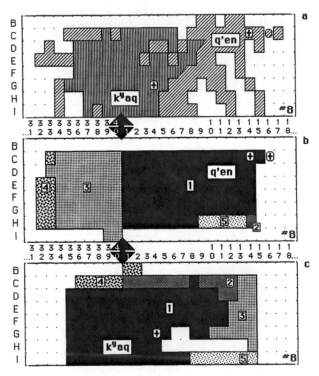

FIGURE 5.1. Uspantec, Las Pacayas, Uspantán, Guatemala, m 74, 1979: (*a*) naming ranges, (*a–c*) foci, and (*b–c*) mappings.

sion differs from near synonymy, in which the mapping of each range covers both elemental hues in a first step, figure 5.9. Attribute 6, intermixture of terms, is exemplified in figure 5.1, where *a* shows slight intermixture at I38, E3, H5, and D8. Either coextensive term may designate any color

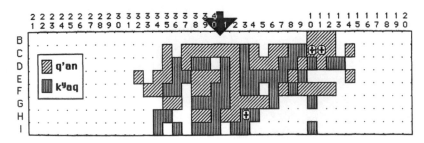

FIGURE 5.2. Aguacatec, Aguacatán, Huehuetenango, Guatemala, m 84, 1978: naming ranges and foci.

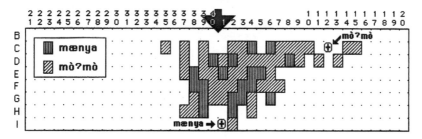

FIGURE 5.3. Tlapanec, Malinaltepec, Guerrero, Mexico, m 22, 1978: naming ranges and foci.

within the category, even though its naming range concentrates around its focus and the elemental color with which it is primarily associated. Attribute 6 varies to the extreme at which some individuals show no intermixture, although their mappings and other data affirm that they relate terms coextensively (figs. 5.4 and 6.4; see note 2 re Zulu). Yet other speakers vary to the opposite extreme, as does the Aguacatec speaker in figure 5.2. He focuses each term near an elemental hue (G1–2 red, C8–9 yellow); yet with each term he names colors beyond the opposite elemental hue.

The Aguacatec speaker of figure 5.2 also provides an example of attribute 7, polarized foci. He selects foci at H3 and C10–11 outside the elemental hues. They are mutually polarized, as if he chose them to stress a distinction. Mutual polarization is rare, although polarizing one focus is common, as the Uspantec speaker has polarized his focus of *q'en* at C14 and C16 (fig. 5.1).

In figure 5.3, a Tlapanec speaker mutually polarizes foci (I1 and C12) beyond the margins of his naming ranges (fig. 6.37*b*, full system). Tlapanec speakers focus *mænya* in reference to red and *mò?mò* in reference to yellow (figs. 6.37, 7.7*b*, 7.17*b*). In general, people polarize a focus beyond its naming range (figs. 4.9*b*, 6.26*a*, 10.3*c*, 10.5*c*) often enough to suggest that not all of them do so by "mistake."[3] It is possible that as subjects focus, they accentuate distinctiveness while suppressing other awareness.

Figure 5.4 shows that another Aguacatec speaker names the warm category with three coextensive terms: *k^y aq* red-focused, *q'an* yellow-focused, and *sq'inko?x* "brown-oriented"; the brown focus was overlooked during the interview. The mapping of each term starts around its focus or at brown and progresses by steps in a direction opposed to those of the other mappings. Frequently used *k^y aq* and *q'an* descend from Proto-Mayan while *sq'inko?x* originates locally.[4]

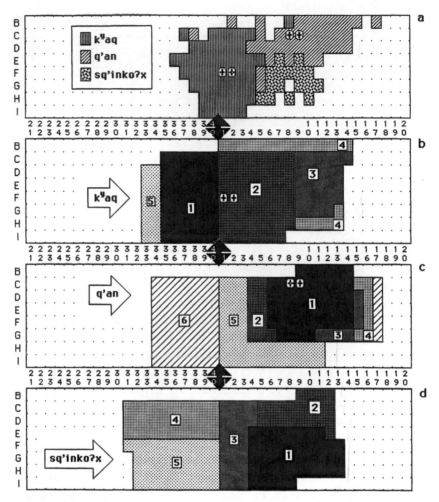

FIGURE 5.4. Aguacatec, Aguacatán, Huehuetenango, Guatemala, f 41; triple co-extensivity: (*a*) naming ranges and foci 1978, (*b–d*) mappings 1980.

5.1.2. Coextension in the Cool Category

The attributes (1–7) that characterize coextension in the warm category also pertain in the cool category, but their form is less dichotomous. In the cool category, (1) coextensive ranges are often named with two terms. In specific languages, however, the cool category is constructed from opposite angles but named with only one term. (Evidence of this "covert coextension" is developed in §§8.2.2.4, 8.5–6). (2) When the cool category is named with coextensive terms, each is associated with a different elemental hue. However, the tie may be weak: at least one coextensive term may be focused in a dual manner in separate reference to each elemental hue, as in figure 5.6, or both terms may be focused in reference to only one of the elemental hues, as in figure 5.7. (3) The weak association is also manifested when the mapping of each coextensive term covers both elemental hues with the first step. (4) The first step can apply disjunctively to pure green and pure blue while leaving turquoise for a subsequent step, as in figure 5.5c, or the first step can apply continuously to both pure colors as well as to the colors between them, figure 5.11. (5) An extensive intermixture of coextensive terms is more common in the cool category than in the warm category, figure 5.8. (6) When coextension is demonstrated by mappings, confinement of either naming range to only part of the cool category is rare, figure 5.5. (7) The foci of coextensive names of the cool category are a little less likely to be polarized than are foci of the same in the warm category. Among the foci of coextensively named cool categories in figure 8.16b, the ratio of laterally polarized-to-nonpolarized foci is 26:156

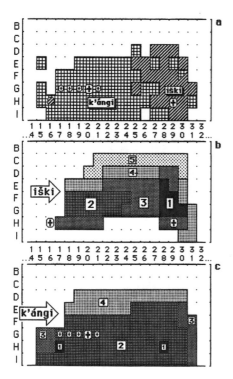

FIGURE 5.5. Otomí, Arenadito, Valle del Mezquital, Hidalgo, Mexico, m 26, 1980: (a) naming ranges and foci, (b–c) mappings.

(16.66% polarized); while among the foci of coextensively named warm categories in figure 6.38 the ratio is 13:71 (18.30%). Four figures exemplify polarized foci of coextensive cool terms: fig. 5.5 at H16; fig. 5.7 at F16, fig. 5.8 at F16, H30, H13–14 and F31; and fig. 5.10 at C15 and G7.

Among all cool categories (fig. 8.16*d*) and warm categories (fig. 6.38 and table 7.1), the ratios of laterally polarized-to-nonpolarized foci are: cool 115:571 (20.31% polarized) and warm 29:93 (31.18%). The amount of polarization is greater than among coextensively named categories because the statistics pertain on the whole to categories in a more advanced phase of division. The difference between ratios evident in coextensive naming pertains to warm and cool categories regardless of how they are named.

In figure 5.5, an Otomí speaker coextensively maps the cool category: *k'ángi* is broadly green-focused through columns 17 to 21 with preference at G20; *iški* (also the name of a beverage) is dual-focused at H16 and H29. The data exhibit all attributes (1–7) of coextension in the cool category except attribute 5, intermixture of terms: (*a*) dual-focused *iški* names only blue in the vicinity of its first mapping step, shown in *b;* the second step of this mapping is applied to green, the third to turquoise, and the last to marginal colors. In *c,* the mapping of *k'ángi* is disjunctive, with the first step occurring only on H17 and H28. Its second step is continuous throughout green, blue, and turquoise; final steps are marginal.

In figure 5.6, Mixtec speaker 1 intermixes coextensive naming of the cool category (5), unlike the Otomí speaker (fig. 5.5). But like the Otomí speaker, the Mixtec speaker focuses one term, $k^{w}\bar{\imath}\acute{\imath}$, on dual colors (G19, F28). Both colors are named with the other term, $^{n}d\bar{e}\acute{e}$, whose single focus is also placed on F28.

In figure 5.7, Mixtec speaker 2 focuses both coextensive terms, $k^{w}\bar{\imath}\acute{\imath}$ and $^{n}d\bar{e}\acute{e}$, only in green (F16/G18, G16). The figure displays (*a*) inter-

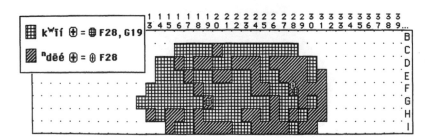

FIGURE 5.6. Mixtec, Santo Tomás Ocótepec, Tlaxiaco, Oaxaca, Mexico, m 75±, 1979: naming ranges and foci, speaker 1.

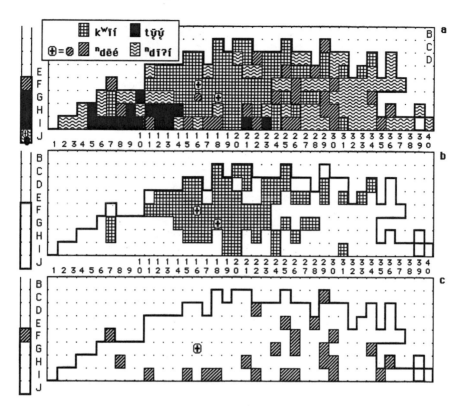

FIGURE 5.7. Mixtec, Ocotepec, m 73, 1979: naming ranges and foci, speaker 2; (*a*) four ranges, (*b*) the range of *kʷīí*, (*c*) the range of *ⁿdēé*.

mixed naming ranges of a black-focused "dark-cool" basic term *ⁿdī ʔí* (JØ), a "black" term *tʊʊ́* (JØ), and *kʷīí* and *ⁿdēé*. This rare case of coextension on the secondary level occurs in a social milieu that encourages differentiation: speakers 1 and 2 are the only two in the sample of 20 from Ocotepec who maintain the cool category, both having adopted coextension. In *b–c*, *kʷīí* concentrates in green, *ⁿdēé* in blue (mismatching its focus G16).

Figure 5.8 compares sets of naming ranges in the cool category from three languages; technically, *a* falls short of coextension at column 28, while *b* and *c* strongly show it.[5] The Nahuatl speaker (*a*) focuses on elemental green F17 *šošoktik* and elemental blue F29 *neštik*. The Paya speaker (*b*) polarizes foci, F16 'sà ʔká and H30 *ᵍwrὰh'ná ʔ*. The Tlapanec speaker (*c*) shows extreme mutual polarization of foci, G13–14 *maša* and F31 *minyüü*. Most Tlapanec speakers apply *maša* to the cool category, *minyüü* to blue-with-purple (figs. 8.36 and 8.28).

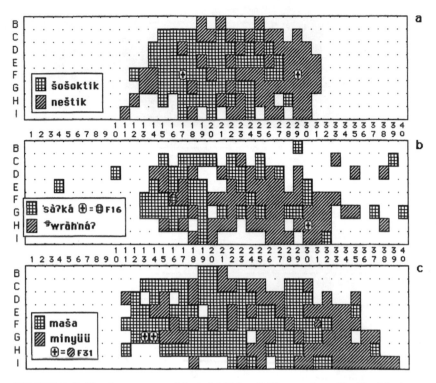

FIGURE 5.8. Naming ranges and foci: (*a*) Nahuatl, Tlaxpanaloya, Puebla, Mexico, m 35, 1978; (*b*) Paya, Pueblo Nuevo Subírana, Honduras, m 23, 1977; (*c*) Tlapanec, Malinaltepec, Guerrero, Mexico, m 30, 1978.

In §4.5.1, figure 4.9 displays coextension in the cool category of a Tenejapa Tzeltal speaker, which is confirmed only by mapping data. A loanword, *selestre,* assumes a coextensive relation with a native word, *yaš.* The ranges contrast by brightness, not by hue: the first mapping step of *yaš* is dark while the first of *selestre* is light; the first steps cover no color in common. The focus of *selestre* (H38) is extremely polarized (as are foci of other individuals, e.g., figs. 5.3 and 5.10). Another loanword, *asul,* makes a case for triple coextension.

5.1.3. Coextension in Two Environments

Table 5.1 summarizes the comparison of coextension in warm and cool categories. Seven (1–7) of the differences have been described as attributes above, partially or fully. Remaining aspects of 1–7 and all of 8–9 will be developed in sections cross-referenced in the table. All attributes

TABLE 5.1. Coextension in two environments

Warm Category	Cool Category
1. Each vantage that composes one category is always named with a different root (§§5.1.1 and 6).	1. Each vantage that composes one category can be named with a different root (§5); or both vantages can be named with the same root (§9.2). Such vantages can be differentiated by a root versus its qualification (§10.4).
2. Each term is focused in reference to a different unique hue. In a category that is constituted by more vantages than there are unique hues, the additional vantages are taken in reference to a complex color, such as brown; and each additional range is focused in reference to such (fig. 5.4).	2. Each term is often focused in reference to a different unique hue, although the link may be weak. The weakness enables at least one of a pair of coextensive terms to be applied from two vantages and, consequently, to be dual-focused in reference to both unique hues. Or, for the same reason, both terms can be focused in reference to the same unique hue (figs. 5.6–7).
3. The mapping of each range encompasses the focus of the opposite range(s).	3. Same as in the warm category
4. The mappings of the two (or more) ranges substantially overlap throughout the category.	4. Same as in the warm category
5. A range is likely to be mapped such that the first step is placed in the vicinity of one unique hue and the other unique hue is mapped by a subsequent step as the mapping progresses in the direction of the most distant margin of the category. The mapping of the second range is likely to progress in similar fashion, but from an opposite starting point and in the converse direction (fig. 5.1; cf. fig. 6.3). Rarely, one range will be mapped over both unique hues by one step (cf. figs. 6.3, 6.7, and 6.10). Both ranges will not be mapped over both unique hues by the first step of each mapping (fig. 5.9).	5. A range is likely to be mapped such that the first step is placed on both unique hues, *either* disjunctively on green and blue with turquoise colors left to be mapped by subsequent steps (fig. 5.5c) *or* continuously throughout green, turquoise, and blue (fig. 5.11). In either case, both unique hues are treated with one performance during the mapping of each range. A mapping of one range over the unique hues by separate steps occurs less (fig. 6.27). Mapping in separate steps commonly coincides with crossover (figs. 10.1–5), item 9 below.
6. The name of any range can be applied throughout the category (fig. 5.1), although the extensive intermixture of co-	6. The name of any range is used with slight preference in the vicinity of one unique hue, although extensive intermix

TABLE 5.1. Continued

Warm Category	Cool Category
extensive terms occurs in about one in ten cases (figs. 5.2, 6.1, and 6.34). A prevailing confinement of each term to the vicinity of opposite elemental hues is common (fig. 5.4).	ture of terms occurs in about one in two cases (fig. 5.8). A prevailing confinement of each term to the vicinity of opposite elemental hues is rare (figs. 5.5 and 11.9).
7. Foci are often polarized to a position between a unique hue and the category margin (fig. 5.1). Foci of opposite ranges can be polarized in apparent opposition to each other (cf. fig. 5.2). In extreme cases, mutually polarized foci are placed on opposite peripheries outside of their naming ranges (fig. 5.3).	7. Foci are sometimes polarized, although seldom to an extreme (figs. 4.9 and 5.8). Rarely, the foci of both ranges are polarized to peripheral positions that are adjacent or virtually the same rather than opposite (fig. 5.10). Such adjacency seems to result from the weakness of association of a range with a particular hue, as detailed under 2. See also 9.
8. Coextension exhibits a dominant-recessive pattern (table 6.1).	8. As in the warm category (see tables 11.2–5), and this is so in spite of crossover (item 9.)
9. During advancing category division, each coextensive range retracts toward its own polarized focus and away from the focus of the opposite range. The coincidence of a term, its mapping, and its focus is unequivocal. Data from different individuals coincide in like ways (§7.1).	9. As in the warm category, except that crossover sometimes occurs between coextensive ranges (§10.1). The relation between green and blue hues may be stressed more than their separate identities (§§10.1–3)

except 3–4 differ between the environments. Each difference implies that red and yellow appear more distinct than green and blue; ethnographic evidence and physiological evidence corroborate one another (§4.1.1).

5.2. Coextension in Relation to Other Semantic Types

The reciprocity of strength between attention to similarity and to distinctiveness entails a typological continuum of semantic relations. Strong attention to similarity and weak attention to distinctiveness produce near synonymy. Strong attention to distinctiveness and weak attention to similarity produce complementation. Between the extremes, emphases closer to equal strength produce coextension, with small shifts producing varia-

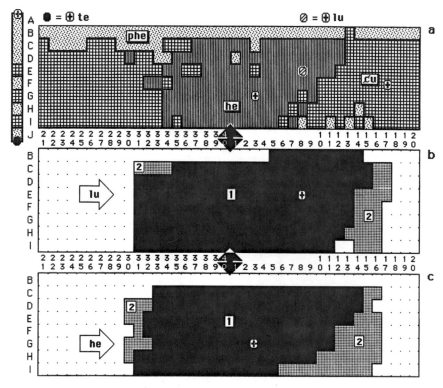

FIGURE 5.9. Jicaque, Montaña de la Flor, Honduras, f 25±: (*a*) naming ranges and foci, 1977; (*b–c*) mappings, 1981.

tion within the type. A decided shift toward distinctiveness produces inclusion. The relations evolve as a category divides.[6]

The following compares near synonymy and coextension and exhibits systems intermediate to pristine forms. Inclusion and complementation are discussed mainly in §7.1.

Figure 5.9 shows the best example of near synonymy within any composite category of the Mesoamerican sample; the type is rare. A Jicaque speaker—the only individual in the sample who named all colors with just three terms—named warm with one term, *he,* that she focused in red (G3). Another nine Jicaque interviewed at Montaña de la Flor used yellow-focused *lu* as well as *he* (figs. 8.28*b* and 11.7). This speaker, because she was asked to do so, focused and mapped *lu* also. Her knowledge exceeded her use of terms. In contrast to the coextensive warm ranges of figures 5.1–4, *lu* and *he* are focused close together and mapped almost alike; the first

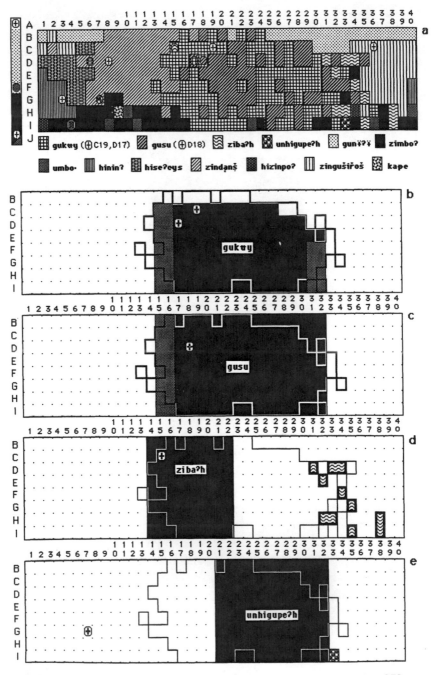

FIGURE 5.10. Chichimeca Jonáz, San Luís de la Paz, Guanajuato, Mexico, f 73, 1981: (*a*) naming ranges and foci; (*b–e*) mappings and foci with naming-range outlines superimposed. Data from Doña Clemencia Ramírez de Matos.

mapping step of each covers most reds and yellows, *including both unique hues*. Since the two terms had almost the same meaning to this speaker, she might have felt that one of them would suffice to name chips. (We shall add to this interpretation in note 14 of §6.2.4.)

In figure 5.10*a–e,* a Chichimeca Jonáz speaker names the cool category with combined traits of coextension and near synonymy. (*a*) Two major terms name the cool category, *gukᵾy* and *gusu;* both are focused in the same polarized vicinity at C19, D17, and D18 (table 5.1, item 2). The terms apply evenly to both sides of column 23: *gukᵾy* (C19, D17) 37 green and 36 blue; *gusu* (D18) 22 green and 24 blue. Each term is mapped continuously. The mappings mismatch on only 24 of the 136 colors they cover.

Minor terms suggest "crossover" of coextension (§10.1): (*d*) *ziba?h* names purple in columns 31–38 but is focused on C15; its mapping corresponds to its focus. In *a* and *e, unhigupe?h* is used once at I33, mapped throughout columns 21–32, but focused at G7 in polarized and crossed-over contrast to its mapping. The mappings of *ziba?h* and *unhigupe?h* are

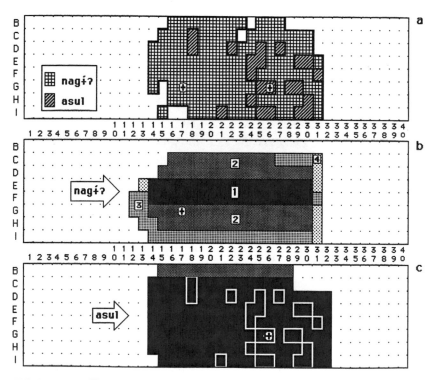

FIGURE 5.11. Zapotec, Santiago Apóstol, Ocotlán, Oaxaca, Mexico, m 57, 1980: (*a*) naming ranges, (*a–c*) foci, and (*b–c*) mappings; speaker 1.

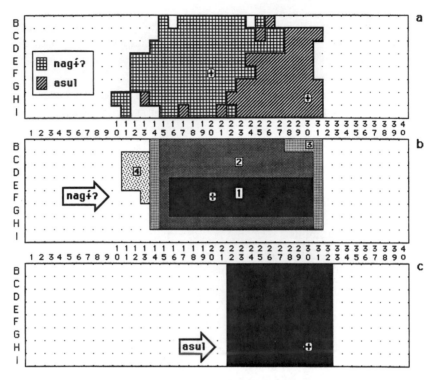

FIGURE 5.12. Zapotec, Santiago Apóstol, Ocotlán, Oaxaca, m 61, 1980: (*a*) naming ranges, (*a–c*) foci, and (*b–c*) mappings; speaker 2.

on opposite sides. Although these minor data appear erratic by themselves, they corroborate the polarized foci of the major terms. The data collectively suggest the Chichimeca speaker is beginning to name the cool category coextensively while maintaining attributes of near synonymy.

Figures 5.11–13 show distinct semantic relations that three Zapotec speakers maintain among green and blue. Figure 5.11 shows coextensive "cool" ranges of *nagɨʔ* and *asul,* a loanword. The native term is more salient. Yet, each is mapped with one step covering green and blue. Figure 5.12 exemplifies a relation of inclusion between *nagɨʔ* 'cool' and *asul* 'blue'. Figure 5.13 shows complementation.

In figure 5.12*a*, speaker 2 applied *asul* beyond its mapping to H13 and I17, which suggests he maintained a semantic relation intermediate to coextension and inclusion, but no sign of this appears in *c* his mapping of *asul.* In figure 5.13*a,* speaker 3 volunteered *nagɨʔ* at C28, suggesting a relation intermediate to inclusion and complementation, but (*b*) the intermediacy is not otherwise evident.

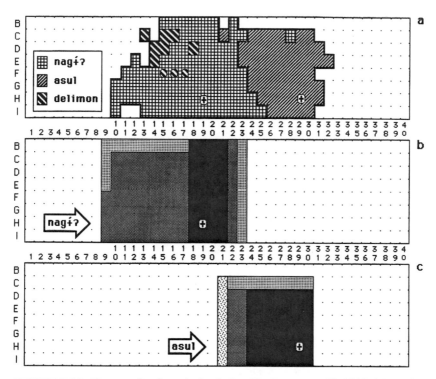

FIGURE 5.13. Zapotec, Santiago Apóstol, Ocotlán, Oaxaca, m 63, 1980: (*a*) naming ranges, (*a–c*) foci, and (*b–c*) mappings; speaker 3.

5.3. Semantic Evolution in Two Environments

As a category divides, it may be named with only one term throughout the process. The shift between attention to similarity and attention to distinctiveness does not compel semantic types to develop; rather, any particular balance between the emphases establishes a *precondition* for the development of a particular semantic type. Whenever an individual first names one category with more than one term, the terms will assume the relation that reflects the prevailing balance. Evolution of semantic relations can begin at any point on the typological continuum, including a very late point. The continuum is one of cognitive preconditions that constrain semantic relations; it is not a semantic continuum in the sense of surface naming.[7]

It is more likely that semantic evolution will begin early on the continuum in the warm category than in the cool category. In the latter, the second term is commonly introduced at the segment that produces inclusion. Rarely, the cool category fully divides before a second term is intro-

TABLE 5.2. Percentages of semantic-relation types
in warm and cool categories

	Warm	*Cool*
Near synonymy	.0196	.0017
Coextension	.6275	.1750
Inclusion	.3529	.1969
Simple use of one name	.0000	.6264

duced, which leaves one hue unnamed. Complementation may emerge as the first relation between two terms in the environment of green and blue (figs. 8.3–4).

The statistics in table 5.2 concern the entire continuum of semantic evolution, comparing the frequencies at which warm and cool categories are named with two terms in different semantic relations. Like the attributes in table 5.1, they conform to the axiom that red and yellow appear more distinct than green and blue. For the 51 warm categories in the Mesoamerican sample, semantic types amount to: 1 near synonymy, 32 coextension, and 18 inclusion. The count for the 589 cool categories is: 1 near synonymy, 103 overt coextension (43) or attested covert coextension (60), 116 inclusion, and 369 named with only one term and no independent evidence of covert coextension.[8]

The reciprocal shift in strength between emphases on similarity and difference establishes a continuum of preconditions for the development of semantic relations between names of a composite color category. In Mesoamerica, types of relations always evolve in the warm category and begin the evolution early on the continuum; in the cool category, the types tend to begin the evolution late, usually with inclusion being the first type to emerge.

5.4. Summary

Coextension is a unique type of semantic relationship characterized by nine traits that, as a complex, distinguish it from three other types. The attributes differ between the warm category and the cool category in consonance with the perceptual axiom that red and yellow appear more distinct than green and blue. Engagement of this axiom with the emphases on similarity and distinctiveness explains (1) evolutionary emergence of the warm category before the cool category, (2) distinctive manifestation of coextension in each, (3) different proportional counts of semantic types among them, and (4) division of warm before cool.

Coextension is a segment of a continuum through which semantic relations evolve from near synonymy through coextension and inclusion to complementation. The evolution is propelled by reciprocal shift in strength between attention to similarity and attention to distinctiveness. The precondition for the emergence of each type is established by a different balance of strength among the emphases. Since the strengths are reciprocal, the evolution is continuous, producing types that are intermediate to ideal forms.

The same reciprocal shift of emphases advances the emergence of basic categories, as discussed in §4.5.1. Thus, basic color-category evolution also progresses continuously rather than by disjunctive leaps.

Each range of a coextensively named category involves a separate weighting or slant on color perception. The perspectives do not inhere in neural response but are rather adopted by the observer and are, therefore, cognitive. Coextensive ranges and category division constitute separate arguments that color categorization is as much cognitive as it is perceptual. A theory of this domain requires axioms of both kinds.

This introduction to coextension has maintained simplicity by emphasizing surface semantics and criterial traits. It has featured seven characteristics of coextension while postponing treatment of others. Chapter 6 develops the evidence that coextensive ranges manifest a characteristic dominant-recessive pattern, and it accounts for the pattern with a cognitive hypothesis.

CHAPTER 6

VANTAGES

Coextension characteristically shows a "dominant-recessive" pattern: one range is usually both broader and more centrally focused than the other. Individuals manifest the pattern to different extents, strongly or weakly. The variations represent minor steps along a continuum of typological change. Competing accounts suggest why the pattern is widely shared, positing physiological determinants, personal habit, or cultural prescription. But the only explanation consistent with all facts concedes the importance of individual cognition: the pattern is entailed by an elemental strategy that each person privately adopts when creating, maintaining, changing, recalling, or using a color category. The strategy may derive from innate knowledge of how to construct a category rather than from social learning.

Coextensive ranges by themselves—independent of their dominant-recessive pattern—suggest that a person names a color category from different points of view, as is consistent with the evidence that, at very least, the category is named with two words from opposite angles. In effect, the category is constructed by analogy to personal experience in physical space. The dominant-recessive pattern, however, is defined by numerical correspondences between naming ranges, foci, mappings, and mapping steps; these are of sufficient detail to suggest that the analogy is more than a general equation between a space and a category. Rather, the affinity is formed between specific spatial and mental coordinates.

The mental coordinates are provided by the same axioms that account for the other observations of color categories, such as continuous change, semantic types, and evolutionary order. This pivotal provision integrates the various observations under one theory that any person constructs a color category by drawing an analogy to real spatial and temporal awareness on the level of the coordinates that constitute a point of view.

In §§8.1–6, I shall argue that any color category is a vantage, not only those that are coextensively named. Most categories are conventionally regarded from only one point of view and, thus, have only one name. But need of explanation is dramatized when a category assumes distinct organizations under different names. The data from Mesoamerican warm categories prove exceptionally useful for presenting the principal points, because most are named coextensively. Moreover, the perceptual difference between red and yellow keeps the two ranges free of complications that mainly pertain in cool categories (§§10.1–5, table 10.1, and item 9 of table 5.1), even though these, too, show the predicted pattern (table 10.2). Cool-category coextension will be fully analyzed in §11.3.5. (tables 11.2–5), after complications are enumerated. This chapter deals principally with warm categories.

The idea that a category is a vantage has implications for a theory of categorization that may exceed the domain of color. Section 6.1 describes data, §6.2 develops theory, §6.3 does both, and §6.4 reviews implications of the theory.

6.1. The Dominant-Recessive Pattern of Coextension

Coextensive ranges of almost any pair differ in size, shape, and organization. The difference can be quantified among independently elicited attributes: (1) size of naming range, (2) centrality of focus, (3) size of mapping, and (4) average size of mapping steps.[1] A dominant range shows higher numbers on at least three of these counts; a recessive range shows lower numbers. The even number of attributes (1–4) enables a test of the null hypothesis that the dominant-recessive pattern occurs only by chance. If it does, then half of the categories in the sample would manifest a coincidence of two high numbers and two low numbers within each coextensive range.

6.1.1. Variation on a Continuum

Variation falls out along a short segment within the continuum of semantic change. "Early phases" of coextension show strong signs of attention to similarity, while "late phases" suggest stronger emphasis on distinctiveness. Figures 6.1 through 6.4 show four systems that seem to represent this shift.

Figure 6.1 shows correspondence of four characteristics for dominant

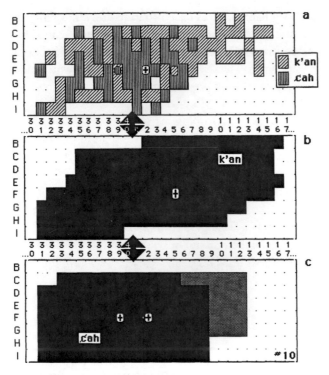

FIGURE 6.1. Tzeltal, Amatenango, Chiapas, Mexico, f 85, 1980: (*a*) naming ranges, (*a–c*) foci, and (*b–c*) mappings.

k'an and recessive *¢ah:* chips named 59/43; centrality of focus F5 (most)/ F2 (least); chips mapped 155/144; average per mapping step 155/72. Since the elemental hue of *k'an* is yellow C8–9 and of *¢ah* red G1–2, the focus of *k'an* at F5 is centralized by three levels of brightness darker than C8–9 and the focus of *¢ah* at F2 by one level lighter than G1–2. Other attributes of early coextension are the breadth of the category, execution of the dominant mapping in one step, extensive intermixture of naming ranges, and foci at close proximity on one level.

Figure 6.2 shows a full correspondence that is easy to count. This example—in comparison to that of figure 6.1—manifests slightly stronger attention to distinctiveness: naming ranges show less intermixture, recessive mapping steps are of equal size, and foci are on separate levels.

Figure 6.3 shows a correspondence of three attributes, again with *k'an* dominant and *¢ah* recessive: naming 56/51, foci D7 (most)/I40 (least), mapping 210/187, average mapping step 23/37. The average size of mapping

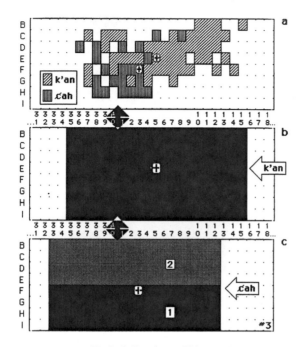

FIGURE 6.2. Tzeltal, Tenejapa, Chiapas, Mexico, m 65, 1980: (*a*) naming ranges, (*a–c*) foci, and (*b–c*) mappings.

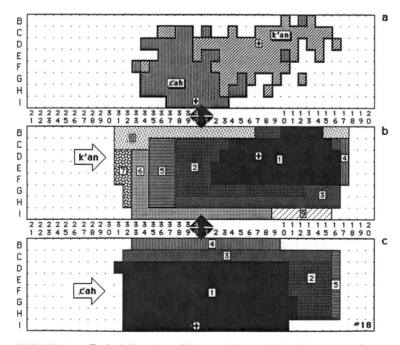

FIGURE 6.3. Tzeltal, Tenejapa, Chiapas, Mexico, f 60, 1980: (*a*) naming ranges, (*a–c*) foci, and (*b–c*) mappings.

steps is smaller in the dominant range. Naming ranges are commingled, but the extent is slight. Both mappings are of multiple steps that progress in converse directions. Foci are placed widely apart. The focus of dominant *k'an* is "centralized" at D7, that is, between the elemental hues; it is one level darker than elemental yellow. The focus of recessive *¢ah* is "polarized" at I40, that is, placed on the category margin and outside of the axis that runs between the elemental hues through the center of the category. These characteristics suggest an attention to distinctiveness that is stronger than any such attention pertaining to the data of full correspondence.

In figure 6.4, *¢ah* is dominant and *k'an* is recessive. Three attributes correspond. The noncorrespondence is the slightly polarized focus of *¢ah*, G39; it is on level with elemental red, G1–2, but outside of the central axis. The focus of *k'an* is within the axis, even though it is on elemental yellow, C8. Numbers that correspond are: naming 73/36, mapping 170/164, average step 43/27. Attributes of strong attention to distinctiveness are naming ranges that show no intermixture whatsoever, widely separate foci, and mappings of multiple steps executed in converse directions. The map-

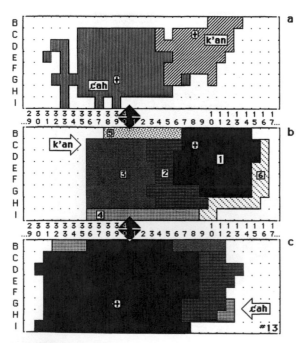

FIGURE 6.4. Tzeltal, Amatenango, Chiapas, Mexico, f 45, 1980: (*a*) naming ranges, (*a–c*) foci, and (*b–c*) mappings.

pings are sufficient to demonstrate coextension, which this speaker shares with her senior cohort, profiled in figure 6.1. They were coworkers at a ceramics kiln where I interviewed them.

6.1.2. The Null Hypothesis

Will the dominant-recessive pattern characterize coextension across languages and cultures? The MCS verified 28 cases of coextension in the warm category, 22 with complete sets of naming ranges, foci, and mappings. Among these 22, 11 pairs of coextensive ranges correspond in all 4 characteristics, 7 correspond in 3, and 4 show a balanced noncorrespondence of two-for-two in each range. The total correspondence includes 65 of the possible 88 characteristics, a significant 74% (p<.01 Pearson chi square), which means that the dominant-recessive pattern of coextension requires an explanation.[2]

The 22 sets of data all happen to be from Mayan languages.[3] Their numbers are summarized in table 6.1. Each row of the table contains data from one individual. For example, the top row identifies a particular individual, number 1., as a speaker of Tenejapa Tzeltal (TT) and cross-references this row to the figure that displays his data (6.14). His dominant range **D** is focused in reference to elemental yellow Y, and his recessive range **R** is focused in reference to elemental red R. His Y range is labeled as **D** dominant, and his R range as **R** recessive, because he named his Y range most (66 times) and his R range least (46) and repeated this pattern of most versus least for centrality of focus (D6 most : H3 least), number of colors mapped (155 : 138), and average number of colors per mapping step (39 : 28). His correspondence is thereby consistent across the four pairs of statistical columns, with the highest number or most central focus on the left and the lowest number or least central focus on the right within each pair. This dominant-recessive pattern is repeated down the column pairs for each individual, regardless of where the dominant range occurs, Y or R. But the individuals identified as 12–18 all show one noncorrespondence, which is highlighted by italics. Individuals 19–22 show no correspondence and, therefore, their statistical columns are all italicized and each is headed with **∅**. Their coextensive ranges are described as "balanced" in regard to the even distribution of high and low numbers among each pair of ranges. They contrast with the other eighteen pairs that show the dominant-recessive pattern of coextension, strongly in rows 1–11 and weakly in rows 12–18.

Each cross-referenced figure in the text refers to its data in table 6.1 with the identification number marked (with #) at lower right.[4]

TABLE 6.1. Numbers pertaining to coextension in the warm category

ID	Lang	Figure	Hue		Naming Size		Centrality of Focus		Mapping Size		Average Step-Size	
			D	**R**	**D**	**R**	**D**	**R**	**D**	**R**	**D**	**R**
1.	TT	6.14	Y	R	66	46	D6	H3	155	138	39	28
2.	TT	6.16	Y	R	59	28	F4–5	I2–3	158	81	17	9
3.	TT	6.2	Y	R	48	21	E6	F3	168	160	168	80
4.	TT	6.17	R	Y	63	39	F4	D8	188	63	27	13
5.	J	7.8	R	Y	66	39	F4	C8	158	59	40	15
6.	TZ	6.23	R	Y	75	40	E5	C8	132	112	19	12
7.	U	6.18	Y	R	79	35	F4	G2	109	27	27	14
8.	U	5.1	R	Y	67	65	G4	C14	150	140	38	35
9.	A	5.4	R	Y	49	37	F1–2	C8–9	214	162	43	27
10.	AT	6.1	Y	R	59	43	F5	F2	155	144	155	72
11.	AT	6.19	R	Y	77	47	F1	C8	248	99	50	25
12.	TT	6.20	Y	R	*45*	*53*	D6	G2	160	73	40	36
13.	AT	6.4	R	Y	73	36	*G39*	*C8*	170	164	43	27
14.	TT	6.12	Y	R	93	60	D7	G38	*134*	*144*	67	36
15.	A	6.15	Y	R	77	38	D7	G2	163	104	27	*104*
16.	TZ	6.21	Y	R	62	52	E4	G2	141	84	*13*	*14*
17.	TZ	6.22	Y	R	54	40	E4	G40	145	117	*10*	*24*
18.	TT	6.3	Y	R	56	51	D7	I40	210	187	*23*	*37*
			Ø	**Ø**	**Ø**	**Ø**	**Ø**	**Ø**	**Ø**	**Ø**	**Ø**	**Ø**
19.	TZ	6.30	Y	R	*32*	*52*	D6	*G1*	*140*	*114*	*46*	*57*
20.	A	6.31	Y	R	*54*	*49*	*C10–11*	*H3*	*35*	*106*	*12*	*21*
21.	TT	6.32	Y	R	*28*	*55*	*G1/H3/I3*	*C8/E5*	*109*	*55*	*52*	*28*
22.	U	6.33	Y	R	*20*	*60*	*I4*	*C12/C9/D7*	*88*	*81*	*44*	*27*

Key:
D dominant range   Italics = noncorrespondence   U Uspantec
R recessive range   Lang Language   A Aguacatec
Ø balanced range   TT Tenejapa Tzeltal   TZ Tzotzil
Y yellow   AT Amatenango Tzeltal   J Jacaltec
R red

6.1.3. Alternative Explanations

Five possible explanations of the dominant-recessive pattern may be considered.

Physiological Determinants. Of the 18 individuals who demonstrated dominant-recessive coextension on the bases of complete sets of data,

11 assigned dominance to the yellow-focused range and 7 assigned dominance to the red-focused range. Nothing in the perception of unique yellow or unique red determines the dominant-recessive pattern.

Personal Predisposition. Perhaps the dominant range is the one that a person favors and, therefore, names most, something like being right-handed or left-handed? But this idea of private bent does not address such dynamics as the more evenly balanced and centrally focused form of the dominant range or the correspondingly skewed and polarized form of the recessive range; it does not relate these forms to other details that accompany the process of change, such as the complexes found by comparing figures 6.1–4, which suggest different strengths of attention to distinctiveness.

Visual Acuity. Perhaps some people, especially elders, do not clearly see the color chips? Chapanis (1950), a perceptual psychologist, demonstrated that color discrimination does not fail with advancing age, even for individuals whose general visual acuity wanes. Further, in Mesoamerica, old and young alike show the dominant-recessive pattern.

Culture and History. The Tzeltal, in particular, tend to assign dominance to *k'an;* however, even close neighbors make opposite choices (figures 6.1 and 6.4). Within the small samples of Uspantec, Aguacatec, and Tzotzil, individuals were almost evenly divided in their preferences (table 6.1). Local culture need not condition the pattern.[5]

The slightly higher occurrence of yellow dominance might have a historical origin if the Proto-Mayan "yellow" term **q'an* named middle-level brightness (compare figs. 6.13 and 2.29). But even if this prehistory took place, it has not established an enduring constraint. Further, there is no link between age and a choice of red or yellow dominance.

Individual Cognition. The remaining possibility is that the dominant-recessive pattern results from individual cognition—that is, some process that each person performs mentally when he or she constructs, maintains, changes, or recalls a color category. Such would imply that every person independently adopts the same cognitive strategy because this is the way people are innately predisposed to categorize; they go about the task without deferring to convention and without having learned the method in childhood from their tutors or peers. This cognitive account provides the research hypothesis.

6.2. Categorization as Spatiotemporal Analogy

There is a great difference between formulating a research hypothesis and testing one. Yet, even at the start, the hypothesis must encompass established observations exhaustively or, at least, more thoroughly than alternative accounts. A first formulation that succeeds to this extent is ipso facto an initial test. Subsequent tests might consist of using the hypothesis to model new observations within the same domain, especially unexpected discoveries; more extensive tests would explore the applicability of the model to data outside of the original domain of research. Ideally, the relation between formulation, testing, and reformulation would continue indefinitely, because no hypothesis, regardless of past performance, is exempt from refutation or need of modification.[6]

What follows is a first formulation of the research hypothesis that the dominant-recessive pattern of coextension manifests individual cognition. In concise terms, a color category is an analogy: people create and maintain a category by drawing an equation between the abstract process of categorization and the process by which they keep their balance in a world of three dimensions or keep their bearings in a physical terrain.

6.2.1. Vantages and Coordinates

For the moment, consider coextension (as described in §5.1.) apart from its dominant-recessive pattern. The simplest explanation of two terms that name one color category with separate emphases and at different angles is that a person constructs the category from two outlooks. He uses a different word to name each perspective because he names the category as a personal point of view rather than as a detached entity. A color category is an analogous spatial vantage whose organization derives from the active participation of the person who composes it.

The model of vantages need not entail literally envisioning oneself as standing in or beside an imaginary field of graded hue, but rather as going about the business of categorizing according to the same procedure by which one would keep track of one's own location in real space-time: by maintaining reference to things that are fixed and to things that are moving or, at least, movable, as congenitally blind people construct their points of view (Hollins and Kelley 1988). Color categorization, perhaps, depends more on visual imagery than does much of other cognition, because sighted people may name color in reference to their memory of elemental hues. But blind people accurately depict the color wheel on the basis of nonvisual information, suggesting that visual memory is only one ingredient within the organization of this domain (Marmor 1978). By "vantage," then, I mean the method by which a person makes sense of some part of his world by picking out specific points of reference and plotting their relation to his own position, a process that is spatial and temporal in the first order but incidentally visual.[7]

An example in real space will introduce some concepts of vantage theory, the hypothesis that categories are constructed by analogy to space-time coordinates. This initial example will ignore the time element. To comprehend the ordinary spatial description "The newspaper is on the living room table," one must locate the living room in relation to the house design, the table in relation to the living room, and the newspaper in relation to the table. One "zooms in" from a broad to a narrow purview by envisioning three relations of figure to ground: living room to house design, table to living room, and newspaper to table. As one narrows concentration through the three levels, one takes the figure from the broadest level to use as the ground on the next level. Thus, the living room is a figure in relation to the house design but a ground in relation to the table, which, in turn, is a figure in relation to the living room but a ground in relation to the newspaper.

Figure 6.5 depicts this mundane spatial operation as zooming in through a hierarchy of three figure-to-ground relations and two transformations between relations. Transformations are indicated by arrows, while each relation resides at a separate level of concentration, numbered 1, 2, or 3.[8] The hierarchy incorporates an allegedly limited human ability to hold foremost in mind only one relation of a figure to a ground at a time. The other relations are kept in memory as presuppositions, "in the back of the mind" so to speak. In this manner, a person remains aware of the multiple figure-ground relations that may compose a particular point of view while managing the information.

Levels of Concentration	Ground Fixed Coordinate	Figure Mobile Coordinate
1	House Design	Living Room
2	Living Room	Table
3	Table	Newspaper

FIGURE 6.5. A vantage of "The newspaper is on the living room table."

In vantage theory, the newspaper on the living room table is a point of view constructed in reference to "fixed" and "mobile" coordinates. The house plan, living room, table, and newspaper are coordinates. They are "fixed" when thought of as a ground and "mobile" when thought of as a figure, even though they do not actually move. Rather, each figure is held in attention against an established background as a moving object would be regarded in relation to a stationary surround. Further, each figure can be moved to the next level of concentration where it is converted to established knowledge and thereby becomes a ground where, in relation to it, a new figure is introduced as the point of active interest. Immediately below, the justification of calling a ground and a figure "fixed and mobile coordinates" will be developed further. Coordinates are highlighted aspects of a landscape that are selected for attention while other parts of the landscape are suppressed. For example, "the living room table is in the corner" constitutes a different selection of points for emphasis and, thereby, produces a distinct point of view, albeit within the same house design.

Coordinates are not precisely things in themselves, such as a table or a newspaper, but a selective emphasis upon certain things at the expense of ignoring other things in the environment (cf. Sahlins 1976, §2.4.3 herein). Although they are represented by real things and based on real things, they are mental points of reference; one who knows the house can find the newspaper blindfolded and, theoretically, without touching anything. This last issue is critical to vantage theory, because some things, such as elemental hues, may have no immediate representatives in an environment—say, in a totally grey room or the dark of night—but they can be called to mind from memory and used as coordinates of a color category. To carry this reasoning further, the coordinates of a paranoid delusion or a benign fantasy may never have had a real existence, but they are used as points of reference as easily as a table sitting in the living room. Regarding all coordinates as thoughts rather than as things, it is easier to accept the fundamental idea of vantage theory—that coordinates can be set up analogically to form a category as a purely mental construction which is, nevertheless, treated as a physical space. The analogy is performed between two systems of thought, not between a couple of things and a system of thought.

The simple digression of figure 6.5 makes progress toward exemplifying the contributions to a spatial viewpoint of coordinates, their bipartite relations, levels of concentration, and zooming in or out. Anyone will manipulate such organization innumerable times each day while moving in and out of enclosed spaces, wending his way though a world of objects, di-

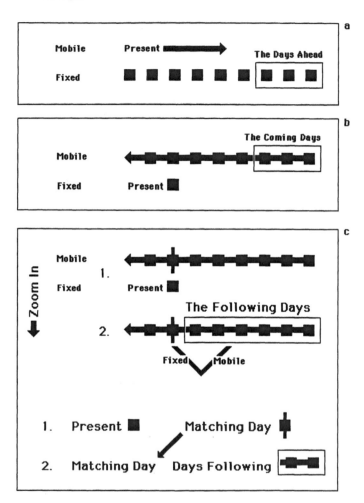

FIGURE 6.6. Three vantages of time in English.

lating and restricting concentration, conversing, or even fantasizing. But in this real world, many things are moving.

   A second example will underscore the manipulations of motion within this scheme derived from space. Figure 6.6 extends this system from space to conceptions of time, still not time in the einsteinian sense but only in the metaphorical sense of Lakoff and Johnson (1980:41–43). Their example merely portrays motion coordinates; they discuss time as moving-object metaphors with front-back orientation. Time is plotted in reference to people, as in "face the future," "weeks ahead" or "the time will come";

or time is plotted in reference to other time, as in "the next week and the week following it." Figure 6.6 separates these expressions as three vantages of time. Part *a* represents units of time on a fixed scale; the present is moving along the scale. Part *b* reverses the relation of fixed and mobile coordinates such that the time line is moving and the present is fixed. Each relation warrants a different expression: "the days ahead" and "the coming days." Part *c* depicts zooming in to a closer level of concentration on the mobile time-line: first, a mobile unit of reference—called a "matching day"—is coordinated with the fixed present; then, this unit is established as a stable point of reference with a mobile coordinate following it. The so-called "matching day" could be "farther off" on the time line, as is "next week" in "the next week and the week following it." Although the unit of reference has become a fixed coordinate on level 2, it is still moving within the metaphor; "fixed" means stabilized as a point of reference at a particular level of concentration, not devoid of other motion. At both levels, motion is accentuated only on the figure.

This example of time concepts illustrates another principle of vantage theory: once a coordinate is regarded as mobile, it need not be treated as moving thereafter. In *c,* on level 1 part of the scene is regarded as moving, whereas on level 2 this part is treated as stationary while the movement is emphasized on another slice of the concept; what is moving on one level can be stopped on another level where what was previously unemphasized can be brought to the fore and treated as moving.

The restricted examples of figures 6.5 and 6.6 highlight some principles of vantage theory but not all of them. Probably the analogy by which color categories are constructed is drawn between that domain and broad experience in space and time. In this wider realm, cognizance of motion is indispensable while time itself is a function of motion. Moreover, the general awareness of space and movement would certainly be shared between humans and other species, including creatures that would not be commonly credited with conceptual abilities, such as a flying insect that alights with precision on the tip of a twig. Unlike the metaphoric conventions of figure 6.6, this primal world of stationary and moving entities is seemingly preconceptual or, at least, requires only primordial sensory abilities to negotiate successfully. If such fundamental experience were the source of analogy, then "fixed and mobile coordinates" would be apt constructs for a theory of categorization.

What kind of coordinates do people select when they make sense of space and time? And what would people select as mental equivalents when thinking of a color category? On the physical side, we have Einstein's classic example of a rock that falls through a trajectory from a moving railway carriage. The trajectory is straight when viewed from the train but parabolic when seen from the ground. Observers in the two places share a fixed reference body of up-down, front-back, and right-left, but their motions differ. Einstein regarded standing still to be a coordinate of time by allowing motion to include its zero point. Any spatial experience is based on awareness of the fixed perpendiculars and of time as a function of relative motion. Alteration of the mobile coordinate changes a point of view.

The data of table 6.1 indicate that the warm category also differs when it is regarded from opposite vantages: it differs in size and internal organization. The difference is consistent across individuals and languages. Moreover, the differences are sufficiently detailed to suggest what the coordinates are: two coordinates consisting of the elemental hues; two coordinates consisting of attention to the similarity and attention to the difference that pertains between the hue points. People construct color categorization by selecting these perceptions as structural equivalents to spatial perpendiculars and motion.

The axioms that provide for universal regularities, individual variation, and continuous change further provide the coordinates by which a color category is composed as a vantage.

6.2.2. Relativity of Coordinates

Since all coordinates are thoughts—that is, awareness, recognition, selection among alternatives, and emphasis upon them—nothing physical obstructs the substitution of one system of coordinates for another as an analogy is formed. However, some coordinates of color categorization have special resemblance to fixed parts of terrain and others have greater likeness to movement.

The elemental hues—once they have been selected—are inherently fixed in the sense that they are stable points determined by perceptual physiology; they have upper thresholds of maximum purity that afford little leeway for mutable emphases. They are like landmarks in real geography or like the unchanging vectors at right angles whose orienting anchor is gravity.[9]

Attention to similarity and attention to difference are selected from a vast continuum. The enormous latitude makes them as inherently mobile as degrees of velocity. Slow-fast and similar-different share three properties upon which an analogy can be based.[10] First, both oppositions consist of points on an absolute axis. Motion ranges from perfect stillness to the speed of light or, from an unschooled standpoint, to as fast as one can imagine. Similarity and difference range from perfect identity to utter disparity. Yet points along each axis are relative when compared. Thus, a train traveling 80 kilometers per hour appears to be traveling 20 kmph to a passenger on a train traveling 60 kmph when both trains move in the same direction on parallel tracks. Likewise, dissimilar sport coats may resemble each other more when both are compared to beach attire. Second, any point on either axis is mutable. What moves slowly can accelerate while similarities and differences between two entities can be picked out for varying emphases. Third, judgments of speed and judgments of similarity-difference are each reciprocal such that what goes fast does not go slow and what is deemed to be a degree of difference, to this degree, is not a similarity. In the physical world, relative speeds of slow and fast are usually judged by a person standing still, whereas similarity and difference, perhaps, are often judged only in reference to each other. Nevertheless, this difference in typical standpoints of judgment may not be sufficient to undermine the bases for an analogy between the two axes.

6.2.3. Formalisms

As a preliminary account, a color category is constituted as a vantage on a "preferred" level of concentration, the degree of concentration that is easiest to hold in mind from that particular point of view. In depictions of models, the preferred level is represented at the top, as "level 1." The "arrangement" of coordinates on subsequent levels falls out from this initial selection. All coordinates in their arrangement constitute the category from one angle of viewing.

Two vantage points of a composite color category are constituted on their preferred levels of concentration by coordinating attention to similarity with one elemental hue and attention to distinctiveness with the opposite elemental hue. This strategy produces the dominant-recessive pattern attested by the data of table 6.1 because, in general, attention to similarity determines that the colors of a category will be viewed as strongly associated with each other, of relatively equal membership, and separated by minimal psychological distance. Attention to distinctiveness determines that the colors will be weakly associated, of precipitously unequal membership, and separated by maximal psychological distance. Specifically, when a category is regarded primarily in reference to similarity between colors, the distance between stimuli will be contracted such that many colors will fit within the purview of the vantage, which will broaden the naming range and mapping on the Munsell array; the category will be centrally focused so as to evenly and equally represent its members. When a category is thought of mainly in reference to differences, the distance between stimuli will be protracted such that fewer colors will enter the scope, which will diminish the naming range and mapping and will encourage a less central focus that favors some of the members in contrast to others. In pronounced cases, the focus will be polarized on the category periphery in contradistinction to most members. Contracted versus protracted conceptions foster large versus small mapping steps.

Figure 6.7 formally models composite color categories that are not coextensively composed, the three most widely reported kinds. They are (a) warm, (b) yellow-with-green, and (c) cool, with (d) modeling any such category of two elemental hues, H₁ and H₂, that is named by one term. Respective ethnographic examples are: (a) figures 2.14, 2.16b, 2.22a–c,

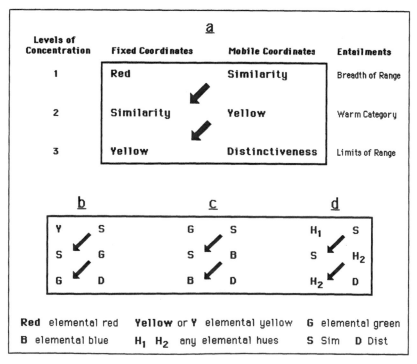

FIGURE 6.7. Formal models representing composite categories of two elemental hues: (a) warm, (b) yellow-with-green, (c) cool, (d) abstract.

2.24*c–d*, 2.25*c*, 2.28*a–c*, 2.34*b;* (*b*) figure 2.33; (*c*) figures 2.15, 2.16*b–d*, 2.17–18, 2.20, 2.22*d*, 2.23, 2.24*a* and *c–d.*

In (*a*), the coordinates are elemental red, similarity, elemental yellow, and distinctiveness. They constitute a single vantage with three levels of concentration. The principles of vantages that have been exemplified outside the color domain in figures 6.5 and 6.6 obtain in figure 6.7: each level consists of a fixed and a mobile coordinate and is related to the adjacent level(s) by the zooming processes; each level consists of two coordinates because, at any moment, only two coordinates can be held foremost in mind. "Mobile" can mean "given special emphasis" in the sense that a figure is accentuated in contrast to its ground. Just as such highlighting is a metonym of motion, a coordinate that is sustained in high relief against a backdrop may be mobile metonymically, that is, in virtual motion. To "zoom in" is to change a mobile coordinate to the fixed status of a background while concentrating on a new mobile coordinate, and to "zoom out" is to reverse the process. Attention to similarity is the mobile coordinate of the preferred level of concentration, while attention to distinctiveness is the mobile coordinate of the most zoomed-in level. Moreover, elemental hues are "inherently fixed," although they may move within the zooming hierarchy and may be treated as mobile on its middle level; whereas attention to similarity and distinctiveness—as selections from an axis—are "inherently mobile," even though at middle-level they may be treated as fixed coordinates.

All levels are held in some degree of awareness, even though full concentration is directed on only one level at a time; for example, one cannot concentrate on similarity without being remotely aware that there is a reciprocal measure of distinctiveness. The order of levels from top to bottom represents the preference of concentration. In most warm categories that are named with only one term, the choice of a best example is placed in reference to elemental red, which, in figure 6.7*a,* is the fixed coordinate on level 1.[11]

In *a,* the *arrangement* of coordinates represents the way a category is cognitively organized. This mental system *entails* various surface behaviors. For example, on level 1, strong attention to similarity entails that the category will be broad enough to include many colors. On level 2, strong attention to similarity—and its *entailment* of breadth—is taken to be established; it becomes a fixed coordinate. The broad range is shaped to include specifically unique yellow, as opposed to "other possibilities" (to be discussed below). Yellow is the center of attention against the backdrop of its similarity to unique red. On level 3, yellow is a fixed assumption against which attention to distinctiveness is actively balanced. The breadth of the category does not supersede the yellow percept, because the coordinate of distinctiveness ensures that the vantage does not extend indefinitely throughout the color domain. Similarity and distinctiveness maintain their reciprocal balance of strength, because each emphasis is presupposed when the other is held in concentration.

Finally, as noted on level 2, the inherently mobile coordinate of attention to similarity is treated as fixed while the inherently fixed coordinate of elemental yellow is treated as mobile. The former is like the treatment of motion as a fixed coordinate in the example featuring temporal designation of figure 6.6c; the latter reverses the relation to hold an essentially fixed notion in high relief, which is equally possible. But the inversion occurs only on level 2, leaving coordinates to evince their inherent fixities and mobilities on levels 1 and 3, which allows their natural relations to predominate in the category.

Figures 6.7b–c extend the same organization to the categories of yellow-with-green (Y,G) and cool (G,B). Any of the three formalisms could place the opposite elemental hue at level 1, creating a yellow focus for warm (as in fig. 2.22c), a green focus for yellow-with-green (fig. 2.33d; MacLaury 1987a: fig. 2), or a blue focus for cool (fig. 2.16c). All such cases are observed in data, and permuted models would pertain to them.

Regarding "other possibilities" than elemental yellow as a coordinate on level 2 of Figure 6.7a, a category that is focused in red and named with one term does not lead to a natural example. The unnatural possibility would be to include elemental blue as a coordinate on level 2 instead of elemental yellow; however, a red-with-blue category has not been observed in any language, perhaps because elemental red and elemental blue appear too distinct (§4.1.1.1). But figure 6.7c makes a realistic demonstration of alternatives, as its level 1 includes elemental green and its level 2 elemental blue. If the latter hue were elemental yellow instead, then a green-focused, green-with-yellow category would result (fig. 2.33d), as reported of Shuswap (MacLaury 1987a: fig. 2) and of three Wakashan languages (MacLaury 1986b: figs. 13–14; Saunders 1992a: 147–151).

All of these switches are theoretical options; some pertain to ethnographically verified categories but none is intended to represent the ways that categories change.[12] For example, most Shuswap speakers focus a yellow-with-green category in yellow, and the one exceptional focus in green is a variant of those (MacLaury 1987a: figs. 1–3). Presumably its maker had rearranged the green and yellow coordinates within the con-

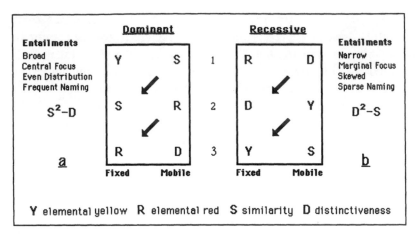

FIGURE 6.8. Formal model representing a coextensive organization of the warm category: (*a*) dominant vantage, (*b*) recessive vantage.

ventional category without entertaining an option outside of it. Similar rearrangement is suggested by the red and yellow foci in the warm categories of figure 2.22.

Figure 6.8 formally models a coextensive organization of the warm category. The dominant vantage is focused in reference to yellow (see figs. 6.1–3), which places on level 1 the coordinates of elemental yellow (Y) and attention to similarity (S). The recessive vantage places on level 1 elemental red (R) and attention to distinctiveness (D). The two displays represent opposite arrangements of one set of coordinates, not different sets of coordinates. For this reason, the arrangements constitute different vantages of one category rather than distinct categories.

6.2.3.1. Different Sizes of Dominant and Recessive Ranges

The dual formalism includes more than attention to similarity and attention to distinctiveness. It represents the multiplicatively reinforced emphases of these inherently mobile coordinates, dominant SS-D or S^2-D versus recessive DD-S or D^2-S: in the dominant vantage, similarity is considered twice, SS—once as a mobile coordinate on level 1 and again as a fixed coordinate on level 2—before distinctiveness is considered on level 3 as a mobile coordinate, D. In the recessive vantage, DD-S expresses the double emphasis on distinctiveness. Since any level of a vantage presupposes the others, keeping the others in the back of the mind enables the multiplicative reinforcement of inherently mobile coordinates that occur on different levels, as S^2 or D^2. As points on an axis, they are essentially quantitative.

Concentrating on levels is unavoidable when calling to mind a category. Thus, concentrating primarily on similarity—placing S on level 1— necessarily entails a broader category (S^2), as placing distinctiveness on level 1 likewise must entail a narrower category (D^2). The size of the category perforce differs when it is regarded from opposite vantages.[13]

Inherently fixed coordinates such as R or Y have no multiplicative power. As isolated apexes, they are intrinsically qualitative; so elemental red saturated to its imaginable maximum cannot get redder. Solely the inherently mobile coordinates provide for change of a category or for perspectival differences in its size and shape.

6.2.3.2. Increase of the Size Differential

Generally, as the balance of emphases shifts toward stronger attention to distinctiveness, both semantic ranges tend to shrink, although the recessive range shrinks faster. These effects become pronounced as the late phase of coextension transforms to inclusion: the dominant range continues to encompass both unique hues while the recessive range retracts to the colors surrounding one unique hue. The dominant double emphasis on similarity (S^2-D) entails a broad range while the recessive double emphasis on distinctiveness (D^2-S) entails retraction. Up to a point, even weak double emphasis on similarity will entail a broad range, even though minor shrinkage will accompany the weakness; whereas, when distinctiveness is doubly emphasized, any increase in its strength will expedite retraction straightway (figs. 6.16–18, 6.20, 7.8). These dynamics appear to account for the trajectory of change through which near synonymy becomes coextension, which, in turn, becomes inclusion before transforming into a relation of complementation between autonomous categories.

The four ideal types of relation are diagrammed in figure 6.9a, wherein strong or weak emphasis on similarity or distinctiveness is represented by depicting S or D as large or small; time is shown as proceeding from right to left while retraction of ranges progresses from bottom to top. The lineal representation of dominant-range shrinkage is slower than the nonlineal recessive-range shrinkage; whereas S^2 retards shrinkage, D^2 accelerates it. Part b pegs the relations of near synonymy, coextension, inclusion, and complementation to the unequal rates at which the two ranges shrink.

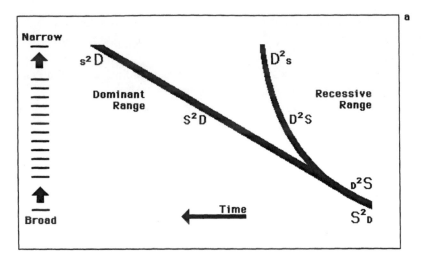

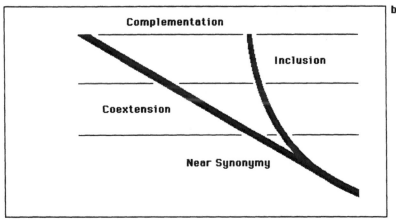

FIGURE 6.9. (*a*) Rates of retraction among dominant and recessive vantages in relation to a shift in emphasis from S similarity to D distinctiveness; (*b*) types of semantic relations resulting from the difference between dominant and recessive retraction rates.

6.2.3.3. Near Synonymy, Coextension, and Inclusion

The formalisms of figure 6.10 depict the dual arrangements of coordinates that would pertain in a relation of near synonymy, of coextension, and of inclusion; the arrangements are structurally identical among the three. (Any of them is the same as that shown in figure 6.8.) The formal difference between them is one of emphasis among inherently mobile coordinates. Strengths are distinguished by sizing S and D. In a relation of near synonymy, attention to similarity is stronger and attention to distinc-

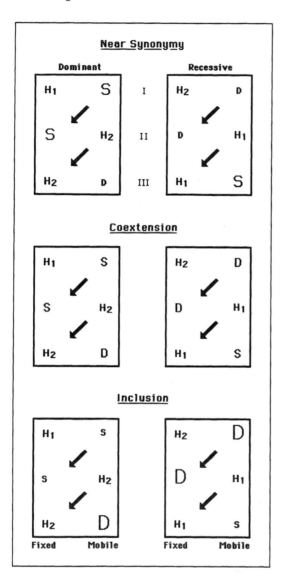

FIGURE 6.10. Formal model representing three types of semantic relation. They share one organization but differ in the balance of strength between emphases on S similarity and D distinctiveness. H_1 and H_2 represent any different elemental hues.

tiveness is weaker, S D; in a relation of inclusion, the strengths have the inverse distribution, s D; in coextension, between near synonymy and inclusion, the strengths are about equal, S D. This is another way of expressing the dynamic shown in figure 6.9.

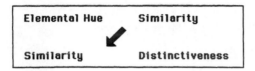

FIGURE 6.11. Formal model representing a category of one elemental hue.

6.2.3.4. Complementation

Figure 6.11 shows another arrangement of coordinates by which a color category can be composed as a vantage. The combination constitutes an elemental basic color category, such as English red. One elemental hue stands against the reciprocal tension between similarity and distinctiveness, which are distributed over two levels of concentration. A "relation" of complementation between separate categories, such as red and yellow, would consist of two such arrangements in autonomous coexistence. This state of affairs differs radically from the three depicted in figure 6.10; near synonymy, coextension, and inclusion share a common structure from which complementation departs. Any two autonomous formalisms will depict complementation, for example, those of *a* and *c* in figure 6.7. Complementation means that two categories do not share coordinates, unlike the relations diagrammed in figure 6.8 or 6.10. In strictly this sense, complementation is a negative relation (even though categories in complementation will be related by contrast if they are of the same domain).

6.2.4. Pragmatics

Why would a person regard a category from optional vantages? Probably it would depend on what one wished to accomplish as the category was invoked. A person might construct a viewpoint in reference to similarity when in a relaxed frame of mind, when actively preferring not to differentiate, or when wishing to convey continuity. The person may assume a view in reference to distinctiveness when remembering a contrast with a similar color or when feeling that exacting identification is appropriate. While naming the random sequence of 330 color chips, a person makes different decisions for a host of private reasons and will accordingly switch back and forth between vantages.[14]

6.2.5. Summation

An individual forms a category as an analogy to a point of view in space-time. The analogy occurs at the level of fixed and mobile coordinates, which the individual arranges in a particular order of preference. A coextensively composed category consists of two such arrangements of the same coordinates, each of which may bear its own name. The maker of the category, in effect, names the ways he constructs it rather than the set of its components as detached from himself; he names his relation with the category as of a given moment. As the observer, or his descendants, may respond to change in the sociophysical environment, any of them may place stronger emphasis on distinctiveness as a means of thinking more analytically and may thereby alter the dynamics of categories across diverse domains, color categories among them. Broad categories will divide into narrower ones and, if they are named with two terms, will pass through typological phases of semantic relations as division progresses. This sequence will begin with the relation suited to the particular balance of emphases that prevails at the time the second term is innovated. No one learns from a tutor how to compose a category; rather, everyone applies this propensity as specialized innate knowledge. Thus, people coextensively name color in accord with the same pattern everywhere.

6.3. Descriptions of Coextension

Individual systems of coextensive ranges fall out along the continuum of early-to-late phases. Figures 6.1–4 and 12–28 attest to substantial variation between individuals and between languages. Yet the dominant-recessive pattern prevails throughout them all in spite of each person's inclination to categorize in a unique way.

6.3.1. Early Coextension

In figure 6.12, a coextensive relation is close to near synonymy; *k'an* is dominant and *¢ah* recessive. Each is mapped over both elemental hues with a first step, C8–9 and G1–2, like the nearly synonymous ranges in figure 5.9. This Tzeltal speaker, age 90, is the oldest of the sample. Yet he mapped dominant *k'an* over 10 fewer colors than he mapped recessive *¢ah*, 134 versus 144, showing incomplete correspondence. Although "early coextension" will often show a four-way correspondence, it may not; there is no single criterion of "early" versus "late."

Figure 6.13 displays again the first coextensive system we elicited; its mappings appear in figure 5.1, which shows full correspondence. However, the dominant range, *kʸaq*, maintains a thin numerical edge throughout the four characteristics: namings 67/65, foci G4/C14–16, mappings 150/140, average size of steps 38/35. The dominant focus, G4, is centralized by only

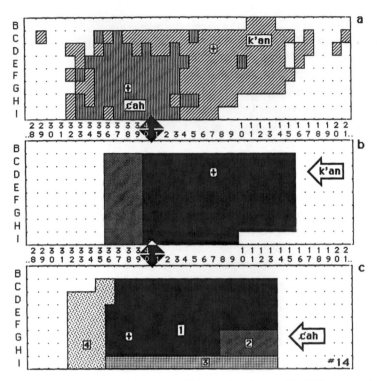

FIGURE 6.12. Tzeltal, Tenejapa, Chiapas, Mexico, m 90, 1980: (*a*) naming ranges, (*a–c*) foci, and (*b–c*) mappings.

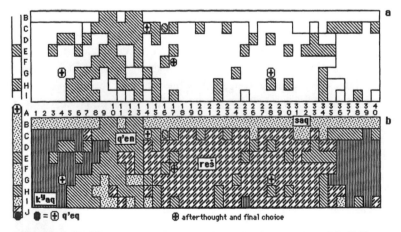

FIGURE 6.13. Uspantec, Las Pacayas, Uspantán, Guatemala, m 74, 1979: (*a–b*) naming ranges and foci (cf. fig. 5.1).

two columns and by no levels of brightness; whereas the recessive focus is polarized at C14 and 16.

This range of *q'en* represents the only apparent remnant of a brightness category among systems collected in Guatemala or Mexico; it is a weak example of the genre (figs. 2.27–32; MacLaury 1992*a:* figs. 11–18). It is focused in yellow and, as shown earlier, it is mapped over yellow, red, and purple; but *q'en* applies sparsely throughout green and blue, including colors that are almost pure, F16, E17, G28, and H30. This exotic range might represent a survival from prehistoric Mayan color categorization, or it might be one man's idiosyncrasy. Yet it presents an immediate problem of quantification. Which uses of *q'en* should be attributed to the coextensive relation with *kʸaq?* I have excluded those not contiguous with the main naming ranges of *q'en* or *kʸaq* or with their foci and that apply to green or blue: F16, E17, I17, C20, H–I22, C23, G24, E25, D26, D28, H28, E30, and H30. If these uses were counted, then the recessive naming range would amount to 79, not 65; the system would represent a weak correspondence of three characteristics, not a strong correspondence of four. Finally,

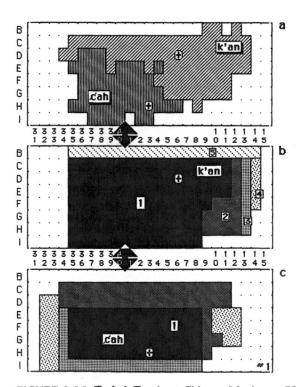

FIGURE 6.14. Tzeltal, Tenejapa, Chiapas, Mexico, m 75, 1980: (*a*) naming ranges, (*a–c*) foci, and (*b–c*) mappings.

if Proto-Mayan *q'an* named a broad brightness category, its vestige might prevail in the current fact that *q'en* or one of its other reflexes (*q'an, k'an, k'on*) names the dominant range in 11 out of the 18 dominant-recessive cases in table 6.1. Among the 18, the mean age for yellow dominance is 62 years and for red dominance 53, which is not significant (p>.05). This isolated hint that *q'an* might have named brightness comes from a system in which its reflex, *q'en,* names a recessive range, weak or strong (see note 9 of §7.2.2).

Figure 6.14 shows full correspondence between dominant and recessive characteristics, *k'an* versus *¢ah.* The dominant range is mapped over both elemental hues with a first step, whereas the recessive mapping covers them with separate steps. There is no intermixture of naming ranges, as there is none in figure 6.4.

Figure 6.15 shows (*c*) the only single-step mapping of a recessive warm-category range in the sample (table 6.1). Figures 6.1–2 show (*b*) single-step mappings of a dominant range.

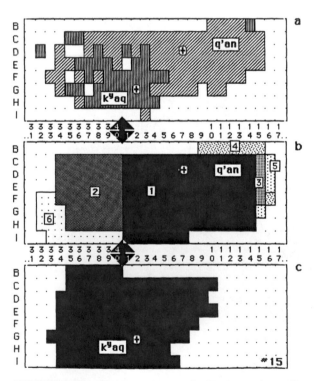

FIGURE 6.15. Aguacatec, Aguacatán, Huehuetenango, Guatemala, m 60, 1980: (*a*) naming ranges, (*a–c*) foci, and (*b–c*) mappings.

6.3.2. Late Coextension

When coextension enters its late phase, it may resemble a relation of inclusion; its ranges may differ substantially in size. Evidence of coextension may only persist in details.

In figure 6.16*a,* the recessive naming range, *¢ah,* applies to yellow at D8, D10, E11, E13, F9, and F12, although its mapping stops short of these yellows at column 7. Secondary loanwords, *rosado* and *morado,* reduce the size of dominant and recessive naming ranges to 59 versus 28. Counting the loanwords as part of the recessive naming range would increase its size to 55. The focus of dominant *k'an* is centralized at F4–5; the focus of *¢ah* is polarized at I2–3 (see fig. 6.3). This late system contrasts with the early system of figure 6.2; the two speakers of Tenejapa Tzeltal differ in age by 30 years. The younger speaker maps each range with nine steps, the elder with one step and two. Late phases of coextension require stronger attention to distinctiveness.

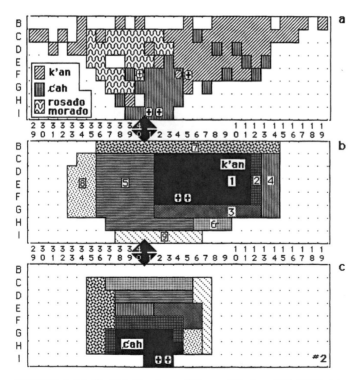

FIGURE 6.16. Tzeltal, Tenejapa, Chiapas, Mexico, f 36, 1980: (*a*) naming ranges, (*a–c*) foci, and (*b–c*) mappings.

In figure 6.17, *ȼah* is dominant and *k'an* is recessive. Although the ranges show extreme difference in size, there is evidence of coextension: the recessive range is named at H3 on the dark side of elemental red and its mapping extends to elemental red at G2. This system shows a dominant-recessive pattern that is the opposite of that shown in figure 6.16, although both originate in Paraje Nabil of Tenejapa.

In figure 6.18, the only evidence of coextension is the meager application of recessive *kʸaq* to C8 and C13—the latter as an alternative to dominant *q'en*. The speaker strongly centralized the focus of *q'en* at F4 as her first choice but, as an afterthought, she changed her choice to elemental yellow, C8–9. The first choice is counted as part of the four-way correspondence (table 6.1), because it was spontaneous.[15] But her second choice coincides with the tendency of the dominant-recessive pattern to break down as coextension evolves toward inclusion. Her mappings suggest inclusion. This system and that of figures 6.17 and 7.8 (in which red is dom-

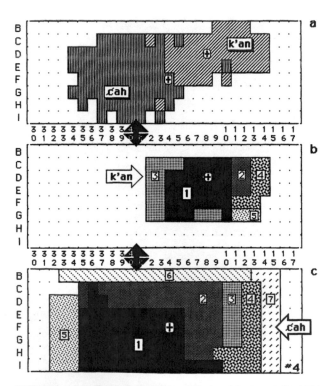

FIGURE 6.17. Tzeltal, Tenejapa, Chiapas, Mexico, f 60, 1980: (*a*) naming range, (*a–c*) foci, and (*b–c*) mappings.

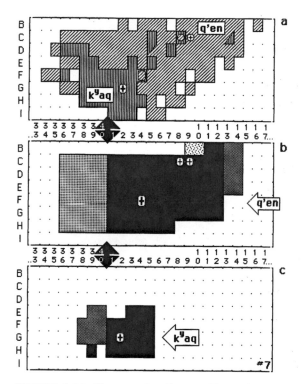

FIGURE 6.18. Uspantec, Las Pacayas, Uspantán, Guatemala, f 70, 1979: (*a*) naming ranges, (*a–c*) foci, and (*b–c*) mappings.

inant and yellow recessive) seem to dramatically manifest the different rates of retraction among dominant and recessive ranges that are modeled in figure 6.9. Figures 5.1. and 6.13 show an Uspantec system in which co-extensive ranges are less retracted and in which dominance is in reference to red.[16]

Figure 6.19 shows the weakest possible evidence of coextension: the recessive range, *k'an*, is named at H3 beyond its mapping and on the dark side of elemental red.

Figure 6.20 shows other weak evidence that two ranges are coexten-sive. The recessive mapping of *¢ah* extends to the focus of the dominant range, *k'an*, but not to elemental yellow. There is no intermixture of terms, and the naming range of recessive *¢ah* is larger than the naming range of dominant *k'an*. Perhaps the system is precisely on the border between co-extension and inclusion. Data from this speaker's daughter show further change, figure 7.3.

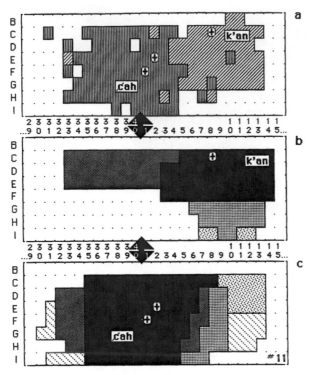

FIGURE 6.19. Tzeltal, Amatenango, Chiapas, Mexico, f 80, 1980: (*a*) naming ranges, foci, and (*b–c*) mappings.

Figures 6.21–23 exhibit a pattern shared by Navenchauc Tzotzil speakers: although coextension survives, the ranges are mapped with more steps than any others of the Mesoamerican sample. The same occurs within their dark-cool category, which, in addition, contains smaller ranges to four levels of embedding, another record number. I compared taxonomic depth and number of mapping steps among Tzeltal and Tzotzil color categories to find that the two qualities correspond (MacLaury 1991a:50–55, figs. 9–10). Thirty years prior to my fieldwork, Navenchauc was skirted by the newly constructed Pan American Highway. The resident Tzotzil have maintained tradition, such as native dress, monolingualism, and broad color categories, although it appears that their intensive contact with the national mainstream has fostered strong attention to distinctiveness.

Figure 6.21 shows an eleven-step mapping of dominant *k'on* and a six-step mapping of recessive *ȼoh*, which reaches elemental yellow, C8. The dominant range is centrally focused at E4, where it coincides with the first mapping step.

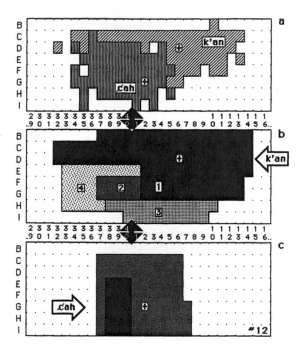

FIGURE 6.20. Tzeltal, Tenejapa, Chiapas, Mexico, f 70, 1980: (*a*) naming ranges, (*a–c*) foci, and (*b–c*) mappings.

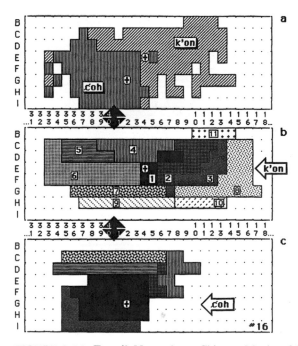

FIGURE 6.21. Tzotzil, Navenchauc, Chiapas, Mexico, f 50, 1981: (*a*) naming ranges, (*a–c*) foci, and (*b–c*) mappings.

Figure 6.22 shows a fourteen-step mapping of dominant *k'on* and a five-step mapping of recessive *¢oh*. This speaker first focused *k'on* at E4, then changed her choice to D9 where the focus matches her first mapping step. Both choices are centralized; whereas her focus of recessive *¢oh* at G40 is outside the axis plotted by elemental hues.

In figure 6.23*a–e*, *¢oh* is dominant and *k'on* recessive. The range of *¢oh* (*a, d*) includes a secondary category that is named coextensively by *morado* and *kafe*. The secondary terms name colors that would otherwise be named by *¢oh*, which diminishes the dominant naming range to 28 colors; its size is 75 when the 47 uses of the secondary terms are also counted (table 6.1). The focus of *¢oh* (*a*) mismatches its naming range at E5 but (*c*) corresponds to the upper right of its first mapping step. Perhaps the very centralized focus was chosen to mark contrast against the secondary category; however, *e* shows that chip E5 is the one color shared by the first step of both mappings. The dominant-range focus may have been strategically placed on the only color that represents maximal membership in both ranges.

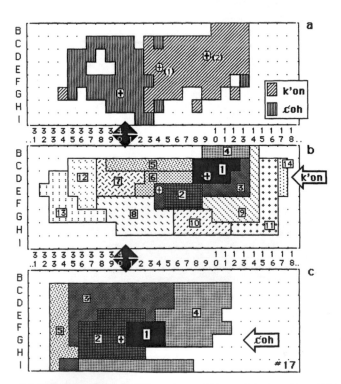

FIGURE 6.22. Tzotzil, Navenchauc, Chiapas, Mexico, f 26, 1981: (*a*) naming ranges, (*a–c*) foci, and (*b–c*) mappings.

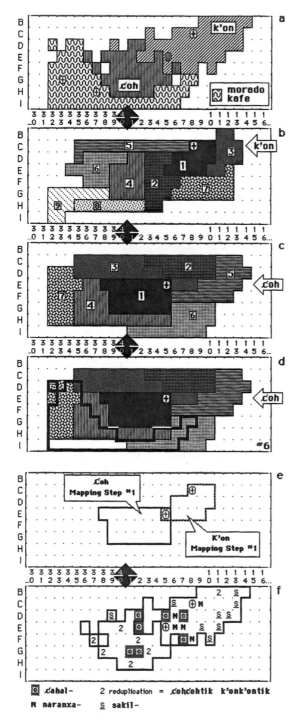

FIGURE 6.23. Tzotzil, Navenchauc, Chiapas, Mexico, f 19, 1981: (*a*) naming ranges; (*a–c*) foci; (*b–d*) mappings; (*e*) first mapping steps and foci (see *b–c*); (*f*) naming-range outlines and qualifiers of roots (see *a*).

6.3.3. Dominant and Recessive Qualifiers

Many individuals do not volunteer qualifiers, which precludes counting such data in table 6.1; yet, qualifiers index the dominant-recessive pattern.

In figure 6.23, *f* outlines the dominant and recessive naming ranges of *a*. Each range is designated by a distinct pair of qualifiers: dominant *¢oh* is qualified by *¢ahal-* or, by reduplication, *¢oh¢oh-tik*, which, respectively, designate good and marginal members of the category from the dominant vantage. Recessive *k'on* is qualified predominantly by *naranxa-* and *sakil-*, designating good and marginal members from the recessive vantage. The root *k'on* is qualified by terms that do not qualify *¢oh*, which is consistent with an attention to distinctiveness. But the qualifiers of *¢oh* also qualify *k'on*—as *¢ahal-k'on* and reduplication *k'onk'on-tik*—which is consistent with an attention to similarity. This practice parallels (*e*) placement of the dominant focus on the one color shared by the first mapping steps of both *¢oh* and *k'on*.

The model of figure 6.24 offers an account of these patterns. This depiction modifies figure 6.8 by omitting arrows that indicate zooming in. In the dominant range (*a*), the two elemental hues are linked by attention to similarity. The linkage would encourage similar treatment of hue. For example, (*e*) the focus of the dominant range would be placed on a color that is shared by the first mapping steps of both ranges; or (*f*) a qualifier that is primarily associated with the name of dominant range might also qualify the name of the recessive range. In the recessive range (*b*), the elemental hues are linked by attention to distinctiveness. The linkage would discourage similar treatment: a qualifier that is primarily associated with the name

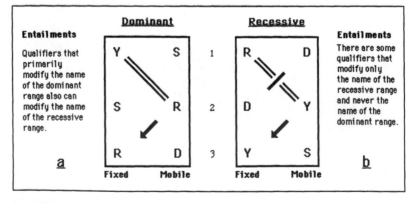

FIGURE 6.24. Formal model linking the asymmetrical relation between dominant and recessive ranges to asymmetry of qualifier distributions.

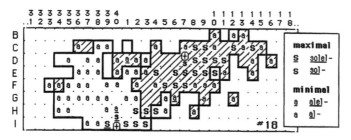

FIGURE 6.25. Tzeltal, Tenejapa, Chiapas, Mexico: naming-range outlines and qualifiers of roots (cf. fig. 6.3a).

of the recessive range would be applied exclusively to that term; the focus of the recessive range would probably be placed at a degree of removal, as in *e–f.*

Figure 6.25 shows qualifiers of dominant *k'an* and recessive *¢ah*, the ranges displayed in figure 6.3. The range of *k'an* is shaded. The focus of *¢ah* is polarized, I40. Both terms are qualified by augmentatives, *solel-* and *sol-,* and diminutives, *alel-* and *al-,* which, respectively, distinguish maximal versus marginal members of the warm category. Both *k'an* and *¢ah* are qualified by more diminutives than augmentatives, but *k'an* is qualified by more augmentatives and fewer diminutives than is *¢ah.* The ratios are 17 augmentatives to 27 diminutives versus 8 to 34 (p<.05 Pearson chi square). On the dominant side, the difference agrees with the entailment of attention to similarity: many colors will be viewed as maximal and equal members of the category. On the recessive side, the difference is entailed by attention to distinctiveness: fewer colors will be maximal members and more will be marginal.

6.3.4. Lexical Borrowing

In figure 6.23*f,* the common qualifier, *¢ahal-,* is native (< Proto-Tzeltalan **¢ax-al,* Kaufman 1972:97, item 095), while the qualifier pertaining exclusively to the recessive range, *naranxa-,* is a loanword (< Sp. *naranja* 'orange'). As a general tendency, it is likely that the recessive range, rather than the dominant, will be named with a loanword as in figures 4.9*a–c,* 5.4*a–d,* 5.11*a–c,* 6.26*a–b,* 6.27 and 6.35*b.* The widespread naming of the recessive range with loanwords requires an explanation. The recessive range may be recently added and, thus, out of sheer historical happenstance, be the range most apt to receive an identifiable foreign name. But *naranx-* replaces Proto-Tzeltalan **k'an-al* (Kaufman, p. 106, item 322).

Perhaps the recessive range, with its emphasis on distinctiveness, is associated with refinement and, thus, is suitably named with a prestigious Spanish term.[17]

Figure 6.26 displays dominant-recessive coextension in the cool categories of Mixtec speakers. Each names the dominant range with native $k^{\omega}\check{\imath}\check{\imath}$ and the recessive range with a loanword, *àsúl* or *asul* (< Sp. *azul*). In *a,* the Diuxí Mixtec speaker focuses $k^{\omega}\check{\imath}\check{\imath}$ at H17, the column of unique green; on the same side of the category, he polarizes the focus of *àsúl* at C15. In *b,* the Peñoles Mixtec speaker also focuses both ranges on one side of the category, centralizing the focus of $k^{\omega}\check{\imath}\check{\imath}$ at G21 and polarizing the focus of asul at D15. Both systems exhibit crossover of coextensive characteristics in the recessive range (item 9 of table 5.1: one kind of complication typifying cool-category coextension). Yet numbers across the Mesoamerican sample do not overwhelmingly indicate that the recessive range is "indeterminate" or less stable than the dominant range; for example, in the recessive range, ambivalent, dual, and crossed-over foci are seen in figures 5.1, 5.5, 5.10, 6.1. 6.26*a–b,* 7.4–5, and in the dominant range the same is seen in figures 5.6–7, 6.18–19, and 6.22, a ratio of 8:5. The speaker from Peñoles (*b*) coextensively names the warm category, but he places its foci in reference to opposite hues, in keeping with the difference between warm and cool (item 2 of table 5.1).

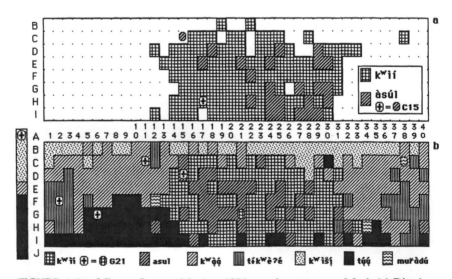

FIGURE 6.26. Mixtec, Oaxaca, Mexico, 1978; naming ranges and foci: (*a*) Diuxí, m 18; (*b*) Peñoles, m 27.

6.3.5. Triple Coextension

Figure 6.27 displays a complex. Mappings of (*a*) *reš* and (*b*) *selest* barely show a dominant-recessive coextensive relation: the last mapping step of *selest* reaches column 17 of unique green. On a finer level of differentiation, *selest* presumably includes (*c*) *asul*, whose focus is polarized at H31 and whose naming range (*a*) concordantly extends to purple, I35–36.

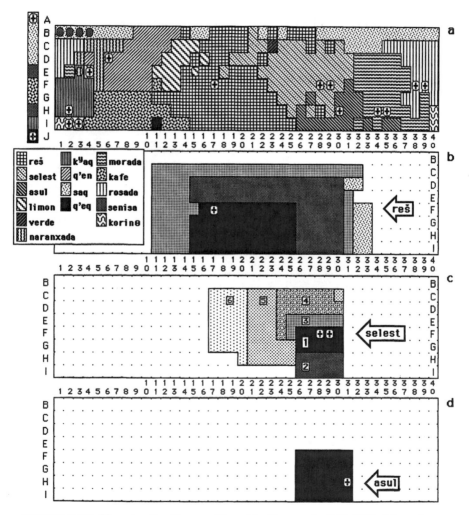

FIGURE 6.27. Uspantec, Las Pacayas, Uspantán, Guatemala, f 40, 1979: (*a*) naming ranges, (*a–d*) foci, and (*b–d*) mappings.

It is presumed that *selest* directly includes *asul* because their ranges are smaller than that of *reš*. The polarization of *asul* in focus and naming would be entailed by very strong attention to distinctiveness within the most restricted range among the three (§7.1.4).

Figure 5.4 shows triple coextension in the warm category, while figure 6.27 shows a coextensive relation under which the recessive range encompasses a third range in a relation of inclusion. As modeled by figure 6.10, both coextension and inclusion are constructed in the same way, except that attention to similarity and attention to distinctiveness assume different balances of strength within each. However, complex relations may be modeled as a chain in which a dominant range is related to a recessive range which, in turn, is related to an ultra-recessive range. There is not a direct relation between the dominant range and the range that is ultra-recessive.

The problem in devising a formalism is that in any balance there are only two cognitive emphases: attention to similarity has one strength while attention to distinctiveness has a reciprocal strength. The balance does not admit a three-way distribution; however, preclusion of a direct linkage between dominant and ultra-recessive ranges allows attention to distinctiveness to play a double role. In the relation between the dominant and recessive ranges, attention to distinctiveness remains squarely that. But in the relation between the recessive range and the ultra-recessive range, attention to distinctiveness plays the part of an attention to similarity *relative* to the even stronger attention to distinctiveness by which the ultra-recessive range is composed. As is discussed in §6.2.2, relativity can pertain among mobile coordinates because they are selections of points on an axis. A selection that emphasizes distinctiveness relative to an emphasis on similarity in turn will become an emphasis on similarity relative to an even stronger emphasis on distinctiveness.[18]

Figure 6.28 depicts the relativity of inherently mobile coordinates on the axis between strong attention to similarity **S** (= unity) and strong attention to distinctiveness **D** (= disparity). A relation between two vantages is a "frame" or closed set of parameters. A frame precludes consideration of a third vantage, even though the latter may exist as a presupposition; in a relation of inverted coordinates, only two arrangements may be attentively convoked at one time. The preclusion is essential to the linking of three vantages as a chain whose first and third link lack a direct connection. The first and third vantages are always and only considered separately from each other, in either frame I or frame II. From a transcendent or abso-

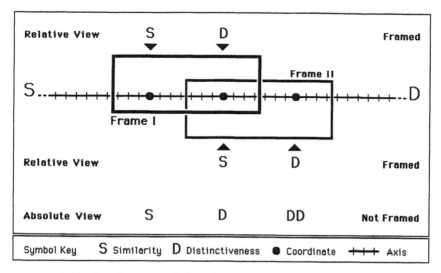

FIGURE 6.28. Coordinates consisting of emphases on S similarity and D distinctiveness selected from the axis between S unity and D disparity; they are relative when framed but absolute when not framed.

lutist view, the two frames include selections of similarity **S**, distinctiveness **D** and doubly strong distinctiveness **DD**. But from the framed views, the coordinates are relative: attention to distinctiveness of frame I becomes attention to similarity in frame II relative to the stronger attention to distinctiveness that is exclusive to this second relation between viewpoints. Here the stronger attention to distinctiveness **DD** serves as does **D** in the first frame, although with a greater polarization entailed. Indeed the emphasis on distinctiveness is strongest in frame II, in spite of its cognitive relativity.

Figure 6.29 expresses the relativity in two other ways, long and short. In *a,* the dominant, recessive, and ultra-recessive vantages are marked, respectively, as 1, 2, and 3; the frames are identified as I and II. In frame I, at a broad level of concentration, the coordinates are defined as in figure 6.8. But in frame II, at closer concentration, the coordinates of vantage 2 are redefined in reference to those of vantage 3, which is only considered here.[19] In *b,* the figure abbreviates the redefinition by depicting only the emphases on inherently mobile coordinates. In frame I, distinctiveness **D** is defined as such in reference to similarity **S**. But the strength to which similarity is emphasized in frame I will not pertain in frame II, **S** > **Ø**. Rather, in frame II, distinctiveness **D** is contrasted against stronger dis-

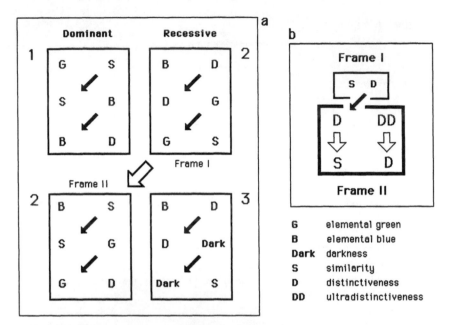

FIGURE 6.29. Formalisms chain-linking triple vantages as relations within two frames: (*a*) full representation, and (*b*) highlighting inherently mobile coordinates.

tinctiveness **DD**, which are both defined in relation to each other: **D** > **S**, **DD** > **D**. In vantage 2 of frame II, **Ø** > **D**.[20]

6.3.6. Balanced Coextension

In table 6.1, four individuals (19–22) equally distribute dominant and recessive characteristics between coextensive ranges, 18% of the 22 fully described cases. The dominant-recessive pattern dissolves as attention to distinctiveness strengthens sufficiently to bring about a relation of inclusion (table 7.1). Here it appears that four individuals have begun this process while they maintain a coextensive relation. Three show coextensive systems of a late phase, while the balanced system of an elder Aguacatec speaker (20) defies being typed as early or late.

Figure 6.30 displays the balanced coextensive ranges of a fourth speaker of Navenchauc Tzotzil, a young relative of those whose data appear in figures 6.21–23. Her balanced coextension occurs in the milieu of rapid culture change and atomization of traditional category ranges. Although it may be a coincidence, this speaker—in addition to rendering balanced coextension—demonstrated four levels of taxonomic depth in her

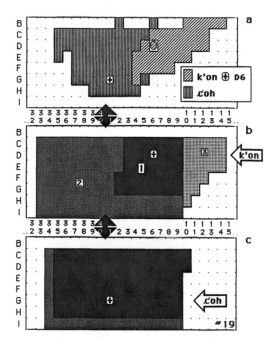

FIGURE 6.30. Tzotzil, Navenchauc, Chiapas, Mexico, f 16, 1981: (*a*) naming ranges, (*a–c*) foci, and (*b–c*) mappings.

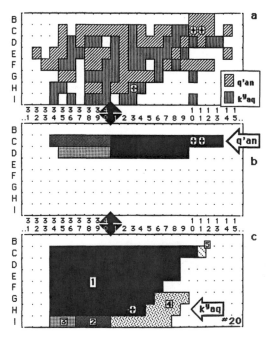

FIGURE 6.31. Aguacatec, Aguacatán, Huehuetenango, Guatemala, m 87: (*a*) naming ranges and foci, 1978, (*b–c*) mappings, 1980 (cf. fig. 5.2).

dark-cool category (MacLaury 1991*a:* fig. 9). Her taxonomy is two levels
deeper than any other in the Mesoamerican sample, save the four-tier systems that her sister and cousins mapped.

Figure 6.31 shows a second case of balanced coextension, that of the
Aguacatec elder (fig. 5.2). His naming ranges (*a*) are thoroughly intermixed
as they would be in an early-phase system, such those of figure 6.34*a–b*.
But he mutually polarized his foci of *q'an* and *kʸaq*, C10–11 versus H3;
he mapped *q'an* (*b*) in three small steps on only rows C–D, stopping short

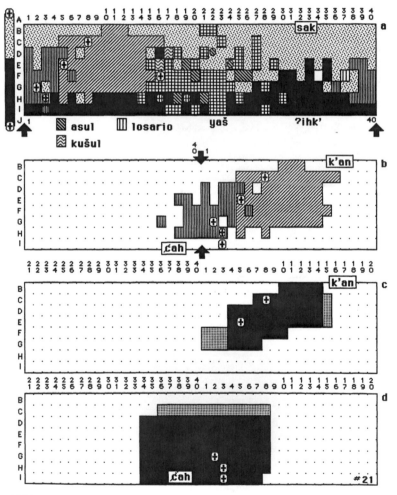

FIGURE 6.32. Tzeltal, Tenejapa, Chiapas, Mexico, f 32, 1980: (*a–b*) naming ranges,
(*a–d*) foci, and (*c–d*) mappings.

of colors that (*a*) he named *q'an* on rows E–H. It seems that he rendered the mapping only in reference to elemental yellow and distinctiveness while ignoring all else. His balanced coextension coincides with this performance.

In figure 6.32*b–c,* the second steps of mappings minimally demonstrate coextension, reaching G1 for *k'an* and C8 for *¢ah.* This woman, age 32, was the youngest Tzeltal interviewed. Her naming of *yaš* is smaller than that of any other cool category in the Mesoamerican sample, yielding to incursions of light *sak* and dark *ʔihk',* although her mapping of the cool

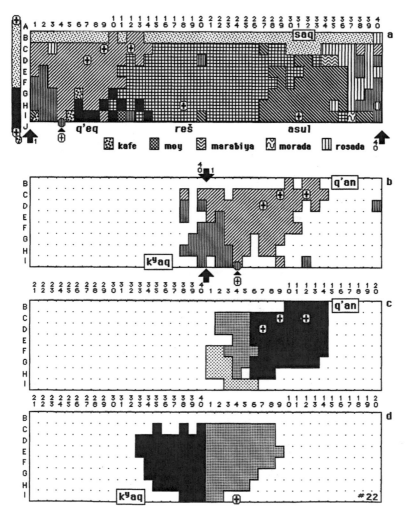

FIGURE 6.33. Uspantec, Las Pacayas, Uspantán, Guatemala, f 78, 1979: (*a–b*) naming ranges, (*a–d*) foci, and (*c–d*) mappings.

category was broad. She shows signs of a strong emphasis on difference, such as multiple foci for every hue category; she attached multifarious qualifiers to each use of every term, for example, *¢ah¢ah-naš-yalal-k'anal-tebuk* at F3 (not just *¢ah*), perhaps the longest responses recorded for any color survey.[21]

Figure 6.33 shows another set of coextensive ranges, squeaking by with a third mapping step at G–H 1–2 and a second step at C8. The multiple foci are unusual, but the naming ranges are of a standard configuration.

6.3.7. Systems Not in Table 6.1

Six individuals who name the warm category coextensively were interviewed only for naming and foci: the 5 WCS cases listed in note 3 plus that

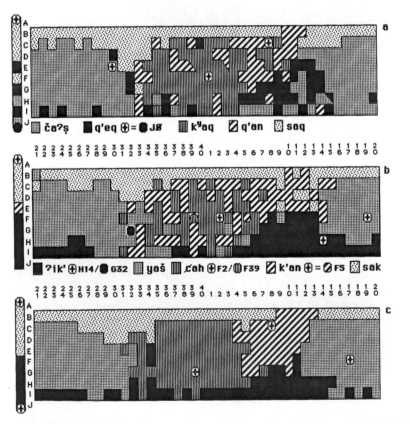

FIGURE 6.34. Naming ranges and foci: (*a*) Mam, Tacaná, Guatemala, f 60, 1979; (*b*) Tzeltal, Amatenango, Chiapas, Mexico, f 85, 1980 (cf. fig. 6.1); (*c*) Tzeltal, Amatenango, f 45, 1980 (cf. fig. 6.4).

of figure 6.34*a*. Lack of mappings makes such data harder to interpret; yet, these data demonstrate additional qualities of coextension.

Figure 6.34*a* displays the system of a Mam speaker who coextensively named both warm and dark-cool. Coextensive dark-cool terms are *ča?ş* and *q'eq*. The focus of *ča?ş* at E30 is slightly polarized to middle-light brightness; the focus of *q'eq* occurs on black JØ, where most Mayan speakers focus this term or its cognate. But JØ is named *ča?ş* while a usage of *q'eq* occurs at D30, on the light side of E30 where *ča?ş* is focused. In *b* and *c* are complete Amatenango Tzeltal systems whose coextensive relations have been displayed, figures 6.1 and 6.4. The two allow comparison of full systems in which occur early and late coextension of the warm category. They differ from the system of the Mam speaker, who named two categories coextensively.

In figure 6.35, a Mixtec speaker may also coextensively compose both the dark-cool category and the warm category. The suggestive evidence is that *kʷìī* is applied to black, JØ, while its focus is polarized at C17. The term *túú*, focused at JØ, would name the recessive range. Coextensive naming of the warm category appears to involve at least two terms, with foci at F4 red *tíʷè?é*, G8–9 brown *kàféé* (< Sp. *café* 'coffee'); it would require a mapping to determine the relation of *kʷàá* (C9) to the other terms.

In figure 6.36, a Mazatec speaker focuses the dominant range, *si³nę¹*, at D1 in pink; it surrounds the recessive range, *?a³ni¹*. The term *tʸa³va³* is

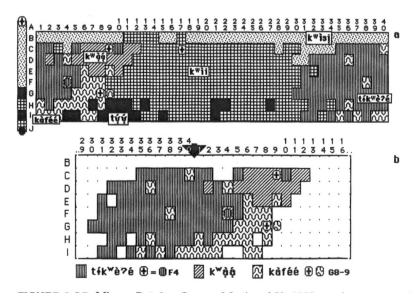

FIGURE 6.35. Mixtec, Peñoles, Oaxaca, Mexico; f 50, 1978, naming ranges and foci: (*a*) obverse and (*b*) reverse.

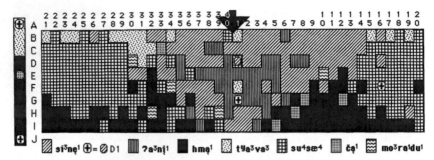

FIGURE 6.36. Mazatec, Chiquihuitlán, Oaxaca, Mexico, m 45, 1977: naming ranges and foci.

focused in white, AØ, although it names bright red at F1. The semantically complex warm category might be encompassed by a white-focused light-warm category, although only mappings would demonstrate this. Such a relation of light-warm to warm might explain why the focus of dominant $si^3 n\varrho^l$ at D1 is triangulated at equal distance from elemental white, yellow, and red.

Figure 6.37 shows four Tlapanec systems. In *a*, both the cool category and the warm category are coextensively named. (Fig. 5.8*c* shows solely cool.) The focus of *mò²mò* is crossed over to elemental red at G2 while the focus of *mænya* is polarized at I1. In the 25 other Tlapanec systems of the Mesoamerican sample, *mò²mò* is focused in reference to yellow. Crossed-over foci are rare in the warm category, unlike in the cool category (figs. 5.5–7, 5.10, 6.26*a*–*b*). In *b*, the two terms of figure 5.3 are shown within a system; *mænya* at D8 falls a chip short of verifying that they are coextensive. Their foci are polarized outside of their ranges, I1 and C12. Another category named with two terms, *šäni* and *ngïdï*, encompasses colors that surround the warm category and extend through pastels. The detached foci of the warm ranges coincide with this anomaly. In *c* is what appears to be a relation of inclusion in the warm category. The range of *mænya* is limited to G1–2 and F4, while the focus of *mò²mò* is markedly polarized at C13 outside its naming range. These data dramatically exemplify the disproportion of size that can develop between two ranges as the relation of inclusion emerges (fig. 6.9), and they exemplify how the focus of the dominant range can become polarized at this phase (table 7.1). Both characteristics differentiate inclusion from coextension. (This warm category is diagrammed by itself in figure 7.7*b*.) In *d*, *mænya* and *mò²mò* name the warm category coextensively, with *mænya* naming C8; its red focus is polarized and extended, H–I1–3.

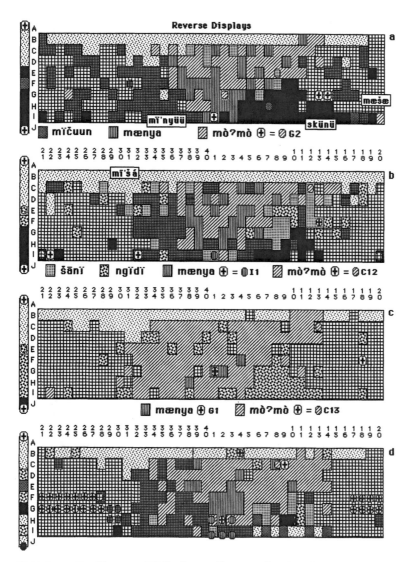

FIGURE 6.37. Tlapanec, Malinaltepec, Guerrero, Mexico, 1978, naming ranges and foci: (*a*) m 30, (*b*) m 22, (*c*) f 50, (*d*) f 60.

6.3.8. Foci of the Warm Category

Figure 6.38 shows all foci of the 32 pairs of coextensive ranges pertaining to warm categories that were elicited in Mesoamerica by the MCS and WCS (see note 3). Each number is the sum of individuals who chose a

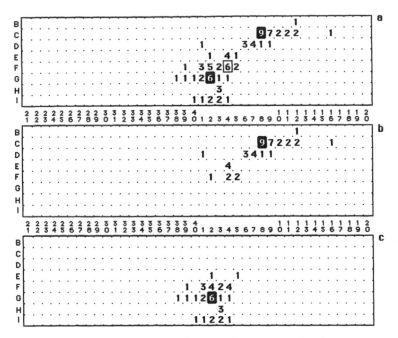

FIGURE 6.38. Focus aggregate of coextensive terms naming the warm category from 32 speakers: (*a*) foci of all "warm" terms; (*b*) foci of "warm" terms that are cognate with the "yellow" terms of advanced systems; (*c*) foci of "warm" terms cognate with "red" terms. Presumably, the foci of (*b*) and (*c*) were placed in reference to yellow and red, respectively.

particular color as the focus of one term. Some individuals placed one focus on two adjacent colors (fig. 6.31 and others) or placed disjunctive foci for one term (figs. 6.32–33 and others). Only foci covering three or more adjunct colors are excluded (fig. 6.37*d* alone).

The foci distribute through an axis constrained by the locations of elemental red and elemental yellow; these are pinpointed at G1 and C9 by steep plurality peaks in separate WCS aggregates of all non-Mesoamerican red-, yellow-, and warm-category foci (MacLaury MS-1:figs. 36–40). The Mesoamerican pluralities in coextensive categories occur as 6 on G2 and 9 on C8. The cognitive emphases on similarity and distinctiveness have pulled the majority of foci away from the perceptual maxima so that they distribute through an arc of centralized and polarized positions. However, the distribution does not imply that the foci are randomly "floating." Foci regarded within individual systems exhibit the dominant-recessive pattern (table 6.1). This focus aggregate from coextensively composed warm categories is more centralized and less polarized than the aggregate from warm categories composed by inclusion, as will be analyzed in §7.1.1 (table 7.1). Vantage theory attributes this difference to the distinct balances between attention to similarity and distinctiveness that produces each relation, including their diagnostic focus patterns. Such statistics make it hard to deny that these dynamics are vital to the composition of the warm category.

6.4. Implications of Vantage Theory

The central implications of vantage theory pertain to accounts of how people categorize, but the theory also brings up questions about the genetic bases of categorization and offers an ingredient for the modeling of cognitive evolution.

6.4.1. Analogy on the Level of Coordinates

The general idea that linguistic categorization is based on spatial analogy goes back to Byzantine scholarship, according to Anderson (1973; cf. Lyons 1977:718–724). Vantage theory adds that the analogy occurs specifically between spatial and mental coordinates. It stipulates further that space is space-time, while time is manifested as motion. Projection of a coordinate to the forefront may substitute for motion as its metonym.

6.4.2. Phylogeny

It is unlikely that the human capacity to categorize evolved among proto-human populations in vacuo without a noncategorical precedent (MacLaury 1986a:81, 207, 410; cf. Lakoff 1990:73). Keeping one's bearings in space and time is a rudimentary aptitude shared by most complex species. Perhaps we differ from other animals in our ability to use analogy as a means to transfer the strategy of spatiotemporal reckoning to methods of abstract thinking, such as our means of forming and using categories. This would enable human categories to be other than direct functions of physical reality. Vantage theory attributes to human categorization that particular primeval origin. Other theories treat categorization in the here and now without linking the capacity to a phylogenic speculation.

6.4.3. Human versus Animal Categorization

Even insects—bees, for example—behave as if they categorize, and they keep their bearings by awareness of coordinates. But if only humans have combined the two capacities through analogy, then how do bees organize a category? Possibly their categories are fuzzy-set identities, like those modeled by Kay and McDaniel (1978). We know little about how intelligent mammals (for example, apes) categorize. How do neonate human infants categorize? Bees, apes, and infants have all been shown to categorize color or, at least, to treat it categorically (Gould and Marler 1987:77, 83; Matsuzawa 1985; Bornstein, Kessen and Weiskopf 1976).[22]

6.4.4. Innateness

Since the dominant-recessive pattern is produced—or can be produced—by each individual independent of cultural prescription or physiological determinacy, one must inquire where the knowledge comes from. Where do people learn how to construct a category by analogy to a vantage in space-time? The only apparent answer is that the propensity is inborn, which implies that it resides in human genes and, thus, is instinctive. It would seem less radical to propose that categorization, irrespective of how it is achieved, is an innate human propensity. But that seemingly safer idea ignores the connection between a category and its making. If categorization is innate, then the method of creating a category, maintaining it, and changing it must also be inborn (cf. Sperber 1980).

6.4.5. Embodiment

On Johnson's (1987) view, people model abstractions after the design of bodily experience with space, force, sensation, and basic-level objects. They transfer such structure to abstract thought by analogy and metaphor. Vantage theory extends Johnson's "embodiment" to commonplace categorization to provide for the active involvement of the individual.

6.4.6. A Vantage Is Always Part of a Category

A category is the sum of its coordinates: for example, a cool category is the sum of elemental green, elemental blue, a particular attention to similarity, and an attention to distinctiveness of converse strength. But a category also must consist of at least one vantage, which is an arrangement of the coordinates and, further, the priorities that produce the arrangement. For example, on the preferred level of concentration, elemental green may be the main fixed coordinate coupled with the mobile coordinate of attention to similarity, and so on through other levels (fig. 6.7c). This singular arrangement is sufficient to ascribe one vantage to the category, and at least one such vantage is unavoidable in any act of categorizing green and blue together. If a second arrangement of the same coordinates is adopted, say, with blue in the fixed position on level 1 and attention to distinctiveness as the mobile coordinate, then the category will have a second vantage. When people construct a category of more than one vantage, they may distinguish the vantages with different terms, or they may name them with only one term. Whatever the case, a category is a dynamic relation among selective emphases, coordinates, and at least one point of view.

6.4.7. Coordinates versus Features

A definition of a category as the sum of its coordinates is almost the same and almost as reductionistic as a checklist definition, as in markerese or feature theory (Katz and Fodor 1963; cf. Fillmore 1975). The minimal difference is that selective emphasis pertains among coordinates. But mainly vantage theory differs from feature theory by stipulating the importance of the way or ways that coordinates are arranged. As the person who forms the category is the only one who can select one or another arrangement among the options, vantage theory connects the person to what he or she forms. Whereas some versions of feature theory imply that selection of features is objective—that is, determined by the natural salience of certain attributes in the external world—both the selective emphases and their arrangements come only and always from the viewer and never from the world outside. This is so even when the natural discontinuities are as blatant as the difference between fire and water. Unlike feature theory or the theory of semantic primitives (Wierzbicka 1972, 1993), vantage theory stresses the agency of people who construct and use categories.

6.4.8. Primary Motivation versus Function

A person's objective in forming a category is to establish a view on the world, a point of view from which to comprehend. There is also the functionalist notion that a category serves to reduce infinite variation to manageable groupings. This function is undeniable; it implies that the human capacity to categorize would be favored by natural selection. The two purposes of categorizing are not at odds, because behavior can be selectively advantageous for reasons apart from what motivates it. However, theory can go astray when function is confounded with motivation. People categorize and change categories in order to create and to refine viewpoints;

they do not feel themselves to be surviving as a species or to be reducing infinite variation. To explain data, a model must phrase theory in terms of the primary objectives of the people who categorize, not only in terms of ultimate results and evolutionary benefits.

6.4.9. Alternative Accounts of Color Categorization

The hypothesis of vantages and coordinates is only one among various models of color categorization. Rosch's prototype concept predicts that the focus of most major color categories, including those of figure 6.38 and table 6.1, will be an elemental color point; deviant focus selections will be random. Thus, the model does not account for coextension or its dominant-recessive constitution, including the predictable pattern of more and less centralized foci. The model by itself cannot explain the observed regularities of variation and continuous change. Since, in Rosch's view, a category functions to manage infinite difference, it must "correspond to the correlational structure of the environment" (see §§1.1 and 6.4.8). This assumption further abuses the functionalist evolutionary view (apart from confounding function with motivation), as it attributes a nonadaptive rigidity to categorization. It ignores that a human population—without undergoing a change of the gene code—may not only divide a category but, as a further adaptation, may reconfigure its range, as when a brightness category is altered to one of hue. The vantage model accords such plasticity to categorization, a property that surely helps the species to cope with external change.

Kay and McDaniel's (1978) fuzzy-set formalism is limited in the same ways as Rosch's prototype notion. Yet it has additional inadequacies, which are enumerated in §§2.4.2 and 6.4.11.

6.4.10. Etic and Emic

Modeling or describing a people's behavior by the analyst's constructs is etic when the constructs are extrinsic to native meaning, whereas modeling in accord with the native view is emic. Vantage theory is an attempt to model emically because its aim is to identify how a person composes a view, maintains it, and changes it. The alternatives to vantage theory equally aspire to be emic, but their constructs are patently etic. Classical logic does not even include a viewer while it asserts that its operations depict how the viewer would think if accurately attuned with the world as it really is; both the operations and this concept of a singular real world are etic. Fuzzy-set logic adds an etic decimal point to these already-etic operations; the decimal is extraneous because it measures membership from the view of the one who makes the model while failing to state why, from the view of the native, membership is as the decimal describes; that is, the descriptive decimal involves no source of explanation apart from itself. Rosch and Mervis (1975:575) define a category as family resemblances of members to a prototype, while they define a prototype as the member of the category that has most resemblances to all other members and least to prototypes of other categories. They break this tautology by saying that the family resemblances and the prototype reside in the correlational structure of the environment. However, the environment in unedited form is external to a cognitive model and, therefore, etic. Consistent with that, Rosch and Mervis do not use the term "cognition." Some or all of vantage theory could be etic as well, although indicating how this is so will be up to its critics. Any model that incorporates an etic construct, however minor, will never represent a native point of view.

6.4.11. Point of View and Fuzziness

In 1965, Zadeh modeled the fuzziness of categories by attaching a decimal to classical logic. The classical framework was the only account of categorization available to him then. But since, he has never contrasted classical logic against another system to argue why the former, as opposed to the other, is the legitimate recipient of the decimal. Vantage theory addresses fuzziness without need of a decimal, because a point of view is intrinsically clearest near the vantage point and vaguest at its outer reaches; any viewpoint, whether spacio-temporal or analogical, implicitly entails gradation and fuzziness. Moreover, the inherently mobile coordinates of category—attention to similarity and difference—naturally establish that its boundary will fluctuate. This system does not have to be accommodated to behavior by imposing a prop, such as a descriptive decimal. The very need for such a measure in fuzzy-set theory betrays its own essential inadequacy as a cognitive model as well as the privation of the logic from which it derives. Although engineers use fuzzy logic to govern a wondrous washing machine, the calculus has nothing to do with human thinking. The difference is that a machine never adopts a point of view unless so instructed by an etic formula, whereas a person always is compelled to construct a viewpoint and always composes it emically.

6.4.12. Boundaries

The fuzzy-set theory of categorization derives its major appeal from empirical recognition that category boundaries are indeterminate. They are said to end abruptly only when they meet a natural disjunction; for example, Kay and McDaniel (1978) portray the red category stopping at unique yellow and unique blue. But to the contrary, although orange and purple are perceived to be reddish, the better examples of neither category double as members of the red category. What curtails the range of "red" substantially short of the neighboring unique hues?

Vantage theory supplies three principles that specify such a definite category boundary independently of any perceived discontinuity while they accommodate graded category membership. The same principles crisply demarcate boundaries between other categorical behaviors that exhibit equally uneven values, such as the separate semantic domains of a color category (e.g., burgundy hue) versus a category of something typically of that color (e.g., burgundy wine). They aid in drawing a line between kinds of cognition, such as categorization and noncategorical thought.

First, the essential formula of a category is $(X \, S^2\text{-}D)$, three coordinates on two levels of concentration, always including S and D. The balance of strength between S^2 and D establishes a category margin; as the balance shifts, the margin moves commensurately. The difference between a category and another kind of viewpoint is that any vantage of a category always contains S and D while a noncategorical viewpoint never does; it cannot do so without becoming a category. For example, a noncategorical figure-to-ground relation only needs F and G as its coordinates.

Second, a recessive vantage $(X \, D^2\text{-}S)$ is derived by inverting the inherently mobile coordinates of a dominant vantage and cannot exist without accompanying dominant $(X \, S^2\text{-}D)$. This is useful for formally distinguishing basic color terms, which always name a dominant vantage; nonbasic terms always name a recessive point of view. The latter are in a relation of near synonymy, coextension, inclusion, or even polarized inclusion with one or another dominant vantage. However, the notion of a basic category is complicated when a vantage participates in two frames of reference, because in one frame the vantage is necessarily recessive while in the other it must be dominant. The dual role is attested by the Uspantec data in figure 6.27 (and by others, e.g., figs. 2.8 and 5.4) and abstracted in figures 6.28–29. From the Uspantec speaker's view, *selest* is nonbasic in the broad frame but basic in the narrow frame. Defining basic terminology in the absolute sense (depicted in fig. 6.28) requires imposition of an etic construct, such as Berlin and Kay's (1969:5–6) four criteria (§2.4). As they have said, their notion of basic as "operational" belongs exclusively to analytical metalanguage (cf. §6.4.10).

Third, S and D, in either order, must always be mobile coordinates on the highest and lowest levels of the zooming hierarchy to retain the multiplicative strength of one of them versus the singular strength of the other. As they are inherently mobile, their strengths are shifted by changing emphases on them without moving them from one level to another. But the strengths of inherently fixed coordinates are shifted by demoting or promoting them between levels, as shown among color-category types A–D in figure VIII.1 (cf. MacLaury 1992a: fig 9). Since inherently fixed coordinates are not selected from an axis, their recognition is all-or-none. If recognized at all, they can only be emphasized or de-emphasized by this promotion and demotion. Demoting one of them below the lowest level, bracketed by D or S, eliminates it from the category. Equally, a new coordinate is introduced on low levels, whence it may begin its ascent to top position. Specifically, it is introduced as a mobile coordinate on the second lowest level and as a fixed coordinate on the lowest level, leaving S or D as mobile on the lowest level.

As a consequence of this principle, coordinates on the way down and on the way up will never occupy the same position in the hierarchy. Thus, one of them will always predominate in shaping a category. For example, among types A–D, a color category can consist of (A) only emphasis on hue, (B) strong emphasis on hue and weak emphasis on brightness, (C) strong emphasis on brightness and weak emphasis on hue, or (D) only emphasis on brightness, but the category will never consist of equal emphases on hue and brightness.

The principle of unequal ranking of coordinates further applies to categories that combine coordinates from among the dimensions of color perception and from elsewhere, as Conklin (1955) reports of the Hanunóo, who combine green with succulence and red with dryness. This means that a category cannot pertain equally to separate domains and, therefore, will always pertain to only one domain. Thus, the substance categories of claret or amber are, respectively, of wine or fossil resin and not of purplish pink or translucent brown-yellow, unless someone will change the original category. Or people might create a derivative category by promoting the color and demoting the substance. The latter has happened with "amber," which consequently names the luminous brown-yellow independently of the fossil resin that characteristically imparts this sense, as in "amber lighting." Although "amber" is not as prevalent among color terms as is "red" or "green," its derived meaning is within the color domain and outside the domain of resin or fossils. Delimiting membership of a domain according to the primary fixed coordinates of its constituent categories gives the domain a clear margin despite the ranking of categories within it. This measure crisply defines, at least, the color domain because its primary coordinates are not ambiguous, unlike "resin or fossils."

6.4.13. Contextualization and Connotation

The inevitable ranking of coordinates assists a further distinction. A category that combines coordinates of color and noncolor will be constituted by any of three formulae: $CH\ S^2\ D$, $HC\ S^2\ D$, and $H\ S^2\ C\ D$. Let C mean "context" and H mean "hue," although brightness or saturation could replace hue. "Claret" exemplifies $CH\ S^2\ D$, which is primarily wine (C) and secondarily its inherent purplish pink (H). As wine is the context of the color and the color the context of the wine, C and H are fused as CH, which represents a complex image; it is like the prototypical image of a bird, which combines feathers, flight, nesting on eggs, and so forth (MacLaury 1995a: fig. 5). Assigning priority to C over H represents that "claret" is viewed as a substance of typical color rather than as mainly the color. "Roan," a color contextualized to horse hair, exemplifies $HC\ S^2\ D$. The ordering of priorities within HC represents that "roan" names a color, while the fusion shows the determinate link between hue and context; "roan" cannot be applied to anything besides a horse's coat. The color term "amber" exemplifies $H\ S^2\ C\ D$ because it can name the yellow-brown of anything, although on occasion it will call to mind its original referent, fossil resin, to those who know of its origin, while even the etymologically naive will evoke "amber" mainly in luminous or translucent settings. In either case, some context abides in the color-term meaning, at least as a connotation. The third position of C in $H\ S^2\ C\ D$ represents the weakness of contextualization, which need not be called to mind every time the term names color. The formulae rank coordinates according to their importance.

A fourth formula, $H\ S^2\ D$, represents a perfectly abstract color term that has either dropped every connotation or has never had any (a simple example might not exist). Quiché *k'el* 'yellowish green parrot-species (Sp. chocoyo)' doubles as a name for green and blue (fig. 11.8), as does its Mam cognate, *č'el* (figs. 10.4a and 10.5c), which suggests that speakers do not remember the green bird when they name blue with these terms. Thus, people may apply one color term according to different formulae. To cover all of the linkages, Spanish "bayo," which derives from Latin *badius* 'spleen' ($CH\ S^2\ D$), names a particular horse color ($HC\ S^2\ D$) or this horse-like color ($H\ S^2\ C\ D$) anywhere (Malkiel 1954); *k'el* names 'a green parrot species' ($CH\ S^2\ D$), 'parrot green' ($H\ S^2\ C\ D$) or 'blue' ($H\ S^2\ D$).

The color terms "amber" and *k'el* were derived as a metonymy from an object of the same name, seemingly transforming their formulae from

CH S^2 D to H S^2 C D while bypassing intermediate HC S^2 D. It makes no sense to designate the color of an object with that object's name, "*amber amber," if the object only comes in one color. Thus, H S^2 C D represents the result of metonymy, HC S^2 D a theory of its fleeting process.

6.4.14. Category Change

A category shifts in size and shape when an individual alters the balance of emphases on similarity and distinctiveness. The balance is adjusted as a way of coping with change in the sociophysical environment that has little or nothing to do with color, such as acceleration of the rate at which novelty impinges. The shift will alter many linguistic categories during an interval of time, and color categories will incidentally be transformed with the rest. Color categories are not altered to directly accommodate changes in kind or amount of colors that people are exposed to, as McNeill (1972) and Casson (1994) suggest. The adjustment of cognitive strategies toward a more analytical view differs from accounts of category change that accompany the prototype concept. These hold that alteration of category structure corresponds directly to physical or social revision specifically of the categorized domains. Kempton (1981) notes that a provincial class of upwardly mobile Mexicans shifted pottery prototypes from rural to mass-produced forms while their country cousins continued to envision local hand-made types. Dahlgren (1985) documents Anglo-Saxon notions of the *thegn*, fourth-ranked land-owning royalty, that changed as the society transformed from a patchwork of tribes into feudalism.

6.4.15. Judgments of Similarity and Difference within Categories

Medin, Goldstone and Gentner (1990, 1993) review the literature on the contribution of judgments of similarity and difference to categorization, showing that, since Hollingworth (1913), psychologists have in the main agreed that these judgments are indispensable to whatever it is that people do to organize a category. However, the specific way that the two emphases contribute to categorization—or, even how they *can* contribute—remains unsettled. Medin, Goldstone and Gentner reply principally to the philosopher Goodman (1972), who dismisses similarity judgment as a useless construct, at least in terms of the gratuitous ways it has been entertained; his criticism would extend automatically to the treatment of difference judgments. As the former (1993) paraphrase Goodman: "similarity, like motion, requires a frame of reference. Just as we have to say what something is moving in relation to, we also must specify in what respects two things are similar." They answer him by detailing cognitive processes that direct attention to respects of similarity, such as alignment of predicates within analogies. Vantage theory picks no quarrel with either side of this contention; a category is inherently a frame of reference based on a spatial analogy that includes the equation between degrees of motion and degrees of emphasis on similarity and distinctiveness. Vantage theory meets Goodman's critique by supplying the construct that he finds wanting (fig. 6.28).

Rosch et al. (1976) investigate respects of similarity through another approach. They find that a complex of seemingly distinguishable percepts contributes to a judgment of similarity between a prototype and a nonprototypical category member. They explore the roles of attributes, motor movements, shape, and expectation versus ignorance of stimuli in the formation of basic-level categories.

Medin, Goldstone and Gentner (1990:66) find that attention to similarity and to difference are not perfect opposites: " . . . the relative importance of attributes and relations shifts substantially . . . with relations being more attended to in similarity judgments and attributes more attended to in difference judgments." Under vantage theory, judgments of similarity and difference can never be perfect opposites to any observer because people always incorporate them within the coordinate system of one or another analogous vantage, which necessarily includes one of the emphases twice and the other only once, S^2-D versus D^2-S, per the arrangements shown in figure 6.8. This kind of frame foreordains the asymmetry that the authors identify.

6.4.16. Judgments of Asymmetry within Categories

Rosch (1975*a:* experiment 2) observes that subjects equate differences between prototypes and nonprototypical category members with increments of spatial distance; they also judge nonprototypes to be more similar to or "closer" to prototypes than are the prototypes to the same marginal members. Rips (1975:experiment 1) and Tversky and Gati (1978) replicate these asymmetries in experiments with diverse categories. However, Rosch and Mervis's (1975) notion of family resemblances to a prototype accounts for neither the persistent equation with space nor the asymmetrical assessments of similarity.

Vantage theory addresses the problem, as shown in figure 6.39, which represents any category; coextension is not required. Here, a prototype and a nonprototypical category member act as coordinates within a point of view. From the dominant perspective, attention to similarity is coordinated with the prototype on the preferred level of concentration, level 1, where the prototype is the fixed reference point of the category; the marginal

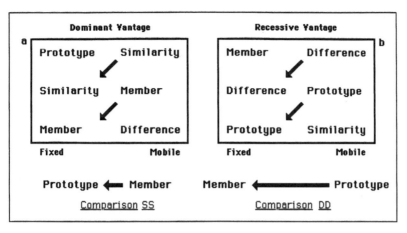

FIGURE 6.39. Formal model of the relation of vantages to asymmetry of similarity judgments when subjects compare (*a*) a nonprototypical category member with its prototype and (*b*) the prototype with the same nonprototypical member.

member is coordinated with similarity on level 2; and distinctiveness ("difference" in the figure) is coordinated with this member on level 3. Membership in the category is usually assessed from such a dominant view: matching of the member against the prototype is mediated across a double consideration of attention to similarity (S^2), which provides the fixed coordinate on level 2 and the mobile coordinate on level 1. From this (*a*) dominant vantage, attention to similarity contracts conceptualized distance in the same way as it does from the dominant vantage of a color category. However, in *b*, when the direction of comparison is reversed, a recessive vantage is temporarily created whereby the prototype is matched against the marginal member across a double consideration of distinctiveness (D^2). As in a recessive vantage of a color category, attention to distinctiveness protracts distance. The equation with distance itself is carried over to the category from the source domain of space-time via the analogy to physical viewpoint by which the category is constructed. Asymmetries occur, in effect, when category members are compared from alternative vantages, one dominant and the other recessive, even though the recessive vantage may be created only for comparing a prototype to a marginal member and dissolved with completion of this task.

6.4.17. Reference Point Reasoning

Rosch (1975*a*) suggests that a prototype serves as a reference point in similarity judgments, as do other canons, such as multiples of ten or vertical and horizontal planes. Her notion of "reference point reasoning" verges on vantage theory. Thus, in figure 6.39a, the prototype is included as the fixed coordinate on level 1. Vantage theory incorporates many of Rosch's main concepts, although it rebuffs her functionalism and naive realist notion that category gradation reflects "correlational structure." Vantage theory adds that a category is an analogy with a viewpoint of space-time conducted on the level of coordinates, that judgments of similarity and difference are equated with motion (as a function of time), that the resulting coordinate system is organized as levels of concentration related by zooming, and that the coordinate system is a frame of reference. These additions allow explanation of further facts about categories: coextension, change, a predictable trajectory of semantic relations, the human propensity to think of comparison in terms of distance, and asymmetrical categorical perceptions that emerge when comparisons are made in opposite directions.

6.4.18. Categorical Perception versus Weber's Law

Harnad (1987:3) regards *categorical perception* as reducing the continuum of senses to discrete groups and viewing the senses within each group as resembling one another more than any resemble senses included in other groups (see Kay and Kempton 1984). Weber's law represents the antithesis of categorical perception. The law stipulates, among other things, that discrimination will be constant for stimuli separated by a fixed ratio of magnitudes. In a single patch of the Munsell array, that which is occupied by reds and yellows, for example, there can be no quibbling about ratios of magnitude, because the colors are the same ones regardless of how they are categorized. Yet, when encompassed within the warm category by a single individual during one uninterrupted two-hour interview under stable lighting, the colors are treated as less separated when regarded from the dominant vantage and more separated from the recessive vantage. This seems to rule out the validity of Weber's law for color categorization with firm finality, as all variables are eliminated except the categorizing thoughts of the lone subject.

6.4.19. Relativity and Universality

There are many ways to organize and categorize the same perceptions of color. Speakers of Tzeltal are not backward or less aware of the world than English speakers when they name red and yellow with coextensive terms. The speakers of both languages have accurately named different points of view. Vantage theory attempts to indicate how their views differ and what principles they share.

6.4.20. Is the Space-Time Analogy Alive or Dead?

Seemingly the analogy itself is alive, or such is implied, at least, by the subjects of asymmetry experiments who speak of similarities between category members by reference to distance. But spatio-temporal reckoning may constitute a general procedure of making sense, first by picking out a fixed reference and building upon it and then by stabilizing the added elements to relate even newer material to those. Indeed this would be a live analogy, but it may underlie a wide range of cognition that both supersedes and includes categorization. Categorization is, then, only a special manifestation of the analogy that occurs when mobile coordinates constitute attention to similarity and difference $(X S^2\text{-}D)$, as in figure 6.11.

6.4.21. Speed and Productivity

In terms of productivity, to ask whether the categorical analogy is alive is like asking whether a phoneme is alive. The ability to produce phonemes is genetically based, indispensable to human behavior, and so automatic that we effortlessly articulate many as fast as we speak—easily a dozen for even an average short sentence. Yet every phoneme is cognitively constituted by coordinating at least three articulations that, in turn, are drawn from a larger, cognitively organized system of articulations. We know that the phoneme and the phoneme system are productively composed because they can change in form and content without loss of function. In that sense, a phoneme is alive, and it is not dead in the sense of being a mere physiologically determined reflex. Likewise, the way we produce a category is genetically based, indispensable to language and culture, and so automatic that several categories can be combined in rapid succession, either in a sentence or apart from speech. And like a phoneme and a phoneme system, a category and a domain of categories may change without loss of meaning or function. The speed with which a category is assembled does not indicate that it is directly determined by physiology or composed in any other way than as a point of view with the space-time analogy as its basis. Shared by a phoneme, a category, and a spatio-temporal vantage is their vital contribution to human survival, their dependence on one process or another of cognition, and the speed at which they are assembled and replaced in a sequence of like cognitions.

6.4.22. Is It Possible to Categorize without Constructing a Vantage?

Perhaps, but the categories would be unstable and adverse to intersubjective sharing, unless they were stabilized by specialized neural processing as, apparently, phonemes are synthesized in Broca's area. Without the arrangement of selected senses and emphases into a hierarchy of priorities, there would be no frame to prevent attention to similarity and attention to difference from rambling throughout the axis of possibilities. When similarity is emphasized without limits, the category could be extended indefinitely, say, from bananas, to apples, to round stones, to rocks of any shape or size, to rocky places, and so on, as children sometimes categorize (Rosch and Mervis 1975:602–603). Or, when difference is emphasized to an extreme, the category would shrink until it ceased to exist. Apes may categorize by such unbound complexes and may share their categories long enough to act upon them collectively. This hypothesis may be falsified if apes could be shown to exhibit asymmetries when they categorize; asymmetrical categorization would suggest that vantages are involved. But if the hypothesis gains support, the evidence could suggest that human categorization differs from animal categorization specifically by the addition of vantages; grouping by similarity is a rudimentary process, while using analogy to put attention to similarity and distinctiveness into a frame constitutes an additional feat. Vantages accord categories with a compromise between plasticity and stability by which they are always changeable but also shareable and memorable in the long term. Categories of this sort are prerequisite to language and culture.

6.5. Summary

The foregoing presents an argument that coextensively named color categories are composed by means of an analogy to the method by which an individual keeps track of her own position in physical space and time. The analogy is formed specifically between reference points of conceptual space-time and the mental coordinates by which a person constructs a category as though it were a vantage. Each person privately and individually uses the analogy to create, maintain, and change a color category. The strategy is independent of cultural prescription, historical precedent, personal habit, or the neurology that determines elemental hues. The strategy is so fundamental to human thought that people do not need to reach an accord, consciously or unconsciously, prior to putting it into practice.

Whether people use the strategy on a general basis to construct categories of perceptions other than color is a separate question. It is also a separate question—and, to say the least, a debatable one—whether humans are genetically predisposed to construct categories by spatiotemporal analogy and, specifically, by the analogy that is stipulated here.

The model of analogous vantages elevates the analysis of Mesoamerican data to higher integration, because the axioms that provide for individual variation, evolutionary order, and continuous change also provide the coordinates by which a person constructs a color category as a vantage. On this plane, all of the dynamic processes of color categorization simultaneously occur as an individual forms and alters a personal point of view. The model specifies how the categorizer is related to the category she creates and maintains, and it attributes all the dynamics directly to that personal agency.

Formalisms express the model starkly. They incorporate the processes of zooming in and zooming out by which people expand and contract levels of concentration as they locate objects, move in and out of enclosures, confine or defray their interest, or wend their way from one point to another. The formalisms specify how a person keeps in mind several coordinates while concentrating on no more than two at a time.

In addition to addressing variation and regular change, the model of vantages further integrates the following observations: coextension per se, the linkage of coextension to other types of semantic relations, the continuous nature of the full typology, early and late phases of coextension, the dominant-recessive pattern of coextension, dissolution of the dominant-recessive pattern late on the continuum of typological change, polarization of foci, disproportion in size of coextensive ranges, accentuation of the disproportion as change advances, overall shrinkage of both coextensive ranges apart from disproportionate changes of size, two different kinds of qualifier distributions, and cases of triple coextension among dominant, recessive, and ultra-recessive ranges.

Other models of color categorization, such as family resemblances to a natural prototype or fuzzy-set logic, cannot account for these various processes. The hypothesis of vantages and coordinates might ultimately be replaced by a more effective model; however, for the moment, it offers the most thorough explanation of observed regularities.

The theory of vantages brings with it some implications regarding the phylogeny of categorization, its nature as an inborn strategy, relativity and universality, the embodied role of the conceptualizer, asymmetry judgments in categorical perception, and the frame of reference within which judgments of similarity and difference may make their acknowledged contribution to categorization.

CHAPTER 7

CATEGORY DIVISION

When does a composite color category start to pull apart? Under the current model, separation originates with the category because categorization intrinsically incorporates attention to distinctiveness. The signs of dividing become blatant as inclusion gives way to complementation, although such division is by far only the culmination. There are significant differences between the coextensive relation and the relation of inclusion apart from the size differential between ranges. The sample of each relational type shows quantifiable distinctions of detail.

Five enigmas accompany category division. First, as inclusion develops, foci of warm categories are polarized randomly and abundantly.

Second, categories in apparent complementation continue to manifest mutually polarized mapping steps and foci, even though complementation supposedly entails that categories be unlinked. What constitutes the lingering connection?

Third, speakers of related languages—even speakers of the same language—show "mirror-image" patterns of inclusion within ranges of dark-cool or warm. For example, one speaker includes a yellow range within a red-focused warm range, whereas her neighbor includes a red range within a yellow-focused warm range. Since the speakers share an ethnic history, how did the inverses develop?

Fourth, the broad dark-cool category assumes at least two kinds of range. While one of them neatly skirts elemental green, blue, and black, the other assumes immense size to amorphously engulf warm hues. How do they differ?

Fifth, the dark-cool category may display ephemeral qualities that make it hard to typologize, or even to specify, its relation to other color categories. What occasions its vagueness?

While these questions are addressed in turn, data are reviewed in the order of yellow-focused warm ranges that include a range of red, red-focused warm ranges that include a range of yellow, black-focused and cool-focused dark-cool categories, and putative vestiges of the light-warm category. The cool category will be taken up in chapters that follow.

7.1. Pulling Apart the Warm Category

Vantage theory answers the first, second, and third questions unequivocally. In general, as differences are emphasized, coextensive ranges pull apart in opposite directions, with the recessive range at the vanguard in this parting of the ways. So, first, as the emphasis increases, the focus of either range may polarize, breaking the pattern that characterized coextension. Second, after two ranges show little overlap of mappings and no commingling of names, they continue to polarize away from each other, as if they were still connected. Probably they maintain the relation diagrammed in figure 6.10, even though mappings and namings reveal no sign of an abiding tie; or at least they would appear to have no tie if we looked only at the colors they cover but not at their contrasting configurations. This issue carries far-reaching implications regarding the nature of category relations, the kinds of data that may indicate them, and the assumptions that have guided experiments with categories. These matters will be resumed in §7.1.4 after data are reviewed. Third, and with less consequence, mirror-image relations of inclusion descend from reverse patterns of dominant-recessive coextension, which, as we have seen in Chapter 6, may distinguish two speakers of one language, even close friends.

"Superordinate" and "subordinate" will describe dominant and recessive ranges that have evolved into a relation of inclusion. These old favorites preserve continuity with terminology long in use; however, superordinate and subordinate ranges are as much vantages as are the ranges in a coextensive relation.[1]

7.1.1. Superordination in Reference to Yellow

Figure 7.1 displays namings and mappings from an Aguacatec speaker. One range is tucked neatly inside the other in accord with orthodox notions of how inclusion should behave. Further, the mapping of the superordinate range corresponds to almost all of its naming, for example E33, C40, and I36. The first steps of the superordinate and subordinate mappings do not overlap, unlike the first steps of most coextensive ranges and of all coextensive ranges at an early phase.[2] The superordinate warm range is focused in reference to yellow and polarized at C12; the subordinate range is focused on elemental red at G2. These foci do not show the dominant-recessive pattern.

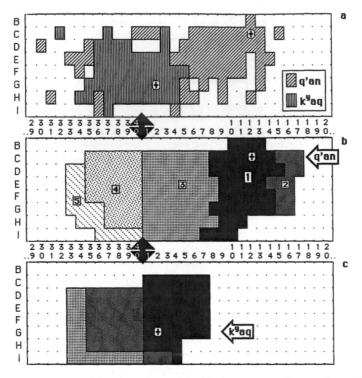

FIGURE 7.1. Aguacatec, Aguacatán, Huehuetenango, Guatemala, m 79, 1978: (*a*) naming ranges, (*a–c*) foci, and (*b–c*) mappings.

This superordinate yellow-focused range shows the pattern of the Aguacatec system in figure 6.15, whose dominant coextensive range is focused in reference to yellow. Its pattern contrasts with the Aguacatec systems of figures 5.4 and 7.16*a,* whose dominant coextensive ranges are focused in reference to red. The four individuals have lived since birth within a kilometer of the Aguacatán market.

In figure 7.2, a Huehuetlán Huastec speaker centrally focuses the subordinate red range, *ȼakni,* at E3 in correspondence with its second mapping step. The unlikely placement might mark contrast against an abutting complex, focused at F35, H40, and G7. The first mapping step of each category is small and slightly polarized; they do not overlap.

In figure 7.3, a Tenejapa Tzeltal speaker focuses a superordinate warm range, *k'an,* at D6–7 and subordinate red, *ȼah,* at I1. She is the only Tzeltal-Spanish bilingual of the Tenejapa sample and the only one whose warm category is not coextensively composed; she lived fifteen years in San Cristóbal de las Casas, an urban center. The warm ranges of her parents represent early and late phases of coextension, figures 6.12 and 6.20. The

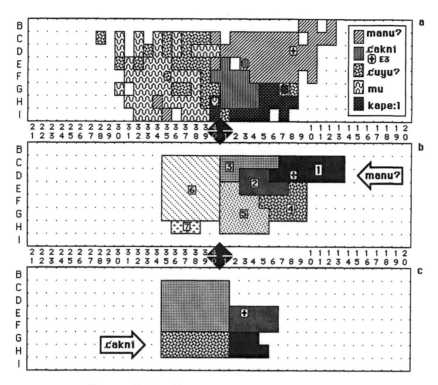

FIGURE 7.2. Huastec, Huehuetlán, San Luís Potosí, Mexico, f 75±, 1980: (*a*) naming ranges, (*a–c*) foci, and (*b–c*) mappings.

warm range of *k'an* is mapped on elemental red, G1–2, and elemental yellow, C8–9. Since this mapping reaches elemental red only with its fourth step, *k'an* and *ȼah* are almost in complementation. Subordination of *ȼah* is shown by confinement of its naming and mapping to rows E–I. The focus of *ȼah* at I1 shows strong polarity. Unlike the subordinate focus of the Aguacatec speaker whose ranges are "well behaved" (fig. 7.1), her subordinate focus is polarized such that it is not encompassed by the superordinate range. The dynamics of polarization cause variable layouts of mappings and naming ranges, witnessed by the difference between data of figures 7.1 and 7.3. Polarity always characterizes inclusion, at least to some extent.

Figure 7.4 shows that an Acatec speaker focuses a superordinate warm range, *k'an,* on elemental yellow, C8–9. The subordinate red range, *kax,* is focused with a first choice centralized at F2 and the final choice polarized at F40 in agreement with the first mapping step. The polarization makes the inclusion of the red category by the warm category appear incomplete.

In figure 7.5, a Sipacapa Quiché speaker—like the Acatec speaker of

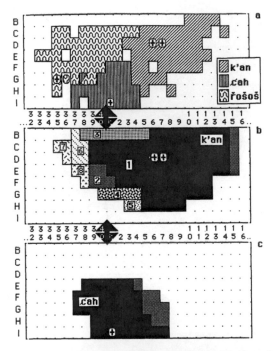

FIGURE 7.3. Tzeltal, Tenejapa, Chiapas, Mexico, f 34, 1980: (*a*) naming ranges, (*a–c*) foci, and (*b*) mappings (cf. fig. 4.8).

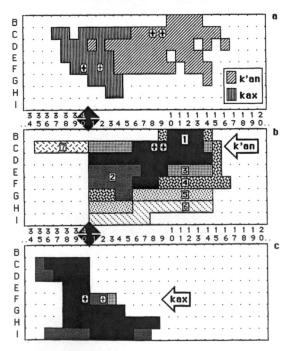

FIGURE 7.4. Acatec, Coyá, San Miguel Acatán, Guatemala, m 32, 1980: (*a*) naming ranges, (*a–c*) foci, and (*b–c*) mappings.

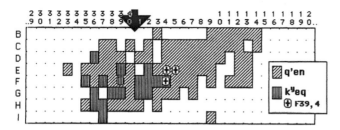

FIGURE 7.5. Naming ranges and foci, Quiché, Sipacapa, Guatemala, f 60, 1978.

figure 7.4—ambivalently centralizes and polarizes foci of subordinate red *k^{y}eq,* F4 and F39. She centrally focuses superordinate *q'en* E4–5.

In figure 7.6, (*a–b*) older and (*c–d*) younger Chinantec speakers, re-

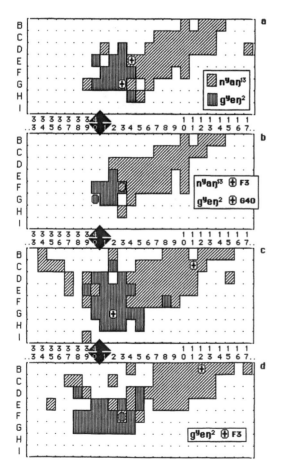

FIGURE 7.6. Chinantec, San Juan Palantla, Oaxaca, Mexico, 1978; naming ranges and foci: (*a*) f 52, (*b*) f 59, (*c*) f 27, (*d*) f 39.

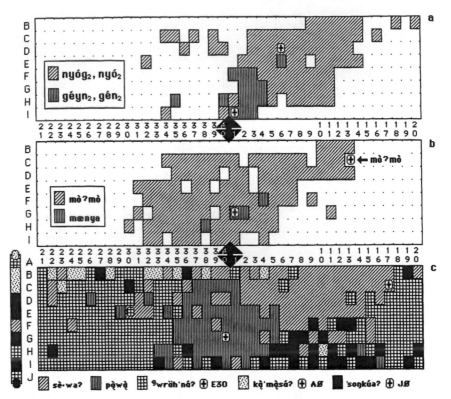

FIGURE 7.7. Naming ranges and foci: (*a*) Chinantec, Tepetotutla, Usila, Tuxtepec, Oaxaca, Mexico, m 69, 1979; (*b*) Tlapanec, Malinaltepec, Guerrero, Mexico, f 50, 1978; (*c*) Paya, Pueblo Nuevo Subírana, Honduras, m 40, 1977.

spectively, centralize and polarize foci of superordinate $n^y a \eta^{13}$, E4 and F3 versus C11 and B12.

In figure 7.7*a*, a Chinantec speaker shows a dominant-recessive pattern among apparent superordinate and subordinate ranges. In contrast, a Tlapanec speaker (*b*) polarizes the superordinate focus at C13; yet, she names the superordinate range 103 times and the subordinate range 4 times (cf. fig. 6.37*c*). The Paya speaker (*c*) mutually polarizes foci, G40 subordinate and C17 superordinate; column 17 contains unique green (cf. fig. 6.35*a* Mixtec: C17 dark-cool focus). A relationship of inclusion cannot be reliably affirmed without mapping data.

7.1.2. Superordination in Reference to Red

Developments seen throughout figures 7.1–7 also befall warm categories focused in reference to red. As coextension transforms to inclusion, the superordinate "red" focus can be either polar or central; the subordinate naming and mapping may be polarized away from yellow and toward green.

Figures 7.8–12 suggest continuous increments of division within warm categories of five Jacaltec speakers, including dominant-recessive coextension, superordination of the red-focused range, and complementation.

In figure 7.8, speaker 1 demonstrates coextension by applying recessive *q'an* to G37 and dominant *kaxh* to C8–9. With *q'an* (focus C9) retracted, her system approaches inclusion.

In figure 7.9, speaker 2 shows no coextension. The mapping of superordinate *kaxh,* centrally focused at F3, scarcely covers elemental yellow, C8–9. Subordinate *q'an* is polarized: it is mapped to column 16 and focused at C10. In columns 12–16, the polarized mapping of *q'an* does not overlap the mapping of *kaxh,* which gives the impression that the relation of inclusion is partial or distorted. In an idealized or logician's preconception of inclusion, a superordinate "category" should fully encompass a subordinate "category." But in a real relation, such as this of speaker 2,

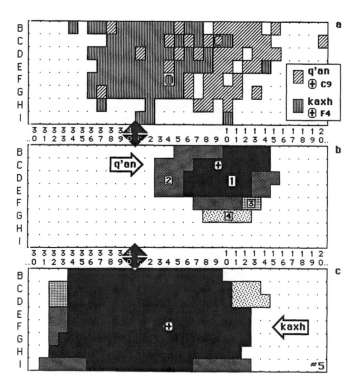

FIGURE 7.8. Jacaltec, Jacaltenango, Huehuetenango, Guatemala, f 50, 1980: (*a*) naming ranges, (*a–c*) foci, and (*b–c*) mappings (cf. table 6.1, #5), speaker 1.

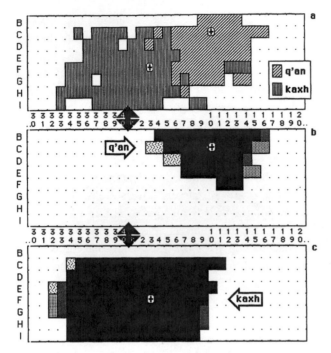

FIGURE 7.9. Jacaltec, Jacaltenango, Huehuetenango, Guatemala, f 86, 1980:
(*a*) naming ranges, (*a*–*c*) foci, and (*b*–*c*) mappings, speaker 2.

countervailing dynamics between ranges promote their nonoverlap. The idealized concept is naively static; it anticipates the bounding of one "category" by another while ignoring polarization or, more pointedly, while remaining ignorant of it. Hardly by happenstance, the logical model lacks the means to account for polarization. The model would seem valid only to one who has never confronted category relations as they actually work.

In figure 7.10, speaker 3 shows further retraction of superordinate *kaxh;* only its second and third mapping steps cover elemental yellow, C8–9. Both foci are polarized, H3 and C10. This inclusion is almost complementation, or it is virtually intermediate. Or, at least, so it appears.

In figure 7.11, speaker 4 has barely accomplished the transformation to complementation, or so it seems on the surface. Her mapping of *kaxh* stops short of elemental yellow, C8–9. Its focus is polarized at G40 while *q'an* is focused on C9.

In figure 7.12, speaker 5 shows fully developed complementation. The mappings of *kaxh* and *q'an* share no colors; each is focused on an elemental hue, G1 and C8.

The data from Jacaltec speakers suggest an evolution of semantic relations. In its middle phases, a dominant-recessive pattern of foci gives way

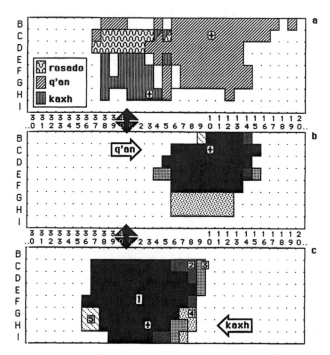

FIGURE 7.10. Jacaltec, Jacaltenango, Huehuetenango, Guatemala, m 37, 1980: (*a*) naming ranges, (*a–c*) foci, and (*b–c*) mappings, speaker 3.

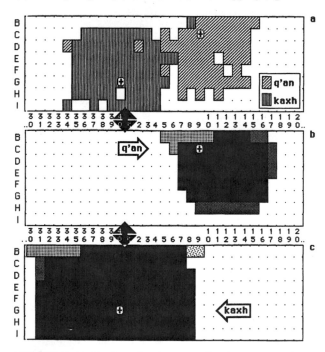

FIGURE 7.11. Jacaltec, Jacaltenango, Huehuetenango, Guatemala, f 42, 1980: (*a*) naming ranges, (*a–c*) foci, and (*b–c*) mappings, speaker 4.

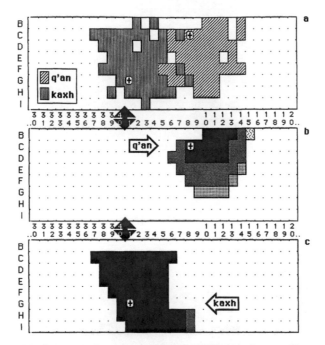

FIGURE 7.12. Jacaltec, Jacaltenango, Huehuetenango, Guatemala, m 43, 1980:
(*a*) naming ranges, (*a–c*) foci, and (*b–c*) mappings, speaker 5.

to unpredictable polarization. The polarizing dynamic creates areas of
nonoverlap that would not pertain in a stationary conception of inclusion.
Polarization persists between categories that ostensibly have separated,
suggesting they remain related in a way that naming ranges do not reveal.

    Figures 7.13–17 exemplify further the relation of inclusion between a
superordinate warm range focused in reference to red and a subordinate
yellow range.

    In figure 7.13, a Mam speaker mapped red-focused superordinate *kaq*
over elemental yellow, C8–9. She polarized the focus and first mapping
step of subordinate *q'an*.

    In figures 7.14–15, Chuj speakers 1 and 2, respectfully, contrast late
inclusion with early complementation. Speaker 1 shows inclusion with mutually polarized foci and a polarized first mapping step of subordinate *k'an*.
Speaker 2 betokens complementation between *čak* and *k'an*. He mapped
čak only to C7, short of elemental yellow, and he polarized the mapping
and focus of *k'an*. The polarization shows that exaggerated differences are
maintained after division is ostensibly completed, implying that *čak* and
k'an remain linked in a way that is not suggested by the distribution of
their names or merely by the colors covered by their mappings.

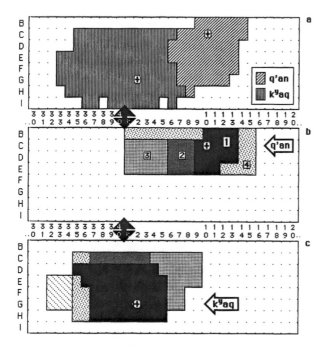

FIGURE 7.13. Mam, San Ildefonso Ixtahuacán, Huehuetenango, Guatemala, f 56, 1980: (*a*) naming ranges, (*a–c*) foci, and (*b–c*) mappings (cf. fig. 10.6).

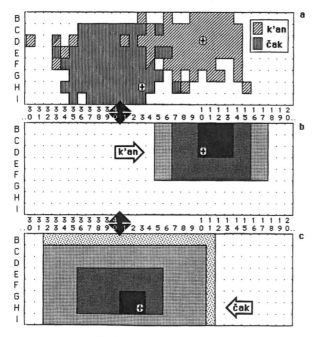

FIGURE 7.14. Chuj, San Sebastián Coatán, Huehuetenango, Guatemala, m 30, 1980: (*a*) naming ranges, (*a–c*) foci, and (*b–c*) mappings, speaker 1.

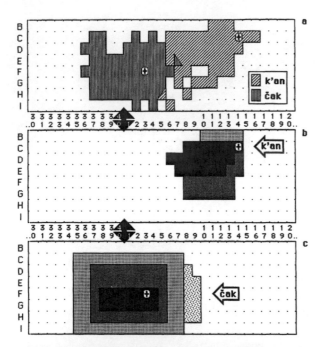

FIGURE 7.15. Chuj, San Sebastián Coatán, Huehuetenango, Guatemala, m 70, 1980: (*a*) naming ranges, (*a–c*) foci, and (*b–c*) mappings, speaker 2.

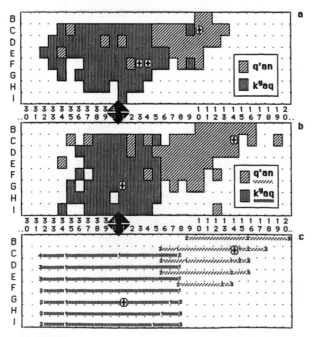

FIGURE 7.16. Aguacatec, Aguacatán, Huehuetenango, Guatemala: (*a*) f 20, 1978, naming ranges and foci; (*b–c*) m 19, 1980, (*a*) naming ranges, (*b–c*) foci, and (*c*) mappings.

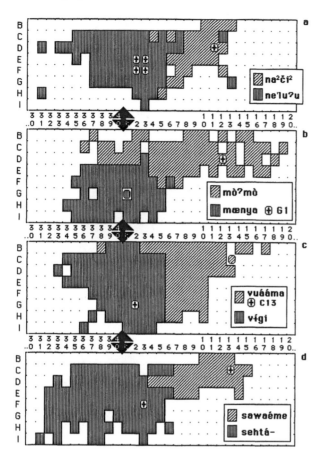

FIGURE 7.17. Naming ranges and foci: (*a*) Zapotec, Santa María Lachixío, Sola de Vega, Oaxaca, f 60±, 1979; (*b*) Tlapanec, Malinaltepec, Guerrero, f 45, 1978; (*c*) Northern Tepehuán, Chihuahua, f 31, 1981; (*d*) Guarijío, Alamos, Sonora, f 20, 1978. All of Mexico.

Figure 7.16 contrasts (*a*) probable coextension with (*b*) a relation that appears to be complementation. Both speakers are Aguacatec. In *a*, the focus of dominant *kʸaq* is centralized F3–4, the focus of recessive *q'an* polarized C10. In *b–c*, the focus of *q'an* is polarized at C14, suggesting that attention to distinctiveness is much stronger here than in the probable coextension of *a*. Again, polarization that persists after the outward achievement of complementation requires a special explanation.

In figure 7.17, speakers of (*a–b*) Otomanguean and (*c–d*) Uto-Aztecan languages show strong polarization of the yellow category in relations of (*a*) inclusion and, going by the appearances of naming, (*b–d*) complementation. In *a*, usages of red-focused *ne'lu²u* at D12 and G13 reveal inclusion.

7.1.3. Inclusion to Complementation

A major characteristic of inclusion is random polarization, which is caused by a stronger attention to distinctiveness than that which fosters co-extension. This polarization differs from the coextensive pattern shown in table 6.1, in which the focus of the dominant vantage is significantly more central than the focus of the recessive vantage (p<.01). Table 7.1 displays the foci of the eighteen relations of inclusion seen in figures 7.1–17, all that were attested within warm categories of the Mesoamerican sample. Among them, 50% show the dominant-recessive pattern in which the most central focus matches the broadest range, meeting only chance expectation. In five of these pairs of ranges, the most central focus is on an ele-

TABLE 7.1. Foci of warm ranges in a relation of inclusion

	Dominant-Recessive				Antidominant-Recessive			
Lang	Figure	Red	Yellow		Lang	Figure	Red	Yellow
		Sub	Super				Sub	Super
TT	7.3	I40	D6–7		AG	7.1	G2	C12
AC	7.4	F40,F2	C8–9*		HC	7.2	E3	D8
SQ	7.5	F39,F4	E4–5		PC	7.6c	G2	C11*
PC	7.6a	G3	E4		PC	7.6d	F3	B12
PC	7.6b	G40	F3		TP	7.7b	G1	C13*
TC	7.7a	I1	D6		PY	7.7c	G40	C17**
		Super	Sub				Super	Sub
JC	7.9	F3	C10		JC	7.10	H3	C10**
IM	7.13	G2	C10*		JC	7.11	G40	C9*
LZ	7.17	E–F2–3	D11		CH	7.14	H3	D10**

Key:
Lang	language	AG	Aguacatec
Red	focused in reference to red	TP	Tlapanec
Yellow	focused in reference to yellow	CH	Chuj
Sub	subordinate range	AC	Acatec
Super	superordinate range	PC	Palantla Chinantec
		JC	Jacaltec
TT	Tenejapa Tzeltal	LZ	Lachixillo Zapotec
SQ	Sipacapa Quiché	HC	Huastec
TC	Tepetotutla Chinantec	PY	Paya
IM	San Ildefonso Ixtahuacán Mam		

*The most central focus is on an elemental hue.
**Both foci are polarized (to the outside of unique hues).

mental hue while the opposite focus is polarized; in three of the pairs, both foci are polarized outside the elemental hues. In table 6.1, among the coextensive ranges, only one pair (13) shows the former (fig. 6.4) and two (20, 22) the latter (figs. 6.31 and 6.33); pairs 20 and 22 do not show the dominant-recessive pattern.[3]

Figure 7.18 complements table 7.1. The figure compares (*a*) the focus aggregate from 32 coextensively named warm categories (from fig. 6.38) and (*b*) the focus aggregate from the 18 warm categories inventoried in the table, all of the 51 warm categories in the Mesoamerican sample except the

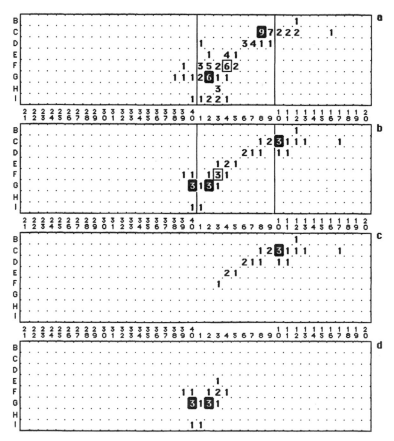

FIGURE 7.18. Comparison of focus aggregates in warm categories composed by different types of relation between vantages: (*a*) the focus aggregate from the thirty-two coextensively composed warm categories of figure 6.38*a;* (*b*) the focus aggregate from the eighteen warm categories composed by a relation of inclusion, those of table 7.1; (*c*) foci of ranges whose names are usually focused in yellow, extracted from (*b*); (*d*) foci of ranges whose names are usually focused in red, also from (*b*).

one composed by near synonymy (fig. 5.9). Vertical lines enclose unique red of column 1 and unique yellow of column 9 plus columns between them; the lines contrast these central columns of the warm category against columns on its margins. In *a*, foci show a central-to-marginal ratio of 69:13, whereas in *b*, the ratio is 22:16 (p<.001 chi square association test). This greater polarization of foci among ranges related by inclusion fits the hypothesis that coextension evolves into inclusion as emphasis on distinctiveness increases. But, further and more fundamentally, this statistic supports the claim that reciprocal emphases on similarity and difference are the inextricable dynamic of categorization: a category fits the dynamic primarily, while it fits the external world strictly as an extension of the dynamic, that is, in accord with the way a person applies the dynamic to his surroundings.

7.1.4. Polarized Inclusion

Other systems not in table 7.1 show relations among red and yellow categories that appear to be in complementation, figures 7.15–17. Yet one focus among each pair is polarized. Why do categories remain polarized after they have divided? The short answer is that they have not divided fully. Although namings and mappings may indicate that the two ranges are in complementation, they remain cognitively related according to the arrangement of coordinates that pertains in a relation of inclusion, figure 6.10. The polarization shows that the "categories" continue to share something. The import, then, is that "category relations" are effectively defined in terms of the cognitive arrangements that produce them instead of by the way that some data—those that logicians have privileged—appear on the surface.

Ranges that look separate can still be vantages of one category—not yet different categories—until their coordinate systems become autonomous. So what do people who name such ranges think they are naming? As sketched in note 4, there is evidence that they think in terms of the juxtaposed reference points: they believe these points are more closely related than certain others; they personify the relation as one of "dominance" and "dependence" (fig. 6.8) and chain-links of such (fig. 6.29; cf. figs. IV.1–5, Russian blues).[4]

7.1.5. Notions of Categorization

The term "inclusion" creates unfulfillable expectations of what data should show. According to time-honored wisdom (Whitehead and Russell 1910–1913), inclusion occurs when one semantic range encompasses another; complementation occurs when two ranges are independent or only overlap at their edges. But in vantage theory, inclusion is a linkage between two points of view that share cognitive coordinates at a particular balance of strength. One view tends to overarch while the other pulls away; even the overarching view can pull away while overarching partially. Inclusion does not become complementation until the cognitive link is broken.

Figure 6.11 shows a two-level arrangement of coordinates that may characterize the composition of a red category or yellow category. Each category is autonomous in that its inherently fixed coordinate does not participate in any other arrangement. Mutual polarization will not occur between independent arrangements, because they provide no common ground on which to oppose difference. The formalism, in this sense, stipulates that complementation is a negative relation.

7.2. Mirror Images of the Dark-Cool Category

Coextensively composed dark-cool categories are rare in the Mesoamerican sample. Possible examples appear in figures 6.34a, 6.35, and 7.7c, none of which is supported by mappings. All full descriptions of the dark-cool category show a relation of inclusion, some with the superordinate term focused in black and others with it focused in green or blue. These are mirror-image systems, like those seen in the warm category, §7.1.1. versus §7.1.2. In the past, probably, Mesoamerican dark-cool categories were commonly named coextensively, but they might have pertained to brightness rather than to elemental color.[5] Regardless, a coextensively composed dark-cool category would divide by retracting first one coextensive range and later the other. In the interim, a relation of inclusion would prevail. The process would parallel that by which warm categories divide.

The final retraction of the superordinate dark-cool range is characterized by ambivalence: some individuals show the superordination in naming but not in mapping; others show it in mapping but not in naming. A dark-cool range focused in green or blue is difficult to distinguish from a range confined only to green and blue.

7.2.1. Categories of Elemental Color

The examples of dark-cool categories shown here are of the kind originally described by Berlin and Berlin (1975) and Kay (1975), figures 2.2 and 2.3 [(3) *mili*]. They categorize primarily the elemental colors of black, green, and blue. They differ from others that emphasize brightness, §7.2.2.

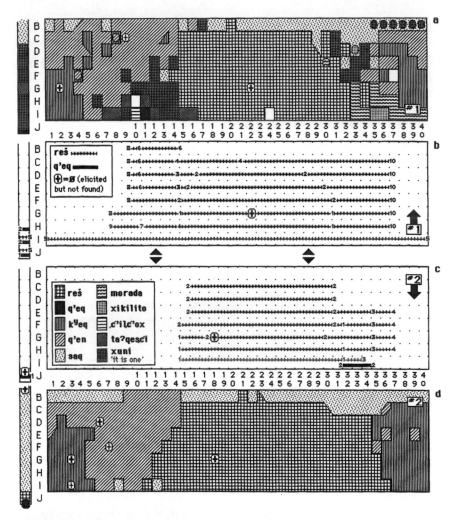

FIGURE 7.19. Uspantec, Las Pacayas, Uspantán, Guatemala, 1979: (*a–b*) speaker 1, f 70 (cf. fig. 6.18); (*c–d*) speaker 2, m 58; (*a, d*) naming ranges, (*a–d*) foci, and (*b–c*) mappings.

The mirror-image relation is found among related languages, such as Tzeltal Mayan and Uspantec Mayan. Figures 4.3–6 document the way that four Tzeltal speakers relate a superordinate black-focused dark-cool range and a subordinate cool range. Figure 7.19 displays the way that Uspantec speakers relate a superordinate cool-focused dark-cool range and a subordinate black range. Eleven Uspantec speakers, ages 30 to 80, were interviewed in Las Pacayas. Five of them—ages 35, 60, 65, 78, and 80—mapped the cool-focused category throughout black of row J on the Munsell array, as did speaker (*a–b*) in figure 7.19. Two of them—ages 58 and 74—extended the cool-focused naming range to row J: they are speaker (*c–d*) in figure 7.19 and another whose data appear in fig. 6.13. Four of them—ages 30, 35, 40, and 50—showed no evidence of a dark-cool category in naming ranges or mappings; data from the two youngest speakers appear in figs. 6.27 and 8.21. None of the eleven demonstrated a dark-cool category in both naming ranges and mappings. The seven who exhibited some evidence of the cool-focused dark-cool category were older than 58 years, except one at 35. The four who showed no evidence were age 50 or younger. (See note 9.)

Figure 7.20 displays mappings with the naming range (*a*) in outline or (*b*) shaded. They are from two Aguacatec speakers, who maintain mirror-image dark-cool categories: one (*a*) named the dark-cool category *ça?ş*, focused in blue at G29–30; the other (*b*) named it *q'eq*, focused in black at JØ. Throughout Mayan languages, most speakers use *ça?ş* and *q'eq* or their cognates to name, respectively and separately, the cool category versus the black category.[6]

Figure 7.21 shows possible mirror-image relations, among which a dark-cool category is difficult to substantiate. In *a–b*, a Chuj speaker mapped a cool-focused dark-cool category but did not apply the 'cool' nam-

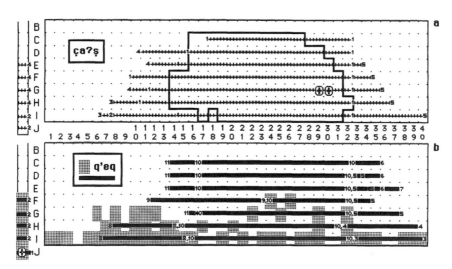

FIGURE 7.20. Aguacatec, Aguacatán, Huehuetenango, Guatemala, 1980 mappings and 1978 foci with naming ranges in outline or shading: (*a*) m 60 (cf. fig. 6.15), (*b*) m 79 (cf. fig. 7.1).

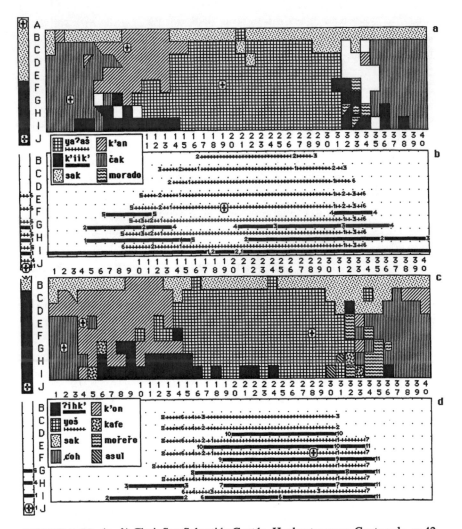

FIGURE 7.21. (*a–b*) Chuj, San Sebastián Coatán, Huehuetenango, Guatemala, m 42, 1980: (*c–d*) Tzotzil, Navenchauc, f 50, 1981 (cf. fig. 6.21); (*a, c*) naming ranges, (*a–d*) foci, and (*b, d*) mappings.

ing range to black. Among the eleven speakers interviewed in San Sebastián Coatán, only he mapped a dark-cool category. A Navenchauc Tzotzil speaker (*c–d*) mapped a black-focused category in ten steps to row D of the Munsell array, but not to rows C and B as did the Tzeltal speakers (figs. 4.3–5). Tzotzil speakers are in a final phase of retracting the dark-cool category toward its black focus; others in Navenchauc also demonstrated a black-focused dark-cool category of low salience (MacLaury 1991*a:* figs. 9–11).

Otomanguean languages, too, show mirror-image inclusion within a hue category. The black-focused dark-cool naming ranges of an Ocotepec Mixtec speaker, figure 5.7, and of a Mazatec speaker, figure 6.36, can be compared with the cool-focused dark-cool naming range of other Mixtecs, figures 6.35*a* and 7.23*b.*

7.2.2. Categories of Brightness

Figure 7.22 displays further cases of naming ranges suggesting cool-focused dark-cool categories, but they radically contrast. In *a*, a Seri speaker focuses a dark-cool naming range on unique green, G17. The range is neatly bounded in conformity to locations of elemental black, green, and blue. In *b*, a Paya speaker applies one term through a massive range, including elemental green F17, blue F29, and red G2, and colors at D8 and D10 adjacent to elemental yellow (C8–9). The category pertains throughout low to medium-high brightness, including elemental black JØ and greys. It appears to be based on a recognition of brightness, whereas the Seri category

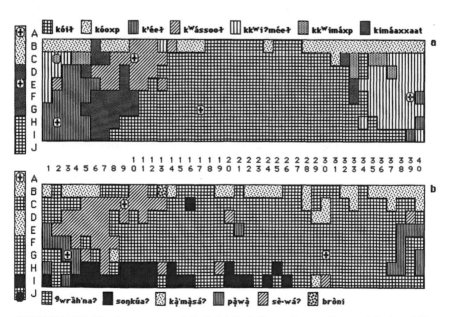

FIGURE 7.22. Naming ranges and foci: (*a*) Seri, Desemboque, Sonora, Mexico, f 25, 1978; (*b*) Paya, Pueblo Nuevo Subírana, Honduras, f 22, 1977.

appears to pertain to hue and elemental black.[7] Paya is located outside Mesoamerica but immediately south of it.

Other Paya speakers seem to have converted the brightness category to one of cool hues, but at a late stage of evolution, Stages IV–V (fig. 11.4; cf. 7.24). Figure 5.8*b* shows a Paya hue category with scattered remnants of emphasis on brightness.[8] Brightness categories assimilate to any of the hue categories found in the 1975 revision of Berlin and Kay's evolutionary sequence (figs. 2.2, 2.11–12; MacLaury 1992*a*).[9]

7.3. The Elusive Light-Warm Category

There is no strong evidence of a Mesoamerican light-warm category. (The data on Stage I systems elsewhere are reviewed in conjunction with figure 2.13 in §2.6.) Proto-Otomanguean color categories can be reconstructed as Berlin and Kay's 1975 Stage I (MacLaury 1986*a:* Appendix II, 1988*a*). Kaufman's (1983 MS) Otomanguean sound correspondences indicate that color terms of diverse meanings might be cognates; possibly a broad ancient category subsumed all. For example, a Proto-Otomanguean light-warm category may be inferred from Chicahuaxtla Trique $ga^3\mathcal{c}i^{54}$ 'white', sixteenth-century Zapotec *nagáchi* 'yellow', Ixcatec $ka^1\mathcal{c}e^3$ 'red'. But the hypothesis of an ancient common category might be wrong. For example, the Trique reflex could have taken on its "white" meaning locally; a change from 'yellow' to 'white' would be plausible if color terms named brightness (see note 7 and figures 2.24–25, 2.26*d–h* [*piila piila* and *karn-tawarra*], and 2.27). Early-stage color categories can warrant many terms (Hage and Hawkes 1975). The Proto-Otomanguean reconstruction includes six color terms, almost as many as are used by its descendants (Merrifield 1971:263–267).[10]

A putative Stage I system is suggested by the foci and naming ranges of one Mazatec speaker, figure 6.36; the warm-category focus is uncharacteristically centralized in pink at D1, while the white-focused term designates red at F1. In figures 4.3*a–b*, a Tenejapa Tzeltal speaker applied the white-focused term to red at G1 and mapped it as a light-warm category, but among the nine interviewed in Tenejapa, only she did so. A Jacque-speaker, who names hue (fig. 5.9), mapped *phe* 'white' and *te* 'black' with ranges that meet on the Munsell array, E–F 8–36 (MacLaury 1986*a:* fig. 7.36).

In figure 7.23, a Mixtec speaker intermixes white-focused (AØ) and pink-focused (D36) naming ranges throughout pastels, yellows, and browns.

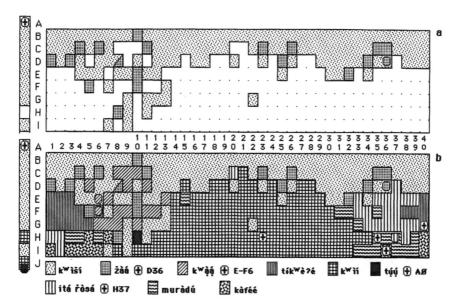

FIGURE 7.23. Mixtec, Peñoles, Oaxaca, Mexico, m 72, 1978: naming ranges and foci, (*a*) partial and (*b*) complete.

Loanwords are focused in a polarized dark cluster at H35, H37, and I36, and their naming ranges designate dark colors in a contrast of brightness. The "yellow" focus is centralized at E–F6, the "red" focus polarized at G40. The focus of the dark-cool category is centralized at H18.

In figure 7.24, a Paya speaker intermixes the white-focused (AØ) naming range throughout warm colors, H33, H36, I1, G5, G8, F36, F8–9. The possible light-warm category co-occurs with a category of brightness, focused at H30 (cf. fig. 7.22*b*).

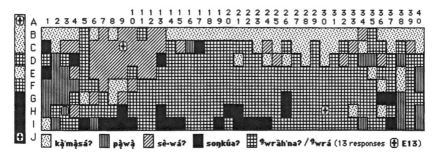

FIGURE 7.24. Paya, Pueblo Nuevo Subírana, Honduras, m 33, 1977: naming ranges and foci.

7.4. Summary

Vantage theory addresses the dynamics of dividing categories. Division begins as a category is initially formed because attention to distinctiveness is intrinsic to its composition; yet, division conspicuously transpires only as inclusion gives way to complementation. In the warm category, coextensive ranges retract, one after the other, toward their respective elemental hues, which produces inclusion and, finally, complementation. The dominant-recessive pattern of foci dissolves as increasing attention to distinctiveness induces random polarization.

Categorization is the engagement of this dynamic with stimuli. It matches "correlational structure" inasmuch as the dynamic emphasizes or suppresses its particulars and discontinuities. As demonstrated by the different shapes of double vantages, there is more than one possible correlation among the same stimuli, perhaps an infinite number. A choice of any one of them is part and parcel of the way a particular dynamic is constituted.

After two ranges have separated by most outward appearances, they may continue to show signs of a close relation: polarized foci and mapping steps seem to be placed in opposition. Probably, in underlying cognition, the ranges still share coordinates in the arrangement common to near synonymy, coextension, and inclusion. In Mesoamerica, people say, "This hue dominates that one," speaking without reference to a notion of boundaries. Complete complementation is based on autonomous arrangements, which may develop at some interval after much of the surface data seem to show separation. Relations within and between categories are properly defined in terms of the underlying arrangement of coordinates rather than select kinds of data.

Dark-cool categories divide much as do warm categories. Both reflect mirror-image relations of inclusion, which are found between cognate languages and among speakers of one language. The opposite patterns derive from antecedent dominant-recessive coextension, which allows variation in the assignment of dominance to a range.

The vagueness of some cool-focused ranges together with the extensive size of a few suggest these qualities are the weakened remnants of what was once a stronger emphasis on brightness.

Light-warm categories are not attested in Mesoamerica.

PART THREE

FURTHER DYNAMICS, REFLECTIVITY, AND COMPLEX CATEGORIZATION

Most cool categories are named with only one term; yet, their dynamics are as complex as those of the warm category. They offer the supreme challenge to models that have appeared to measure up when pitted against data that are comparatively simple.

The cool category manifests five major processes: skewing, darkening, transference, detachment, and crossover. Chapter 8 substantiates the first three of these and separately ties each to the vantage model. Chapter 9 examines effects of submerged perspective versus reflective overview in categorization. Chapter 10 addresses crossover, which emerges when the balance of attention on similarity and difference receives more emphasis than the hues themselves. As shown earlier, some complex categories are constructed as framed relations between vantages. But in certain crossover categories, emphases on similarity and difference prevail within one frame while emphasis on hue predominates in another. The combination produces the most complex semantics to be found in a color category.

In Chapter 11, the Mesoamerican data on categories of green-with-blue are set in the context of worldwide data to evaluate in depth hypotheses of areal diffusion versus universal process.

CHAPTER 8

SKEWING AND DARKENING

Most color categories of the Mesoamerican sample are named with only one term; however, the categories with a single name undergo processes that suggest they, too, are composed as an analogous vantage. The principle of space-time analogy is not confined to relations between two or more ranges. It pertains to the construction of any color category.

The dynamic processes of common color categorization can be verified statistically, which is preliminary to integrating them into a theory. The cool category is the natural choice for this demonstration, because the Mesoamerican sample yields 589 of them; their conspicuous regularities are easy to measure and to compute.

In Mesoamerica, cool categories are of more than one kind. For example, we have seen a cool category that is based as much on brightness as on hue (figs. 6.13, 7.22 and 7.24). Herein I analyze only the most common kind of cool category in Mesoamerica: that in which individuated green and blue hues are valued above all else (Hue + S^2-D). In Chapter 10, I shall examine a rare kind of cool category in which the relation between hues is stressed more than are the hues as separate sensations (S^2-D + Hue). Nevertheless, within the kind of cool category that I analyze here, the relation between hues is critical to dynamics. These consist of three processes: skewing, darkening, and transference. Although they operate predictably when hue is of primary interest, they may not prevail as strongly when other values predominate, as when relations are the priority.

The sole departure from the present restriction on data will obtain among focus aggregates, which are from all Mesoamerican cool categories. Often the precise typology of a particular cool category is anyone's guess, especially when data exclude mappings. Since this discussion develops theory regarding processes that should mainly, if not exclusively, transpire in cool categories that feature hue, adding to aggregates the foci from other kinds of cool categories may push statistics toward nullity. Yet this laxity does not undermine statistical results, which emerge as positive in spite of this bias against them.

Skewing and darkening are the main processes. Vantage theory provides a separate explanation of each. Transference will be considered as an alternative to areal diffusion to explain widespread skewing toward green. It, too, might be explained by vantage theory, but only if it recurs widely beyond Mesoamerica and only if its nonoccurrences are explicable. These issues are not settled here but will be revisited in Chapter 11.

Skewing means that any noncoextensive cool category (1) has only one focus and (2) this focus is placed on either the green or blue side of turquoise column 23. As division progresses, (3) the focal side corresponds with the most abundant use of the category name, the first mapping step, and the most frequent use of maximal or augmentative qualifiers, and (4) the focus becomes even less centralized if not polarized. As division culminates, (5) the historical "cool" term is confined to what used to be the focal side while the other side becomes a separate basic category and is named with a new term. The simplest explanation is that the cool category is composed from a single vantage point established on one side of the category in reference to the preferred fixed coordinate of a particular elemental hue. Even a secondary cool category will be skewed. Increase of attention to distinctiveness exaggerates the skew until the category divides completely.

A cool category darkens as its focus and highest values of membership shift away from middle brightness toward black. The shift becomes pronounced as category division concludes, showing highest frequency among basic categories of green and blue. Under the current hypothesis, as attention to distinctiveness increases sufficiently to divide the cool category, attention to similarity weakens to the extent that many individuals reinforce the vantage point by emphasizing a coordinate of darkness. They choose darkness rather than lightness because elemental green and blue are perceptually closer to black than to white; or, perhaps, darkness effectively counterbalances attention to distinctiveness by obscuring discrimination.

Most cool categories in the Mesoamerican sample are skewed toward green. This might result from either of two processes, although they need not exclude each other. One is areal diffusion, and the other is transference. Transference occurs when people who traditionally focus the cool category in blue reassign the focus to green. Most speakers of a language may transfer the focus within a generation. The green and blue options entail, at least, a temporary maintenance of dual vantages that are not overtly named with different terms, that is, "covert coextension."

Within the cool category, green should become more attractive than blue when people place more importance on difference. Stressing difference would heighten contrast between categories, as between cool and red. The red category is exceptionally salient, as witnessed by its early emergence in languages everywhere (Berlin and Kay 1969; figs. 2.14–33 herein). Green is the perceptual opponent of red; the two cannot blend. The opponency of green versus red may excite a stronger sense of definition within the cool category than will the opponency of blue with yellow. The cardinal stature of red and its natural opposition to green constitute a fifth axiom, in addition to the four introduced in Chapter 4.

Skewing and darkening are attested by statistics below the .01 level of probability. Transference is attested below .05. The hypothesis that areal diffusion produced the widely practiced skewing toward green involves complications. For example, diffusion in Mesoamerica might have removed certain deterrents of transference that seem to operate in other regions of the world, a subject to be pursued in §§11.3.1–6.

To model the cool category, I use the formalism depicted by figure 6.7d. One elemental hue (H_1) and attention to similarity (S) are, respectively, the fixed and mobile coordinates of level 1, while the other elemental hue (H_2) and attention to distinctiveness (D) are the coordinates of level 3. The open-ended model would allow the addition of a dark segment on the brightness scale as a fifth coordinate, although another coordinate may not be needed to account for every case of darkening within the cool category. People may darken a focus to reinforce attention to similarity vis-à-vis attention to distinctiveness, because it is harder to distinguish dark colors than light colors. The darkening of a category would then be an entailment of strong attention to distinctiveness, not the result of adding a coordinate.

I introduce skewing with individual examples (§8.1), verify statistically the existence of skewing, darkening, and transference (§8.2), and present individual and language-specific examples of darkening (§8.3), skewing of qualifiers and focal aggregates (§§8.4–5), and transference (§8.6). Findings are summarized in §8.7.

8.1. Skewing

Every cool category manifests skewing toward either green or blue. Enhancement of skewing divides the cool category.

8.1.1. Degree of Skewing

Individuals vary. Those who skew slightly tend to focus the cool category between its unique hues, although to one side of column 23; they tend to map with a *continuous* first step that covers both unique hues and turquoise. Those who skew greatly tend to focus on a unique hue or to polarize the focus, and they are inclined to map with *disjunctive* steps: the first step covers only one unique hue; or it covers both unique hues but not turquoise, and it covers more colors around one unique hue than the other. The examples shown by figures 8.1–11 all are skewed toward green.[1]

In figure 8.1, a Nahuatl speaker mapped the cool category continuously; he focused at F22 between the unique hues, one hue to the green side

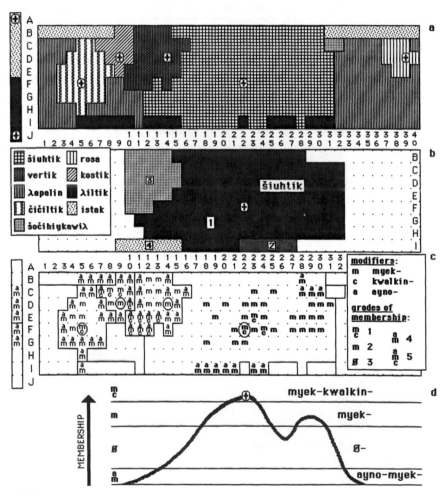

FIGURE 8.1. Nahuatl, Santa Buenaventura, Puebla, Mexico, m 32, 1979: (*a*) naming ranges and foci, (*b*) mappings, (*c*) qualifiers, (*d*) abstract depiction of membership gradation.

of column 23. In *c,* this evidence of slight skewing toward green is corroborated by distributions of qualifiers: maximal qualifiers cluster at the focus; medium-grade qualifiers are bimodally distributed in a large, central cluster around the maximal qualifiers and in a small cluster around elemental blue; minimal qualifiers are peripherally placed. In *d,* a curve approximates the gradation of membership suggested by the correspondence of the focus and qualifier distributions. Depiction of minimal qualifiers is abstract: they cover two peripheral areas, not the entire periphery of the category as the curve would suggest.

In figure 8.2, a K'ekchí speaker continuously mapped and centrally focused the cool category. He focused it in column 23 but then reconsidered and placed his final choice at H21 with slight skewing toward green.

In figures 8.3–4, two Tecpan Cakchiquel speakers declined to name several colors. They differ in the ways they value membership. In figure 8.3, speaker 1 named and mapped the cool category disjunctively and focused with slight centralization, G18. He first mapped 23 greens but only 9 blues and then mapped turquoise with a second step. In *c,* a curve represents the likely gradation of membership with green the highest value. In figure 8.4, speaker 2 mapped the cool category disjunctively and focused it on H17 in the column of unique green in correspondence with his first mapping step. He mapped unique blue only with a fourth step and turquoise with a sixth step. The curve depicts green and blue apexes with the green

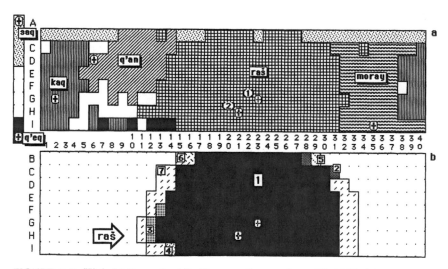

FIGURE 8.2. K'ekchí, Lanquín, Alta Verapaz, Guatemala, m 30, 1980: (*a*) naming ranges, (*a–b*) foci, and (*b*) mapping.

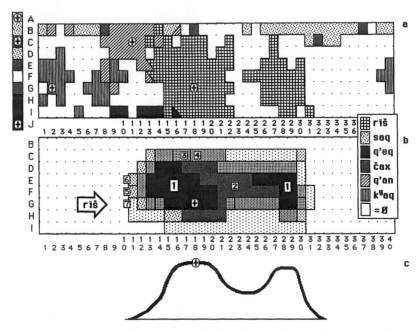

FIGURE 8.3. Cakchiquel, Panajabal, Tecpan, Guatemala, m 27, 1980: (*a*) naming ranges, (*a–b*) foci, (*b*) mapping, and (*c*) membership values; speaker 1.

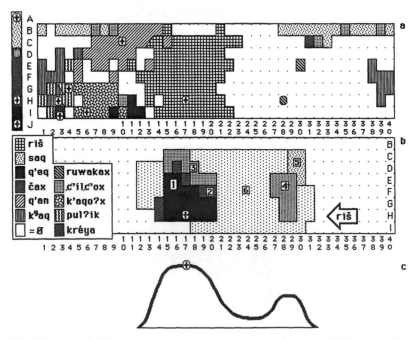

FIGURE 8.4. Cakchiquel, Panajabal, Tecpan, Guatemala, m 34, 1980: (*a*) naming ranges, (*a–b*) foci, (*b*) mapping, and (*c*) membership values; speaker 2.

value highest. He declined to name blues, except one at D30 that he called *ruwakax*, 'sky'. The greater skewing of speaker 2 corresponds to his focus in column 17, whereas the lesser skewing of speaker 1 corresponds to his slightly centralized focus. Speaker 2 named fewer colors than speaker 1 but used more terms.

In figure 8.5, a Northern Tepehuán speaker focused the cool category on unique green and mapped disjunctively green first and blue fourth. The curve shows one green apex with values declining through blue. The mappings by two Cakchiquel speakers and the Northern Tepehuán speaker all are disjunctive, but their different configurations suggest distinct degrees of skewing.

In figure 8.6, a Momostenango Quiché speaker focused the cool category on unique green; like the Northern Tepehuán speaker, he mapped in steps from green to blue. He named and mapped secondary blue categories that correspond to the latest steps of his cool mapping. The large curve depicts values named and mapped for cool; the small curve depicts the relation of one blue category to lowest values.[2]

In figure 8.7, a Chiquimula Quiché speaker demonstrated a cool cate-

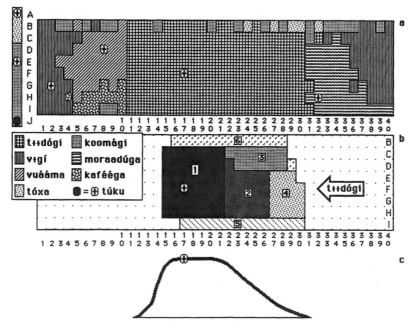

FIGURE 8.5. Northern Tepehuán, Baborigami, Chihuahua, Mexico, f 50, 1981: (*a*) naming ranges, (*a–b*) foci, (*b*) mapping, and (*c*) membership values.

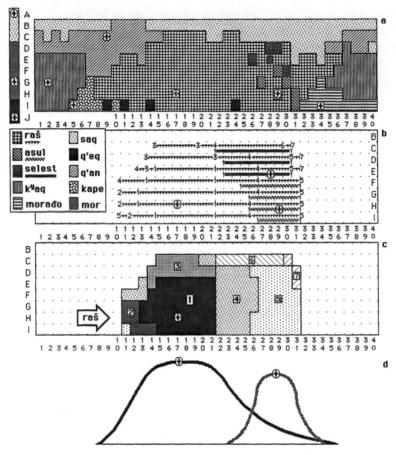

FIGURE 8.6. Quiché, Momostenango, Guatemala, m 29, 1980: (*a*) naming range, (*a–c*) foci, (*b–c*) mappings, and (*d*) membership gradations within *raš*.

gory with a naming response only at G29, which his mapping did not reach. It seems he maintained the cool category in blue at a value lower than those maintained by the speakers of Northern Tepehuán and Momostenango Quiché. Correspondingly, he polarized the focus, F16, one hue to the outside of unique green. The curve depicts steep skewing.

In figure 8.8, a Chinantec speaker, like the Chiquimula Quiché speaker, showed scant evidence of the cool category in blue (E29, I30), and she, too, polarized the cool-category focus, F16. She named a secondary blue category with maximum salience. The left curve projects precipitous decline of values in relation to this secondary category, represented by the right curve.

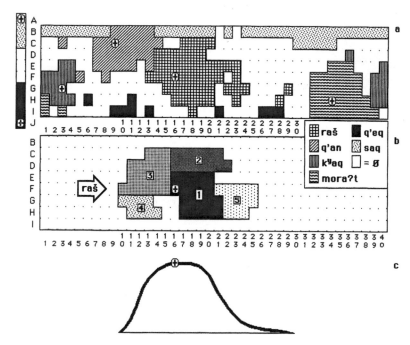

FIGURE 8.7. Quiché, Santa María Chiquimula, Totonicapan, Guatemala, m 38, 1980: (*a*) naming ranges, (*a–b*) foci, (*b*) mappings, and (*c*) membership values.

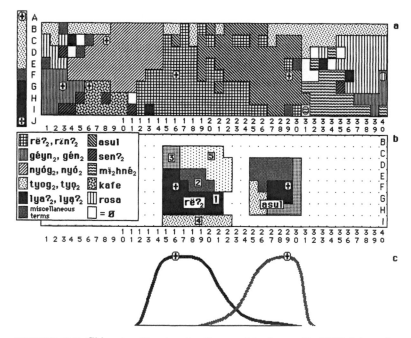

FIGURE 8.8. Chinantec, Tepetotutla, Oaxaca, Mexico, m 31, 1979: (*a*) naming ranges, (*a–b*) foci, (*b*) mappings, and (*c*) membership values.

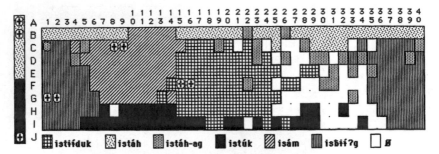

FIGURE 8.9. Tepecano, Atzqueltán, Villa Guerrero, Jalisco, Mexico, m 84, 1979: naming ranges and foci. Dennis Holt's interview of Lino de la Rosa Escobedo, the last known Tepecano speaker.

Figures 8.9–10 show naming ranges of a Tepecano speaker and a Santiago Tilapa Otomí speaker. Their cool categories are like those of the Chiquimula Quiché and the Chinantec speaker, except polarized foci suggest even greater skewing.

In figure 8.11, a Mezquital Otomí speaker named and mapped basic green and blue categories and focused each on a unique hue. Other Otomí speakers name the cool category *k'ángi* (figs. 5.5 and 8.10), which implies that this green category derives from skewing.

Figure 8.12 displays the curves of membership from figures 8.1, 8.3, 8.4, 8.5, 8.6, 8.7, and 8.8. Broken lines represent Munsell column 17 of unique green and column 29 of unique blue. Differences among the curves suggest a process by which the cool category skews increasingly as attention to distinctiveness augments, resulting in basic green and blue categories (fig. 8.11). The focus moves from near center, to a unique hue, to a polar position; values remain high on the focal side but diminish to zero on the other side. The cool category always skews.

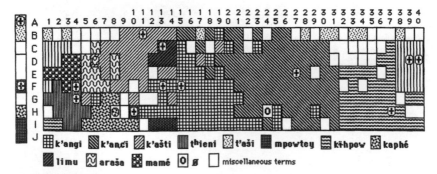

FIGURE 8.10. Otomí, Santiago Tilapa, Sierra de las Cruzes, Mexico, Mexico, f 48, 1979: naming ranges and foci.

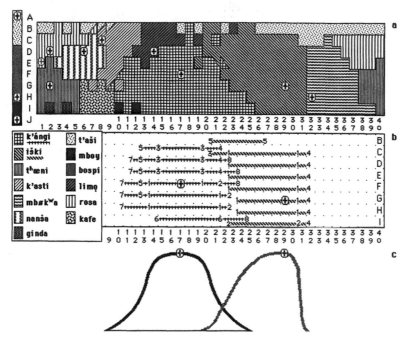

FIGURE 8.11. Otomí, Julián Villa Grande, Valle del Mezquital, Hidalgo, Mexico, f 33, 1981: (*a*) naming ranges, (*a*–*b*) foci, (*b*) mappings, and (*c*) membership values.

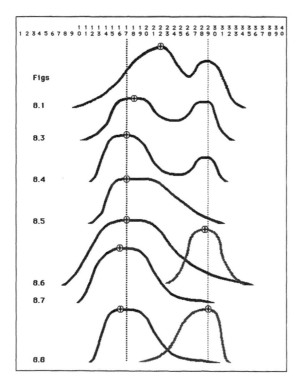

FIGURE 8.12. Foci and membership curves in relation to the unique-hue columns of the Munsell array representing degrees of skewing toward green.

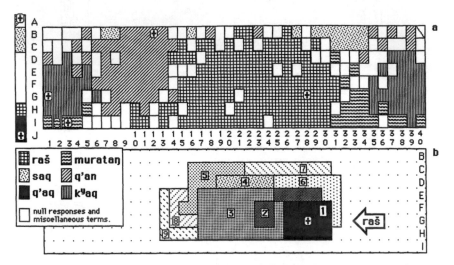

FIGURE 8.13. Sacapultec, San Juan Sacapulas, El Quiché, Guatemala, m 78, 1980: (*a*) naming ranges, (*a–b*) foci, and (*b*) mapping.

8.1.2. Direction of Skewing

About 25% of the cool categories in the Mesoamerican sample are skewed toward blue, as exemplified by figures 8.13–14.

In figure 8.13, a Sacapultec speaker named and mapped the cool category. His focus, G28, is slightly central to the inside of unique blue, column 29.

In figure 8.14, a Pima speaker skewed the cool category toward blue while naming green *s-ʔíiwagi*. The cool-category focus is on unique blue, F29; the focus of the "green" term was not elicited.

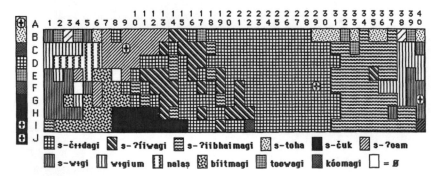

FIGURE 8.14. Pima, Gila River, Arizona, f 62, 1978: naming ranges and foci.

8.2. Quantification

Throughout the Mesoamerican sample, statistics substantiate the tendencies exemplified by individual data in §8.1 and §§8.3–4: (1) three times as many individuals skew the cool category toward green as toward blue (p<.01); (2) continuous mapping of the cool category corresponds with a centralized focus, and disjunctive mapping corresponds with a focus that is either in the column of a unique hue or polarized (p<.01); (3) foci of the basic green and basic blue categories are darker than foci of the cool category (p<.01); (4) foci of the cool category exhibit a dominant-recessive pattern with centralization in green (p<.01) and polarization in blue (p<.01); (5) a greater proportion of cool categories is focused in blue at the earliest phase of the division process than at the latest phase (p<.05). The statistics indicate that (1) Mesoamerican languages predominantly skew the cool category toward green, (2) skewing increases as category division progresses, (3) foci darken after division, (4) covert coextension is widely maintained, and (5) transference of foci from blue to green accompanies category division.

8.2.1. Outline of Major Numbers

The statistics are embedded in a broader array of numbers that characterize the cool category within the Mesoamerican sample: 589 individuals used the cool category; 527 focused it on one or two adjacent colors, 23 focused it on more than two adjacent colors, and 39 were not asked to focus it. Thirty-two individuals included the cool category within the range of a dark-cool category. Two hundred sixty cool categories were mapped, 33 of which are not used in calculation: 5 are focused on more than two adjacent colors and 28 were not focused. Of the 151 mapped cool categories composed by one vantage, 70 are mapped continuously and 81 disjunctively. (See tables 11.3 and 11.4 for inventories of coextensively named cool categories.)

8.2.2. Descriptions and Analyses

Statistics are described and analyzed in relation to direction of skewing (§8.2.2.1), degree of skewing (§8.2.2.2), darkening (§8.2.2.3), covert coextension (§8.2.2.4), and transference (§8.2.2.5). Formulae are the binomial proportion Z score (ZS), the functionally equivalent Pearson chi square (CS), and Pearson chi-square independence test (IT).

8.2.2.1. Statistics on the Direction of Skewing

Figure 8.15 displays the number of times each color of the Munsell array was selected as a focus for different classes of cool categories. A selec-

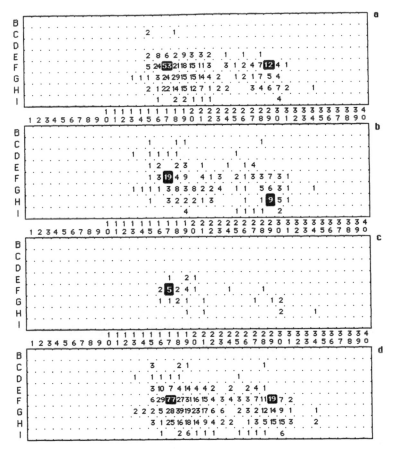

FIGURE 8.15. Aggregates of cool-category foci in the Mesoamerican sample:
(*a*) basic categories composed from one vantage, (*b*) basic and secondary coextensively composed categories, (*c*) secondary categories composed from one vantage,
(*d*) all categories (*a–c*). Foci on more than two adjacent chips are excluded.

tion is one individual's designation of a color as a focus; designation of two
adjacent colors constitutes two selections. Thus, the total number of selections is greater than the number of categories in the sample. The figure aggregates only individual choices of one color, two adjacent colors, or nonadjacent colors; 23 foci that cover three or more adjacent colors are omitted.
Part *a* displays focus selections for the 399 basic cool categories that show
no evidence of coextensive composition. Part *b* shows the aggregate for the
98 secondary and basic coextensively composed categories, whether named
with two terms or one. Many of the latter are focused only on one side,
usually green, which is one of the reasons that there is not an equal number
of choices on each side of column 23. Part *c* shows the aggregate for the

30 secondary categories that are not coextensively composed. Part *d* combines all choices of no more than two adjacent colors recorded in the Mesoamerican sample. Elemental hues attract the most foci: 77 at F17 in green, 19 at F29 in blue. Such pluralities are highlighted against dark background.

Figure 8.16 expresses as histograms the data of figure 8.15, with parts *a–d* matching between figures. Each cell represents a Munsell column. Number of focus selections per column appears at bottom. The figure re-

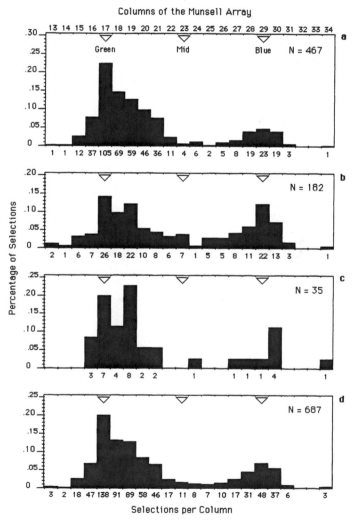

FIGURE 8.16. Frequency distributions across Munsell columns of aggregated cool-category foci in the Mesoamerican sample, those of figure 8.15: (*a*) basic categories composed from one vantage, (*b*) basic and secondary coextensively composed categories, (*c*) secondary categories composed from one vantage, (*d*) all categories (*a–c*).

veals that at least three times as many individuals focused the cool category on green as on blue. On each side of column 23, the numbers are:

(a) single-vantage basic categories   377:86
(b) coextensively composed categories   106:69
(c) single-vantage secondary categories   26:9
(d) all categories   509:167 (p<.01 ZS)[3]

In (b), the ratio is smallest because this aggregate, from 98 categories, includes foci of 44 categories that are composed of separately named coextensive ranges of which many were focused on opposite hues. The skewed aggregate of cool-category foci (d) and the aggregate of foci combined from basic green and blue categories in figure 8.19c show the expected difference between distributions (p=.00000 ZS).

8.2.2.2. Statistics on the Degree of Skewing

Continuous mappings correspond with central foci and disjunctive mappings correspond with foci that are placed on a unique hue or polarized between a unique hue and the cool-category margin. The correlations reflect the sequence represented by figure 8.12.

Figure 8.17 displays all foci of cool categories that are both composed from only one vantage and mapped. All mappings are either continuous or disjunctive in the manner exhibited by figures 8.1–2 versus 8.3–8 and 8.13.

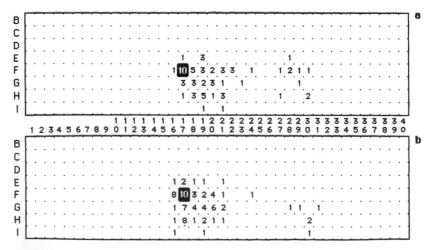

FIGURE 8.17. Aggregated foci of cool categories mapped (a) continuously and (b) disjunctively.

Part *a* aggregates foci of categories continuously mapped, part *b,* foci of categories disjunctively mapped. Figure 8.18 plots the same foci, *a* and *b,* respectively, as two distributions across Munsell columns. There is no probability (p=.00000 IT) that their difference is independent of the continuous and disjunctive patterns by which the categories were mapped. Foci of continuously mapped categories were selected at 69.94% between unique hues and 30.06% on or outside unique hues; foci of disjunctively mapped categories were selected 45.70% between and 54.30% on or outside.

Foci tend to migrate away from the center of the cool category and toward its unique hues and margins as attention to distinctiveness is enhanced and as the category approaches division.

After division, foci of basic green and basic blue categories do not migrate away from each other. The process of polarization transpires before the cool category divides; insignificant polarization increases after division. But basic green and blue categories show no less polarization than do cool categories that are disjunctively mapped.

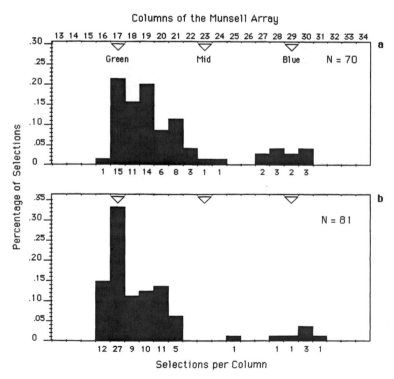

FIGURE 8.18. Frequency distributions of foci chosen for cool categories mapped (*a*) continuously (fig. 8.17*a*) and (*b*) disjunctively (fig. 8.17*b*).

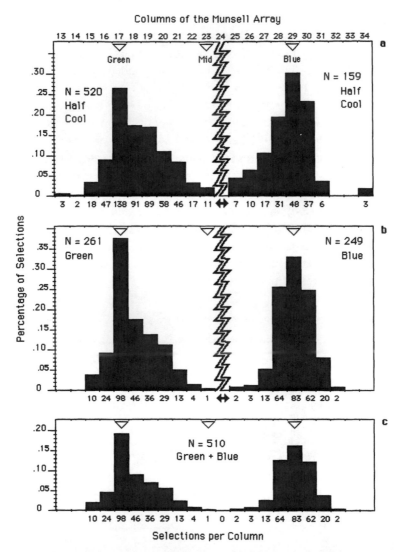

FIGURE 8.19. Frequency distributions: (*a*) cool-category foci (from fig. 8.16*d*) with percentages calculated from separate totals on either side of column 24 to facilitate comparison with (*b*); (*b*) separate focus aggregates of basic green and basic blue categories of the Mesoamerican sample (fig. 8.20*b*); (*c*) focus aggregates of basic green and basic blue categories with percentages calculated from one total to facilitate comparison with figure 8.16*d*. Since no basic green or basic blue categories are focused in column 24, division occurs there instead of at column 23 in *a* and *b*. Foci on more than two adjacent chips are excluded.

In figure 8.19, part *a* divides the cool-category focus distribution of figure 8.16*d* into its green foci of columns 13–23 and its blue foci of columns 25–34, which enables their comparison with data of part *b*. The latter displays foci distributions of the basic green and blue categories of the Mesoamerican sample, which are naturally distinct. Part *c* combines distributions of (*b*) foci for basic green and blue categories to facilitate their comparison, in turn, with those of cool categories, figures 8.16*d* and 8.18, as in table 8.1.

Table 8.1 shows how distributions of foci vary between cool categories continuously mapped, cool categories disjunctively mapped, and the artificially constituted aggregate from basic green and basic blue categories. Polarized foci outside unique-hue columns 17 and 29 increase across the three classes of aggregate. Foci on these columns also increase. Selections between these columns decrease.

TABLE 8.1. Foci of cool categories (a) continuously and
(b) disjunctively mapped

	Green		*Blue*	*Totals*
Continuous mappings, fig. 8.18*a*				
Polarized	1.48		4.29	**5.77**
Unique hues (UH)	21.43		2.86	**24.29**
Polarized + UH	22.91		7.15	**30.06**
Between UH		69.94		**69.94**
Disjunctive mappings, fig. 8.18*a*				
Polarized	14.81		4.93	**19.74**
Unique hues	33.33		1.23	**34.56**
Polarized + UH	48.14		6.16	**54.30**
Between UH		45.70		**45.70**
Basic green and basic blue, fig. 8.19*b*				
Polarized	6.66		16.46	**23.12**
Unique hues	19.21		16.27	**35.48**
Polarized + UH	25.87		32.73	**58.60**
Between UH		41.30		**41.30**

Percentages that contribute directly to statistical analysis are in boldface type.

Skewing increases as the cool category divides. The significant numbers are derived in figure 8.18 from comparison of foci in categories mapped (*a*) continuously and (*b*) disjunctively. In *b*, a higher proportion of foci are placed on unique green or polarized (p=.01037 IT). As might be expected, a difference pertains between the focus distributions of all cool categories and those of basic green and basic blue categories. A comparison of the green halves of figure 8.19, parts (*a*) and (*b*), and a comparison of their blue halves show that the difference between focus distributions in green columns 13–23 is moderately significant (p=.02909 IT), in blue columns 25–34 highly significant (p=.00156 IT).

Skewing ceases upon division of the cool-category and does not regress after division. This is shown by comparing foci distributions between disjunctively mapped cool categories and basic categories of green or blue; the former are closer to the end of the division process than are continuously mapped cool categories. Distributions of foci from the green side of the disjunctively mapped cool category (fig. 8.18*b*) and the basic green category (fig. 8.19*b*), columns 16–21 in both distributions, show no significant difference (p=.82435 IT). The difference between shortened distributions through blue columns 24–32 of the same figures is also insignificant (p=.61816 IT), although the 7 blue foci of disjunctively mapped categories are almost as few as can validly be compared.

8.2.2.3. Statistics on Darkening

Darkening is the movement of a focus toward black. People darken foci away from middle brightness when they divide the cool category into basic green and blue. Figure 8.20 compares (*a*) the distribution of foci within the comprehensive cool-category aggregate (fig. 8.15*d*) with (*b*) a distribution of foci across separate aggregates within the basic green and the basic blue categories (fig. 8.19*b*). The figure sums frequencies and represents them as histograms across the Munsell rows from light to dark, each row providing a cell. The foci of *b* are much darker than those of *a* (p=.00000 IT).

Significant darkening occurs after skewing has ceased. As shown in §8.2.2.2., there is a difference in skewing between continuously and disjunctively mapped cool categories but none between the latter and basic categories of green or blue. Whereas foci of continuously mapped and disjunctively mapped cool categories (fig. 8.17) are of the same light-dark value (p=.42106 IT), foci of basic green and blue categories (fig. 8.20*b*) are darker than foci of disjunctively mapped cool categories (fig. 8.17*b*) to a significance of p<.05 (=.04503 IT). Foci of basic green and blue

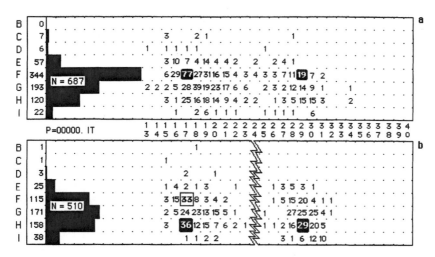

FIGURE 8.20. Focus aggregates of (*a*) all cool categories, figure 8.15*d*, and (*b*) all basic green and basic blue categories. Both *a* and *b* include a frequency distribution of foci across Munsell rows from light to dark.

categories are darker than foci of continuously mapped cool categories (fig. 8.17*a*) at a significance of p<.01 (=.00280 IT).

8.2.2.4. Statistics on the Dominant-Recessive Pattern

The distribution of all cool-category foci in figure 8.16*d* shows significantly more central in green (than in blue) and significantly more polar in blue (than in green). The pattern suggests prevalence of a dominant green vantage and a recessive blue vantage, regardless of whether they are separately named. A parallel overall difference appears between focus distributions in green columns 13–23 versus blue 31–23 (the 11 foci of column 23 are divided 5.5/5.5 between the two calculations) (p=.00012 IT).[4]

Cool-category foci are central significantly more in green than in blue. Central foci are counted as those placed on columns 18–19 and 27–28, the first and second columns to the inside of each unique hue. In green, there are 180 foci in columns 18–19 and 334.5 in columns 13–17 and 20–23 (p<.01, critical value 2.58, Z value 6.101083). In blue, there are 48 foci in columns 27–28 and 124.5 in columns 23–26 and 29–31 (p>.05 or specifically 1.0, critical value 1.96, Z value 1.703929). The difference between the ratios is insignificant (p>.05, critical value 1.96, Z value 1.728082).

Cool-category foci are polar significantly more in blue than in green. Polar foci are counted as those on column 16 in green or 30 in blue, the first column to the outside of each unique hue. In green, there are 47 foci in column 16 and 464.5 in columns 13–15 and 17–23 (p>.05 with chance expectation 46.45). In blue, there are 37 foci in column 30 and 135.5 in columns 23–29 and 31–32 (p<.01, critical value 2.58, Z value 2.920902). The difference between the ratios is also significant (p<.01, critical value 2.58, Z value 4.237734).

8.2.2.5. Statistics on Transference

Transference is the practice of permanently changing the focus of the cool category from blue to green. It occurs in conjunction with advancing category division. This is established by comparing foci distributions of categories at the earliest and latest phases of division, the secondary cool categories of figure 8.16c and the disjunctively mapped cool categories of figure 8.18b, in which the green-to-blue ratios of foci are 29:9 in the former and 74:7 in the latter, p<.05 (critical value of 1.96, Z value of 2.24476, CS). However, the two distributions share data from six individuals who mapped a secondary cool category disjunctively. These are five young Tzotzil speakers, whose data are discussed in reference to their other uncommon corollaries (MacLaury 1991a: figs. 9–10), and one Aguacatec speaker. Eliminating these, the ratios become, respectively, 24:5 and 72:3, p<.05 with the critical value 1.96 and Z value 2.2725. The latter falls short of a critical 2.58 required for p<.01.

This significant statistic matches the direction of two others that are not significant. Both obtain in comparisons by which we may expect to find an effect of transference; both regard a difference between two ratios of foci in green to foci in blue. Figure 8.16 (a) and (c) shows such ratios in basic versus secondary cool categories, respectively, of 377:4:86 versus 26:9 (81.16% to 18.84% versus 74.3% to 25.7%), p=.48069 IT. Figure 8.18 (a) and (b) show such ratios in continuously versus disjunctively mapped cool categories of 58:1:11 versus 74:7 (83.57% to 16.43% versus 91.35% to 8.65%), p>.05 CS (critical value 1.96, Z value 1.009).

8.2.2.6. Miscellaneous Statistics

A plurality of foci are placed on unique green and unique blue; foci placements are constrained by the locations of unique hues and do not occur at random on the Munsell array. In figure 8.16d, 138:376.5 (p<.01 CS with critical value 2.58, Z value 6.9672) is the ratio of foci in column 17 of unique green to surrounding green columns 13–16 and 18–23 with the 11 foci of column 23 counted as 5.5; 48:124.5 (p<.01 CS with critical value

2.58, Z value 4.237013) is the ratio of unique blue column 29 to blue columns 23–28 and 30–34, with 5.5 in cell 23.

Some numbers are of interest, although I offer no interpretation. For example, the frequency distributions of foci in basic green versus basic blue (fig. 8.19b) differ significantly (p=.00000 IT). (See note 4.)

8.2.3. Synopsis

Five patterns pertain to skewing of cool categories in the Meso-american sample.

1. The cool category is predominantly skewed toward green.

2. Skewing increases as the cool category divides. Skewing does not continue to increase after the cool category divides, although it does not decrease after division.

3. Darkening increases as division culminates. It mainly progresses after skewing has ceased.

4. The dominant-recessive pattern prevails among foci of cool categories that are named with a single term, suggesting that many are composed by covert coextension. This condition is a prerequisite for transference.

5. Transference of foci from green to blue occurs as division of the cool category progresses.

8.3. Darkening

Vantage theory accounts for darkening. Complete division of the cool category requires very strong attention to distinctiveness, because green and blue are perceived to be more similar to each other than are any other pair of unique hues. Such strong attention to difference produces reciprocal weakening of attention to similarity to the extent that, perhaps, many people feel that it no longer suffices by itself as a coordinate. They reinforce the vantage by selecting a third coordinate from the continuum of brightness. They choose a dark point of reference rather than a light one, probably because elemental green and blue are perceived to be more similar to black than to white (see §4.1.1). Addition of a coordinate of darkness to a vantage pulls values of membership toward black.[5]

Darkening is subject to variation from its normal co-occurrence with emergence of basic green and blue. Some people darken the cool-category focus without showing signs of advanced division; others focus the basic green and basic blue category at middle brightness in spite of the statistical tendency to darken them. Figures 8.21–23 supplement the statistics by showing individual systems.

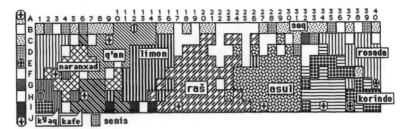

FIGURE 8.21. Uspantec, Las Pacayas, Uspantán, Guatemala, m 30, 1979.

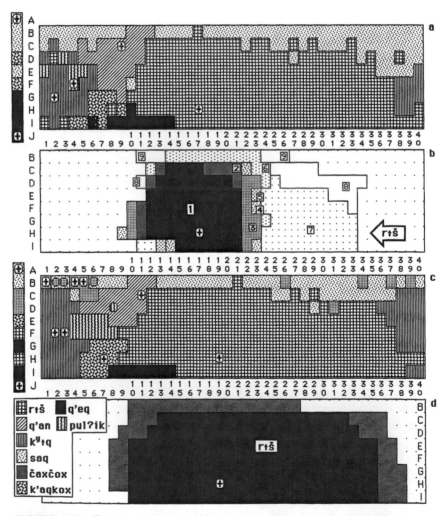

FIGURE 8.22. Cakchiquel, Patzún, Chimaltenango, Guatemala: (*a–b*) speaker 1, f 29–30; (*c–d*) speaker 2, f 15–16; (*a, c*) naming ranges and foci 1978, (*b, d*) mappings 1979.

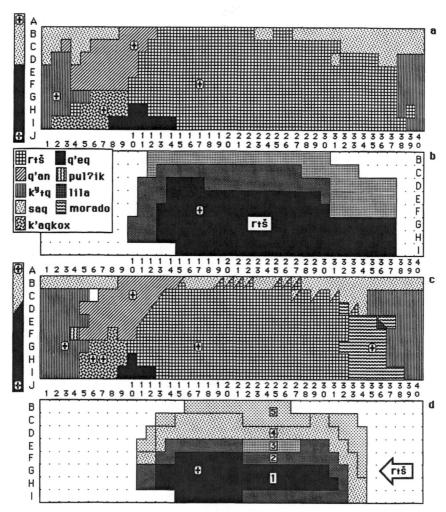

FIGURE 8.23. Cakchiquel, Patzún, Guatemala: (*a–b*) speaker 3, f 24–25, 1978 (*a*) and 1979 (*b*); (*c–d*) speaker 4, m 28, 1979; (*a, c*) naming ranges and foci, (*b, d*) mappings.

Figure 8.21 shows the advanced system of an Uspantec speaker who darkens most foci, including those of green and blue. Darkening applies generally to categories whose ranges include colors at middle brightness. Examples from Tzeltal, Sacapultec, and Paya appear in figures 4.9*a*, 8.33*c*, and 11.4*d*. Harkness (1973: fig. 6) finds that Mam-speaking children focus the cool category on Munsell row E while Mam adults focus it on row G.

In figures 8.22–23, four Cakchiquel speakers darken the cool-category focus, its first mapping step, or both. In figure 8.22, (*a–b*) speaker 1 darkens her focus but maps from green to blue; (*c–d*) speaker 2 only darkens her focus. In figure 8.23, (a–b) speaker 3 and (c–d) speaker 4 map both unique hues with the first step while skewing it toward darkness, which is rare. Speaker 4, who maps from dark to light with finest discrimination, adds a purple category.

8.4. Qualifiers and Skewing

Burgess, Kempton, and MacLaury (1983, 1985) present the original study of color qualifiers as indices of skewing, which is extended here. A monolingual speaker of Western Tarahumara, speaker 1, was interviewed twice, first in January 1978 in his native village, Huicochi, after he had become literate in Tarahumara and had worked as a translator, and second in December 1979 at Mitla, Oaxaca, the day he had finished a four-month intensive linguistic workshop. He had advanced the skewing process during the interim. Figures 8.24–25 display data from both of his interviews and from a speaker of Central Tarahumara, speaker 2, a younger linguistic assistant from Samachique.

Figure 8.24 shows naming ranges and foci from (a) the first and (b) second interview of speaker 1. During the first, he centralized his cool-category focus at F19 and named the category 70 times on the green side of column 23 and 76 times on the blue side. During the second, he focused the category on unique green at F–G17 and named it 78 times on its green side and 77 times on its blue side. The correspondences among the focus and the naming range suggest a slightly greater skewing toward green during the second interview. This apparent subtle advancement of skewing over a two-year interim is not significant by itself; however, it corroborates stronger correspondences among qualifiers that differentiate high and low values of category membership.

Figure 8.25 shows uses by speaker 1 of (a–b) obligatory postposed qualifiers. During both interviews, he postposed to the root, siyó-, only -kame or -name, which designate high and low membership, respectively. During his first interview, (a) he used -kame 90 times and -name 55 times, a ratio of 1.000 to 0.633. During his second interview, (b) he used -kame 79 times and -name 82 times, 1.000 to 1.048. He showed keener discrimination by assigning higher value to fewer colors and lower value to more (p=.022 CS). During the second interview, he differentiated further by using three optional preposed qualifiers that he did not use during the first: bánaga- 'focal green', čoname 'dark', čokame- 'very dark'. These usages are not diagrammed.

Figure 8.24 depicts (c) the disjunctive mapping of the cool category that

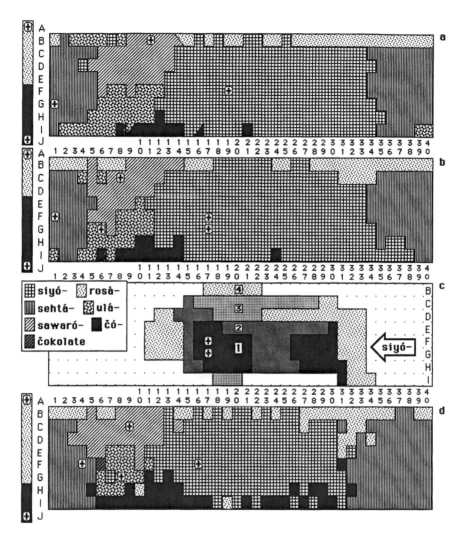

FIGURE 8.24. (*a–c*) Western Tarahumara, Huicochi, Chihuahua: speaker 1, m 31, (*a–b*) naming ranges and foci, (*a*) January 1978, (*b*) December 1979, (*c*) mapping 1979; (*d*) Central Tarahumara, Samachiqui, Chihuahua, Mexico: speaker 2, m 25, 1978, naming ranges and foci.

speaker 1 rendered during his second interview. Mappings were not elicited during the first. The mapping shows slight skewing toward green: the first mapping step covers 20 greens and 17 blues, the last step 21 greens and 25 blues (from Burgess, Kempton, and MacLaury 1983:fig. 7, 1985:fig. 11).

In figure 8.24*d,* naming ranges and foci of speaker 2 show greater skewing toward green than any data from speaker 1. Speaker 2 applied the cool-

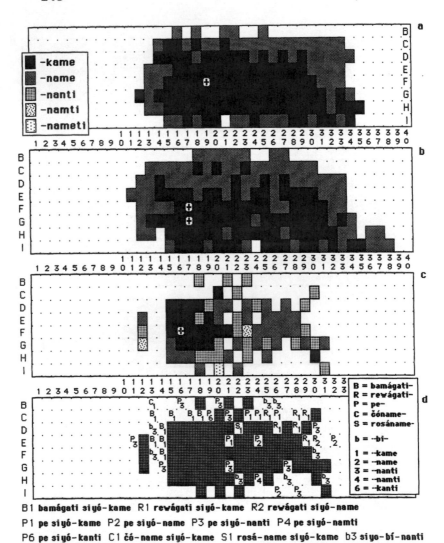

FIGURE 8.25. Tarahumara: qualifiers and foci, same speakers and dates as in figure 8.24; (a–b) Western Tarahumara, speaker 1, (c–d) Central Tarahumara, speaker 2.

category root, *siyó-*, to fewer colors than did speaker 1: he applied it 69 times to green and 46 times to blue, and he polarized the cool-category focus at F16, one chip to the outside of elemental green. The ratio of usages in green and blue, the paucity of usages, and the polarity suggest that speaker 2 attended more strongly to differences among cool colors than did speaker 1 during either of his interviews.

In figure 8.25*c–d,* the distribution of qualifiers from speaker 2 corroborates this suggestion: he used five optional preposed qualifiers, one optional postposed qualifier of first order, *-bi-,* and six obligatory postposed qualifiers. In *d,* the obligatory postposed qualifiers assume more peripheral meanings when combined in a phrase with the optional qualifiers, for example, P_3 = *pe siyó-nanti* (E11), b_3 = *siyó-bi-nanti* (D13), R_1 = *rewágati siyó-kame* (C28), B_1 = *bamágati siyó-kame* (C13). This use of qualifier combination to displace meaning toward lower membership is of rare sophistication. Further, (*c*) the distribution of simple postposed usages shows maximal membership, *siyó-kame,* in green and a predominance of lesser membership, *siyó-name* and *siyó-nanti,* in blue. Minimal membership, *siyó-namti* and *siyó-nameti,* occurs in turquoise at F23 between unique hues and on marginal colors, G12 and I20.

In sum, the speaker of Western Tarahumara shows slightly greater skewing after two years of diverse experience; it matches other indications of stronger attention to distinctiveness, such as elaboration of qualifier classes. The speaker of Central Tarahumara shows much greater skewing among all data while he uses an intricate system of qualifiers, suggesting even stronger attention to difference.

8.5. Aggregates of Foci in Specific Languages

Figures 8.26–27 depict aggregates of cool-category foci from speakers of single languages. The aggregates differ. The cases complement the statistics on skewing and on the prevalent dominant-recessive pattern, §8.2.2.1. and §8.2.2.4.

Figure 8.26 displays foci from (*a*) Santa Buenaventura Nahuatl and (*b*) Chiquimula Quiché, 10 speakers of each. The Nahuatl foci are centralized on the green side of column 23 and the Quiché foci are placed on or outside column 17 of unique green. All the Nahuatl speakers mapped the cool category continuously, as in figure 8.1; all the Quiché speakers mapped disjunctively, as in figure 8.7.

Figures 8.26*c–d* and 8.27 display cool-category foci, respectively, from (*c*) 22 Palantla Chinantec speakers, (*d*) 23 Texmelucan Zapotec, (*a*) 19 Papago, (*b*) 4 Pima, and (*c*) 6 Lacandón. Each aggregate shows less interspeaker agreement than do those of Nahuatl or Quiché. Two Zapotec speakers focused the cool category on its blue side, as did 7 of the Papago, 3 of the Pima, and all 6 Lacandón. Lacandón is the only Mesoamerican language in which all recorded speakers skewed toward blue (fig. 11.14).

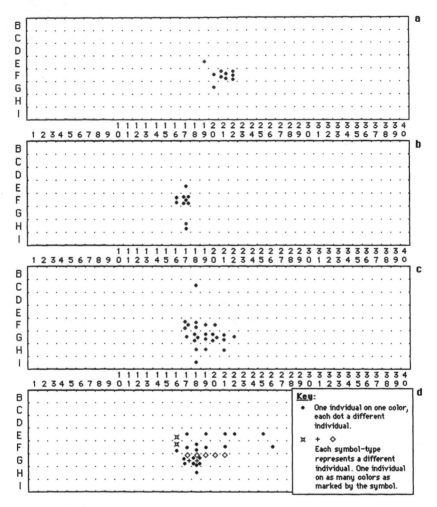

FIGURE 8.26. Aggregated cool-category foci: (*a*) Nahuatl, Santa Buenaventura, Puebla, Mexico, 1979, (*b*) Quiché, Chiquimula, Totonicapan, Guatemala, 1980, (*c*) Chinantec, San Juan Palantla, Tuxtepec, Oaxaca, Mexico, 1978, (*d*) Zapotec, San Lorenzo Texmelucan, Sola de Vega, Oaxaca, Mexico, 1978.

In figure 8.28, (*a*) Tlapanec and (*b*) Jicaque speakers extend foci (fig. 11.6). The Tlapanec focus is skewed toward green, covering unique green of column 17 but not unique blue of column 29. The Jicaque focus covers unique blue but not unique green. In spite of their breadth, extended foci may show skewing.

Subsequent discussion and analyses will refer to these focus aggregates of figures 8.26–28.

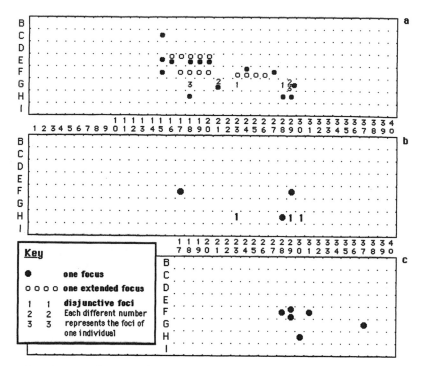

FIGURE 8.27. Aggregated cool-category foci, 1978: (*a*) Papago, southern Arizona, U.S., and northern Sonora, Mexico; (*b*) Pima, Gila River and Casa Grande, Arizona, U.S.; (*c*) Lacandón, Nahá, Selva de Lacandón, Chiapas, Mexico.

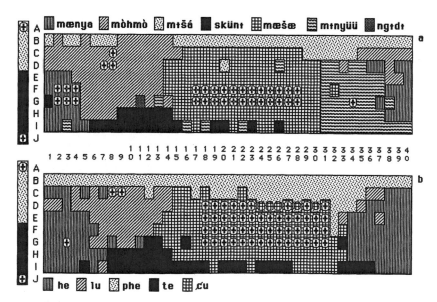

FIGURE 8.28. Naming ranges and foci: (*a*) Tlapanec, Malinaltepec, Guerrero, Mexico, m 55, 1978; (*b*) Jicaque, Montaña de la Flor, Honduras, m 25, 1977.

8.6. Transference versus Areal Diffusion

We need a hypothesis that might tie together statistics: (1) at least three times as many cool categories are skewed toward green as toward blue ($p<.01$); (2) the aggregate of all cool-category foci manifests the dominant-recessive pattern with significant proportions of green foci centralized and blue foci polarized ($p<.01$); (3) secondary categories that are continuously mapped show a greater percentage of foci in blue than do basic categories that are disjunctively mapped ($p<.05$), that is, categories in the earliest phase of division versus categories in the latest phase.

One hypothesis is areal diffusion: a cultural value favoring green pervades Mesoamerica. Traits of color categorization can indeed diffuse; for example, in the Pacific Northwest, Salishan and Wakashan languages share a yellow-with-green category (MacLaury 1986*b*, 1987*a;* Kinkade 1988; Saunders 1992*a*), even though it is rare throughout the world. However, the area covered by the Mesoamerican Survey ranges from the Papago in southern Arizona to the Paya of Honduras, more than ten times the territory of the Pacific Northwest. As a result of the Spanish Conquest, trade routes and exchanges among native peoples were reduced to regional market systems (Wolf 1962: Chapter 10); thus, if pre-Columbian diffusion had produced skewing toward green, the practice would have been retained at innumerable local points throughout the vast area for the past 500 years. But even more formidable questions arise. Would areal diffusion explain why significantly more cool categories are skewed toward blue at the earliest phase of division? And would it account for the prevalent dominant-recessive pattern? Such subtleties are unlikely to be picked out for widespread popularity, if even noticed.

The preference for skewing the cool category toward green, especially during its final phase of division, might be a panhuman proclivity that people throughout Mesoamerica exercise independently of each other. I call the second hypothesis "transference," a universal process by which people who focus the cool category in blue transfer the focus to green as they increase attention to distinctiveness.

The explanation is based in the neurology of color perception. Green is the opponent of red, while red is probably more salient than any other hue (see §§2.4.2 and 4.1.1.2). Contrast between red and cool categories would encourage people to focus the latter in green.[6] Observers would place increasing importance on contrast as they emphasized differences more. Transference coincides with category division, because both of these processes are provoked by increasing emphasis on distinctiveness, but division itself does not cause transference.

Transference entails that a person will construct the cool category from two points of view as he transfers a focus from blue to green. In effect, a person will construct the category from coextensive vantages while naming each perspective with the same color term. The period of maintaining this "covert coextension" might be short; it would differ from overtly named coextension only in its duration, if at all. Statistics in §8.2.2.4 indicate that covert coextension is prevalent in Mesoamerica and seems to be established in the cool category of some languages.

The prerequisite of double viewpoints would explain details of the transference process. First, a focus is canceled on the blue side of the category and newly planted in green; it does not migrate across the category such as to occupy column 23 for a time along its way. Second, aggregates of cool-category foci from single languages manifest the dominant-recessive pattern when placed in both green and blue (fig. 8.34*a–b*). Green foci show the centralized dominant pattern, and blue foci show the polarized recessive pattern that would result from an underlying coextension.

Figures 8.29–32 may catch transference on the wing, while figures 8.33–38 show its prerequisite and its result.

In figures 8.29–30, data appear to capture transference in progress among three speakers of Northern Tepehuán. In figure 8.29, (*a–b*) speaker 1, age 81, skews the cool category toward blue, and (*c–d*) speaker 2, age 50, skews it toward green. Neither speaker evidences coextension. In figure 8.30, (*a–b*) speaker 3, age 52, focuses his cool category in green at G18 but maps it with a first step in blue. Each datum indicates skewing toward an opposite side of the category. Speaker 3 appears to represent the intermediate phase between the skewing toward blue of speaker 1 and the skewing toward green of speaker 2. According to the hypothesis of transference, speaker 3 focuses a dominant vantage but maps a recessive vantage. Parts (*c–c'*) displays the focus aggregate from the 11 Northern Tepehuán speakers who contributed foci. In *c*, 8 foci fit the dominant-recessive pattern with green dominating: 6 centralized in green of column 18, 2 polarized in blue. In *c'*, 2 foci fit the dominant-recessive pattern with blue dominating: an extended focus centralized and a green focus polarized, G16. A third focus on elemental green at F17 may fit either pattern, *c* or *c'*.

Figures 8.31–32 display data from four Pocomchí speakers. In figure 8.31*a–b*, speaker 1 produces a naming range and focus skewed toward blue; her mapping is continuous. In *c*, speaker 2 focuses and disjunctively

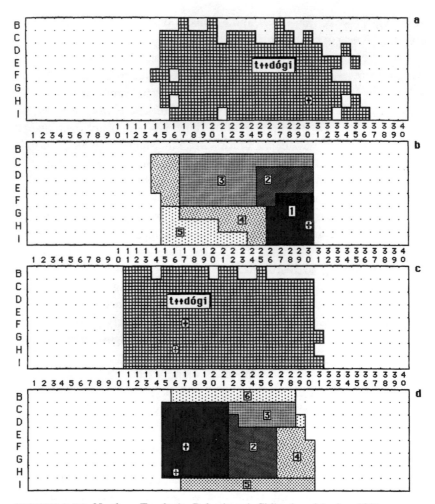

FIGURE 8.29. Northern Tepehuán, Baborigami, Chihuahua, Mexico, 1981; (a–b) speaker 1, f 81 (c–d) speaker 2, f 50; (a, c) naming ranges, (a–d) foci, and (b, d) mappings.

maps the cool category with skewing toward blue. As he was hesitant to respond to any elicitation, he mapped few colors in four steps; his naming ranges were too sparse for meaningful display. In figure 8.32a–b, speaker 3 names the cool category 48 times in green and 74 in blue, but his focus and disjunctive mapping are skewed toward green. He appears to manifest an intermediate phase of transference. His disjunctive mapping suggests a stronger attendance to distinctiveness than does the continuous mapping of speaker 1, who skews toward blue in all data. The discrepancy in skewing

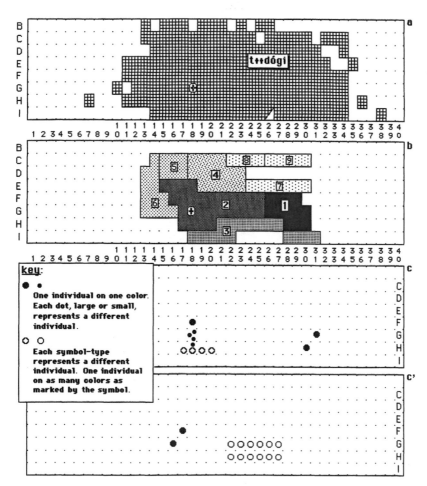

FIGURE 8.30. Northern Tepehuán, Baborigami, Chihuahua, Mexico: (*a–b*) speaker 3, f 52, 1981, (*a*) naming range, (*a–b*) focus, and (*b*) mapping; (*c–c'*) focus aggregate from 10 speakers.

between the naming range and focus of speaker 3 is greater than that produced by the first interview of Tarahumara speaker 1, figure 8.24*a*, who named the cool category 70 times in green and 76 in blue but focused it in green. In figure 8.32*c*, a younger Pocomchí speaker named only green with the term that older speakers 1–2 used to name a cool category skewed toward blue.

Figure 8.33 displays data from Sacapultec speakers 1 and 2, ages 72 and 17. Data from a third man, age 78, appear in figure 8.13. The latter maps and focuses the cool category with skewing toward blue, while here

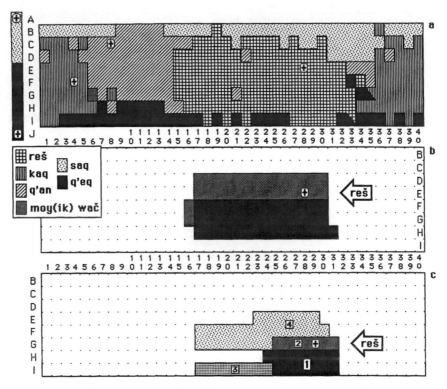

FIGURE 8.31. Pocomchí, San Cristóbal Alta Verapaz, Guatemala, 1979: (a–b) speaker 1, f 40; (c) speaker 2, m 70; (a) naming range, (a–c) foci, and (b–c) mappings.

speaker 1 focuses the category with the same skewing. Speaker 2 names only green with the term that the older men use to name both green and blue, the result of transference and division. Two other Sacapultec interviewees, ages 28 and 55, also applied the historical "cool" term only to green (MCS files).

Figure 8.34 displays aggregates of foci from four languages whose speakers appear to be undergoing transference of skewing within the cool category. The Tzeltal foci (a) are from one dialect of an agricultural people who live in small sedentary settlements. All Seri (b) speak the same dialect; most stay throughout the year at the seaside settlement where these foci were elicited, although some move between fishing sites. The Guarijío speakers (c) share one dialect, Lowland Guarijío. The Guarijío and some of the Tarahumara are transhumant. The Tarahumara foci are from two strong dialects, Western (d) and Central Tarahumara (d'). Two population centers of each are represented.

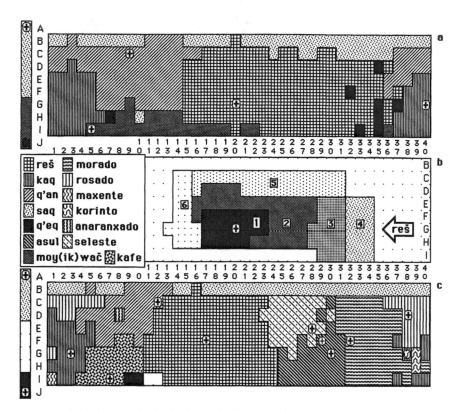

FIGURE 8.32. Pocomchí: (*a–b*) San Cristóbal Alta Verapaz, Guatemala, speaker 3, m 30, 1979; (*c*) Chialli, Tactic, San Cristóbal Alta Verapaz, Guatemala, speaker 4, m 17, 1978; (*a, c*) naming ranges, foci, and (*b*) mapping.

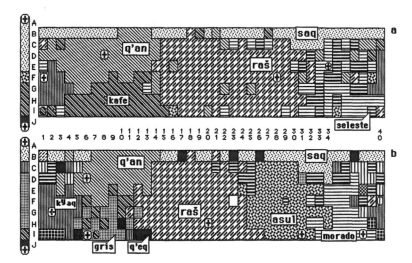

FIGURE 8.33. Sacapultec, San Juan Sacapulas, Guatemala, naming ranges and foci, 1979: (*a*) speaker 1, m 72, (*b*) speaker 2, m 17.

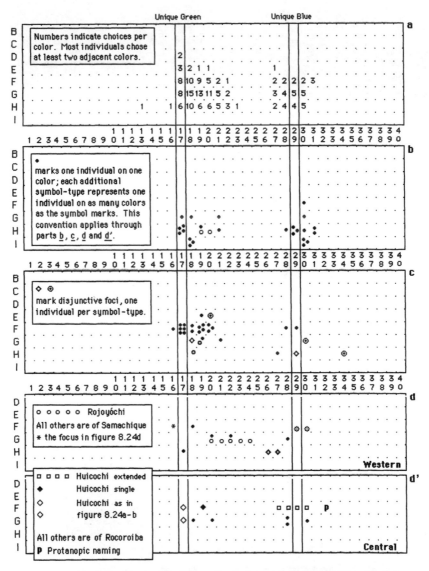

FIGURE 8.34. Aggregates of foci from the cool category: (*a*) Tenejapa Tzeltal (Brent Berlin 1968 MS-1), (*b*) Seri of Desemboque, (*c*) Lowland Guarijío, (*d*) Western Tarahumara, and (*d'*) Central Tarahumara.

Brent Berlin (MS-1) in 1968 elicited these foci from 40 Tzeltal speakers (*a*) with the original array of contiguous rectangular chips. The contiguity of stimuli encouraged 27 individuals to volunteer extended foci (cf. fig. 2.5). Each number represents selections of its corresponding color. This way of representing the data differs from Berlin and Kay's (1969:131, figs. 2–3) normalization of the same foci with single dots (which show only the green foci). Thirty-one Tzeltal focused the cool category in green, 9 in blue. The foci show the dominant-recessive pattern: on the green side, 2 (1.47%) choices are polarized, 27 (19.70%) are in column 17 of unique green, and 108 (78.83%) are centralized within columns 18–23; on the blue side, 15 (34.40%) are polarized, 11 (25.00%) are in column 29 of unique blue, and 18 (40.09%) are centralized within columns 27–28 (p<.001 IT). The numbers suggest that the Tzeltal covertly maintain coextension, constructing the dominant vantage in reference to green. Berlin recorded one individual who polarized his focus in blue at E–G30 but then reviewed his choice, canceled it, and centralized his final choice in green at G20. These Tzeltal foci are not included in figure 8.16*d* or in any other calculation herein (cf. MacLaury 1986*a:* fig. 8.52*a* by permission of Brent Berlin).

In (*b*), the foci of 25 Seri distribute like those of Tzeltal. Thirteen individuals focused in green, 5 on unique-hue column 17 and 8 in a centralized position; among blues, 11 individuals polarized foci or focused on unique-hue column 29, and one centrally focused in column 28. The significantly distinct ratios are 5:8 versus 11:1 (p=.00000 ZS and Fisher exact test).

In (*c*), foci of 25 Guarijío speakers pattern in green like those of Tzeltal and Seri; however, only 5 speakers focused the cool category in blue, 2 with foci in a dual pattern of two or three. The two foci are centralized at G18 and placed on the unique-blue column, H29; the three are centralized at E20 and ambivalently polarized at G30 blue and H34 purple, probably a recessive choice with equivocal placement.

In (*d*), 16 speakers of Western and Central Tarahumara show less pat-

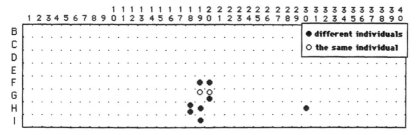

FIGURE 8.35. Aggregate of cool-category foci, 9 Acatec speakers, San Miguel Acatán, Huehuetenango, Guatemala.

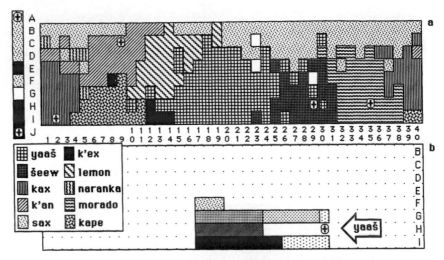

FIGURE 8.36. Acatec, San Miguel Acatán, Huehuetenango, Guatemala, m 58, 1980: (*a*) naming ranges, (*a–b*) foci, and (*b*) mapping.

tern, especially among blues, than do the speakers of Tzeltal, Seri, and Guarijío. Burgess, Kempton, and MacLaury (1983:143–144) observe that these blue foci mismatch a prevailing tendency to skew high-membership qualifier distributions toward green (figs. 8.24–25). Such mismatching is the trademark of transference (figs. 8.30, 8.32 and 8.36). They also observe marginal uses of the high-membership qualifier in purple, G34 and F36 (1985:fig. 7), which are consistent with the polarization of best-example rating that would occur in a recessive vantage.[7]

None of the nine Acatec speakers in the sample from Acatán produced the diagnostic correlation between foci and mappings of the cool category (§8.2.2.2., figs. 8.17–18). All mapped disjunctively with a first step in green, but eight centralized their foci in green and one polarized his focus in blue, figure 8.35. Figure 8.36 shows the blue-focused system, figures 8.37–38 green-focused systems. However, this extreme ratio of 8:1 manifests the same dominant-recessive pattern as do foci of Northern Tepehuán, Tzeltal, Seri, and Guarijío, figures 8.30c and 8.34a–c. As they differ in ratio but not in pattern, they suggest phases of transference that share the cognitive underpinning of dominant-recessive vantages.[8]

In sum, covert coextension is prerequisite to transference of a cool-category focus from blue to green. Covert coextension in Mesoamerica is statistically attested in both the overall aggregate (fig. 8.16d) and in singular dialects of sedentary settlements, such as Tzeltal and Seri. Enhanced

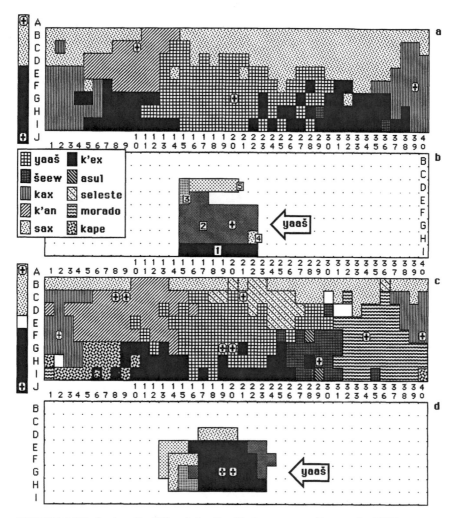

FIGURE 8.37. Acatec, San Miguel Acatán, Huehuetenango, Guatemala, 1980: (a–b) f 30, (c–d) m 30; (a, c) naming ranges, (a–d) foci, and (b, d) mappings.

emphasis on difference probably directs attention to the opposition between categories, which is epitomized by the antagonism between red and green. Green, then, more readily identifies the cool category than blue. The alternative is that a green focus is widely diffused as a cultural value, which ignores subtleties that likely are beneath consciousness and beyond social sanction, such as the penchant to focus green during advanced phases of division or to link green with the dominant vantage.[9]

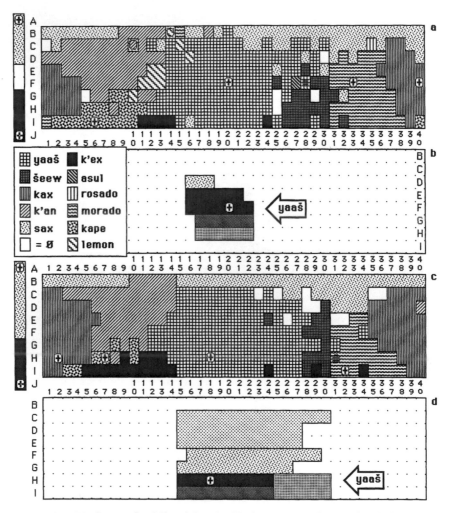

FIGURE 8.38. Acatec, San Miguel Acatán, Huehuetenango, Guatemala, 1980: (*a–b*) m 73, (*c–d*) m 40; (*a, c*) naming ranges, (*a–b*) foci, and (*b, d*) mappings.

8.7. Summary

The cool category is always constructed by analogy to a vantage in space-time, whether it is named with one term or coextensive terms. Cool categories that are named with a single term are constructed from two covert vantages or from only one. In either case, the analogy between spatiotemporal coordinates and those of perception and cognition is essential to the categorization of cool colors.

To argue this point, I have presented statistical evidence that three processes pervade the cool category: skewing, darkening, and transference. I have used vantage theory to formulate a separate hypothesis of each process and a subsequent account of how the three are related. Skewing is produced by establishing a vantage point in preferred reference to one elemental hue. Skewing increases as attendance to distinctiveness gains strength; the process coincides with category division. Darkening occurs at the end of division when attendance to similarity weakens sufficiently to encourage many people to reinforce the vantage point by selecting a coordinate from the brightness continuum; they select darkness rather than lightness because black is perceived to be closer than white to elemental green and blue. Or, perhaps, darkness is emphasized to counteract the nullifying effect of strong differentiation upon the category. Transference occurs as strong emphasis on difference accents contrast between categories of cool versus red hue, singling out green as the antagonist of red.

While I have presented transference as a universal process, I note that data from around the world show that cool categories are commonly skewed toward blue. This issue is the subject of Chapter 11.

Skewing, darkening, and transference emerge when people stress hue as their main interest, the only provisory constraint upon the three. Otherwise, they are the by-products of a single process of progressive differentiation that is automatically set into motion as people construct categories by analogy to viewpoint.

CHAPTER 9

SUBMERGED VERSUS REFLECTIVE CATEGORIZATION

Individuals who categorize from a "submerged" perspective are involved in this one position to an extent that they do not envision alternatives. But others categorize "reflectively": not only have they created optional points of view, but they show that they are aware of all the possibilities at one time. Yet others seem to shift their perspective from submerged to reflective during an interview as they realize options one after another. Questions concerning the relation of "mental acuity" to color categorization were introduced by W. Wundt and W. H. R. Rivers around 1900, and similar issues have been raised since in anthropological, linguistic, and psychological subfields. Yet the problems remain intractable: What differentiates subjective from objective thought? How can the difference be demonstrated through psychological testing? How can it be modeled?

Here, I attempt to model the distinct patterns by which speakers of different languages focus the cool category. I hypothesize that an explanation may lie in certain variant degrees to which people engage with or detach from the categories they construct. I offer no independent psychological tests of my proposals; they have come about as a result of my post-survey ruminations on the curious differences among data. My purpose is not to press particular assertions, but to illuminate the problem. Further, I shall pursue one particular line of inquiry as far as it can be taken under the existing limitations. At least it may benefit color ethnography to frame the issue and to underscore its importance. At the very least, an integrated assembly of all the facts as I know them will highlight the need to resume the kind of program that Wundt and Rivers sought to establish.

Members of specific communities share a preference for volunteering single, dual, or even triple foci of the cool category. Preferences differ among communities. People who favor multiple foci may even share a priority for the order of placement: for example, most of the members of one particular community first place a green focus, whereas members of another community usually place multiple foci by starting with blue. They do so even when each is interviewed privately. Doubtless, people do not entertain customs that prescribe how they should focus the cool category when visited by an anthropologist. Rather, the shared behavior within each community may reflect some specific approach to categorizing color—or to categorizing anything—while the disparities between communities may reflect different approaches.

My specific working hypothesis, then, is that people who choose multiple foci categorize from a reflective standpoint, while others who choose a single focus are immersed in a particular position. The tentative status of this idea must be born in mind.

Vantage theory specifies the necessary conditions for assuming degrees of lesser or greater detachment while constructing a cool category: strong attention to distinctiveness should be preconditional to detachment. Yet single, dual, and triple foci occur in different languages under what appear to be like conditions of strong differentiation. The vantage model does not specify why some people share a practice of categorizing from a remote overview while others who would seem to be equally motivated do not.

A cool category that harbors covert coextension may display one, two, or three widely separated foci. Because a single focus will be placed in reference to a dominant or a recessive vantage, dual foci are more accurately called the "single foci of separate vantages" on one category. In Mesoamerica, in keeping with the tendency to assign the dominant vantage to green, a focus in green is usually more central than a focus in blue within a dual pair. True triple foci include one focus in blue, one in green, and another in turquoise. Three foci in themselves do not comprise a triple set; what is really a dual choice of green and blue may involve two ambivalent decisions in green or blue, one more polarized than the other—pseudo triple foci (fig. 8.34c).

While covert coextension accounts for the dominant-recessive pattern and, in part, explains dual foci, other questions remain.[1] As merely thinking analytically may not instigate a choice of more than one focus, what other cognition is required? What motivates triple foci? Why in one community do people focus the first of a multiple series in green while in another they begin with blue? What accounts for different patterns of single foci?

9.1. Single Foci

Patterns of single foci differ among languages. Some do not manifest covert coextension, while others manifest its pattern at different phases of transference. Santa Buenaventura Nahuatl and Chiquimula Quiché place tight clusters of exclusively green foci, the former centralizing all and the latter placing them on or outside unique green (fig. 8.26, also figs. 8.1, 8.7, and 11.14). Neither shows corroborating evidence of covert coextension, as opposed to the systems of Tzeltal, Seri, Acatec, and Guarijío (figs. 8.34–35); stronger evidence would consist of foci in both green and blue. Similarly, Lacandón speakers place single foci exclusively in blue, polarizing three of six (figs. 8.27 and 11.8). Tzeltal and Seri speakers always place a single focus in either blue or green, showing on the aggregate the dominant-recessive pattern (figs. 8.34a–b). Most Acatec speakers centralize single foci in green, except one who polarizes the focus in blue (fig. 8.35). Only half of Guarijío speakers centralize foci in green while the others polarize green foci, choose a blue focus, or select dual foci (fig. 8.34c).

Although the Lacandón have not transferred any foci to green, the polarization in blue suggests a recessive vantage and, thereby, might imply covert coextension.[2] The Seri and Tzeltal are in the middle of transference; the Guarijío and Acatec have almost completed it. The Buenaventura Nahuatl might have taken transference a short step beyond Acatec by merely not focusing an abiding covert vantage at blue. The Chiquimula Quiché may have dissolved the perspective from blue, if they ever maintained it.

9.2. Dual Foci

Speakers of a given language place dual foci in the cool category (1) when they maintain covert coextension and (2) as they begin to attend strongly to distinctiveness; however, these events do not fully address the data. Speakers of some languages place dual foci and speakers of others place single foci, even though all seem to attend to distinctiveness with about the same strength, that is, the languages represent about the same stage of color-category evolution. For example, 20% of Futunese speakers at Stages IIIa and IV focus the cool category in both green and blue (Dougherty 1975; see §2.4.2 and fig. 2.7). Yet the Tenejapa Tzeltal and Seri, who represent Stages II through IV, place only single foci on either green or blue. The Guarijío represent Stages IIIb and IV; 23 of them placed single foci in either green or blue, and 2 placed dual foci. The Guarijío as a rule separately name brown and grey (*sáwčame* and *móčame*), while the Tzeltal do not; but the Seri use many derived color terms (fig. 7.22). The correlation between dual foci and probable emphasis on distinctiveness is seemingly demonstrable in only some cases.[3]

Figure 9.1 shows naming ranges and foci of four Guarijío speakers, who name the cool category *siyó-name* and with other qualifications of *siyó-* (figs. 3.1–3 and 3.9–10). Speaker (*a*) places three foci in a dual pattern (pseudo triple foci), one on green E20 and two on blue-purple, G30 and H34, a dominant-recessive distribution. Speaker (*b*) also places dual foci with this pattern. It appears that speakers (*a*) and (*b*) maintain covert coextension and focus both vantages. Speakers (*c*) and (*d*) centralize a

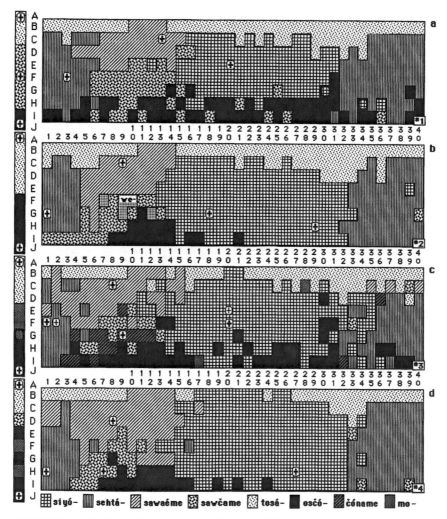

FIGURE 9.1. Guarijío, Alamos, Sonora, Mexico, 1978: naming ranges and foci; (*a*) speaker 1, f 20, (*b*) speaker 2, m 50, (*c*) speaker 3, m 48, (*d*) speaker 4, m 55.

single focus, (c) in green F20 and (d) in blue H27, which together show no pattern.

In figures 9.2–6, thirteen speakers of Tecpan Cakchiquel show strong correlations. Eleven individuals placed dual foci; two placed a single focus, both in green (figs. 8.3–4). Their shared preference for dual foci corresponds throughout the community with a second exceptional tendency to decline to name colors, but the number of colors not named corresponds with the direction of skewing in mappings. Speakers who place dual foci and

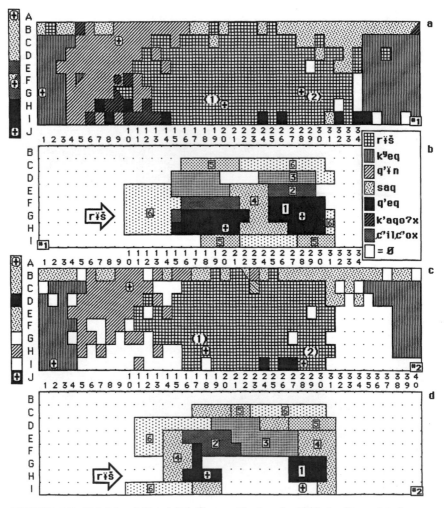

FIGURE 9.2. Cakchiquel, Panajabal, Tecpan, Guatemala, 1980: (a–b) speaker 1, m 32, (c–d) speaker 2, m 20; (a, c) naming ranges, (a–d) foci, and (b, d) mappings.

skew toward blue name the most color chips; those who place dual foci and skew toward green name fewer, and those who place only one focus in green name the fewest. Speakers 1, 2, 4, and 5 (figs. 9.2, 9.3*b–d*) mapped the cool category with skewing toward blue and averaged 33 null responses in naming (= [7 + 84 + 41 + Ø] ÷ 4) out of 330 chips; speakers 3, 6, 7, 8, and 9 (figs. 9.3*a*, 9.4–5) mapped the cool category with skewing toward green and averaged 83 null responses (= [17 + 130 + 136 + 45 + 76] ÷ 5); the 2 speakers of figures 8.3–4, who focused only in green, mapped with

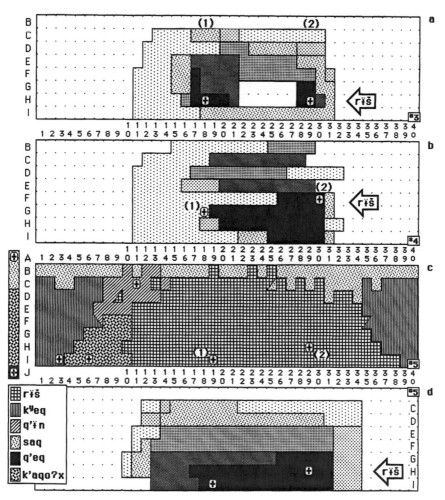

FIGURE 9.3. Cakchiquel, Panajabal, Tecpan, Guatemala, 1980: (*a–b*) speakers 3 and 4, m 50 and m 19, mappings; (*c–d*) speaker 5, f 20, (*c*) naming ranges, (*c–d*) foci, and (*d*) mapping.

skewing toward green and averaged 160 null responses (= [161 + 158] ÷ 2). Speakers 10 and 11 are not counted because they mapped continuously and without skewing.

People offer excessive null responses when they attend strongly to distinctiveness. Words that earlier generations applied broadly to many colors seem inadequate after differences are emphasized, and the new generation will leave some colors unnamed; an interim may elapse before people re-

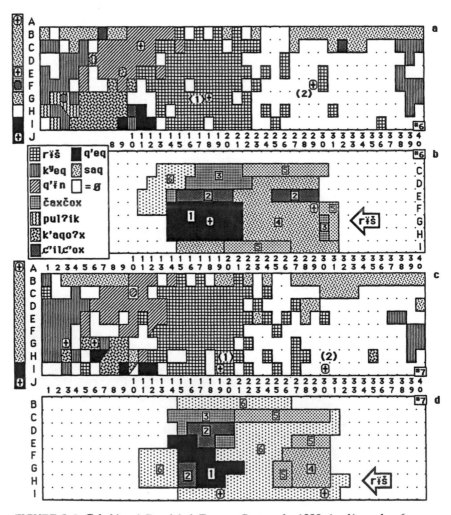

FIGURE 9.4. Cakchiquel, Panajabal, Tecpan, Guatemala, 1980: (*a–b*) speaker 6, f 25, (*c–d*) speaker 7, m 20; (*a, c*) naming ranges, foci, and (*b, d*) mappings.

name them with loanwords or coinages. A shared analytical outlook may have encouraged eleven individuals to focus both of two covert coextensive vantages.[4] Further, skewing toward blue corresponds with the weakest index of attention to distinctiveness, skewing toward green with a stronger index; no evidence of dual vantages accompanies the strongest index of attention to distinctiveness, figures 8.3–4.

These correspondences suggest that transference occurs from skew-

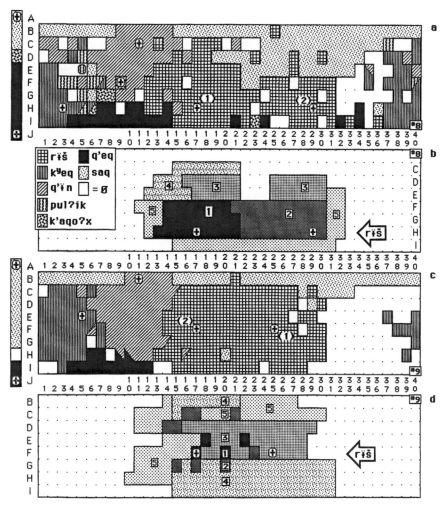

FIGURE 9.5. Cakchiquel, Panajabal, Tecpan, Guatemala, 1980: (*a–b*) speaker 8, m 20, (*c–d*) speaker 9, m 25; (*a, c*) naming ranges, foci, and (*b, d*) mappings.

ing toward blue to skewing toward green as attention to distinctiveness increases. Dual vantages are maintained during the process, while each is
disjunctively focused. Yet the dual foci occur only within a segment of the
complete range of this increasing emphasis on difference. At the strongest
end of the range, the two individuals who attend most to distinctiveness
choose only one focus.

Although speakers 10–11 (fig. 9.6) render continuous mappings,
speaker 11 centralizes his blue focus and names his cool category broadly,

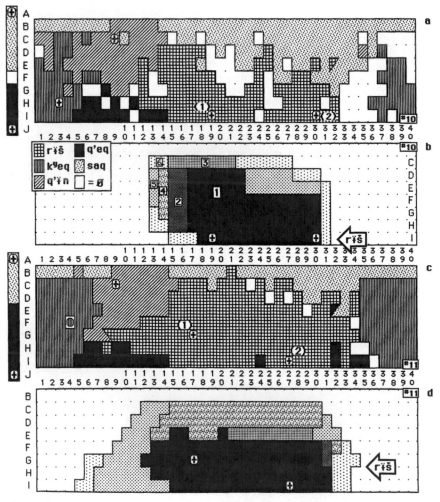

FIGURE 9.6. Cakchiquel, Panajabal, Tecpan, Guatemala, 1980: (*a–b*) speaker 10,
m 31, (*c–d*) speaker 11, m 18; (*a, c*) naming ranges, foci, and (*b, d*) mappings.

while speaker 10 centralizes his green focus and names his cool category sparely.[5]

Figure 9.7 arrays the 11 sets of dual foci. Nine form a dominant-recessive pattern, (*a*) 7 green-central and (*c*) 2 blue-central. Two form no dominant-recessive pattern (*b*). Nine speakers focused green first (speakers 1–2, 4–8, and 10–11), 2 blue first (3 and 9).

In sum, an analytical outlook that occasions substantial null responses corresponds with pervasive dual foci of the cool category. More foci are centralized in green and chosen first in green. Skewing toward green becomes more decisive as indices of attention to distinctiveness increase. The dual foci—and seemingly two covert vantages—are related to a determinate strength of emphasis on difference, although it may be a precondition rather than a definitive motivation for selecting dual foci. Speakers of other languages in a late phase of dividing the cool category focus it only once and name color chips with zero nulls (figs. 8.14 and 11.9).

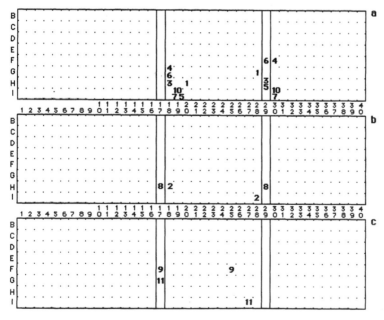

FIGURE 9.7. Dual foci of the cool category selected by 11 speakers of Tecpan Cakchiquel, 1980; numbers key to speaker-numbers of figures 9.3–8, while each pair of identical numbers represents one individual's foci: (*a*) 7 sets of dual foci showing a dominant pattern in green and a recessive pattern in blue, (*b*) 2 sets of dual foci not showing a dominant-recessive pattern, (*c*) 2 sets of dual foci in a dominant-recessive pattern the inverse of *a*.

9.3. Triple Foci

Santa María Tonantzintla and San Pedro Tonantzintla are a main polity and barrio related by exogamous marriage. The urban sprawl of San Andrés Cholula has engulfed them. The elderly individuals who provided the data in figures 9.8–12 had stopped speaking Nahuatl in public during the 1940s and, since their middle years, had become fluent in Spanish. Each

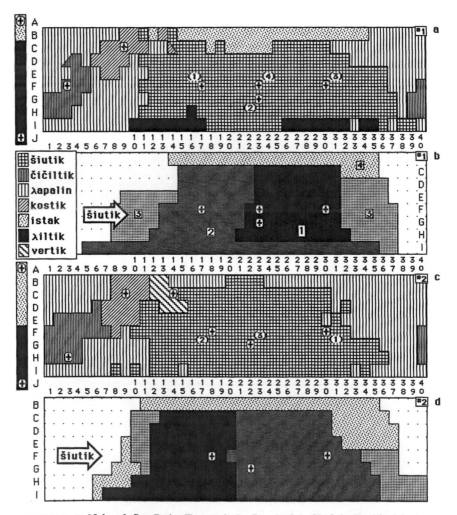

FIGURE 9.8. Nahuatl, San Pedro Tonantzintla, San Andrés Cholula, Puebla, Mexico, 1980: (*a–b*) speaker 1, f 82, (*c–d*) speaker 2, m 84: (*a, c*) naming ranges, foci, and (*b, d*) mappings. *λapalin* 'painted' is a null response.

prolonged the interview to about four hours as he or she recovered the dormant Nahuatl color-naming system. Under these unusual circumstances, each independently volunteered all or part of a distinctive triple-focus pattern for the cool category. On the whole, it appeared that they recalled their cool category while not forgetting their forty years of separately naming green and blue with Spanish *verde* and *azul.* Speakers 2, 3, and 7 focused

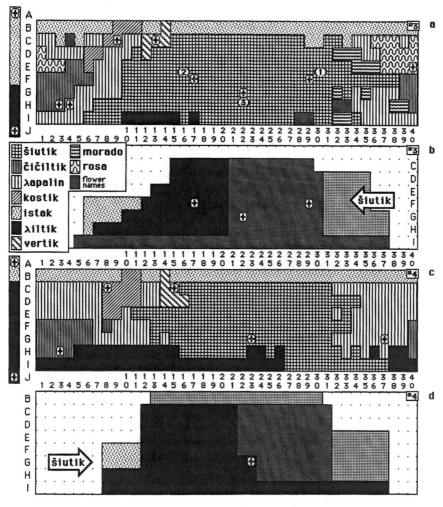

FIGURE 9.9. Nahuatl, San Pedro Tonantzintla, San Andrés Cholula, Puebla, Mexico, 1980: (*a–b*) speaker 3, m 82, (*c–d*) speaker 4, f 66; (*a, c*) naming ranges, foci, and (*b, d*) mappings.

blue first, green second, and turquoise third, figures 9.8*c–d*, 9.9*a–b*, and 9.11*c–d*. On two other trials, speaker 7 manifested fragments of this pattern, figure 9.11*a–b*, as did speakers 4, 5, and 6 on their only attempts, figures 9.9*c–d* and 9.10. Speaker 1 focused green first, turquoise second, and blue third, but then she backtracked and, like speakers 2, 3, and 7, she focused turquoise last, figure 9.8*a–b*.

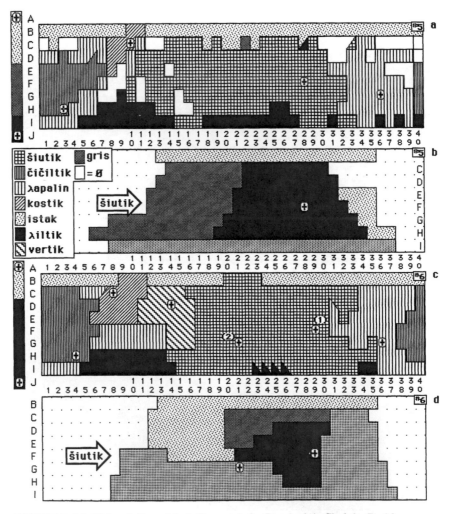

FIGURE 9.10. Nahuatl, Santa María Tonantzintla, San Andrés Cholula, Puebla, Mexico, 1980: (*a–b*) speaker 5, f 70, (*c–d*) speaker 6, m 70; naming ranges (*a, c*), foci, and mappings (*b, d*).

Figure 9.12 aggregates their foci. It appears that either vantage is possible—in reference to green or to blue—as speakers 2, 3, 4, and 7 (figs. 9.8*c–d*, 9.9, and 9.11) favored green with their first mapping step while speakers 1, 5, and 6 (figs. 9.9*a–b* and 9.10) mapped blue first. Probably their triple foci were accompanied by covert coextension, as well as by the perspective afforded by their knowledge of Spanish and, presum-

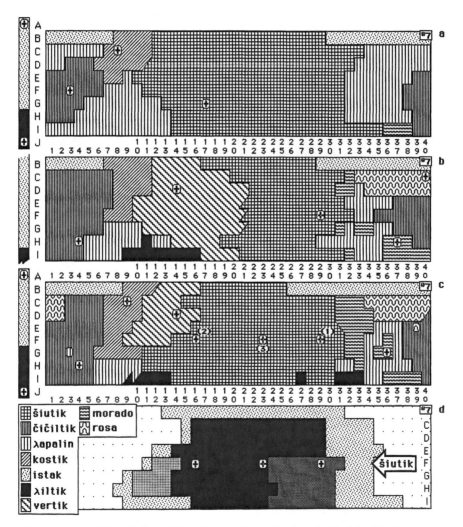

FIGURE 9.11. Nahuatl, Santa María Tonantzintla, San Andrés Cholula, Puebla, Mexico, speaker 7, f 79, 1981: 3 elicitations on different days (*a, b* and *c–d*); (*a–c*) naming ranges, (*a–d*) foci, and (*d*) mapping.

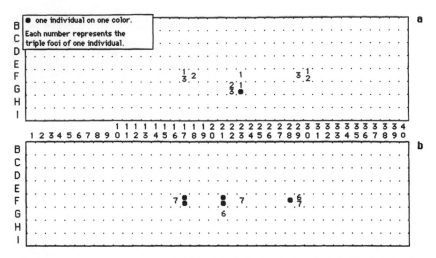

FIGURE 9.12. Focus aggregates, Tonantzintla Nahuatl, San Andrés Cholula, Puebla, Mexico, 1980: (*a*) San Pedro, (*b*) Santa María.

ably, by an analytical outlook they had adopted as urban residents who had undergone tremendous cultural and linguistic change since their younger years.

9.4. Overviews of Viewpoints

Assuming that the Lacandón, Tzeltal, Acatec, Guarijío, Cakchiquel, and Tonantzintla Nahuatl all are focusing one or both of a pair of covert coextensive vantages, the problem is to explain the differences in patterns among single foci and among single, dual, and triple foci.

Differences in placement of single foci in blue, in green, or in either color reflect different phases of transference: (a) not having undertaken it, (b) some individuals having undertaken it but others not, or (c) all individuals either having undergone the process or having always focused in green.

Differences among single, dual, and triple foci probably reflect different strengths to which people attend to distinctiveness. But if this were the only requirement, the three patterns would emerge predictably one after the other in many languages as the cool category divided. Yet, most languages never manifest more than single foci; the dual pattern is rare, and the triple pattern is reported in no other language on earth besides Tonantzintla Nahuatl. The patterns, then, may correspond with different extents to which people attain introspective overviews of how they construct a category. Although attention to distinctiveness seems to be a prerequisite, adopting a vantage on categorization from a degree of removal requires an additional achievement of mind in which only some people participate collectively. I shall attempt to model this process, first in common terms and second with a formal model from vantage theory.

9.4.1. Kinds of Thinking

Fathoming degrees of cognitive detachment is a venerable aim shared by anthropologists (Evans-Pritchard 1937; Goody 1977; Hallpike 1979), cognitive linguists (Langacker 1990a), sociolinguists (Bernstein 1971), developmental psychologists (Bruner, Oliver, and Greenfield 1966; Luria 1976; Price-Williams 1962; Vygotsky 1962), specialists in applied literacy (Gombert 1992; Greenfield 1972; McNaught 1992), ethnomethodologists (Mehan 1990), and historians (LePan 1989), who, respectively, distinguish kinds of thinking as "contextualized-decontextualized," "subjective-objective," "restricted-elaborated," "concrete-abstract," "descriptive-conceptual," "oracular-logical" and "Medieval-modern." To descry whether these oppositions all refer to the same genres of cognition would make a life's work. I draw only from my background in color research, cognitive linguistics, fieldwork with Zapotec, and anecdotal encounters during the Mesoamerican Survey to surmise the kinds of thinking that may be among the necessary conditions for the differences to arise between focus patterns in the cool category. Yet, I suspect this limited task may serve the cross-disciplinary effort, because color categorization can be observed with exceptional control. Further, in the above-cited works and others of their bracket that I have checked, the only formal models that oppose any kind of thinking to another are those proposed by Langacker (1990a) and coworkers (Casad 1982; Vandeloise 1986). This is a deficiency that I hope to offset slightly, invoking Langacker as my departure point. As color is measurable, it is an apt site for the attempt.

Langacker (1990a) finds that "subjectification" accompanies semantic change and grammaticalization, for example, deriving an adverb (e.g., "ahead") from a noun (e.g., "head"). He gauges "subjectivity" in terms of a speaker's nonawareness of viewpoint. But, paradoxically, the awareness increases and subjectivity decreases as viewpoint moves from outside a viewing area likened to a theatrical stage (the "scope of predication") to its spotlighted center along an axis of potential positions. Langacker's claim is paradoxical because he does not mention that the increase in objectivity requires implicitly that a second vantage be maintained on the outside from which to regard the inner viewpoint as "on stage"; otherwise, the increasing attribution of parts of the objective scene to the viewpoint would render meanings more subjective. In brief, a person must simultaneously maintain at least two vantages to command an overview of his or her own thinking, both the position of viewing and an involvement in the thoughts themselves.

Vantage theory posits four echelons of viewpoint that range from egocentricity to omniscience. Each has scalar variants when identified in the real world, although the four are diagnostically disjunctive when defined in ideal terms. They are symbolized as VP-1, VP-2, VP-3, and VP-4. VP-1 is a special deictic viewpoint, confined to the first person, whose location is coterminous with both coordinates. It will not figure in this analysis of color categorization. VP-2 is ideally a deictic viewpoint whose location is coterminous with either the fixed or the mobile coordinate, but VP-2 has a scalar variant in which the viewpoint is merely closer to one coordinate than to the other, or the view is otherwise partial to one coordinate. Such partiality may indeed pertain within color categories, for example, as between the vantage point and the elemental hue that supplies the preferred fixed coordinate. This looser version of VP-2 is used below. VP-3 is a deictic viewpoint whose location is canonically anchored in relation to coordinates but without closer proximity or partiality to either. VP-3 is more remote from its purview than is VP-2. VP-3 has a couple of variants, one of which uses VP-2 as a coordinate; this variant is used below. VP-4 is an omniscient viewpoint whose location in relation to coordinates is unspecified and free to float. It is the most detached or remote of the four kinds. It has a variant whose location is known but situated in a second frame of reference, which makes it substantive but even more remote. I use VP-4 in the latter capacity to analyze native color categories that are reconstituted in accord with the norms of a foreign language.

Countless acts and expressions involve setting up two kinds of vantage points, then conceptualizing from one in reference to the other; for example, the act of driving through a landscape, VP-2, in reference to a road map, VP-3. The four degrees to which a viewpoint can be involved in a vantage correspond to Langacker's subjectivity differential. But vantage theory attributes maximum separation to VP-4 and maximum involvement to VP-1.

Any descriptive statement would represent VP-4, for example, "A dog is in the yard." Although there must be a point of view from which to envision the scene, its location is unspecified or unimportant. *Yesterday, tomorrow,* and *last year* are examples of VP-3 because they are vantages on segments of time removed from the present, but they are constructed from a viewpoint that is anchored in the current moment. In terms of the zooming hierarchy, the definite meaning of "yesterday" is constituted as in figure 9.13.

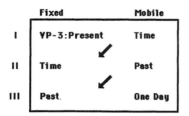

FIGURE 9.13. The definite sense of "yesterday" as an example of an anchored vantage point that stands in equal proximity to all its coordinates (i.e., VP-3).

Herein, (M) will signify a mobile coordinate, (F) a fixed coordinate. The indefinite meaning of "yesterday" is achieved by extending (M) One Day to include an immediate past that is more recent than "last year," (M) X-Days. The meaning of "last year," which only is definite, is produced by replacing (M) One Day with (M) One Year. Indefinite "yesteryear" is created by analogy with indefinite "yesterday" by replacing (M) One Year with any length of more remote time, possibly (M) Historical. VP-3 is coterminous with the first fixed coordinate in the zoom-in process, but not with the coordinates on the lowest level of concentration, such as (F) Past (M) One Day. In contrast, "here" and "now" are examples of VP-2, because the deictic anchor partially composes the lowest level. "Here" consists of only *Level I* (F) VP-2:Present (M) Space. "Now" consists of *Level I* (F) VP-2:Present (M) Time. Finally, vantage theory poses VP-1, the self, by collapsing viewpoint and coordinates into an egocentric singularity that warrants "I," "me," "my," "mine," and "myself." These lexemes distinguish relations of VP-1 to other coordinates of a sentence, as when VP-1 is a figure, a ground, an owner, or a ground that duplicates a figure.

The above examples suggest that the viewer's involvement in a vantage intensifies through the axis of VP-4, VP-3, VP-2 and VP-1. But, in order for the intensification to foster an increase in objectivity, construction of more than one vantage point is essential. So the next example addresses the transfer of viewpoint to multiple points of reference, a problem examined by Vandeloise (1986). Langacker (1990*a:* fig. 3) cites "The rock is in front of the tree." Vantage theory treats this statement as a zoom-in plus a "subroutine," a conventional procedure for dealing with an event.

In figure 9.14, on Level I the speaker establishes the deictic viewpoint of VP-3 in relation to a tree. On Level II, the tree is ascribed an orientation according to a culture-specific subroutine by which an object without an inherent front and back is thought of as facing the vantage point, VP-3; the projected orientation gives the tree a vantage point, VP-2.[6] On Level III, the front of VP-2 is selected from among other possibilities, such as its

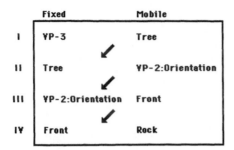

FIGURE 9.14. A vantage (VP-3) that enhances the objectivity of another vantage (VP-2) by incorporating the latter as a coordinate.

back or side. On Level IV, the rock is located in reference to the front of VP-2. Throughout the process the viewer maintains VP-3, which lends to the depiction of VP-2 an objective quality; that is, VP-2 is regarded more objectively than if it were occupied by the viewer, as it is in "now" or "here" or "that's a rock in front of me."

The next and final examples relate degrees of viewpoint to the anthropological distinction of contextualized versus decontextualized thinking. Figure 9.15 represents sentence processing in (*a*) Zapotec and (*b*) educated

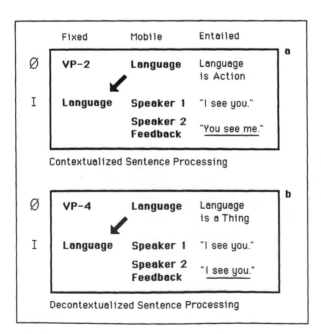

FIGURE 9.15. Different views of language evidenced by feed-back tests, (*a*) deictic and (*b*) detached.

English. During linguistic fieldwork (MacLaury 1970), I quoted sentences in Spanish that I wanted my assistants to feed back to me verbatim in Zapotec. But, for example, when I requested "I see you," they said "You see me," and so forth. I adjusted to my helpers by reversing the pronouns of any such sentence that I wanted them to utter. In *a*, a Zapotec speaker pegs his own view to the appropriate pronouns, VP-2, which submerges both speaker and listener into the flow of ongoing speech. Thus, first- and second-person pronouns refer to those who are present; they will be fed back by any interlocutor with the inverted syntax. In *b*, English speakers may remove their viewpoints from their language, VP-4, which allows them to discuss the language apart from themselves. If requested, one will feed back the other's sentences word for word, including the pronouns.[7] This example underscores the link between kinds of viewpoint and the inclination to adopt an overview of one's own activities. My Zapotec friends did not grasp that the alternative view was possible even after they diligently listened to me explain it.[8]

While with the Zapotec, I saw innumerable examples of contextualized thought. They name *lòptîw* 'upgrade' apart from *bzè* 'downgrade' but have no term meaning "slope." They define words by describing a human relation to the referent rather than its physical properties, for example, "*nīlà²a* is the little animal that swarms before it rains and gets caught in one's hair" or "*dam* is a bad bird; it foretells that someone will die." When greeting any large group of Zapotecs, as when passing on a trail, I learned to very distinctively comment to all in the second person *plural: žan b-dìd-lo̱ ǰe-štì²-lo̱* ("How did y'*all* pass your-*plural* day?"). Early in my visit I had erred by only waving and saying *čaž ba* "hello" (literally, "We go, eh?"), which caused each of a dozen people to expect an individual salutation.

Throughout Mesoamerica I had one eye-opening encounter after another with people who were disinclined to supersede the immediate and the literal. In Guatemala, I was driving over a narrow dirt road, trying to reach Cunén. Each time I stopped to ask the distance to the town, people along the way gave progressively greater distances. No one told me that I had taken a wrong turn at Sacapulas and was headed toward El Quiché. On another dirt road in the mountains of Chiapas, I stopped my car and leaned out the window with the engine running to ask a man how long it would take to reach Palenque, figuring about an hour. The man said "one day," the time it would take him to walk it. In Mexico City, I was interviewing a man of rural origin at the living-room table of an anthropologist colleague. The man's nephew sat idly by. When I noticed that the lad was penning his name into the table top, I said, "Please don't write your name on the table." But while his uncle and I were busy, he engraved "Don Timoteo," my colleague's name. Speakers of various Mayan languages refused to map the Munsell array until I turned it "with white on the bottom." (I had presented it to them with black at bottom as an English speaker would view it and as it is accordingly lettered and numbered.) Then they insisted on mapping white first.

Contextualized, concrete, and particularizing thought is evident in various studies of color naming. Kuschel and Monberg (1974) find that the Bellonese name color with three basic terms while using 26 contexualized terms to specify colors of vegetation, fruit, ripening, roots, soil, body-part invectives, tattooing, weather, healing, bone, shell, coral, hair, and complexion. Many African languages name few basic color categories while naming livestock with dozens of color-pattern terms (see item 6 in note 3 of §3.3). The link between a language and a frame of reference is evident in Magnus's (1880:10) account, interpreted by Berlin and Kay (1969:141): ". . . the Ovaherero are herders and have innumerable color designations . . . of livestock. . . . it should surprise us even more that two such characteristic colors as green and blue are handled in such a stepmotherly manner and that even to have specific terms for these colors is declared silly."

Stepping into a novel frame universally sparks humor (Babcock 1978). A frame may shut out other views so thoroughly that a view confined to one frame can seem self-absorbed when regarded from an exalted vantage. Frame-bound thinking as well as liberation from it are integral to cognitive variability between cultures. Both must figure into any model of color categorization.

9.4.2. In Common Terms

Overviews are enhanced as the observer disengages from frames of reference enough to detect alternative ways to discern a sociophysical scene or a form of thinking. Color categorization involves at least two frames, the color category and the language that sanctions it. If the category is constructed from two vantages, then it offers optional frames that cannot be occupied simultaneously. A third viewpoint outside the category must be available—even if it is only occasionally and momentarily employed—if the options are ever to be acknowledged and alternatively taken.

In ordinary terms, (1) people who focus covert coextension on only one color or another are both inside their category and inside their language; (2) people who choose dual foci are outside their category but still may be inside their language; (3) people who choose triple foci are both outside of their category and outside of their language. Group (1) is maximally

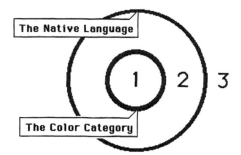

FIGURE 9.16. Disposal of cool-category foci in relation to points of view taken from inside or outside of the category and from inside or outside of the native language: 1 single focus, 2 dual foci, 3 triple foci.

subjective, group (3) is maximally objective, and group (2) is between the maxima. The relation among the three degrees of objectivity is diagrammed in figure 9.16, in which "1, 2, and 3" represent the vantage points of people who place, respectively, single, dual, and triple foci, and the inner and outer circles represent the cool category and the native language, respectively. "Inside the category" means that a person occupies a vantage without immediate awareness of an opposite vantage; the person is enveloped in the one perspective, like following road signs to reach a destination without comprehending one's location in relation to compass points, landmarks, or alternative routes. "Outside the category" means that a person is aware of the complete construction of the category, including the choice between points of view, over and above the vantage point occupied at a given moment; a dual focus communicates the nature of the total structure as though an individual were plotting sites on a map, not just following a road on the ground. "Inside the language" means that a person is unaware that green and blue could be treated in any other way than that which the native language sanctions, as in Magnus's report of the Ovaherero. "Outside the language" means that a person is both (1) aware that another language categorizes green and blue separately and (2) thinks of the cool category from the alien perspective.

Thus, the single focus results from not being able to envision options within a coherent scheme. The dual focus results from treating the whole scheme as the category. The triple focus also results from understanding the category as the scheme, but the scheme is matched against the split categories of green and blue in Spanish; thus, a person recognizes that the conjoining of green and blue itself is an option and marks this special quality with a third focus at the conjunction.

In Tecpan Cakchiquel, most people probably first focus the dominant green vantage without awareness of the abstract scheme but then invoke the overview and focus the blue vantage. They elevate their level of objectivity after placing the first focus and before placing the second. In Tonantzintla Nahuatl, perhaps people construct their erstwhile cool category while using their current familiarity with Spanish as a ground of reference: they first recall the joining of green and blue; they next note salient green; they last note recessive blue; finally they begin to place foci at this deepest point of analysis. Thus, they focus in an order that reverses the sequence by which they analytically constructed the category: first a blue focus, then a green focus, and finally the conjoint focus in turquoise, working backward toward their ultimate reference point in Spanish.[9]

Single, dual, and triple foci require progressively stronger degrees of attention to distinctiveness. Analysis, in general, depends upon differentiation. Separating oneself from a singular vantage point so as to place dual foci requires more analysis than does, say, remaining unaware of the options within a complete scheme. Assessing the cool category from the vantage of another language requires even greater analysis. The data that accompany color categorization in Tzeltal, Tecpan Cakchiquel, and Tonantzintla Nahuatl are consistent with the likelihood that speakers of Tzeltal emphasize distinctiveness least, speakers of Nahuatl emphasize it most, and speakers of Cakchiquel emphasize it to an intermediate extent.

9.4.3. In Formal Terms

The simple three-place model makes headway, although it fails to address why all speakers of some languages, such as Tzeltal and Seri, focus only one or the other of covert coextensive ranges while almost all Tecpan Cakchiquel speakers focus both.

Figure 9.17 depicts models of different valuations of vantage points VP-2, VP-3, and VP-4 that may proffer distinct focus choices. They are (1) <u>VP</u> most likely to be taken, (2) VP *either* an option among two equally probable alternatives that is most likely to be taken one way or the other as opposed to some less-likely third choice *or* the only viewpoint possible, (3) (VP) less likely, and (4) ((VP)) least likely. "Likely" refers to the vantage point that most speakers of a language will assume and, hence, the one that will account for the predominant *pattern* within their focus *aggregate,* to underscore this distinction. In some languages more than in others, speakers will vary in their inclinations (figs. 8.26–27 and 8.34). Variation occurs to the extent that speakers differ in how they rank and relate points of view and, thereby, in the views they usually assume.

The seven models in the figure address seven focus patterns, 1 through 7

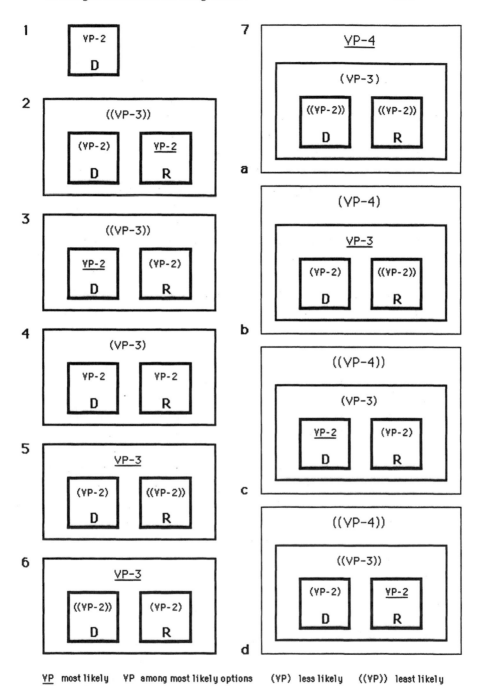

YP̲ most likely   YP among most likely options   (YP) less likely   ((YP)) least likely

FIGURE 9.17. Formal models specifying degrees of overview and subsequent relations among vantages that motivate single, dual, or triple foci and their selection according to particular orders and patterns.

respectively. In the abstract, orders and patterns are: 1. always the same hue, 2. always polarized, 3. always centralized, 4. either one hue or the other but never both and with a dominant-recessive pattern on the aggregate, 5. dual with the most central focus chosen first, 6. dual with the least central focus chosen first, 7. triple with the most polarized focus chosen first, a focus slightly closer to center second, and a focus dead on center third. Concretely in Mesoamerica, a centralized focus is usually green and a polarized focus is usually blue (as are the preferred coordinates of, respectively, dominant and recessive ranges). Examples of the respective patterns are: 1. Chiquimula Quiché (fig. 8.26*b,* also figs. 8.7 and 11.7); 2. Lacandón (fig. 8.27*c,* also fig. 11.9); 3. Acatec (fig. 8.35, also figs. 8.36–38); 4. Tzeltal (fig. 8.34*a,* also figs. 4.2–9); 5. Tecpan Cakchiquel (fig. 9.7, also figs. 9.2–6); 6. Individuals (order of choice not recorded, e.g., Papago, fig. 8.27*a* [depictions of Papago dual-focused systems in MacLaury 1986*a:* fig. 9.13]); and 7. Tonantzintla Nahuatl (fig. 9.12, also figs. 9.8–11).

Each model pertains to all speakers that manifest a respective pattern, not necessarily to all speakers of a particular language. In model 1, speakers construct the cool category always as one and the same vantage and focus it as such, VP-2, either in green or blue, depending on which hue constitutes its preferred fixed coordinate. This vantage, like any that lacks a coextensive counterpart, is automatically dominant, symbolized as **D**. The cool categories of Patzún Cakchiquel (figs. 8.22–23) are of this pattern.

In model 2, speakers construct two vantages but they assume the recessive vantage, *VP-2* **R**, at least during the Munsell interview, as did three among six Lacandón speakers (figs. 8.27*c,* 11.14). Certainly some third-order viewpoint, at least ((VP-3)), is critical to any pair of coextensive vantages, as it would be impossible to invert one set of coordinates, that is, to derive a recessive vantage from a dominant vantage, unless people on occasion distanced themselves from their thoughts sufficiently to recognize options. Yet occupying ((VP-3)) doubtless is wholly unconscious and very transitory, adopted only long enough to recognize a potential for the opposite view.

In model 3, ((VP-3)) serves as unapparently as in model 2. But in model 3, speakers assume the dominant vantage, <u>VP-2</u>, as in Acatec (figs. 8.36–38) and Tantoyuca Huastec (fig. 2.6), and as is commonly practiced throughout Mesoamerica (§8.2.2.4.). Both model 2 and model 3 license the lesser option to adopt (VP-2); perhaps one speaker of both Acatec and Huastec took this course, the lone individuals who focused blue, although each (as well as others) may think in terms of model 4.

Model 4 represents languages, such as Tenejapa Tzeltal or Seri (figs. 8.34*a–b*), in which speakers always choose one focus that is either dominant or recessive, but they are ambivalent about which, and they never choose both. In Tzeltal the odds favor green over blue 3 to 1, whereas in Seri they are even. Indecision may be more likely among individuals who think in terms of model 4 than among those who act according to model 2 or 3. For example, Berlin (MS-1, 1968) interviewed a Tzeltal speaker who first chose blue but then *canceled this choice* to choose green instead. Thus, model 4 represents the options equally as VP-2 and VP-2, while it represents (VP-3) as less likely to be maintained than either of the other two. Although Berlin's consultant adopted this overview, he did not dwell on it long enough to realize that dominant and recessive options could warrant separate foci, a dual choice, and that his cancellation was not compulsory. According to his way of relating and ranking the vantages, occupying **D** required him to quit **R**, while the third alternative of taking an overview was not evident to him. The absence of any dual cool-category foci in Tzeltal after 40 interviews by Berlin in 1968 and 12 by myself in 1980 suggests that few if any speakers abided at the neutral vantage (VP-3) during those years.

In models 5 and 6, speakers are likely to assume VP-3 by placing themselves outside of both **D** and **R**. They maintain this overview. Looking in upon their own constructions from the vantage of an outsider, they remain aware of both options simultaneously and, therefore, they focus green and blue, in turn, by choosing dual foci. In model 5, most speakers regard the dominant vantage as the most likely view, and they focus it before focusing the recessive vantage. Thus, most speakers of Tecpan Cakchiquel focus green before blue because they skew the dominant vantage toward green. The minority who focus blue before green may slant the dominant vantage toward blue. Or, they may represent model 6, in which people place the first of dual foci from the recessive vantage. Although in the Mesoamerican sample individuals might do this, no language represents model 6.[10]

One model can change to another within a language. Model 4 is likely to become model 3 as transference progresses, or model 4 may become model 5 if people become exceptionally analytical while two vantages remain in force. Although Tecpan Cakchiquel speakers are predominantly of model 5 (figs. 9.2–7), two of them represent model 1 (figs. 8.3–4). A language may always represent model 1, as perhaps has Patzún Cakchiquel (figs. 8.22–23), or some of its speakers may evolve model 1 in advance of their peers, as the two in Tecpan Cakchiquel apparently have done.

Model 7 reiterates in formal terms the account of the Tonantzintla

Nahuatl cool category (figs. 9.8–12). In *a,* VP-4, the present vantage, is located in the conceptual realm of Spanish, whose speakers separately categorize green versus blue; this starting point is outside of Nahuatl and outside of the cool category. Here the former speakers recall that, in Nahuatl (VP-3), green ((VP-2)) and blue ((VP-2)) are both named *šiutik.* In *b,* speakers transport themselves to the Nahuatl perspective, VP-3, as much as is possible after forty years of thinking differently. From that position, green (VP-2) appears to be a better example of *šiutik* than does blue ((VP-2)). Green stands out for its strong antagonism to red, as it does throughout Mesoamerica and elsewhere. In *c,* the speakers step inside the category to assume a view from the dominant vantage, green VP-2. They relive the way they used to experience *šiutik.* Blue (VP-2) is the recessive vantage, opposed to the green view and not yet occupied. Finally, in *d,* speakers complete their reconstruction, assuming the recessive vantage of blue, VP-2, while quitting the green angle (VP-2). When they are asked to point to the chip that is "the most *šiutik,*" they reconstitute the category through this process, then begin to back out through their layers of constructed memory toward their present point of orientation ((VP-4)), choosing a focus from the perspective of each layer: first (*d*) blue VP-2, second (*c*) green VP-2, and third (*b*) the union of the two VP-3, before (*a*) re-emerging as Spanish speakers VP-4.

9.5. Distinguishing Closely versus Customarily Taking an Overview

Attention to distinctiveness is only a prerequisite to choosing dual foci, not its determinant. A person must do more than only think analytically before he or she will lastingly regard two covert vantages on the cool category from an overview. Various groups, such as the Acatec (fig. 8.36–38) and Chiquihuitlán Mazatec (fig. 10.12–16), appear to strongly attend to distinctiveness, while no individual among them places dual foci (figs. 8.35 and 10.12). It appears that while they distinguish closely, they do not scan their own thoughts when categorizing green and blue. The Tecpan Cakchiquel share a cognition among themselves that they do not hold in common with the Acatec or the Mazatec (fig. 9.7).

As figure 6.8 shows, the recessive zooming in begins with the ground-figure relation at which the dominant zooming in ends, whereas the attention to similarity at the end of the recessive zooming in occurs within the analytical context of the levels that precede it. In concrete terms, dominant zooming in begins at a preferred level of naive lack of discrimination but ends with extreme analysis, whereas recessive zooming starts at this latter state but continues toward synthesis.[11] The synthesis will put the analyzed fragments back together into an abstraction, a theory, or systemic understanding. Although the recessive synthesis ends by incorporating attention to similarity, this view of the world is not naive, as is that which is adopted on the preferred level within the dominant vantage. The sophisticated, synthetic view may encourage the viewer to distance himself from the subject of observation; as depicted in figure 6.39, polarization of the recessive vantage automatically relegates the viewer to the margin.

Nevertheless, extreme analysis from the dominant vantage need not provoke an individual to adopt a recessive vantage, even though such analysis would be a prerequisite. Likewise, formidable synthesis from the recessive vantage need not induce a viewer to assume a remote perspective, even though this, too, would be a precondition. The sequence of dominant vantage to recessive vantage to remote vantage may model, or at least describe, a sequence of intellectual development. But the question remains as to why some people leap from one stage to the next while others do not, even when both groups have satisfied the requirements.

9.6. Summary

Categorization of cool colors involves single, dual, and triple foci, different orders of selecting them, or other shared preferences, such as focusing either green or blue but never both. Additional modeling is required to contend coherently with such differences. It seems that people construct and use categories at degrees of removal, ranging from submerged to detached points of view. Although both analytical and synthetic outlooks may be prerequisite to categorizing from an overview, speakers of many languages show they acutely differentiate within color categories without displaying any sign of reflective cognition, such as dual foci. Although grades of removed viewpoint may be formally expressed, it is not clear what instigates them. Immersion and disengagement in categorization appear to be coupled with other long-appreciated dichotomies of thought, such as contextualized versus decontextualized, subjective versus objective, concrete versus abstract, literal versus imaginative, or egocentric versus receptive. Color ethnography today comes back to the ground plan of W. H. R. Rivers, pioneer in this field, who urged with small success that such questions become a cornerstone of anthropology.

CHAPTER 10

CROSSOVER

In Mesoamerica, cool categories are of two kinds, each of which behaves and divides in its own way. In previous chapters we have seen only the first kind. People construct this type of cool category by devoting predominant attention to hue. They also keep in mind the balance of strength between attention to similarity and attention to difference. This balance is vital to the coherence and definition of the category and, naturally, has profound influence on its size and shape; yet, people's interest in hue proper has more influence on their treatment of this kind of category than it does on their treatment of the second kind. In the latter, people care more about the balance between attention to similarity and difference than they do about hue. Certainly, they keep hue in mind as well; their awareness of a special link between green and blue gives the category its identity. Yet their interest in the balance of strength between similarity and difference prevails over their discernment of hue enough to have a singular effect: neither green nor blue by itself shapes the category as much as does the manner in which their relation is constructed. In the abstract terms of vantage theory, this means that the name of a dominant vantage signifies mainly an arrangement of coordinates in itself, s^2-D, without assigning priority to either green or blue. Concretely, the effect is "crossover": during one performance (one interview procedure) the vantage will be skewed toward green while during another it will be skewed toward blue. In any category of a single vantage, this sole construction is always dominant, but it will cross over if the category is of the second kind.

If this kind of category is composed of coextensive vantages, both will cross over. If they are separately named, the terms will retain their meanings of "dominant" or "recessive," regardless of whether either happens to be skewed toward green or blue during a particular naming, mapping, or focus selection. "Dominant" (S^2-D) or "recessive" (D^2-S) appears to be their main meaning, while priorities are assigned randomly, or at least loosely, to green or blue. The dominant-recessive pattern is retained even though each vantage is skewed toward opposite hues during different performances.

Thus, cognitive order is maintained even though the surface data appear chaotic, especially to the thinking of an English speaker, who will value specific hue over all else when categorizing color. But in a cool category that fosters crossover, its naming range may pertain to green while its mapping covers only blue and its focus may favor either. The second term, if there is one, may cross over with an opposite design. Different speakers will compound the options, convincing the English speaker once and for all that they are unable to communicate.

The first and second kinds of cool-hue category are distinguished formulaically by (1) the *transference formula* $H + S^2\text{-}D$ and (2) the *crossover formula* $S^2\text{-}D + H$. "H" means hue; the order of symbols (unlike ordinary mathematics) signifies priority of emphases, hue versus the relation between attention to similarity and attention to difference. In other words, the emphasis can favor inherently fixed coordinates or inherently mobile coordinates. The emphases operate over and above those by which attention to similarity and distinctiveness are given reciprocal weightings, or those that arise from positioning similarity and distinctiveness differently in a zooming hierarchy (fig. 6.10).

By naming the formulae after transference and crossover, I underscore that these processes are opposites. While transference moves unidirectionally from blue to green, crossover moves randomly between these hues. A person who stresses hue may transfer a focus after appreciating the cardinal contrast between red and green, while a person who stresses relations within a category will be less so inclined. These preferences do not preclude that the dominant range of a *crossover category* will tend to favor green, just as they do not foreordain that transference will occur under the right conditions. A predominant stress on either hue or relations will not totally govern dynamics; the other important parts of a category can and will be recognized. Yet the predominant stress will influence dynamics more than will any weaker emphasis. The formulae or the categories based on them may also be distinguished as *hue-stressing* versus *relation-stressing*.

To complete this distinction between formulae, stressing must be characterized differently from attending to coordinates. In §9.4.1, a scalar variant of deictic VP-2 is introduced, by which a viewer is "closer to" or partial toward either a fixed or a mobile coordinate. In the present expression, the partiality translates to either $H\,S^2\text{-}D$ or $S^2\text{-}D\,H$. "Stress" is the partiality of VP-2, which is entirely other than the strength of attention placed on S or D. As we shall see, the partiality or stress applies to all the fixed or all the mobile coordinates of a vantage.

10.1. Crossover and Coextension

Crossover among coextensive ranges in the cool category gives them a scrambled appearance. Data from eleven speakers of San Ildefonso Ixtahuacán Mam exemplify the exotic result, figures 10.1–7. Although such systems appear chaotic, they will show pattern throughout if we know what to look for. The description will be followed by an analysis.

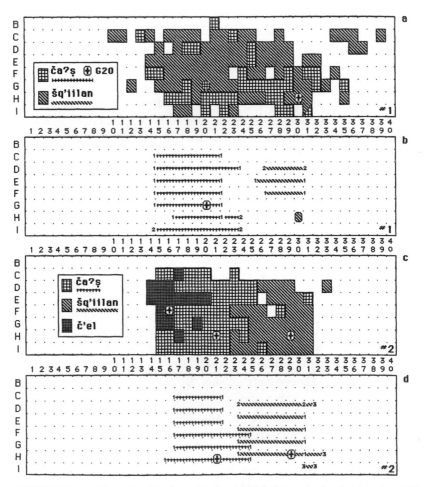

FIGURE 10.1. Mam, San Ildefonso Ixtahuacán, Huehuetenango, Guatemala, 1980: (*a–b*) speaker 1, m 48, (*c–d*) speaker 2, m 40; (*a, c*) naming ranges, foci, and (*b, d*) mappings.

In figure 10.1*a*, speaker 1 demonstrates coextension with intermixed naming ranges. But he maps each range (*b*) on an opposite side of the cool category, exhibiting his tendency to confine them. Speaker 2 (*c–d*) predominantly confines naming ranges and mappings to opposite sides of the cool category, *ča?ṣ* to green and *šq'iilan* to blue. The mappings and foci of speakers 1 and 2 are alike. In *c*, applications of *ča?ṣ* at E31 and F28 are the only evidence that speaker 2 maintains the cool category. It suggests inclusion rather than coextension.

In figure 10.2, speakers 3 and 4 predominantly apply *ča?ṣ* to blue and

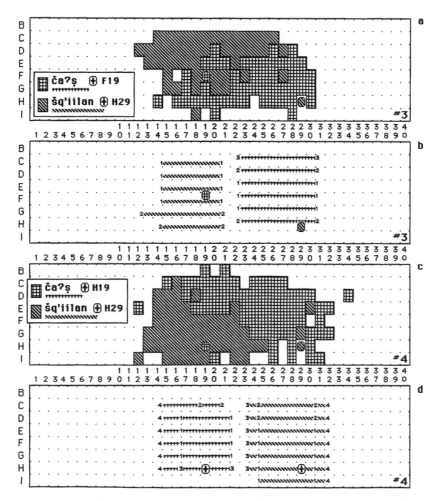

FIGURE 10.2. Mam, San Ildefonso Ixtahuacán, Huehuetenango, Guatemala, 1980: (*a–b*) speaker 3, m 38, (*c–d*) speaker 4, m 48; (*a, c*) naming ranges, (*a–d*) foci, and (*b, d*) mappings.

šq'iilan to green (*a* and *c*), a pattern reversing that of speaker 2. Yet, speakers 1, 2, 3, and 4 focus the terms in almost the same way. Otherwise, speakers 3 and 4 differ. In *a–b,* speaker 3 matches the predominant naming range of each term with its mapping, *šq'iilan* in green and *ča?ṣ* in blue. Mappings and naming ranges mismatch foci. In *c–d,* speaker 4 applies *šq'iilan* to green but maps and focuses the term in blue; he applies *ča?ṣ* to blue but maps and focuses it in green.

In figure 10.3, speakers 5 and 6 further demonstrate coextension. In

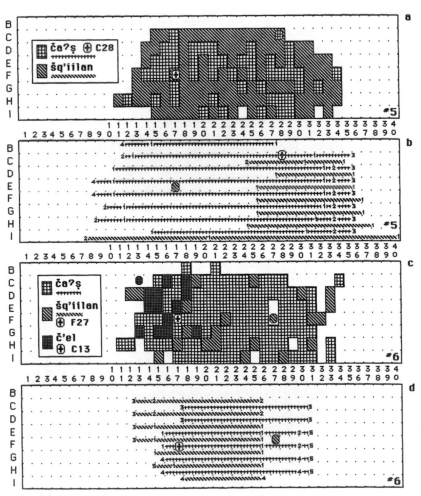

FIGURE 10.3. Mam, San Ildefonso Ixtahuacán, Huehuetenango, Guatemala, 1980: (*a–b*) speaker 5, m 42, (*c–d*) speaker 6, m 35; (*a, c*) naming ranges, foci, and (*b, d*) mappings.

a–b, speaker 5 confines the mapping of *šq'iilan* to blue but focuses the term in green at E17. In *c–d,* speaker 6 confines the mapping of *šq'iilan* to green but focuses the term in blue at F27. Both map *ča?ṣ* throughout green and blue, although speaker 5 marginalizes the focus of *ča?ṣ* in light blue at C28 while speaker 6 focuses *ča?ṣ* on elemental green at F17.

In figure 10.4*a,* speaker 7 applies *č'el* to G30, which minimally shows coextension, but the range of *šq'iilan* falls short. Speaker 8 (*c–d*) shows no evidence of coextension. Their mappings are roughly alike; however,

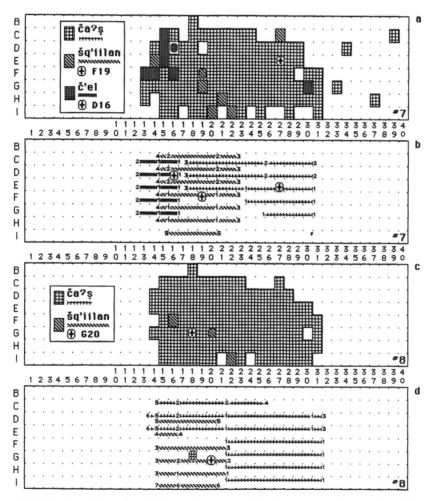

FIGURE 10.4. Mam, San Ildefonso Ixtahuacán, Huehuetenango, Guatemala, 1980: (*a–b*) speaker 7, f 49, (*c–d*) speaker 8, m 26; (*a, c*) naming ranges, (*a–d*) foci, and (*b, d*) mappings.

speaker 7 focuses *ča?ṣ* in blue at E27 and speaker 8 focuses *ča?ṣ* in green at G18. Both map *šq'iilan* on the opposite side of the category as do speakers 2–5, but on the same side as do speakers 1 and 6.

In figure 10.5, speakers 9 and 10 show coextension in naming ranges. Speaker 9 (*a–b*) maps and focuses the terms in a pattern similar to that of speaker 8. Speaker 10 (*c–d*) shows probable triple coextension with uses of *šq'iilan* at only H15 and D28 but of *ča?ṣ* and *č'el* throughout. However, the mapping and focus at D13 of *č'el* are polarized and confined to chartreuse.[1]

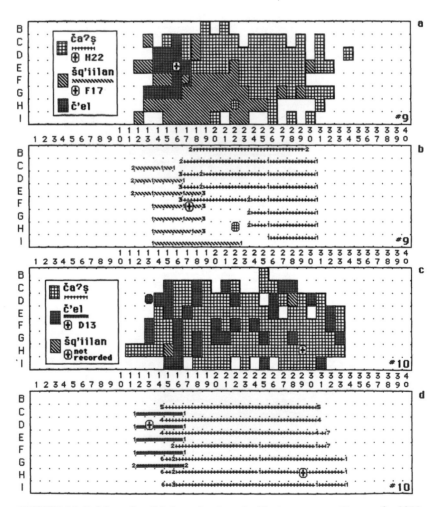

FIGURE 10.5. Mam, San Ildefonso Ixtahuacán, Huehuetenango, Guatemala, 1980: (*a–b*) speaker 9, f 32, (*c–d*) speaker 10, f 29; (*a, c*) naming ranges, (*a–d*) foci, and (*b, d*) mappings.

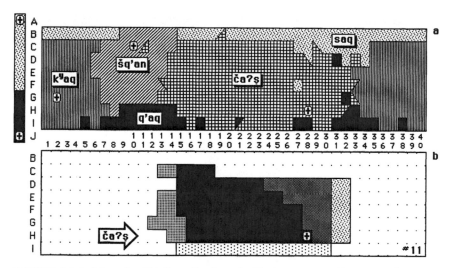

FIGURE 10.6. Mam, San Ildefonso Ixtahuacán, Huehuetenango, Guatemala, f 56, 1980: (*a*) naming ranges, (*a*–*b*) foci, and (*b*) mapping.

Figure 10.6 displays data from the oldest Mam speaker among the eleven interviewed in San Ildefonso Ixtahuacán. Although she names the cool category with only one term, she places her focus on H28 at the bluest edge of her first mapping step, which, in turn, predominantly covers green. She, too, exhibits crossover.

Table 10.1 summarizes as blue (BU), green (GN), or yellow-green (YGN) the entire or main application of each individual usage that pertains to part or all of the cool category in figures 10.1–6. The seemingly random biases toward blue or green throughout the usages indicate that crossover is pervasive. Usages of *ča?ş* favor blue over green by a negligible edge, 16:17; *šq'iilan* favors green over blue by 17:10, an apparent tendency which is, however, insignificant in proportion to this small sample. Because *č'el* is preponderantly centered in yellow-green, it will not be considered again beyond statistically tabulating the two cases of its coextensive application to blue (see note 1).

Table 10.2 quantifies the data on coextensive ranges from figures 10.1–5, itemizing size of naming range, centrality of focus, size of mapping, and average size of mapping steps. Fifty-four quantities show the dominant-recessive pattern while only twelve traverse it. In spite of the speakers' bent to cross over the ranges between procedures of the interview, the pattern is highly significant when compared with chance (54:12 versus 33:33, p.<001 chi square); and, as a further manifestation of stability, *ča?ş* names the dominant range in all seven of the pairs that show the

TABLE 10.1. Evidence of crossover: the sole or main
applications of naming, focus, and mapping
that pertain to the cool category in Mam of
San Ildefonso Ixtahuacán

Figure	Term	Skew of Naming	Focus	Skew of Mapping
10.1a-b	ča'ṣ	BU	GN	GN
10.1c-d	ča'ṣ	GN	GN	GN
10.2a-b	ča'ṣ	BU	GN	BU
10.2c-d	ča'ṣ	BU	GN	GN
10.3a-b	ča'ṣ	GN	BU	BU
10.3c-d	ča'ṣ	BU	GN	BU
10.4a-b	ča'ṣ	GN	BU	BU
10.4c-d	ča'ṣ	GN	GN	BU
10.5a-b	ča'ṣ	BU	GN	BU
10.5c-d	ča'ṣ	BU	BU	BU
10.6c-d	ča'ṣ	GN	BU	GN
10.1a-b	šq'iilan	GN	BU	BU
10.1c-d	šq'iilan	BU	BU	BU
10.2a-b	šq'iilan	GN	BU	GN
10.2c-d	šq'iilan	GN	BU	BU
10.3a-b	šq'iilan	GN	GN	BU
10.3c-d	šq'iilan	GN	BU	GN
10.4a-b	šq'iilan	GN	GN	GN
10.4c-d	šq'iilan	GN	GN	GN
10.5a-b	šq'iilan	GN	GN	GN
10.4a-b	č'el	YGN	YGN	YGN
10.5c-d	č'el	GN	YGN	YGN

Sums: ča'ṣ GN 16, BU 17; šq'iilan GN 17, BU 10
Key: BU blue, GN green, YGN yellow-green

pattern. In sum, *ča'ṣ* always names the dominant point of view, the relation of S^2-D, while it does not consistently single out green or blue as the preferred coordinate. Correspondingly, *šq'iilan* or *č'el* names the recessive view, the relation of D^2-S, while *šq'iilan* does not show a singular preference for green or blue.

The illusion of chaos among these data might stem from our culturally engendered preconception that the range of a color term should pertain in a regular way to a particular hue or set of hues. Nothing in our background

TABLE 10.2. The dominant-recessive pattern of coextension coinciding with crossover

| Figure | Term | Naming | | Mapping | Average | Pattern |
		Size	Focus	Size	Step	
10.1a-b	*ča²ṣ*	36	G20	53	26.5	Dominant
	šq'iilan	82	H30	13	7.5	Recessive
10.2a-b	*ča²ṣ*	48	F19	48	*16.0*	Dominant
	šq'iilan	47	H29	38	*19.0*	Recessive
10.2c-d	*ča²ṣ*	65	H19	*41*	10.25	Balanced
	šq'iilan	51	H29	*55*	13.75	Balanced
10.3a-b	*ča²ṣ*	47	G28	196	49.0	Dominant
	šq'iilan	90	F17	96	31.0	Recessive
10.3c-d	*ča²ṣ*	80	*F17*	86	17.2	Dominant
	šq'iilan	21	*F27*	82	16.4	Recessive
10.4a-b	*ča²ṣ*	83	E27	51	17.0	Dominant
	č'el	7	D16	20	10.0	Recessive
10.5a-b	*ča²ṣ*	61	H22	75	25.0	Dominant
	šq'iilan	44	F17	40	13.33	Recessive
10.5c-d	*ča²ṣ*	88	H29	122	17.43	Dominant
	č'el	35	D13	25	12.5	Recessive

Key: Italicized data pairs traverse the pattern of *ča²ṣ* naming the dominant range.

helps us to realize that stressing relations constitutes an option. As it turns out, this option attains an equal or even tighter regularity than does the means of organization that most languages adopt.

Figure 10.7 reviews the consequence of such stress on relations for a model of categorization. (This figure and other graphics will be called "diagrams" to avoid confusion with "figure-ground.") Here, as in diagrams 6.7–8 and 6.10–11, coordinates are arranged in a hierarchy of figure-to-ground relations. But here the stress is overtly represented, whereas in the other models stress is left implicit, even though it is as important there as here. In the earlier diagrams, as in this one, stress falls on the column of coordinates at the left. However, within each vantage of the models presented in Chapter 6, the stressed coordinates comprise two hues but only one emphasis on either similarity or difference; all of them are grounds and none are figures. In contrast, each vantage in the model displayed by diagram 10.7 stresses both the emphasis on similarity and the emphasis on difference but stresses only one of the two hues; all the stressed coordinates are figures and none are grounds. Thus, in the former model the van-

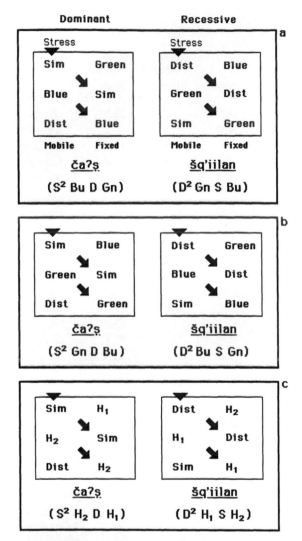

FIGURE 10.7. Formal models representing coextension in a cool category that stresses the relations between hues: (*a*) etic model with the dominant range focused in blue; (*b*) etic model with the dominant range focused in green; (*c*) emic model with ranges unrelated to specific hues.

tages stress the grounds and mainly the hues, while in the latter model the vantages stress the figures and mainly the relations. The inversion of stress from grounds to figures requires the proviso of turning the transformational arrows to point rightward in diagram 10.7, but this is merely mechanical. The order of zooming is identical in both the hue-stressing model and the relation-stressing model. They differ essentially by placement of stress.

Stress placement has consequences for the hue-stressing and relation-stressing models alike, in particular, for the formulae that differentiate the consequent kinds of categories. In models that stress hue, as in diagrams 6.7–8 and 6.10–11, the order of stressing coincides with the order in which ground-figure relations are arranged through the hierarchy. For example, in the dominant vantage of a composite color category, the order follows, first, the primary fixed coordinate—that is, hue H_1—then attention to similarity S^2, then the second hue H_2, and finally attention to difference D, combining in the formula $H_1 S^2 H_2 D$. In the recessive vantage, the formula is reversed as $H_2 D^2 H_1 S$. By contrast, as diagram 10.7 shows for the dominant vantage of a relation-stressing category, the stress bypasses the primary fixed coordinate. Thus, H_1 receives the weakest stress and commensurately assumes the final position in the formula: $S^2 H_2 D H_1$. The recessive vantage is likewise modeled with its primary fixed coordinate at the end, $D^2 H_1 S H_2$. When hue is stressed, the the order of zooming and the order of stressing are isomorphic, but when relations are stressed the orders are distinct.[2]

This formal difference between models, in turn, addresses three characteristic differences between cool categories that undergo transference and those that cross over. First, in the former kind, green is naturally favored because it provides the cardinal opposition with red and, therefore, is often the primary fixed coordinate. But in a crossover category, the favoritism and the dual role of green are at odds. To the extent that green is promoted to the position of H_1, it will be bypassed by the stress on figures. Thus, blue in the position of H_2 will be favored in relation-stressing categories more than in hue-stressing categories; in the former, the dominant vantage may even be focused more in blue than in green.

Three sources of data bear on this first consequence of the crossover formula. Table 10.1 shows that dominant *čaʔṣ* definitely does not favor green and negligibly favors blue; *šqʼiilan* favors green, but not enormously. Figure 10.8 displays green-to-blue ratios of foci from figures 10.1–6: dominant *čaʔṣ* 7:4; recessive *šqʼiilan* 4:4. Green is more frequently focused than blue, although blue is often chosen. Table 10.3 displays an independent datum on the meaning of *šqʼiilan* in San Ildefonso Ixtahuacán Mam, which appears in line 7 of a list originally compiled by Kaufman (1970) in a comparative sketch of 29 Mayan languages (Proto-Mayan and Yucatec were added by England [1992: 153]). The list is unusual because it itemizes words that name a contrived gloss, specifically "green," rather

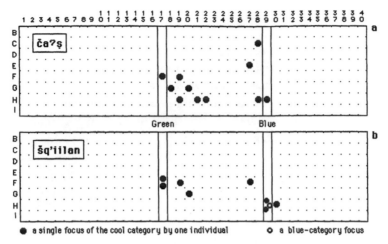

FIGURE 10.8. Mam, San Ildefonso Ixtahuacan, Huehuetenango, Guatemala; focus aggregate for two terms with which speakers name the cool category: (*a*) focus of *ča?ṣ* from eleven speakers; (*b*) foci of *šq'iilan* from nine of the eleven with one range confined to blue.

than their natural meanings, such as "green, blue." Words that name blue are not considered as such in Kaufman's comparison, whether they are the same or different than those on the list. Of interest is that *šq'iilan* is the only noncognate among the thirty words meaning "green," that is, the only term failing to reflect the Proto-Mayan form; the proper Mam cognate *ča?ṣ* was rejected as the better name for "green." Probably the entry of *šq'iilan* was contributed by just one or only a few Mam-speaking linguistic technicians who represented San Ildefonso Ixtahuacán on the project that compiled Kaufman's data (Proyecto Lingüístico "Francisco Marroquín"). Whatever intuitions lead to the entry, it agrees with the tendency shown in table 10.1 and may presage the future of color naming in San Ildefonso if its cool category divides.

Second, among Mesoamerican cool categories, stressing hue is far more common than stressing relations. Perhaps this is because it is easier to stress coordinates in the order of their hierarchical arrangement, as H_1 $S^2 H_2 D$ rather than as $S^2 H_2 D H_1$. Bypassing stress on the primary fixed coordinate (H_1) might be the most complicated alternative. Kaufman's list is additionally valuable for independently suggesting how rare crossover is among the cool categories of Mayan languages, because seemingly the 29 Mayan cognates name a hue-stressing category that favors green. (In fact, 25 of the listed communities were visited by the MCS and confirmed to name the cool category or its green remnant and to decidedly stress hue.)

TABLE 10.3. Naming of green in Mayan languages*

The Proto-Mayan form (unglossed):	*ra²š

Contemporary terms that name green,
regardless of how blue is named:

1. Chuj (San Mateo Ixtatán)	ya²aš
2. Kanjobal (Santa Eulalia)	yaš
3. Acatec (San Miguel Acatán)	yaaš
4. Jacaltec (Jacaltenango)	yaš
5. Teco (Tectitlán)	ča²ṣ
6. Mam (Ostuncalco)	ča²ṣ
7. Mam (San Ildefonso Ixtahuacán)	šq'iilan
8. Aquacatec (Aguacataán)	ča²ṣ
9. Ixil (Chajul)	ča²ṣ
10. Uspantec (Uspantán Centro)	raš
11. Quiché (Santa Catarina Ixtahuacán)	raš
12. Quiché (Totonicapán)	raš
13. Quiché (Momostenango)	raš
14. Quiché (Santa María Chiquimula)	raš
15. Rabinal Achí (Rabinal)	raš
16. Sipacapeño (Sipacapa)	raš
17. Sacapultec (Sacapulas Centro)	raš
18. Tzutujil (San Juan La Laguna)	res
19. Tzutujil (Santiago Atitlán)	raš
20. Cakchiquel (San Andrés Itzapa)	riš
21. Cakchiquel (Patzún)	riš
22. Cakchiquel (Tecpán)	riš
23. Cakchiquel (San Martín Jilotepeque)	riš
24. Pocomam (San Luís Jilotepeque)	raš
25. Pocomchí (San Cristóbal Verapaz)	reš
26. K'ekchí (San Juan Chamelco)	raš
27. K'ekchí (Cahabón)	raaš
28. Mopán (San Luís Petén)	ya²aš
29. Yucatec (Place unspecified)	ya²š
30. Chortí (Jocotán)	yašyaš

*From Kaufman (1970:69–149), supplemented by England
(1992:153).

Yet we shall see that crossing over of the cool category occurs throughout
certain diffusion areas. Crossover may, however, represent marked cognition, whereas hue-stressing will always occur in default when the rarer

thinking is not pursued. Thus, widespread crossover may result from diffusion while recurrent hue stressing may only suggest that nothing of consequence has diffused in regard to the cool category.

Third, stressing of relations will foster fluid interchange of H_1 and H_2 by minimizing the importance of their distinct identities. While H_1 and H_2 would always symbolize distinct hues in a hue-stressing formula, in a relation-stressing formula the symbols will only mean that two hues participate and that they will be the same two on different days. The implication is important: symbols do not carry immutable etic values but rather acquire emic values from their place in a system (§6.4.10); they assume different meanings in different formulae. Thus, in diagram 10.7, a and b are etic representations while c is emic: a and b distinguish opposite angles of skewing for *ča$^{\gamma}$ṣ* and *šq'iilan* while c suggests that H_1 and H_2 represent green and blue in either order and that both hues will partake in each of two relations. Presumably, a and b represent how an analyst would dissect recorded observations of the Mam cool category while c shows how a Mam-speaker would view it. In c, the opposite arrangements in which H_1 is the dominant primary coordinate and H_2 is the recessive primary coordinate might imply that H_1 and H_2 must constitute different hues, but this expectation is etic. To the native, dominant H_1 and recessive H_2 could be the same hue, as is indicated in figure 10.4c–d where both foci are green; or they could as well be different hues, as is found among other systems throughout figures 10.1–5. Emically, H_1 and H_2 differentiate hues only within one vantage, not between two vantages, providing the relation-stressing formula obtains.

The effect of formulaic context on the symbolic value of H_1 or H_2 is highlighted by comparing the dominant-recessive patterns of focus distribution between figures 8.34a–b and 10.8. The former figure shows a focus pattern in cool categories that stress hue; the hues are differentiated such that foci are centralized to the inside of unique green but polarized to the outside of unique blue. The latter figure shows a focus pattern in cool categories that stress relations; the dominant range is focused nine times between unique hues and twice on them, 9:2, whereas the recessive range is focused three times between and five times on or outside, 3:5 (the two outside foci of *č'el* are excluded). Neither the centralization nor the polarization occurs in reference to a particular hue.

In figure 10.6, the data of elder speaker 11 show crossover but not coextension. It seems that speakers of San Ildefonso Ixtahuacán Mam have stressed relations over hue in the cool category at least as long as they have named it coextensively.[3]

10.2. Crossover and Inclusion

A cool category that crosses over can encompass one or two secondary ranges. When there is only one superordinate and one subordinate range, both cross over; but—at least in the present data—when there are two subordinate ranges, one always pertains to green and the other always to blue, that is, both stress hue and hold to an externally ascertainable meaning, while only the superordinate range crosses over, apparently because it stresses relations. The differences call for further modeling.

We shall begin with the kind of inclusion in which both ranges cross over, "crossover inclusion." We have already seen three questionable examples in San Ildefonso Ixtahuacán Mam. In figure 10.1c, *čaʔṣ* includes *šqʼiilan* but without evidence of crossover, although hue stressing would be exceptional in this language. As figure 10.4a shows probable coextension between dominant *čaʔṣ* and recessive *čʼel, šqʼiilan* would be subordinate to *čʼel*, if *šqʼiilan* itself doe not name an unattested coextensive range. Figure 10.4c–d shows the strongest evidence from San Ildefonso of crossover inclusion between *čaʔṣ* and *šqʼiilan*, which both are focused in green.

Figure 10.7c almost provides the formal model of crossover inclusion, except that in inclusion attention to difference must be stronger than attention to similarity, $(s^2 H_2 D H_1)(D^2 H_1 s \{H_2\})$. Even if $\{H_2\}$ were dropped from the recessive coordinate system, the interchangeable identities of H_1 and H_2 would allow the remaining hue, H_1, to be either green or blue. The weak identity of hues in a crossover formula has been addressed (§10.1).

Figure 10.9 displays two examples of crossover inclusion in Chiquihuitlán Mazatec. Superordinate *suʼsæʼ* descends from Proto-Mazatec (Kirk 1966:set 444) while subordinate *suʼsæʼ* derives from *suʼsæʼ* by change of tone. In both examples, *suʼsæʼ* is focused in blue and *suʼsæʼ* in green, but *suʼsæʼ* names green in *a* and blue in *b*. Although *suʼsæʼ* does not cross over in these examples, it is focused in green or blue in figures 10.12–16. Of the 25 data sets from Chiquihuitlán, 5 show a cool category named only with *suʼsæʼ*, 18 show *suʼsæʼ* superordinate to hue-stressing *verde* and *asul*, while *suʼsæʼ* appears only in the two systems shown here; its only affirmed usage is as a crossover hyponym.

The two Mazatec cases and the putative examples from Mam are the sole instances of crossover inclusion in the Mesoamerican sample. Why is the type rare? Probably, as attention to distinctiveness becomes strong enough to transform coextension to inclusion, the stress on relations changes to stress on hue in specifically the subordinate range, D^2-S; here the reinforced emphasis on difference would encourage cognitive separa-

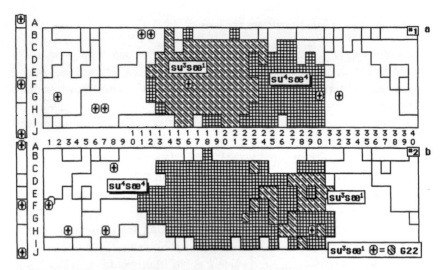

FIGURE 10.9. Mazatec, Chiquihuitlán de Benito Juárez, Cuicatlán, Oaxaca, Mexico: naming ranges and foci, 1977: (*a*) speaker 1, f 34, (*b*) speaker 2, m 40.

tion of hues. In Mazatec, the subordinate hue-stressing ranges are always named with the loanwords and never with *su³sæ¹*. Distinct terms name the dissimilar kinds of vantage (as elsewhere dominant and recessive vantages of the same kind are named differently).

When a subordinate term names part of a cool category that stresses hue, the term always names the hue opposite the cool-category focus. But this unfailing regularity is radically transgressed by the pattern seen in figure 10.9*b*, which underscores the extent to which hue-stressing and relation-stressing effect categorization differently.

Matlatzinca and Chiquihuitlán Mazatec cross over the range of the cool category and name it with a native term, while they name green and blue separately with Spanish loanwords whose ranges do not cross over. Languages that stress hue in the cool category, such as those analyzed in Chapter 8, separately name only one of the hues with a subordinate term, exclusively blue in almost all Mesoamerican cases; they never name both hues separately.[4] Because a crossover cool range is not constructed in reference to a particular hue as a primary fixed coordinate, it does not preclude secondary naming of one hue or the other but rather accommodates the discrete naming of both. This provides another demonstration of how hue-stressing and relation-stressing effect categorization differently.[5]

In figure 10.10*a–b*, Matlatzinca speakers 1 and 2 name and focus the cool colors. In *c–d*, speaker 2 maps *ʔin-čoyə* 'cool', *ʔasúl* 'blue', and *verde*

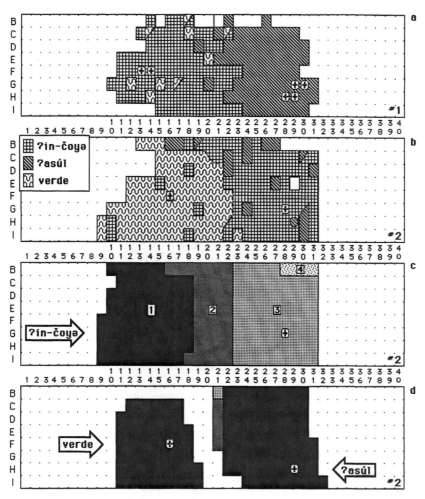

FIGURE 10.10. Matlatzinca, San Francisco Oxtotilpan, Mexico, Mexico, 1979: (*a–b*) naming ranges, foci, and (*c–d*) mapping; (*a*) speaker 1, m 35, (*b–d*) speaker 2, f 48.

'green'. Roberto Escalante and I interviewed speaker 2 for only naming ranges and foci, but nine months later we elicited her mappings. We did not obtain mappings from speaker 1. He applies *ʔin-čoyə* only to green and *ʔasúl* to blue; he sparely names green *verde*. Speaker 2 predominantly applies *ʔin-čoyə* to blue, minimally to green. She mainly names green *verde,* and sparely names blue *ʔasúl,* the opposite of speaker 1. Yet she patterns her mappings in reverse of her naming ranges and cool focus, as she maps the cool category with a first step in green and a last step in blue; commensurately, her mapping of *ʔasúl,* 'blue', covers more colors than her mapping of *verde,* 'green'. Her data of different dates show crossover, but only the data regarding *ʔin-čoyə. Verde* and *ʔasúl,* respectively, retain stable reference to green and blue between the two interviews. To offer an interpretation, *ʔin-čoyə* names a stress on relations and thereby crosses over, whereas *verde* and *ʔasúl* name a stress on hue and thereby do not cross over. The theoretical problem, then, is to combine a relation-stressing formula and a hue-stressing formula in a model that links two frames.

Figure 10.11 introduces this model in two parts, (*a*) etic and (*b*) emic. Part *a* pertains strictly to the naming and foci in figure 10.10*b,* ignoring the

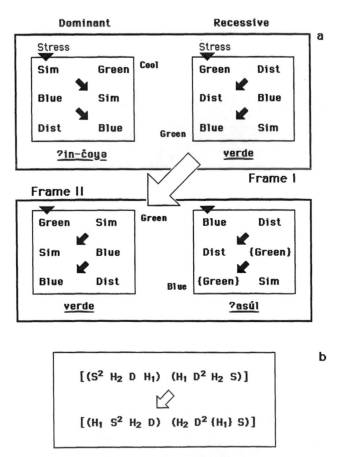

FIGURE 10.11. Formal models representing a color category of which the dominant vantage stresses relations between hues while recessive and ultra-recessive vantages each stress an opposite hue: (*a*) etic model with the superordinate range focused in blue; (*b*) emic model not specifying a superordinate focus in terms of a particular hue.

mappings for the moment. Throughout the model, all dark transformational arrows point toward the fixed coordinates; "fixed" and "mobile" are distinguished only in that way. In Frame I, in the vantage named $?in$-$čoyə$, green is the primary fixed coordinate but the stress on relations (throughout the column of mobile coordinates) incidentally favors blue, which entails that $?in$-$čoyə$ will mainly name blue during the interview, as it does in figure 10.10b. In Frame I, in the vantage named $verde$, the complete set of coordinates is retained (as is addressed in §7.1.5), even though $verde$ does not name blue in figure 10.10b. Herein, green is also the primary fixed coordinate but the stress is on hue (throughout the column of fixed coordinates). The two vantages differ by an inversion of mobile coordinates from S^2-D to D^2-S and by a shift in stress from mobile to fixed coordinates, that is, from relations to hues (which may be envisioned as, respectively, "vertical" versus "horizontal" movements in terms of the way the diagram is oriented). The latter "horizontal" shift in stress is different from a "vertical" inversion of hue coordinates of the kind distinguishing dominant and recessive vantages that both stress hue (fig. 6.9), but, when this shift is combined with the "vertical" inversion of mobile coordinates, the total result is identical to that which would pertain among any pair of hue-stressing vantages: a dominant formula completely and symmetrically inverts to a recessive formula. This result is shown on the top line of figure 10.11b, wherein dominant relation-stressing $S^2 H_2 D H_1$ inverts to recessive hue-stressing $H_1 D^2 H_2 S$. This top line is the emic representation of Frame I. It ostensibly represents the thinking of the Matlatzinca speaker who inverts the vantages. She senses no contradiction in viewing the same two hues in terms of their relations versus their separate identities, as long as she can consistently and thoroughly achieve the inversion.

In Frame II of figure 10.11a, the vantage of $verde$ becomes dominant via the process demonstrated for chain relations (fig. 6.28–29); $?asúl$, then, is ultra-recessive in accord with the inversion that is standard between hue-stressing vantages, $(H_1 S^2 H_2 D) (H_2 D^2 \{H_1\} S)$, as is represented on the second line of figure 10.11b. In this ultra-recessive vantage, the second coordinate, etic {green} or emic {H_1}, is optional, because here extra strong attention to distinctiveness may shrink the category range to the point at which H_1 is dropped from the coordinate system, and a coordinate of darkness may replace H_1 (as is modeled in fig. 6.29). In figure 10.10b, the focus of $?asúl$ is dark.

Figure 10.11b emically accommodates the native view of the two possibilities for crossing over $?in$-$čoyə$. These are not recognized as such by Matlatzinca speakers because, in a crossover formula, H_1 and H_2 only represent different hues without pegging each to its own separate identity (as was discussed in §10.1). Thus, the one formula depicts both the naming of *ʔin-čoyə* in figure 10.10*b* and its mapping in *c;* there is no need to present a second etic depiction that systematically mirrors figure 10.11*a* by reversing the order of all the hue coordinates. (The reversal that is evident between figure 10.10*b* and *c–d* would be etically diagrammed in Frame I with *ʔin-čoyə* of *c–d* having green as H_2 and blue as H_1 and, therefore,

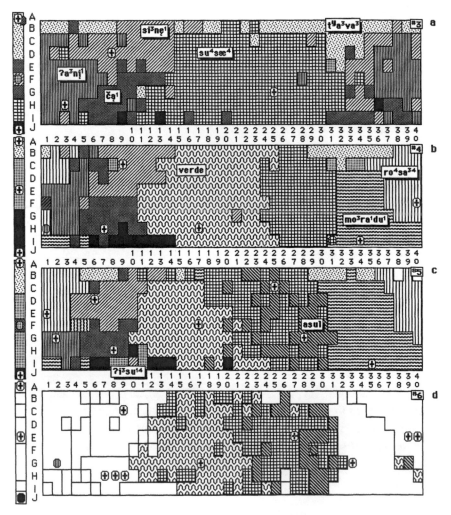

FIGURE 10.12. Mazatec, Chiquihuitlán de Benito Juárez, Cuicatlán, Oaxaca, Mexico, naming ranges and foci, 1977: (*a*) speaker 3, m 20, (*b*) speaker 4, m 49, (*c*) speaker 5, f 29, (*d*) speaker 6, f 35.

with ʔasúl naming the recessive vantage while having H₁ as blue, and in
Frame II with ʔasúl dominant and *verde* ultra-recessive.) The emic model
projects that the two possibilities are unconscious to the native even though
they appear conspicuously in figure 10.10 and are blatant to the analyst.

Figures 10.12–15 show Mazatec systems in which two secondary
terms replace the original cool term; the latter may be skewed toward either
green or blue. Chiquihuitlán yields conservative systems among elders
(fig. 6.36), hinting that its variable complexes emerged with the recent
generation.

Figure 10.12 shows four Mazatec cool categories skewed toward blue,
all named *su⁴sæ⁴*. Speaker 3 uses only the "cool" term, *su⁴sæ⁴*. Speaker 4
names green *verde* and blue *su⁴sæ⁴*. Speakers 5 and 6 name green *verde*
and blue *asul* but *verde* is more salient. Figure 10.13 shows three cool categories skewed toward green, again named *su⁴sæ⁴*. Speaker 7 uses only

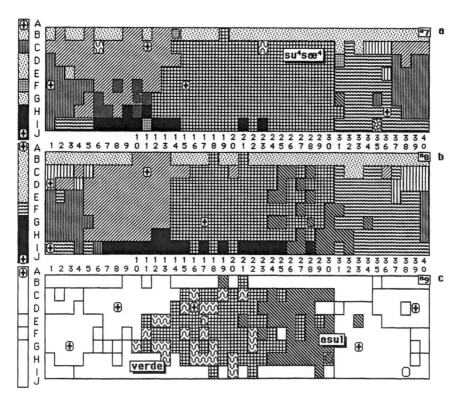

FIGURE 10.13. Mazatec, Chiquihuitlán de Benito Juárez, Cuicatlán, Oaxaca,
Mexico, naming ranges and foci, 1977: (*a*) speaker 7, m 61, (*b*) speaker 8, m 40,
(*c*) speaker 9, m 28.

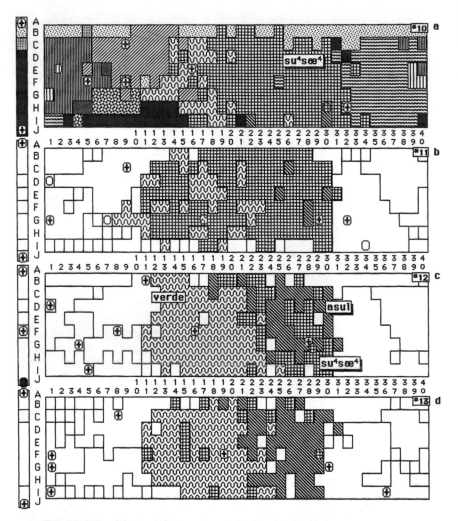

FIGURE 10.14. Mazatec, Chiquihuitlán de Benito Juárez, Cuicatlán, Oaxaca, Mexico, naming ranges and foci, 1977: (*a*) speaker 10, m 35, (*b*) speaker 11, f 50, (*c*) speaker 12, f 38, (*d*) speaker 13, f 35.

su⁴sæ⁴. Speakers 8 names blue with secondary *asul;* speaker 9 uses *asul* with greater salience than *verde*. Figures 10.14–15 show increments by which *verde* and *asul* gain salience to replace completely original *su⁴sæ⁴*. Speakers 10–14 focus *su⁴sæ⁴* in blue, speaker 15 applies it once at D10, and speaker 16 names green and blue only with *verde* and *asul*.

Figure 10.16 shows the focus aggregate for *su⁴sæ⁴* of the 15 Mazatec who apply this term to both green and blue. Only 4 of the foci are central,

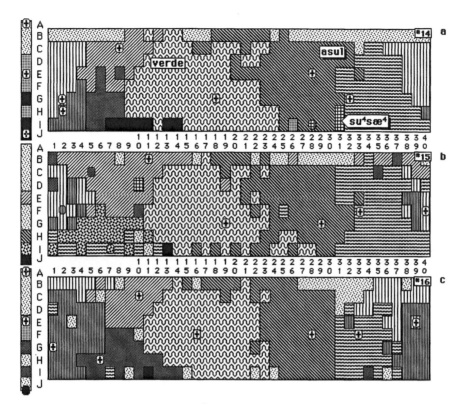

FIGURE 10.15. Mazatec, Chiquihuitlán de Benito Juárez, Cuicatlán, Oaxaca, Mexico, naming ranges and foci, 1977: (*a*) speaker 14, f 22, (*b*) speaker 15, m 39, (*c*) speaker 16, m 38.

5 are on a unique hue, and 6 are polar, which suggests strong emphasis on distinctiveness. In spite of this, none of the 15 chose dual foci.

In figure 10.17, a Zapotec speaker (*a*) names and focuses *ngya* 'cool', *verde* 'green', and *asul* 'blue', and he (*b*) maps *ngya*. Mappings of *verde*

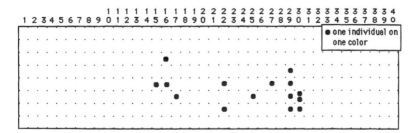

FIGURE 10.16. Mazatec, Chiquihuitlán de Benito Juárez, Cuicatlán, Oaxaca, Mexico: foci of the cool category *su⁴sæ⁴* selected by 15 speakers, 1977.

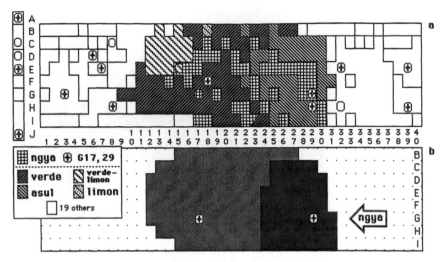

FIGURE 10.17. Zapotec, San Juan Mixtepec, Mihuatlán, Oaxaca, Mexico, m 26, 1979: (*a*) naming ranges, foci and (*b*) mapping.

and *asul* were not elicited; these terms name secondary ranges more saliently than *ngya* names the inclusive range. The latter is dual-focused on G17 and G29, named 19 times on the green side and 16 times on the blue side of column 23, but mapped with the first step covering blue and the second step green. One other Zapotec in San Juan Mixtepec focused *ngya* in blue and 5 others focused it in green; they showed no dominant-recessive pattern among the foci (unlike Acatec, fig. 8.35) but exhibited little positive evidence of crossover in other data. In the present system, there are a few suggestions that *ngya* crosses over: (1) the mismatch of its predominant naming in green and first mapping step in blue, (2) two secondary hue names, one green and the other blue. These traits resemble those among most of the Chiquihuitlán Mazatec systems (figs. 10.12–15). But, in theory, a single crossover cool range will never be dual-focused because it always must be composed as a single vantage, never as two covert vantages; the latter may pertain only to a range in which hue is stressed (figs. 8.34*a–b*). So what sort of system is this?

Possibly, the Zapotec-speaker stressed relations as he named and mapped *ngya* (S^2-D H) but stressed hue when he focused (H S^2-D); when he named and mapped, he adopted an engaged perspective, VP-2, in which he was partial to relations, but, when he focused, he adopted a detached perspective, VP-3. Either this made him partial toward hue or lead him to take a neutral stance toward all dynamics in his category. Or he may have maintained VP-3 throughout the procedures. Perhaps by no coincidence, this individual had undergone analytical training. He was the head assistant for the missionary team at San Juan Mixtepec, was fully bilingual and literate in both Zapotec and Spanish, and had conducted linguistic analysis as his daily job for three years.

Figure 10.18 summarizes the stresses and formulae that obtain in the cool categories of the Mam, Mazatec, Matlatzinca, and Zapotec dialects.

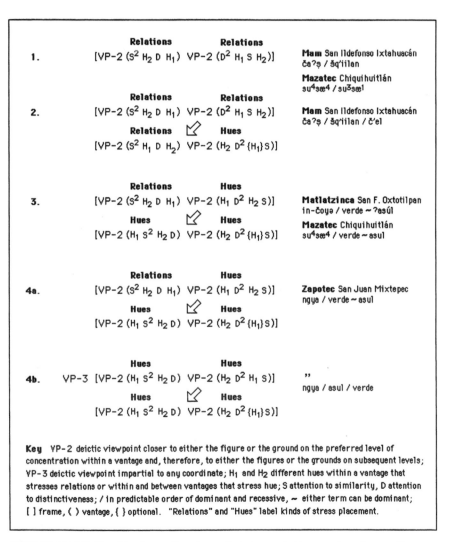

FIGURE 10.18. Combinations of vantages that stress relations or stress hues articulated with partial and impartial deixes.

The representation of coordinates, which is expounded in Appendix VIII, is less important to this summary than are the gross options: (1) stressing relations versus stressing hue; (2) deictic viewpoints, attached VP-2 and detached VP-3. First, relations are more commonly stressed in Frame I (upper part of each formula), hue in Frame II (lower). Stressing the independent identity of hues is compatible with the stronger emphasis on distinctiveness that prevails in Frame II. Mam (formula 2) is an exception: *šq'iilan* continues to stress relations in its linkage with *č'el,* which, in turn, always stresses hue as the ultra-recessive vantage. Second, all vantages are taken from an engaged perspective wherein the viewer regards either the figures or the grounds to be closest; such engagement with vantages at VP-2 is the source of stress. Zapotec (formulae 4*a* and 4*b*) is exceptional in precisely that respect, as the viewer may assume VP-3. The Zapotec formulae represent the hypothesis that relation-stressing converts to hue-stressing when a detached viewpoint is taken or, perhaps, stress weakens, becomes ambivalent, or is evenly distributed between figure and ground. The prospects might be resolvable by interviewing a sample of such speakers twice and in different months or years. Any of the possibilities would add a dimension to the complexity of modeling.

Hereafter, I shall merely describe the complex categorization of Mazahua and Huastec, some of which might require models even more involved than those in figure 10.18. The purpose thus far has been to outline principles. Advanced analyses could require specification of VP-2 and VP-3 in conjunction with more than two frames.[6]

10.3. An Areal Study

Complex semantics of the cool category can recur throughout an area where it shows up in mutually unintelligible languages. Perhaps the practice diffuses from language to language; or conditions favoring it prevail throughout the region, although none have been identified.[7]

Here, we shall survey a 10,000 km² (3,900 mi²) area of south-central Mexico. Donald Stewart interviewed 25 Mazahua speakers in 19 of the 20 villages plotted on the map of figure 10.19 by (*a*) name and (*b*) zone. San Francisco Oxtotilpan (bottom of the map) is Matlatzinca-speaking, whose complex we have seen (fig. 10.10). To the north of Matlatzinca, Mazahua dialects show another five distinct complexes of terms among their cool categories. Particular intricacies of word choice and cognitive organization characterize, respectively, each of five zones. The complexities of some exceed those shown by the Chiquihuitlán Mazatec, 350 kilometers (220 miles) to the southeast (off the map).

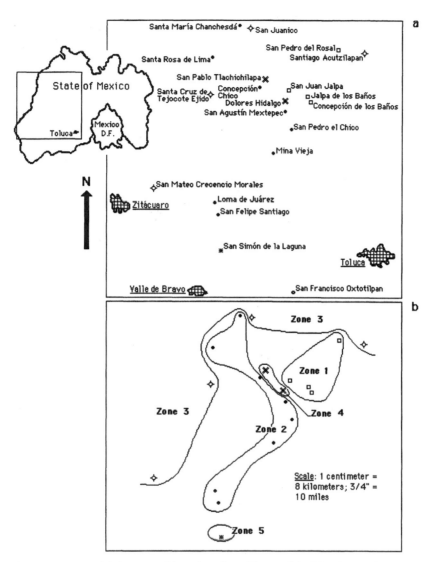

FIGURE 10.19. (*a*) A map and inset locating villages of the Mazahua region where interviews were conducted (San Francisco Oxtotilpan is Matlatzinca-speaking); (*b*) zones between which Mazahua speakers differ in the way they name and focus green and blue.

Figures 10.20–23 represent the five Mazahua compositions with 14 systems. Each shows unique detail, but all appear to have developed as did those of Matlatzinca and Mazatec, with an original "cool" term crossing over while secondary hue terms gain salience. Mazahua *k'ạnga* and *k'ạngï* are dialectical variants that descend from Proto-Otomí-Mazahua *k'angi* 'cool' (1994 letter from Doris Bartholomew). An apparent derivative, *¢'anga* or *¢'angɨ,* refers to a blue dye (Stewart in a 1994 letter recalls *¢'an-ga¢iʔi*).

Zone 1 includes speakers 1–4 of Concepción de los Baños, Jalpa de los Baños, San Pedro del Rosal, and San Juan Jalpa, figure 10.20. All apply

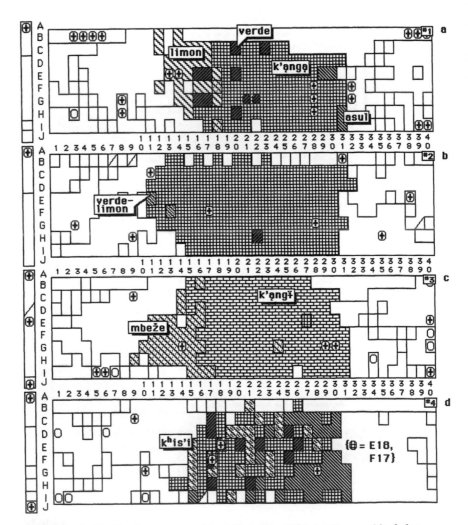

FIGURE 10.20. Naming ranges and foci, Mazahua, 1978: (*a*) Concepción de los Baños, speaker 1, f 70, (*b*) Jalpa de los Baños, speaker 2, m 36, (*c*) San Pedro del Rosal, speaker 3, f 38, (*d*) San Juan Jalpa, speaker 4, m 69.

the original "cool" term, *k'anga* or *k'angɨ,* throughout green and blue. Speakers 1 and 3 focus the cool term only in blue, and speaker 4 focuses it only in green at E18 and F17. Speaker 2 places dual foci and speaker 4 names coextensive vantages, applying *verde* and *asul* in addition.

Zone 2 includes speakers 5 and 6 of Concepción Chico and San Agustin Mextepec, figures 10.21*a–b;* ten individuals were interviewed in Zone 2.

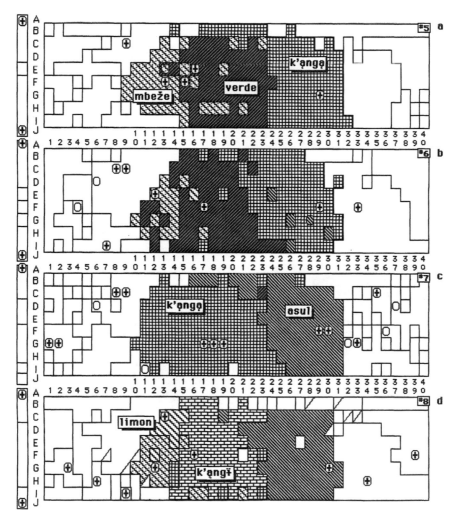

FIGURE 10.21. Naming ranges and foci, Mazahua, 1978: (*a*) Concepción Chico, speaker 5, f 34, (*b*) San Agustin Mextepec, speaker 6, f 45, (*c*) Santiago Acutzilapan, speaker 7, m 37, (*d*) San Juanico, speaker 8, m 37.

All mainly apply the original "cool" term to blue and name green with another salient term.

Zone 3 includes speakers 7 and 8 from Santiago Acutzilapan and San Juanico, two of four villages on the periphery of the Mazahua region, figure 10.21c–d. One individual was interviewed in each of the four. The four speakers mainly or exclusively apply the original "cool" term to green.

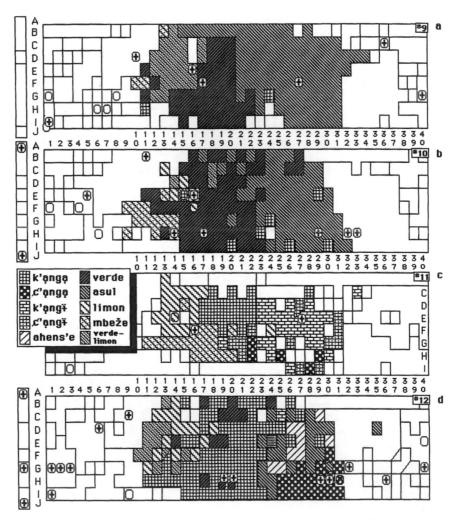

FIGURE 10.22. Naming ranges and foci, Mazahua, 1978: (*a*) San Pablo Tlachichilapa, speaker 9, f 22, (*b*) SP Tlachichilapa, speaker 10, f 40, (*c*) Dolores Hidalgo, speaker 11, m 53, (*d*) Dolores Hidalgo, speaker 12, f 53.

Zone 4 includes speakers 9 and 10 from San Pablo Tlachichilapa and speakers 11 and 12, two of three interviewed in Dolores Hidalgo, figure 10.22. Zone 4 consists of two microzones that show distinctive compositions. Speakers 9 and 10 have almost supplanted the original "cool" term with salient secondary terms (as in Mazatec, fig. 10.15). The focus of the "cool" term was not elicited from speaker 9; speaker 10 focused it in green at E15. Speakers 11 and 12 mainly name green with the original "cool" term *k'anga* and name blue with *k'angï,* and with the blue-dye derivatives, *¢'anga* or *¢'angï.* Speaker 11 uses all four forms, speaker 12 uses three. The focus of *k'anga* was not elicited from speaker 11; speaker 12 focuses it in green at H19–20. The complexity of their compositions is equivalent to that of speaker 4 of San Juan Jalpa, Zone 1, five kilometers north of Dolores Hidalgo (fig. 10.20*d*).[8]

Zone 5 includes speakers 13 and 14, San Simón de la Laguna, figure 10.23. Like 9 and 10, they have virtually supplanted the original "cool" term with names for green and blue, but both new terms are native.

Figure 10.24 displays the focus aggregate of the 11 Mazahua cool categories attested by one name that covers both green and blue, *k'anga* or *k'angï.* The bipartite cluster suggests alternative vantage points but not a dominant-recessive pattern. The prospect of two viewpoints constitutes an

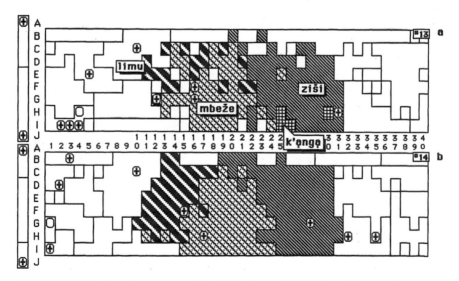

FIGURE 10.23. Naming ranges and foci, Mazahua, 1978: (*a*) San Simón de la Laguna, speaker 13, f 37, (*b*) San Simón de la Laguna, speaker 14, f 40.

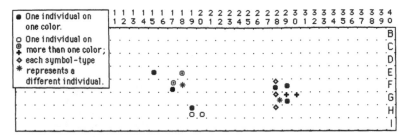

FIGURE 10.24. Foci of the cool category selected by 11 Mazahua speakers, 1978.

outsider's illusion: if relations are more important than hues [S^2-D + H], then there is only one point of view with its trivial consequence of crossover. Of the 11 foci, 5 are on a unique hue and 2 are outside, opposed to the 5 on a unique hue and 6 outside among 15 Mazatec (fig. 10.16). The Mazatec foci also do not show the dominant-recessive pattern. These two focus aggregates differ in this way from those of Tzeltal and Seri (figs. 8.34*a–b*), whose speakers stress hue in the cool category.

10.4. Qualifier Coextension

Although coextension is usually either covert or named overtly with head lexemes, Huehuetlán Huastec names the vantages of its cool category with a head lexeme and its qualifications. Yet both lexical classes manifest traits that typify coextensive names of the cool category: dual foci, mismatching of focus and first mapping step, mappings of distinct terms whose steps progress in different directions, and secondary ranges of green and blue. The peculiarities stem from the underlying organization of vantages rather than from any property unique to either of the lexical classes that name vantages.[9] Although crossover is among these characteristics, there is less evidence of it in Huastec than in Mam (figs. 10.1–7). Some Huastec may engage in crossover, while others may not. Regardless, they set the record for complex construction of the cool category.

The ten speakers of Huastec in Huehuetlán, San Luís Potosí, name vantages with *yašuˀ*, the unqualified name of the cool category, and with *yašu:l, yašušu:l,* and *yašašu:l,* any in combination with *k'ayˀla:l* 'sky' and *ȼ'oho:l* 'herb'.

In figure 10.25, speaker 1 names triple coextensive vantages with *ya-šuˀ, yašušu:l,* and *k'ayˀla:l*. In figure 10.26, speaker 2 ascribes dual foci to *yašuˀ* and names two additional vantages with qualified forms, *yašu:l* and

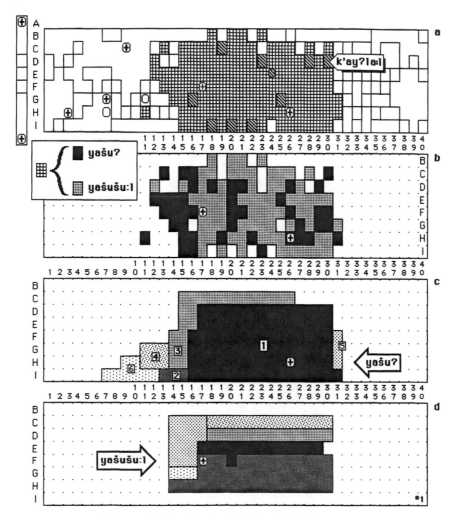

FIGURE 10.25. Huastec, Huehuetlán, San Luís Potosí, Mexico, speaker 1, m 55, 1979: (*a*) naming ranges of the root and of an unrelated stem, (*b*) distributions of unqualified versus qualified root, (*a–d*) foci, and mappings of (*c*) unqualified and (*d*) qualified root.

yašušu:l. A third qualification, *yašašu:l,* may name a green range. Neither *yašašu:l* nor yašušu:l was mapped.

In figure 10.27, speaker 3 names coextensive vantages with *yašuꞋ* and *yašušu:l.* Their foci and first mapping steps mismatch. Green and blue are separately named with *ȼ'oho:l* and *k'ayꞋla:l.* Blue also is named *yašu:l.*

In figure 10.28, speaker 4 names coextensive vantages with *yašuꞋ,*

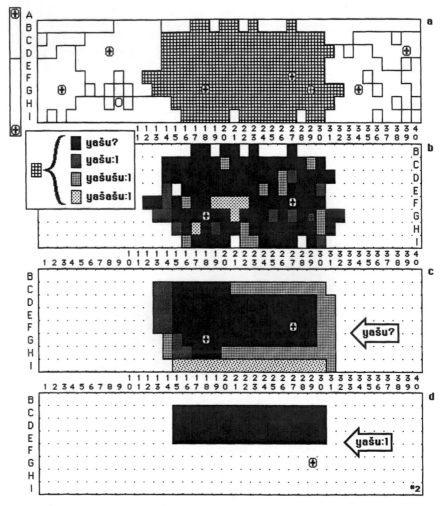

FIGURE 10.26. Huastec, Huehuetlán, San Luís Potosí, Mexico, speaker 2, f 25, 1980: (*a*) naming range of the root, (*b*) distributions of unqualified versus qualified root, foci, and mappings of (*c*) the unqualified root and (*d*) one of its qualifications.

yašu:l, and *k'ay^ʔla:l.* This and *yašušu:l* are mapped on opposite sides, where each mismatches its focus. The crossover is like that of San Ildefonso Mam (figs. 10.1–5). Although probably *yašušu:l,* too, names a co-extensive vantage, its bluest indication at F26 falls short (see note 5 of §5.1.2).

Figure 10.29 displays the cool-category qualifiers of a Tantoyuca

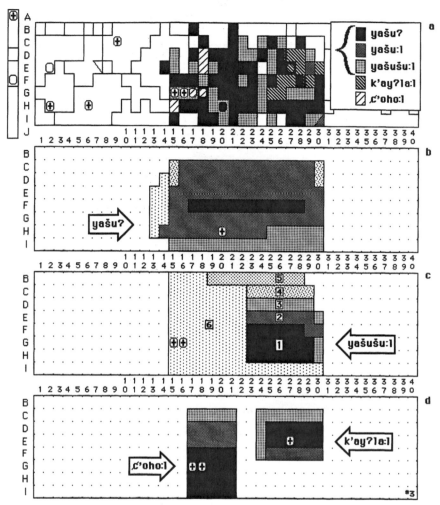

FIGURE 10.27. Huastec, Huehuetlán, San Luís Potosí, Mexico, speaker 3, m 45, 1980: (a) naming ranges of a root and of two unrelated stems and distribution of two qualifications of the root, (a–d) foci, and (b–d) mappings of (b) the unqualified root, (c) one qualification of the root, and (d) the stems.

Huastec speaker, Veracruz, who uses them differently than do the Huehuetlán Huastec speakers. She distinguishes light and dark and applies the reduplication, *yašušu:l,* only to light colors. Perhaps in Huehuetlán Huastec *yašušu:l* was readapted to coextension while Tantoyuca retains older usage; qualifier coextension is rare while qualifiers meaning "light" versus "dark" are common across languages.[10]

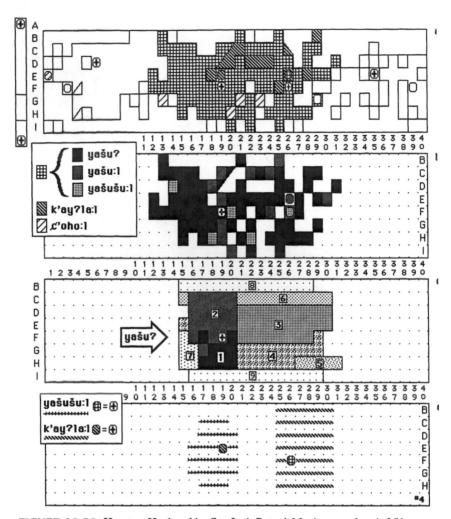

FIGURE 10.28. Huastec, Huehuetlán, San Luís Potosí, Mexico, speaker 4, f 51, 1980: (*a*) naming ranges of a root and of two unrelated stems, (*b*) distributions of unqualified versus qualified root, (*a–d*) foci, and mappings of (*c*) the unqualified root and (*d*) one of its qualifications and one of the stems.

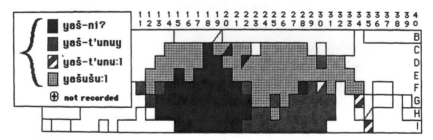

FIGURE 10.29. Huastec, Xiloxuchil, Tantoyuca, Veracruz, Mexico, f 55, 1978: qualifier distributions on one root.

10.5. Brightness Coextension

Among the 51 cases of overtly named cool-category coextension in the Mesoamerican sample (tables 11.3–4), 5 speakers of as many languages juxtapose vantages on the axis of dark-versus-light, figures 4.9 and 10.30–33. Figures 10.30–32 present examples from mutually unintelligible Zapotec languages. Among the 486 cool categories of the Mesoamerican sample that seem to be composed from only one perspective, a coordinate of darkness is included in the vantage point of several, as in Patzún Cakchiquel (fig. 8.22; cf. fig. 8.15d). But the light-dark coextensive systems are rare.

Finally, isolated individuals apply and map a term throughout exclusively the darkest cool colors, Munsell row I or rows H–I only, which suggests an exceptional sort of category. But the term may be under-revealed. It might name a coextensive vantage that is both recessive and constructed in reference to darkness. In figure 10.33a, a Mixtec speaker focuses both a

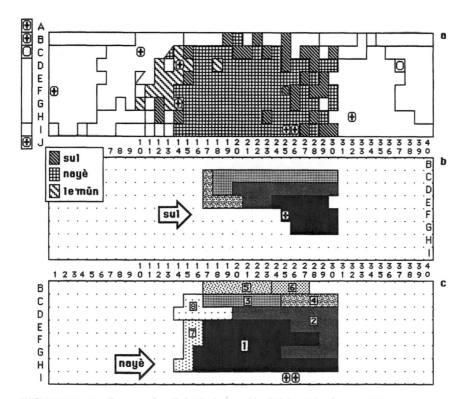

FIGURE 10.30. Zapotec, San Cristóbal Amatlán, Miahuatlán, Oaxaca, Mexico, m 55, 1981: (a) naming ranges, (a–c) foci, and (b–c) mappings.

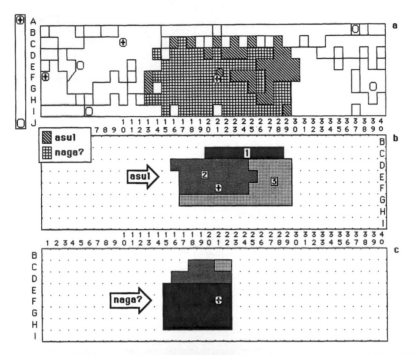

FIGURE 10.31. Zapotec, San Baltazár Chichicapan, Ocotlán, Oaxaca, f 80, 1980: (*a*) naming ranges, (*a–c*) foci, and (*b–c*) mappings.

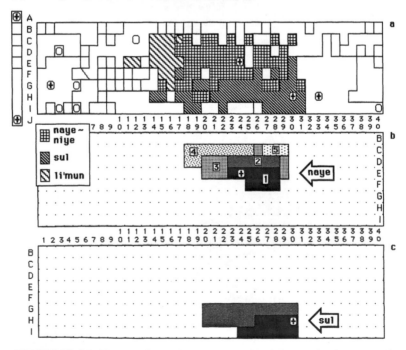

FIGURE 10.32. Zapotec, Santo Domingo Amatlán, Miahuatlán, Oaxaca, m 32, 1981: (*a*) naming ranges, (*a–c*) foci, and (*b–c*) mappings.

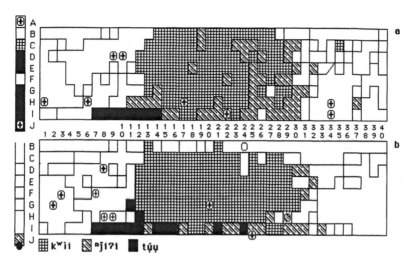

FIGURE 10.33. Mixtec, Santa María Peñoles, Etla, Oaxaca, Mexico, 1978: naming ranges and foci; (*a*) f 38, (*b*) f 59.

dominant and a recessive "cool" term in reference to darkness but applies them broadly. In *b,* her senior compatriot concentrates the recessive range on row I and polarizes it to JØ black.

10.6. Summary

Cool categories of hue manifest two kinds: those that stress hue (H + S^2-D) and those that stress the relations that bind and juxtapose the hues (S^2-D + H). The former are given to relations of covert coextension and subsequent transference, while the latter encourage crossover of dominant viewpoint with little regard to which of the two hues provides the main point of reference. The two ways of constructing the cool category have distinct effects on the way it divides. When hues are stressed, the category divides by skewing; but when relations are stressed, the main term is replaced by dual secondary terms as both gain salience.

Coextensive terms may retain a dominant-recessive relation in spite of crossover, which implies that they name dominant or recessive vantages rather than particular hue preferences; in a vantage, the arrangement of coordinates, including emphases on similarity and difference, may be at least as important as a preferred hue when the hues are as similar as green and blue.

Much of the complexity is handled by models of chain relations between vantages, in which each link provides a separate frame. The frames may bracket either sort of composition: stress on hues or stress on their relation. Both kinds may obtain within a category if they are separately framed; however, change tends to favor the former type of meaning, usually as two new terms replace one old one.

Complex categorization shows distinct patterns of distribution in linguistic geography, different options among head lexemes and their qualifications, and alternative emphasis on hue or brightness.

Complex categorization may stymie certain models of the category, such as the fuzzy-set union or family resemblances to a prototype. In general, color categorization is a complicated process requiring various cognitive capacities. It involves far more than applying words to colors whose notability is predetermined by perceptual neurology.

CHAPTER 11

TRANSFERENCE VERSUS DIFFUSION: MESOAMERICA COMPARED WITH THE WORLD

In Mesoamerican languages, the majority of speakers transfer the focus of the cool category from blue to green if the focus is originally singular and blue, as is established in §8.2.2.5 and discussed in §8.6. Transference is unlikely to be diffused over an area for its own sake: switching a focus from blue to green within the cool category at a certain point in its development hardly seems to be the sort of behavior that would be noticed and rewarded. Yet transference is not a cognitive linguistic universal. Many languages outside Mesoamerica skew the cool category toward blue (fig. 2.5). Some name only blue with the historical "cool" term after the composite category has divided. Perhaps transference is a universal in the sense that it always occurs under specific conditions, which, nevertheless, do not prevail everywhere; that is, transference is predictable if certain prerequisites are in place or, better, if nothing in particular discourages it.

A comprehensive review of data on the cool category may identify conditions that will impede transference and distinguish them from those that will not. Unlike prior chapters, this exploration considers data from wherever they have been collected; Mesoamerica will be regarded as one region among many. We shall identify the linguistic areas in which transference occurs and ask if they share some exceptional societal property that may foster a kind of color categorization hospitable to this process.

To specify kinds of color categorization, we shall review the potential influence on transference of six common and major characteristics of the domain. These are crossover (§11.3.1), brightness categories focused in blue (§11.3.2), brightness categories focused in yellow (§11.3.3), yellow-with-green hue categories (§11.3.4), coextensive naming of the cool category (§11.3.5), and incipient transference (§11.3.6). Do some of these practices correlate negatively with transference? Are they absent in such areas as Mesoamerica where green is the focus of choice among cool categories?

11.1. The Cool Category in Global Perspective

Table 11.1 (at end of chapter) provides a comparative overview of the cool category as it is observed in Mesoamerica and throughout the world. The comparison features the direction of skewing. Three columns contain names of languages in the Mesoamerican sample, the World Color Survey, and the literature.[1] The table partitions four major classes of data: classes I and II list cool categories skewed toward blue, classes III and IV list categories skewed toward green. (Classes V and VI put in perspective classes I–IV by listing languages that name green and/or blue in other ways.) Under the headings Mesoamerica, World Survey, and Literature, the languages that skew or used to skew the cool category toward green number, respectively, M 108, W 46, and L 18; languages that skew cool toward blue number M 11, W 27, and L 23. Skewing toward green is a Mesoamerican trait (ratio 108:11),[2] although even here it does not predominate in every language. The WCS also finds more skewing toward green than toward blue, but the ratio is smaller (46:27). The literature reports more skewing toward blue (18:23).

Other ratios may be compared with those of table 11.1. Figure 11.1 contrasts the exhaustive aggregates of cool-category foci from (a) Mesoamerican languages in the MCS and WCS (fig. 8.15d) to (b) other languages in the WCS. Ratios of green-to-blue chips most frequently focused are Meso-

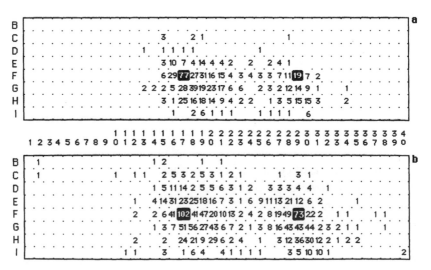

FIGURE 11.1. Focus aggregates of cool categories in: (a) Mesoamerican languages of the MCS and WCS, (b) non-Mesoamerican languages of the WCS. Foci on more than two adjacent chips are excluded.

america 77:19 and elsewhere 102:73. Overall ratios of green:mid:blue are, respectively, 491:11:185 versus 945:12:474 (or .7147:.0160:.2693 versus .6604:.0084:.3312). In figure 11.2, these focus aggregates are shown as frequency distributions, *a* and *b*, using as cells the Munsell columns on the hue dimension. In *c*, using the rows of brightness as cells, frequency distributions of the same data show that the Mesoamerican aggregate is darkest. On the average, Mesoamerican cool categories are skewed toward green and toward darkness more than are cool categories throughout the rest of the world.

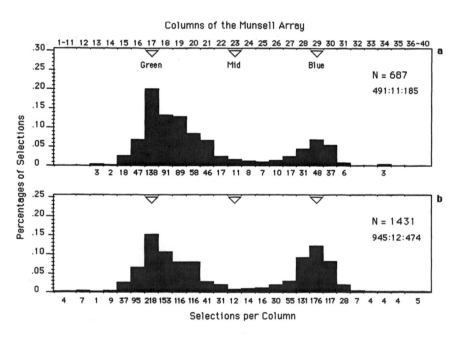

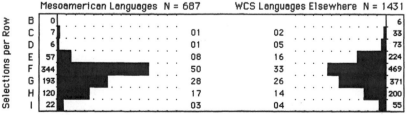

FIGURE 11.2. Frequency distributions of foci in (*a, c*) Mesoamerican and (*b–c*) non-Mesoamerican languages of cool-category foci: (*a–b*) hue columns and (*c*) brightness rows of the Munsell array. The foci are shown in figure 11.1. The same foci compose both the hue and the brightness distributions for each sample.

Skewing involves two kinds of *systemic corollaries:* the results of skewing (§11.2) and the conditions that may influence its direction (§11.3). To compare data effectively, both types must be understood. In this text and in table 11.1, data are identified by the name of the language that yields them, and they are classified according to the kind of corollary they suggest. Language names in text are keyed to the table by reference to class and subclass, for example, Teribe (class I2B). Not all speakers of a language under a class will show the corollary featured in the class heading. For example, under class III1 "A yellow-focused yellow-green(-blue) category overlaps the cool category in green" indicates that this relation is maintained among speakers of the languages listed. My minimum is 3 speakers in any sample of 25 or less, although in most languages of any class more speakers than 3 show its diagnostic—often many, and sometimes almost all. Always enough speakers meet specifications (see note 5 of §5.1.2) to ensure that all are exposed to the practice. I place no language under more than one class and classify each by the corollary that it manifests most.

11.2. Results of Skewing

Skewing will always pertain to a cool category composed by the transference formula ($H + S^2$-D). Two results are predictable, although only in this kind of cool category.

First, a secondary term that names one unique hue, green or blue, only names the nonfocal side of the cool category; secondary terms naming only the color focused for the superordinate range are seldom if ever observed (classes I1B and I2B; see fig. 11.8).

Second, skewing leaves a remnant, as we have seen in figures 8.11, 8.21, 8.32*c,* and 8.33*b* (and will see in figs. 11.5*d,* 11.9*d,* and V.1*b*). After all speakers of a language or dialect have divided the cool category, its historical term—if retained at all—will name the unique hue toward which the category was formerly skewed. We infer the earlier "cool" meaning by examining cognate languages that still name the cool category or, at least, did so when they were described. Thus, we may reconstruct the skewing of a cool category that ceased to exist in a particular community before its color naming was recorded. In languages of classes I2B and III4B–C, some speakers name the cool category while others confine the name to one hue.

11.3. Conditions That Affect Skewing

Transference may prevail in Mesoamerica because systemic corollaries that avert skewing toward green are largely absent from this region. Six characteristics of color categorization that may affect the direction of skewing are reviewed here.

11.3.1. Crossover

Although data are minimal (§9.1–4), cool categories composed by the crossover formula (S^2-D + H) might skew toward blue in more cases than not. Composition of the cool category in San Ildefonso Ixtahuacán Mam (class III2) differs from the usual procedure in Mesoamerica sufficiently to make the language stand out among all its relatives on Kaufman's word list (table 10.3); its recessive range is named more on green but focused with even distribution while its dominant range is evenly named but focused more in green. Matlatzinca (fig. 10.10), Mazatec (figs. 10.9, 12–16), and Mazahua (figs. 10.20–24), all of class II4, show no greater skewing toward blue than would occur by chance, although these languages also eschew a bias toward green. Six Tzotzil focus *yoš* 'cool' with a ratio of 3 green to 3 blue (MCS files; MacLaury 1991*a:* figs. 9–11). Mazatec speakers focus the crossover "cool" term with 6 green to 9 blue; as the Mazatec "cool" term vanishes, it lingers longer in blue. In San Juan Mixtepec Zapotec (class II4), blue is favored in some data but not all, and mainly by one unusually literate speaker. In table 11.1, under class II4, the literature reports that speakers of Futunese, Tikopia, Machiguenga, Burushaski, and Korean prefer to focus a crossover cool term in blue; Futunese, Machiguenga, and Korean apply the term only to blue after the cool category divides. Tyson (1994) shows that some Koreans, like some Mazatec and a few Mazahua, especially young people, do not use the original cool term to name Munsell chips.

Baxter (1983) finds in Ancient Chinese texts that dominant *qīng* and recessive *cāng* coextensively named the cool category from 770 B.C. to A.D. 220; present-day Chinese languages use terms unrelated to this pair to separately name "green" and "blue," while no forms of the original words survive as common color names. Baxter, a thorough scholar, provides no data suggesting whether dominant *qīng* was skewed toward green or blue as it was being replaced. His information might assign Ancient Chinese to class II4. Shorter studies of Chinese color terms agree with him (Beffa 1978; J. Gernet 1957; MacLaury 1986*a:* fig. 9 of Appendix I). Contemporary Malayo-Polynesian languages on Taiwan name green and blue separately but retain a "cool" term that they focus in blue (Lü 1985: 13–17), which assigns them to class II4 as well. Apart from the work with Korean (Kim 1985; Tyson 1994), little else seems to be reported in Western literature of color categorization on the East Asian mainland. As crossover is shared by Matlatzinca and Mazahua dialects throughout a tiny area of central Mexico (§10.3), it could be shared between languages over a vast area in Asia. Because $[S^2\text{-}D + H]$ is both cognitive and semantic, it can be diffused as readily as any other meaning. Presently there is no account of why stressing relations would be diffused when stressing hue is simpler.

Crossover "cool" terms may favor blue because a green range shows countervailing favoritism on the secondary level, as diagrammed in figure 10.9. The secondary loanwords in, at least, Mazatec are composed by the hue-stressing formula, $H + S^2\text{-}D$, which licenses the accent on green per its cardinal opposition to red. This opposition would also encourage the establishment of green as a ground in the inclusive range, which would leave blue among figures. Stressing figures produces crossover. Cool categories in which crossover occurs might be shown to significantly favor blue if enough data were collected.

11.3.2. Brightness Categories Focused in Blue

A brightness category that includes all of yellow, green, and blue may be focused in blue by most speakers (MacLaury 1992a: fig. 16). This initial condition may develop into permanent skewing of the cool category toward blue if, subsequently, a certain kind of interspeaker variation emerges. The trajectory of events may unfold as follows: When people form a category in reference to brightness, hue may not influence their choice of focus (fig. 2.29). When they begin to emphasize hue, they may collectively prefer one hue over another, although the perceptual properties of green versus blue may not constrain their choice, which could as well be blue. At this phase, most speakers of some languages will settle on blue. When some individuals convert such a brightness-hue category to one of exclusively cool hues, they may, nevertheless, keep its blue focus to preserve maximum communality with the majority of their cohorts who continue to apply the category name to blue-focused brightness. A few individuals then divide this cool category, retaining the blue focus and the blue range of the original term while naming green with an innovation. They preserve a core of meaning in common with the majority, but they also establish the pattern of the future when all individuals will shift their emphasis wholly to hue and when more of them will name green and blue separately. Languages that narrow the composite range of a term only to blue may share precisely this history of three-tiered variability. The process, then, is socially motivated; it is not exclusively driven by interaction of hue perception and selective emphasis on similarity and distinctiveness.[3] This situation has not been found in Mesoamerica and is uncommon elsewhere.

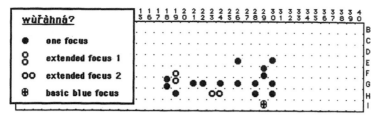

FIGURE 11.3. Paya, Pueblo Nuevo Subírana, Honduras, 1977: aggregated cool–category foci of 17 speakers.

Paya of northern Central America presents a putative example. Its naming pattern is unlike any described within Mesoamerica. Figure 11.3 arrays foci seventeen Paya speakers selected for a category that includes green, blue, often black, and a strong emphasis on brightness, *wùràhnâ?*. The foci occur primarily in blue, although they show the dominant-recessive pattern with all green foci centralized and three blue foci polarized in column 30 (figs. 5.8*b*, 7.22*b*, 7.24). In figure 11.4*a*, the category extends across all the hues and encompasses black (cf. MacLaury 1992*a:* fig. 14 Mundu). In *b*, the category is more confined, approaching the configuration of a dark-cool category. In *c*, the category applies mainly to cool colors but also to dark red, H2–3. In *d*, the category applies only to blue, while green and blue foci are dark.

The evolutionary path taken by Paya has been diagrammed in figures 2.11–12, which depict brightness categories merging into Berlin and Kay's 1975 hue sequence. The merger can occur at any of their five main stages. In Paya it occurs at Stage V, the late extreme. The confinement of the original broad brightness term exclusively to blue depends on such a late merger. If, after merging, the former brightness term had named only a cool category at hue Stage IIIa or IV, then nothing would have discouraged transference of its focus to green. Moreover, if not for the large ratio of (1) a majority of conservative speakers using a blue-focused brightness category to (2) a few progressives at hue Stage V, then the conservatives would have had less influence on progressives while the latter would have been less swayed to retain a core of blue meaning for the original term. The incentive to reassign the original term to green might have prevailed if the majority had named solely a blue-focused hue category, because people who categorize only hue place more importance on the cardinal opposition between green and red than do those who emphasize brightness.

Figure 11.5 contrasts the diachronic trajectories through which people may develop distinct directions of skewing. The figure plots two such paths through which a language may develop a cool category focused in blue and

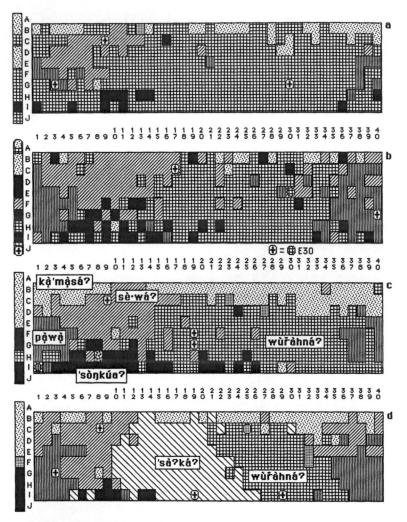

FIGURE 11.4. Paya, Pueblo Nuevo Subírana, Honduras, 1977: naming ranges and foci; (*a*) f 22, (*b*) m 40, (*c*) f 46, (*d*) f 19.

eventually restrict the original "cool" term to blue. It charts the one sequence that produces transference in the cool category from blue to green. It excludes categories that are focused in green throughout their careers.

First, we use figure 11.5 to trace the hypothetical process suggested by the Paya data, which show one speaker (fig. 11.4*d*) naming only blue with the term that her cohorts apply to a blue-focused brightness category (fig. 11.4*a–c*). In figure 11.5, *a* diagrams the *range, emphasis,* and *focus* of a category, which are, respectively, yellow-green-blue, brightness, and

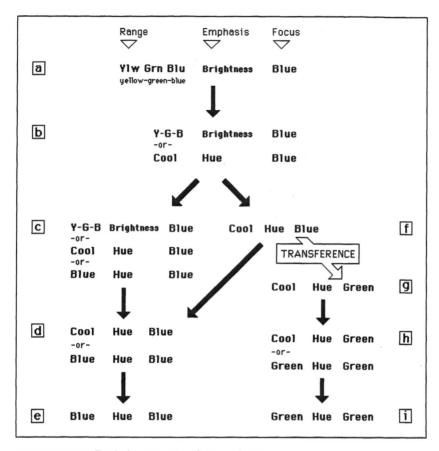

FIGURE 11.5. Evolutionary paths of the cool category.

blue. Part *a* represents a hypothetical language in which all speakers maintain such a category; Chacobo comes very close to this ideal (class I2C of table 11.1; MacLaury 1992*a:* fig. 16). (The labels of *range, emphasis,* and *focus* indicated in [*a*] apply equally to [*b–i*].) Part *b* represents a language in which different individuals name either this brightness category or a blue-focused cool hue category, all with the same term; examples are Shipibo and Chayahuita (class I2C). Paya (figs. 11.3–4; class I2C) represents *c*, and Candoshi (I2B) and Teribe (I2B) represent *d*. Part *e* is a historical projection that, in a given language, the contemporary "blue" term earlier and by itself named cool. Japanese *ao* might provide an example (?class I2C); its prehistory might be as in *c* or even as in *a*, as, for example, is that of Ainu *siwnin* (class I2C), now only on Hokkaido but anciently in contact with Japanese on Honshu. Kunihiro (1970:note 11) cites Takesi Sibata's reconstruction of four color terms in primitive Japanese, including *awo* 'yellow, green, blue'. They are of the same range that Hattori (1964) reports for the four Ainu color terms.

Thus, in the sequence of $a > b > c > d > e$ (fig. 11.5), we assume that (*e*) Japanese was formerly like Teribe and Candoshi are now; (*d*) Teribe and Candoshi were formerly like (*c*) Paya is today; Paya was formerly like (*b*) Chayahuita and Shipibo actually are, and they were once like (*a*) latter-day Chacobo. Hypothetically, the Teribe and Candoshi speakers who represent Stage V maintain the original "cool" term as a contemporary "blue" term because the pattern was established at least a generation ago when innovative speakers divided a cool category while simulating the core meaning of a blue-focused brightness category. The latter is now extinct in those languages but it resembled the current Paya usage (fig. 11.4*a*). The contemporary users of the Teribe or Candoshi "cool" term represent what is left of the intermediate generation. After another generation or two, Teribe and Candoshi speakers will all have divided the cool category to instantiate type (*e*), a process that Japanese has largely completed (Stanlaw 1987: 14–16, 18–19, 107–108, 429, 455, 461, 480).

Figure 11.5 shows a second sequence, $a > b > f > g > h > i$, which is hypothesized for Mesoamerica. Systems *a* and *b* are shared with the first sequence, but system *f* diverges. Unlike system *c* of Paya, system *f* discontinues the yellow-green-blue brightness category while the blue hue category is not innovated, which leaves only a cool hue category focused in blue. Some current Mesoamerican systems are like this: for example, Tzeltal, Seri, Guarijío, and Tarahumara partially (fig. 8.34; classes III3A–B) or Lacandón fully (figs. 8.27*c* and 11.14; class I1A). Among these, no tradition of separately naming blue has been established, nor is there pressure to retain communality with users of a blue-focused brightness category. Apparently nothing dissuades speakers from transferring the cool-category focus from blue to green as they attend more to distinctiveness, as is represented by system (*g*), a process actually ongoing in Mesoamerica. Systems shared throughout many Mesoamerican communities instantiate (*g*), (*h*), and (*i*) (classes III3–4; figs. 8.1–11 and 8.21–25, and 8.29–37).

The ideal systemic prerequisite of transference is (*f*) preservation of only the cool hue category over generations without other kinds of categories abiding among green and blue colors. In a community or throughout the region, speakers must attend strongly enough to difference to encourage exclusively hue categorization but not enough to fully divide the cool composite. That is, individuals must experience relatively uniform exposure to complexity, novelty, and rate of change to avoid (*c*) the variable range between brightness systems at early stages and hue systems at Stage V, such as that shown by Paya (fig. 11.4).

The Mesoamerican sequence of $g > h > i$ does not preclude a starting point prior to system g that is focused in green (fig. 2.21; MacLaury 1992a: figs. 14–15, 17). Figure 11.5 merely contrasts two sets of conditions surrounding (1) transference in Mesoamerica versus (2) its absence in other regions (classes I2B–C). Most of these regions are of lesser societal complexity than contemporary Mesoamerica. Japan in its insular setting and proximity to the territory of Ainu stands apart from these, as do the homelands of medieval Germanic languages (classes I2C and II1A). These exceptions will be brought up again in §11.3.3.

Finally, figure 11.5 offers a third sequence: $a > b > f > d > e$, which also accommodates Teribe and Candoshi. It predicts transference in these two languages at its phase f, while it offers no account of why either language evolves to phase d instead of phase g. Did either of them cross over the cool term? Do they belong in class II4? This third route is impossible to prove or disqualify with present data. Thus, the figure shows why such languages as Paya, Teribe, and Candoshi are not necessarily counterexamples of the transference hypothesis while leaving moot their potential as contrary evidence in future research.

11.3.3. Brightness Categories Focused in Yellow

A brightness category may include all of yellow, green, and blue (figs. 2.27–32). Various languages focus this kind of category in yellow (class II1A) while its range partially or fully overlaps the cool category. Some speakers of these languages skew the cool category toward blue, perhaps to mark contrast against the overlap;[4] yet, no trend among them is definite enough to preclude transference.

Jicaque, also located in Northern Central America immediately south of Mesoamerica, offers an equitable example (class II1A). Its yellow-focused category overlaps its cool category throughout green; while the former shows slight emphasis on brightness, the latter only pertains to hue. The Jicaque yellow-focused category does not extend to blue, unlike brightness ranges in certain other languages (figs. 2.29a–b, 2.30a, 2.31a, 2.32a–c). Figure 11.6 displays cool-category foci from ten Jicaque speakers; one focus covers four chips while two foci cover many (fig. 8.28b): three are green, four are blue, and one is on column 23. The lightest extended focus is skewed toward blue, the darkest covers both unique hues. In figure 11.7, three Jicaque systems include the yellow-focused hue-

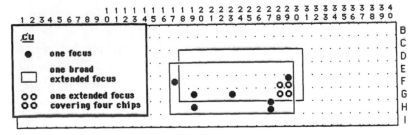

FIGURE 11.6. Jicaque, Montaña de la Flor, Honduras, 1977: cool–category foci of 10 individuals.

brightness category, *lu*, that intergrades with the cool category, *¢u*. (In *b* and *d*, other signs of the emphasis on brightness are uses of red-focused *he* in columns 24 and 25.) Naming ranges of *b* are mapped in *c*, showing overlap of categories in unique-green column 17 and a focus in column 23, an unusual placement (fig. 11.1). In Jicaque, the broad yellow-focused category does not determine that the focus of the cool category will be blue, although blue is focused in five of the nine assayable systems [GN 3:1:5 BU].

Certain languages have two ranges of yellow-green-blue that are coextensive, one focused in yellow and the other focused in blue, as does Cayapa (fig. 2.29). Or elders may retain this trait from a bygone era, as does elder Slave (m 75) in *a* of figure 2.30. Thus, in middle-aged Slave (m 40), the original terms contrast as yellow versus blue-focused cool (*b*), in young Slave (m 22) as yellow versus blue (*c*); a term meaning "plant" takes over green. McNeill's (1972) cognate sets suggest that Proto-Indo-European related the original ranges of yellow and blue in the pattern of elder Slave's brightness terms (see §2.4 quotation; see note 26 of §2.6). Then, much later, Germanic (class II1A) languages underwent the phases exhibited by middle-aged and younger Slave so that English represents the final result with "yellow" and "blue" as disjunctive hue terms, "green" deriving from reference to "growth" of plants (Old English *blawæn* 'dark blue' might have been replaced by *hæwen* 'blue, grey' which in Middle English was replaced by French *bleu* [Biggam 1993]). Yellow versus blue categories may result from a such a contrast of brightness ranges, as will be discussed further in §11.3.4 regarding Salishan and Northern Athapascan. Neither of the original two terms is ever focused in green, not even as speakers shift their emphasis to hue.

In spite of these events in Slave and among Indo-European languages, yellow-green-blue brightness categories do not predict that the cool category will be focused in blue. Classes II1A, II2, and III1A–B exhaustively

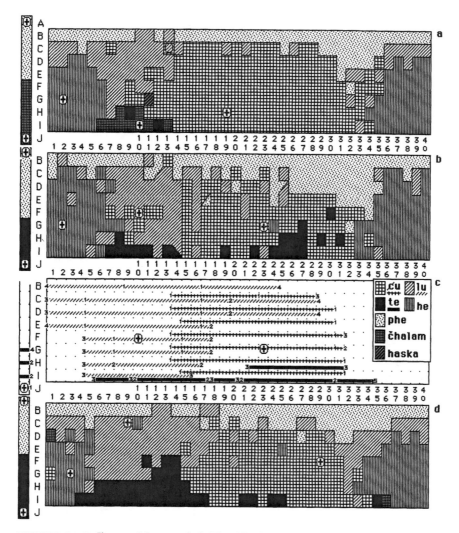

FIGURE 11.7. Jicaque, Montaña de la Flor, Honduras, 1977: (*a–b*, *d*) naming ranges, (*a–d*) foci, and (*c*) mapping; (*a*) m 20, (*b–c*) m 35, (*d*) f 18.

include the languages known to overlap the cool category with a yellow-focused composite. In the languages of II1A–B and II2, most speakers focus the cool category in blue, while in III1A–B most focus it in green. The former includes 18 languages, the latter 9 (p>.05 chi square against chance). Thus, presently we have no basis to claim that a yellow-green-blue brightness category induces people to skew the cool category toward blue, even though more data (if ever collected) may enhance the ratio to significance. Speakers of some languages are inclined to skew the cool category

toward green in spite of the overlapping category focused in yellow, providing that the yellow-focused composite is not focused in green and/or
formed solely in reference to hue. This is why the Jicaque case [3:1:5] of
figures 11.6–7 equitably represents the world.[5] See Appendix V.

11.3.4. Yellow-with-Green Hue Categories

A hue category may include all of yellow and green (fig. 2.33). In
Aguaruna (fig. 2.5; class II1A) and many Salish languages (fig. 2.33; class
II1A), a yellow-focused composite category may instigate a blue focus in
the cool category of almost every speaker. The Aguaruna yellow-with-
green category is coextensively named and focused as often in green as in
yellow (Berlin and Berlin 1975: figs. 5–7), which may encourage a skewing of the cool category toward blue that is more consistent than that found
in Jicaque. The skewing of Salishan cool categories—or leaving their
retracted ranges in blue—is invariable across those Salishan languages
that name yellow-with-green; their invariability coincides with the strong
emphasis on hue manifested by Salishan yellow-with-green categories
(fig. 2.33; MacLaury 1991*b:* figs. 1 and 10). The Salishan emphasis on hue
is stronger than that of Jicaque, whose less consolidated ranges suggest
moderate stress on brightness (figs. 2.33 versus 11.7; cf. 2.29–30).

In figure 11.5, the third sequence—$a > b > f > d > e$—characterizes
the probable development of the cool category in the foregoing languages
of class II1A, which (as discussed in §11.3.2) for Candoshi (class I2A) and
Teribe (class I2B) is only possible. Ray (1953: fig. 1) reports a yellow-with-
green category in Athapascan Chilcotin (class II1B), although it was not
maintained among the four speakers I interviewed (MacLaury 1986*b*). Yet
they may know of it; or, at least, they participate in a tradition of focusing
the cool category in blue that may have been established by contrasting
cool with the yellow-focused composite. The Chilcotin live adjacent to the
Shuswap Salish, who sport a yellow-with-green hue category par excel-
lence (MacLaury 1986*b:* figs. 1–8, 1987*a:* figs. 1–3; fig. 2.33 herein). As
influence of one or the other origin is likely, Chilcotin is classed as having
a "covert" or unnamed yellow-with-green category (II1B). In my data, three
Chilcotin speakers confined the original "cool" term to blue while naming
green with the regional "plant" cognate (MacLaury 1986*b:* figs. 10–12), as
do Athapascan Slave and Hare (class II1A). One Chilcotin speaker applied
the plant term and the original term coextensively to green and blue, focusing both terms in green but mapping the plant-term with a first step in
green and the original term first in blue (MacLaury 1986*b:* fig. 9).

Speakers of languages that overlap a yellow-with-green hue category and a cool hue category will likely focus the latter in blue. So will people who have bilingual knowledge of the practice, and they will influence monolinguals. Transference is unlikely to occur in such languages or in the languages that neighbor them.

11.3.5. Coextensive Naming

Would coextensive naming mitigate transference? Speakers of many languages construct the cool category coextensively (classes II2, II3, and III2). We will assume that most of these speakers do not categorize according to the crossover formula (S^2-D + H), but rather with the transference formula (H + S^2-D). Regardless, coextension may provide people with an evenly weighted option to select green or blue as the main point of reference for either coextensive range, be it dominant or recessive. Conversely, more coextensive ranges may be focused in green than in blue, and more dominant coextensive ranges may be skewed toward green than toward blue. Both of the latter events would suggest that the same process acts upon coextensively named cool categories as upon cool categories that develop a bias toward green while named with one term. Certainly, then, coextensive naming would not hinder transference. The data on coextensively named cool categories in the WCS and MCS are numerous enough to decide the question.

We can derive a coarse approximation from table 11.1 wherein 33 languages skew most coextensive terms toward green (class III2 [plus Tecpan Cakchiquel of class III3A and Guambiano of class I2B; Guambiano is exceptional, as noted in table 11.2]) and 14 skew most of them toward blue (classes II2 and II3A–B). My gross assumption here is that all of the terms apply to a cool category that is at least covertly constructed from two points of view. This measure allows me to include in my count Yupik (class II3B), Tecpan Cakchiquel (III3A), and San Pedro Tonantzintla Nahuatl (II3B), whose dual and triple foci evidence covert coextension in data from many or most individuals. I preclude languages, such as Northern Tepehuán, Pocomchí, Tzeltal, Seri, Guarijío, and Tarahumara (figs. 8.29–34), whose dominant-recessive pattern of focus aggregates suggests covert coextension but lacks abundant dual or triple foci. Since all covert systems that I preclude are predominantly skewed toward green, I keep this slant out of the sample. Yet the green-to-blue ratio among languages is 33:14 (p<.01 chi square). This casual test indicates that coextension does not inhibit transference.[6]

Thorough statistics afford a rigorous test of the possibility that coextensively named cool categories are skewed toward green. Tables 11.2 through 11.5 (end of chapter) constitute a series. Table 11.2 arrays numbers regarding all coextensively named cool categories in the non-Mesoamerican languages of the WCS, those not listed in table I.1. Tables 11.3 and 11.4 show numbers regarding coextensively named cool categories from Mesoamerican languages, those listed in table I.1 from both the MCS and WCS. The data in table 11.3 consist only of naming ranges and foci because no mappings were collected during these interviews, whereas the data in table 11.4 include naming ranges, foci, and mappings. Table 11.5 summarizes the totals from tables 11.2, 11.3., and 11.4 and includes statistical analyses of grand totals. The tables include all the data on coextensively named cool categories in the WCS and MCS.

Are more coextensive ranges focused in green than in blue? Each table, under the shared heading of All Foci, enumerates the foci of coextensive ranges as either GN (green) or BU (blue). Table 11.2 provides a column between those of GN and BU for foci in turquoise of Munsell-array column 23, as explained in note *b* of that table; whereas the data in the other tables do not comprise turquoise foci. In table 11.2, the green-to-blue ratio of foci among coextensive cool ranges is $254:216$ (p>0.5 chi square), which is not significant. In tables 11.3 and 11.4 the equivalent ratios are, respectively, $23:16$ and $31:22$, which too are insignificant. In table 11.5, however, the sum of the ratios is $306:252$ (p<.05), which is significant by the minimal standard. Taken together, the data expose a pattern. It reveals that in coextensively named cool categories around the world there is a tendency to focus two ranges in green and none in blue, which suggests, further, that coextension does not nullify transference. Mesoamerican examples of two coextensive cool ranges focused in green are seen in figures 5.5, 5.7, 5.10, 6.26a–b, 10.5a, and 11.8. Figure 5.6 shows two coextensive cool ranges focused in blue. In figures 5.5 and 5.6, the dual foci of one coextensive range are divided between green and blue, which are counted, respectively, in tables 11.3 and 11.4.

Before we ask if dominant coextensive ranges are more frequently skewed toward green, we must ask whether coextension in the cool category even shows the dominant-recessive pattern. Are dominant ranges statistically meaningful in this environment? This query was prefigured in note 3 of §6.1.2; but the numbers are fully developed here in the left pair of columns under the heading of "Ratios," which is shared throughout tables 11.2, 11.3, 11.4, and 11.5. These columns tally for each language the ratio of coextensive relations in the cool category that show the dominant-recessive pattern to those that are "balanced," that is, which do not show the pattern (see table 6.1). The ratio is called "dominant-recessive to balanced" in the four tables here. In table 11.2 of non-Mesoamerican languages, this ratio is 149:113 (p<.05), which is minimally significant. In tables 11.3 and 11.4 the ratios are, respectively, 14:5 (p>.05) and 28:6 (p<.001) which are significant when computed together or when the latter is computed. In table 11.5, the summed ratio of 191:122 (p<.001) shows that significance increases as sample-size augments.[7] (These numbers are critical to the arguments of Chapter 6 as much as to the following account.)

If dominant coextensive cool-category ranges more frequently skew toward green than toward blue, then this statistic would agree with the account of transference posing that green provides the strongest opposition to red. Green would be the optimal point of reference for the dominant vantage, as this view of the category—as opposed to the recessive vantage—is commonly adopted and strongly identified with the category throughout; green provides the effective standpoint from which to define the categorical unit vis-à-vis others.

The tables present the data from exclusively dominant ranges in their middle group of columns under the heading "Dominant Foci," GN (green) versus BU (blue). For non-Mesoamerican languages, table 11.2 shows the green-to-blue ratio of 87:61 (p<.05 chi square), which is significant. In tables 11.3 and 11.4, the green-to-blue ratios of, respectively, 13:2 and 16:2 are too weak on the blue side to calculate, at least when only naming and foci are considered. In table 11.4, however, a third column-pair adds ratios that are based on naming, foci, mapping, and average size of mapping steps (as calculated in table 6.1). Between the second and third column-pair the symbols < (gain), = (hold), or > (lose) indicate whether augmenting the data with mappings adds to a ratio (gain), leaves it unchanged (hold), or reduces it (lose). The mappings produce more gains than losses, which brings the summed ratio to 24:7 (p<.001) for Mesoamerican languages alone. In table 11.5, the summed green-to-blue ratio of skewing among dominant naming and focusing of cool categories in the WCS and MCS is 116:65 (p<.001). The double or triple options for skewing that are putatively afforded by coextension in the cool category are apparently swayed by the same cognitive dynamic that drives transference. The evidence refutes the hypothesis that coextension impedes transference.

Figures 11.8–13 display all the remaining examples of coextensively named cool categories collected by the MCS (exclusive of those collected by the WCS) to provide complete access to these data. Kay, Berlin, and Merrifield (in preparation) will publish the systems that are listed in tables 11.2 and 11.3 according to their WCS identifications, which will make all data on coextension in the cool category accessible (See MacLaury 1995*a:* fig. 2

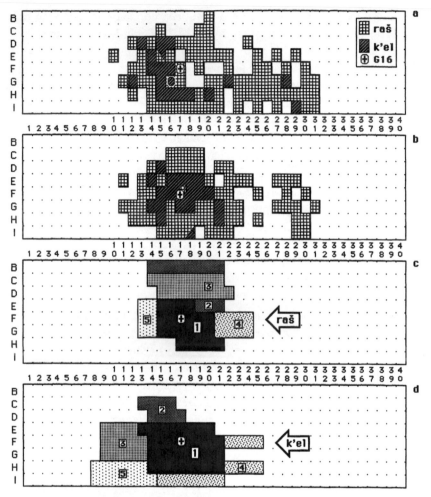

FIGURE 11.8. Quiché, Santa María Chiquimula, Totonicapan, Guatemala, 1980:
(a) m 70, (b–d) m 28; (a–b) naming ranges, (a–d) foci, and (c–d) mappings.

and MS-2 for coextension in Zulu). Figure 11.8 displays (a) coextensive
terms focused in green, *k'el* and *raš*. In *b–d*, *k'el* names only green while
both terms are mapped only in green; *raš* names green and blue but its mapping is undersized. Probably both coextensive terms are focused in green
because the focus of *raš* was transferred from blue: *k'el* refers primarily to
a species of green parrot (Sp. *chocoyo*), whereas *raš* is the common cognate of Mayan "cool" terms, which are often focused in blue (figs. 4.4, 4.6,
7.20a, 7.21c, 8.13, 8.31, 8.33a, 8.35, 9.1, 9.2–7, 10.5d, 10.6, and 11.14).
In Amuzgo (class III4C), coextensive "green" terms appear to have origi-

nated by the same process while its "grey" term took over blue (Merrifield 1971:263–264). These examples suggest how transference of any coextensive term, dominant or recessive, will produce a pair that both name only green after the cool category divides.

Figure 11.9 exhibits two Chinantec systems that exemplify specifications I rely upon to identify coextensive relations within the cool category and to verify or disaffirm its dominant-recessive pattern.[8]

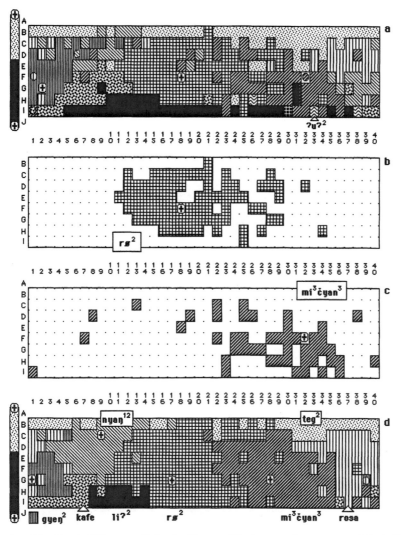

FIGURE 11.9. Chinantec, Palantla, Oaxaca, Mexico, naming ranges and foci, 1978: (*a–c*) f 57, (*d*) m 28.

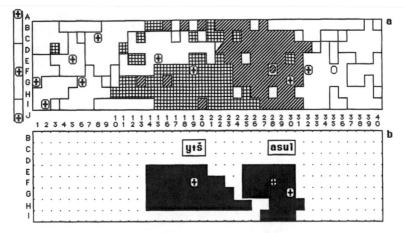

FIGURE 11.10. Chontal Mayan, Mesaman, Tabasco, Mexico, 1979, m 16: (*a*) naming ranges, foci, and (*b*) mappings.

Figures 11.10, 11.11, and 11.12 show cases that qualify as coextension in the cool category by only the naming of two chips, G16 and E30 (fig. 11.10), E14 and G28 (fig. 11.11), F16 and H29 (fig. 11.12a), and G17 and F30 (fig. 11.12b).

In figure 11.13, a Totonac-speaker names the cool category coextensively with *stakningi* and *spupuku,* which are, respectively, dominant and recessive. In turn, *spupuku* and *łpupuko* appear to share a root. As *łpupuko* names the cool colors throughout row D, it technically qualifies as a "cool" term (see note 5 of §5.1.2). However, the rest of its range and its mapping suggest that it names desaturated color plus two saturated blends, olive and purple; the latter colors are occasionally included within desaturation categories (Greenfeld 1986). Of the nine other Totonac-speakers of this local sample (Zapotitlán de Mendez and Tetela de Ocampo, regionally "Nanacatlán Totonac"), three do not use *łpupuko,* while two apply it to

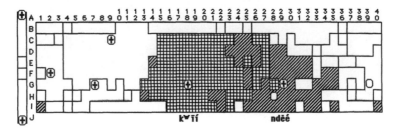

FIGURE 11.11. Mixtec, Santo Tomás Ocotepec, Tlaxiaco, Oaxaca, Mexico, 1979, f 35: naming ranges and foci.

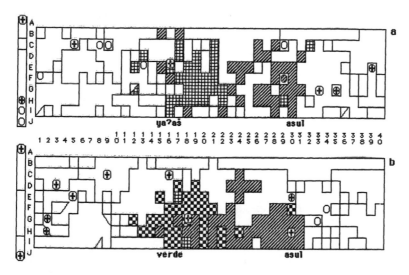

FIGURE 11.12. Mopán Maya, San Luís, San Luís Petén, Guatemala, 1978: naming ranges and foci; (*a*) f 32, (*b*) f 66.

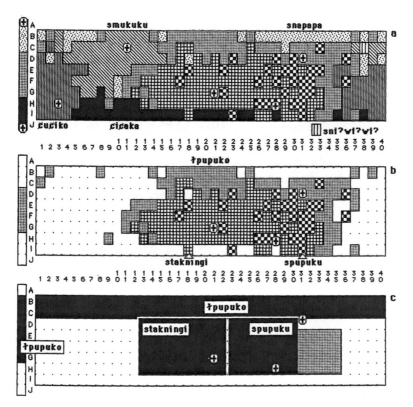

FIGURE 11.13. Totonac, Zapotitlán de Mendez, Puebla, Mexico, 1980, m 70: (*a–b*) naming ranges and foci, and (*c*) mappings.

light blue and purple, one to very light blue, one to light blue and grey, one to grey and all pale shades, and one with a light desaturated range but focused in dark grey and applied minimally to dark turquoise. Eight focus *spupuku* in blue, one in purple; all apply it to both colors.

11.3.6. Incipient Transference

In some languages, speakers focus the cool category in blue even though all categorize only hue. In table 11.1, some languages may pertain to class I2A only because speakers have not yet initiated transference: Wao [GN 3:20 BU], Cofan [8:1:17], Hupa [1:2], and Micmac [2:7]. But others focus the cool category in blue while encompassing a green category within it, for example, Keres and Breton of class I1B. These two are asserted to do so in all individual systems, although neither report is as unabridged as are the WCS and MCS studies. For example, Tiffou and Morin (1982: 372–373) dispense with Breton in one sentence without a citation: "Il est intéressant de noter que le même phénomène s'observe en breton: *glas* était le nom de la couleur composite «bleu-vert», qui s'est ensuite divisée en deux couleurs de base *gwer* «vert» et *glas* «bleu», bien que l'herbe continue d'être *glas*." None of the WCS or MCS studies shows the same. Navaho and Fijian, also class I1B, focus cool in blue in most cases and name a green hyponym in some, but there are exceptions.[9] In class I2B, at least one speaker of each language focuses the cool category in green: Pima ([1:4] fig. V.1*a*), Teribe [2:1:10], Mikasuki [7:16], Candoshi [1:10], and Guambiano [6:14]. In Pima, Mikasuki, and Guambiano, the option may remain open to transfer the "cool" term to green, even though green is already named with a secondary term; but in Teribe the skewing toward blue appears to be entrenched, as discussed in §11.3.2. Probably Candoshi is also like this. Two Candoshi speakers confine the blue-focused term to blue (WCS 9 and 11) and 8 include the nascent "green" term within the blue-focused "cool" range (WCS 1–7,10–11); all 11 speakers of the sample name only hue. None of these languages indicate crossover, except possibly Micmac and Mikasuki. Some Micmac fail to name green while others fail to name blue. Some Mikasuki name green with a secondary term while a few name blue with another secondary term, although none uses both terms.

Lacandón [0:6] is the only language in class I1A. Three of the six speakers interviewed at Nahá focus the cool category with a recessive pattern polarized to the outside of unique blue, figure 8.27*d*, and all skew its naming range toward blue and focus it there, figure 11.14. Wao [3:20] po-

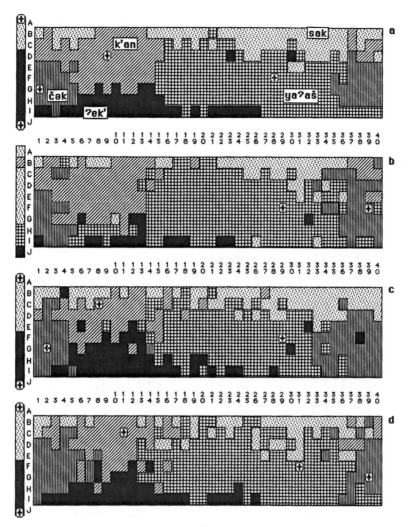

FIGURE 11.14. Lacandón, Najá, Selva Lacandón, Chiapas, Mexico, 1978: naming ranges and foci; (*a*) m 27, (*b*) m 82 Chan K'in I ti' Najá T'o'ohil, (*c*) m 28±, (*d*) m 25± (cf. Bruce 1975:88n.13, 1979:137).

larizes 9 of its 20 blue foci, a percentage comparable to the 3 among 6 Lacandón, although other Wao categories show strong emphasis on brightness while no Lacandón categories do so. Thus, in the depths of Mesoamerica—where green is widely favored—we find the only language reported throughout the world in which all individual interviews substantiate blue-focused cool. Someday Lacandón speakers may transfer the focus to green, although current data do not predict this outcome. The Lacandón are legendary for what, until quite recently, was their isolated jungle transhumance and inbreeding, not to mention their white robes, shoulder-length hair, and continued use of the bow-and-arrow (Duby 1961; Soustelle 1935; Tozzer 1907). They properly represent "internal marginals," peoples who inhabit the inaccessible pockets of vast areas whose main arteries are populated and trafficked by state-level societies. Surrounded minorities may routinely adopt a recessive view throughout many practices—color categorization constituting only one example—and they may reinforce their identity by behaving in ways counter to the trends of those who beset them. Internally marginal peoples whose color naming has been reported include the Toda (Rivers 1905b, 1906; see his quotation in note 9 of §4.3) and the Paliyan (Gardner 1972; Casson and Gardner 1992) of Tamil Nadu.[10]

11.4. Transference in State Societies

Brightness categories are virtually absent throughout contemporary Mesoamerica, with weak possible remnants (figs. 6.13, 8.31a, 8.33a, and 10.30–33). Transference cannot be preempted in Mesoamerican languages, as may occur in Paya (figs. 11.3–4); nor is it likely deterred in any of them, as may happen to some extent in Jicaque (fig. 11.6–7). The composite categories in the MCS sample represent Berlin and Kay's evolutionary Stages II, IIIa–b, and IV (fig. 2.2), of which practically all instantiations are hue systems. Crossover is rare in Mesoamerica. Moreover, Mesoamerican peoples may attend more strongly to distinctiveness than do peoples in areas of less societal complexity or of less assimilation into nation states. The analytical outlook would not only reduce brightness categories to hue categories (through the process represented by figs. 2.11–12), but it would simultaneously establish the precondition of transference—that depicted in figure 11.5 as phase f in the sequence $a > b > f > g > h > i$. Thus, transference commonly operates in Mesoamerica such as to almost always leave the historical "cool" term to name a basic green category after any system evolves to Stage V (class III4).

Transference is a universal process in the sense that it is predictable, even though it is not ubiquitous; it transpires predictably where preconditions are favorable. We can predict that skewing toward green will pervade areas which, like Mesoamerica, are densely settled at the complex levels of social organization that fit definitions of civilization and, at least, of the preindustrial state (Carneiro 1970). Table 11.1 affords a fleeting check of this hypothesis. The areas of predominantly simplex societies covered by the WCS and by the literature are Central America, the Amazon Basin and its headwaters, the Great Basin, the Sonoran Desert, the Colorado Plateau, the Pacific Northwest, Australia, New Guinea, Polynesian outliers, the Sahara Desert, the West African Coast, the Philippines, and Hokkaido. These areas yield the majority of cases skewed toward blue (classes I–II). Besides Mesoamerica, the reported areas of complex societies are India, China and the Korean Peninsula, Indonesia, the Upper Nile, the Mediterranean Basin, the High Andes, and Honshu. These areas yield the majority of cases skewed toward green (class III).

There are exceptions. Thus, in detail, India yields 2 cases skewed toward blue, Habli ([GN 11:14 BU] class II1A) and Burushaski (II4), and 5 skewed toward green, Vasave ([23:1] III1A), Kokoni ([22:2] III2), Mawchi ([23:2] III2), Bhili ([23:2] III3A), and Toda (III4A). Indonesia yields: 2 dialects of Batak with coextension dominating in blue, Toba (II3A) and Pardembanan (II3A); 2 languages with coextension dominating in green, Berik ([22:1] III2) and Kemtuik ([19:1] III2), and 3 skewed toward green, Tabla ([14:11] III1B), Bauzi ([15:16] III3A), and Javanese (III4A). Latin (III4A), Coptic (III4A), and Quechua (III4C–D), all languages of state societies, skewed the cool category toward green, Quechua until recently. Arabic (III4A) on the Upper Nile does the same. The exceptions are Habli (class II1A) and Burushaski (II4) of India, Toba (II3A) and Pardembanan (II3A) of Indonesia. Only Habli hails from the WCS; the other three are from literature. Habli harbors at least 4 brightness systems at an early evolutionary stage (WCS 6, 9, 12, 15) and 2 based on brightness with a yellow-green-blue category (WCS 21–22). As both areas are ethnographically complex, any or all of the four systems may be of internally marginal peoples, like the Lacandón in Mesoamerica.

The critical exceptions are Early Germanic (I2C and II1A) and Japanese (I2C). Germanic, like other Indo-European languages, may have evolved color naming through the trajectory represented by contemporary variation in Slave (fig. 2.30), leaving open the question of whether any Germanic peoples had attained state-level organization when the evolution occurred (notes 25 and 27 of §2.6). Japanese, as discussed, may leave *ao* in blue as the result of a similar change, not excluding the sequence of $a > b > c > d > e$ shown in figure 11.5. Ancient Japanese shared Honshu with other languages, including Ainu (class I2C), whose early twentieth-century color naming instantiates this sequence. Korean (class II4) shows crossover with the "cool" focus either green or blue, although the original "cool" term now names only blue or is not used. This crossover may be widely diffused in Asia, notably in China, as Baxter (1983) reports that the "cool" term and the category it named have vanished in Chinese languages;

his data derive from texts rather than from fieldwork among unlettered folk. Finally, ancient languages of Anatolia and the Tigris Valley, both within a culturally advanced area, may have named a yellow-with-green hue category as do the contemporary Salish (fig. 2.33), which predisposes the cool category to be skewed toward blue.[11]

Mesoamerica was a complex area for at least 2,000 years prior to the Conquest; it included a network of highly developed regional cultures as well as marginal groups. This specific milieu at once encouraged attention to difference and averted the Paya-style recourse that could deflect transference (class I2C). Salish-style obstacles to the process were probably never adopted (class II1A). Korean-style crossover is rare (class II4). Perhaps conditions in colonial and contemporary Mesoamerica have been as favorable to the shift in primary meaning from blue to green within the cool category as they have been anywhere in the world during any era. Although Mesoamerican cultures may never have aesthetically valued green over blue, nothing in the region diverted the universal yen to single out green as the difference between hues gained import.[12]

11.5. Summary

Transference occurs as increasing emphasis on difference accents contrast between categories of cool versus red hue, singling out green as the antagonist of red and the point of strongest identity within the cool category. But, for transference to occur, its obstacles must be absent. These include crossover or, specifically, a stress on the relation between green and blue rather than on the hues themselves, brightness categories focused in blue with accompanying variation to Berlin and Kay's hue Stage V, and a yellow-with-green hue category or, with less effect, a yellow-green-blue category. The deterrents to transference are most often absent in areas of civilization, although there are exceptions, such as those reputed of ancient Assyria, evident in Japanese and Old English, current in Korea, and possibly diffused throughout China. Positive examples are Mesoamerica, the Andes, India, Indonesia, Arab provinces, Ancient Egypt, and the Roman Empire. The strong analytical outlook typical of state societies often couples with categorization of a hue-stressing kind. Wherever this precondition is met, transference of the cool category will be automatic when people pick out among other senses the opponency of green versus red. Transference is predictable if the variables are understood.

People marginal to a culturally complex area may traditionally adopt a covert recessive vantage that opposes the mainstream norm, which invokes a hypothesis of a special viewpoint in relation to ethnic identity among speakers of minor languages, such as Lacandón or even Welsh.

Coextensive names of the cool category favor green overall, which suggests that transference holds sway even when it seems that random probability would cancel bias toward green or blue. Most dominant ranges are focused in green and, at lower significance, more coextensive terms are focused in green than in blue. People are inclined to transfer the hue reference of a dominant range from blue to green more than from green to blue. Mesoamerican languages assign coextensive dominance to the view from green more than do languages elsewhere, which keeps pace with the advanced state of transference in noncoextensive cool categories throughout Mesoamerica.

The inclination to transfer primary meaning from blue to green need not be diffused. Rather, its preconditions may be nurtured by the analytical cast of the cognition that typifies complex societies and the diffusion areas that envelop them.

TABLE 11.1. Cool-category skewing in the MCS, WCS, and literature

Mesoamerica[a]	World Survey	Literature

I. The cool category is skewed toward blue without apparent cause internal to the system.

  1. All recorded cases

    A. Cool only

      Lacandón

    B. Some speakers include a green category within the cool category.

		Keres (New Mexico; White 1943:559)
		Breton (France; Tiffou and Morin 1982:373)
		Navaho (Arizona; Lander et al. 1960; Ervin 1961)
		Fijian (Melanesia; Geddes 1946:34)

  2. Most cases

    A. Cool only

	Wao (Ecuador)	Hupa (N. California; MacLaury MS-1)
	Cofan (Ecuador)	
	Micmac (E. Canada)	

    B. Some speakers name green separately and retract the original "cool" term to blue.

Pima (Arizona)	Teribe (Panama)	
Hopi (Arizona)	Mikasuki (Florida)	
Guambiano (Colombia)		
Candoshi (Peru)		

Mesoamerica	*World Survey*	*Literature*

C. Some speakers use/used the same term to name a blue-focused blue-green-yellow category.

Paya (Honduras; figs. 11.3–4)	Gunu (Cameroon; fig. 2.28)	Germanic *blau (see II1A)
	Shipibo (Peru)	?Japanese *awo (Kunihiro 1970:note 11)
	Chayahuita (Peru)	Ainu *siwnin* (Hokkaido;
	Chacobo (Bolivia;	Hattori 1964:282–283)
	MacLaury 1992:fig. 16)	Karuk θukin-kuniš, 'bite-like'
	Carib (Guatemala)	(N. California; MacLaury 1992b)

II. The cool category is skewed toward blue with apparent cause internal to the system.

1. A yellow-focused yellow-green(-blue) category overlaps the cool category in green.

A. Named

Jicaque (Honduras; figs. 8.41–42)	Habli (India)	Aguaruna (Peru; Berlin and Berlin 1975)
	Podopa (New Guinea)	Salishan (W. Canada; MacLaury 1986b,
	Cree (E. Canada)	1987a, 1991b; MacLaury and Galloway
	Slave (N.W. Canada;	1988; Galloway 1993)
	fig. 2.30)	Numic (Great Basin; Nichols 1980; Hill
	Abidji (Ivory Coast)	and Hill 1970; Berlin MS-2)
		Hare (N.W. Canada; Broch 1974)
		?Germanic *blau (see I2C) vis à vis
		*gel-, PIE **ghel- (Ademollo G. 1985:
		8–9; Jacobsohn 1915:175)

B. Covert

| | | Chilcotin (W. Canada; MacLaury 1986b; |
| | | Ray 1953) |

Mesoamerica	World Survey	Literature

2. A yellow-focused yellow-green-blue category overlaps a coextensively named cool category.

	Ngäbere (Panama)	
	Arabela (Peru)	
	Sursurunga (New Guinea)	
	Maring (New Guinea)	
	Mampruli (Ghana)	
	Bete (Ivory Coast)	

3. The cool category is coextensively constructed with foci and dominant ranges favoring blue.

   A. Named

	Guajibo (Colombia)	Eskimo (Arctic; Heinrich 1972:227, note 7; 1974)
	Kuna (Panama)	Toba Batak
	Djuka (New Guinea)	Pardembanan Batak (Indonesia; Bartlett 1928)

   B. Covert

| Nahuatl (Santa María Tonantzintla) | Yupik (Alaska) | |

4. A single cool-category name crosses over and is focused in blue more than in green; the term may encompass secondary ranges of green and/or blue; either it will be replaced by them or it will name blue after the cool category divides.

| Mazahua (figs. 10.20–22) | | Futunese (Pacific; Dougherty 1975, 1977; fig. 2.7 herein) |
| Matlatzinca (fig. 10.10) | | |

Mesoamerica	World Survey	Literature
Mazatec (Chiquihuitlán; figs. 10.12–16) Tzotzil (MacLaury 1991*a*: figs. 9–11) ?Zapotec (San Juan Mixtepec; fig. 10.17, an ambivalent case)		Tikopia (Pacific; Monberg 1971:353–354) Machiguenga (Peru; Johnson, Johnson, and Baksh 1986) Burushaski (N.W. India; Tiffou and Morin 1982:372) Korean[b] (Kim 1985; Tyson 1994) ?Ancient Chinese (Baxter 1983, difficult to classify)

III. The cool category is skewed toward green.

1. A yellow-focused yellow-green(-blue) category overlaps the cool category in green.

   A. All are skewed toward green.

Mesoamerica	World Survey	Literature
	Konkomba (Ghana) Vasave (India) Tboli (Philippines) Kuku-Yalinji (Australia)	

   B. Most are skewed toward green.

Mesoamerica	World Survey	Literature
	Cayapa (Ecuador; fig. 2.29) Apinaye (Brazil; MacLaury 1992: fig. 17) Cavinena (Bolivia) Yaminahua (Peru) Tabla (Indonesia)	

2. The cool category is named coextensively with dominant-range foci favoring green.

Mesoamerica	World Survey	Literature
Chichimeca Jonáz Quiché (Chiquimula)	Yucuna (Colombia) Buglere (Panama; fig. 2.19)	Papuan (Is. Mabuiag; Rivers 1901*a*:47)[c]

Mesoamerica	*World Survey*	*Literature*
Zapotec (San Juan Guelavía, Ayoquesco [MacLaury 1970], San Cristóbal Amatlán)	Siriono (Bolivia)	
Huastec (Huehuetlán)	Ticuna (Peru)	
Mixtec (Ocotepec, Peñoles)	Amarakaeri (Peru)	
Otomí (Mezquital)	Kemtuik (Indonesia)	
Mam (Tectitlán, San Ildefonso (Ixtahuacan; figs. 10.1–7 crossover as in II4)	Berik (Indonesia)	
	Agta (Philippines)	
	Kamanokafe (New Guinea)	
	Ampeeli (New Guinea)	
	Angaatiha (New Guinea)	
	Behinemo (New Guinea)	
	Kalam (New Guinea)	
	Saramaccan (Surinam)	
	Kriol (Australia)	
	Kokoni (India)	
	Mawchi (India)	

3. Transference toward green is in progress within a category named with one term.

A. Early

Pocomchí	Colorado (Bolivia; fig. 2.15)	
Cakchiquel (Tecpan)	Ese Ejja (Bolivia)	
Sacapultec	Tacana (Bolivia)	
Seri	Ocaina (Peru)	
Apache (Cibecue, East Fork; fig. 2.18)	Tucano (Colombia; fig. 2.16)	
	Patep (New Guinea)	

Mesoamerica	*World Survey*
	Menye (New Guinea; fig. 2.20)
	Iwam (New Guinea)
	Agarabi (New Guinea)
	Bhili (India)
	Bauzi (Indonesia)
	Walpiri (Australia)
B. Late	
Aguacatec	Murle (Sudan)
Acatec	Zulu (South Africa; fig. 2.21)
Guarijío	Múra Pirahá (Brazil; fig. 2.24)
Huastec (Tantoyuca)	
Jacaltec	
K'ekchí (Lanquín)	
Mam (Tacaná)	
Mixe (Coatlán [Hoogshagen	
and Halloran de Hoogshagen	
1993: Appendix E])	
Nahuatl (San Pedro Tonantzintla)	
Papago	
Northern Tepehuán	
Quiché (Sipacapa)	
Tarahumara	
Tzeltal (Tenejapa)	
Uspantec	
Zapotec (Lachixillo, Texmelucan)	

Mesoamerica	World Survey	Literature

4. The cool category is skewed toward green without an exception reported.

A. Cool only

Mesoamerica	Literature
Cakchiquel (Santa María de Jesús, Patzún)	Javanese (Indonesia; Bartlett 1928)
Chinantec (Palantla, Usila, Tepetotutla)	Malagasy (Madagascar; Bartlett 1928:11–12)
Chontal de Tabasco	Toda (S India, Rivers 1905:324–328)
Chuj (San Mateo Ixtatán, San Sebastián)	Luri (Iran; Friedl 1979:61, fig. 8)
Ópata (Lombardo 1702:26–27)	Arabic (Upper Egypt; Rivers 1901b: 232–233)
Ixil	Uráli (India; Rivers 1903)
Kanjobal (Santa Eulalia)	Bellonese (Kuschel and Monberg 1974:232)
Mam (Todos Santos)	Binumarien (New Guinea; Hage and Hawkes 1975:295, table 3)
Mixtec (Diuxi, Coatzospan)	Mursi (Chad; Turton 1980:308, 334)
Mopán Maya	Gusii (Kenya; Whiteley 1973)
Nahuatl (Santa Buenaventura Coxcatlán)	Hanunóo (Philippines; Conklin 1955)
Otomí (Ixtenco, Santiago Tilapa)	Latin and Rural Italian (Roman Empire and Italy; André 1949: 185–186,194; Kristol 1980a–b)
Pocomám	Coptic and Egyptian (ancient and medieval Egypt; Schenkel 1963:142; Weeks 1979: 66–68; Baines 1966:283)
Popoloca	Koryak (northeastern Siberia; Jochelson 1908:415)
Quiché (Momostenango)	
Tepecano	
Tzeltal (Amatenango)	

Yucatec
Zapotec (San Pablo Ozolotepec)
Zoque

B. Some individuals name only green with the term the others use to name the cool category.

Chortí
K'ekchí
  Cobán
  Chamelco
  Carchá
Tlapanec
Tojolabal
Zapotec (Chichicapan, Santiago Apóstol)

C. Most speakers name only green with the term that a few still use to name the cool category.

Amuzgo (San Pedro, Xochistlahuaca)
Huave
Huichol
Nahuatl (Tlaxpanaloya)
Ocuiltec
Otomí (San Antonio el Grande)
Quiché (Santa Catarina Ixtahuacán)
Rabinal Achí
Totonac
Trique (San Juan Copala, San Andrés Chicahuaxtla)

Camsa (Colombia)
Yakan (Philippines)

Misquito (Honduras; Wattenwyl and Zollinger 1978:62–63)
Quechua (Ccachin, Peru; Johansen 1992)

Mesoamerica	World Survey	Literature
D. All name only green with a historical "cool" term whose original range is reconstructible.		
Chatino (Panixtlahuaca, Nopala)		Quechua (Chinchero, Peru; Johansen 1992)
Chinantec (San Juan Lealao, Tlacoatzintepec, Comaltepec; Merrifield 1971:264)		
Cócopa		
Eudeve (Smith 1861)		
Mam (Ostuncalco)		
Mazatec (Jalapa de Diaz)		
Mixe (San Juan Guichicovi, Sayula de Alemán)		
Mixtec (Atatlahuca, Xayacatlán)		
Tepehua (Tierra Colorada, Huehuetlán)		
Totonac (San Juan Aguacatán, Xicotepec)		
Tzutujil		
Yaqui		
Zapotec (Atepec, Santa Catarina Cuixtla, San Agustín Loxicha, Guevea de Humboldt, Santiago Choapan, San Pedro Cajonos)		

Mesoamerica	World Survey	Literature

IV. One term names green ostensibly by itself while another names at least blue and black together.

1. Weak: a green-focused term and a black-focused term name blue to varying extents.[d]

Guarijío (figs. 3.1–9, 9.1)	Iduna (New Guinea; fig. 2.23)	Batak (Bartlett 1928:37)
Tzeltal (Berlin and Kay 1969:32; see figs. 4.3–10)	Chumburu (Ghana)	
	Ifugao (Philippines)	

V. Yellow-with-green opposes blue-with-black.

1. Yellow-with-green is probably focused in yellow.

Nuba (Faris 1972:59–64)

2. Green-with-yellow is focused in green; blue-with-black was reported long ago.

Wakashan (Saunders 1992a:143–176; MacLaury 1986b)

VI. "Green" and "blue" basic terms *might* appear right after Stage II, but these reports are not ascertained with Munsell interviews.

Samoan (Pacific; Snow 1971)

Pukapuka (Pacific; Beaglehole and Beaglehole 1938)

Tongan (Pacific; Beaglehole 1939)

a. Includes Mesoamerican results from World Color Survey.

b. "The Korean language has ... *phalaha* for *chensayk* 'blue' and *noksayk* 'green' ... *chensayk* and *noksayk* are interchangeably used.... *chengkaykuli* ... is ... 'blue frog' ... *noksayk* ... was ... borrowed later." (Kim 1985:430–431).

c. "There was a fairly definite term for green, 'ildagamulnga,' which was, however, sometimes used for blue, and there was a term for blue, 'maludgamulnga,' which was not infrequently used for green." [Classification as III2 is based only on Rivers's choice of words and order of presentation.]

d. Reports of strong cases—a green category contrasting with a black-with-blue category—are suspicious (Bornstein 1973a: table 1; Bartlett 1928:46; Kay Berlin, and Merrifield 1991b: fig. 3; Rivers 1901c:56); see figure 2.23 and attendant discussion.

TABLE 11.2. Coextensively named cool categories in non-Mesoamerican languages of the WCS

Language	All Foci			Dominant-Range Foci			Ratios		WCS ID Numbers[a]
							Dom-Rec:		
	GN	ts	BU	GN	ts	BU	Balanced		
Abidji	2	·	0	1	·	0	1 :	0	5
Agarabi	7	·	7	2	·	2	4 :	3	1, 4, 18, 19, 20, 23, 24
Agta	9	1	8[b]	3	·	2	5 :	4	1, 3, 4, 6, 7, 8, 17, 19, 24
Amarakaeri	6	·	2	0	·	0	0 :	4	3, 4, 5, 6
Ampeeli*	16	·	10	5	·	3	8 :	8	3, 4, 5, 11, 12, 13, 15, 18, 19, 24, 25, 26
Angaatiha	9	·	5	3	·	1	4 :	3	8, 9, 10, 11, 13, 14, 21
Arabela*	9	·	14	1	·	8	9 :	4	3, 4, 6, 8, 9, 11, 12, 15, 16, 19, 20
Behinemo	11	·	9	3	·	2	5 :	5	1, 4, 5, 9, 10, 12, 14, 18, 19, 20
Berik	12	·	4	3	·	1	4 :	4	1, 6, 7, 15, 16, 17, 21, 25
Bete	1	·	1	0	·	1	1 :	0	1
Buglere	14	·	12	5	·	1	6 :	7	4, 8, 9, 10, 12, 13,15, 17, 18, 20, 21, 22 (fig. 2.19)
Camsa	1	·	1	1	·	0	1 :	0	20
Candoshi	1	·	1	0	·	1	1 :	0	10
Carib	1	·	1	0	·	1	1 :	0	12
Djuka*	9	1	11	2	·	2	4 :	8	2, 7, 12, 14, 17, 19, 21, 22, 24, 25
Guajibo*	14	·	28	10	·	12	22 :	11	1, 2, 3, 5, 7, 8, 9, 10, 12, 13, 17, 18, 20, 24, 25
Guambiano[c]	6	·	4	3	·	1	4 :	1	1, 11, 14, 18, 26
Ifugao	2	·	0	0	·	0	0 :	1	12
Kalam	9	·	6	2	·	4	6 :	3	4, 6, 9, 10, 14, 17, 20
Kamanokafe[d]	4	·	5	3	·	0	3 :	1	13, 15, 21, 22

	GN	ts	BU	GN	ts	BU			
Kemtuik	11	·	1	2	·	0	2 :	4	2, 3, 8, 10, 17, 18
Kokoni	9	1	10	8	1	1	10 :	0	1, 7, 8, 9, 13, 15, 16, 17, 21
Kriol	2	·	0	1	·	0	0 :	1	19
Kuna*	4	·	13	2	·	2	4 :	6	4, 9, 10, 12, 13, 19, 24, 25
Mampruli	5	·	5	2	·	0	2 :	3	6, 10, 11, 13, 24
Maring*	3	·	2	0	·	2	2 :	2	9, 19
Mawchi	5	·	1	3	·	0	3 :	0	4, 6, 20
Micmac	1	·	1	1	·	0	1 :	0	6
Ngäbere	11	·	11	0	·	3	3 :	8	2, 4, 6, 7, 9, 10, 12, 13, 15, 19, 25
Patep	2	·	0	1	·	0	1 :	0	13
Saramaccan	3	·	5	2	·	1	3 :	1	1, 4 , 10, 24
Siriono*	7	·	8	3	·	2	5 :	4	5, 6, 8, 11, 17, 18, 24
Surs urunga	2	·	4	0	·	3	3 :	0	4, 5, 10
Tboli	2	·	2	1	·	0	1 :	1	2, 7
Teribe	2	·	2	1	·	0	1 :	1	17, 19
Ticuna	31	1	14	7	1	5	13 :	10	1, 2, 3, 5–14, 16, 17, 20–25
Walpiri*	4	·	1	1	·	0	1 :	3	1, 17
Yucuna	7	·	5	5	·	0	5 :	1	2, 5, 7, 22, 23, 25
Yupik	0	·	2	0	·	0	0 :	1	5
Totals	254	:	216	87	:	61	149 :	113	
chi square		p>.05			p<.05		p<.05		

Key:
GN   green
ts   turquoise
BU   blue
Dom-Rec   dominant-recessive

*This language includes at least one triple coextensive relation, which causes the sum of its ratio (two columns under Ratios) to amount to more than half the sum of its foci (three columns under All Foci). In an ordinary case, every coextensive relation involves only two ranges and each range has one focus; there will be two foci for every relation. As Ratios displays the number of relations and All Foci the number of foci, the former will amount to exactly half the latter.

[a]WCS ID numbers identify results of individual interviews in the WCS database. These interviews are independently numbered within each language, usually from 1 through 25. Figure 2.19 exemplifies coextensive WCS data.

[b]The column labeled "ts" is occupied by an occasional focus placed on the turquoise Munsell-array column 23; absence of foci in this position is shown with a dot. Only the Ratios columns contain ratios that are naturally binary, while the foci represented in the remaining columns are on a continuum between green and blue that allows turquoise foci at the midpoint of each column group. The rare mid-point foci are excluded from calculations to compute the two largest sums as binary ratios within the left

column-group and the middle column-group.

    [c] In the WCS, four Guambiano speakers name the cool category with only one term that they all focus in blue. Six speakers name cool with this term, also focusing it in blue while they name green with a secondary term. Twelve speakers confine one of these terms to blue and the other to green. Thus, Guambiano appears in table 11.1 as class I2B, "The cool category is skewed toward blue. . . ." However, three of the five speakers who name the cool category coextensively focus the dominant term in green.

    [d] Kamanokafe has nine foci rather than eight, because one of its foci is dual. Any number in the left column under Ratios always equals the sum of the numbers on the same row in the middle three columns under Dominant-Range Foci, because there is always one dominant-recessive relation for each dominant-range focus. As the dual foci of Kamanokafe are both green, they are counted as one in the middle columns. Whereas numbers in the left three columns separately tally disjunctive foci, numbers in the middle three columns only quantify whether the dominant range is focused in green and/or blue and/or between, regardless of whether the focus is single, dual, multiple, or extended.

TABLE 11.3. Mesoamerican coextensively named cool categories
          without mappings

| Language | Source | Naming Ranges Only | | | | Ratios Dominant-Recessive to Balanced |
| | | All Foci | | Dominant Foci | | |
		GN	BU	GN	BU	
Aguacatec	WCS 19[a]	1	1	1	0	1 : 0
Chinantec						
Palantla	11.9	1	1	1	0	1 : 0
Huave	WCS 22	1	1	1	0	1 : 0
Mixtec						
Ocotepec	5.6	1	2	1	0	1 : 0
	11.11	1	1	1	0	1 : 0
Diuxí	6.26a	2	0	1	0	1 : 0
Peñoles	6.26b	2	0	1	0	1 : 0
	10.31	2	0	1	0	0 : 1
	WCS 10	1	1	1	0	1 : 0
	WCS 24	2	0	0	0	0 : 1
Mazahua	10.18d	2	0	1	0	1 : 0
Mopán Maya	11.12a	1	1	1	0	1 : 0
	11.12b	1	1	0	0	0 : 1
Otomí						
Stgo. Tilapa	8.10	1	1	0	1	1 : 0
Paya	5.8b	1	1	0	0	0 : 1
Tlapanec	5.8c	1	1	0	0	0 : 1
	6.37d	1	1	1	0	1 : 0
	WCS 16	1	1	1	0	1 : 0
Zapotec						
Texmelucan	WCS 8	0	2	0	1	1 : 0
Totals	19	23	16	13	2	14 : 5
chi square		p>.05		NA		p>.05

[a]Numbers containing a decimal refer to figures herein. WCS ID numbers refer to data and their respective figures in the WCS database (Kay, Berlin, and Merrifield 1991*a* and in preparation). For example, "WCS 19" means "WCS Aguacatec data-set 19." Huave, Peñoles Mixtec, Tlapanec, and Texmelucan Zapotec also are marked with WCS numbers.

TABLE 11.4. Mesoamerican coextensively named cool categories
with mappings

Languages	Figures	Naming Ranges Only					Add Mappings		
		All Foci		Dominant Foci			Dominance by 4 Criteria		Ratios
		GN	BU	GN	BU		GN	BU	Dom-Rec:Bal
Tzeltal	4.9	0	2	0	0	< gain	2	1[a]	3 : 0
Otomí									
Mezquital	5.5	2	1	1	0	= hold	1	0	1 : 0
Mixtec									
Ocotepec	5.7	2	0	1	0	> lose	0	0[b]	0 : 1
Chichimeca									
Jonáz	5.10	4	0	5	0	=	5	0	5 : 1
Zapotec, Stgo.									
Apostol	5.11	1	1	0	0	<	1	0	1 : 0
Uspantec	6.27	1	1	0	0	<	1	0	1 : 0
Mam, San Ildefonso									
Ixtahuacán	10.1*a,b*	1	1	0	0	<	1	0	1 : 0
	10.2*a,b*	1	1	1	0	=	1	0	1 : 0
	10.2*c,d*	1	1	0	0	=	0	0	0 : 1
	10.3*a,b*	1	1	0	0	<	1	0	1 : 1
	10.3*c,d*	1	1	0	0	<	0	1	1 : 0
	10.4*a,b*	1	1	1	0	=	1	0	1 : 0
	10.5*a,b*	2	0	1	0	=	1	0	1 : 0
	10.5*c,d*	1	1	0	1	=	0	1	1 : 0
Huastec									
Huehuetlán	10.23	1	2	0	0	<	2	1[c]	3 : 0
	10.24	1	2	1	1	=	1	1	1 : 0
	10.25	2	0	1	0	<	1	1	1 : 0
	10.26	1	1	0	0	=	0	0	0 : 1
Zapotec									
San Cristóbal									
Amatlán	10.28	0	2	0	0	<	0	1	1 : 0
Chichicapan	10.29	2	0	0	0	<	1	0	0 : 1
Santo Domingo									
Amatlán	10.30	1	1	1	0	=	1	0	1 : 0
Quiché									
Chiquimulas	11.8	2	0	1	0	=	1	0	1 : 0

Languages	Figures	Naming Ranges Only			Add Mappings	
		All Foci	Dominant Foci		Dominance by 4 Criteria	Ratios
		GN BU	GN BU		GN BU	Dom-Rec:Bal
Chontal Mayan	11.10	1 1	1 0	=	1 0	1 : 0
Totonac	11.13	1 1	1 0	=	1 0	1 : 0
Totals	24	31 22	16 2	<	24 7	28 : 6
chi square		p>.05	NA		p<.001	p<.001

[a] Tzeltal figure 4.9 shows triple coextension, although the mapping of the ultra-recessive range, *asul*, is not depicted. It covers in two steps chips F29–31, G27–31 and H–I27–32 (MCS Tenejapa Tzeltal file #4).

[b] Ocotepec Mixtec figure 5.7 does not show mappings, which were collected twice. In the first set, $k^{\omega}\bar{\imath}$ covers B–I13–40 in one step, $^{n}d\bar{e}\acute{e}$ A–J15–40 in five. Both mappings, especially that of $^{n}d\bar{e}\acute{e}$ seem to be based on brightness. In the second set, $k^{\omega}\bar{\imath}$ covers E13–29, F-G15-31 and G16–31 in four steps, and $^{n}d\bar{e}\acute{e}$ covers C20–33, D17–33, E20–30, F17–35 and H17–31 in four steps. As a further indication that this speaker categorizes brightness, he spanned the spectrum with mappings of two other terms (MCS Ocotepec Mixtec file #19).

[c] Huehuetlán Huastec figure 9.31 omits the mapping of *k'ayˀla:l* 'sky,' which covers C–D 17–26 in two steps.

TABLE 11.5. Summary and computation of totals from tables 11.2, 11.3, and 11.4

Table	Naming Ranges Only		Ratios Dominant-Recessive to Balanced
	All Foci	Dominant Foci	
	GN BU	GN BU	
11.2	252 : 214	87 : 61	149 : 111
	(p>.05)	(p<.05)	(p<.05)
11.3	23 : 16	13 : 2	14 : 5
	(p>.05)		
11.4	31 : 22	16 : 2	28 : 6
	(p>.05)		(p<.001)
Grand totals	306 : 252	116 : 65	191 : 122
chi square	(p<.05)	(p<.001)	(p<.001)

PART FOUR

CONCLUSION

Vantage theory ties together disparate observations of Mesoamerican color categorization, which any other account of the same data
must also integrate coherently. This final chapter lists the empirical
particulars, accommodates them to an informal summary of the
explanations that have been expressed as formal models, and, last,
highlights implications of the theory for color and beyond.

CHAPTER 12

COLOR AND CATEGORIZATION

Languages in Mesoamerica categorize color with common character-istics, and they share them with languages throughout the Sonoran Desert to the Gila River in southern Arizona. The traits consist of emphasizing hue, naming the warm category with two terms, skewing the cool category toward green, and knowing at least five salient color terms. Elsewhere, lan-guages may emphasize brightness, name the warm category with one term while adopting only red as a point of reference, skew the cool category to-ward blue, and regularly use only two, three, or four color terms or, con-versely, use many, as do latter-day cosmopolitan languages. The question is whether the Mesoamerican characteristics diffused as such or emerged independently at many locations as universal reflexes of the particular strength at which people attend to distinctiveness throughout the region. Is it this degree of attention that pervades Mesoamerica, rather than color-naming traits per se? The current analytical outlook engenders change among color categories in most Mesoamerican languages, which is proba-bly accelerated by incorporation of communities into the modern nations that govern them (Dehouve 1978); however, the pace might have been gathering for at least a millennium. Color terms in contemporary Meso-american languages may name compositions that starkly diverge from those that were named by their proto-languages; the erstwhile categories may leave vestiges too meager to support reconstruction. The present milieu fosters composite and primary color categories that neatly fit the evolution-ary hue sequence proposed by Berlin and Kay in 1975. As the sequence was, at least in part, inspired by Berlin's pioneering Munsell measurements of Tzeltal color categories, Mesoamerica is a safe place to conduct such wider tests.

12.1. Three Levels of Analysis

During and after the Mesoamerican Color Survey, I combined an improved use of the Munsell instrument with systematic observation, other people's findings and theories, and fifteen years of thinking about what I saw native consultants do and say during interviews. The results support my conclusion, which separates into three levels of analysis: the observations by themselves, the theory I devised to account for them comprehensively, and broader implications of the theory for a science of cognition. The results are summarized in that order herein.

12.1.1. Raw Observations

The present survey returns scores of replicable and quantifiable observations of how color categories are organized and how they change. Such details provide closer insight into this aspect of Mesoamerica than has been previously accessed. Probably most of the scrutinized processes shape color categories elsewhere. Accordingly, this analysis of regional data offers a study of color-category composition, variability, and dynamics that may interest theorists of categorization across disciplines. Appendix VII lists 100 observations and cross-references them with the chapters where they were introduced.

12.1.2. A Model of Color Categorization

Color is an attribute with no form of its own other than its unique hues and other perceptual properties, such as brightness and saturation. Color differs in this way from material domains of, for instance, plants, animals, or body parts, that consist of substance, occupy space, and project shape. But no less than any sensible experience, color is constructed cognitively. The mental processes that impart its coherence are largely independent of the masses and substances that reflect or emanate light. Color offers almost a perfect medium to study cognition in freedom from such extraneous variables.

Throughout this study, the 100 observations of Appendix VII have been integrated into a theory on the basis of a fundamental idea: Color categorization is an analogy to the fixed and mobile coordinates by which people make sense of their positions in space-time; they use the analogy to make sense of an experience that sustains no substance or movement by itself. In the following digest of this explanatory scheme, each observation is keyed by a number in parentheses to its place in Appendix VII as I relate it to the others.

12.1.2.1. Axioms and Dynamics

First are the axioms of six elemental colors, the different perceptual distances between pairs of the colors, and the selective emphases that each person places upon similarities and differences within each pair (§§4.1–2). The two emphases are reciprocal such that strengthening one weakens the other proportionately. Other axioms are added: the primacy of elemental red; the different speeds of neural channels. As red is more notable than other hues, its opponency with green activates the strongest contrast among hues. Channels conveying information to be interpreted as lightness or luminance—popularly termed "brightness"—are faster than those conveying chromatic information. Thus, the first impression to be apprehended of any colored object, however brief the interval between this initial signal and those that follow it, is its brightness. As selective emphases are cognitive, they may be discussed separately from the sensory reflexes of wavelength; indeed they may have a separate neural origin. But no sense can be separated from emphasis if the latter is to be regarded as ranging from zero to the maximum possible, even though the weakest emphasis on a sense would render it unimportant to the person who imposes selections.

Another kind of axiom regards motivation: as people are increasingly challenged by their social and physical environment—a notion reducible in theory to the rate at which novelty impinges—they emphasize similarity less and difference more. The shift induces differentiation throughout much of language and culture, including color categories (30). The evolution of color categories is incidental to a blanket process that pervades many domains.

The shift of emphasis from similarity to difference does not drive the evolution of color categorization with equal predictability across all of its compositions. Brightness categories transform to hue categories while the reverse does not occur (1). But brightness categories merge into any of Berlin and Kay's hue Stages I–V (5–6), suggesting that hue-category evolution and the merger of brightness categories into it are not governed to the same extent (4). A likely reason is that, although both hue and brightness are inherently fixed relative to the mutable qualities of attention to similarity and difference, brightness probably affords more latitude than hue for emphasis and de-emphasis. Hue must be promoted or demoted within the hierarchical organization of a vantage to change its influence on the composition of a category; whereas the influence of brightness may be intensified or reduced to some extent without promoting or demoting this coordinate within the ranking. The elasticity of brightness may, in some cases, absorb the effect of increased emphasis on difference enough to delay a demotion of brightness coordinates. Such flexibility may render the conversion from brightness to hue more sporadic than events pertaining to hue alone. This account assumes that changing the rank of a coordinate is of greater consequence to category makeup than is a shift of emphasis without a change of rank.

The Dani of Irian Jaya name hue with just two abstract terms, meaning 'light-warm' and 'dark-cool'; their warm and cool boundaries circumscribe hue. But speakers of other minor languages, such as the Anbarra, prefer to apply their color terms to brightness rather than to hue (7). Brightness meanings may be joined with others, such as luster, gloss, scintillation, shimmer, flicker, or any light in combination with rapid movement, as, for example, among the reconstructed glosses of Proto-Indo-European names of the light sense (notes 22 and 26 of §2.6). Or qualities of brightness may be separately categorized, such as lightness versus illumination, which Gardner reports of Paliyan (Casson and Gardner 1992:397–99). In sum, early stages may consist of either hue or brightness categories, and the brightness categories may involve additional meanings; but, at later stages, brightness categories convert to hue categories (1–2) and they shed their rich connotations. Most Mesoamerican color categories are too evolved to show strong emphasis on brightness (§8.1).

Once speakers of a language recognize hue as the predominant object of color categorization, the order proposed by Berlin and Kay takes effect (19, 37–41; cf. 1–14), figures 2.11–12. As people increasingly emphasize differences, they separately categorize the most distinct hues prior to the very similar hues: for example, red versus yellow before green versus blue (3, 20 and 38). But, simultaneously, they also contract the ranges of hue categories, leaving colors of weak membership at margins or even refusing to name such colors (40). Shrinkage of the system especially occurs among binary colors, such as brown, purple, pink, orange, and grey, whose complexity causes indecision about which category they belong to and, in turn, encourages retraction of abutting hue ranges away from them (8). The final strategy is to name the binary colors separately, while thinking of them either as mixtures of hues or as areas of depressed saturation, particularly in grey, brown, lavender, and beige. The former tactic produces binary categories, while the latter course creates a desaturation category (Dougherty 1975; Greenfeld 1986); both strategies can be adopted within one system (figs. 2.16, 2.18, 7.22*a*). It is likely that people will take one or both of these paths only after brightness categories have transformed to hue categories and, under yet an additional constraint, after Stage II of the 1975 hue sequence has emerged. But nothing further determines precisely when binary color categories will ensue (8). Berlin and Kay originally predicted their emergence after Stage V, but actually such a system of exclusively six elemental hue categories rarely occurs—at least in Mesoamerica—because, by the time the cool category divides, one or a few binary categories have entered the system. Although a desaturation category may begin to form at Stage III*a*, it will grow to full size only at Stage IV; and thereafter it will shrink in range (e.g., *dun*) to grey and brown or to pale color, it will migrate to blue (Biggam 1993), or it will disappear (13).

The mainspring of change—shift of emphasis from similarity to difference—propels division of all composite hue categories at once, even though they will complete the process in sequence and each will show a different phase of progress (2–4, 21, 32, 36–37 and 41). As attention to distinctiveness is inherent in categorization, any color category will begin to divide—albeit inappreciably—at the moment it is created (61); its division will become blatant only at a later time (if ever), perhaps after many generations. The division of a category is integral to its underlying dynamics, which will determine three ideal types of semantic relation, near synonymy, coextension, and inclusion, if and when people name the colors of one category with two or more terms (24, 25, 48). A fourth type is complementation, which pertains between autonomous categories. The four types represent different balances of emphases on similarity and distinctiveness (45). Near synonymy is produced by the strongest emphasis on similarity while complementation results from strongest attention to distinctiveness. Coextension is invoked by favoring similarity at intermediate strength, inclusion by a fairly strong preference for distinctiveness (47 and 49). Most real semantic relations pertaining to single categories lie at an interval between two of the ideal types (46). Many categories may be named with one term throughout their division and, in rare cases, only this term will serve by itself even after division to name only half of its former range of colors, while the other half will be left unnamed (50, 51; fig. 8.4). But whenever someone adds a second name, it will assume—with its older counterpart—the semantic relation dictated by the prevailing balance of emphases on similarity and distinctiveness (52, also 31 and 39). Usually the relation will emerge as near synonymy, coextension, or inclusion, but it can enter a system as complementation when the new term is coined to name colors that have been deserted by other ranges (40).

Since shift in the balance is continuous, division will proceed with like continuity even though it may progress quickly (22). When two names are involved—as usually they are—final division consists of converting a relation of inclusion to a relation of complementation (23, 26 and 35). As this occurs, a person conceives of both categories on the basic level (32); the category that was formerly included is now used more often while its range broadens (33, 34). However, this range will shrink again later, when difference is emphasized even more (27). People who favor differences define category margins more crisply than do their compatriots who bide at earlier stages (29); people at the different stages do not vary in the value they place on accuracy but rather their preconception of accuracy sharpens as change advances.

Coextension (42) manifests itself differently in environments of warm versus cool colors. Warm categories display coextension more dichotomously (43): fewer naming ranges are extensively intermixed, more foci are polarized, mappings of opposite ranges tend to progress from opposite sides, and foci, namings, and mappings almost always match. Cool categories show more commingling of naming ranges while manifesting less the other three characteristics. Coextension in the cool category is such that two ranges may be focused on the same side or one of them may be focused on both sides (72; figs. 5.6–7). Both mappings may cover both unique hues with the first step (figs. 5.10–11). All individuals in the Mesoamerican sample who name a warm category can name at least part of it with two terms, and almost all of them actually did so when interviewed (fig. 5.9); but most of those who named a cool category could name it or its parts only with one term (50). The differences are consistent with greater perceptual distance between red and yellow, less between green and blue. They complement the categorization of red versus yellow before green versus blue in Berlin and Kay's evolutionary order.

12.1.2.2. Points of View and Frames of Reference

The axioms are adequate to account for the observations sketched above. But the dominant-recessive pattern of coextension requires a statement about category organization that addresses more of the data and consequently will have farther-reaching implications for cognitive theory (52–54). Similarity and difference can contribute to a category only if they are conceptualized within a frame of reference that circumscribes their comparison within the category while limiting assessment to the selected balance of strength (fig. 6.28). Otherwise, since both similarity and difference are relative points on a vast axis, either could be compared to any such point that a person picks out from an unbounded realm of experience. Co-extension by itself suggests that the frame is of a specific kind, namely a point of view. Such would be sufficient to explain why certain Mesoamerican color categories seem to be named with two terms from different angles. However, the dominant-recessive pattern implies, further, that each vantage is organized by reference to specifically the constructs provided by the axioms: elemental hues and emphases on similarity and difference. Each perspective incorporates these perceptions as coordinates.

The perspectives assume distinct sizes and shapes because each incorporates the coordinates in a different arrangement, one giving priority to a particular hue and attention to similarity and the other to an opposite hue and attention to distinctiveness (64). The arrangements can be expressed with a simple mathematic devised for the task (figs. 6.7–11 and 6.28–29; Appendix VIII). Its implication for categorization is that people construct color categories by analogy to the viewpoints they maintain of real space and time; they draw the analogy specifically at the level of fixed and mobile coordinates, setting up mental equivalents to physical points of reference. The model has further implications concerning the phylogenesis of categorization in paleoanthropic populations and the genetic basis of the method by which people construct categories, as it seems that adults do not teach children to constitute categories by spatiotemporal analogy. Regarding the axioms, then, of hues and emphases, the only reason that any of them are brought to bear upon an act of categorization is that a person selects these hues and emphases as points of reference to make sense of color experience in the same way that one would make sense of one's relation to a terrain. Any event that occurs among categories of the color domain takes place at such a vantage point, whether the act involves construction, maintenance, alteration, or dissolution. Color categorization is essentially this one viewing process founded upon the ability to analogize.

Coordinates are arranged in such a way that similarity plays a double role in the dominant vantage while distinctiveness does equivalent duty in the recessive vantage, which may multiply the force of each emphasis to its exponent (fig. 6.9). The converse arrangements not only account for the difference between ranges in their size and skewing (52) but further explain their different rates of retraction, with the recessive range leading as division progresses (57). The model addresses not only the dominant-recessive size difference but the typological trajectory of semantic relations in which coextension becomes inclusion before complementation emerges at the final phase (47).

Triple coextension (55) involves two frames of reference, dominant/ recessive versus recessive/ultra-recessive, with the recessive vantage playing the dominant role within the second relation while it separates the other two vantages, functioning like the middle link of a chain (63). Since the balance of strength among coordinates is relative and fully bounded within each frame, strong, weak, and ultraweak emphases on similarity (and three emphases on distinctiveness of opposite force) can distribute through the chain-linked system, even though only two emphases can counterbalance each other within one relation (figs. 6.28–29).

As a semantic relation in the warm category transforms to inclusion, the dominant-recessive pattern among foci disintegrates (14 and 58–59); polarization of foci becomes more common than in cases of coextension (table 7.1). The dispersal of foci reflects stronger attention to distinctiveness. In some relations of inclusion, properly called "polarized inclusion," data pertaining to the subordinate category are polarized such that the superordinate range only encompasses some of them (60 and 62). As the ranges pull apart, they remain connected by the same system of reversed coordinates that connect coextensive vantages (fig. 6.10). The dynamics of pulling apart are unlike the logician's portrayal of inclusion as a small category tucked under the umbrella of a large one (60). Whereas reality departs from this simple-hearted image, the vantage model addresses what actually occurs (63). Two naming ranges that have retracted from each other's foci may appear to represent complementation, the complete independence of vantages; however, their foci commonly remain polarized in mutual opposition. This is not independence. Probably they remain connected by one system of inverted coordinates, which will break apart and undergo independent revisions only later (if ever). A category relation is emically definable in terms of an arrangement of coordinates and weightings among them, but not in reference to surface data and certainly not in reference to only some data to the exclusion of others.

12.1.2.3. Simplex and Complex Categorization

Most hue-stressing categories are named with one term, especially cool categories (65). Many consist of one vantage; the preferred fixed coordinate is the hue on whose side the category is focused (74). As distinctiveness is emphasized, the range of the cool category shrinks toward the focused side (66), leaving the colors of the other side to receive another name (26). Foci that are placed closer to one edge of the category correspond with disjunctive mappings, while foci placed closer to the center correspond with continuous mappings (68), as would be expected if both a focus and a mapping were rendered in reference to emphases that favor distinctiveness as division proceeds.

After the cool category divides into basic categories of green and blue, their skewing ceases to progress (69) but their foci darken (67). This occurs because an emphasis on distinctiveness that is strong enough to divide the cool category entails simultaneous weakening of attention to similarity to an extent that, to many people, it no longer serves easily as a coordinate. To thwart disintegration of the category, they reinforce their views of green and blue with a coordinate of darkness; or, at least, they darken their vantages to counteract the differentiation. The affinity of green and blue with black rather than with white conforms to the lesser differentiation between any two percepts in darkness, colors included, keeping in mind that in the real world—which is only imitated by reflective Munsell pigments—the brightness dimension is luminous. This affinity is echoed by the abiding coherence of the dark-cool category through Berlin and Kay's Stages I, II, and III*b,* after white and warm or even red and yellow have been separately categorized.

Many cool categories are constructed from two points of view but named with one term, a "covert coextension." Usually the dominant range is constructed in reference to green, perhaps because green and red contrast more than any other hue pair while red is the most appreciable hue. The dominant-recessive pattern surfaces in aggregates of single foci that cluster in two groups, one centralized in green and the other less centralized or even polarized in blue (70). Covert coextension—at least its temporary maintenance—is critical to the transference of foci from blue to green (71), which does not involve migration of a focus through turquoise but rather a saltant relocation as if switched from one vantage to another. Foci will be transferred in categories that originally were focused in blue as attention to difference increases (73). However, languages in many regions of the world predominantly focus the cool category in blue (94). Either they have not begun to transfer foci or transference has been diverted or blocked (95–96).

Transference may not occur when crossover prevails, as in Mazatec, Korean, and possibly Ancient Chinese. Transference is diverted when a minority of speakers at Stage V retain an original term in blue to preserve core communication with a majority who use the term to name a blue-focus brightness category (97); the term continues to name blue after the minority becomes the majority. Paya, Karuk, and possibly Ancient Japanese seem to reflect this process (98). Transference is blocked by a yellow-with-green composite category that either pertains to hue or is focused in green or both. Mesoamerica shares its proclivity for a green focus of the cool category with other areas of preindustrial civilization, such as the Andes, Indonesia, India, ancient Egypt, the Roman Empire, and the Arab world (100). Societies of these regions were sufficiently complex to engender stronger attention to difference than that which others may have exerted in less developed localities (95), including the cultural backwaters and peripheries of advanced zones. Nothing prevents a people from retaining the blue focus as an insignia of tribal identity vis-à-vis dominant societies that abut them. The inhabitants of a beleaguered enclave may indeed attend to differences as a requirement of survival. A recessive blue focus would aptly symbolize the way a minority perceives itself in relation to hegemonic neighbors (99).

Individual speakers of different languages, acting in concert with other members of their own group, chose either a single focus or dual foci or triple foci for the cool category, when no convention that pertains specifically to color prescribes that members of each group will share one or another pattern (76 and 80). Some groups that place a single focus may merely construct the cool category from one vantage. But other groups who maintain covert coextensive vantages still place a single focus, although, among some of them, each member may choose either green or blue (73). These groups differ from others whose members usually place dual foci (82), and both groups differ from a third whose members place triple foci. Most people who place dual foci choose green first and blue second (78), while the few who place triple foci choose blue first, green second, and turquoise last (81). The members of each group that prefers one, two, or three foci probably share among themselves a certain will or ability to assess their own processes of categorization from an outsider's standpoint, and inclination differs between the groups. It may range from no such ability to a highly developed reflectivity. The standpoints may vary from one that is situated both inside the cool category and inside the language, to one that is outside the category but still inside the language, to one that is both outside the category and outside the language, that is, in another language. People who maintain coextension, overt or covert, must maintain at least the first two kinds of viewpoint, although most will adhere to a preference for the innermost option. They will not occupy the outer view long enough to contemplate the prospect of dual foci, but will only use it as a way station while switching from one submerged perspective to the other.

Of those who select dual foci in reference to covert coextension, most focus the dominant vantage first, which in Mesoamerican languages is usually constructed in reference to green (77, 78); then they focus the recessive vantage, usually blue. The only people who placed triple foci had abandoned their language years before to take up Spanish; they labored overtime to resurrect their native color naming (80). Probably they assembled viewpoints on the original system from the perspective of Spanish, which separates green from blue. Then they worked their way toward their present position from the depths of the remembered system, first focusing the recessive range in blue, next the dominant range in green, and then representing both ranges with a focus between them. This last selection was a way of marking the integrity of the cool category in contrast to their current predisposition to categorize its halves distinctly (17). They worked from a standpoint outside of the original frame of vantages on cool colors and outside of the relic language that had sanctioned the frame.

Thought may develop through stages of analysis, synthesis, and assuming a reflective overview (objectivity); each stage is a prerequisite to the stage that follows. The stages correspond to the adoption of dominant, recessive, and detached vantages (note 11 of §9.5). Taking a dominant vantage, the viewer zooms in from naive attention to similarity to analysis; taking a recessive vantage, the viewer zooms in from analysis to synthesis and, likely, to abstract formulation (fig. 6.8). As the recessive vantage is polarized at greater distance from the subject under scrutiny (fig. 6.39), it provides the opportune platform from which to step outside of one's standpoint to command a reflective overview (75 and 78). Is this step to the outside an inevitable consequence of zooming in toward synthesis, or does it require a special leap from here to there that, for whatever reason, some people take and others do not? In the former event, vantage theory would incorporate the advent of objective thought, but in the latter it would only describe steps to the threshold.

Single noncoextensive names of the cool category may cross over (83), showing mismatches of different data (table 10.1). Terms that undergo crossover and terms that undergo transference differ in meaning (86–88). The deference is formally expressed as $(S^2\text{-D Hue})$ for crossover and $(\text{Hue } S^2\text{-D})$ for transference. The formulae convey by order of symbols priorities of stress on either figures or grounds (fig. VIII.1). People who cross over their "cool" term care more about the arrangement of inherently mobile coordinates, $S^2\text{-D}$. People who transfer their emphasis from blue to green care more about the arrangement of inherently fixed coordinates, Hue (90). Crossover seems chaotic and contradictory to those of us who think in the latter way. Nevertheless, all people who categorize color care about both kinds of coordinates; they merely differ in what they stress.

As a crossover cool category transforms from coextension to inclusion, correspondence between naming ranges, mappings, and foci may appear to disintegrate; data that seemingly should match each other appear on opposite sides of the category (44). Two processes work together to produce this false appearance of chaos (84). To divide the cool category, attention to difference must be exceptionally strong, which confines specific performances, such as naming and mapping, to one side of the category. But crossover continues, nevertheless, which can confine the naming and mapping of one term to opposite sides, an apparent contradiction. The hidden order persists in the arrangement of coordinates, which remain as the standard inverse priorities that actuate coextension and inclusion among neat-looking data and disheveled-looking data alike (85). But, in the seemingly contradictory cases, it is dominance that crosses over, S^2-D, not an emphasis on one or another of the hues (table 10.2). That is, the dominant formula can incorporate the unique hues in either of two ways, (S^2 BU D GN) or (S^2 GN D BU), whose difference is inconsequential to the native viewer (Appendix VIII expounds the principles of formulae, e.g., why hues are last in a crossover formula). The term that names the dominant vantage continues in this role regardless of which hue supplies the preferred coordinate. The term means "mainly dominant and incidentally one and another hue." Likewise, the recessive relation, D^2-S, may cross over inversely; its name, too, continues its main meaning of "recessive," that is, "a special quality of view," the ranking of green and blue or blue and green being irrelevant to the viewer, at least in theory.

In fact, in a cool category of coextensive crossover, the recessive range may favor green, albeit moderately, showing that hue has some influence in spite of crossover (tables 10.1 and 10.3). A dominant range may favor blue if its primary fixed coordinate is green because this coordinate will be stressed least (fig. 10.7), but the favoritism might be very slight. A noncoextensive "cool" term that crosses over may favor blue for the same reason and to the same slight extent (88; also 87 and 89). Hue-stressing cool categories divide by skewing until the original term names only one hue (94), always green in Mesoamerica, usually green elsewhere (table 11.1), and always opposite a new term whose range takes over the other hue. But the name of a crossover cool category can be replaced by a pair of salient hue-stressing ranges that do not cross over, one naming only green and the other only blue (87). As the green range, in its cardinal opposition to red, expands faster than the blue range, the original cool range will most often skew toward blue before it disappears. Rarely a lone subordinate term is of the relational kind of meaning, even though it seems to name one hue at any particular moment; but it crosses over between green and blue (89), sometimes naming the same side of the category on which the superordinate term is focused (fig. 10.9). Such processes compound the complexity of the cool category.

Hue stressing and relation stressing is caused by the deictic partiality of the engaged point of view, VP-2, in which viewers situate themselves closer to the ground or to the figure on the preferred level of concentration. Only when a viewer constantly maintains the disengaged deictic, VP-3, will a category seem to show neutral or ambivalent stress (fig. 10.17). This notion of stress specifies the link between the composition of vantages and degrees of engagement.[1]

12.1.2.4. Flip-Flop

In §2.6, a problem was identified. The various Martu Wangka systems are registered as exceptions to any of the schemes proposed heretofore (9–12), notably the typologies set forth by Berlin and Kay over the years (figs. 2.1, 2.2, and 2.10). The exceptions pertain to the predominant focusing of *yakuri yakuri* in columns 14–16 on the yellow side of unique green column 17 (fig. 2.26), the flip-flopping of its range from green-with-yellow to green-with-blue (g), and the occurrence of these anomalies in communities that use Stage I and Stage II systems ($a–d$), occasionally name brightness (e), and show variable ways of naming yellow ($f–h$). How would vantage theory address the Martu Wangka complex? First, we shall assume that *yakuri yakuri* usually names a hue category in accord with the hue-stressing formula but, at Stage I and Stage II, similarity is emphasized very strongly. The elaborated formula, then, is ($H_1 S^2 H_x$ D). Here H_1, the preferred hue, is always green, but the strength of emphasis on similarity makes the specific identity of the second hue less important; mainly it matters that H_x be other than green and, to most people, some particular hue (yellow or blue being the neighboring candidates). Very strong similarity minimizes differences sufficiently to create this laxity, even between yellow and blue and especially on a level of concentration that is not the preferred level. The laxity, however, is anything but rampant, as almost all subjects chose yellow as the second hue coordinate when they focused the category and when they named it. The indefinite identity of the second hue—minor though this indefiniteness may be—is expressed with the subscript $_x$ (H_x) to contrast its slightly indeterminate status vis à vis the definite identity of the primary fixed coordinate, which is distinguished by its numerical subscript (H_1).

The choice by all speakers of yellow as H_x when they focused accounts for the consistently yellowish foci in columns 14–16; this choice determines that the foci are pulled by strong similarity away from unique green toward the category center between green and yellow. The weaker identity of H_x explains the occasional flip-flopping of the range during the naming elicitation when a sustained overview of all colors is prevented by turning the array face-down; people are less likely to exercise their weak preference for yellow when yellow and blue cannot be contrasted within one field of vision. In figure 2.26f and h, *yakuri yakuri* is focused in columns 16 and 15, respectively, even though its naming does not cover yellow; however, the range might be shown to cover yellow if it were mapped. Throughout the figure, yellow is named in five ways, which suggests that Martu Wangka supplies no conventional alternative to naming yellow with a term other than *yakuri yakuri*. In figure 2.26e, *yakuri yakuri* appears to name a brightness category, which may only mean that this individual constructs the category differently than do the others, using a brightness coordinate in lieu of H_x.

Vantage theory provides that certain speakers of Martu Wangka and Lani represent typological Stage I' or Stage II' (fig. 2.12), and it explains why the attendant complex, including occasional flip-flopping, should be expected at these stages (7). The theory shows how explanation facilitates typology while the earlier efforts to merely classify would only confound typology if forced beyond their limit.[2]

12.1.3. A Theory of Categorization

Most observations of Mesoamerican color categorization are tied together under a model of the method by which people construct categories. They categorize by drawing an analogy between fixed and mobile physical coordinates and backgrounded and highlighted mental complements, thereby constituting a category as they do a vantage of space-time. Since this tactic does not seem to be taught or even unconsciously imparted, humans may inherit physically both the technique and—equally crucial—the irrepressible drive to apply it. This adaptation may be one of the major qualities that sets our species apart from other creatures, even though they too keep track of their spatiotemporal bearings by reference to coordinates. The other critical constructs of this model are linkages of frames and degrees of engagement.

Models of categorization espousing prototypes or logical sets cannot begin to tie these some 100 observations into a coherent system (Appendix VII). Although vantage theory may not offer the final word on the findings, any account that supersedes it must explain all the observations more cogently and economically and should accommodate at least a few more that no other theory can address.

People would be untypically wasteful of their cognitive resources if they used the analogy of spatial coordinates only to categorize color while categorizing all else by other means. Yet the notion of categories as analogous viewpoints has scarcely been considered outside the color domain (Aoyagi 1995; Hill and MacLaury 1995; Lansing 1995; MacLaury 1995*a,b;* M. MacLaury 1989; Preston 1993; Taylor 1992; Taylor and MacLaury 1995).

Modeling categories as points of view incorporates a commitment to what categorization is and to what it is not. It is a process that a person undertakes, maintains, and changes in order to comprehend the world. It is a way of organizing what one senses by continuously projecting oneself. It is a method consisting of specific procedures. It wholly depends on human agency. It is not a metaphorical container, nor is it a neural reflex that deserves a name; it has no existence apart from the person who produces it on the basis of an edited selection of external reality. The selections are not arbitrarily taken from a boundless store of equally weighted possibilities; rather, they are limited by the organs of perception and motivated by social and physical environments, such as those that are easy to live in versus others that demand close attention to difficulties and unpredictable events.

Vantage theory offers a modest array of dividends to the interdisciplinary attempt to understand categorization. They are, first, that, although human categorization helps us to survive as a species, the people who categorize are forming points of view; theory may address this primary impetus apart from its adaptive benefit. Second, vantage theory specifies how the people who categorize are engaged in their creations and why the engagement is continual, mutable, and active. The specification adopts a deeper cognitive commitment than other efforts to tie conceptualizers to their cognitions, such as the models that represent points of view by tacking arrows on diagrams. Third, vantage theory ventures to propose how and why categories change, even though human physiology changes appreciably less or, perhaps, not at all, and even though the physical stimuli and viewing conditions remain proportionately stable over immense time. Finally, this theory of categorization addresses such long-standing questions as how judgments of similarity and difference can participate in a reference frame, what such a frame would consist of, and why comparisons of stimuli within categories are asymmetrically distanced when conducted from opposite starting points. These issues and others are on the table for debate.

Above all, this study shows how a small part of language and culture has been systematically understood, keeping in view the potential of extending some of the principles uncovered here to broader relevance. Other domains will offer even tougher challenges, but they will be easier to meet if we thoroughly explore the areas of cognition that are exceptionally accessible. The proven approach depends on use of an instrument, innovation of replicable method, quantifiable observations, imaginative hypothesizing, testable theoretical models, and the means to represent them formally. With personal commitment and the support of society, basic science will contribute endlessly to our knowledge of who we are and why we think as we do.

INVENTORY OF DATA, COLLABORATORS, LANGUAGES, AND LOCATIONS

Table I.1 inventories the Mesoamerican sample. It lists sources of data and acknowledges collaborators and their institutions, abbreviated as follows: the Summer Institute of Linguistics of Mexico (SIL-M), Central America (SIL-CA), and North America (SIL-NA); Centro de Estudios Mayas of the Universidad Nacional Autónoma de México (CEM-UNAM) and Instituto de Investigaciones Antropológicas, also of the Universidad Nacional Autónoma de México (IIA-UNAM); Instituto Nacional de Antropología e Historia (INAH); Universidad de San Carlos (U de SC); Proyecto Lingüístico "Francisco Marroquín" (PLFM); Southern Methodist University (SMU); the University of California at Berkeley (UCB) and at Los Angeles (UCLA). The World Color Survey (Kay, Berlin, and Merrifield 1991*a*) is credited as WCS. The total number of naming elicitations is greater than the total of individuals interviewed because some were interviewed twice, marked with a dash when under different surveys. Figure I.1 links table I.1 to the map.

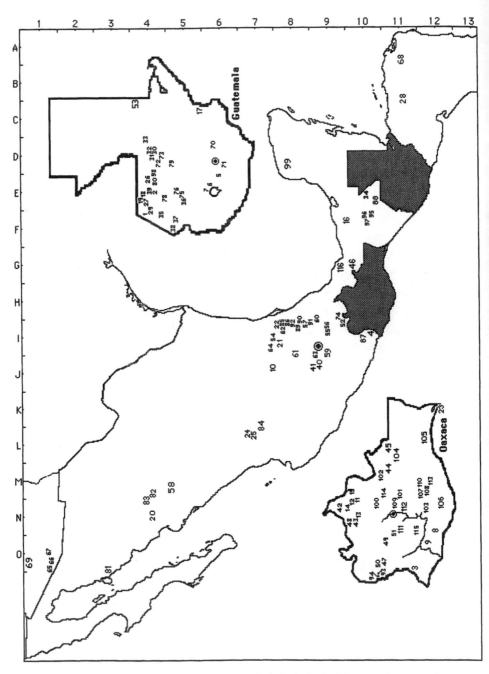

FIGURE I.1. Locations of the languages included within the Mesoamerican sample, keyed by number to table I.1.

TABLE I.1. The Mesoamerican Sample

Language	Location	Key to Fig. I.1	Survey	Collaborator and Institution	Interviewees	Naming Elicitations	Mapping Elicitations
1. Acatec	San Miguel Acatán, Huehuetenango, Guatemala	F4	MCS	José Juan Andrés, PLFM; Arvid Westfall, SIL-CA	19	19	19
2. Aguacatec	Aguacatán, Huehuetenango, Guatemala	E4	WCS	Harry McArthur, SIL-CA	35	35	0
			MCS	SIL-CA	—	0	5
3. Amuzgo	San Pedro Amuzgos, Putla, Oaxaca, México	N12	WCS	Susana Cuevas	5	5	4
			MCS	INAH			
4. Amuzgo	Xochistlahuaca, Guerrero, México	I10	WCS	Amy Bauernschmidt	25	25	0
			MCS	SIL-M	—	1	1
5. Cakchiquel	Santa María de Jesús, Sacatepequez, Guatemala	E6	MCS	Stephan Stewart, U. de San Carlos	12	12	12
6. Cakchiquel	Patzún, Chimaltenango, Guatemala	E6	MCS	Stephan Stewart, U. de San Carlos	10	10	8
			WCS	Débora Ruyán & Joanne Munson, SIL-CA	30	30	0
7. Cakchiquel	Tecpan (Aldea Panabajal), Chimaltenango, Guatemala	E6	MCS	Wenceslao Tucubal S., PLFM	13	13	13
8. Chatino	Santo Reyes Nopala (Cerro de Aire), Oaxaca, México	M12	MCS	Allen Lachmann, SIL-M	1	1	1
9. Chatino	San Miguel Panixtlahuaca, Juquila, Oaxaca, México	M12	MCS	none	1	1	1
10. Chichimeca Jonáz	San Luís de la Paz, Guanajuato, México	J8	MCS	none	1	1	1

Language	Location	Key to Fig. 1.1	Survey	Collaborator and Institution	Interviewees	Naming Elicitations	Mapping Elicitations
11. Chinantec	San Juan Lealao, Comaltepec, Choapan, Oaxaca, México	L10	MCS	James Rupp, SIL-M	1	1	1
12. Chinantec	San Juan Palantla, Tuxtepec, Oaxaca, México	L10	WCS	Allen & Patricia Anderson, SIL-M	25	25	0
13. Chinantec	Tepetotutla, Usila, Tuxtepec, Oaxaca, México	L10	MCS	David Westley, SIL-M	11	11	11
14. Chinantec	Tlacoatzintepec, Cuicatlán, Oaxaca, México	L10	MCS	Mabell Lewis, SIL-M	1	1	1
15. Chinantec	Tuxtepec, Oaxaca, México	L10	MCS	Leo Skinner, SIL-M	1	1	1
16. Chontal	Mesamán, Tabasco, México	F10	MCS	Jorge Raul de Moral Mena, CEM-UNAM	1	1	1
17. Chortí	Jocotán (Aldea Pelillo Negro), Chiquimula, Guatemala	C5	MCS	Vitalino Perez, PLFM	5	5	4
18. Chuj	San Mateo Ixtatán, Huehuetenango, Guatemala	E4	MCS	none	1	1	1
19. Chuj	San Sebastián Coatán, Huehuetenango, Guatemala	E4	MCS	Mateo Felipe Diego, PLFM	11	11	11
20. Guarijío	Los Alamos, Sonora, México	N4	WCS	Ron & Sharon Stolzfuz, SIL-M	25	25	0
			MCS		—	1	1
21. Huastec	Huehuetlán, San Luís Potosí, México	I8	MCS	María Angel Ochoa Peralta, INAH; Daniel Wilcox, SMU	10	10	10
22. Huastec	Tantoyuca (Xiloxuchil), Vera Cruz, México	I8	MCS	María Angel Ochoa Peralta, INAH	4	4	3
			WCS	James & Mary Walker, SIL-M	25	25	0

Language	Location	Key to Fig. I.1	Survey	Collaborator and Institution	Interviewees	Naming Elicitations	Mapping Elicitations
23. Huave	San Mateo del Mar, Tehuantepec, Oaxaca, México	I13	WCS	Glenn & Emily Stairs, SIL-M	25	25	0
24. Huichol	Santa Catarina, Jalisco, México	L7	MCS	Glenn Gardener, UNAM	1	1	1
25. Huichol	San Sebastián, Mezquitic, Jalisco, México	L7	MCS	Dennis Holt, UCLA	4	4	3
26. Ixil	Chajúl, El Quiché, Guatemala	E4	MCS	Dwight Jewett, SIL-CA	1	1	0
27. Jacaltec	Jacaltenango, Huehuetenango, Guatemala	E4	MCS	Baltazar Hurtado Díaz, PLFM	10	10	10
28. Jicaque	Montaña de la Flor, Francisco Morazán, Honduras	B11	WCS	Ron & Lynn Dennis	10	10	0
			MCS	SIL-CA	—	0	5
29. Kanjobal	Santa Eulalia, Huehuetenango, Guatemala	F4	MCS	Juan Diego Diego, PLFM	6	6	5
30. K'ekchí	Carchá, Alta Verapaz, Guatemala	D4	MCS	Stephan Stewart, U. de San Carlos	1	1	1
31. K'ekchí	Cobán, Alta Verapaz, Guatemala	D4	MCS	Stephan Stewart, U. de San Carlos	3	3	0
32. K'ekchí	Chamelco, Alta Verapaz, Guatemala	D4	MCS	Stephan Stewart, U. de San Carlos	1	1	1
33. K'ekchí	Lanquín (Yutbál), Alta Verapaz, Guatemala	D4	MCS	Pedro Tiul, PLFM	10	10	6
34. Lacandón	Najá, Selva Lacandón, Chiapas, México	E10	MCS	Robert Bruce, INAH	6	6	0
35. Mam	San Ildefonso Ixtahuacán, Huehuetenango, Guatemala	F4	MCS	Juan Ortíz Domínguez, PLFM	11	11	11

Language	Key to Fig. 1.1	Survey	Collaborator and Institution	Interviewees	Naming Elicitations	Mapping Elicitations
36. Mam	San Juan Ostuncalco, Quezaltenango, Guatemala	E5	MCS	David Scotchmer	2	2	1
37. Mam	Tacaná, San Marcos, Guatemala	F5	MCS	Tom Godfrey, SIL-CA	5	5	2
38. Mam	Tectitlán (Tichumel), Huehuetenango, Guatemala	F5	MCS	Eleanor Beach, SIL-CA	7	7	4
39. Mam	Todos Santos, Huehuetenango, Guatemala	E10	MCS	Richard Reimer, SIL-CA	1	1	0
40. Matlatzinca	San Francisco Oxtotilpan, Temascultepec, México, México	J9	MCS	Roberto Escalante, INAH	3	3	1
41. Mazahua	Nineteen locations (see fig. 10.19)	J9	WCS	Donald & Shirley Stewart, SIL-M	25	25	0
42. Mazatec	San Felipe, Jalapa de Díaz Tuxtepec, Oaxaca, México	L10	MCS	Terry & Judy Schram, SIL-M	1	1	0
43. Mazatec	Chiquihuitlán de Benito Juárez, Cuicatlán, Oaxaca, México	L10	WCS	Carole Jamieson, SIL-M	25	25	0
44. Mixe of Coatlán	a) Santa María Natavitas de Coatlán, Santiago Lachiquirí	K11	MCS	Searle Hoogshagen, SIL-M	2	2	2
	b) San José Paraiso (a ward of Santa María Natavitas de Coatlán)				2	2	2
	c) Santiago Isquintepec, Isquintepec, Zacatepec				2	2	2

Language	Location	Key to Fig. I.1	Survey	Collaborator and Institution	Interviewees	Naming Elicitations	Mapping Elicitations
45. Mixe	San Juan Guichicovi, Juchitán, Oaxaca, México	J11	MCS	Norman Nordell, SIL-M	1	1	1
46. Mixe	Sayula de Alemán, Veracruz, México	G10	MCS	Roberto Escalante, INAH	1	1	1
47. Mixtec	San Esteban Atatlahuca, Tlaxiaco, Oaxaca, México	M11	MCS	Betty Forshaw, SIL-M	1	1	1
48. Mixtec	San Juan Coatzospan, Teotitlán, Oaxaca, México	L10	MCS	Priscilla Small, SIL-M	5	5	3
49. Mixtec	San Juan Diuxí, Nochixtlán, Oaxaca, México	M11	MCS	Joy Oram, SIL-M	17	17	14
50. Mixtec	Santo Tomás Ocotepec, Tlaxiaco, Oaxaca, México	N11	MCS	Betty Forshaw, SIL-M	20	20	13
51. Mixtec	Santa María Peñoles, Etla, Oaxaca, México	M11	WCS	John & Margaret Daly, SIL-M	25	25	0
52. Mixtec	Xayacatlán de Bravo, Acatlán, Puebla, México	I9	MCS	Kenneth Wistrand, SIL-M	1	1	0
53. Mopán Maya	San Luis, San Luis Petén, Guatemala	C4	MCS	Matt & Rosemary Ulrich, SIL-CA	10	10	0
54. Nahuatl	Coxcatlán, Ciudad Santos, San Luís Potosí, México	I8	MCS	none	1	1	1
55. Nahuatl	Santa Buenaventura Nealtican, Nealtican, Puebla, México	I9	MCS	Tim Knab, IIA-UNAM	10	10	10

Language	Location	Key to Fig. I.1	Survey	Collaborator and Institution	Interviewees	Naming Elicitations	Mapping Elicitations
56. Nahuatl	a) Santa María Tonantzintla, San Andrés Cholula, Puebla, México	I9	MCS	Tim Knab, IIA-UNAM	8	13	5
	b) San Pedro Tonantzintla (a ward of Santa María Tonantzintla)	I9	MCS	Tim Knab, IIA-UNAM	3	6	3
57. Nahuatl	a) Tlaxpanaloya, Puebla, México	I8	WCS	Earl Brockway, SIL-M	5	5	0
	b) Iczotitla, Puebla, México	I8	WCS		1	1	0
58. Northern Tepehuan	Baborigami, Guadalupe y Clavo, Mina, Sonora, México	M5	MCS	Burt Bascom, SIL-M	12	12	11
59. Ocuiltec	Santa Lucía, México, México	I9	MCS	none	2	2	1
60. Otomí	San Juan Ixtenco, Ixtenco, Tlaxcala, México	I9	MCS	none	1	1	1
61. Otomí	Valle del Mezquitál, Ixmiquilpan, Hidalgo, México	I8	MCS	Donald & Isabelle Sinclaire, SIL-M	3	3	3
62. Otomí	San Antonio El Grande, Huehuetla, Hidalgo, México	I8	MCS	Katherine Voigtlaner & Artemisa Echegoyen, SIL-M	16	16	1
63. Otomí	Santiago Tilapa, Santiago Tianguistengo, México, México	I9	MCS	Sergio Vivanco, INAH	1	1	0
64. Pame	Santa María Acapulco, Santa Catarina, San Luís Potosí, México	I7	MCS	Lorna Gibson, SIL-M	1	1	1

Language	Location	Key to Fig. 1.1	Survey	Collaborator and Institution	Interviewees	Naming Elicitations	Mapping Elicitations
65. Papago (O'odham dialect)	Poso Verde, Sonora, México; Santa Rosa, Topawa, and San Xavier, Arizona, U.S.A.	O1	WCS	Dean & Lucille Saxton, SIL-NA	7	7	0
66. Papago (Ko-loodi dialect)	San Miguel and Sells, Arizona, U.S.A.	O1	WCS	Dean & Lucille Saxton, SIL-NA	4	4	0
67. Papago (Totogwuañ dialect)	San Xavier, Topawa, Covered Wells, and San Pedro, Arizona, U.S.A.	O1	WCS	Dean & Lucille Saxton, SIL-NA	9	9	0
68. Paya	Pueblo Nuevo Subirana, Olancho, Honduras	A11	WCS	Steven & Pamela Echerd, SIL-CA	20	20	0
69. Pima	Gila Crossing and Casa Grande, Arizona, U.S.A.	O1	WCS	Dean & Lucille Saxton, SIL-NA	5	5	0
70. Pocomám	San Luís Jilotepeque, Jalapa, Guatemala	D6	MCS	Thomas Smith-Stark, Tulane	1	1	0
71. Pocomám	San Antonio Palín, Palín, Escuintla, Guatemala	D6	MCS	Otto Schumann, CEM-UNAM	1	1	0
72. Pocomchí	San Cristóbal Alta Verapaz, Alta Verapaz, Guatemala	D4	MCS	Ted & Gloria Engles, SIL-CA	3	2	3
73. Pocomchí	Tactíc, Alta Verapaz, Guatemala	D4	MCS	Stephan Stewart, U. de San Carlos	1	1	0
74. Popoloca	San Felipe Otlaltepec, Puebla, México	H9	MCS	Ann Williams, SIL-M	2	2	0

Language	Location	Key to Fig. 1.1	Survey	Collaborator and Institution	Interviewees	Naming Elicitations	Mapping Elicitations
75. Quiché	Santa María Chiquimula, Totonicapan, Guatemala	E5	MCS	Gaspar Pú Tzunux, PLFM	10	10	10
76. Quiché	Momostenango (Xequemeyá), Totonicapan, Guatemala	E5	MCS	Pedro Sanic Chanchavac, PLFM	11	11	11
77. Quiché	Santa Catarina Ixtahuacán, Sololá, Guatemala	E5	MCS	Manuel Isidro Choxtum, PLFM	11	11	11
78. Quiché	Sipacapa, San Marcos, Guatemala	E4	MCS	Susan Hoiland, SIL–CA	10	10	0
79. Rabinal Achí	San Miguel Chicaj, Baja Verapaz, Guatemala	D5	MCS	Rodrigo & Carol Barrera, SIL–CA	5	5	5
80. Sacápultec	Sacapulas, El Quiché, Guatemala	E4	MCS	Jack DuBois, UCLA	5	5	5
81. Seri	Desemboque, Sonora, México	O3	WCS	Beckie Moser, SIL–M	25	25	0
82. Tarahumara (Central)	a) Samachique, Chihuahua, México	M4	WCS	Don Burgess, SIL–M	8	8	0
	b) Rojoyochi, Chihuahua, México				1	1	0
83. Tarahumara (Western)	a) Rocoroiba, Chihuahua, México	N4	WCS	Don Burgess, SIL–M	6	6	0
	b) Huicochi, Chihuahua, México		MCS	Willett Kempton, UCB	1	1	1
84. Tepecano	Atzqueltán, Villa Guerrero, Jalisco, México	L7	MCS	Dennis Holt, UCLA	1	1	0
85. Tepehua	Tierra Colorado, Tlachichilco, Chicontepec, Veracruz, México	I8	MCS	James Watters, SIL–M	1	1	1
86. Tepehua	Huehuetla, Hidalgo, México	I8	MCS	Susan Edgar, SIL–M	7	7	7
87. Tlapanec	Malinaltepec, Guerrero, México	I10	WCS	Mark Weathers, SIL–M	25	25	0

Language	Location	Key to Fig. 1.1	Survey	Collaborator and Institution	Interviewees	Naming Elicitations	Mapping Elicitations
88. Tojolabal	Santa Margarita Agua Azul, Chiapas, México	E10	MCS	Jorge Raul de Moral Mena, CEM-UNAM	3	3	0
89. Totonac	Zapotitlán de Mendez, Puebla, México	I8	MCS	Betty Aschmann, SIL–M	6	6	6
90. Totonac	Tetela de Ocampo, Puebla, México	I8	MCS	Betty Aschmann, SIL–M	4	4	4
91. Totonac	San Juan Aguacatán, Zacatlán, Puebla, México	I9	MCS	Antonia Espinoza & Blanca Garcia, U. Veracruzana	1	1	0
92. Totonac	Xicotepec, Apapantilla, Puebla, México	I8	MCS	Ruth Bishop, SIL–M	1	1	0
93. Trique	San Andrés Chicahuaxtla, Putla, Oaxaca, México	N11	MCS	Claud & Alice Good, Franconian Missions Society	11	11	0
94. Trique	San Juan Copala, Juxtlahuaca, Oaxaca, México	N11	MCS	Bruce & Barbara Hollenbeck, SIL–M	3	3	0
95. Tzeltal	Amatenango del Valle, Chiapas, México	F10	MCS	none	3	3	3
96. Tzeltal	San Ildefonso (a.k.a. San Alonso) Tenejapa, Chiapas, Mexico	F10	MCS	none	9	9	9
97. Tzotzil	Navenchauc, San Lorenzo Zinacantan, Chiapas, México	F10	MCS	none	6	6	6
98. Uspantec	Las Pacayas, San Miguel Uspantán, El Quiché, Guatemala	D4	MCS	Stanley & Margot McMillen, SIL–CA	11	10	11
99. Yucatec	Yaxtzabá, Mérida, Yucatan, México	D8	MCS	William Pulte, SMU	1	1	1

Language	Location	Key to Fig. 1.1	Survey	Collaborator and Institution	Inter-viewees	Naming Elici-tations	Mapping Elici-tations
100. Zapotec	Atepec, Ixtlán de Juárez, Oaxaca, México	L10	MCS	Neil Nellis, SIL-M	3	3	1
101. Zapotec	San Baltasar Chichicapan, Ocotlán, Oaxaca, México	L11	MCS	Joseph & Mary Benton, SIL-M	14	14	8
102. Zapotec	Santiago Choapan, Choapan, Oaxaca, México	K11	MCS	Larry Lymann, SIL-M	1	1	0
103. Zapotec	Santa Catalina Cuixtla, Miahuatlán, Oaxaca, México	L12	MCS	Jane Ruegsegger	2	2	1
104. Zapotec	Guevea de Humboldt, Tehuantepec, Oaxaca, México	K11	MCS	Barbara Morse, SIL-M	1	1	1
105. Zapotec	Juchitán de Zaragoza, Juchitán, México	J12	MCS	María Villalobos, SIL-M	5	5	3
106. Zapotec	San Augustín Loxicha, Pochutla, Oaxaca, México	L13	MCS	Jerry Gutierrez	2	2	1
107. Zapotec	San Cristóbal Amatlán, Miahuatlán, Oaxaca, México	L12	MCS	none	4	4	4
108. Zapotec	Santo Domingo, San Alefonso Amatlán, Miahuatlán, Oaxaca, México	L12	MCS	none	1	1	1
109. Zapotec	San Juan Guelavía, Tlacolula, Oaxaca, México	L11	MCS	none	1	1	1
110. Zapotec	San Juan Mixtepec, Miahuatlán, Oaxaca, México	K12	MCS	Roger Reeck, SIL-M	10	10	10

	Language	Location	Key to Fig. I.1	Survey	Collaborator and Institution	Inter-viewees	Naming Elici-tations	Mapping Elici-tations
111.	Zapotec	Santa María Lachixío, Sola de Vega, Oaxaca, México	M11	MCS	Dave & Jan Persons, SIL-M	10	10	0
112.	Zapotec	Santiago Apostol, Ocotlán, Oaxaca, México	L12	MCS	Donald Olson, SIL-M	3	3	3
113.	Zapotec	San Pablo Ozolótepec, San Juan Mixtepec, Miahuatlán, Oaxaca, México	K12	MCS	Roger Reeck, SIL-M	1	1	1
114.	Zapotec	San Pedro Cajonos, Villa Alta, Oaxaca, México	L11	MCS	Don Nellis, SIL-M	1	1	0
115.	Zapotec	San Lorenzo Texmelucan, Sola de Vega, Oaxaca, México	M12	WCS MCS	Chuck Spec, SIL-M	25 —	25 1	0 1
116.	Zoque	San Pedro Soteapan, Veracruz, México	G9	MCS	Roberto Escalante, INAH	1	1	1
	Totals					894	904	362

APPENDIX II

LINGUISTIC RELATIONS

Table II.1 outlines the genetic affinities of Mesoamerican languages, including their relatives outside the area. The estimate of "more than 100 indigenous languages" in Mesoamerica referred to in the preface is conservative. "It would seem, so far, that only about 50 of 300, or 17%, of Mesoamerican indigenous languages (including Mexico) . . . are likely to be moribund" (Hale et al. 1992:5). It is difficult to count these languages, especially when having to distinguish between languages and dialects. Mesoamerican languages comprise three stocks (Otomanguean, Mayan, Uto-Aztecan), two families (Mixe-Zoquean, Totonacan), and nine isolates, if one includes Xinca, Lenca, Paya, Jicaque, and Seri, which are outside of Mesoamerica but under its influence. The latter two, with Chontal of Oaxaca, might be part of the Hokan stock, most of which is in California. Oaxacan Chontal, Huave, Tarascan, and extinct Cuitlatec are inside Mesoamerica. Uto-Aztecan has many members north of Mesoamerica, and extinct Mangue of the Otomanguean stock was south of Mesoamerica. Many entities represented as languages, such as "Mixtec," are subfamilies, of which several members are represented in the MCS.

At least 200 non-Mesoamerican languages contribute to this study, either from the WCS, my own files, or the literature. Precise information on the genetic classification, location, number of speakers, and typology of most of the extant languages in the world may be found in Grimes (1984), its sequel (Pittman, Grimes, and Evans 1988), or Moseley, Asher, and Tait (1994). Grimes is a member of SIL, which furnished all of the WCS data and more than half of the MCS data; her information is exhaustive for the languages of both surveys. With the exception of Anbarra, she covers the nonMeso-american languages diagrammed in figures 2.13–33 as shown (with minor deletions and additions) in table II.2.

TABLE II.1. Indigenous Language Families in and near Mesoamerica

Otomanguean (Kaufman 1983)	Mayan (Kaufman 1974)	Uto-Aztecan (Steele 1979)	Isolates, Outliers, and Small Families
Amuzgoan	Huastecan	Numic†	Isolates
Amuzgo*	Huastec*, Chicomuceltec°	Western	Huave*
Mixtecan	Maya	Paiute, Paviotso, Mono	Tarascan
Mixtec*, Cuicatec	Yucatec*, Lacandón*	Central	Cuitlatec°
Trique*	Itzá, Mopán*	Shoshone, Gosiute	Xinca†
Popolocan	Western	Comanche°	Lenca†°
Chocho, Popoloca*	Cholan	Southern	Paya†*
Ixcatec°, Mazatec*	Chol, Chontal*	Southern Paiute, Ute	Jicaque†*
Manguean	Chortí*, Choltí°	Chemuhuevi, Kawaiisu	
Chiapanec°	Tzeltalan	Panamint	Hokan outliers
Mangue†°	Tzeltal*, Tzotzil*	Tubatulabal†	Chontal of Oaxaca
Zapotecan	Chujean	Hopi†	Seri†*
Zapotec*, Chatino*	Chuj*, Tojolabal*	Takic†	
OtoPamean	Kanjobalan	Kitanemuk°, Serrano°	Mixe-Zoquean (Kaufman 1974)
Otomí*, Mazahua*	Kanjobal*, Acatec*	Cupan	Zoquean
Matlatzinca*	Jácaltec*, Motozintlec*	Cahuilla, Cupeño	Zoque*
Ocuilteco°	Tuzantec°	Luiseño°, Gabrieleño°	Sierra Popoluca*
Chichimeca Jonáz*	Eastern	Pimic†	Texistepec
Pame*	Mamean	Papago*, Pima*	Mixean
Chinantecan	Mam*, Teco*,	Northern Tepehuán*	Mixe*, Tapachultec°
Chinantec*	Aguacatec*, Ixil*	Southern Tepehuán,	

Otomanguean (Kaufman 1983)	Mayan (Kaufman 1974)	Uto-Aztecan (Steele 1979)	Isolates, Outliers, and Small Families
Tlapanecan	Quichean	Tepecano*°, Pima Bajo	Totonacan
Tlapanec*	Uspantec*	Taracahitic†	Totonac*
Subtiaba†°	Rabinal Achí*	Tarahumara*, Guarijío*	Tepehua*
	Quiché*	Ópata°, Yaqui, Mayo	
	Sipacapa*	Eudeve°	
	Sacapultec*	Aztecic	
	Tzutujíl*, Cakchiquel*	Nahua	
	Pocomamean	Classical Aztec	
	Pocomam*, Pocomchí*	Central*, Western	
	Kekchí*	Eastern*, Pipil, Pochutec°	

Key:
* in Table I.1
° extinct
† outside Mesoamerica

TABLE II.2. Non-Mesoamerican languages represented by figures

Genetic Classification	Typology	Number of Speakers	Location
Agta (Dumagat)	Northwestern Austronesian	1,000 (1979)	Luzon, northern Philippines
Anbarra (Gidjingali)	Australian	100–150 (1973)	Northern Arnhem Land, Australia (Jones and Meehan 1978)
Apache (Western)	Na-Dene, Southern Athapascan, Apachean (White Mountain, Cibecue, Tonto dialects)	1,100	East central Arizona (data from Philip Greenfeld)
Buglere (Bokotá)	Macro-Chibchan (unclassified)	2,000	Mountains of western Panama
Cayapa	Macro-Chibchan, Chibchan, Barbacoan, Cayapa-Colorado	3,000	Ecuador, Esmeraldas Province, Cayapas River and tributaries, north coastal jungle
Colorado	Macro-Chibchan, Chibchan, Barbacoan, Cayapa-Colorado	1,100	Ecuador, Santo Domingo de los Colorados, northwestern jungle west of Quito
Ejagam (Ejagham)	Niger-Kordofanian, Niger-Congo, Benue-Congo, Bantoid, Bantu, Ekoid	a) 35,000 b) 45,000	a) Cameroon b) Nigeria
Gunu (Yambassa)	Niger-Kordofanian, Niger-Congo, Benue-Congo, Bantoid, Bantu	60,000	Cameroon
Halkomelem	Salishan, Central Salish (Chehalis, Chiliwak, Sumas, Tait dialects)	50, elderly	Southwestern British Columbia, Canada (Galloway 1993)
Konkomba (Likpakpaln)	Niger-Kordofanian, Niger-Congo, Gur, Central Gur, Oti-Volta, Gurma	a) 170,000 b) 27,000	a) Ghana b) Togo

411

Genetic Classification	Typology	Number of Speakers	Location
Kriol (Roper River Kriol)	English-based creole	10,000 (as first language) 20,000 (as second language)	Northern Territory, Australia
Kuku Yalinji (Guguyalanji)	Australian, Pama-Nyungan, Pama-Moric, eastern Pama	no data	Bloomfield River, Queensland, Australia
Kwerba (Airmali)	Papuan, North Papuan, Upper Tor, Kwerba	2,000	around Apiaweti, Irian Jaya, Indonesia
Iduna (Vivigana)	Austronesian, Oceanic, Papua Austronesian, Bwaidoka	4,900	Papua New Guinea, Milne Bay Province, North Coast, Goodenough Island, Esa'ala Subprovince
Lani	Dani-Kwerba, Southern Dani	150,000	Irian Jaya, Central Highlands, west from Baliem Grand Valley, Indonesia
Lillooet	Salishan, Interior Salish	500, age 40 or older	Lillooet River and middle Fraser River, southern British Columbia, Canada
Martu Wangka (Mantjiltjara, Kartutjara)	Australian, Pama-Nyungan	250–500	Jigalong area, western Australia
Menye (Menyama)	Papuan, Central New Guinea, South New Guinea, Angan	13,000	Morobe Province, Papua New Guinea
Múra Pirahá	Language isolate	110, mostly monolingual	Amazona, western Brazil
Murinbata (Murrinh-Patha)	Australian, Garaman	800	Fort Keats, Northern Territory, Australia

Genetic Classification	Typology	Number of Speakers	Location
Sechelt	Salishan, Central Salish	15 elderly	British Columbia coast north of Vancouver, Canada (MacLaury 1991b)
Shuswap	Salishan, Interior Salish	500, middle-aged or older	upper Fraser River, Southern British Columbia, Canada (MacLaury 1987a)
Slave (Slavi, Slavey)	Na-Dene, Athapascan, dialects: Slave, Mountian, Hare, Bearlake	4,000	Hay River and middle Mackenzie River, Northern Alberta and Northwest Territory, Canada
Tifal (Tifalmin)	Papuan, Central New Guinea, Central and South New Guinea, Ok, Mountain Ok	2,800	West Sepik Province, Papua New Guinea
Tucano (Dasea)	Tucanoan, eastern Tucanoan	a) 1,500–2,000 b) 2,400	a) Colombia b) Brazil (Upper Papuri River)
Walpiri (Warlpiri)	Australian, Pama-Nyungan, South West, Ngara, Yuendumu	no data	Hooker Creek, Northern Territory, Australia
Zulu (Isizulu)	Niger-Kordofanian, Niger-Congo, Benue-Congo, Bantoid, Bantu, Nguni	a) 5,421,000 b) 37,500 c) 5,700 d) 11,500	a) South Africa (mainly Natal Province; MacLaury 1995a) b) Malawi c) Lesotho d) Swaziland

TECHNICAL INFORMATION

An abbreviated description of colorimetric standards will put the Munsell system in perspective while providing background for arguments advanced in §4.1.1 regarding physiological evidence of perceptual axioms.

Color Solids

There are two three-dimensional systems of color perception, one composed of spectral light and the other of reflective samples. Natural sources of the former are few, for example, the sun, hot things, and bioluminescence. (The moon, a rainbow, or a translucent material with the light behind it are peculiar cases, as they appear to be luminous and are so for practical purposes, but they do not generate light; nor does the sky, which looks blue because photons from the sun rebound at short wavelength from molecules of the atmosphere.) No material system of standards represents spectral light, although there is talk of attempting to develop one with CRT technology. Most light that stimulates color perception reflects from a surface, as that of soil, a person's skin, or foliage (if no light shines through it toward the viewer). The material Munsell standards comprise only reflective samples.

Normal experience of reflective color would involve some average saturation, which may vary slightly according to latitude and season. Yet, because of the little-understood property of perception called "color constancy"—the ability of visual neurology to compensate—latitudinal and seasonal variations may have no effect on color perception (Maloney and Wandell 1986). No worldwide average reflective saturation has been computed (independent personal communications from Nick Hale and David Miller, 1993), apart from those composing the 18% grey card that photographers use (a secret of Eastman Kodak). My attempt to incorporate such averages into the axioms of §4.1 proved futile; I had expected to be able to say, for example, that the average experience of reflective green is more saturated than the average experience of reflective blue. Apart from the minimal data available, however, we have little indication whether average experience or memorable experience most influences cognition, if, indeed, there is a difference. And who knows how *average* and *memorable* are related?

Nickerson and Newhall (1943: table 1) represent the "Chromas at theoretical pigment limits for 40 hues, Munsell values 1/ through 9/," which are transposed to a two-dimensional format in figure III.1. The figure represents reflective colors at the most saturated levels at which people theoretically can see them. However, in figure 1.2, the maximum levels of saturation within the material Munsell color solid are those attainable with current pigment technology, which not only are less than the theoretical levels of figure III.1 but are less than the levels visible in nature, as, for example, the purple-red of a fuchsia blossom.

Nickerson and Newhall (1943) and Newhall, Nickerson and Judd (1943) specify the theoretical psychological color solid and the material Munsell color solid in terms of eleven levels of brightness, of which nine are chromatic, 1.0/ through 9.0/—the nine shown in figure III.1. This figure (and the table that it depicts) omits their lightest level of 10/ and their darkest level of 0/. In figure 1.2, levels 2.0/ through 9.0/ correspond to the same of figure II.1; however, level 1.0/ is omitted. Figure 1.2 specifies a lightest level as 9.5/N (N = "neutral," that is, zero saturation), "white," a darkest level as 0.5/N, "black." These lightest and darkest levels comprise single chips (cf. Jones 1943).

It seems that Lenneberg and Roberts (1956: fig. 6) used only levels 1.0/ through 8.0/ when they introduced the array to linguists and anthro-

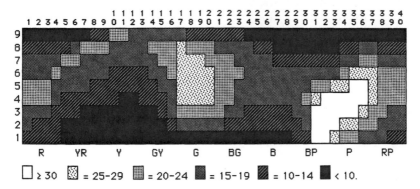

FIGURE III.1. Saturations at a theoretically visible maximum within the psychological color solid of reflective samples.

pologists. At least this is implied by their figure 6, but their presentation of stimulus materials is terse and informal (for example, in their figure 5, they wrongly assign twelve levels of brightness to the Munsell color solid). Whatever we must infer, their field array included only the 40 hue columns and eight brightness levels. Berlin and Kay (1969) adopted this 320-chip format, although they included brightness levels 2.0/ through 9.0/. Because the chips of level 9.0/ are easier to distinguish than those of level 1.0/, to exclude the latter was the right choice. They can hardly be distinguished, even at their maximum saturation; thus, they could hinder fieldwork while adding little data. Berlin and Kay added chips 1.0/N through 9.0/N as the achromatic column, augmenting the format to 329 chips. Nick Hale added chip 9.5/N when he prepared the color array that was used in the field by Berlin and Berlin (1975) and Dougherty (1975), which therein and thereafter appears in publications as the display format of 330 chips. Berlin, Kay, and Merrifield changed chip 1.0/N to 0.5/N in 1976 while preparing for the WCS. Not having noticed, I misrepresented level 0.5/ of my field array as 1.0/ (MacLaury 1986*a:* fig 1.3, 1987*a: l*fig 10), corrected here in figure 1.2.

Tristimulus Values and the 1931 CIE Chromaticity Chart

The Commission Internationale de l'Eclairage (CIE) has set various standards for the specification of color stimuli, ultimately definable by the wavelengths that compose them. Since wavelength occurs outside of the body and color sense occurs in the cortex, color stimuli and their appearance do not have a predictable relation. Yet in §4.1.1.2, evidence in support of axiom 3—that some pairs of elemental colors appear more distinct than others—relies upon two of the CIE standards, "tristimulus values" and the "1931 CIE Chromaticity Chart." Before I address the discrepancy between stimulus and sense, a thumbnail history of standards is in order.

Helmholtz (1896) showed that, when given three light sources of a single wavelength each (W_1, W_2, W_3), a fourth (W_x) could be added to any one of the three so as to match the mixture of the remaining two $(W_x + W_1 = W_2 + W_3)$, providing that none of the three by itself will match the mixture of the two others. Any such triad of wavelengths are called "primaries." Their choice can be arbitrary if the provision is observed. Helmholtz chose red, green, and blue; printers use magenta, cyan, and yellow.

Wright (1928–1929) conducted matching experiments with human subjects to demonstrate empirically the proportions of the primaries 650nm red, 530nm green, and 460nm blue that the subjects required to match all spectral colors. Wright devised a two-dimensional horseshoe-shaped chart of the "chromaticity space" that showed the amounts of each primary relative to the total of the three. One axis, C_1, represented amounts of red, and another axis, C_2, amounts of green. The third proportion, C_3, was not charted, although it was derivable from C_1 and C_2. See figure III.2.

In 1931, the CIE adopted Wright's system as a means of describing colors by trichromatic composition, specifying a standard observer and a standard illuminant. To eliminate Wright's negative values and to attain other advantages, the CIE adopted primaries of 700nm, 546.1nm, and 435.8nm. Figure 4.1 displays the 1931 CIE chromaticity chart. The CIE replaced Wright's axes with a commensurate Yxy system, by which the tristimulus values of any color match are expressed in wavelength. Two values, x and y, are attributed to any point of color within the prismatic parabola from coordinates of the chart; the third value, Y, is derived from the other two.

The Munsell system and the matches obtained in the CIE chromaticity chart together constitute the means of specifying pigments in science and industry. For example, the tristimulus values of the Munsell color 2.5 Y 8/16 are Y = .4957, x = .4800, y = .5910. The Munsell color solid differs from the CIE chart by including psychological spacing and luminance information. The relationship between the two systems is detailed by Newhall, Nickerson, and Judd (1943; see also Boynton 1979:19, 97–158; Hurvich 1981:270–297; Agoston 1987:Chapters 7–8).

As argued in conjunction with figure 4.1, the confusion lines of different kinds of color blindness contribute to an account of why green and blue appear more similar than any other pair of elemental hues. The confusion lines crosscut the chromaticity diagram; however, the diagram represents

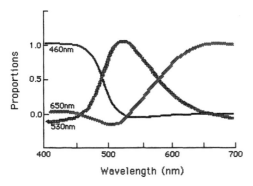

FIGURE III.2. Wright's proportions of primaries for achieving color matches.

not color appearance but color stimuli and the wavelengths that compose them. There is no relation between stimuli and appearance in terms of a predictable correlation, because at least three conditions may alter the appearance of a stimulus while no specific condition constitutes an absolute. First, color appearance depends on the viewing conditions of a stimulus; for example, the same grey stimulus will appear reddish against a green surround but yellowish against a blue surround. "Same" means having one set of chromaticity coordinates and identical spectrophotometric reflectance curves. Second, the same stimuli appear bluer or yellower under higher illumination but redder or greener under lower levels of light, an effect called the Bezold-Brücke shift. Third, there is a possible influence of rods on the fovea as an observer adapts to darker lighting, for example, as when entering a room from outdoors in daylight; this is one aspect of an adjustment called the Purkinje shift.

So why, in figure 4.2, do I mislead the reader by labeling color appearances, such as "red," "yellow," "green," and "blue," on the chromaticity space when the chart tells us nothing about appearance? These labels very crudely name one of the sets of senses that are registered in the cortex in response to neural processes initiated in the retina by wavelengths reflected from the corresponding stimuli in the chart. I must take this shortcut to give the reader some idea of the senses that a normal observer may derive from the stimuli that are connected by the confusion lines of color-blind observers. Otherwise, I would be unable to communicate the argument based on confusion lines without writing a treatise at the magnitude of the works cited above. This quick fix is intended only for the immediate purpose of getting across one idea to an audience who might not be predisposed to take a university course in vision science.

I note that others, some with sterling reputations in the vision field, have followed precisely this route, although subtly in cases (Boynton 1979: fig. A.3, imaginary primaries; Cornsweet 1970:227–231:n. 4, figs. 10.2–3, color plate; Gouras 1991: color plate 10; Padgham and Saunders 1975: fig. 7.10; Schrödinger 1970: fig. 15). For informed objections, see Hurvich and Jameson's (1969) review of Sheppard (1968: fig. 13 and frontispiece), who presents the chromaticity diagram partitioned into Kelley's (1949) twenty-two "color designations" plus a breath-taking color plate of Louis M. Condax's oil painting of hues on the chart (from the December 1965 *Official Digest/Journal of Paint Technology and Engineering*). Gouras (1991: plate 4) again reproduces this painting. Finally, in MacLaury (1987*a*), with permission of Sinauer Associates, I combined my figure 4.2 with other diagrams credited to Dr. Leo M. Hurvich. He informs us that he would not have condoned it had either of us notified him. It was an unwitting mistake.

A COGNITIVE CEILING OF ELEVEN BASIC COLOR TERMS

JOHN R. TAYLOR, HENRIETTA MONDRY, AND ROBERT E. MACLAURY[1]

A fresh answer to an old question is possible if we define category relations as the arrangements and balances of strength among the coordinates of a spatial analogy. Have some languages evolved more than eleven basic color terms? Specifically, certain languages relate distinct and salient categories of blue and light blue, as reported for Russian (Istomina 1963), Japanese (Uemura and Yamazaki 1950), and Central and South American Spanish (Bolton 1978*a*:293–294), but how do the languages constitute this relation? Berlin and Kay (1969:35–36) associate this question with another regarding two Hungarian terms for red.

> Hungarian presents a special case. It has basic terms for the ten basic categories exclusive of red and two basic terms for red. If this finding is borne out by further research, it may be possible to suggest a developmental stage other than those already mentioned. Similarly, Russian, as well as several other Slavic languages, is reported to have two basic terms for blue: *sinij* 'dark-blue' and *goluboy* 'light blue'. The status of *goluboy* as a basic color term is less clear. The work of Istomina (1963) shows *goluboy* to be less salient and less well understood by Russian children than the Russian terms for red, green, yellow, dark-blue (*sinij*) . . . Our own interviews with Russian-speaking informants are not conclusive but suggest that, for some speakers at least, *sinij* marks two categories—one includes *goluboy* and one contrasts with *goluboy*. Thus, depending on context, *sinij* has two senses,

---

1. J. R. Taylor and H. Mondry collected the Russian data from immigrants on their arrival to the Republic of South Africa. Mondry (professor of Russian studies, translator for the Russian Embassy, and originally of Latvia) arranged the interviews and provided further information on the language (Mondry and Taylor 1992). This study will be expanded into a comparison of method and theory between our research and that of the Surrey group.

'blue' and 'dark-blue'. . . . If this formulation is generally correct, *goluboy* must be considered a secondary term in Russian. The same argument may perhaps apply to Hungarian *vörös* 'dark red'.

Although Hungarian red has not been examined closely until the present (MacLaury, Almási, and Kövecses, in press), the researchers at Surrey have extensively studied Russian blue and light blue. They conclude that both categories are "basic," which implies that they are related by complementation.

> Russian is an interesting language. . . . Instead of the supposed maximum of eleven basic terms, it has twelve, including two . . . for 'blue', *sini* . . . and *goluboj*. . . . *fioletovyj* 'purple' emerged as a basic term at least five hundred years later than either *sinij* or g*oluboj*. . . . Russian has not only more basic terms than the maximum allowed by theory, but has also developed them in a different order from that predicted by the theory (Moss 1989*a*–*b*). [Moss, Davies, Corbett and Laws 1990:314]

The conclusions from Surrey are based on appraisals that *sinij* and *goluboj* are both highly salient and more salient than Russian terms for purple, yellow, or brown; using techniques introduced by Dixon (1982:23–24), Battig and Montague (1969), and Boynton and Olson (1987), the Surrey researchers quantify salience from word counts and native response during experiments. Their criteria include the extent of derivational morphology, frequency in literature, listing tasks, reaction time, inter-subject agreement (consensus), and intrasubject stability of reference (consistency) (Corbett and Morgan 1988; Morgan and Corbett 1989; Moss, Davies, Corbett, and Laws 1990). Yet, their conclusions differ from those that we shall put forth. The difference results, in part, because mapping with rice measures category relations more revealingly than methods designed mainly to determine salience. Two categories are basic when in complementation; one of them is secondary when the two share coordinates. In the latter case, the two terms may be nearly synonymous or coextensive, or they may be pulling apart in keeping with the dynamics of inclusion. The Surrey group assumes that salience alone will signal basicness, not acknowledging that salient terms can bear any relation and, perhaps, without coming to grips with the gamut of relations that can occur. To investigate whether blue and light blue are both basic, it is most effective to measure category relations directly. Figure IV.1 shows a Pame speaker's naming ranges and her mappings

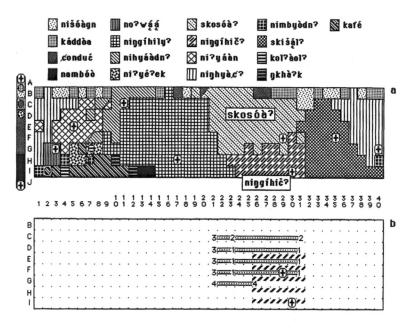

FIGURE IV.1. Pame, Santa María Acapulco, San Luís Potosí, Mexico; f 17, 1981: (*a*) naming ranges, (*a–b*) foci, and (*b*) mappings.

of *niŋgíhič* 'dark blue' and *skosóà* 'blue'. The dark blue range, focused at I30, is mapped over and beyond the focus of the blue range, F29, showing a relation of inclusion. The mapping of *skosóà* in light rows D and E and turquoise columns 21–25 is independent, showing that this relation of inclusion is advanced toward complementation. However, complementation has not been realized.

The Pame system parallels the conclusion of Uchikawa and Boynton (1987:1829) regarding the relation of Japanese *ao* 'dark blue' and *mizu* 'light blue' (< 'water').

> *Mizu* was used by the ten subjects with 90% consensus at 64% consistency (both greater than for *ki* and *ao*) . . . However, of the 79 samples named *mizu*, 61 (77%) are also named *ao*. Among the eleven basic color terms, those most strongly linked in this way are *aka* and MOMO, where 60% of samples named *aka* were also named MOMO. Thus *mizu* is not used quite as independently as the basic color terms.

Zollinger (1988*b*) corroborates this relation in Japanese with different methods. For the equivalent word-pair in Peruvian Spanish, van der Hoogt (1975:16) lists *celeste* as a hyponym of *azul* without even raising a question.

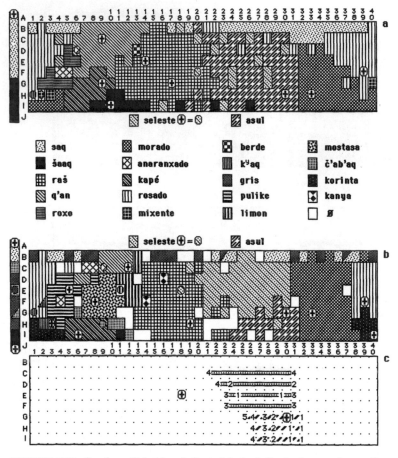

FIGURE IV.2. Southern Cakchiquel, Santa María de Jesús, Sacatepéquez, Guatemala: (*a*) m 56, 1978; (*b–c*) m 39, 1980; (*a–b*) naming, (*a–c*) foci, and (*c*) mapping.

Figure IV.2 shows naming ranges from two speakers of Southern Cakchiquel, including those of the loanwords *asul* 'blue' and *seleste* 'light blue' (< Guatemalan Spanish). Speaker (*a*) polarizes both foci at F20 and H30 and relates the terms coextensively. Speaker (*b*) also polarizes both foci, but applies the terms separately to dark and light blue, as does the Pame speaker of figure IV.1. But unlike the latter, Cakchiquel speaker (*b*) maps the terms separately with no overlap, suggesting that dark and light blue categories are in complementation. However, both Cakchiquel speakers polarized the focus of *seleste* outside of its naming range, F20 and E18, indicating that in both systems the dark and light blue categories remain linked and in opposition. Probably, speaker (*b*) maintains a relation of inclusion between *asul* and *seleste,* although it may have advanced toward complementation. This latter Cakchiquel case offers the strongest evidence of two basic blue categories among any of that collected by the three-part method in Mesoamerica or from Russian (Mondry and Taylor 1992), Japanese (Uchikawa and MacLaury 1986:MCS files), or Quechua (Johansen 1992). Yet it fails to show beyond a doubt that the categories are cognitively autonomous.

The data from Russian, Japanese, and Quechua indicate that speakers of these languages relate their two categories of blue in the same way as do speakers of Pame and Cakchiquel; they show individual variation but not patterned differences between the languages. Only Russian data are shown below, because the Russian terms have been most frequently cited in discussion of the blue-versus-light blue issue (e.g., Forbes 1979:296; Frum-

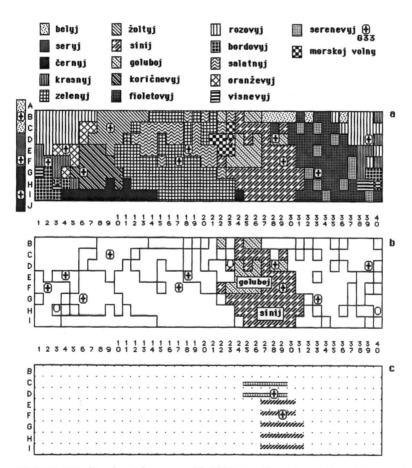

FIGURE IV.3. Russian, Moscow, m 25, 1992; (*a–b*) naming, foci, and (*c*) mappings (collected by John R. Taylor).

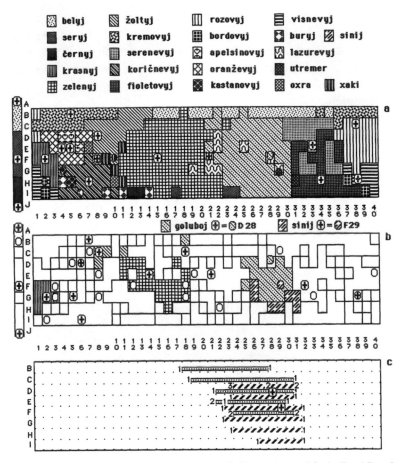

FIGURE IV.4. Russian, 1992: (*a*) Moscow, f 48, naming and foci; (*b–c*) Latvia, f 37, naming, foci, and mappings (collected by Henrietta Mondry).

kina and Mikheev 1983; Vamling 1986:231; Wierzbicka 1990; Zollinger 1972:5); the Surrey researchers base their claims only on Russian.

In figure IV.3, naming ranges show that *sinij* includes *goluboj*, even though they are mapped without overlap.

In figure IV.4*a*, a Russian speaker names all of blue only as *goluboj*; at least one Russian counters Berlin and Kay's projection (quoted above) that *sinij* will be the superordinate term. This speaker was not asked to map *sinij*. Some individuals may opt to name colors with only one of two terms when the two are related by near synonymy (fig 5.9). In *b*, a Russian speaker names colors with 36 roots, many with small ranges. Some are hatched in the diagram. However, her mappings are broad; those in *c* show that *sinij*

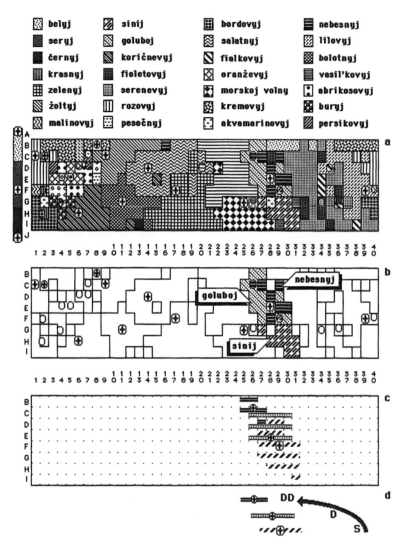

FIGURE IV.5. Russian, Moscow, f 28, 1992: (*a–b*) naming, (*a–c*) foci, (*c*) mapping, and (*d*) abstract depiction of relations between ranges (collected by John R. Taylor).

and *goluboj* bear a relation intermediate to coextension and inclusion. The focus of *sinij* corresponds to the naming range of *goluboj,* F29; the focus of *goluboj* is polarized beyond its naming range, D28.

In figure IV.5, a Russian speaker uses 28 terms, naming blues with *sinij, goluboj,* and *nebesnyj.* The foci of both *sinij* and *nebesnyj* co-occur with the naming range of *goluboj,* F29 and C26. The mapping of *sinij* includes the focus of *goluboj* E28, and the mapping of *goluboj* includes the

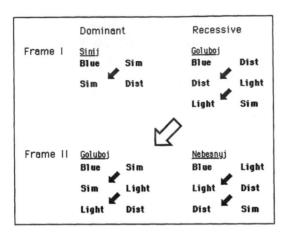

FIGURE IV.6. Formal model of blue, light blue, and ultralight blue categories as points of view in chain-linked frames, as among Russian *sinij, goluboj,* and *nebesnyj* or Japanese *ao, mizu,* and *sora.*

focus of *nebesnyj;* the mappings decrease in size through that order while distance between foci—that is, polarization—commensurately increases. This stepped configuration suggests the linked relation between superordinate and subordinate ranges diagrammed in figure 6.29; the relation can pertain to triple coextension, to triple inclusion, or to a combination (figs. 5.4, 6.27–29, 6.35*b*). In *d,* the diagram shows three levels of categorization in relation to predominant attention to similarity S, predominant attention to distinctiveness D, and ultrastrong attention to distinctiveness DD; these different emphases of D and DD match the degrees of distance between foci. Figure IV.6 repeats the formalism of figure 6.29, except that its coordinates include Light; category relations constitute two frames of reference, enabling transformations in the second frame: D > S, DD > D.

In the environment of blue, the dominant and recessive roles of *sinij* and *goluboj*—or their equivalents in other languages—may interchange substantially. The interchange makes it difficult to determine whether the relation obtains between categories of dark blue versus light blue or of blue versus light blue. Polarization further obscures the question. I have favored the latter opposition, which conforms to Istomina's (1963) observation that Russian children learn *sinij* before *goluboj;* since the recessive vantage derives by inversion of the dominant vantage (figs. 6.8 and 6.11), the dominant vantage necessarily is prior. Children would have no reason to favor dark blue over elemental blue when they originally construct *sinij.*

The Hungarian red categories, *piros* and *vörös,* are coextensive, as shown in figure IV.7. In this example, *vörös* is dominant and *piros* recessive; *piros* warranted a slightly smaller mapping and a polarized focus.

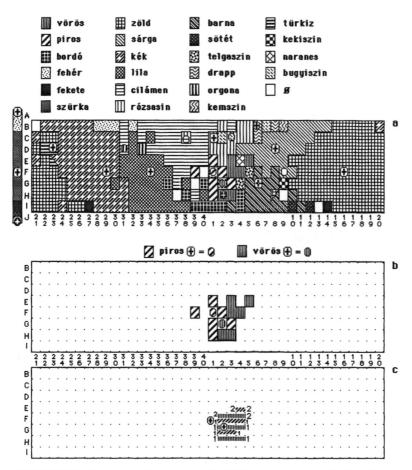

FIGURE IV.7. Hungarian, Budapest, m 45, 1991: (*a–b*) naming, foci, and (*c*) mappings.

(Our other interviews in Budapest showed that *vörös* is usually recessive; *vörös* is used metaphorically more than *piros* [citation above]; Grossmann 1983:1339; Mátray 1910:22–23, 46–47; Selényi 1946). The discussion that treated this relation as a mystery occurred before coextension was recognized or, at least, publicized (Forbes 1979:296; Frumkina 1984:117; Moss 1988:168–169, 1989*b*:315, 319; Wierzbicka 1990:100).

In the environment of brown, Forbes (1979) describes a coextensive relation in French of dominant *marron* and recessive *brun;* the focus of *brun* is polarized. Although she does not give the relation its own name, she notes that it departs from conventional wisdom and describes it for that reason (see note 1 of §5.0). French speakers tend to apply *brun* to contexts warranting aesthetic taste or delicacy, as when referring to paint, an ani-

mal's coat, or race. But they switch to dominant *marron* to purvey the ordinary or the indelicate, as in "un énorme rat marron." My two French
consultants used only *marron* to name color chips (MacLaury 1986*a:* Appendix I, figs. 5–6; 1992*a:* fig. 5). Forbes traces the historical emergence
of *marron's* salience and notes that some of her consultants distinguish
marron from *brun* more than others (as MacLaury, Almási, and Kövecses
[in press] find among Hungarian reds). Corbett and Morgan (1988:45, 58;
cf. Morgan and Corbett 1989:121) note that Russian brown terms *kori-
čnevyj* and *buryj* (cf. fig. IV.4*a*) are related in almost the way that Forbes
reports of *marron* and *brun.* They find the same kind of relation among
multiple Russian purple terms (p. 45), and Moss (1989*a*:151–152) determines that *fioletovyj* is basic with *sirenevyj* the next runner up; *fioletovyj* is
more prosaic than poetic. Their near-synonymous and coextensive relations appear with *fioletovyj* dominant in figures IV.3–4 and *sirenevyj* dominant in figure IV.5, showing synchronically the same shift that *marron* and
brun underwent over time. Malkiel (1954:179–180) notes that medieval
Spanish *bayo* and *bazo,* both meaning 'brown', are "more sharply distinguished by different frames of reference (horsehair, human skin) than by
clashing colors." Corbett and Morgan (1988: table 4, pp. 45, 49) and Wade
(1985:51–52) find that *goluboj* predominates in literary prose, as is in
keeping with the stronger analytic-synthetic tenor of a recessive point of
view (see note 11 of §9.5).

   In §2.4.2 (point 6), I criticize the fuzzy-set model for its inability to
impose a cognitive ceiling on the number of basic color terms without mon-
grelizing its epistemology of naive realism. The three-part interview has
yielded no evidence that any system will comprise more than the eleven
basic color categories that Berlin and Kay (1969) enumerated, regardless
of how many secondary terms abound. The latter will be related to the basic terms by near synonymy, coextension, inclusion, or even polarized inclusion that has advanced toward complementation, but no twelfth term
will be related to the basic eleven by complementation. The Surrey group
confirms that more than eleven terms can become highly salient, but the
data of figures IV.1–5 suggest that some are satellites of others. Vantage
theory models their derivative relations in terms of shared coordinates. At
the ceiling, terms become salient without becoming independent. Probably
the ceiling is imposed by human perception, which between blue and light
blue is too minimal to be comfortably overtaken by our capacity to distinguish on the basic level. The same inborn limitation probably pertains
among all colors in excess of the eleven that are distinguished over and
again by fully evolved basic systems. (See note 4 of §7.1.4.)

Postscript: A basic color term names a dominant vantage (X S^2-D). Such totally constitutes its cognitive definition. Normal people can construct the color domain from up to eleven dominant vantages. Any other color term names a recessive vantage or an ultra-recessive vantage (X D^2-S) and is, therefore, nonbasic. Its range and focus will show surface signs of its dependence, such as polarization, at least among most speakers of any language. The few who manifest no such sign will represent a percentage of the sample too small to prove that they construct autonomous categories—that is, too small to discount the likelihood that they maintain the dependence without showing it (Johansen 1992). Berlin and Kay's four operational criteria of a basic color term are limited, because they attempt to define a cognitive construct in noncognitive terms. The discrepancy has left such broad latitude as to enable opposite conclusions between this short exposition and the methodologically impeccable experiments of the Surrey group.

NORTH AND SOUTH
OF MESOAMERICA

Color naming typical of Mesoamerica (§12.0) exceeds the northern boundary of the area proper, which has fluctuated in the vicinity of Hidalgo for a millennium (Kirchhoff 1943). The common practices are found throughout the desert to south central Arizona; however, the shared complex stops abruptly at the southern perimeter of Mesoamerica in northern Honduras. Color naming beyond these margins contrasts with the Mesoamerican system of traits. This work considers color-naming systems north and south of these limits over a distance of about 1,500 kilometers (900 to 1,000 miles) in each direction.

North. Pima and Papago are, respectively, northern and southern dialects of the same language, occupying riverine alluvium versus the high desert in southern Arizona and northern Sonora. In figure V.1*a,* a Pima speaker skews the cool category toward blue and names green with a secondary native term. A Papago speaker (*b*) has divided the cool category after skewing it toward green and naming blue *s-ʔañíilimagi* (< Sp. *añil* 'indigo, anil'). In figure 8.27, (*a*) 19 Papago speakers focus the cool category with a green-to-blue ratio of 11:7; 2 foci are dual. The Pima (*b*) favor blue, 1:4. North of Pima, most speakers of indigenous languages skew the cool category toward blue, while south of Papago, skewing toward green extends to the southern edge of Mesoamerica near the Honduran border. The northern divide is at Casa Grande in Arizona.

North and northeast of the Pima are, respectively, the Navaho and the Apache, who speak closely related Athapascan languages. Lander, Ervin, and Horowitz (1960) and Ervin (1961) used 29 Munsell chips to determine that Navaho speakers volunteered their "cool" term with lowest response latency in blue and highest in green, suggesting that most skew the cool category toward blue; older speakers applied a secondary term to green, while juveniles did not (see note 9 of §11.3.6). Greenfeld (1986, cf. 1977), working with the Mesoamerican Survey, interviewed 22 Western Apache

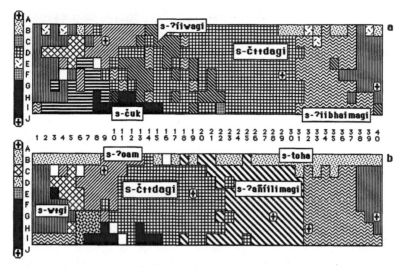

FIGURE V.1. Naming ranges and foci: (*a*) Pima, Gila River, Arizona, f 62, 1978;
(*b*) Papago, Tótogwuañ dialect, Big Fields, Arizona, m 42, 1978.

speakers at three locations; their cool-category foci are 10 green, 10 blue,
one dual, and one with a first choice in blue and a re-elicited choice in
green (fig. 2.18). One Apache interviewee suggested covert coextension by
mapping in steps from green to blue while focusing in blue (as did Northern Tepehuán speaker 3, who mapped from blue to green but focused
in green, fig. 8.30); covert coextension is the prerequisite of transference
(§§8.2.2.3–4.). All Apache have been located south of the Navaho for at
least 400 years; traditionally the Apache were nomadic, the Navaho sedentary or transhumant. The Western Apache marauded deep into Mexico,
camping for periods in the Sierra Madre and along the Yaqui River; they
incurred decimation and forced settlement during the late nineteenth century (Basso 1971; Opler 1973). This history placed the Western Apache in
contact with the green-skewing languages to the south, such as Yaqui and
Guarijío (figs. 8.34c and 9.1), and it may have aroused the stronger attention to distinctiveness that accompanies transference. Either their southern
contact or their harsh history would foretell that the Apache skew the cool
category toward green more than the Navaho.

Hopi, an Uto-Aztecan enclave language among Navahos, skews the
cool category toward blue while naming green with a secondary term
(David Shaul, MCS data). But Hopi shares skewing toward blue with
northern Uto-Aztecan languages, including Numic languages (class II1A
of table 11.1) of the Great Basin immediately north of Hopi. Nichols (1980;

1974:250–281) finds a complex situation among Numic languages that occupy a chain of locations across the desert. At the southeastern end, languages name the cool category with blue-focused *sakʷa* and, at the northwestern end, with blue-focused *puhi* or its derivative. In the center, languages use both terms coextensively, although the central southeastern languages focus *sakʷa* in blue and *puhi* in green, while the central northwestern languages focus *puhi* in blue and *sakʷa* in green. The pattern appears to be one of blue-focused dominance throughout, while central languages name the cool category from its green-focused recessive vantage with one or another interdialectical borrowing.

The Numic preference of blue may have been established in response to an Uto-Aztecan category of yellow-green-blue (§11.2.3). The widely used Central Uto-Aztecan *sawa* 'yellow' and its cognates look like *sakʷa* 'cool'; Uto-Aztecan etymological alternations of *w* and *kʷ* are common (Nichols 1980:162; cf. Miller 1967). According to Berlin (MS-2), the C. Hart Merriam vocabularies show that two Numic languages name yellow and green with one term (Archaeological Research Facility, UC Berkeley). The prospect of a widely shared Uto-Aztecan category of yellow-green-blue is supported by cognates, such as Cupeño *kənəkənəʔəš* 'green, blue' and Luiseño *kunóknuš* 'yellow' in Southern California (Hill and Hill 1970:233–234).

The influence of an Uto-Aztecan yellow-with-green category could impinge on Navaho through the adjacent Southern Paiute language, or the fourteenth-century common ancestor of Navaho and Apache could have used a yellow-green-blue category. The latter is suggested by Athapascan cognates from Northern California Hupa *łitsow* 'blue, green' (MacLaury 1992*b:* figs. 4–5; class I2A) or Mattole *łitsow* and Chasta Costa *łaθo* 'yellow, green, blue' (Greenfeld 1980: table 2, citing Sapir [1914:295, 297], Li [1930:10], and Hoijer [1963:11]), Navaho *łitso* 'yellow' (Lander, Ervin, and Horowitz 1960:371), Apache *łitsog* 'yellow' (Greenfeld 1986:909), Slave *detθoi* 'yellow, green, blue' (fig. 2.30*a*) or 'yellow' (figs. 2.30*b–c*), and western Canadian Chilcotin *delȼow* 'yellow' (MacLaury 1986*b:* figs. 9–12; class II1B); Ray (1953:102) measured the range of Chilcotin *deltsow* (*Teltso°'* by Ray) as covering yellow and green. Most speakers of Slave and Chilcotin, who are in the final phase of dividing the cool category, leave the original "cool" terms in blue, *diX̌ee* and *dilʒan* (fig. 2.30; MacLaury 1986*b:* figs. 9–12); they name green with a botanical term (cf. Broch 1974:193 on Athapascan Hare; see §11.3.4).

Salishan languages (class II1A of table 11.1) are located to the west and south of Chilcotin throughout the Pacific Northwest. They name a yellow-with-green category and focus the cool category in blue or restrict its current range entirely to blue (fig. 2.33; MacLaury 1986*b*, 1987*a*, 1988*b*, 1990, 1991*b*: figs. 1, 10; MacLaury and Galloway 1988; Galloway 1993: Appendix; Saunders 1992*a*: table 14.2). Kinkade (1988) reconstructs a Proto-Salishan category of yellow-green-blue.

Hokan Karuk (class I2C) abuts Athapascan Hupa on the upper Klamath River. As Hupa probably once did, Karuk presently focuses in blue a yellow-green-blue category that may earlier have had a range as broad as that of the equivalent Paya category (figs. 7.22, 7.24, and 11.4). West of Hupa on the lower Klamath, Algonquian (Ritwan) Yurok names yellow-with-green (MacLaury 1992*b*). WCS data from eastern Canada show that Algonquian Cree (class II1A) speakers separately name yellow-with-green and cool-hue categories, consistently focusing the latter in blue. Most Micmac (I2A) speakers, also Algonquian and east of Cree, skew the cool category toward blue.

In sum, it seems that at least Uto-Aztecan, Athapascan, and Salishan languages have a yellow-green-blue category in their prehistory which corresponds with the tendency of daughter languages to skew the cool category toward blue. The tendency persists as an areal trait in the regions where these language families diversified. Daughter languages such as Uto-Aztecan Pima and Athapascan Navaho seem to represent the southern outposts of this tradition. The closest relatives of Pima and Navaho, respectively Papago and Apache, show stronger inclination to skew toward green; they are located farther south. Uto-Aztecan languages on the Sonoran Desert south of Papago for the most part skew toward green, as do Yaqui (Brown 1983), Huichol (MCS files), and Tepecano (fig. 8.9), or they show late transference toward green, as do Tarahumara, Northern Tepehuán, and Guarijío (figs. 8.24–25, 8.29–30, 8.34*c–d'*, 9.1).

South. Among the small WCS sample of Central American languages that name the cool category, only Buglere favors green while six others favor blue. Carib [foci 6:7], Jicaque [3:5], and Paya [6:11] are the first attestations of brightness categories south of Mesoamerica. In Panama, Kuna [9:24], Ngäbere [14:17], and Buglere [21:16] coextensively name the cool category; Teribe [2:1:10] names it with one term.

In the Upper Amazon Basin—in the interiors of Colombia, Ecuador, Bolivia, Brazil, and Peru—14 languages in the WCS skew mainly toward green and 9 toward blue, showing a higher proportion of the latter than do Mesoamerican languages (table 11.1). In others, a strong emphasis on brightness precludes the cool category, as in Culina and Ucayali Campa, or cool-category foci are so extended that they cannot be identified as only green or blue, as in Mayoruna.

DATA ORGANIZATION METHODS

Figures VI.1–5 display the field notes elicited from Guarijío speaker 1, and figures VI.6–10 demonstrate the procedures by which these data were organized prior to analyzing them or depicting them in figures 3.1–10. The procedures apply to the organization of any data elicited by the MCS method (MacLaury 1988b). Figures VI.1–10 are drafted by hand rather than by machine to wholly portray the manual approach taken by the MCS. Certain procedures can be performed with a computer, as is exemplified by the WCS result in figure VI.11.

Current commercial database programs can accommodate the MCS organizing technique for head lexemes, qualifiers, and foci. Laptop computers and printers are easily carried to the field (not so when the MCS and WCS were conducted). But the manual method will stand in when the batteries die or hardware goes on the blink. Electronic organization of mappings may require custom programming, if even feasible yet. Although it takes six hours to organize a set of data by hand, during the process the analyst cultivates a familiarity with his subject that can be critical to developing an effective theory of it.

Figure VI.1 shows names applied to randomly ordered Munsell chips numbered 1–330 throughout four sheets. Conventions of notation appear among the data: for example, in response 18, a dash followed by a space before the name flags a hesitation, and a question mark in parentheses after the name registers an expression of doubt; in 63, a slash separates alternative responses while three dots signify a pause; in 70, square brackets enclose a canceled response while the name outside of brackets is the final decision; in 87, parentheses enclose an afterthought. Elsewhere, as in 168 *siyó-name,* a head lexeme and qualifier are separated by a hyphen, which was applied at the whim of the interviewer and is therefore not used consistently throughout the data (see 310 *siyóname*). Guarijío always modifies its native basic color terms with one of the qualifiers listed in figure VI.7. As the sheets were double-sided, identification occurs once on each sheet, twice in a data set.

Figure VI.2 shows the foci of qualified head lexemes. The interviewers were uncertain of which qualifications named a whole category and which named only a part, so they attempted to elicit foci for all qualifications (see note 5 of §3.4.4). The focus [D39] of *wa·rósa* is canceled in favor of D35. The second focus of *wetapáeme,* FØ, was spontaneously volunteered later by the consultant as he mapped this category.

Figure VI.3 lists the prompts used to encourage the consultant to map all of each category.

Figure VI.4 records the consultant's mappings. The interviewers had guessed, correctly as it turned out, that head lexemes qualified by *-name* designate all of a category. They did not elicit mappings of other qualifications. Let us take as an example *siyóname*. The consultant mapped this category in four steps, numbered I–IV. He placed his first grain on G19. The interviewer's statements at each step are indicated by a parenthetical number referring to the prompts listed in figure VI.3. The consultant's remark is recorded in slashes. Throughout all the mappings, the first prompt is used initially but the subsequent order of prompts is optional and, in particular mappings, one or another prompt is repeated while others are skipped. Mapping steps volunteered without prompts are labeled /spontaneous/.

Figure VI.5 shows the form used to record the consultant's background. Notes distinguish place of the interview from place of origin and indicate that the consultant was interviewed by the WCS while at home in 1978. In 1980, with an improvement of this form, investigators separately recorded places of interview and origin, even though they often were one and the same.

Figure VI.6 displays the seven sheets used to derandomize all naming data from the original encoding (fig. VI.1) and to situate foci (fig. VI.2) in relation to them. The seven sheets together represent the Munsell array, each sheet a specific segment of it. Letters and numbers of the rows and columns in the derandomizing sheets correspond to those in the Munsell array. Each cell of these sheets matches a chip on the array as well as its duplicate in the loose set. The cell also corresponds to the numbered response to this chip that is transcribed on one of the four encoding sheets of original data (fig. VI.1). The number of the response, in turn, occurs in the lower right of the cell. This provision enables the analyst to copy the data from the four encoding sheets (fig. VI.1) to the seven derandomization sheets (fig. VI.6). For example, in figure VI.6, cell B1 contains number

129. In figure VI.1, the response to chip 129 is *tohsáname*. This response is written into cell B1. In this way, numbers and data all match between the two sets of sheets.

Conventions used in the derandomization sheets are these: a head lexeme is underlined to distinguish it from its qualifiers; a focus is marked as an encircled X when it corresponds with its name on a chip, as in AØ, but when the focus and name fail to correspond, as in G17, the encircled X is labeled with the name and enclosed in double square brackets. In G-17, *siyomúrame* is focused on a chip named *siyóname*. In F25, the foci of two terms fail to correspond with the term that names the chip. The conventions described in connection with figure VI.1 are transferred in tact from encoding sheets to derandomization sheets. (Section 3.3.2 contrasts corresponding and noncorresponding foci in reference to the two foci of *wetapáeme* in figure 3.1, seen as well in cells FØ and E11 of figure VI.6.)

Figure VI.7 shows symbol keys that represent (*a*) head lexemes, (*b*) preposed qualifiers, and (*c*) postposed qualifiers. The symbols, which depict terms with only one or two letters, are devised in preparation for subsequent parts of the organizing procedure and some aspects of graphic display.

Figure VI.8 uses the symbols to present the data from figure VI.6 in compact displays on a single sheet that matches the Munsell array. Such condensed charts allow the analyst to discern at a glance the derandomized distributions of (*a*) head lexemes, (*b*) preposed qualifiers, and (*c*) postposed qualifiers. In *b* and *c,* visualization is aided by carbon-copying the outlines of head lexemes from *a,* which shows the relation of the qualifiers to the latter. The carbon-paper method can be applied to any compact diagram to extract selected data; for example, those in figures 3.2–3 and 3.10*b–c* were redrawn from such an intermediate chart. Figure VI.8*a* is redrawn as figure 3.1.

Figure VI.9*a* organizes the mappings of the basic terms from figure VI.4. Ordinarily, lines are drawn with colored pencil to distinguish different mappings with red, yellow, green, and such; but for the purposes of this demonstration, colored lines are replaced with hatching. This sketch is redrawn as figure 3.5, in the context of which the conventions of a mapping display are described. The head-lexeme outlines from figure VI.8*a* are superimposed on the mappings in figure VI.9*b,* as is depicted with partial re-drawings in figures 3.6*a* and 3.8.

Figure VI.10 shows a condensed array of the random number-to-chip correspondences that link the cells of figure VI.6 to the responses of figure VI.1. The compact key is used for checking data within displays against original transcriptions.

Figure VI.11 shows the result of computerized data organization by the WCS from the 1978 interview of Guarijío speaker 1.

language: Guarijío Bajo de Sonora   _Informant No._ #1

(a)

#		#		#		#	
1.	seyomúriame	21.	-tisa setamúrame	41.	sehtaname	61.	kawe sehtaname
2.	teesa siyóname	22.	wa'reherame	42.	warosahérame	62.	tiisa siyomúrame
3.	sehtaname	23.	setamurame	43.	ohčoname	63.	tiisa/ te esa... setamúriame
4.	ohčoname	24.	tisa očomúriame	44.	tosamúrame	64.	tiisa... tisa siyoname
5.	-siyoname	25.	tisa siyomuriame	45.	siyomúriame	65.	setapóčame
6.	wa'rósa	26.	ka'we siyoname	46.	wetapáeme	66.	tosapóčame
7.	ca'we siyóname	27.	tisa tosaname	47.	ohčomurame	67.	siyomúriame
8.	setamuriame	28.	tisa sehtaname	48.	wa'rósahérame	68.	setamúriame
9.	warosaherame	29.	tisa siyoname	49.	siyomúrame	69.	tiisa...wetapáeme
10.	ca'we siyóname	30.	čokonáhéame	50.	ka'we ohčoname	70.	(tosapóčame) tosaničame
11.	-očomuriame	31.	siyomúrame	51.	tisa wetapáeme	71.	--tosa sehtaname
12.	sa'waime	32.	setapóčame	52.	tosa múrame	72.	siyóname
13.	-tisa ohčoname	33.	-siyomúrame	53.	setapóčame	73.	setapóčame
14.	ka'we ohčoname	34.	ka'we siyomuriame	54.	-siyomúriame	74.	tisa siyóname
15.	geta počame	35.	sawa murame	55.	tisa si'yóname	75.	ohčoname
16.	tosa počame	36.	očomurame	56.	tisa warósa herame	76.	tiisa warósahérame
17.	tisa sehtáname	37.	tisa siyomúriame	57.	očomurame	77.	siyóname
18.	-ohčoname (?)	38.	sehtaname	58.	wetapáeme	78.	setapóčame
19.	tisa siyomuriame	39.	siyoname	59.	tosapočame	79.	[sa'we] ohčoname// očomurame
20.	ka'we siyoname	40.	siyomurame	60.	-ohčoname	80.	siyomurame
						81.	tiisa siyoname

(b)

#		#		#		#	
82.	siyóname	103.	tisa warósa	124.	sawamúrame	145.	si'yóname
83.	tisa warósa	104.	teesa siyoname	125.	tiisa sawamúriame	146.	wa'rósa
84.	tiisa warósa hérame	105.	teesa sehtaname	126.	tiisa sehtamúriame	147.	si'yóname
85.	kawe siyoname	106.	tesa sa'waeme	127.	očomurame	148.	ka'we sehtáname
86.	setapóčame	107.	tohsáname	128.	sawamúrame	149.	tiisa si'yoname
87.	(ka'we...) ohčoname	108.	tisa tosamúriame	129.	tohsáname	150.	ohčoname
88.	tisa sehtáname	109.	tiisa ohčoname	130.	ohčoname	151.	setapóčame
89.	ohčoname	110.	wa'rósa	131.	setamúrame	152.	tiisa wa'rósahémme
90.	očomúrame	111.	tisa očomúriame	132.	setapóčame	153.	siyočáme
91.	tiisa sawamúriame	112.	sehtamúrame	133.	siyočáme	154.	tisa wetapáeme
92.	tisa tosamúriame	113.	ohčoname	134.	ohčoname	155.	tisa čokorá
93.	siyomúrame	114.	siyočáme	135.	tisa sehtáname	156.	si'yóname
94.	-ohčoname	115.	sehtáname	136.	siyóname	157.	tisa čokorá hérame
95.	-tosamúrame	116.	tosapóčame	137.	tisa siyočáme	158.	tohsáname
96.	wa'rosa hérame	117.	ka'we ohčoname	138.	tiisa si'yóname	159.	sawamúrame
97.	? siyočáme	118.	tisa setamúriame	139.	tosamúrame	160.	setapóčame
98.	sehtáname	119.	ka'we siyoname	140.	ka'we si'yóname	161.	siyomúrame
99.	tisa setamúriame	120.	tohsáname	141.	tohsáname	162.	sehtáname
100.	tisa siyomúriame	121.	setamúrame	142.	tisa tohsáname	163.	si'yóname
101.	ka'we sehtáname	122.	siyóname	143.	tisa si'yóname	164.	siyočáme
102.	tiisa siyóname	123.	tisa siyóname	144.	ka'we ohčoname	165.	tiisa wetapáeme

FIGURE VI.1. Names volunteered in response to 330 randomized Munsell color chips by Guarijío speaker 1: (*a*) 1–81, (*b*) 82–165, (*c*) 166–249, (*d*) 250–330.

166. ačo-múriame	187. sawamúriame	208. wetapáeme	229. tesa si·yó-name
167. tesa-múriame	188. siyomúrame	209. si·yo-čame	230. tiisa wa·rósa
168. siyo-čame	189. tosa-múriame	210. –setapóčame	231. seta póčame
169. tiisa si·yó-name	190. seta-múriame	211. tiisa siyoname	232. tiisa wetapáeme
170. ohčó-name	191. si·yo-name	212. sawamurame	233. ti·sa siyomúriame
171. tiisa wetapáeme	192. setapóčame	213. ti·sa siyomúriame	234. si·yó-name
172. tohsá-name	193. [sawamúriame] sawamúrame	214. [sawamuridme te·sa] ti·sa sawamuriame	235. siyo-čame
173. seta-póčame	194.	215. ti·sa sehtá-name	236. tiisa sawamúrame
174. sa·waeme	195. ka·we sehtáname	216. ačo-murane	237. tiisa warósa(herame)
175. tiisa si·yó-name	196. siyo-čame	217. [setamariame tiisa] tiisa setamuriame	238. siyo-čame
176. tiisa sehtaname	197. tosa-wičame	218. tiisa sawamuriame	239. seta-póčame
177. sawamurame	198. setapóčame	219. tosa-múriame	240. –kawe wetapáema
178. siyočame	199. ohčó-name	220. siyo-čame	241. tohsá-name
179. ka·we sehtáname	200. tosa-púčame	221. tosa-púčame	242. sawamúrame
180. si·yó-name	201. setapóčame te·sa	222. seta púriame	243. seta-múriame
181. wa·rósa	202. si·yó-name	223. si·yé-name	244. tosa-púčame
182. seta-póčame	203. seta-muriame	224. tiisa [tohsá-name] tosa murame	245. setapóčame
183. tiisa čokorá	204. ohčóname	225. tiisa čokorá	246. siyomúriame
184. tiisa seta [murjame] –mučame	205. ačomurame	226. ka·we si·yó-name	247. ti·sa si·yóname
185. tiisa čokorá-hérame	206. tosa-múrame	227. ohčo-name	248. ohčó-name
186. si·yo-murame	207. setapóčame	228. ačo-múriame	249. si·yočame

(c)

250.– [si·] ačomurame	270. wa·rósa	290. wa·rósa hérame	310. si·yoname
251. tiisa siyočame	271. ohčóname	291. siyočame	311. ačomúriame
252. tosapóčame	272. tohsáname	292. setapóčame	312. ohčóname
253. tiisa si·yóname	273. setapóčame	293. tosapóčame	313. ka·we ohčóname
254. tiisa siyomúriame	274. tohsáname	294. tiisa tohsáname	314. tosapóčame
255. ohčóname	275. teesa wa·rósa	295. wetapáeme	315. tiisa si·yóname
256. setapóčame	276. setamúriame	296. siyočame	316. siyomúriame
257. ačomúriame	277. siyočame	297. (ka·we)sa·waeme	317. setamúrame
258. sawamúriame	278. tiisa sawamúriame	298. setamúrame	318. sawamúrame
259. setamúriame	279. siyočame	299. tiisa siyóname	319. tohsáname
260. sawamuriame	280. tiisa si·yóname	300. tiisa wetapáeme	320. tiisa wetapáeme
261. tiisa wa·rósa	281. ka·we si·yóname	301. si·yóname	321. setapóčame
262. tohsáname	282. ki·ka·we si·yóname	302. tosapóčame	322. tiisa si·yóname
263. tesa wetapáeme	283. tiisa wa·rósa	303. tiisa si·yoname	323. siyočame
264. tiisa si·yóname	284. tiisa tohsáname	304. tiisa wa·rósa	324. tosapóčame
265. siyočame	285. ...tiisa setamúrame	305. tiisa sehtáname	325. setamúriame
266. setapóčame	286. tohsáname	306. tiisa siyomúrame	326. sawamúrame
267. ačomúrame	287. wa·rósa	307. siyočame	327. tosamúriame
268. si·yoname	288. ´setamúrame	308. setapóčame tiisa	328. siyočame
269. setamúriame	289. siyomúrame	309. ačomúrame	329. wa·rósa
Idioma; lenguage: Guarijio Bajo de Sonora		No. del informante informant No. # 1	330. tosapóčame

(d)

Guarijío Bajo 9/29/79
Foci

siyomúriame   F25   wa·rosa herame   E6
sehtáname   H40   čokorá   E8
ohčóname   J39   wetapáeme   E11/F0
siyóname   F25   tosa wíčame   C33
wa·rósa   [D39]D35   seta póčame   E38
sa·waeme   C8   očomúrame   I32
tohsáname   A   sawamurame   C10
setamúrame   F38   siyomurame   G17

FIGURE VI.2. Foci of the qualified head lexemes listed in figure VI.1.

Guarijío Bajo
Mapping Prompts

1. Piiripi a'rosi yachasa yòma (sehtaname) = (x)
   Put rice on all the red   = (x)

2. Yachasa epeche … yooma (x).
   Put on more …. all (x).

3. ¿ toina (x)?
   Are there any (x) left?

4. ¿ intun epeche?
   Are there more?

5. kawe unatepa.
   Think well

6. yoomaja?
   Is that all?

FIGURE VI.3. Mapping prompts in Guarijío.

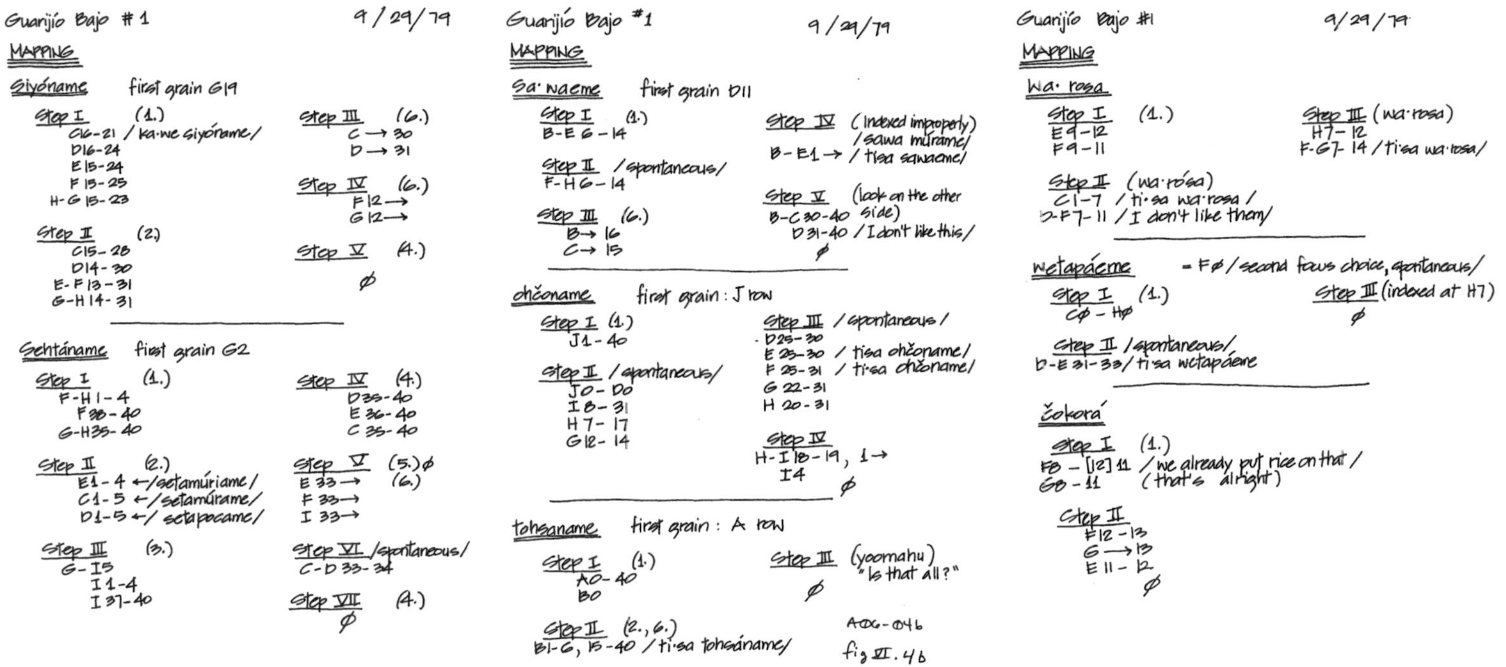

FIGURE VI.4. Mappings of Guarijío terms that name whole color categories: (*a*) *siyóname* and *sehtáname*, (*b*) *sa·wéeme*, *ohčóname*, and *tohsóname*, (*c*) *wa·rósa*, *wetapáeme*, and *čokorá*.

(a)

(b)

(c)

Información Demografica/Demographic Information

1. Informante No. / Informant No. 1 fecha/date: 9-29-79

2. Nombre de Investigador(es) / Investigator's Name(s) Ron Stoltzfus, Robert MacLaury

3. Idioma/Language: Guarijio ;dialecto / dialect Bajo

4. Iluminación/Lighting: inside - afternoon - 100 wt incandescent

5. Localidad de estudio/Locality of Study:

País/Country: Mexico ;Distrito/state / County District Sonora

Municipio Alamos Pueblo/Village La Junta

Aldea, barrio u otra unidad pequeña/ sub village unit dispersed population

ú otro tipo de localidad/ Other locality-type

6. Nombre del Informante/ Name of Informant Jesús Valdez Enrique

7. Edad aproximada/ Approximate age 35 8. Sexo/ Sex Male

9. Oficio/ Vocation Peasant Farmer . si suele de trabajar con tejido, bordado, u otras materiales de color, explique/ if informant regularly works with color materials, specify:

—

10. ¿Nacio en la localidad de estudio?/ Was informant born in locality of study? Yes
Si no, entonces ¿donde?/ If not, where?
¿y cuanto tiempo tiene en la localidad de Estudio? and how long has informant lived in locality of Study? all life

11. ¿Cuales otros idiomas o dialectos habla?/ What other language or dialects does the informant speak?

Spanish

12. ¿De donde proceden sus padres?/ Where are informant's parents from?

madre/mother close to Setajaqui ; padre/father Mesa Colorado

13. ¿Cuales otros idiomas o dialectos habla(ba)n? What other languages or dialects do/did they speak?

madre/mother none ; padre/father little Spanish

14. Comentaria opcional (p. ej., escuela, experienca afuera, rasgos exceptionales)/Optional comments (e.g., schooling, foreign contact, exceptional characteristics): (otro lado/over)

Jesus Valdez first interviewed by WCS August 1978 in Sonora as Speaker # 19, giving origin as Masacopa and age as 35. Present interview in Ixmiquilpan, Hdgo., Mex. at SIL workshop. Gave origin as La Junta and birthdate as 24 May 1944.

FIGURE VI.5. Identification sheet.

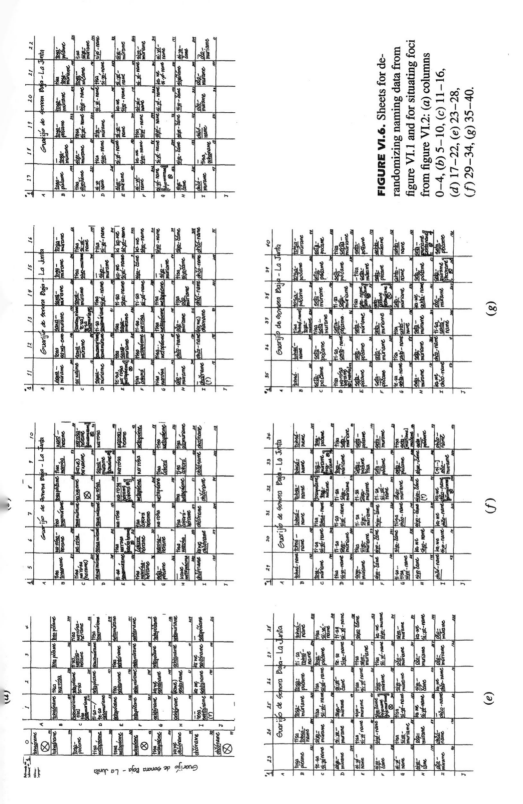

FIGURE VI.6. Sheets for derandomizing naming data from figure VI.1 and for situating foci from figure VI.2: (a) columns 0–4, (b) 5–10, (c) 11–16, (d) 17–22, (e) 23–28, (f) 29–34, (g) 35–40.

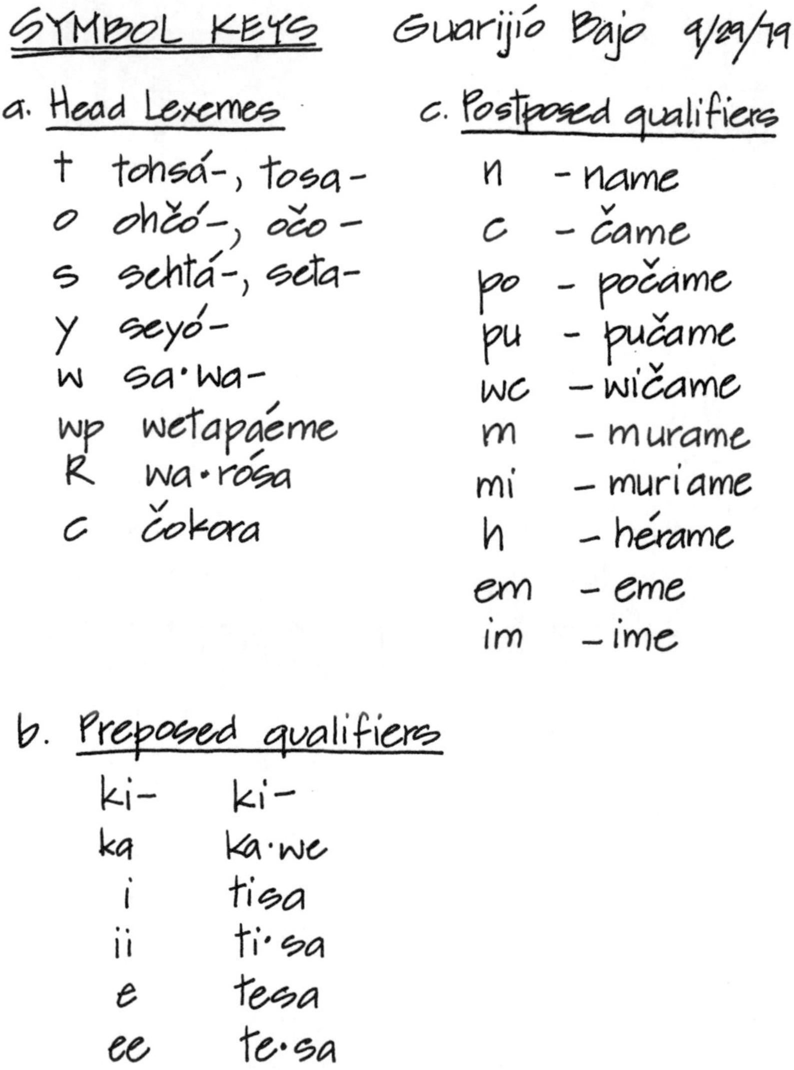

SYMBOL KEYS   Guarijío Bajo 9/29/79

a. Head Lexemes   c. Postposed qualifiers

  t   tohsá-, tosa-   n   – name
  o   ohčó-, očo –   c   – čame
  s   sehtá-, seta-   po   – počame
  y   seyó-   pu   – pučame
  w   sa·wa-   wc   – wičame
  wp wetapáeme   m   – murame
  R   wa·rósa   mi   – muriame
  c   čokora   h   – hérame
                               em   – eme
                               im   – ime

b. Preposed qualifiers

  ki-   ki-
  ka   ka·we
  i   tisa
  ii   ti·sa
  e   tesa
  ee   te·sa

FIGURE VI.7. Symbol keys: (*a*) head lexemes, (*b*) preposed qualifiers, (*c*) postposed qualifiers.

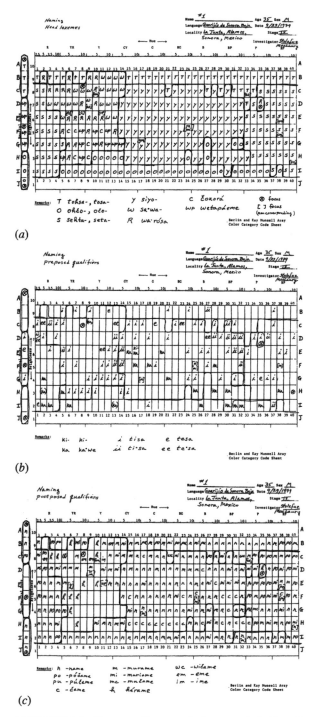

FIGURE VI.8. Compact diagrams that use symbols from figure VI.7 to condense an overview of naming data and foci from figure VI.6: (*a*) head lexemes, (*b*) preposed qualifiers, (*c*) postposed qualifiers.

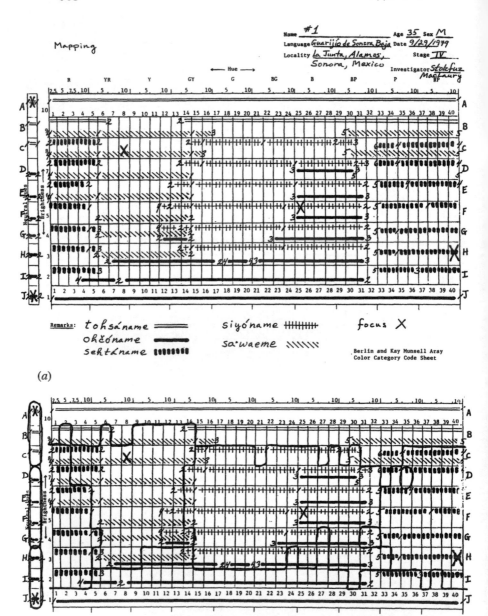

FIGURE VI.9. Compact diagrams of mappings from figure VI.4 and foci from figure VI.2: (*a*) basic color categories with (*b*) head-lexeme outlines superimposed from figure VI.8*a*.

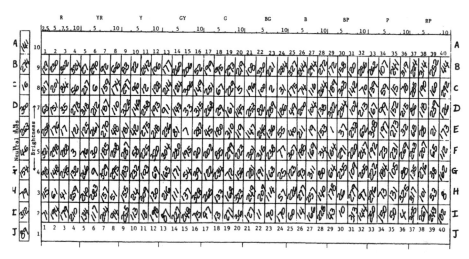

FIGURE VI.10. A key linking color chips as they are positioned in the Munsell array to the random order by which they are presented during a naming elicitation, as in figure VI.1; a compact display of the cell-numbers in figure VI.6.

OVERVIEW INVENTORY: GUARIJIO LANGUAGE MEXICO

```
              Terms chosen by speaker #19
                 1         2         3         4
     01234567890123456789012345678901234567890
  A  !!!!!!!!!!!!!!!!!!!!!!!!!!!!!!!!!!!!!!!!!!!  A
  B  !!!!!!!!!!/!$$$!$!!!%!%!!!!!!!!!!!!!!!!!!!!  B
  C  !#,$/$$$$$$$$%%%%%%%%%%%%!%%%!!!!!######  C
  D  !###$$$$$$$$$$$%%%%%%%%%%%%%%%%!!######  D
  E  %###$$/$$/$$$$%%%%%%%%%%%%%%%%%#######  E
  F  "###$$/''$/$%%%%%%%%%%%%%%%%%%%#######  F
  G  "###'''//'$%$$%%%%%%%%%%%%%%%"#%######  G
  H  "###'''/''""%"%%%%%%%%%%%%%%"%%#####,#  H
  I  "###"""""""""""""%%%%"""""""""%"""""#"###  I
  J  """"""""""""""""""""""""""""""""""""""""""  J
(a)
              Focal points for speaker #19
                 1         2         3         4
     01234567890123456789012345678901234567890
  A  !!!!!!!!!!!!!!!!!!!!!!!!!!!!!!!!!!!!!!!!!!!  A
  B                                               B
  C              $                                C
  D              /                                D
  E              '                                E
  F                   %                           F
  G      #                                        G
  H                                               H
  I                                               I
  J  """"""""""""""""""""""""""""""""""""""""""  J
(b)
```

FIGURE VI.11. Electronically organized results of the 1978 WCS interview of Guarijío speaker 1, therein speaker #19 (from Kay, Berlin, and Merrifield 1991a): (a) head
lexemes are symbolized as ! *tohsá-,* " *oscó-,* # *sehtá-,* % *siyó-,* $ *saawa-,* / *waarósa,*
and ' *cokorá* (WCS orthography differs from MCS transcription); (b) the symbols
represent foci of ! *tohsáname,* " *oscóname,* # *sehtáname,* % *siyóname,* $ *saawaeme,*
/ *waarósa,* and ' *cokorá.*

INVENTORY OF OBSERVATIONS

Chapter 2: Issues in Color Ethnography

1. Brightness categories merge with the hue sequence, but not the reverse.
2. Color-category evolution can consist of reconfiguring brightness categories to hue categories rather than of dividing categories and adding categories.
3. Hue categories evolve by division and addition.
4. The sequencing of evolutionary stages of hue categories is more predictable than the timing by which brightness categories will merge with the hue sequence.
5. Any brightness system may merge with the hue sequence one category after another; it may complete its merger with a total hue configuration representing any of Stages I–V.
6. Each brightness category in a system incrementally shifts its emphasis to hue (allowably over more than one generation); unless all categories of the system recognize only brightness, each will exhibit a different increment. The system may be individual or shared in accord with the extent of local variation.
7. In a Stage I system of strong emphasis on brightness, the range of one term may cover almost all of the Munsell array while the other correspondingly covers only a row or two. In some languages, such terms may be abruptly converted between hue and brightness meanings by one individual in response to different procedures (say, naming and mapping) during a single two-hour interview.
8. Binary categories may appear after Stage II of the 1975 hue sequence. Addition of binary categories and desaturation categories can parallel assimilation of brightness categories to an emphasis on hue.
9. Categories of yellow-with-green can descend from sources outside of

the 1975 hue sequence and will remain as exceptions to the sequence, even though they categorize hue.

10. Hue categories constituting exceptions to the 1975 hue sequence are far fewer than hue categories that fit the sequence.

11. Three Polynesian languages are reported to evolve directly from Stage II or Stage IIIb to Stage V (table 11.1, class VI). They name green and blue with descriptive compounds, atypical of basic color terms. No mappings have been collected. A WCS language, Vagla, uses compounds in this way to name secondary categories within a Stage II system (see 22), but the stage could only be ascertained by corresponding with the investigator who collected the data.

12. Martu Wangka speakers all focus a variable green-with-yellow or green-with-blue range in yellowish green. The range flip-flops between speakers. Some Lani speakers name such a range. Speakers of both languages represent early stages. Hanunóo is reported to similarly focus a more restricted range, and, as far as classicists can determine, Homeric Greek so focused a salient term with a range of pale, green-to-yellow, and honey color.

13. Desaturation categories commonly accompany Stage IV. They may be named coextensively. They include levels of brightness and perceptual mixture in many combinations; their ranges are more variable than are those of hue categories; after Stage V, they disappear or they become binary basic categories or a blue category, and they manifest states of transition.

14. Foci never "float." They show patterned differences between categories, stages of evolution, and languages.

Chapter 3: Descriptive Method

15. Most individuals add to a mapping when asked to include more colors of X-name.

16. The lexeme that names the entire category is used most frequently to name colors near its focus.

17. An individual who focused on an elemental hue while at home focused between unique hues while away from home and during analytical training (see 80).

18. One elemental hue can be a member of two categories that are focused in reference to other hues they do not share. Its membership is greater in one of the categories.

Chapter 4: Axioms

19. Opponent hues will never be combined in a hue category. They may be covered by a brightness category but incidentally, as hue is not what a brightness category mainly pertains to.
20. The warm category divides before the cool category.
21. Division pertains to all categories at once but shows different progress in each.
22. Division is continuous, not saltant or punctuated (see 11).
23. Division may consist of changing a relation of inclusion to complementation.
24. There are different types of semantic relations.
25. Different semantic relations correspond with distinct degrees of category division.
26. A composite category divides by retracting its range toward its focus while another category takes exclusive dominion over colors that are farthest from the original focus and left outside the retracting range (see 87).
27. A category, at least when it is newly basic, will have a broader range than when included by another category. Basic ranges shrink as evolution progresses.
28. The later the stage of a system, the more secondary categories it will include.
29. Category boundaries assume a sharply bounded appearance at later stages but appear diffuse at earlier stages.
30. Color-category evolution excels in environments of novelty, which are complex or otherwise demanding; members of simple societies can represent a late evolutionary stage.
31. Bilinguals mainly accommodate loanwords to native notions, not native categories to foreign ones; color terms are defined anew as they cross a linguistic boundary.
32. The extent of differentiation with which people are comfortable in unmarked circumstances increases as part of evolutionary advance.
33. Secondary terms become basic as differentiation increases.
34. A category can be salient but encompassed by another category; it becomes "basic" gradually as the encompassing range retracts. Salience is relative.
35. A system can incorporate fewer basic categories than salient terms.
36. A system retains vestiges of its past and projects its future.
37. Change occurs in spite of fixed panhuman perceptual neurology.
38. Languages differ in their number of basic terms.

39. Speakers of the same language differ in their number of basic terms, even within a small community and within the same generation.
40. Newly added terms usually assume a relation of coextension or inclusion, although a new term can solely name a basic category of colors that were previously left unnamed by the shrinkage of an established range.
41. Change may move toward reconfiguration or greater differentiation. Change never decreases differentiation without reconfiguration; for example, terms may be lost in the transition from emphasizing brightness to emphasizing hue, as occurred in Zapotec and Old English.

Chapter 5: Coextensive Semantic Ranges

42. Some categories are named with two terms whose ranges overlap each other's foci and that each overlap two unique hues when the category includes two hues. Their mappings on average share much of their combined coverage and proceed from opposite directions. One or both foci can be polarized, sometimes to an extreme beyond the naming ranges. Their naming ranges can be fully commingled, slightly intermixed, or seemingly separate.
43. Coextensive ranges show greater dichotomy in the warm category than in the cool category regarding polarization, separation of naming ranges, direction of mappings, placement of foci, and infrequency of crossover.
44. Foci or mappings sometimes do not match other data, such as a confined mapping or an extremely polarized focus, or such as a naming range and its mapping that occur on opposite sides of a category.
45. The four ideal types of semantic relation are near synonymy, coextension, inclusion, and complementation.
46. The semantic typology is continuous; pristine types mark points on the continuum, while real systems represent points between the ideals.
47. Semantic types evolve in a predictable order.
48. Evolution of semantic types and evolution of basic categories unfold together.
49. Semantic types later on the continuum show independent evidence of stronger attention to distinctiveness.
50. In the warm category, semantic evolution begins early on the continuum, whereas in the cool category the evolution tends to begin later or, in some cases, occurs after a category has divided by leaving one unique hue unnamed.

51. Semantic types consisting of two terms need not occur; or an individual on a given day may choose not to use all of the names that he or she would use on another day.

Chapter 6: Vantages

52. Coextension manifests a dominant-recessive pattern defined by centrality of foci and sizes of naming ranges, mappings, and mapping steps.
53. There is evidence that the dominant-recessive pattern of coextension is not neurally determined, culturally prescribed, attributable to poor vision, or established by habit of using one term more than its counterpart.
54. In spite of substantial variation throughout coextensively named warm categories, the dominant-recessive pattern pertains to over 70% of them (note 2). Coextensive cool categories show 60% predictability, although they, too, vary in nearly every other respect (table 11.5).
55. Coextension is rarely triple; inclusion can be of three levels; two ranges can be coextensively related while the recessive range includes a third range. Tzotzil speakers showed four levels of inclusion, and they accompanied this unprecedented feat with a record number of mapping steps per category.
56. Qualifiers conform to the dominant-recessive pattern. All qualifiers modifying the dominant term can modify the recessive term, but the recessive term can be modified by a qualifier that pertains exclusively to it. The dominant term will be modified by more augmentatives and fewer diminutives than the recessive term.
57. The ranges of two names for one category shrink as their relation evolves, but the recessive range shrinks faster than the dominant range.

Chapter 7: Category Division

58. As coextension becomes inclusion, its foci lose their dominant-recessive relation to become randomly polarized.
59. Foci of ranges related by inclusion are more often polarized than foci of coextensive ranges.
60. Rare cases of inclusion resemble the logicians' preconception of one range tucked within another, although even these show polarization; usually both ranges pull in opposite directions with the superordinate range partially overarching.
61. Any category, even a nonbasic category, shows at least some sign of

dividing, such as skewing, although it may never fully divide. But its dissolution will become conspicuous if inclusion transforms to complementation.

62. Categories remain in polarized opposition after naming ranges and mappings cover separate colors with little overlap.

63. Speakers of various Mesoamerican languages describe both geopolitical relations and category relations in terms of points rather than boundaries and in terms of dominance and dependence and of chains of such. Their anthropocentric analogy aptly captures the relation between large and small ranges that overlap partially with foci wide apart.

64. Mirror-image relations of inclusion obtain in the warm and dark-cool categories, as shown by comparing related languages or even speakers of one language.

Chapter 8: Skewing and Darkening

65. Most cool categories are named with a single term.

66. When people stress hue, the cool category skews as it divides. After division, the original "cool" term names the hue that skewing formerly favored (see 94).

67. The foci of basic green and basic blue categories darken.

68. Categories continuously mapped are focused more centrally than categories disjunctively mapped.

69. After the cool category divides, skewing stops advancing. But basic green and blue categories are no less skewed than cool categories in the final phase of division.

70. The focus aggregate of cool categories in specific languages shows a dominant-recessive pattern of more centralization in green and more polarization in blue.

71. As division of the cool category progresses, blue foci transfer to green. Dominant coextensive ranges favor green.

72. A skewed "cool" term may encompass a secondary term, but only one that names the hue that is opposite its direction of skewing (see 89).

73. Different languages show distinct distributions of single foci, some polarized in blue, some with each choice in either green or blue but none in both, some centralized in green, and others polarized in green. Separate languages distribute foci in green and blue at different proportions, often showing the dominant-recessive pattern (see 86).

74. In the aggregate of all cool-category foci, pluralities occur on unique hues.

Chapter 9: Submerged versus Reflective Categorization

75. Evidence of strong differentiation accompanies dual foci, but it may also accompany single foci.
76. Nothing predicts dual foci, which are somewhat rare.
77. The one aggregate of dual foci from a Mesoamerican language shows the dominant-recessive pattern.
78. In that language, most dual foci were placed in green first and blue second.
79. Null responses are indices of skewing toward green and, in the one language, correspond with dual foci. Dual foci disappear in correlation with the highest frequency of null responses.
80. Triple foci are vary rare. The only reported case coincides with vast social change, the speakers' midlife switch to the national language, and demise of the native language (see 17).
81. In the sole case of triple foci, they are placed on blue first, green second, and turquoise last.
82. In some languages that focus the cool category in green and blue, such as Tzeltal, no dual foci were volunteered after many interviews, 52 for Tzeltal. In such languages, rare individuals canceled a focus on one hue while choosing a final focus on an opposite hue.

Chapter 10: Crossover

83. In some cool categories, the naming range of a single term may be skewed toward one hue and its mapping skewed toward the other. The focus may land anywhere.
84. Coextensive naming ranges and mappings, too, may mismatch each other on opposite hues of the cool category, and each may show an opposite pattern. Different speakers of the same language will compound the muddle with their own ways of criss-crossing responses to different interview procedures.
85. Crossed-over coextensive ranges maintain the dominant-recessive pattern as do coextensive ranges that do not cross over.
86. Focus aggregates of single crossover "cool" terms in any language that sanctions them will show individual choices in green, blue, or both; but they will not show a dominant-recessive pattern, unlike focus aggregates of single "cool" terms in languages that do not sanction such crossover (see 73).
87. Some crossover "cool" terms encompass a "green" term and a "blue" term. The two gain salience as the "cool" term loses salience, which

culminates in disuse of the "cool" term and division of the cool category. This kind of division differs from that which is accomplished by the skewing of cool categories whose names do not cross over (see 26).

88. Cool terms that divide by skewing leave the original cool term in green. Any noncoextensive "cool" term that shows crossover is confined randomly to either green or blue before it is replaced or, in a rare case, before its range stabilizes on one hue. Although data for a test are presently insufficient, it appears that more of these terms are confined to blue than to green when last seen in use. Concordantly, it seems the secondary "green" term is named with greater salience than the "blue" term more often than the reverse. In consistency with this, the dominant range is more often skewed toward blue in systems of coextensive crossover.

89. In a very rare relation, a crossover cool term encompasses another crossover term that is confined to one hue at any time but to opposite hues at different times. Unlike "cool" terms that skew in one direction and that include a secondary term (see 72), the superordinate and subordinate terms may at any time be focused on the same hue. This rare relation tends to be supplanted by one that retains the superordinate crossover term but replaces the subordinate crossover term with two that each name an opposite hue without crossing over (see 87).

90. Cool categories of the skewing type can often be shown to have a history of transference, while transference has not been attributed to cool categories of the crossover type.

91. When a root and its qualifications name the cool category coextensively, they cross over in the same way that separate coextensive roots may cross over.

92. A few coextensive ranges of the cool category are juxtaposed as light versus dark.

93. While some speakers of a language narrowly apply a term to only the darkest edge of the cool category, others focus it with dark polarity while they apply it to a recessive "cool" range in a coextensive relation with the dominant "cool" term. In some languages, a few speakers name the dark edge of the cool category while other speakers of their community do not show coextension.

Chapter 11: Transference versus Diffusion: Mesoamerica Compared with the World

94. Skewing the cool category toward green rather than toward blue is more common in Mesoamerica than in many other areas, although

its greater frequency at the final phase of division does not in itself seem to be a diffusible trait (see 66).

95. Mesoamerican color categories stress hue over other options.

96. In Mesoamerica, transference of foci from blue to green occurs in the virtual absence of specific kinds of categorization found elsewhere: (1) a crossover "cool" term, as in Korean, Taiwanese, and, according to texts, Ancient Chinese; (2) brightness categories, (3) yellow-with-green categories. Conversely, these kinds of systems occur in the absence of transference.

97. In certain non-Mesoamerican languages, many individuals focus a brightness category in blue, some focus a cool category in blue, and a few separately categorize green and blue, although all name their blue-focused category with the same term. Paya, Karuk, and Ainu show this variation. Japanese, anciently in contact with Ainu, confines *ao* to blue, although the term is reputed to mean "cool" to elderly speakers.

98. Slave and Germanic languages confine a term of former blue-green-yellow range to blue and a term of erstwhile yellow-green-blue to yellow. Latin did the same with crossed-over cognates of the Germanic terms.

99. Lacandón is the only language studied in which all recorded speakers focus the cool category in blue, the more remarkable for its location in the depths of Mesoamerica. But the Lacandón comprise sparse and marginal populations in the forests of Chiapas and the Petén. They mark their ethnic identity with salient cultural practices not seen elsewhere in contemporary Mesoamerica. Their cool-category foci and naming ranges not only show invariant bias toward blue but prevalent polarization.

100. Most recorded cool categories of state societies and areas in their orbit are (or were) focused in green: Mesoamerica, the Andes, Indonesia, India, ancient Egypt, the Roman Empire, and the Arab world. Japanese, Korean, and Chinese appear to offer exceptions (see 96).

FORMULAE

In various sections, kinds of color categories and their subtypes have been distinguished by some of the formulae in tables VIII.1–2. (Two formulae are newly specified here.) The formulae are intended to represent kinds of color categories emically, as is discussed in §6.4.10. Figures VIII.1–2 exhibit the bases of formulae selected from the tables to highlight principles common to all. (Hereafter, the graphic that is labeled a "figure" will be called a "diagram" to avoid confusion with "ground-figure.")

In table VIII.1 and diagram VIII.1, formulae express the order of zooming through a hierarchy of ground-figure relations. In table VIII.2 and diagram VIII.2, formulae express the priorities by which coordinates are stressed throughout the ground-figure hierarchy. We note, for example, that the "type A hue composite" formula in diagram VIII.1 and the "hue-stressing" formula in diagram VIII.2 are identical. The former name highlights the type of coordinates that are included in the zooming process while the latter calls attention to the stressing of hue as opposed to the stressing of relations. The hue-stressing formula shares with all formulae in diagram VIII.1 the quality of stressing grounds as opposed to figures within the respective hierarchies. Thus, marking stress throughout these formulae would be wholly redundant if it were not for the stress upon figures in the relation-stressing formula of diagram VIII.2. This exceptional inversion of stress constitutes the sole reason to separately highlight zooming versus stress among the formulae. Although the two processes usually match, they are not the same process nor must they coincide.

In table VIII.1 and diagram VIII.1, sizing of S and D not only contrast formulae but represent the reason why certain formulae differ. For example, in the "type A hue primary" category, weak S and strong D restrict the range to a single hue, whereas in the "type A hue composite" category, S and D of equal strength extend the range to include two hues; in the "flip-

TABLE VIII.1. Formulae of zooming

Formula	Kind	Section
$H\,s^2$-D *or* $H\,s^2\,D$	Type-A hue primary	2.5, 6.2.3
$H_1\,S^2\,H_2\,D$	Type-A hue composite	6.2.3
$H_1\,S^2\,H_x\,{\scriptstyle D}$	Flip-flop	12.1.2.4
$(H\,S^2$-$D)(H\,D^2$-$S)$	Two vantages on one primary category or on a composite category, abbreviated	6.2.3
$(H\,S^2$-${\scriptstyle D})(H\,D^2$-$S)$	Near synonymy	6.2.3
$(H\,S^2$-$D)(H\,D^2$-$S)$	Coextension	6.2.3
$(H\,s^2$-$D)(H\,D^2$-${\scriptstyle s})$	Inclusion	6.2.3, 7.1.3
$(H_1\,S^2\,H_2\,D)(H_2\,D^2\,H_1\,S)$	Two vantages on one composite category, generalized	6.2.3
$(H\,S^2$-$D)(H\,S^2$-$D)$	Complementation	6.2.3.4
$T\,S^2\,B\,D$	Desaturation-brightness	new
$B\,S^2$-D *or* $B\,S^2\,D$	Type-D brightness	2.5
$B\,S^2\,H\,D$	Type-C brightness-hue	2.5
$B\,S^2\,H_1\,\{H_2\{H_3\}\}\,D$	Type-C brightness-hue, elaborated	2.5
$H\,S^2\,B\,D$	Type-B hue-brightness	2.5
$H_1\,S^2\,\{H_2\{H_3\}\}\,B\,D$	Type-B hue-brightness, elaborated	2.5
$CH\,S^2\,D$	Nonchromatic but typically colored	6.4.13
$HC\,S^2\,D$	Metonymic or strongly contextualized	6.4.13
$H\,S^2\,C\,D$	Connotative or weakly contextualized	6.4.13
	Many elaborations of the last three formulae are possible, including use of B brightness.	
$[(H_1\,S^2\,H_2\,D)(H_2\,D^2\,H_1\,S)]\,[(H_2\,S^2\,H_3\,D)(H_3\,D^2\,H_2\,S)]$		6.3.5
	Triple coextension or inclusion, generalized and composite. Many elaborations are possible.	

Key: H hue, H_1 preferred hue of the dominant vantage or its recessive inversion, $H_1\,H_2\,H_3$ different hues, H_x indeterminate hue exclusive of others in the formula, S attention to similarity, D attention to distinctiveness, T desaturated color, B brightness, C nonchromatic context, { } add or subtract, ( ) separate, [ ] frame. Size differences between S and D (or D and S) symbolize strong (= large) and weak (= small) emphases, but only in formulae that require this information.

flop" category, very strong S and very weak D establish that the second hue will be indeterminate, which, in turn, is what allows the flip-flopping of the range. The desaturation-brightness formula, by including B, allows for the characteristic variability of desaturation categories across the gamut of brightness, as is shown in figures 2.16 and 2.18. Types B, C, and D of,

TABLE VIII.2. Formulae of stressing

Formula	Kind	Section
$H\,S^2\text{-}D$ *or* $H\,S^2\,D$	Hue-stressing, abbreviated	10.0
$H_1\,S^2\,H_2\,D$	Hue-stressing	10.1
$S^2\text{-}D\,H$ *or* $S^2\,D\,H$	Relation-stressing, abbreviated	10.0
$S^2\,H_2\,D\,H_1$	Relation-stressing	10.1
$(S^2\,H_2\,D\,H_1)(D^2\,H_1\,S\,H_2)$	Relation-stressing coextensive*	10.1
$(s^2\,H_2\,D\,H_1)(D^2\,H_1\,s\,\{H_2\})$	Relation-stressing inclusion	10.2
$(S^2\text{-}D\,H)(D^2\text{-}S\,H)$	Relation-stressing coextensive or inclusion, abbreviated	new
$[(S^2\,H_2\,D\,H_1)(H_1\,D^2\,H_2\,S)]\,[(H_1\,S^2\,H_2\,D)(H_2\,D^2\,\{H_1\}\,S)]$	Dominant relation-stressing in frame 1, recessive hue-stressing in frame 1 and throughout frame 2	10.2

*Symbols are keyed in table VIII.1, adding here the etic stipulation that, in a relation-stressing formula, H_1 and H_2 differ within a vantage but not necessarily between vantages; in the negative case, H_1 and H_1 or H_2 and H_2 will differ between vantages (§§10.1–2). Anything etic is for the benefit of the analyst but meaningless in the native view (§6.4.10).

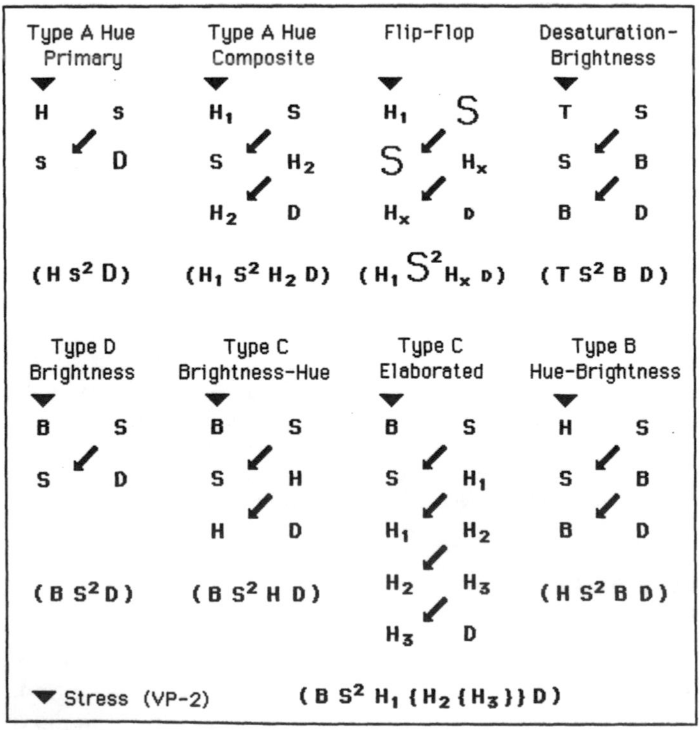

FIGURE VIII.1. The bases for formulae of zooming.

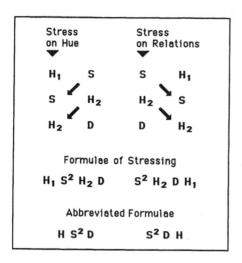

FIGURE VIII.2. The bases of hue-stressing and relation-stressing formulae.

respectively, hue-brightness, brightness-hue, and brightness represent the degrees to which hue and brightness participate in a category, as discussed in §2.5. The elaborated type C category is a full-blown representation of the usual case in which the category covers yellow, green, and blue. Type B could be similarity elaborated. The formulae capture the principles of depicting any color category in terms of its hierarchical arrangement without pretending to represent every variety that may occur. (This may be carried out by anyone motivated to apply the principles exhaustively.)

Diagram VIII.2 shows the bases for the full and the abbreviated formulae for a hue-stressing and a relation-stressing category. Both kinds of category maintain the same hierarchy and zooming order; only their stresses are inverted. The full hue-stressing formula directly matches the order of zooming, $H_1 S^2 H_2 D$. (Herein H_1 is the primary fixed coordinate; then S is transformed from a figure to a ground; then H_2 is so transformed; and finally D is incorporated.) Conversely, the full relation-formula, $S^2 H_2 D H_1$, mismatches the hierarchy. Because H_1 is never stressed, it comes last in this formula, even though H_1 is the primary fixed coordinate.

This difference between formulae may mean that relation-stressing categories are less natural and more difficult to maintain, which might be why they are rarer than hue-stressing categories in the MCS and WCS. Because the full formulae represent priorities of stressing instead of orders of zooming, the placement of H_1 at the end of the relation-stressing formula does not require that D receive an exponent; D or S would automatically receive the exponent only when positioned in the middle or at the top of a zooming hierarchy. The full relation-stressing formula further reveals that one of the hues, H_2, is stressed to some extent—albeit not as much as are relations—which helps to explain why hue continues to constrain any relation-stressing category. Also, the stress on H_2 may enhance its prominence within the category over unstressed H_1. Yet, in the cool category, H_1 is likely to be green because its primary position in the zooming hierarchy places it at the point of maximum contrast with the red category. Thus, moderately stressed H_2 is likely to be blue. This may help to explain why blue is favored over green in relation-stressing cool categories in spite of the primal contrast between green and red (§11.3.1).

The abbreviated formulae H S^2-D and S^2-D H merely show whether hues or relations are stressed the most. They elude the need for the foregoing sort of exegesis but also forbear imparting the implications expressed by the full formulae.

Finally, figure 10.18 integrates degrees of engagement with formulae of vantages and frames. Without representing any particular individual's system, the following formula combines omniscient VP-4, impartial deictic VP-3, and partial deictic VP-2, excluding egocentric VP-1:

$$VP\text{-}4\ll VP\text{-}3|VP\text{-}2\{[(H_1 \, S^2 \, H_2 \, D)(H_2 \, D^2 \, H_1 \, S)][(H_2 \, S^2 \, H_3 \, D)(H_3 \, D^2 \, H_2 \, S)]\}|\gg$$

Meanings of brackets are ( ) vantage and [ ] frame, with { }, | |, and ‹‹ ›› setting off degrees of detachment greater than VP-2, which, in turn, applies within any vantage or frame. VP-3 enables the viewer to be aware of all his frames in relation to each other; the Zapotec-speaker is similarly depicted in figure 10.17, but only with a detached overview specified for frame I. VP-4 enables the viewer to comprehend his frames in relation to those of another language, as the Tonantzintla Nahuatl-speakers reconstitute their dormant cool category in reference to their present view from a Spanish-speaking perspective (§9.3; figures 9.8–12). VP-4 is also the analyst's perspective on hue-stressing and relation-stressing presented in §10.1–2, countering the assumption that hue-stressing is the only way to categorize color, our own VP-2.

NOTES

1. CONCEPTUAL AND MATERIAL EQUIPMENT

1. As the stimuli omit Munsell row 1.0/, it would express the gap to omit "J" and instead refer to Munsell level 0.5 as "K." I retain "J" to stay consistent with the WCS and most publications.

2. The attached copy of the Munsell color array was prepared by Nick Hale in collaboration with R. E. MacLaury. To purchase copies by the lot, write Hale Color Consultants, 3 Starlight Farm Drive, Phoenix, MD 21131, U.S.A. The Hale plate appears in Kay, Berlin, and Merrifield (1991a), Berlin and Kay (1991), Galloway (1993), and Hoogshagen and Halloran de Hoogshagen (1993). The latter two append diagrammed interview results in native American languages, which serve as models for anyone wishing to add a specialized section on color to a dictionary, ethnography, or other work. N. Hale (when president of the Munsell Color Company) also prepared the large plate published as a loose insert with Berlin and Kay (1969), which his present version improves upon. As no paper reproduction of color is accurate (e.g., elemental yellow at C9 is printed orange; some reds look alike), only genuine Munsell chips (or equivalent standards) can be used for research.

2. ISSUES IN COLOR ETHNOGRAPHY

1. Interest in color blindness (Dalton 1798; Holmgren 1877; cf. Boynton 1979: 337) antedated color ethnography but intersected with it by producing Holmgren's wools, which doubled as a color blindness test and the first ethnographic stimulus materials. They helped to inform the debate and to initiate systematic surveying.

Gladstone, who was Prime Minister four times during Queen Victoria's reign, had proportional influence on scholars, which is exemplified by Stack's (1880) analysis of Maori color naming:

> Stack quotes Gladstone with regard to the limited colour-sense of the Greeks ... Stack speaks of the historical development of the colour-sense, the first stage after complete blindness being reached when the eye is able to distinguish between red and black; in the next stage both red and yellow, with their

shades, are discerned; in the third, green is discernible; and finally, blue is distinguished. He seemed to think that the Maori was still in the second stage, for he had names for only white, black, and red: he recognized yellow and green, not as abstract conceptions of colour, but only as they were associated with objects; he thought blue was not recognized, as no word existed to represent it; and he said no words were found in Maori to express violet, brown, orange, and pink colours. In support, he cited the Maori translation of the Bible (Andersen 1942:5–6).

2. The debate stimulated *discussion* (Lubbock 1882; Furrell 1885; Pouchet 1888; Myers 1908) and traditions of (1) *linguistic reconstruction* (Weise 1878, 1888; Schwentner 1915, 1925) and (2) *analysis of color terms in literature* (Brumeister 1859; Roesler 1868; Bastian 1869; Ewald 1890; Boehmer 1872; Delitzsch 1878, 1888, 1896; Clerke 1892:294–302; Jeoffroy 1882; Hopkins 1883; Price 1883; Veckenstedt 1888; Blümner 1889*a–b*, 1892; McCrea 1894; Basset 1895; Ellis 1896; Pratt 1898; Meylan-Faure 1899; Ott 1899; Smyth 1900; Mead 1899, 1901; Charencey 1899; Loewenthal 1901; Mulvany 1901; Toynbee 1902; Willms 1902; Euler 1903; Schultz 1904; Wood 1902, 1905; Scheinert 1905; Schulze 1910; Kranz 1912; Jacobsohn 1915; Phillips 1919; Platnauer 1921; Müller-Boré 1922; Levengood 1927; König 1927; Wallace 1927; Schwyzer 1929; Cunliffe 1931; Kober 1932, 1934; Mayer 1934:294–302; Davis 1945; André 1949, 1957; Cole 1952; Herne 1954; Moorhouse 1954; Meyerson, ed. 1957 including Filliozat, Gernet, and Guillaumont; Tarrant 1960; Schenkel 1963; Mugler 1964; Innes 1972; Irwin 1974; Maxwell-Stuart 1981). Portal (1837), Linton (1852), and Göbel (1855) are *predecessors,* Werner (1814), Hay (1846), and Lucas (1859) of historical interest. Buck (1949: 33–38) and Pokorny (1959) are the major sources on development of color terms in *Indo-European.*

3. Titchener (1916), another psychologist, drafted a penetrating critique on what by then had become the famous experiments in Torres Straits. As he wished to demonstrate how concern with method had sharpened in so few years (cf. Mollison 1913), he pleaded for a point-by-point reply. But Rivers was on his way to serve in the Great War; on his return he planned his candidacy for Prime Minister but died unexpectedly in 1922 (Slobodin 1978).

Hickerson (1972, 1975) analyzes Rivers's measurements of hue and brightness terms. Klineberg (1935:139–151) provides an overview of all work on the senses both in the Torres Straits and at the St. Louis Fair. Slobodin (1978:87–99) and Mandelbaum (1980) relate Rivers's psychological program to the history of anthropology. Herne (1954), after outlining Gladstone and Magnus, combines etymological techniques and ethnographic analogy to reconstruct a sequence of color-term evolution for the Slavic linguistic family (cf. Priestly 1981:note 5). Rivers (1901*c*:44–50, 53–55) and Hickerson (1983) review early evolutionary work, both touching on Darwin's (1877) minor contribution, Rivers on Bénaky's (1897) inferences about the ancient color sense from painted monuments and art, and Hickerson on Gladstone's intellectual milieu. Rivers (1901*a*:48–49) sketchs a few early highlights. Woodworth (1910*a*:178–179), Parsons

(1915:145–151), Thurnwald (1922:167–169), Bartlett (1928:2–3, 45–46), Segall, Campbell and Herskovits (1966), Berlin and Kay (1969:134–149), and Dougherty (1975:4–8) summarize color research from Gladstone through Rivers. Rivers's assertion regarding pigmentation anticipated similar claims by Bornstein (1973a), who sought possible correspondence between latitude and "cool" or "dark-cool" terms, hypothesizing that eye pigmentation increases toward the equator, where it impedes discrimination of green and blue. But his sample is skewed toward European and circum-Mediterranean languages at northern latitudes, which divide the cool category in keeping with the complex cultures of that area. After counting those cases as one, the languages that Bornstein plots on the world map do not show a significant match between latitude and ways that cool colors are named. Ember (1978) compiles statistics suggesting that a latitudinal effect is evident in samples from only complex societies. But why would societal complexity beget many basic color terms only if eye pigmentation is light? Ember's statistical observation requires scrutiny because the very complex societies might be northern. Van Wijk (1959) claimed that brightness categories prevail near the equator where sunlight is intense. But his small sample omits northern brightness systems, such as those of Ainu (Batchelor 1926:451; cf. Hattori 1964:283), Chukchi (Almqvist 1883:47) and Karuk (Bright 1952:56). Like Geddes and Klineberg (quoted §2.3), Van Wijk regards cognition as selective emphasis (130–132).

4. One can compare Ray's (1953) spectroscopic measurement of Songish responses with Samish responses to Munsell chips (MacLaury 1991b: fig 3). These neighboring Central Salish dialects are almost identical. The comparison shows how the measurements match and what the spectroscope omits.

5. Brown and Lenneberg initiated an enduring tradition in color ethnography whose proponents have used controlled procedures to test specific aspects of the linguistic relativity hypothesis and to develop it (e.g., Lenneberg 1953, 1957, 1961, 1967; Lantz and Stefflre 1964; Stefflre, Castillo Valles and Morley 1966; Brown 1976, 1978; Lucy and Shweder 1979, 1988; cf. Garro 1986; Lucy 1985, 1992; Collier 1963, 1966). As Roger Brown was Eleanor Rosch's mentor (Rosch 1988), her experimental methods derive from this tradition (§1.1). Gellatly (1995:203–204) relates the research to a larger scheme of developments.

Other literature of the 1960s consists of a synopsis (Shemiakin 1959), a technical overview (Chapanis 1965), more on the classics (Mangio 1961; Young 1964; Merker 1967; Osborne 1968; Halleux 1969), and analyses of color naming in a particular language (Moskovich 1960; Lander, Ervin, and Horowitz 1960; Ervin 1961; Goodman 1963; Koch 1965; Bulmer 1968; Kopp and Lane 1968).

6. Durbin (1972:268–269) analyzes Berlin and Kay's hypothesis as seventeen propositions, but our differences are minor.

7. Mary Haas (letter to Kay 1972, UC Berkeley) described yellow-with-green in Creek and Natchez and M. Dale Kinkade (letter to Kay 1972, UCB) confirmed the same in several Pacific Northwest languages. Kay cites Haas's data in a footnote (1975: 260; cf. Branstetter 1977:3). Berlin (MS-2) found two Numic yellow-with-green terms in the C. Hart Merriam files.

8. NSF Grant BNS 76-14153 to Kay, Berlin, and Merrifield, 1976, was renewed in 1978, 1980, and 1994. "All data will be placed on inexpensive microfiche making them readily available for scholars throughout the world" (page 9 of their 1975 proposal to NSF). Merrifield (1992:164) provides the purchasing address.

9. Aguaruna names dark-cool and yellow-with-green at lower salience than warm and cool (Berlin and Berlin 1975:figs. 3 versus 5–7, 10, 14); five speakers name a yellow-green-blue category (figs. 5–6, 7), focusing it throughout its range.

10. After 1969, linguistic reconstructions of color terms address the Berlin and Kay order (Baxter 1983; Branstetter 1977; Greenfeld 1980; Hickerson 1988; MacLaury 1982, 1986a:Appendix II, 1988a; Moonwomon 1983; Shields 1979; Wescott 1975a) or proceed with knowledge of it (Biggam 1993; Brenner 1982; Hamp 1980b; Kinkade 1988; Maxwell-Stuart 1981; Priestly 1981).

11. For more complete accounts, see MacLaury (1987a:112–116) or Albright (1991:267–268). They explain that each class of opponent cell is of two types. The RG class consists of type +R-G, which conveys a signal to be interpreted as red when firing fast and a signal to be interpreted as green when firing slow, +R versus −G; its −R+G type conveys this information with opposite rates of firing, −R slow versus +G fast. The YB class correspondingly consists of types +Y−B and −Y+B. Hurvich and Jameson (1957) introduced opponent-process theory to vision research by translating it from the nineteenth-century writings of Ewald Hering (1920 [1878]), which had been neglected. Prior to 1957, vision science followed the Young-Helmholtz tri-receptor theory by which the three retinal photopigments were thought to be directly linked to the brain (Young 1802; Helmholtz 1856–1866). After 1966, it was thought that ganglia cells behind the retina transformed the three cone inputs into opponent processes. After 1975, many investigators found that neural activity between the retina and the cortex is infinitely more complex than R. De Valois's lineal model suggested. Yet opponency as a functional explanation has remained embedded in vision research while no rival model has gained a footing. Hardin (1988, 1993) likens the present period to seventeenth-century astronomy when there were gaps of knowledge, unassimilated observations, apparent contradictions, and a growing body of findings, but no respectable astronomer any longer doubted that the planets revolve around the sun. Among the interesting complications of theory are different modulations in the lateral geniculate nucleus in response to distinct genre of stimuli (Young 1986). Contrary to De Valois's data, Derrington, Krauskopf and Lennie (1984) find evidence that the yellow-blue channel might derive in the brain such that monitoring at lower sites in the lateral geniculate nucleus will produce poles "closer to violet and chartreuse," as Albright reports (1991:267). Teller (1991) provides an accessible review of these and other problems. De Valois and De Valois (1993) present a much revised model of post-retinal color processing, their first since 1975. Zollinger (1988a) outlines events that led to the revision.

A "unique hue" is one of four pure or irreducible hue sensations that crosscut the spectrum from light to dark through red, yellow, green, and blue. The Munsell array approximates unique hues in columns 1 pink-red, 9 yellow-brown, 17 light-to-dark green, and 29 light-to-dark blue. (Technically, the purest pink-red under normal conditions contains a slight sensation of yellow, which, however, can be offset in a laboratory with an equal increment of blue light so as to produce a sense of unique red.) An "elemental hue" is a point of maximally vivid or most intense hue within a unique hue, which the Munsell array approximates at G1 red, C9 yellow, F17 green, and F29 blue. As pure white and pure black are not hues, they do not warrant this appellation. But, contrary to what every child is taught in school, I call white and black "colors," as I do red, yellow, green, and blue. I call the purest, most intense perceptions of these six colors "elemental colors" or, for emphasis, "elemental color points." (Speakers of my American dialect linguistically recognize the elemental colors as "fire-engine red," "chrome yellow," "kelly green," "true blue," "snow white," and "jet black.")

"Elemental hues" follows Miller and Wooten (1990), but "elemental colors" is my coinage. Although the opponent-process model explains the universality of unique hues as well as of elemental white and elemental black, I find no account of why the elemental hues are universal or even of why they exist. They are not of equal brightness, nor are they pegged to saturation; Collier et al. (1976) found that subjects preferred them as foci even on a Munsell array whose chips were all of chroma 2/. A plurality of subjects in the MCS and WCS selected them as foci (fig. 11.1; MacLaury MS-1).

Johnson-Laird (1983) calls the six elemental color points "the landmark colors"; the expressions "pure" and "primary colors" are also used. I avoid all three expressions for minor reasons. Others have called these six the "focal colors" (e.g., Heider 1971), which is misleading and tautological; the term anticipates that an elemental color will be chosen as the focus of any category that contains at least one of them. But the focus of a category is whatever color(s) an individual chooses as its best example, nothing more. While foci vary between individuals, human perception of elemental colors varies far less.

12. Fuld, Wooten, and Whalen (1981) replicated with purple Sternheim and Boynton's (1966) experiment with orange. Saunders (1992b) argues that the pioneering state of visual physiology voids Kay and MacDaniel's appeal to the opponent-process model; yet, whatever the problems with the model, the unique hues are an empirical fact. Without conjuring any evidence from De Valois and co-workers, Sternheim and Boynton's work alone shows that some color sensations are irreducible while others are complex. MCS and WCS foci cluster on specific Munsell chips: AØ, JØ, G1, C9, F17, and F29 (fig. 11.1; MacLaury MS-1), a cross-linguistic vote on preferred colors. Although the research on neural pathways is fascinating, no one need evoke it to support the premise that elemental color perception is everywhere the same.

13. Kay and McDaniel did not distinguish elemental colors and unique hues as I do in note 11. They suggest as much with "unique hue" versus "unique hue point," but they apply the latter to white and black, which are not hues. I accepted their vagueness in the absence of decisive terminology (MacLaury 1992a), but Saunders (1992b) and Hardin (personal communication) rightfully protested. Hence, note 11.

14. Instead of the fuzzy-set terms "derived" and "primary," in discussion apart from this model I call the same color categories "binary" and "elemental." I retain "composite color category." "Binary" suggests that only two elemental colors con-

tribute to a blended category, which may be so with grey and orange, but pink, purple, and brown may be more complex. "Blended category" is a fine synonym.

15. Appendix IV (mainly germane to §7.1.3) examines the question Can a language have more than eleven basic color terms? in reference to Mesoamerican, Japanese, Russian, and Hungarian data. Russian blue and Hungarian red categories have been cited in support of various claims regarding basic color terms (e.g., Wierzbicka 1990:100, 114, 121–122, 142). In 1986, K. Uchikawa and I interviewed six Japanese adults with the three-part method (§3.2) but did not verify the additional basic color terms that Stanlaw hypothesized (1987:111–116, 139–146, 178–190, 241). Researchers at the University of Surrey claim that Russian speakers treat light blue as a basic term (Corbett and Morgan 1988; Morgan and Corbett 1989; Moss 1989*a–b;* Moss et al. 1990; Davies et al. 1991; Morgan and Moss 1991; Corbett and Davies in press; Laws and Davies in press). However, the Surrey group collects and analyzes data by different methods than those described in §3.2. They mainly consider salience. In response to widespread but arbitrary favoring of salience as an indicator of basic categorization, I argue that category relations are an equally important criterion (MacLaury 1991*a*).

16. Notable studies of 1970–1985 (plus a few that continue the same topics into the 1990s) are:

Historical analyses of literature: Barley 1974; Burnley 1976; Staehelin 1977.

Salience testing: Bolton 1978*a–b;* Bolton and Crisp 1979; Bolton, Curtis and Thomas 1980; Hays et al. 1972.

Descriptions supporting Berlin and Kay's 1969 hypothesis or suggesting modifications and counterexamples: Berman 1979; Brunner-Traut 1977; Callaghan 1979; Caprile 1971; Caskey-Sirmons and Hickerson 1977; Décsy 1981; Dunn 1985; Friedl 1979; Frish 1972; Giacalone Ramat 1978; Gimple 1979; Hardman 1981; Hazaël-Massieux 1973; Heinrich 1977; Iijima, Wenning and Zollinger 1982; Johnson 1986; Kristol 1978, 1980*a–b;* Menges 1965; Monberg 1971; Pollnac 1972, 1975; Royer 1974; Schaefer 1983; Tanaka and Mizuno 1983; Wattenwyl and Zollinger 1978.

Arguments addressing theory or method: Cairo 1977; Collier 1973; Collier et al. 1976; Crawford 1982; Hacker 1986; Heinrich 1978; Michaels 1978; Ratner 1989; Terusuke 1984; Vallier 1979; Wattenwyl and Zollinger 1979; Weeks 1979; Zimmer 1984.

Studies contrasting two languages: Buchholz 1977; Duczmal 1979; Garmadi Le Cloirec 1976; Loffler-Laurian 1983; Schmitz 1983; Solta 1966; Zaręba 1981.

Treatments of synesthesia: Ryalls 1986; Wescott 1975*b*.

Studies of sex differences: Graham 1994; Jaffe, Pringle, and Anderson 1985; Mollon 1986; Nowaczyk 1982; Rich 1977; Simpson and Tarrant 1991; Steckler and Cooper 1980; Swaringen, Layman, and Wilson 1978; Thomas, Curtis, and Bolton 1978.

Special topics: Bender 1983; Boggess 1981; Bousfield 1979; Gamst 1975; Leach 1970:21–25; Proulx 1988; Wattenwyl and Zollinger 1981; Whitefield 1979; Zollinger 1976, 1984, 1989. See Ferreira Brito and Siqueira 1989; Woodward 1989.

Tornay ed. (1978*a*, reviewed by Hickerson 1980) anthologizes thirty-four papers, most of which answer Berlin and Kay with relativist views. Wyler (1992) represents a late case of taking Berlin and Kay's 1969 model as current. Work primarily on Russian color categories at the University of Surrey is cited in note 15 and selectively reviewed in Appendix IV. Earlier, others investigated acquisition of color categorization by verbal children (Bartlett 1976; Bornstein 1985a–b; Conley and Cooper 1981; Cruse 1977; S. Davis 1982; Dougherty 1975, 1977, 1978a–b; Fijalkow 1974; Harkness 1973; Istomina 1963; Johnson 1977; Kepner 1905; Mervis, Catlin and Rosch 1975; Mills 1976; Molrieu 1957; Raskin, Maital and Bornstein 1983; Schefrin and Werner 1990) and infant response to color (Bornstein 1975a–b, 1985a–b; McDougall 1908; Teller and Bornstein 1987; Peeples and Teller 1975; Staples 1932; Suchman 1966; Valentine 1914). Grossmann (1988) supplies a 1,469-item bibliography on these and other color-term topics with 653 sources dating between 1970 and 1985. For overviews, see Bornstein (1987), Lyons (1977:245–250, in press), and MacLaury (in press).

17. Eco (1985: fig. 7), referring to Sahlins, diagrams Conklin's (1955) analysis of the Hanunóo parity of color categories with oppositions between light and dark, dry and moist, firm and faded. Berlin or Kay may still disagree with Sahlins's argument. Working with another domain, Berlin (1992:8) remains consistent with his position of 1969: "When human beings function as ethnobiologists, however, they do not construct order, they discern it."

18. Boynton and his coworkers investigated categorical color perception with 424 OSA samples in a laboratory, finding evidence of no more than eleven basic color categories in English and Japanese (Uchikawa and Boynton 1987; Boynton and Olson 1987). We compared his techniques and stimuli with those of the Mesoamerican color survey (Boynton, MacLaury and Uchikawa 1989).

19. Van Brakel and Saunders share with environmental determinists a belief in human malleability. The latter's argument surfaces frequently in discussion of color categorization (e.g., McNeill 1972:23–29; Van Wijk 1959:127). Believing in environmental determinism requires an assumption that goes beyond naive realism in holding that people are molded by what they see. But there is no evidence that conspicuous colors in one's environment will prompt development of corresponding color categories. Rather, people will coin vocabulary when they are mentally ready to innovate categories; then they may metonymically extend to hue their words for fruits, flowers, dyes, unripeness, or the like. English and Anbarra have incorporated pigment terms into secondary color vocabulary (Casson 1994; Jones and Meehan 1978); whereas Coptic kept its abstract color categories to only four over the millennia, even though Egyptian pigment technology was vast (Baines 1986; Lucas and Harris 1962). Karuk (of the Hokan stock) derives all color terms directly from nouns denoting natural phenomena but without favoring terms for dyes or paints; Hupa (Athapascan) inhabits the same environment as Karuk but names colors after a different selection of natural surrounds; and, unlike Karuk, Hupa uses abstract color terms as well (MacLaury 1992b). Thus, three views dominate this debate: environmental determinism, dominant-culture determinism, and selective emphasis without external instigations more specific than the rate at which change impinges. Hewes, Van Brakel, Saunders, and I elaborate this three-sided debate (MacLaury 1992a: all four in the comment-reply section).

20. Languages of people whose thinking is not routinely analytical across domains of experience may, nevertheless, show vast lexical elaboration in specific domains, especially those of economic interest. For example, the Ayoquesco Zapotec, among whom I did my first fieldwork, used at least 19 words for types of grasshoppers (MacLaury 1970:72, 148, 150, 160, 164, 166), because the insects were regularly gathered, roasted, and eaten. Yet the language has no prepositions; instead, its speakers optionally employ body-part nouns to express the shape of space in which action takes place, as lip-river for "river side" (MacLaury 1989). Zulu used rich context specific vocabulary to identify cattle by color and pattern (Bryant 1949:333), but its prepositions are sparse compared to those of English and its traditions of description make the teaching of academic subjects, such as chemistry, less effective than when undertaken in English; to give a simple example from among many more complex instances, "The same construction is usually used for concepts such as 'on, in, to, at' etc., in Zulu. This means that distinctions such as 'in the flask/on the flask' are not always made." (Mc-Naught 1993:237). Kuschel and Monberg (1974) document extensive contextualized color categories among surviving traditional Bellona speakers, although their abstract color vocabulary exemplifies the three-term system of Berlin and Kay's Stage II. The traditional Maori too named color with three basic terms (Best 1905), but the complexity and specificity of Maori color qualifiers were phenomenal (Colenso 1882; see Andersen 1942:12–16 for a moderated view). Context-specific elaborations may pervade realms of cultural focus, such as the Zapotec terms for supernatural beings (MacLaury 1970:23–29) or Totonac terms for aromas (Aschmann 1946). Yet as small societies join the orbit of worldly ones, the context vocabulary depletes: "Similar was it with cattle-colours. Until recent years there use to be all manner of colour-forms, which we no longer notice" (Bryant *ibid.*).

21. Boynton (1979:308) finds that "the opponent-color channels have a more sluggish temporal response than do the luminance channels. . . . Ample evidence in support of this assumption now exists." Experimental evidence that the visual system can follow higher frequencies of modulation of luminants than of color is consistent with the idea that the system carrying chromatic information is not only slower but induces a measurable drop in performance (e.g., Dreher, Fukada, and Rodiek 1976; Lange Dzn 1958; De Valois et al. 1986). The observable difference in the ease with which people process brightness perception and hue perception may discourage hue naming in milieus that do not motivate people to differentiate keenly on a routine basis.

Peralta (1980:53), reporting the three-category brightness naming of the I'wak on Luzon, explains the shift to hue naming with an account compatible with my hypothesis of the relation between channel speed and analyticity. He proposes that—since light-dark sensitive rods are peripherally distributed on the retina while wave-sensitive cones cluster in the *fovea centralis* to the exclusion of rods—light-dark perception is easier than hue perception: it takes "considerable concentration of effort" to direct most of the incoming light on the fovea. Because hue perception and the discernment of detail both require sustained confinement of light to this pinpoint target, hue naming would supersede brightness naming as people attend more to difference. Peralta (p. 57) notes further that Berlin and Kay's "point over volume" conception of categorization cannot account for I'wak brightness terms, of which each range meanders over various pure hue points. As a dividend, Peralta's model may help to explain why hue-naming peoples think of white and black as though these sensations were hues—as "object color" in Conklin's (1973) phrase: predominant use of wave receptors would commit viewers to this equation of brightness with hue—a cognitive strategy—because it would be easier for them to maintain a steady state of concentration than it would to candidly acknowledge all the properties of light by switching constantly between a concentrated and a dilated state. Peralta and I share the premise that color naming will be effectively explained only with a model that combines psychophysical response with cognition.

22. To appreciate the semantic complexity of terms naming broad ranges, we can look back 1,000 years upon our language to a time from which Old English texts survive (Barley 1974; Bragg 1982; Biggam 1993; Cameron 1968; Casson and Gardner 1992; König 1957; Lerner 1951; Mead 1899, 1901; Scheinert 1905; Schwentner 1915, 1925; Willms 1902; Wyler 1984). The fragments suggest multiple meanings for single terms, including combinations of hue with various levels of brightness and saturation (cf. MacLaury 1992a for the principles of a model). For example, Lerner (1951:247) notes that *faelwe wegas* refers to waves during a night storm; but the 1971 OED cites similar forms that associate plowed soil, its color, the color of withered vegetation, and the color of animals, as a fallow deer.

As basic color terms evolve from few to many, they may become semantically simplex. Blommaert (1985) shows that each of sixteen Stage II Bantu languages attaches rich metaphoric and contextualized meanings to its three color terms; but he finds such connotations to be absent among the color-term senses in the Stage VII system of market Swahili, a creole derived from Bantu.

Anbarra applies alternating brightness terms to waves of the sea: "One night in July we were camped at Waiyal, looking east over the sheltered sea towards Milingimbi, and a full moon rose over the lapping waters. We sat for a long time looking at the view as black water tipped through silver into black again. One of our companions (J. Butjarraga) said quietly, pointing with pursed lips at the sea, there, *'gun-gungundja gun-gungaltja; gun-gungundja gun-gungaltja'* rocking his hand back and forth in time with the swell" (Jones and Meehan 1978:28).

Regarding the penchant of ancient minds to pick out brightness from their surrounds, we can count such terms in this passage from *Iliad* XIX (Rowe 1974:339), which portrays a world seemingly aflame (emphasis added):

". . . *brightly gleaming* helmets poured from the ship, bossed shields, plated
cuirasses and ashen spears. A *flash* went up to the heaven and all around
the earth laughed with the *gleam* of *bronze,* and rang to the feet of marching
men. In the midst of them the noble Achilles fitted on his armour. His teeth
gnashed, his *eyes blazed like fire* . . . Over his shoulder he threw the *silver-
studded* sword with its *bronze blade;* then he took the great thick shield which

flashed into the distance like the moon. As when sailors see the *flash of a blazing fire* which *burns* high up in the mountains on a lonely farm."

Wallace (1927:29) painstakingly counted hue versus value terms in ancient and modern literature to deliver this comparative overview:

> 83% of the color-words in the *Iliad* are those words expressing value rather than hue, and 60% in the Odyssey. It may seem unfair to count all words alike, since so many are otiose epithets. So I shall give the percentages again, after subtracting the commonest, i.e., 'rosy-fingered Dawn' and 'tawny-haired Menelaus' from the words of actual color, and 'black ships' and 'white-armed' from the value words. The percentages now stand, value-words in the *Iliad* 86% and in the *Odyssey* 65%. So the use of black-and-white words is actually far greater than that of red-to-violet words in the poems.[7]

[7] In the last ten books of Pope's *Odyssey,* where inspiration at the time was low for him as well as for Homer, he uses 48 color-words—37 of hue, 11 of value, or only 23% value-words. In the same books, Homer has 79 color-words—25 of hue, 54 of value, or 68% value-words. In Pope's *Windsor Forest* the value words are about 15%. Byron, in the first 22 pages of *Childe Harold's Pilgrimage,* Canto II, uses 50% value-words. So, though the proportions may vary widely, if these three widely different poets may be taken as representative, we may say that the modern tendency is to use words of hue in poetry oftener than words expressing black-and-white.

23. Descriptions of Stage I with Munsell chips do not meet present standards. Anyone who has contact with people using a Stage I brightness or hue system and who would be willing to describe it via Munsell-chip interviews should write to me, regardless of the year, at my address as published in the American Anthropological Association Guide or c/o Dr. Jane Hill, Anthropology, University of Arizona, Tucson, AZ 85721 USA.

24. See MacLaury 1992*a,* figure 18, upper left, which represents with arrows that type D light or dark ranges may fluctuate over the Munsell array with either expanding massively while the other retreats to almost nothing. (Imagine a novel light-over-dark window shade that operates on a scroll.) Figure 2.12 was adapted from that depiction with responses commingled and arrows removed.

25. Probably these data were accurately recorded and processed (fig. 2.27), as the 19 other Kuku Yalinji systems in the WCS fit brightness typology while 13 commingle broad ranges.

26. Some Indo-European reflexes might have descended from categories of brightness. Pokorny (1959:118–24, 429–32, 872) reconstructs ****ĝhel-* 'yellow, green, blue' and ****bhel-* 'blue, green, yellow, grey.' From this, Watkins (1969) reinterprets their primary meanings as "to shine." Compare these glosses with the data of figures 2.16*a,* 2.27, 2.28*d,* 2.30*a,* 2.31*a–c* and 2.32*a–c,* but especially 2.29*a–c.*

27. Slave *et'ǫ* 'plant' becomes a "green" basic color term through a three-step process (*a'–c*). Karuk, which also has a blue-focused brightness term, adopts "plant"

to "green" by first incorporating it with a "yellow-with-green" meaning (MacLaury 1992*b:* fig. 9).

28. In Germanic, **blēwaz* became confined to blue (cf. figs. 2.28 and 2.30), while in Latin or the predecessor of Latin, a cognate, *flāvus,* was confined to yellow (cf. figs. 2.29 and 2.31–32). This difference suggests as much variability in range and focus of the Proto-Indo-European common form, ***bhel-.* The Tifal brightness term (fig. 2.31), which is focused in yellow or green, shows less variability, although this is of the range that Berlin and Kay (1969: fig. 13c) would have to have found in several languages in order to justify their Stage III*b*. The examples of Stage III*b* that they cite, such as Bisayan 'yellow', Homeric Greek 'green-yellow', and Arunta 'yellow-green-blue', are not accompanied by the evidence of internal variation that would show all to be of the Tifal type; rather each language presents a separate type.

29. Researchers report yellow-with-green at different stages in various languages: Stages I′ and II′ in Martu Wangka (figs. 2.26*b–c*), always with a yellowish green focus; Stages II′ and III*a*′ in Aguaruna (Berlin and Berlin 1975: figs. 5–8), although green-focused or yellow-focused, coextensively named with terms of low salience relative to others, and varying to assume a yellow-green-blue range; possible Stage III*a*′ in Shuswap and Lillooet (MacLaury 1986*b:* fig. 1, 1987*a:* fig. 3, 1988: files 9–10); possible Stage III*b*′ in Classical Sanskrit (Van Brakel 1992 from Hopkins 1883 and Schulze 1910), Nuba (Faris 1972: 59–64), and Wakashan early in the twentieth century and before (Saunders 1992*a:* diagrams 12.1–6, tables 13.1–4 plus text); definite Stage IV′ in Shuswap (MacLaury 1986*b:* figs. 3, 5–6, 1991*b:* fig. 10) and Assyrian (Allen 1879: 213; cf. MacLaury 1991*b:* 38); definite Stage V′ in Shuswap, Halkomelem, Lillooet, and Sechelt (MacLaury 1986*b:* figs. 2, 4, 7–8, 1990, 1991*b;* MacLaury and Galloway 1988; Galloway 1993: Appendix), Creek (Gatschet 1879*b;* Kay 1975: 260 n), and Natchez (Kay); unspecified stages in Chukchi (Almqvist 1883: 47; see §2.4), Numic (Berlin n.d.), Ainu (Batchelor 1926: 451), Hittite, Akkadian, Sumerian, and Biblical Hebrew (see Ch. 11, n. 11). There is evidence that some systems of stages III*a*′–*b*′, IV′ and V′ descend from systems containing yellow-green-blue brightness categories. In Stages I′ and II′ of Martu Wangka, the range flip-flops from green-with-yellow to green-with-blue (fig. 2.26). Wesley Dale found that some Lani speakers show the same variability of such categories in the context of Stage I (fig. 2.13).

In other WCS data, Vagla of Ghana appears to evolve toward Stage V directly from Stage II or Stage III*b*, at least bypassing the cool category of Stage IV. But Vagla names secondary color categories within a basic Stage II system; the system names them with compounds, such as *aah lugo susau* 'yellow' ("red like powder of the dawadawa tree"), *biri lugo korriihuu* 'green' ("black like fresh grass"), and *biri lugo burgu* 'blue' ("black like blue dye"). Vagla children have attended elementary school since 1960, but even elderly adults use the compounds (Marjorie L. Crouch, letter 1995). Snow (1971) reports that Samoan of Polynesia skips Stage IV while naming green and blue with productive compounds, but Samoan color categories have not been investigated with Munsell-chip methods. Beaglehole (1939) reports equivalent compounds in Tongan color naming. Dyimini (WCS) of Ivory Coast, in the same area as Vagla, names blue *bra* and green *wetapiiri* within the dark-cool range of *wolo;* one speaker (WCS 5) names a cool category *bra,* another so names black-with-blue (WCS 16), and others use alternative terms. No rumor of a language that skips hue stages is compelling.

30. Studies of Mesoamerican color terms and categories cover the gamut of symbolism, cognition, historical reconstruction, acquisition, and cultural practice; they do not lend themselves to singular theoretical discussion. The dozen treatments of color-direction symbolism are reviewed under item 6 in note 3 of §3.2. In an impressive compilation from Tlapanec, Mixtec, and Nahuatl, Dehouve (1978) delves into the intricate Mesoamerican color symbolism, which appears to have been richer in pre-Columbian eras than it is now (Beyer 1921). For example, in my own queries on color symbolism in Ayoquesco Zapotec (MacLaury 1970), I learned that black represented (=) harsh, dire conditions, white = death, yellow = sickness, red = rage, green = newness, rawness, and unripeness, and the desaturated color = disorder, its name forming the root of the verb 'to scatter'. Gesche (1927) experimentally identifies color preferences of Spanish-speaking Mexicans; they rank yellow and white lowest, red and green highest, matching the values of the indigenous symbolism. Anawalt (1992), in a study of the royal Aztec textile design, finds contextualized color and pattern symbolism of the magnitude that Dehouve reports. Kieffer (1974) compares the relation of color and emotion in Tzutujíl Mayan to that in Spanish. Disselhoff (1931) analyses reference to color in Mexican Spanish poetic imagery. Moser (1964) documents Seri preparation of blue paint from minerals in northwestern Mexico while Peirce (1964) adds discussion and cites earlier sources on similar pigment industries deep in Mesoamerica. Laudermilk (1949) and Arnold (1967) also report on Mesoamerican dyeing and pigment manufacture. In the tradition reviewed under note 5, Collier (1963, 1966) uses the Farnsworth 100-hue samples to correlate color-term lexical composition and probabilities of color-term use in Tzotzil, and he compares these with Lenneberg's (1961) probabilities of English color-term use. In the same tradition, Stefflre, Castillo Valles, and Morley (1966) measure and compare separate accuracies in communication and in memory between Yucatec and Spanish speakers, conducting experiments at the University of Yucatán. Kopp and Lane (1968) find that English- and Tzotzil-speakers alike differentiate standard color stimuli more acutely between than within their categories, even though the two groups categorize color differently from one another: "hue discrimination may not depend exclusively on the inborn sensory mechanism of the observer but on his linguistic habits" (p. 61). Kay and Kempton (1984) replicate Kopp and Lane's experiments, findings, and conclusions by comparing the ways English- and Tarahumara-speakers discriminate Munsell chips. Burgess, Kempton, and MacLaury (1983, 1985) with Tarahumara data show that color categories are skewed and the skewing leads to category division, after which the original term names the colors formerly favored by the skewing (discussed further in item 7 of §2.4.2). Brown (1983) adds that the Yaqui 'green' term took this route. Kaufman (1964) and Rensch (1976) reconstruct forms of Mayan and Otomanguean color terms, respectively. I presented a

conference paper on the possible ranges of Proto-Otomanguean color categories (MacLaury 1988*a*) but did not investigate problems regarding brightness-to-hue discussed here in regard to Mayan. The contemporary data from Mayan in Chapters 4 through 8 imply that the common ancestor named no more than three color categories, although with five salient terms. But unusual data, such as those of figure 6.13, open the question of whether the proto-terms named categories of hue or brightness; since color categories can radically reconfigure from brightness to hue without gain, loss, or replacement of terms (figs. 2.29–32; MacLaury 1992*a:* figs. 11–18), reconstructing a former disposition of such categories from only contemporary lexical data is equivalent to projecting the historical position of sand dunes (MacLaury 1982; cf. Hamp 1971, 1980*a:*272). Witkowski and Brown (1981:17–21) reconstruct Proto-Mayan as hue-stage II, which I criticize on methodological grounds without reference to the brightness problem (MacLaury 1986*a:* Appendix II, n. 2), but the likelihood that brightness categories can shift to hue categories without leaving evidence of the change relegates to the background other quandaries surrounding the reconstruction of prehistoric color categories (cf. fig. 6.13). Berlin and Kay (1969) classify seven Mesoamerican languages as Stage IV and devote special discussion to Berlin's (MS-1) forty acetate interviews of Tzeltal speakers (cf. Berlin 1970); they cite Mayers's (1966:284–285, 311) color glosses of five terms in twelve Mayan languages and six terms in Xinca. Mayers is a fine example of the many sources that have listed Mesoamerican color terms in passing (also Holmer 1956:159, 163) or in compilations (also Gimple 1979). Merrifield (1971) adds to Berlin and Kay's inventory "cellophane mappings" on the paper array of color terms in nine Otomanguean languages. Wattenwyl and Zollinger (1978), using a restricted Munsell series, compare color-term frequencies in K'ekchí and Misquito, mounting a solid argument that color categorization may be based on hue perception (cf. Wattenwyl and Zollinger 1979:282; Zollinger 1979:3). Hill and Hill (1970) provide Mesoamerican color-term compendia to suggest that Uto-Aztecan "grey" terms emerged earlier in sequence than Stage V. Harkness (1973) compares color-category acquisition between Mam- and Spanish-speaking populations in Guatemala. MacLaury and Stewart (1984) summarize 750 Mesoamerican survey cases accessible at that time to show that basic binary terms usually emerge before the cool category divides and, in some cases, before the warm category divides; binary terms tend to emerge in the order of brown, purple, pink, orange, and grey; purple is often included in a category with blue. My other studies of Mesoamerican color categories are integrated into the present analysis (MacLaury 1986*a*, 1987*b*, 1991*a*, 1991*b:* fig. 9, 1992*a:* figs. 3–5).

3. DESCRIPTIVE METHOD

1. Descriptive method is briefly reported in MacLaury (1986*a–b*, 1987*a–b*, 1991*b*, 1992*a*, 1992*b;* Burgess, Kempton and MacLaury 1983, 1985; MacLaury MSS 1–2; Greenfeld 1986; MacLaury and Galloway 1988). MacLaury (1986*a:* Chapter III) enumerates rules of thumb and details. MacLaury (1988*b*) includes a pamphlet on manually transferring raw data to organized graphs, "Comprehending Lillooet Color Data."

(The same information is provided in Appendix VI.) MacLaury (1991a) replies to referees' questions on method. MacLaury, McMillen and McMillen (1979) exemplifies the method after developing it in the field.

2. Each loose swatch of pigmented, cast-coated paper is cut to a 1.2 × 1.6-cm rectangle, mounted on a 2.5 × 2.5-cm neutral matte (with chip number written on back), and encased in a 4.0 × 6.0-cm lamination of clear acetate. An array consists of a 35.5 × 12.7 × 0.1-cm matte of neutral cardboard to which 330 discoidal chips (plus the extra rows of 40 white and 40 black chips), cut with a ¼-in. punch, are affixed in spectral order and aligned ¹⁄₁₆-in. apart horizontally and vertically; the array is covered front and back by plexiglass separated by a 0.2-cm gasket and secured by neutral tape. The equipment is inexpensive to assemble and easy to carry; the lamination hermetically seals the chip from dust, moisture, and mold, and it arrests outgassing from the pigment, which clouded the glass of WCS chips in slide binders (MacLaury 1987c).

3. Critics of this mapping method express six concerns (MacLaury 1991a: Appendix). Each involves some unspoken assumption about science, vision, or human nature.

(1) *Prompting an individual to expand a mapping may produce a distortion if consultants are anxious to please or ill-at-ease.* People were relaxed and assertive as they performed the mundane act of laying rice on the colors of a particular name, much as Senft (1987:318) found when interviewing similarly in the Trobriand Islands: "Although the standardized introduction and questions, the list, and the tape-recording marked the situation as quite formal, my informants in general did not seem to be bothered at all, but were highly cooperative, even the children, to whom the whole test seemed to be a kind of new game."

The analysis of individual cognition involves cross-checks of accuracy, such as matching independent data. Quantitative checks are performed, such as those shown among the Tzeltal data in §4.5.1 or among the data of tables 6.1, 7.1, 8.2, 10.2, and 11.2–5. Finally, comparison of systems often reveals that individuals share features within a community that they do not share with anyone from another community (e.g., fig. 2.26, yellowish green focus). Every experiment in social science could be impugned on grounds that its procedures *might* influence its result; no formal procedure is "natural." We do not halt experiments because of such possibilities.

(2) *The samples from each community are too small.* When the naming, foci, and mappings are collected from each individual, a sample of ten usually demonstrates shared regularities as well as systematic differences (e.g., table 10.2). Even a smaller sample can bring out the same if it is collected from a tightly knit group, such as a family or hamlet (MacLaury 1991a:44–46; Saunders 1992a:143–51; MacLaury, Almási, and Kövecses, in press). The procedures are adapted to exploring a few people in depth. This tactic differs from that employed by Jernudd and White (1983), who interviewed 173 subjects by asking each to name 18 colored pencils. Jernudd and White studied variation in choice of terms, whereas the MCS analyzed and compared individual cognition. Distinct procedures and sample sizes suit different objectives. Dougherty (1975, 1977) and Kay (1975) note that community-wide samples reveal that variation is the

rule rather than the exception; thus, the MCS targeted samples that were adequate to discover the shared and variable characteristics of micropopulations within larger societies. This plan was backed by the area-wide sample, which affords an overview of similarities and differences between the local samples. The strategy is reinforced further by the backdrop of comparison provided by the WCS and Pacific Northwest Color Survey. Appendix IV compares results of separate studies of Russian "blue" categories: (a) ours, which is based on the descriptive method and theory derived from this Mesoamerican analysis and (b) another that is based on methods established in psychology and on Berlin and Kay's conception of color categorization. We use a small sample and the other uses a large one. The reader may weigh the merits of the two.

(3) *Interviews were not conducted under one standard of illumination.* The eye is remarkably flexible; it discriminates color in the same way under a range of lightings that exceeds the possibilities of an outdoor interview (Boynton 1988; De Valois and De Valois 1975; Hurvich 1981:195; Werblin 1973; Maloney and Wandell 1986). Moreover, any perception of color is a response to ratios of cone-type inputs, not to quantities of photons (see §4.1.1.2). Although photon quantities vary during the day, the ratios remain constant. For these reasons, color discrimination is unaffected by normal variation of ambient daylight, differences in latitude, or seasonal change. During the MCS, most interviews were conducted by day outside in the shade and near direct sun, or inside with the interviewee's back to a window or open door. The few interviews by night were conducted under a 100-watt incandescent bulb. We did, however, uncover a lurking danger in the preponderance of tinted eyeglasses; since their advent, the most artful tact has been required to persuade consultants to remove them or to find their old clear bifocals.

(4) *Interviewees were not screened for color blindness* (e.g., Ishihara 1971). Color-blind individuals usually know that they cannot distinguish certain colors, and they warn of it when invited to an interview. Yet, during the MCS, two men who were apparently red-green blind (protanopic) slipped through the gate. Their data were "retired," because they were blatantly aberrant and contrasted unequivocally with others of their communities and from most others of the three surveys. The chip naming is itself a crude color-blindness test.

Color blindness is rarer among some non-Western populations than among Europeans (Adam, Mwesigye and Tabani 1970; Clements 1930; Ishak 1952; Mann and Turner 1956; Post 1962; Rivers 1901a:90–91; Simon 1951; Squires 1942). Yet these studies found percentages higher than did the WCS, which inadvertently interviewed 10 obvious protanopes: Aguacatec 29, Chavacano 7, Esse Ejja 13 and 15, Gunu 12, Konkomba 25, Ngäbere 23, Tabla 5, Tarahumara 4, Teribe 14. Perhaps the percentage in our results is low because color-blind people declined the interview, although color blindness can be mild enough to escape detection in an interview result. In 1992, I incorporated nonliterate Farnsworth F-2 and Portnoy Plates into my interview to identify all orders of color blindness (MacLaury 1992b; Haegerström-Portnoy 1990). I also collected skin-cell samples by asking subjects to rub a sterile Q-tip against the inside of each cheek; then I froze these samples for genetic analysis (Zegura: experiments in progress at the University of Arizona). Since then, more effective genetic markers have been collected during color interviews by a physician. Nathans (1989) argued that normal and anomalous color vision is determined by 17 different gene combinations. But Neitz and Neitz (1995) developed new methods which reveal that an enormous variety of genotypes produce normal phenotypes and, in turn, the genotypes may alter to produce color vision defects of innumerable sorts. The difference between normal and color-blind vision is more complicated than we anticipated when the tradition of Munsell-chip interviews began (Chapanis 1968:335–336). Although the MCS and WCS survived without color blindness testing, future interviews will include them.

(5) *The Munsell array predetermines the way that people will categorize it.* Collier (1973) projected that maximum saturation would determine Berlin and Kay's universal foci, but Collier et al. (1976) found to the contrary. The Munsell colors are only a measurement and a prerequisite to replicable experiments. Any interviewee is free to categorize them in any manner. Regularities in color data result from people's active engagement of sensation and cognition with the metric rather than from its molding effect on passive minds. The latter notion presupposes a radical folk theory of human abilities.

(6) *The Munsell array elicits decontextualized color categorization devoid of its rich relation to culturally prescribed values and to color symbolism.* Since color is an attribute domain, it is impossible to experience decontextualized color. Even a color chip is a context. The stream of research on color symbolism, color metaphor, color affect, color in poetry, and color in specialized domains that has been flowing since the late nineteenth century suggests that these worthy topics are not neglected; however, this broad range of research has produced no generalizations, which are found only by restricting the realm of observation. The research addresses the following topics: *Color symbolism:* Armstrong 1917; Bonser 1925; Bruce 1937; Christoffel 1926; Dana 1919; de Vries 1965; Dourgnon 1946; Faris 1972; Filton Brown 1962; Izutsu 1974; Jordan 1975; Kees 1943; Luckiesh 1919; Mackenzie 1922; Manniche 1982; Meltzer 1975; Stephenson 1973; Tornay 1978b; Turner 1966, 1967, 1973; Winck 1963; Wright and Rainwater 1962; Zahan 1974; *Color metaphor:* Bennett 1988; Derrig 1978; Dronke 1974; Eisiminger 1979; Jacobs and Jacobs 1958; Monro 1983; Tarrant 1960; Wescott 1983; *Color affect:* Adams and Osgood 1973; Bullough 1907, 1908; Cerbus and Nichols 1963; D'Andrade and Egan 1974; Eysenck 1941; Harbin and Williams 1966; Johnson, Johnson and Baksh 1986; Kobayashi 1974; Nagasaki 1974; Osgood et al. 1975; Osgood 1975; Pérez de Barradas 1932–1933; Stanlaw 1987; Tsukada 1978; Whitefield 1979; Williams 1964, 1966; Williams et al. 1970; Young 1971; *Color in poetry:* Cian 1894; Cole 1952; Davies 1914; Davis 1945; Ellis 1896; Levengood 1927; Phillips 1919; Schulbaum 1930; Tivoli 1893; *Color in African cattle husbandry and of other livestock:* Beek 1977; Bryant 1949:333–334; Dyson-Hudson 1965: 96–103; Evans-Pritchard 1933–1935, 1969:41–48; Fukui 1979; Lienhardt 1961: 12–15; Maffi 1984; Radloff 1871; Tornay 1973:87–91; Turton 1980.

Pre-Columbian Mesoamerican cultures and their neighbors symbolized four cardinal directions, up and down, and a central zone with colors, often of five names (H. Berlin and Kelly 1961; Dixon 1899; La Farge and Byers 1931; Marcus 1973; Martí

1960; Mooney 1891:359; Matthew 1907; Nowotny 1969; O'Neale and Dolores 1943: 391; Reichard 1983:187–239; Riley 1963; Thompson 1934; Titiev 1972:290, 367; Tozzer, ed. 1941; Urry 1969; Voth 1912:135; Waterman 1908). These studies give no evidence that color-direction symbolism has channeled development of basic color categories in any language. Conversely, cognitive and statistical approaches support the hypothesis that color terms name analogous points of view, which would suit them to symbolizing directions (§§6.1–7.4).

4. Kay and Kempton (1984), preparing for their experiments with Tarahumara, established with English and Japanese speakers that Munsell column 23 divides green and blue perceptions; but they report the Tarahumara results while leaving the green-blue divide implicit.

5. "It would be surprising if the best examples of categories were not highly associated with the category name, and it is not surprising that best examples of categories elicit the category name as a superordinate more frequently than do peripheral examples" (Rosch 1973a:139). The focus of *siyóname* at G17 was elicited during a WCS interview in Alamos, Sonora, a year prior to the MCS interview in Ixmiquilpan, Hidalgo. During the latter, *siyóname* was focused at E25. The WCS focus was used in this demonstration of method because it agrees with the other data in the simplest way. Mixture of data between results of different interviews is inadmissible for all other purposes.

The WCS focus agrees with Rosch's statement. The Guarijío speaker might have placed the MCS focus on a central turquoise (E25) because it equally represents the application of *siyóname* to all colors of the cool category; during that interview, he focused *siyomúrame* at G17, unique green. At the time of the MCS interview, the speaker was involved in a linguistic workshop outside of Guarijío territory. His analytically oriented employment might have inspired him to consider additional possibilities as he focused, such as an abstract representation at a central point as opposed to the less reflective tendency that Rosch describes. A formal account of abstract categorization is developed in §§9.4–5. In §8.4, figures 8.24–25, Tarahumara speaker 1 shows a different kind of discrepancy between a focus choice he made at home and another he made away from home at the close of a linguistic workshop. See §9.3 regarding a socially shared practice of choosing three cool-category foci, the last choice on turquoise.

4. AXIOMS

1. Many psychologists use "sensation" and "perception" to designate what I prefer to call "perception" and "cognition" (Kinnear and Deregowski 1992:163–164). I borrow the meanings from cognitive linguistics and adapt them to color categorization (Langacker 1990b: index). Bickerton (1990), as his main theme, differentiates these two sides of consciousness as "primary representation" and "secondary representation."

2. The physiological mechanisms of color vision are precortical and, hence, beyond the reach of feedback from, or modification by, activity within the cerebral cortex. Photochemical reactions in the retina and neuronal firing in the lateral geniculate nuclei (LGN) transform distal stimuli of radiant energy into proximal stimuli. But both orders

of stimuli originate prior to detection in the visual cortex and, hence, prior to sensation, conscious or unconscious. Even though neural signals fire within the body, they are as external to experience as are the wavelengths that initiated them. Experiments with decorticalized monkeys emphasize the lack of reciprocity between the precortical mechanisms and cortically mediated sensation. Hull (1967) nullified the cortex of monkeys of all receptive activity by means of both anesthesia and temperature reduction. Yet she found that the cones and the LGN cells continued to respond in their normal manner to light of all wavelengths as it was directed on the retina. Peripheral physiology automatically sent impulses to an unreceptive cortex.

On reaching the cortex, neural response triggers reflexes that are detected as sensation. Again, the sensory reflexes are automatic and—within a narrow tolerance of individual variation—universal. The reflexes themselves constitute perception, although they derive directly from neural outputs that, in turn, are invariant transformations of events in the external world. In this manner, the external world is directly sensed. Although color perception differs among, say, a frog, a cat, and a human, each species perceives wavelength in the manner for which it is equipped. After perception has occurred, within an instant so brief that it might be immeasurable, color perception and cognition interact.

The species-specific nature of precortical perceptual physiology cannot be invoked as an argument that color categories are "embodied" in the sense in which Johnson (1987) has developed that concept (§§1.1 and 6.4.5). To him, embodiment is an analogy (or a metaphor) between physical experience and more abstract domains of reasoning. In order to construct any analogy whatsoever, a person must be aware of both its source and its target, at least unconsciously if not consciously. But, in either capacity, it is impossible to be aware of peripheral neural events that are free of feedback from the cortex. Although color categories are indeed embodied, their species-specific neurology does not foster that status. Yet Lakoff (1987:29 [emphasis original]) offers this argument: "Color concepts are *embodied* in that focal colors are partly determined by human biology." Any evidence that will demonstrate the embodiment of categories must feature cognition (see §6.4, especially §§6.4.5–22.).

Here we encroach on the realm of philosophy (Hardin 1988; Saunders and Van Brakel 1988b), which is otherwise bypassed here and throughout. Yet vantage theory by virtue of its commitment to a specific concept of color categorization is aligned with one or another ontology regarding color experience and what people name when they refer to it. Tolliver, ed. (1992) reviews a spectrum of the articulated knowledge systems, for example, Johnston (1992), Thompson (1992), Hilbert (1992; 1987), and Hardin (1992). These philosophers argue issues that go back to Aristotle (Anglicus 1582; Gottschalk 1964; Lovejoy and Foster 1913; Sorabji 1972) and that have been addressed by Wittgenstein (1953, 1977), by his analysts (McGuinn 1991; Westphal 1987), and by many others whose numbers have swelled since Goethe (1810) criticized the optical theories of Sir Isaac Newton. For overviews see Hickerson (1980b) and C. Riley (1995:20–69).

3. Information in Appendix III will aid reading of §4.1.1. The review of visual physiology at the top of §2.4.2 is highly pertinent here.

4. Disproportionately reduced discrimination between black and middle-bright-

ness green and blue seems plausible if one deems black to be darkness or absence of spectral light and white to be full spectral light (see Appendix III). Discrimination between any two stimuli is more difficult in darkness than in light. The Munsell array represents the light-to-dark axis of color perception with black and white pigments, a reflective and nonspectral source, whereas real color perception, as categorized by natural language, is likely to be spectral on this axis. In Berlin and Kay's evolutionary order, the early division of light-warm and later division of dark-cool may result from enhancement of differences by light. In my correlation of centrality of foci and size of coextensive naming ranges across the cool categories of the WCS (MacLaury MS-1), I found statistical significance high among focus placements at middle lightness but found no significance among foci placed on rows H and I of the Munsell array. Seemingly, discrimination was insufficient among dark colors to foster the pattern found at middle and high lightness.

5. In 1994, Willett Kempton distributed his program from the Center for Energy and Environmental Policy, College of Urban Affairs and Public Policy, University of Delaware, Newark, DE 19716-7301, U.S.A.

6. The aggregate of focus choices from all color categories of the Mesoamerican sample show that these four colors were chosen most. The WCS foci favor the same chips, except that G1 is chosen more than G2. Both samples select C8 abundantly and with a frequency second only to that of C9 among yellows. Thus, G1–2 and C8–9 are counted as elemental hues in the analysis of Mesoamerican data (fig. 6.38). In stricter calculations of coextension across the WCS, only G1 and C9 are so counted (MacLaury MS-1: figs. 38–42).

7. Also, the comparison of inputs is infinitely more efficient in differentiating minute grades of stimuli than would be a system that devoted a specialized set of neurons for the conveyance of each gradation of stimulus that might occur.

8. Hurvich (1981:132, fig. 4) proposes a slightly different model of cone-to-cell interactions. The difference among models is not critical because the cone inputs have not been affirmed, especially the inputs into $+B-Y$ and $+Y-B$ cells. All models embrace the comparison of inputs.

9. Is attention to similarity a default mode in which people do not devote energy to making distinctions? Or are the emphases on similarity and distinctiveness asserted with equal energy? My guess is that attention to similarity would be asserted less. Yet any individual will prefer to maintain a specific balance of strength between the emphases and will assert this preference. Medin, Goldstone, and Gentner (1990) find that judgments of similarity stress relations while judgments of difference single out attributes.

10. Rivers does not identify the people of tropical climes to whom he compares the Eskimo. He interviewed the latter while they were visiting London. His publication date of 1901 succeeds the 1898 Torres Straits Expedition. Five years later, he subjected 507 Toda speakers to various tests of mental and sensory acuity, finding that their early-stage color categorization correlated with general aptitudes. His inferences about them parallel his comparison of people in luxuriant places with the Eskimo: "They lead a simple existence, their lives being devoted chiefly to the care of their buffaloes, and during a long period of isolation on the Nilgiris they have had no keen struggle for ex-

istence. At one time they seem to have lived largely on roots and berries, but this source of food supply has for a long time been replaced by grain and rice procured from other tribes; and even when they had to seek out their food it was probably easy to find. They have had neither the arduous search for food nor the necessity of being continually on guard against enemies, human and animal, which have done so much to develop the powers of observation possessed by such races as the Australians and American Indians" (1905*b*:321–322).

Rivers, as part of all he did to establish scientific anthropology as an independent field in Great Britain, attempted to initiate within anthropology methods of psychological testing as well as of investigating social organization (Rivers 1906; cf. Slobodin 1978, Mandelbaum 1980). But he succeeded exclusively in the latter, while rigorous approaches to exploring mental aspects of non-Western peoples were pursued by fewer researchers (e.g., Segall, Campbell, and Herskovits 1966; Segall 1979; cf. Lévy-Bruhl 1923; Price-Williams 1961, 1962; Langham 1981; Deregowski 1967, 1989). As Rivers regarded the comparative approach to such qualities as primary, he undertook the study of color categories as a means of accessing them. Conversely, I have taken color categories as foremost but have run head-on into the need to understand mental differences as a means of building models. Since color categories indeed undergo vast change, the driving forces must be addressed. In §9.4, I revisit Rivers's question about the relation of mental acuity and color naming, adding to it some of what has been recognized since 1906 about contextualized and abstract thinking (note 7 of §9.4.1).

11. Jochelson (1908) describes hue naming at Stage IV for the Koryak in Siberia. In Patagonia, hunter-gatherer Tsoneca speakers represented Stage VI (Musters 1897:321).

12. Regarding the pace and acceleration of innovation in the ancient world, archaeologist Schmandt-Besserat (1993) attests the development of writing from clay tokens (10,000 to 5,000 B.P.) to two-dimensional pictographs (5,000 to 3,500) to phonetic writing (3,500 B.P. forward) (cf. Falk 1992:184–188).

13. The specific conditions that favor brightness-naming may include a slow-changing society. The elder Karuk on the Klamath River in Northern California were born into such society, but since the 1940s logging roads and then paved highways thrust them into the modern English-speaking world. During my interviews of Karuk speakers (MacLaury 1992*b*), they named unique yellow, green, and blue with one term, *θukín-kuniš,* but sorted triads of equally distanced color chips according to hue discrimination rather than brightness. Karuk no longer is spoken socially. It appeared that my elderly helpers revived the term for my interviews, although they no longer practiced the emphasis on brightness that might once have justified its broad meaning. They remarked on the term, joked about it, and even apologized for it.

14. Tenejapa Tzeltal offers the appropriate starting point of the Mesoamerican analysis, because in 1968 Berlin conducted Berlin and Kay's first full-dress study of basic color terms by collecting acetate mappings from forty speakers of the Tenejapa dialect. This method revealed five salient terms—*sak* 'white', *ʔihk'* 'black/(blue)', *¢ah* 'red', *k'an* 'yellow', and *yaš* 'cool'—which led Berlin and Kay (1969) to classify Tenejapa Tzeltal color naming at Stage IV; cool-category foci were placed thrice as often in

green as in blue; some speakers applied both *yaš* and *ʔihkʼ* to blue. The current study confirms Berlin's findings, although it warrants further conclusions pertaining to various evolutionary stages and to the forces that drive change. The additions owe to improvement of descriptive method.

5. COEXTENSIVE SEMANTIC RANGES

1. Spense (1989: 482–483), investigating Forbes's (1979) report that French *marron* and *brun* name the same colors with different emphases, had fifty French speakers complete a questionnaire on the relation between these terms. Her reactions echoed our own in Mesoamerica when she too was confronted with coextension among color terms.

> Some replies seemed very illogical: one respondent, for instance, indicated that *marron* was a kind of *brun*, that *brun* was a kind of *marron*, that they were synonyms and also that the two colours were independent of each other. . . .
> Answers seemed to demonstrate that many speakers (including some lexicographers) are vague. Either that, or the whole idea of classifying colours in terms of hyponymic relationship to superordinates (basic categories) is suspect.

2. Zulu speakers rendered coextensive mappings of the warm category and of others, even though none of 50 interviewees intermixed warm-category terms (MacLaury MS-2). MacLaury (MS-1: table II), after tightening criteria, finds 43 cases of warm-category coextension among the namings and foci of the 111 World Color Survey languages, 5 Mesoamerican and 38 non-Mesoamerican; application of equally strict criteria to the WCS cool categories (MS-1: table 1) reveals 12 Mesoamerican coextensive systems versus 260 non-Mesoamerican. Although 18 languages in and around Mesoamerica contribute 16.3% of the individual systems in the WCS (421 Mesoamerican ÷ 2,580 total in WCS), they produce 5.40% of its coextensive relations among warm and cool ranges, or 11.60% of the warm cases and 4.40% of the cool. Coextension is less common in Mesoamerica than in certain other regions. Had the WCS collected mappings, coextension would be demonstrated between many more pairs of terms naming warm or cool categories.

3. In this analysis of Mesoamerican color data or any others that I conduct, subjects do not make "mistakes" but only behave in ways that either fit a hypothesis or do not.

4. The divide between mapping steps at columns 40 and 1 results from the interviewer using only the obverse array. The breach of procedure probably produced distortions, such as the mismatch of a focus and first mapping step in figure 5.4*b;* however, major features, such as the different directions by which mapping steps were laid down, seem to be reliable.

5. The criterion for ensuring that a term names some particular type of category is that it must name the unique hue(s) that the type would include, if not an even broader range. At middle brightness, rows D–G, I accept a range as naming the cool category even if it falls short by one column, say, extending—in a case that is curtailed to the extreme—from columns 18 to 28. Coextension in the cool category is identified when both ranges span at least this width. Thus, in figure 5.8, the ranges in *a* are not properly

coextensive, while those in *b* and *c* are. Criteria for use in hypothesis testing were tightened in my study of the WCS (MacLaury MS-1). Assessment may include mappings and foci; for example, in figure 4.9, only the mapping of *yaš* technically identifies this term as a name of the cool category, even though all other Tzeltal who were sampled manifest its "cool" meaning in naming data (figs. 4.3–8, 4.10 and 6.32). Tightened criteria for identifying coextension in the warm category require responses on or outside of both G2 and C8 for each range. The four systems of figures 5.3 (6.37*b*), 6.35, 6.36, and 7.16*a* are putatively coextensive, even though one range of each falls short of the opposite elemental hue; each involves a circumstance described in conjunction with its figure that makes it difficult to class as either coextension or inclusion. Note 8 of §11.3.5 elaborates use of criteria to enumerate semantic ranges of cool categories.

6. Hage and Hawkes (1975:298–299) describe this semantic evolution and recognize its relation to basic-category evolution:

> An examination of individual protocols reveals . . . steps in the transition
> of one phase to the next. . . . one group . . . had a stable focus . . . but not
> bounded GRUE, i.e., the GRUE category matched the dark-cool or BLACK
> category in range [*Coextension*]. (Informant 1 lacks even a GRUE focus
> [*Near Synonymy*].) A second group . . . has a bounded GRUE, which is
> subordinate to a large BLACK category [*Inclusion*]. A third group . . . has
> a bounded GRUE which contrasts with a restricted or 'shrunken' BLACK
> [*Complementation*]. . . . a more advanced system results from a redefinition
> of the taxonomic relations between old categories rather than the . . . sudden
> introduction of a new category. [Words in square brackets are added.]

7. In vantage theory, preconditions for semantic types are analyzed as a sequence of two prerequisites: first, a particular balance of attention to similarity and distinctiveness prevails; second, these emphases are organized into two (or more) viewpoints. When (at least) two vantages are organized, a second term (or other terms) may be recruited to name the additional point(s) of view. As distinctiveness is emphasized increasingly, the likelihood of two (or more) vantages increases; and, because of this and on top of it, the probability of double (or multiple) naming of a category increases.

8. WCS data may show different numbers. My figures 2.14, 2.16, 2.22, 2.24*c–d*, 2.25*c*, 2.26, and 2.28 show non-Mesoamerican warm categories named with one term. All 51 warm categories of the Mesoamerican sample show that at least one elemental hue is named with two terms while 32 are named coextensively. Figure 5.9 shows the only case of even a quasi-exception, since two ranges are known but only one is named. Warm categories, however named, are rarer in Mesoamerica than in many other regions. See note 2.

6. VANTAGES

1. Only 3 and 4 result from the same elicitation procedure; however, in table 6.1 they exhibit such a weak correlation that elimination of 4 would improve statistics.

2. Among the 88 possible correspondences, there are 65 successes and 23 failures (Group I) as opposed to 44 and 44 expected by chance (Group II). I count as successes only correspondences of 4 or 3 characteristics among data from any individual. In my first account (MacLaury 1987b), I overlooked two negative cases, figures 6.32–33, that both attest coextension by a second mapping step on C8 only. In note 3, another five cases are indexed; they are named and focused but not mapped. Figure 6.34a shows a sixth such case. As five of them are positive, they add 10 successes and 2 failures to the ratio, changing 65:23 to 75:25 (p<.001).

This computation of each characteristic as a success or failure differs from the all-or-none reckoning used to compute the non-Mesoamerican sample from the WCS, which proffers only namings and foci. Therein, a largest naming range and most central focus either coincide or they do not; ties are negative, as between ranges of the same size or foci that are equally central.

3. Certainly this local sample cannot show that coextension and its dominant-recessive pattern occur globally. To test this hypothesis, I scoured the WCS to find 41 warm and 240 cool categories coextensively named (MacLaury MS-1), including 17 cases of triple coextension. The latter add two coextensive relations to any category to which they pertain ($17 \times 2 = 34$), bringing coextensive relations to 43 ($41 + 2$) warm and 272 ($240 + 32$) cool. (The difference between one relation within a pair of coextensive ranges and the three relations within a triple set may be envisioned as the difference between one line connecting two dots versus the three lines that connect the points of a triangle.) The dominant-recessive pattern obtains between any two coextensive ranges of a category among which the most abundantly named range is most centrally focused. Calculating such relations in the WCS, the ratios of positive-to-negative results are 31:12 warm and 158:114 cool (both p<.01 chi square).

To refine these numbers within the WCS, I segregate coextensively named warm categories in Mesoamerican languages, which show four positive cases (Jicaque WCS 4 [fig. 11.7d], Mazatec WCS 25 [fig. 10.3], Tlapanec WCS 19 and 24 [figs. 6.37a and d]) and one negative (Mixtec WCS 21 [fig. 6.26]). Then I calculate for the non-Mesoamerican remainder: positive (Bete WCS 1, 9, 25; Bhili 23; Buglere 5 [fig. 2.19], 7, 22, 21, 22; Carib 3; Chumburu 2, 5, 24; Ifugao 19; Kriol 20, 24; Mawachi 21; Menye 11, 13 [fig. 2.20]; Tboli 1; Ucayali Campa 6; Vagla 22; Vasave 4; Yaminahua 3, 21) and negative (Buglere 25; Kokoni 2; Mawachi 24; Menye 21; Tboli 20, 21, 25; Teribe 11; Vasave 11; Wao 18). Bhili 25 shows triple coextension, with 2 relations positive and 1 negative. The total WCS non-Mesoamerican positive-to-negative ratio is 27:11 (p<.05). Under ratios in table 11.5, coextensive ranges in cool categories are separately analyzed for non-Mesoamerican and Mesoamerican languages, respectively showing (p<.05) and (p<.001).

Figures 5.3 (elaborated as 6.37b), 6.35–36, and 7.16a might show coextensive ranges, but they fall a fraction short of criteria (see note 5 of §5.1.2). They complete the total of 32 listed in §5.3. Their foci are in the aggregate of figure 6.38 and contribute to quantification pertaining to it (§7.1.1); their polarity pushes numbers toward nullity, although to no avail. Elsewhere the four are not used to test the dominant-recessive pattern of coextension, although they would provide positive statistics. Therefore, all 32 cases of coextension reported in Mesoamerican warm categories (including the marginal four) are accessible in the diagrams indexed above or in table 6.1. The stronger statistics in Mesoamerica match a strong emphasis on hue throughout the region in comparison with languages elsewhere that stress brightness (see note 5 of §11.3.3). Centrality of foci is computed in reference to elemental hue, which is a critical diagnostic of the dominant-recessive pattern of coextension. Therefore, the pattern is bound to be weakest among populations that value brightness more than hue. Coextension in non-Mesoamerican languages is exemplified in figures 2.19 (warm and cool), 2.20 (warm and dark), 2.29a–b (yellow-green-blue), 2.30b (cool), and MacLaury (1992a: figs. 14 [middle brightness], 16 [middle brightness], and 17 [yellow-green-blue]).

Finally, there are 1,535 cool categories in the WCS of which 1,246 are non-Mesoamerican (i.e., not from languages in table I.1) and 289 are Mesoamerican (in table I.1). Of the former, 19.26% (240 ÷ 1,246) are coextensively named. The latter 289 constitute part of the 589 cool categories of the Mesoamerican sample (§8.2.1). Among these 589, coextension is demonstrated by naming and/or mapping among 43 or 7.30% (52 relations in table 11.5 less 9 among triple and multiple coextension in Chichimeca Jonaz, Tzeltal, and Huastec, table 11.4). Of the 455 non-Mesoamerican warm categories in the WCS, 36 or 7.91% are coextensively named (38 relations minus 2 from Bhili triple coextension). Mesoamerican warm categories combined from the WCS and MCS show 28 among 51, or 54.9% coextensively named and/or mapped. Mapping reveals more coextension than does naming alone, and only the MCS collected mappings. These percentages are too high to attribute coextension to accidents during interviewing or confusion on the part of a few people. Furthermore, accidents or confusion are unlikely to produce at significance the dominant-recessive pattern.

4. A pair of coextensive ranges are dominant-recessive when one of them shows a "most" in, at minimum, three of the four criteria. Thus, such ranges warrant the labels **D** and **R**. Some individuals show dominance **D** in the range that is focused in reference to yellow Y, and others show dominance **D** in the range that is focused in reference to red R. Thus, in the former case, **D** heads the Y range throughout the column pairs, while in the latter case **D** heads the R range throughout. Yet this relation is manifestly symbolized only in the first column pair to be headed by **D** and **R**, whereas the relation applies to the four statistical columns that follow to the right where it need not be indicated over and over.

In rows 12–18, in columns where the dominant-recessive pattern is transgressed in one criterion or another, the divergent numbers are italicized while the headings of **D** and **R** remain constant. This is so because the ranges, nevertheless, retain their pattern when it is contradicted only once. But in rows 19–22 there is no pattern—the outcome of two disparities within each pair of ranges—wherein every column must be headed by **Ø** rather than by **D** or **R**. To be consistent throughout rows 19–22, the left column of each pair quantifies the Y range and the right column the R range. All data are italicized here to indicate the absence of pattern.

5. A child may learn the pattern from its mother, which is an untested proposition. But then why do mothers differ from one another when they and their ancestors origi-

nate in the same small village? This pushing back of the question forces one to suspect that children do not always copy their care-giver's pattern.

6. MacLaury (1992*a:* figs. 11–18) tests the model as a means of accounting for brightness categories and their merger with Berlin and Kay's 1975 version of the evolutionary sequence (figs. 2.2, 2.12–13 here); examples of brightness categories appear in figures 2.15*a*, 2.24*d*, 2.26, 2.27*b–d*, 2.28*a–b*, 2.29*a*, 2.30*a–c*, 2.31*a–c*. MacLaury (see note 3) demonstrated that the dominant-recessive pattern of coextensive color naming is not local to Mesoamerica but worldwide. Taylor and MacLaury (1995) anthologize case studies that apply vantage theory to issues in discourse analysis and semantics unrelated to color (see Aoyagi 1995; Hill and MacLaury 1995; Lansing 1995; MacLaury 1995*a;* Preston 1993; Taylor 1992). See M. MacLaury 1989 for a nonlinguistic use of vantage theory.

7. I further use "vantage" as meaning "a view from a position composed by an intersection of coordinates" as well as the standpoint itself; it is an analogous view on the world, an understanding, or a category. In ordinary usage, "vantage" means only the position or vantage point, not the purview commanded from it. I use "purview" or "scope" as distinct from the position.

8. In the idiom of vantage theory, "concentrate" refers to fixating mentally on one level within a hierarchy of coordinates; "attend to" refers to emphasizing a coordinate; "focusing" refers to choosing a best example of a category. "Concentration," "attention," and "focus" denote the state or result of each act, respectively. Although in ordinary English these near synonyms are often interchangeable, in discussion of vantage theory they are used with these separate meanings.

See Preston's (1993:217) example of "zooming" that he bases on Fillmore's (1982) frame semantics of "back" and "front" from inside and outside views on a church.

9. "Once they have been selected" alludes to categories featuring coordinates of brightness rather than of hue, which abound outside Mesoamerica (figs. 2.16*a*, 21, 25*d*, 27–30; MacLaury 1992*a*). This presentation of theory is simplified by neglecting brightness coordinates. Degrees of brightness are more movable than hue points, as the axis from light to dark is continuous rather than segmented by perceptual maxima. Selection of a level of brightness as a coordinate allows expansion or restriction as well as some room to slide toward either pole (figs. 2.13*a–b*, 2.25, 2.26*a*, 2.27*a;* see note 24 of §2.6). Yet, the range of selection is not immensely more ample than the one allowed by the hue band or, at least, it is latently less than the span accorded by similarity and difference. Although selection of brightness coordinates produces a more fluid, variable, and wide-ranging category than hue coordinates, the two kinds fulfill the same role of a relatively fixed point of reference (MacLaury 1992*a:* fig. 8). Yet Cotton (1950) argues that motion and brilliance may be equated.

10. Which is analogous to emphasis on similarity, slow or fast? A slow pace of life in a small society like the one the Dani inhabit encourages emphasis on similarity (§4.3, K. Heider's quotation). To simplify discussion, I follow this intuition, even though it may be wrong. Slowness affords finer differentiation while speed blurs acuity, which would justify equating speed and similarity. The question need not be resolved to describe the vantage model.

11. The WCS shows that, over the world, most warm categories are named with one term, which is usually focused in reference to red (figs. 2.14, 16*b*, 22*a*–*b*, and 28 versus fig. 2.22*c*).

12. I entertained the idea of eliminating one elemental hue from a category while adding another, calling it the "flip-flop hypothesis" (MacLaury 1986*b:* fig. 1, 1987*a*:109, 1991*b*:31, 1992*a:* n. 17), which addressed Salishan cognates meaning "yellow, green" in one language and "green, blue" in another, such as the systems in figures 2.33*a*–*b* (also MacLaury 1987*a:* fig. 3, 1991*b:* fig. 10). But Kinkade's (1988) reconstruction of a Proto-Salishan category covering all of yellow-green-blue accounts for the current patterns straightforwardly. Flip-flop is again considerd in §12.1.2.4.

13. Two alternative models avoid the foregoing imperatives, but both require that a category somehow be conceptualized independently of the person who forms it. In the first, all coordinates are regarded at once from a transcendental stance. In the second, the broad and narrow ranges are depicted by a singular formalism that an earthly viewer regards from either of its two ends. In both models, the arrangement of coordinates remains the same regardless of the viewing angle. The dominant-recessive pattern of coextension underscores the need for a third model specifying how conceptualizer and category engage.

14. In figure 5.9, the Jicaque speaker may have named the warm category with only one of her near synonyms because using a second term with almost identical meaning mattered little. But then why retain the alternative? The mappings and foci suggest that the word she uses, *he*, names the recessive range, which may be the appropriate form for marking the occasion of being interviewed by a fair-faced foreigner.

15. Whenever an individual focuses one coextensive range twice and the other once, only first choices can be compared; the second choice lacks a counterpart in the opposite range (cf. MacLaury 1995*a:* fig. 2 plus text).

16. The variation in relative size between coextensive ranges is reflected throughout the thirty-two coextensively named warm ranges. Differences between individuals can be modeled as difference between multiplicative and additive formulae: $(S^2\text{-D }D^2\text{-S})$ for a great discrepancy between range sizes versus (SS-D DD-S) for a small one. Formulae may be manipulated as $(S^{1.5}\text{-D }D^{1.5}\text{-S})$ or (Ss-D Dd-S) or many other combinations. Two people need not relate coordinates in the same way. Such manipulations not only express distinct ratios of range size but different slopes of membership value, which also differ between individuals. Formulae afford potential for all sorts of description through such minor manipulation.

17. Forbes (1979) and the WCS (Carib [12] and Ngäbere [2, 4, and 19]) show dominant coextensive terms that are more recently innovated than recessive terms; WCS Mampruli and Patep show the opposite, as found in Mesoamerican cases and Zulu (MacLaury 1995*a*:§2.3). See Appendix IV regarding Russian "purple" and "brown" terms and Forbes's work with French.

18. In §2.4.2. (item 2), failure to "provide embedded frames of reference" is listed as a problem of the fuzzy-set model.

19. In figure 6.29, the ultra-recessive vantage incorporates a coordinate of dark-

ness, as discussed in §8.3. However, the darkness may be entailed by DD and, therefore, it need not be modeled within the coordinate system. If the ultrastrong attention to distinctiveness shrinks the vantage toward nullification, a person may reduce the differentiation by darkening the vantage. In this capacity, darkness may reinforce the integrating effect of attention to similarity.

20. Regarding concepts, "vantage" and "range" are not synonymous, even though they refer to the same behavior. The difference between terms comes to the surface here, as an objective observer—such as the reader who inspects the data in figure 6.27—can consider several ranges at the same time as well as their relations. But a person who constructs such vantages can only relate two to each other. "Vantage," opposed to "range," includes the participation of the categorizer in its meaning. That only "vantage" accurately designates semantic relations from a speaker's perspective becomes evident when discussing the relations as framed.

Regarding data, in figure 2.8, Binumarien exhibits two frames of reference with a coextensive relation in the first and a relation of inclusion in the second. Figure 6.35 shows a Mixtec example in which the ultra-recessive range is not quite coextensive. Figure 4.9 shows a Tzeltal example of triple coextension between *yaš, seleste,* and *asul* that is complicated by a dark-to-light contrast between *yaš* and *seleste.* This contrast is unlikely to be an entailment of strong attention to distinctiveness; rather, it would result from coordinates of dark and light. (See note 19 for the opposite interpretation of a different category.) At G18, the Tzeltal-speaker's use of *asul* barely qualifies this range as coextensive (see note 5 of §5.1.2).

21. This woman and a few other consultants in the MCS demonstrated outlooks that seemed more imaginative, analytical, or philosophical to me than the impressions I usually gathered from interviewees. These exceptional individuals were, nevertheless, confined to the cultural and linguistic resources of their local societies. The elderly woman who contributed the data in figure 6.33 also was such a person. I note further that the coextensive warm ranges of both these women are among the four in table 6.1 that do not show the dominant-recessive pattern, and that they are the only two among the twenty-two in the table who chose multiple foci for warm ranges. Yet there is no objective method to distinguish anomalous systems from ordinary ones in an opportunistic sample. The effects on this sample of variation among personalities have been attenuated by collecting abundant data.

22. Savage-Rumbaugh and coworkers (1985; esp. Essock 1977) at Yerkes Regional Primate Center show in their experiments with pygmy chimpanzees that these intelligent animals use and flexibly revise categories of objects. What model would pertain—a fuzzy set, family resemblances, a complexive class, a vantage, or other?

7. CATEGORY DIVISION

1. See note 4, third paragraph, for a quotation by Hage and Hawkes that contains conventional usage of "superordinate-subordinate relations between categories." In vantage theory, a "category" consists of its coordinates, the emphases upon them, and

their arrangement, while a "vantage" is strictly the latter. Coextensive vantages consist of (at least) two arrangements of the coordinates that constitute one category. Both arrangements persist in a relation of inclusion, changing only in accord with emphases, wherein the vantages on this category differ greatly in the size of their purviews or ranges. A person who assumes a recessive vantage ceases to think in terms of the dominant vantage, which allows the two to coexist in spite of their difference. (I regard this interpretation to be emic.) Nevertheless, researchers have traditionally regarded a relation of inclusion to pertain between subordinate and superordinate *categories,* not between a retracted view and a broad view of one category that are separately named. (To me, the interpretation of two categories is etic. And probably, as a further obstacle to communication, certain entrenched ways of thinking may identify a category—a cognition—with the stimuli that are categorized—a noncognition.) I try to make this dichotomy between my theory and conventional theory easier for the reader to navigate by calling the two vantages subordinate and superordinate *ranges* while leaving "category" out of the terminology. I introduce this measure here in Chapter 7, in which I feature inclusion, but did not do so in Chapter 6 when addressing coextension. There it was easier to impart the idea that two vantages provide different perspectives on one category, because coextensive ranges share many colors; but here it is harder to convey the same idea when ranges related by inclusion typically share fewer colors and, thus, appear markedly different. As diagrammed in figure 6.10, one kind of relation obtains between ranges or vantages in both coextension and inclusion; their difference is purely one of emphasis. Dissolution of the link defines a relation of complementation, figure 6.11. See note 4 regarding the way indigenous Mesoamericans refer to linked ranges. If Westerners spoke and thought likewise (instead of speaking and thinking in terms of set theory), then terminology would pose no problem. See also Hage and Hawkes's quotation in §2.4.2, in which they express their decision to consider coextensive terms to be names of one category, which is an easy choice compared to deciding the same about ranges related by inclusion.

2. Seventeen pairs of coextensive warm ranges show overlapping first mapping steps (figs. 5.1, 6.1–4, 6.12, 6.14–15, 6.17–19, 6.21, 6.23, 6.30–32, 7.8), five do not (figs. 5.4, 6.16, 6.20, 6.22, 6.33); all are listed in table 6.1. Four pairs of warm ranges related by inclusion show overlapping first mapping steps (figs. 7.3, 7.9–11), five do not (figs. 7.1–2, 7.4, 7.13–14); these are listed in table 7.1 with another nine that were not mapped.

3. Table 7.1 excludes the four systems of figures 5.3 (6.37*b*), 6.35, 6.36, and 7.16*a,* whose foci are counted among coextensive systems (fig. 6.38; also see note 5 of §5.1.2). Respectively, their data show foci at: (fig. 5.3) I1 and C12 (I1 is most polarized with smallest naming range); (fig. 6.35) F4 and C9 (C9 is most polarized with smallest range); (fig. 6.36) G1 and D1 (D1 is off the central axis but with largest range); and (fig 7.16*a*) F3–4 and C10 (C10 is most polarized with smallest range). Three of the four show the dominant-recessive pattern.

4. I found that people throughout Mesoamerica could easily discuss category rela-

tions. But they always said that one category "commands" another; the latter "hangs from" the former; or the two are "apart" or almost "the same." As Joseph Benton (1979 MCS fieldnotes) recorded while eliciting Chichicapan Zapotec color terms, *nya kun kolor de rosa* 'red commands pink'. These concepts, which emphasize points of reference instead of boundaries, are compatible with the notions put forth by vantage theory of near synonymy, coextension, polarized inclusion, and complementation. Hollenbach 1969:263) notes that the Trique discuss geopolitical relations between larger and smaller polities always in terms of points in space, never boundaries, with middle-sized units intermediating between larger and smaller (cf. fig. 6.29).

> The relationship between two towns is usually expressed in terms of dominance. A larger, more important town is said to rule smaller, less important towns. Smaller, less important towns are said to follow larger, more important towns. The verb *noko?*[3] here glossed 'follow' may also be glossed 'hang' or 'be dependent on'. Thus, the Copala Trique view of political geography is a hierarchy in which a large centered unit dominates smaller centered units, which in turn dominate still smaller centered units.

Speakers of Mesoamerican languages invoke geopolitics as a metaphor to discuss categorization or, less likely, appeal to the general theme of dominance and dependency to talk about geopolitical and categorical relations in the same terms. Either means would be perfectly apt to describe polarized inclusion between superordinate and subordinate ranges wherein the superordinate range loses dominion while the subordinate range pulls away toward autonomy, with some of its sectors becoming autonomous before others. (Wardhaugh [1992:27, 36] describes an ethnic political struggle wherein predominating Serbs define a Serbo-Croatian language while minority Croats differentiate themselves by defining their speech as a separate language.)

Hage and Hawkes (1975:288), while eliciting native color categories in Papua New Guinea, found that "superordinate-subordinate relations between categories were determined by how they mapped rather than by asking the standard question, 'Is X a kind of Y?' ('Is scarlet a kind of red?, etc.'). This question appeared to make little or no sense to Binumariens." Berlin and Berlin (1975:62) discovered the same to be true of Aguarunas in eastern Peru. Black (1969:167) underscores a need to learn "the logic of the culture under study," but this methodological tradition of ethnoscience only mustered well-intended probes while it never delineated a clear case in point (sources cited by Black).

The indigenous Mesoamerican folk concept of category relations appears to be more compatible with real categories than are the concepts of classical or fuzzy logic or the prototype notion. The folk concepts coincide with key constructs of vantage theory. Our conventional image of categories as containers is but one of the innumerable ethnic "subroutines" found throughout the world; it is no less arbitrary than the method by which Eastern Nilotic Chamu speakers determine the true front side of a tree (note 6 of §9.4.1), and it is even more imaginative. Yet, our belief in category boundaries guides entire schools of language philosophy. Even theoreticians of fuzzy logic or prototypes are obsessed with the vagueness of boundaries (which they treat as a path-breaking discovery), shaping themselves around this natural aspect of a category as if it were either a monumental problem or a cause for celebration (e.g., McNeill and Freiberger 1993). In contrast, the Mesoamerican concept of category relations takes fuzziness for granted.

5. Hage and Hawkes (1975:297), quoted in connection with figures 2.9*a–b* (§2.4.2), describe dark-cool coextension in Binumarien.

6. Harry McArthur (pers. comm. 1980; see table I.1 Aguacatec) told me of hearing an Aguacatec man refer to the lush green of a corn field as *q'eq,* a term that is usually focused in black, figure 7.20. Stanley McMillen (pers. com. 1979; see table I.1 Uspantec) told me that Uspantec speakers refer to grey-coated animals and to dark moist soil as *reš,* a term which is always focused in either green or blue or between them, figure 7.19. (Regarding inclusion of grey in the cool category, see note 5 of §8.3 and discussion of Turton [1980] in §2.4.3.)

7. Coordinates of a brightness category are formally represented as points or segments of the continuum connecting white and black (MacLaury 1992*a:* figs. 8–10), which includes no natural disjunctions equivalent to unique hues.

8. WCS results show thirteen widely dispersed languages in which at least five speakers use strong examples of a major brightness category, thirty-two languages with at least one speaker doing so (figs. 2.16 and 2.29–32). But as color-category evolution progresses, brightness categories become one or another of the universal-hue categories (MacLaury 1992*a:* figs. 11–14).

9. The Uspantec speaker of figure 6.13 might show remnants of a yellow-green-blue brightness category named coextensively by yellow-focused *q'en* and cool-focused *reš* (*q'en* is applied to F17, F29, JØ and I40, *reš* to C7; cf. figs 8.31*a* and 8.33*a* for *q'an* applied to cool), as seen, for example, in Cayapa, figure 2.29*a*. Cool-focused brightness ranges commonly fluctuate in width to encompass black, as in Paya, figure 7.22*b* (but not in fig. 7.24), or farther afield in Gunu, figure 2.28*d* (see MacLaury 1992*a:* fig. 14, Mundu). A lingering emphasis on brightness in Uspantec *reš* may explain why its range ambivalently covers black, as in figure 7.19. Extraordinarily broad or unusually formed Mayan cool categories (figs. 8.22–23 and 11.14) hint that these, too, may descend from an enormous brightness range (also MacLaury 1986*a:*235, fig. 7.21, Lanquín K'ekchí; MCS file A, Cobán K'ekchí. MacLaury 1982 reconstructs Proto-Mayan hue Stage II, which is more of a statement about knowledge in 1982 than about Mayan).

10. Naming data from Otomanguean languages appear in figures 5.3, 5.5–7, 5.10–13, 6.26, 6.35–37, 7.6, 7.17a–b, 8.8, 8.10–11, 8.28*a*, 10.9–10, 10.12–17, 10.20–23, 10.30–33, and 11.9. Binumarien uses 2, 4, and 6 terms to name, respectively, white, red, and yellow (Hage and Hawkes 1975:290). Researchers (cited in note 22 of §2.6) document a substantial Old English color vocabulary that included brightness terms, most of which are now transformed to hue or are obsolete. In §2.6, see notes 22, 25–26, and 28 and figures listed in note 26 for evidence of the mutability of brightness terms and their ranges.

8. SKEWING AND DARKENING

1. Here and throughout §§8.1–6, "unique hue," a Munsell column, is more appropriate than "elemental hue," one particular chip. The terms are used in contrast, as in the discussion of figure 8.1.

2. "Secondary category" is used loosely here. See note 1 of §7.1 and note 4 of §7.1.4. "Membership" and its curves are heuristics held over from fuzzy-set theory with no commitment to that model. In vantage theory, skewing would be depicted by increasing the value of **D** in a model, for example, by enlarging the symbol to **D**. Secondary categories are recessive vantages. The heuristics serve this description while the theory will aid explanation later.

3. This count of foci and the figures 8.15 and 8.16 were prepared in 1985 (MacLaury 1986a: figs. 8.17–21). Since then, six more cases of coextensively named cool categories have turned up in the MCS sample, raising their number from 44 to 50, as reported in note 3 of §6.1.2. As I kept no record of which systems were newly recognized, I would now have to count the data from 589 cool categories over again to make figures 8.15 and 8.16 consistent with that note and with tables 11.3–5. As about twelve foci from six systems will not transmogrify inferences based on figures 8.15 and 8.16, I leave them as they were originally compiled.

4. This and other comparisons of distributions in green and blue require reversal of cells within one of them, as 13–23 versus 23–31 must be calculated as 13–23 versus 31–23; within the cool category, the central and polar cells of each green versus blue color are ordinarily in mirror-image order.

5. Investigators of specific languages have observed that the cool category (Turton 1980:326; Johnson, Johnson, and Baksh 1986:676; Woodworth 1906:25) and the green category (Furrell 1885:328) include grey; Tzeltal speakers who are beyond Stage II apply *yaš* 'cool' to middle grey, figures 4.5–9. See note 6 of §7.2.1 regarding Uspantec *reš*. This practice is not universal. In no case does it appear that the "cool" or "green" term originally meant only "grey." Conversely, Amuzgo *ȼa³* 'mold' and Trique *dah⁵³* (< *yah⁵³* 'ash') show steps by which a "grey" term extends to pale colors and ultimately to blue or even entirely and exclusively to blue as the retraction of the "cool" term to green reaches its final phase. Biggam (1993) demonstrates similar change in Old English *hæwen* 'mold' from grey to blue (cf. Hamp 1982:187, 189).

Sivik and Taft use the three-dimensional Swedish Natural Color System (NCS) to measure the ranges of color terms throughout this solid, including its least saturated chips. They show that in Swedish and Croatian the green category at its highest value of membership reaches lowest saturation over a broader range of brightness than does any other hue category, including blue (1994:154; Taft and Sivik 1994: figs. 4–5). However, the high membership of Croatian blue is disjunctively distributed between grey and medium-to-high saturation, as is likewise suggested by the semantic migration of "grey" terms to blue in Amuzgo, Trique, and Old English.

6. I thank David Miller for pointing this out to me. He found that subjects almost always refer to red when they guess the meaning of a color term they are unfamiliar

with. Almost none of the WCS systems has a term focused in yellow unless it has a term focused in red. The examples in figures 2.14, 2.16*b*, 2.22*b*, and 2.28 versus fig. 2.22*c* are representative (see note 11 of §6.2.3 regarding same; see also §§2.4.2 and 4.1.1.2). Transference of a cool-category focus from blue to green as occasioned by enhanced attention to contrast is the kind of explanation that Rosch (1978:42) called for when she wrote, ". . . the categories once given would appear maximally distinctive from one another and such that the more prototypical items would appear even more representative of their own and less representative of contrastive categories."

Two Otomanguean languages linguistically recognize the contrast of red versus green with tone pairs (lowest number = highest pitch): Chatino *nga?a*^{32} 'red' versus *nga?a*^{31} 'green'; Trique *mare*^{53} 'red' versus *mare*^{35} 'green' (San Miguel Panixtlahuaca and San Juan Copala dialects). Chatino and Trique are separated by 80 kilometers (50 miles) of Zapotec and Mixtec territory. To my knowledge no other language is reported to contrast tone pairs to name colors (including Zapotec and Mixtec, respectively, the closest genetic relatives of Chatino and Trique), and none opposes its terms for yellow versus blue in this way. (In figure 10.9, Mazatec *su*^{4}*sæ*^{4} and *su*^{3}*sæ*^{1} contrast superordinate and subordinate "cool" terms, marking closeness of meaning rather than extreme opposition.)

7. Mismatching is also the trademark of crossover, the topic of Chapter 10. Crossover precludes a dominant-recessive focus pattern when it involves a noncoextensive range, because the range is always dominant (fig. 10.24 and attendant discussion). But the polarized Tarahumara data suggest that two vantages are in force, which enables transference. The data in figures 8.24–25 reveal no sign of crossover.

8. Covert coextension counteracts the Mesoamerican tendency to correlate a disjunctive mapping with a highly skewed green focus (fig. 8.18), although it does not eliminate the significant difference between foci of disjunctively and continuously mapped categories (§8.2.2.2). Ostensibly, foci that contribute most to this statistic occur in cool categories that are not composed coextensively. For example, figures 8.26*b*–27*a* show 8 foci outside unique-green column 17.

9. Nothing discounts the possibility that pre-Columbian cultures positively sanctioned blue as a cool-category focus despite or even because of the recessive constitution of that view. In some populations, a vestige of this putative value might persist as an unquestioned convention or even as an emblem of identity. The Lacandón—a population of Mayan tribes at the subsistence level (at least until recently)—polarize a blue focus that they unanimously focus in blue (figs. 8.27*c* and 11.14). Anawalt (1992) finds that the Aztec symbolized the central concept of state rulership with blue motifs on the robe of the highest lord, above and apart (Hill and MacLaury 1995).

9. SUBMERGED VERSUS REFLECTIVE CATEGORIZATION

1. Kay and McDaniel (1978) cited dual foci of the cool category as evidence in support of the fuzzy-set union model of composite color categorization (§2.4.2). But this model is inconsistent with triple foci: it cannot address the different orders in

which foci are placed; it cannot explain the dominant-recessive pattern in any of its manifestations, including that within focus aggregates (figs. 8.34–35).

2. Centralized foci in green or in blue, or polarized foci in green, could well be of a single noncoextensive vantage; however, in Lacandón, polarized foci in blue suggest recessive opposition to an unfocused dominant vantage in green rather than division that is about to culminate with the original "cool" term retracting toward blue. It is unlikely that the conservative Lacandón system of five terms would include a cool category on the verge of dividing. Nowhere in the Mesoamerican sample has the cool category divided prior to addition of binary terms to the system, such as names for 'brown' or 'purple' (cf. figs. 2.17–18, 3.1, 4.7–9, 7.19*a*, 8.5–6, 8.8, 8.10, 8.14, 8.22–24, 8.33, 8.36–38, 9.1, 9.2*a*, 9.3*c;* MacLaury and Stewart 1984), or of abundant null responses (8.3–4, 8.7, 8.9, 8.13, 9.2*c*, 9.4–6). It is possible—but not probable!— that the Lacandón foci are a rare exception manifesting only a noncoextensive vantage skewed toward blue.

3. Among the 25 Yupik-speakers (Alaska) of the WCS, 23 focused the cool category (2 at Stage IIIa and 21 at Stage IV; none used binary terms). Six females (mean age 47 years) chose dual foci. Eight men and 8 women (mean ages m 56 and f 49) chose foci in only green or blue. Respondents are too few for calculation, but in general Yupik who choose dual foci may be female and younger. See §4.3 on Eskimo acuity in color naming and note 6 of §11.3.5 on Eskimo coextension. Yupik qualifications listed under the stem of its "cool" term in the WCS hint that the Yupik share "qualifier coextension" (§10.4). Unlike the Tecpan Cakchiquel (fig. 9.2–7, also 8.3–4), who preferred dual foci but who—among half the interviewees—declined to name certain chips, the Yupik offered not a single null response among them.

4. The rare tendency of a majority of individuals in a community to offer substantial null responses was also shown by 8 of the 11 Mam speakers of San Ildefonso Ixtahuacán, who named coextensive vantages while crossing them over (figs. 10.1–5). Twenty Ocotepec Mixtec speakers, among whom only three retained the cool category, declined to name many chips: one chose dual foci for a coextensive range while another focused both coextensive ranges in green (figs. 5.6–7; cf. fig. 11.11).

5. The naming ranges of speakers 3 and 4 are excluded from the figures because they were elicited together. Their null responses are counted because ignoring them would improve statistics. The other 11 speakers were interviewed separately.

6. In the Hausa language of Nigeria, the subroutine for orienting objects is to regard them as facing away from the vantage point, as though the viewer and the viewed object were arrayed in single file (Hill 1975). "Among the Chamus, an Eastern Nilotic-speaking group of the Maa people, the front of a tree is located on the side toward which its trunk is inclined. If the trunk is . . . absolutely vertical then the front is in the direction of either where the biggest branch or the largest number of branches are, in that order" (Heine, Claudi, and Hünnemeyer 1991:124).

7. As a minor refinement, the upper tier of the zooming hierarchy is labeled "level Ø," because it includes the viewpoint itself over and above the coordinates that compose it. Figures 6.9 and 6.11 of color categorization include only the latter sort of cog-

nition, not the viewpoint itself. To keep matters simple, I avoided level Ø in the "yes-terday" and "rock-and-tree" examples, but they should incorporate it.

8. Surely the views on language from VP-2 versus VP-4 would profoundly affect literacy programs in preliterate languages. The pronoun feedback test may provide a crude preliminary litmus for determining how subjects of a color study think. One might predict that none who reverse pronouns would place dual foci, although those who feed them back verbatim may focus in any way. Such testing could be refined and the results correlated with those of color interviews. This program would reintroduce the designs of W. H. R. Rivers, with modification, though, as knowledge and method have accrued for another ninety years (§2.2; see note 9 of §4.3). The goal is as worthy now as then, but now it can be more effectively achieved. The Zapotec who feed back reversed pronouns name at least eight basic color categories, seven of hue and one of desaturation: *nàgăty* 'white', *yáʔas* 'black', *žnyê* 'red', *gùč* 'yellow', *nagèʔe* 'green', *àsŭl* 'blue', *kàfě* 'brown', *mòră d* 'purple', and *yàʔač*, 'desaturation'; *bzāč* refers to the yellow of corn (MacLaury 1970:17). Any number of basic terms by itself may not pro-vide a corollary.

9. I stress the hypothetical nature of this account and offer no independent test. Tim Knab interviewed these consultants (Knab 1977, 1980; Knab and Hasson de Knab 1979), many or all of whom must be gone by now.

10. Some or many Papago may represent model 6 (fig. 8.27*a;* cf. MacLaury 1986*a:* fig. 3 showing four dual-focused cool categories). Recording of the order in which speakers place dual foci was not requested in the WCS instruction booklet.

11. The process of developing expertise in a field may require one to master a recessive vantage while shedding the life-long habit of approaching the world from the dominant vantage. Novices are initially inclined to zoom in on distinctiveness, but, with experience, they learn to zoom in on similarity while maintaining presupposi-tional awareness of the differences. The latter can be quite taxing and unnatural prior to training.

> When a young naturalist commences the study of a group of organisms quite
> unknown to him. . . . His general tendency will be to make many species. . . .
> he has little general knowledge of analogical variation in other groups and in
> other countries, by which to correct his first impressions. . . . But if his obser-
> vations be widely extended, he will in the end generally be enabled to make
> up his own mind which to call varieties and which species; but he will suc-
> ceed in this at the expense of admitting much variation (Darwin 1968:106).

Petyt (1980) chronicles how the field of dialectology paralleled the process that Darwin observed of individuals. Nineteenth-century fieldworkers transcribed so much phonetic detail that resultant isogloss maps were massively entangled. Twentieth-century structuralists found closer agreement between isoglosses and demographic his-tory after they tailored data-collection to phonemic principles, fitting the detail into sys-temic abstractions.

John Gage, Chair of the Art History Department at Cambridge, observes "R. E. MacLaury has recently argued for an emphasis on brightness or value in colour-language as reflecting a belief in unity, and an emphasis on hue as indicating a belief in perceptual diversity. Yet Bridget Riley shows . . . that, at least for the specialised class of painters, hue itself has often been a tool for unification" (Gage 1995:192; cf. MacLaury 1992*a*). Riley (1995:32–34) finds that "In European painting, a remarkable development occurred in Venice at the beginning of the sixteenth century, which introduced an entirely new approach to colour . . . Previously and in other traditions, painters had used what is termed *relational colour* . . . This means thinking of colours as individual hues and placing them in the picture on a system of balances—a red against a blue, or a soft shade against a brilliant one, or one pale colour against another. Whatever the color may be, it is treated as a separate item and given a specific role of its own . . . [Whereas] Titian . . . uses colour all together as one single element . . . through the entire composition. . . . Monet's approach came from a different corner, but it arrives nevertheless at the same point . . . a perceptual *'enveloppe,'* as he called it." To transform Dr. Gage's words into mine, I attribute nonanalytical or moderately analytical outlooks to people who categorize brightness while they emphasize similarity, whereas impressionist masters innovated a way of achieving synthesis by use of hues only after an extraordinary ability to analyze hue had developed throughout the history of art (cf. Malkiel's and Duncan's quotations, §2.5). In terms of vantage theory, the people who name brightness assume a dominant vantage and may accompany it with a recessive vantage, but they seldom zoom in within either. Titian and those who followed him routinely assumed a recessive vantage, as did their predecessors in art, but, unlike their predecessors, they zoomed in to its most concentrated level when they painted. People who assume a dominant vantage begin with naivety and zoom in toward analysis; people who assume a recessive vantage begin with analysis and zoom in toward synthesis. (People may take many generations to prefer viewing the world from such extremes of concentration, or so they did during slower eras than the modern one.) Development of viewpoint beyond synthesis requires disengagement from vantages, which art historians might find among later painters.

10. CROSSOVER

1. The categorical meaning of *č'el*,, which primarily names a kind of parrot (C) typically yellow-green (H_2), is expressed with this formula, $CH_2 S^2 D$ (§6.4.13); C represents context, that is, the image of the parrot; H_2 represents the color of the image; and the contiguity of CH_2 represents the inseparability of C and H_2 within the image. (H_2 is used instead of H_1 to link the color category to the formula that expresses its decontextualized usage, which features H_2 because the usage happens to be an ultrarecessive vantage that stresses hue, $H_2 D^2 H_1 S$. Section 6.4.13 elaborates on this formula, although there it is convenient to use H without a subscript and to express the formula as though it represented a dominant vantage of one hue, $H S^2 C D$. The relation of S and D to formulae is irrelevant to both demonstrations, which concern only H and C). In figures 10.1*c*, 10.3*c*, and 10.5*a*, Mam speakers confine *č'el* to only yellow-green, $H_2 D^2 C S$, as though they remembered C. But in figure 10.4, *č'el* is applied once to blue as well as to yellow-green; and in figure 10.5*c*, *č'el* is applied extensively to

yellow-green, green, and blue, as if C were forgotten and another hue added, $H_2 D^2 H_1 S$—a complete decontextualization of $\check{c}'el$. Yet the foci and mappings of $\check{c}'el$ in figures 10.4a–b and 10.5c–d suggest that $H_2 D^2 C S$ is in force within the minds of the same speakers who decontextualize $\check{c}'el$ when naming chips. They may invoke different formulae for $\check{c}'el$ on separate occasions, contextualizing when mapping and focusing but decontextualizing as they name chips.

Formulae of $\check{c}'el$ stress hue rather than relations because no data directly indicate that $\check{c}'el$ stresses relations, unlike the data regarding $\check{c}a^{\prime}\!\!_\text$ and $\check{s}q'iilan$. Likely, the interaction of these three categories as shown in figures 10.4a and 10.5c is more complex than will be revealed in §10.1, even though the analysis adequately treats $\check{c}a^{\prime}\!\!_\text§$ and $\check{s}q'iilan$. The statistics of table 10.2 are sufficiently robust to eliminate $\check{c}'el$ from the data without consequence for the arguments. Figure 10.18 includes full formulaic representation of the relation between the three terms.

2. Appendix VIII distinguishes formulae of zooming and formulae of stressing, for example, $H_1 S^2 H_2 D$ versus $S^2 H_2 D H_1$; there it is explained why D or S (without exponents) must occur in the penultimate position of the latter when relations are stressed but only in the final position for all cases of the former.

3. Why are relations stressed more than hues in some cool categories? Probably the close similarity of green and blue helps to make their difference seem less consequential than their conjoint participation in one category, although people's motives for selecting this quality as more important than their separate identities are not understood. Most people stress the latter if they group green and blue in one category.

Why are data pertaining to one term confined to opposite colors, for example, as $\check{c}a^{\prime}\!\!_\text§$ may name only green while it is mapped on only blue? To divide the cool category, an attention to distinctiveness is required that is strong enough to supersede the perceived similarity. Its strength is great enough to confine a naming or a mapping to one side of the category while, nevertheless, crossover persists. Underlying this incomplete division, two hues must be included within a single set of coordinates, such as $S^2 H_2 D$ H_1 and $D^2 H_1 S H_2$. Figure 6.10c posses equivalent underlying relations among coordinates for hue-stressing categories that appear to have divided but whose two ranges remain mutually polarized, $H_1 S^2 H_2 D$ and $H_2 D^2 H_1 S$ (§7.1.5).

4. Table 11.1 (under I1B, I2B, III4A, and III4C) lists languages adhering to this rule: Keres, Breton, Navaho, Fijian, Javanese, Rural Italian, Misquito, and Quechua. Mesoamerican languages that name the cool category with one term follow suit (figs. 5.12, 6.33, 10.1c, 8.36–38, and 11.9).

5. A brief review of concepts may help, which are in the glossary and foregoing sections: apparent complementation (§7.1.5); chain relations, links, and frames (§6.3.5); and "vantage" versus "category" (note 1 of §7.1, note 4 of §7.1.4).

6. Dougherty's (1975) description of Futunese cool categories reveals crossover of a main term, its dual foci (fig. 2.7 herein), and some borrowed hue-stressing terms that are coextensive with it in some systems or separately name green and blue in others.

7. Baxter (1983) in Ancient Chinese and Tyson (1994) in modern Korean analyze data that suggest crossover in the cool category was shared across languages over a vast

area of Asia and persists in Korean (cf. Berlin and Kay 1969:96, 124; Kim 1985). Lü (1985) clearly describes the symptoms typical of crossover in the color naming of two Taiwanese languages (Malayo-Polynesian). Lewitz (1974:154–155) sketches possible crossover in Old Khmer (Austo-Asiatic) less clearly (cf. Thongkum 1992).

8. Mazahua speakers 11 and 12 use terms borrowed from a second Mazahua dialect to enhance color semantics. Local and borrowed terms differ only by final vowels, yet their meanings contrast. Figure 19 locates Dolores Hidalgo at the center of the Mazahua region. Speakers in other towns do not oppose terms from two dialects.

9. Mayoruna (WCS, Peru) names the cool category *umumbo* and *umuumumbo* and the warm category *piumbo* and *piupiumbo*, both showing qualified coextensivity of a root (*umu-*, *piu-*) and its reduplication. Mayoruna foci are too extended for impartial calculation, which excludes them from the compilation in table 11.2.

10. The MCS yields voluminous data on color-term qualification (e.g., figs. 6.23–25 and 8.25; fig. 6.32 text; Burgess, Kempton and MacLaury 1983, 1985; MacLaury and Stewart 1984: fig. 5), which remain largely unanalyzed.

11. TRANSFERENCE VERSUS DIFFUSION: MESOAMERICA COMPARED WITH THE WORLD

1. The heading "Mesoamerica" includes the Mesoamerican languages described by the MCS and the WCS as well as six Mesoamerican languages reported in literature: Coatlán Mixe (class III3B) data were collected by the MCS; Ópata (class III4A) and Eudeve (III4D) were reported prior to their extinction, respectively, by Lombardo (1702) and "Anonymous" (Smith 1861; Lionnet 1986:8–9); Comaltepec Chinantec (class III4D) was described by Merrifield from interviews using Berlin and Kay's paper chart and acetate method (§1.2.1); Ayoquesco Zapotec was described by MacLaury (1970: 17–18; unpublished paper-chart experiments conducted in 1972); and Tenejapa Tzeltal was described both by Berlin and Kay (1969; Berlin MS-1) and by MacLaury (1991a). Berlin and Kay's publication on this dialect is included in class IV1 while my data are referenced as class III3B, because our reports differ. "World Survey" comprises the non-Mesoamerican languages in the WCS. "Literature" covers languages whose non-Mesoamerican system of color categorization was addressed as a main topic in a publication or unpublished manuscript. Not included are innumerable dictionaries and ethnographies that define color terms in passing. As the literature often reports the cool category, it is a rich source for this table. Descriptions of composite light-warm, dark-cool, and warm are far fewer and less detailed.

2. Ratios of green-to-blue foci are represented as green:blue, green at left and blue at right. Numbers indicate choices in green or blue. Any single focus counts as 1 regardless of how many chips it covers. Dual foci count as 2 when one is green and the other blue. Dual or multiple disjunctive foci on one side of turquoise column 23 count as 1, a single vote for green or blue. Rare tripartite ratios that include a focus or foci on column 23 are expressed as green:mid:blue. An extended focus is counted as green or blue according to the color that it most pertains to (fig. 8.28, (*a*) green versus (*b*) blue).

A focus on only two adjacent chips, one of which is in column 23, is counted as green or blue in accord with the second chip (e.g., fig. 11.3, H23–24 blue).

3. I distinguish a different socially motivated process from the same purely cognitive one to account for a disparity between Tzotzil and Tzeltal color categorization (MacLaury 1991*a*).

4. When two terms are focused, respectively, in yellow and in blue but both cover green, then speakers may feel disinclined to switch either focus to green, as green is accorded low membership from either viewpoint. Likewise, see figures 3.7–10 with attendant discussion of low membership of blue shared by distinct black-focused and green-focused categories.

5. Green-to-blue ratios of cool-category foci for languages of classes II1A and II2 are listed here (see note 2 for conventions). Also specified is whether the yellow-focused composite category pertains mainly to brightness or hue: Jicaque 3:1:5 hue-brightness, Habli 11:14 brightness, Podopa 2:7 brightness, Cree 2:23 hue, Slave 0:5 younger hue but elder brightness, Abidji 3:12 brightness, Ngäbere (term-1) 4:14 (term-2) 10:3 brightness, Arabela (term-1) 1:6 (term-2) 0:17 (term-3) 6:1:2 brightness, Sursurunga 8:19 brightness, Maring 11:14 brightness, Mampruli 9:14 brightness, Bete 1:3 brightness.

For classes III1A-B the ratios are: Konkomba 7:0 brightness, Vasave 23:1 brightness, Tboli 25:0 brightness, Kuku Yalinji 6:2 brightness (fig. 2.27), Cayapa 27:21 brightness (fig. 2.29), Apinaye 10:5 brightness (MacLaury 1992*a:* fig. 17), Cavinena 19:6 brightness, Yaminahua 15:1:7 brightness, Tabla 14:11 brightness.

6. Seven cases of blue-dominant coextension are supported by the literature on the cool category (class II3A–B), although no author speaks in these terms. Heinrich describes regional variants of Eskimo: "His *sunga-* responses . . . refer to Green . . . but sometimes . . . to Bluish chips. . . . His *tungu-* responses tend . . . toward Blue but include . . . Greenish chips . . . (1974:69, system E)." "At Cape Prince of Wales . . . Green remains *suNaqtuaq,* but blue becomes *suNaaqtuaaq.* What this will do to *tuNaquaq* . . . I do not know (1972:227, n. 7)." Yupik (class II3B), in the area of Nome, names cool with only *sunga-* plus its qualifiers; covert coextensivity is shown by the combination of 12 foci in blue, 5 foci in green, and 6 dual foci in green and blue. The one overtly named case of coextension in Yupik (WCS 5) focuses both terms in blue. In 2 cases (WCS 4 and 11), *sunga-* names only blue while another term names green. Rivers (1901*d:*46) reports that another Eskimo dialect reserves *tungu-* (*tungojoktak*) as the only term for blue.

Bartlett (1928:8, 18, 24, 27) provides lists of color terms showing that dialects of Malay and Batak apply *idjo* and *na rata* (or *biroe*) coextensively to cool, but (*a*) *idjo* shows more qualifiers in green than does *na rata* in blue and (*b*) *idjo* is the older color term (p. 45). These facts point to blue-dominance, because (*a*) the range that extends farthest will warrant the most elaborate qualification at its outer reaches, and (*b*) with exceptions (e.g., Forbes 1979), the oldest term of a coextensive pair is usually dominant when the relative ages of the terms can be established (see MacLaury [1995*a:* fig. 2*f–g*] for such a case in Zulu). *Na rata* has a second meaning of 'fresh' while *idjo* means only 'blue, green'.

Machiguenga (Johnson, Johnson, and Baksh 1986), Futunese (Dougherty 1975, 1977), and Burushaski (Tiffou and Morin 1982) show dual foci and separate qualifiers on the green and blue sides of the cool category, but qualification predominates in green. The latter hints that the blue angle is dominant. JJ&B's Machiguenga report is hard to interpret regarding assignment of dominance: they discuss the "green" qualifier more than the "blue" qualifier but "green" has fewer phonemes. Futunese speakers focus the "cool" term more in blue than in green and leave it on the blue side after dividing the cool category. Tikopia speakers focus the cool category in both green and blue, but they favor blue and apply more qualifiers when using the "cool" term to name green (Monberg 1971:353–54). Younger speakers leave the term in blue after separately naming green with a word meaning "unripe."

7. It appears that Mesoamerican languages show the dominant-recessive pattern of coextension in the cool category more readily than do non-Mesoamerican languages, even though the coextensive naming of cool in Mesoamerica occurs less than its average frequency among WCS languages. Brightness categories are common outside Mesoamerica but almost nonexistent therein (see note 5 for non-Mesoamerican systems). An emphasis on brightness and a de-emphasis of hue may attenuate the pattern, or at least this will weaken my basis for identifying the pattern, as I use unique-hue locations to compute centrality of foci. As discussed in §2.5 in regard to the evolutionary sequence, categories that stress brightness are overall less predictable than those based on hue recognition.

8. Specifications for identifying any type of category are that its range must cover the unique hues that the category would include, allowing for the cool category that responses may pertain only to columns 18 and 28 in rows D–G. Criteria are sketched in note 5 of §5.1.2. Tables 11.2–5 enumerate data from all coextensive cool ranges of the WCS and MCS while distinguishing dominant-recessive relations from those that are balanced (see table 6.1). Some of the assessments are wholly exacting and involve more criteria than I have listed in brief. Here I assess a tenuous system to convey an idea of what an assessment may involve.

In figure 11.9 $(a–c)$, a Chinantec speaker names the cool category with $r\phi^2$ focused in green and $mi^3\check{c}yan^3$ focused in blue-purple. The range of $r\phi^2$ is easy to identify as "cool," as it covers unique-hue columns 17 and 29. But $mi^3\check{c}yan^3$ covers cool colors only by its naming of chip E18, one column short of unique green but within middle brightness rows D–G. Another use of $mi^3\check{c}yan^3$ at C13—outside of middle brightness—is too light to corroborate the minimal approbation, while those at D8, F7 and I1 are on or between red and yellow unique hues and, therefore, are too distant from green or blue to verify a cool category. If any of these had pertained to elemental yellow at C8–9 or elemental red at G1–2, the range of $mi^3\check{c}yan^3$ would be disqualified as a designation of cool hues and instead classified as naming brightness. Thus, this is the most marginal acceptance of a "cool" range that could occur.

A focus (or other response) may be *horizontally polarized* to the outside of the unique hue columns, *vertically polarized* on rows C or B or on rows H or I (lighter or darker than middle brightness rows D–G), or both. Vertical polarization is likely to occur whenever foci darken prior to category division (figs. 8.22–23). Thus, a row of vertical polarization counts for less in the assessment of a dominant-recessive pattern than a column of horizontal polarization, although two rows count for more than one column. The Chinantec speaker centralizes her focus of $r\phi^2$ at F18 but horizontally polarizes her focus of $mi^3\check{c}yan^3$ at F32. This, in combination with $r\phi^2$ showing the largest range, identifies their relation as dominant-recessive rather than as balanced.

To provide contrast with this coextensive relation, in figure 11.9d, a second speaker shows a relation of inclusion between $r\phi^2$ and $mi^3\check{c}yan^3$. His focus of the latter at G28 is central, that is, inside unique-blue column 29. This suggests that $mi^3\check{c}yan^3$ is not conventionally a blue-purple category; it is polarized in the first speaker's system.

9. Ervin (1961:239) reports that elder Navaho include a secondary "green" term (*tatLqid*) within the range of their "cool" term (*dotLquizh*), although "younger Navahos do not know the word tatLqid ($p<0.005$ by the *t*-test)." Response latencies across generations indicate a Navaho preference for a blue "cool" focus (Ervin fig. 1).

10. Paya speakers focus their brightness category with recessive polarization in blue (fig. 11.3), although with less accord among them than the Lacandón show. The Paya too have for centuries been marginal to complex societies of Mesoamerica but do not live in their midst as do the Lacandón.

11. Examples are Hittite of Anatolia (Neu 1983:269 [yellow-with-green]; Sturtevant 1936:22, 44, 102–03, 127, 130, 150–51:139 [complete system of color terms]) and Akkadian of Mesopotamia (Friedrich 1946:86, 100, 109, 111; Allen 1879:213 quoted in MacLaury 1991*b*:38 [yellow-with-green vs. cool]). Landsberger (1967:140) finds that Sumerian, too, named the yellow-with-green category. Hittite used *andara* and *mitas* with an apparent brightness contrast that cautious scholars translate as 'red' and 'blue' while attaching question marks, as when the terms refer in ritual texts to contrasting wools that in their natural condition would be light and dark (Sturtevant and Bechtel 1935:100, 106–07; Sturtevant 1936:22, 103). Landsberger (1967:155–73) reviews this enigmatic naming of wools with putative hue terms, including a conjecture of purple-dyeing. The probability that such very ancient languages emphasized brightness (in spite of their role in high civilization) weakens their force as counterexamples to the hypothesis that societal complexity predicts transference in the cool category when its hues are featured more than brightness or more than are the relations between the hues.

On a later horizon of the Near East, Gradwohl (1963) finds that color-term referents in the Old Testament imply a yellow-with-green category, hence suggesting this practice endured throughout a diffusion area. Brenner (1982:102–105), in a second study of the same texts, submits that "the cognates supply a wide range: from 'pale', 'silvery', to 'yellow', 'gold', and 'green'" (cf. Delitzsch 1878, 1896; Jannsens 1957).

12. Table 11.1 lists Class IV, the naming of green apart from a category of black-with-blue (fig. 2.23*a*). Bornstein (1973*a*: table 1) lists 26 languages reputed to be of this type out of his sample of 128 from the literature. He describes 9 as having both a cool category and a category of black-with-blue, 9 which name green by itself apart from black-with-blue, 5 that name green-with-yellow with one term and black-with-blue with another, and 2 without a record of how green is named. The MCS includes various

languages, such as Tenejapa Tzeltal, Guarijío, and Chuj that intermix a black-focused dark-cool term and a green-focused cool term throughout blue colors, as in figures 3.8, 4.4–6, and 7.21a. Some systems that Bornstein lists are probably of this type; for example, he includes Tzeltal on the basis of Berlin and Kay's (1969:32) account. Three of the 9 that contrast green versus black-with-blue are from Rivers's measurements with Lovibond's Tintometer. The WCS found none of the latter variant, even though Iduna, Ifugao, and Chumburu might lend the impression of green versus black-with-blue if individuals had not named Munsell chips (fig. 2.23). In table 11.1, Iduna can be reclassified as III3B, "Late transference toward green is in progress" and Ifugao and Chumburu fit class III4, "The cool category skewed toward green without an exception." Probably the reports of "green" versus "black-with-blue" neglect that the green-focused term may apply to blue; or, in some languages, the restricted "green" term may be secondary and only developing into a term for a cool category that is itself incipient. No system reported as yellow-with-green versus black-with-blue has been investigated with Munsell chips or other decodable stimuli. The descriptions of current Waskashan languages show they name blue and black with separate basic terms.

12. COLOR AND CATEGORIZATION

1. Sundry observations remain to be tied in. Individuals add steps to a mapping because they view category membership as graded, with better members closest to a vantage point (15). For the same reason, the form of a term that names the entire category—if the term is qualified in different ways—also names more color chips in the vicinity of the vantage point (16). Elemental blue can be named by green-focused and black-focused categories that earlier were related by inclusion (18). The green-focused category gains salience while the black-focused category retracts toward its focus, abandoning green before blue. Elemental blue will be a weaker member of the latter category than of the former. Secondary categories abound in advanced systems (28), which are produced by strong differentiation (Casson 1994; MacLaury MS-1).

There are yet other complications among cool colors. Northern Huastec names different vantages with one root and its qualifications (56, 91). A few languages construct and separately name coextensive vantages of the cool category on the axis of light-to-dark (92), manifesting unusual lexical patterns with a light-dark split or a recessive naming range that skirts the darkest cool colors and, in some cases, polarizes in black (93). In some languages, such as Tecpan Cakchiquel, the number of null responses increases as transference toward green progresses (79) and as dual foci emerge and then disappear; these three processes may accompany enhanced attention to distinctiveness, but only when people throughout a community, for whatever reason, share a detached view of their own categorization.

2. Kinkade (1988) rejects my flip-flop hypothesis (MacLaury 1986b, 1987a, 1991c; cf. fig. 2.33 herein) in his reconstruction of Proto-Salishan color categories, specifically in reference to his reconstruction of a yellow-green-blue category, which is the better bet because (1) Sechelt Salish shows moribund remnants of a yellow-green-

blue range (MacLaury 1991*b*) and (2) this category is far more common in contemporary languages worldwide than is the green-with-yellow to green-with-blue flip-flop.
The latter is attested only by 3 among 25 Martu Wangka interviews and 2 among 10 of
Wesley Dale's Lani results. I recorded yellow-with-green to yellow-with-red flip-flop
between the naming and mapping of a Shuswap Salish-speaker (MacLaury 1986*b:* fig.
1*c–e,* 1987*a:* fig. 3 [naming only]), who performed the red-with-yellow mapping on the
obverse array one day and on the reverse array another day, which inspired me to consider the possibility that some Salishan languages flip-flopped yellow-with-green to
green-with-blue.

GLOSSARY

Terms are defined in the normal glossarial function of assisting the reader. They are interdisciplinary (unmarked) or from color ethnography (CE), anthropology (A), linguistics (L), philosophy (Ph), cognitive linguistics (CogL), philosophy of language (PhL), psychology (Psy), vision research (VR), or vantage theory (VT). Definitions regarding the latter provide a systematic statement of constructs critical to the present version of vantage theory. M. MacLaury's (1989) and Preston's (1993) contributions to vantage theory are credited to them.

abstract (adj): analyzed and reintegrated to comprise essentials only. See *concrete, objective,* and *decontextualized.*

activate (v): to concentrate on a level (VT); *activation* (n). See Preston (1993:219); *level of concentration.*

afterthought (n): information that a consultant adds to a reply during an interview after first responding in briefer fashion, such as "green . . . ," but then "dark green."

agent (n): the person or thing that generates the impetus of a dynamic, such as an observer who constructs a category from a point of view; *agency* (n). See *dynamic* and *observer.*

aggregate (n): responses from more than one individual; such responses displayed in relation to each other.

alternative foci (n, pl): foci placed on different color chips in response to separate requests, often during different interviews (CE). See *dual foci* and *ambivalent focus.*

alternative (response) (n): a reply that a consultant volunteers during an interview as an option to another reply, such as "I can call it blue or I can call it green."

ambivalent focus (n): a choice of a best example on disjunctive color chips on one side of a composite category without a decisive final commitment to one or both, unlike *dual foci* (CE).

analogy (n): an equation between the dynamic relations of a *source domain* and those of a *target domain,* as speakers of Zapotec describe category relations by saying that "red dominates pink" or "pink depends on red" by analogy to relations between geopolities (PhL, CogL, L); analogize (v), analogous (adj). See *metaphor.*

apparent complementation (n): see *polarized inclusion* (2).

arrangement (n): an order of preference for concentrating on specific coordinate pairs of a category (VT). See *level of concentration*.

array (n): the 330 Munsell chips of anthropological interviewing arranged by their positions in the spectrum; part of the stimulus set used in data collection; a graphic display in the format of the array; a *grid* (CE).

ascent (n): the movement of a coordinate as it is promoted (VR). *ascend* (v); see *promote* and *introduce*.

asymmetry (n) *or asymmetry judgment* (n): a subject's assessment that central and marginal members of a category are more related when comparing the latter to the former and less related when comparing the former to the latter (Psy). Vantage theory attributes this difference to the dominant and recessive views that produce like asymmetries between coextensive ranges. See *dominant-recessive pattern of coextension*.

attend to (v tr): to emphasize (Psy); to place emphasis on a coordinate (VT); *attention* (n) is emphasis, formerly called "attendance" (MacLaury 1991*a*). The latter is seemingly not widely used in psychology. In vantage theory, *attend to* contrasts with *concentrate on* (v) and *focus* (v).

attribute (n): a feature of an entity or concept that qualifies it as having a degree of *membership* in a *category* (Psy, Rosch). See *feature*.

axiom (n): a maxim or postulate that underpins a theory and that is not necessarily demonstrated. For example, vantage theory postulates six elemental colors and the dynamic balance of strength between attention to similarity and difference; fuzzy-set theory postulates that categorization consists of four operations plus an observer-independent fit between the operations and the world.

axis (n): a continuum of senses or possible points from which one point is selected as a coordinate; for example, the continuum between standing still and the speed of light with relative judgments of slow and fast as intermediate to the poles, or the continuum between unity and disparity with relative judgments of similarity and difference as intermediate (VT). See *mobile coordinate* and *continuum*.

balanced coextension (n): a coextensive relation that does not show the dominant-recessive pattern (VT).

basic color term (n): (1) the name of a color category that, to an individual, is of the simplest form among color terms, easily coming to mind, of broadest range, and applicable to anything; to a society, it is all of this plus widely shared; the name of a basic color category (CE, Berlin and Kay); (2) the name of a dominant vantage, minimally $X S^2$-D, when X is a point of hue, brightness, or saturation (VT). See *dominant vantage*.

basic level of categorization, the (n): the categories a person prefers to use under usual conditions that demand neither maximum generalization nor exacting specificity, for example, English speakers would ordinarily prefer to say "red" rather than "warm tone" or "vermilion." Rosch defined the basic level as the most inclusive on which it is possible to envision a prototype, say, "lizard" rather than "reptile."

Both in Rosch's thinking and in vantage theory, the basic level varies between individuals and languages. In vantage theory, it varies in accord with the balance of emphasis that an individual places on attention to similarity and distinctiveness (A, Psy, CogL, VT).

Berlin-and-Kay hypothesis (n): Basic color terms are universally focused on the same colors but may number from two to eleven in a language; their meanings are predictable from their number, which implies they evolve in a constrained order in any language. As normal people see color in only one way, all will name what they see accordingly as an augmentation of societal complexity invokes the functional need (CE).

binary color category (n): a color category composed of a blend of at least two elemental colors while excluding the purest perception of both (VR). "Binary" may mislead: some blends, such as purple, may include contributions of more than two elemental colors. *Blended color category* may be used as a stylistic synonym (CE). See *derived color category.*

bottom (n): See *up.*

breadth (n): coordinates plus their entailments. See Preston (1993:217); see *depth.*

brightness (n): (1) To anthropologists and linguists, brightness is the intensity of light in relation to a stable surround, which may itself be of any fixed intensity. Vision researchers prefer "lightness," the quantity of light in relation to a similarly illuminated area perceived as white; lightness may vary from light to dark. True lightness is *luminant,* emanating directly from an object. The Munsell array substitutes reflective brightness or value, the admixture of white or black. These colors, respectively, reflect all wavelengths and reflect none. In ethnographic data, brightness is seldom named per se but is usually a coordinate fixed at a particular intensity by an individual: it may vary from light to dark between individuals, and it may contribute to a category in combination with coordinates of hue, saturation, and various surface effects, such as shininess, and with noncolor coordinates such as dryness, ill-omened, or virtually anything (cf. Cotton 1950). As a brightness coordinate may occupy a high or a low *level of concentration,* it will contribute to a color category strongly or weakly. No psychological tests have been performed with users of "brightness categories," strong or weak, to determine what they actually categorize. The "brightness coordinate" is postulated on the basis of the apparent preference of speakers to apply a term to particular levels of the Munsell array without any regard or without complete regard to hue or desaturation. Thus, its definition is eliminative, based on an assumption that exclusively hue, saturation, and brightness are the cardinal directions of color sensation. In the making of exotic color categories, the role of saturation per se as opposed to that of hue is unexplored. Hunt (1977) defines "colorfulness" as the capacity of some chromatic colors to stand out against others relative to the average brightness of all, and he claims that this quality is as important to color perception as saturation and chroma. Although Hunt himself does not address

ethnographic findings, speakers of certain languages may pick out this compound
property when they name yellow, green, and blue with one term; (2) Scholars of
Old English grapple with the problem of "brightness" by adopting descriptive
terms such as "pale" and "tone" (Biggam 1993). In color ethnography, brightness
is a general rubric meaning "not hue or desaturation." This is fine for the purposes of vantage theory, which addresses the problem specifically by combining
brightness with other coordinates. But Old English specialists regard "brightness" as an uncritical cover term when it is not qualified by analysis. See *color,
color category, color term, surface effects, shiny, connotative coordinate.*

brilliance (n): lightness in high contrast, as with reflection from the moon (VR); a
combination of high saturation with translucence, luminance, or certain *surface
effects,* such as iridescence or shininess (CE); some languages qualify brilliance
in contrast to brightness, as does Panoan Cashinahua (d'Ans and Cortez Mondragón 1973); *brilliant* (adj).

cancel (v): (1) to spontaneously void a datum that one has volunteered in the capacity
of an informant, usually seconds after having offered it; (2) *Cancellations* are an
invaluable genre of data (CE).

canceled focus (n): a focus that an individual spontaneously nullifies prior to making
another choice (CE). See *single focus.*

category (n): (1) in classical logic, a group of entities that fit a set because they share
at least one common property; the identity of such a set or the union or intersection of such sets; (2) In fuzzy-set logic, a group of entities that are of one set
because they share a property, each to some degree; the identity, union, or intersection of such a set or sets; (3) In prototype theory, a group of entities that bear
family resemblances to a prototype; (4) In vantage theory, a selection of fixed
and mobile coordinates, counterbalancing emphases upon them, their arrangements, and the frame that these relations create for the viewer. There must be at
least three coordinates, two of which always consist of attention to similarity and
attention to distinctiveness. These reciprocal attentions distinguish a category
from other cognition, including other kinds of viewpoint. The emphases, arrange-
ment(s), and frame define the category as an extension of the viewer and define
the viewer as an inextricable part of the category. In theories 1, 2, and 3, any
term that names a range names a category, that is, each range is a category. In
vantage theory (4), the ensemble of coordinates, emphases, arrangement(s), and
frame(s) constitute the category, while a term names one of these facets, such as
an arrangement, a hue or the hues (the inherently fixed coordinates), the relations
between coordinates (the inherently mobile coordinates), or the frame. While 1,
2, and 3 consider included ranges to be *secondary categories,* vantage theory (4)
calls them *arrangements* or *vantages.* See *arrangement, vantage, coordinate,
fixed coordinate, mobile coordinate, inherently fixed coordinate, inherently
mobile coordinate, selective emphasis, frame,* and *secondary category.*

category dynamics: See *dynamics.*

central (adj): in reference to the middle of a category or, in a composite hue category, between unique hues; the degree to which a response is executed in reference to a middle point (CE). See *polar.*

centralize (v): to place a response closer to the center of a category or more equally distanced between unique hues in comparison to another response (CE); *centralized* (adj). See *polarized.*

centroid (n): an average of responses from more than one subject to a fixed set of stimuli that are evenly spaced (such that the number of responses is divided by the number of stimuli that invoked them); this average may approximate the center of the evenly spaced set of color chips named with a certain term by subjects during an experiment; the average near the center of an aggregated semantic range within an evenly spaced grid or solid, such as the OSA System (Boynton, MacLaury, and Uchikawa 1989:7) (VR). Centroids cannot be calculated from responses to chips from the Munsell solid because its spacing varies by row and saturation level.

chain relation or *chain-linked relation* (n): a relation between a dominant vantage, a recessive vantage, and an ultra-recessive vantage in which the first and last links are not directly connected; each direct relation constitutes a frame, which enables the balance of attention between similarity and distinctiveness to be assessed independently between any two vantages that are linked (VT); *chain-link* (v) and *chain-linking* (n). See *frame* and *ultra-recessive.*

chip (n): a color chip; cast-coated paper replicably pigmented in accord with a patented formula (CE).

classical category: See *category* (1).

classical logic: See *logic* (1).

classical theory of categorization: See *category* (1).

closely related (adj): of two categories that share a coordinate but are not related by full inversion of an arrangement. For example, "orange (the fruit)" and "orange (the color)" are closely related by sharing a coordinate of yellow-red color sense; this relation pertains regardless of whether the latter category may have derived long ago from the former by partial inversion, as "amber (the fossil resin)" and "amber (the yellow-brown color)" currently appear to be closely related. The latter relation is *polysemous* (VT). See *polysemy; invert* (1, 2).

coextension (n): (1) the state of being *coextensive;* (2) a coextensive *relation.*

coextensive (adj): (1) overlapping substantially; said of words that share almost their entire gamut of *extensions* but whose *best examples* differ widely; (2) In a composite color category, of two ranges that are focused on or in reference to opposite unique hues while each range covers both hues; or, by the loosest standard, of two ranges that cover each other's focus; (3) said of inversions of one set of *coordinates* when the set includes emphases on similarity and difference that are almost of equal strength; said of *vantages* that are named *coextensively* (VT). See *vantage.*

coextensive semantic range (n): The extensions of a term that names a coextensive vantage. See *coextensive, semantic,* and *range.*

cognate (n): one of two or more words in different but related languages that *reflect* an ancestral form. For example, *yaš, yoš, ya?aš, raš,* and *ča?ṣ* presently name the cool category in the respective Mayan languages of Tzeltal, Tzotzil, Chuj, Quiché, and Aguacatec; the forms reflect hypothetical Proto-Mayan **ra?š* (Kaufman 1983 letter; England 1992:153), whose meaning may have been different from any found today (L); *cognate* (adj). See *form, reflex, protoform,* and *etymology.*

cognition (n): (1) the mental editing of sensation after its receipt in the cortex; selective suppression, recognition, or emphasis on what is sensed; *cognitive* (adj) (VT); (2) an integrating process, such as *analogy, metaphor, metonymy,* and *categorization* (L, PhL, VT). See *sensation, perception, continuum, axis, suppression, recognition, selection.*

color (n): (1) any sense of hue, saturation, or brightness, or a combination, etic or emic (cf. Burtleson 1972; Jones et al. 1943) (VR); (2) in categorization and only emically, any or all of the three plus surface effects, such as shininess, or connotations having nothing to do with light or the color solid; but at least one of the three dimensions of color must predominate within a category to define it as mainly of color rather than as mainly of something else (CE). See *etic* and *emic.*

color category (n): (1) a category whose inherently fixed coordinates are of color such that one of them occupies the preferred level of concentration in a vantage. As it is impossible for two inherently fixed coordinates to occupy this position, a vantage is either mainly of color or mainly not of color, which endows the color domain with a clear margin. For example, Hanunóo *latuy* will name a color category if elemental green occupies its preferred level of concentration, keeping its coordinate of succulence in lesser prominence on a level of secondary meaning or connotation; (2) A category emphasizing *surface effects* over *color.* Speakers of a few languages, such as Australian Anbarra, may favor shininess and dullness over other sensations, although they include hue or brightness in the same categories; they categorize Munsell chips only in this way (§2.6). (Vels Heijn [1951: 80–81, 119–120, 125] submits that Latin *candidus* referred to the shininess of white "with a distinct double character." Indo-Europeanists reconstruct glosses of "to shine" for the protoforms of contemporary hue-term cognates.) In vantage theory, surface effects differ from *contextualized coordinates,* because the former inhere in the behavior of wavelength while the latter are extraneous to wavelength. People who attend strongly to distinctiveness separate surface effects from sensations of hue, saturation, and brightness, and they name the surface effects separately; but people who attend strongly to similarity may combine surface effects and color sensations as coordinates of one set, even featuring a surface effect as the preferred fixed coordinate. Any category that so features a surface effect is a *color category,* because the surface effects are wavelength-dependent, not derived from extraneous sensation. Thus, the name of a *surface-effect category* may be applied generally and abstractly to all wavelengths reflected in the special manner, not to wavelengths reflected only by objects that fit classes unrelated to wavelength, as "claret" pertains only to wine, as the widely reported African terminologies apply only to cattle, or as Old English *wann* named only the color of gloomy states. While both *surface effects* and *contextualized coordinates* tend to accompany the color categories of people who emphasize similarity, only surface effects may supersede color coordinates (on levels of concentration) without disqualifying a category from the color domain. In the one or two languages in which surface-effect categories are known to be the only color categories, the surface effects are ubiquitous, such as shininess, rather than rare, such as metallic, frosty, or Day-Glo®, although the categories might lump some rare effects with the common ones (VT). Lyons (1995:196–201) further distinguishes the psychophysical definition of color from the emic definition of color categories. See *color domain, color term, surface effect, contextualized coordinate, emic, etic.*

color domain (n): the totality of color categories in a language. Color categories may be ranked as to the degree that each pertains to color, although only those pertaining mainly to color are of this domain; its boundaries are not fuzzy (VT). See *color category, color, surface effects,* and *connotative coordinates.*

color term (n): a name designating all or part of a color category (VT). For parts, see *vantage, arrangement, crossover formula, hue-stressing formula,* and *frame.*

column (n): a vertical segment of the ethnographic Munsell array one chip in width and including all chips from lightest to darkest of either zero saturation or of one hue at maximum saturation; chips identified by a number on the array (CE). See *row.*

complementation (n): (1) a relation between autonomous categories (PhL); (2) a relation between two categories within one domain that share no coordinates other than those universally essential to categorization (S versus D), that is, sharing no inherently fixed coordinates (VT); (3) a nonrelation of categories in separate and unlinked frames that share no coordinates (VT). See *frame, link, domain, near synonymy, coextension, inclusion,* and *closely related.*

composite color category (n): In fuzzy-set theory, the result of a fuzzy union operating on two unique hues, producing a category such as "green-or-blue"; or the result of a fuzzy union operating on two hues plus white or black. As "composite" itself carries no metaphysical baggage, it is readily accommodated to any theory. In vantage theory, as elsewhere, a composite color category includes three or two elemental colors, such as light-warm, dark-cool, warm, cool, or yellow-with-green (CE). See *derived-* and *binary color category, primary-,* and *elemental color category.*

concentrate (v): to hold in mind a particular level of an arrangement or zooming hierarchy while relegating other levels to the realm of presuppositions; *concentration* (n). In vantage theory, *concentrate* and *concentration* pertain exclusively to the levels of an arrangement, as opposed to "attend to a coordinate" or "focus a category" (VT). See *attend* and *focus* (v).

concrete (adj): whole and unanalyzed; regarded in physical entirety without opposing essentials to nonessentials. See *abstract.*

connotation (n): a quality accompanying a main meaning, as green *connotes* vigor or newness; *connotative* (adj).

connotative coordinate (n): a coordinate extrinsic to color that occupies the *bottom* level of an *arrangement* or *zooming hierarchy* of a *color category;* an ancillary meaning of a *color term* that is of insufficient prominence to *contextualize* the term (VT). See *contextualize, contextualized coordinate, arrangement,* and *zooming hierarchy.*

contextualize (v): to link intention with a concrete but open class, for example, yellow but specifically of corn (A, CE); regarding a color term, to introduce an open class as a noncolor coordinate on the second level of concentration within an arrangement; the open-class coordinate must not have any relation to a specific color, as amber does to yellow-brown or succulence does to green (VT). See *decontextualize, subjective* and *objective, concrete,* and *abstract,* and *closely related.*

contextualized (adj): to be integrated with surrounds or with a usual co-occurrence, as are terms of color-pattern in cattle in many African languages (A, CE).

contextualized coordinate (n): a coordinate from a domain other than that of the category that incorporates the coordinate, for example, a point of reference, such as newness or horsehair, combined in an *arrangement* with coordinates of color to constitute a *category.* On a lower *level of concentration,* a contextualized coordinate may be an abstract quality that gives a color category a *connotation,* as "green" is associated with newness; or, if the contextualized coordinate is an open class and extrinsic to color, it links the category to that class, as "ruddy" is confined to complexion or "roan" to horsehair. On *the preferred level of concentration,* a contextualized coordinate cannot occur, because preferred coordinates define the domain, as "claret" means mainly a type of wine, albeit of a specific color only (VT); herein wine is contextualized to color, not color to wine. See *contextualized, connotative coordinate, color category* (2), and *category.*

continuous (adj): of a mapping step that covers two elemental colors, as in "continuous mapping" (CE). See *disjunctive.*

continuum (n): (1) a scale between poles; a trajectory of change from one extreme to another that generates types of *forms* or *relations* in chronological series, as from *near synonymy* through *coextension* to *inclusion;* a scalar typology of pristine forms or relations and intermediate variants; (2) see *axis* (VT).

contrasting (adj): having a relation (as opposed to a nonrelation) in which distinctiveness is a point of interest, regardless of how strongly similarity is ordinarily emphasized (VT). Synonym: *contrastive* (Psy). See *relation* (3–5).

co-occur (v): to occur at the same time and place; to occur simultaneously in a single system (VT).

coordinate (n): one point of reference among at least two that serves as either a figure or a ground; one among a set of reference points with which a person constructs a vantage. A coordinate may conglomerate smaller units, for example, as up-down, front-back, and right-left comprise a fixed-reference body in Einstein's scheme, as articulatory features compose a phoneme, or as selected degrees of lightness and saturation constitute a particular brightness (VT).

coordinate (v): to establish a position in reference to points or to points and movement or, more specifically, to establish a position in reference to an awareness of them;

they may be landmarks and degrees of motion or they may be images, concepts, or emphases that constitute metaphors and metonyms of points and movement or awareness of them (VT).

correlational structure (n): graded membership of a prototype-based category that matches the similarities and discontinuities of an observer-independent environment, an intrinsic contradiction (Psy). See *observer* and *prototype*.

covert vantages (n, pl): two or more established vantages of a category that are not named separately (VT).

crossover (n): random fluctuation in the maximal membership of a cool category between green and blue; application of its name, focus, and mapping to one or the other hue without more than chance agreement between performances (VT). See *crossover category* and *crossover formula*.

crossover category (n): a hue category that people construct by ascribing more importance to the relation between hues than to the hues as individuated percepts; a cool category whose name randomly switches foci and direction of skewing so as to reduce the likelihood of *transference* (VT). In a *coextensively named crossover category*, both vantages so fluctuate, but without losing their dominant-recessive relation. See *hue-stressing category* and *transference*.

crossover formula (n): $S^2\text{-}D + H$, which expresses the emphasis defining a *crossover category*; order of symbols represents the observer's priority of valuing relations or inherently mobile coordinates over hues or inherently fixed coordinates; in spite of this priority, both emphases are represented (VT); synonym: relation stressing formula. See *transference formula* or *hue-stressing formula*.

dark (adj): closer to black than to middle lightness or closer to black than a third point; the degree to which luminance is absent; Munsell values 0.5/ through 5/ for reflective samples (Appendix III).

darkening (n): shifting toward black the most important or representative members of a hue category (CE); bolstering attention to similarity with a coordinate of darkness as the former weakens, usually during final division of the cool category (VT, CE); the means to counter the nullifying effect on a category of strong attention to distinctiveness and, therefore, an entailment of this attention rather than a coordinate (MacLaury, Almási, and Kövecses, in press) (VT). See *nullify*.

decontextualize (v): to separate intention from particular classes extraneous to an essential class (A, L, CE); to demote a noncolor coordinate within an arrangement (VT). See *contextualize*.

decontextualized (adj): applicable or conceivable independently of particular surrounds, expectation or classes apart from an essential one (A, CE).

default (n) a situation in which there is pressure neither to differentiate exceedingly nor to abstract or generalize beyond the normal call; therein, people take the route of least expenditure, resting on the *preferred level of concentration* within a *vantage* or on the *basic level of categorization* within a *taxonomy* or a *chain-relation* (Psy, CogL, VT).

degree of skewing (n): the difference in values of membership between the side toward which the cool category is skewed and the side away from which it is skewed (CE). See *direction of skewing.*

deixis (n): a word or affix whose meaning includes the speaker's point of view, such as demonstratives (e.g., this, that), pronouns, verb tenses, directional verbs (e.g., come, go), some terms of space or time (e.g., here, now), some honorifics, and others; deictic (adj) (L).

demote (v): to move an inherently fixed coordinate "downward" through an arrangement and, thus, to decrease its emphasis within a category (VT). See *decontextualize.*

depth (n): a zooming hierarchy. See Preston (1993:217). In earlier versions of vantage theory, mobile coordinates were recruited from the entailments of higher levels of concentration. Nothing presently precludes this, as Preston demonstrates. In the current version, mobile coordinates need not be derived from entailments, which makes the theory more flexible. See also *breadth.*

derive (v): to take material from a source to establish a new entity; *derivation* (n). For example, a recessive vantage derives from a dominant vantage by inversion of coordinates; a category derives from a recessive vantage by reconfiguring some of its coordinates into an autonomous system while eliminating others (VT). This usage coexists with but differs from *derived color category.* See *basic color category* (2).

derived color category (n): a fuzzy-set intersection derived from two unique hues or one unique hue and a white or black extreme of value, mainly, brown, purple, pink, orange, and grey (CE); the intersection precludes unique hues, white, or black at their irreducible maxima. A *derived color term* names such a category. A *derived basic color category* is formed by doubling the values of membership within the intersection, but without the sanction of Zadeh's fuzzy-set formalism (Kay and McDaniel 1978) (CE). See *composite-, primary-,* and *binary color category.* See *member* and *logic* (2).

desaturated (adj): on or below Munsell saturation level /6; the closer to /0, the more desaturated (VR, CE).

desaturation category (n): a category that includes color of no greater chroma than Munsell /6 but which has substantial membership above /0. It typically appears discontinuously on the anthropological array throughout grey, brown, lavender, and beige with its focus in any of these colors, varying among speakers of a community; it usually includes a brightness coordinate, which different individuals will anchor at distinct values, adding light-to-dark variability; it may evolve to include pale blue and then to become the category blue hue; it may become a category of grey or brown, or it may disappear. It may undergo more than one process at the same time (VT).

descent (n): the movement of a coordinate as it is demoted (VT); *descend* (v). See *ascend* and *demote.*

describe (v): to record data and to discern their patterns prior to relating them to theory; description (n) and descriptive (adj). See *theory* and *extension.*

detachment (n): the state of maintaining an overview of alternative viewpoints that one has constructed, both of the standpoint currently occupied and of other vantages outside it. Detached perspectives may reside within the worldview of a particular language and its community or they may situate in the foreign community of a bilingual. Strong attention to distinctiveness is a precondition of detachment but not its instigation. See *submersion, similarity, distinctiveness, worldview,* and *precondition* (VT).

deuteranope (n): one who lacks the medium-wave photopigment and thereby has a variety of red/green blindness (VR); deuteranopic (adj). See *dichromat.*

dichromat (n): one who lacks a photopigment and, hence, the ability to discriminate certain hues (VR). See *trichromat, monochromat, protanope, deuteranope,* and *tritanope.*

difference: see *distinctiveness.*

diffusion area (n): a region in which cultural, mental, and linguistic traits spread between otherwise diverse societies to an extent that characterizes it beside other areas.

direction of skewing (n): a bias in values of membership in the cool category that favors either green or blue or, rarely, darkness; an equivalent bias in any category (Burgess, Kempton, and MacLaury 1983) (CE, VT). See *values of membership.*

disjunctive (adj): of a mapping that covers two elemental colors with separate steps or with a single step that is executed on two separate groups of color chips (CE). See *continuous.*

distinctiveness (n): an assessment of affinity based on qualities unique to each half of the comparison; a stress on disparity rather than unity, on discordant attributes rather than relations (Psy, VT). Synonym: *difference.* See *similarity.*

division (n): splitting a whole into segments; splitting one category into two; an effect deriving from the essential role of attention to distinctiveness in categorization; a process ongoing throughout the career of a category from its inception to its complete fission (CE, VT). See *final division.*

domain (n): two or more categories that feature a common genre of coordinates, such as coordinates of color (VT). See *color domain* and *feature* (v).

dominant: See *dominant vantage.*

dominant formula: See *dominant vantage.*

dominant range (n): the larger and more centrally focused of two ranges that share most of their extensions (VT).

dominant-recessive pattern (n): a configuration among the semantic ranges of two names for a single category in which one range is larger and more centrally focused than the other; its status as a pattern is derived statistically from a sample of categories named by two terms. The pattern may prevail only in coextensive relations. In relations of inclusion, the configuration is defined loosely (without a statistical test) as one in which the recessive range is smaller and more polarized in mapping and naming; relations of near synonymy have not been observed in sufficient number to determine whether they show a pattern (VT). See *relation.*

dominant-recessive pattern of coextension (n): a regularity among coextensive ranges in which one, the dominant range, is larger and more centrally focused than the other, the recessive range; the pattern is usually repeated by mappings wherein that of the dominant range will be broader and rendered in steps of larger average size; *qualifiers* will show the pattern in that the name of the dominant range will be qualified by more augmentatives and fewer diminutives than the name of the recessive range, or certain qualifiers will pertain exclusively to the latter while the former is qualified by an equivalent class applied to both. The dominant-recessive pattern of coextension is statistically significant among the categories that manifest it throughout the MCS and WCS and, therefore, it constitutes the instigating source of evidence for vantage theory (VT). See *dominant, recessive, pattern,* and *balanced coextension.*

dominant vantage (n): an arrangement of coordinates with attention to similarity on the preferred level of concentration and attention to distinctiveness at the *bottom* level; a vantage constructed by the dominant formula S^2-D; a primary arrangement that is not derivative of another and that is essential to any category; in the second frame of a chain relation, the vantage that was recessive in the first frame (VT). See *recessive vantage, frame, first frame, second frame, chain relation, preferred level of concentration, zooming hierarchy, arrangement.*

down: See *up.*

dual foci (n, pl): a selection of two *disjunctive foci* for a category in response to one request, or such a response on opposite hues of a composite category (CE); one focus on each of two *covert vantages* (VT). See *single focus, triple foci,* and *ambivalent focus.*

dynamics or *category dynamics* (n): the relation between a observer and a category; the selections, emphases, and arrangements that an observer projects into a category as he creates it, modifies it, or dissolves it; what the observer projects into a category in response to sociophysical pressures (VT). See *observer* and *motivation.*

elemental color (n): either an elemental hue or the lightest and the darkest extremes of neutral value, that is, pure white and black. There are six elemental colors that speakers of some English dialects call "snow white," "jet black," "fire-engine red," "chrome yellow," "kelly green," and "true blue." The focus aggregate of all MCS and WCS interviews show pronounced pluralities at AØ, JØ, G1, C9, F17, and F29 (CE). See *elemental hue* and *unique hue.*

elemental hue (n): a point within a unique hue that the viewer experiences as being more intense than others (VR). There is no explanation of why this point stands out to people universally. See *unique hue* and *elemental color.*

eliminate (v): to demote a coordinate to such an extent that it is no longer recognized; to push it out of a category from the *bottom* level of concentration into zero emphasis (VT). See *introduce, demote, recognize,* and *level of concentration.*

emic (adj): meaningful to a native by virtue of having a place in a linguistic or cultural system, as a unit of sound may distinguish words when it is part of a phon*emic* system; considered as a systemic whole and on its own terms (A); a construct of a model that is meaningful to a native (A, L, VT), as the coordinates of a vantage have been portrayed (VT); psychologically real (A), nonobjectivist (Ph), experiential (VR); examples may be terminological, such as emic "vantage" versus etic "range" (see note 20 of §6.3.5), propositional, such as "similarity is emphasized sufficiently among coextensive vantages that they pertain to major stimuli in common, such as opposite unique hues," or formulaic, such as "coextension involves nearly equal emphases on S and D" or "a basic color term names a categorical vantage that is minimally composed as X S^2-D"; emically (adv). See *etic*.

emphasize (v, tr): to focus attention on something; *emphasis* (n). In vantage theory, *emphasize* is the generic term covering *attend, concentrate,* and *stress,* which, contrary to ordinary usage, are restricted in meaning so as never to overlap.

entailment (n): a consequence or necessary accompaniment, for example, strong emphasis on similarity *entails* a broad category. In vantage theory, *entailment* refers only to the consequences of particular choices, emphases, and arrangements of the coordinates that constitute a vantage. See *presupposition* and *systemic corollary*.

epistemology: See *logic*.

etic (adj): of an analytical unit extrinsic to or isolated from a meaningful system, as is a phon*etic* unit outside the phonology of a language (L); of a crosscultural comparison singling out a specific practice (A); an analyst's construct that has no meaning in any capacity to a native user of the system under analysis (A), as logical operations, the fuzzy-set decimal, adaptive function, or "the correlational structure of the environment" fail to have meaning for the user of a category (VT); objectivist (Ph), operational (CE), or heuristic (A, L); examples may be terminological, such as etic "range" versus emic "vantage," propositional, such as "the two Tzeltal words for warm colors have different ranges," or propositional and prescriptive, such as "ranges must overlap by at least 75% to be called coextensive" or "a basic color term is monolexemic, nonhyponymous, salient, and noncontext-specific"; *etically* (adv). See *emic*.

etymology (n): (1) a history of a word and an account of its origin; (2) the science of demonstrating word origins (L) (e.g., Arias Abellán 1994; Hamp 1984; Lehmann 1964; Malkiel 1953, 1956; Machek 1951, 1957; Miklosich 1886; Rečeva 1984; Vasmer 1955; Walde and Hofmann 1938). See *cognate* and *protoform*.

evidence (n): patterned observations that bear upon a hypothesis so as to sustain or contravene its predictions. See *prediction*.

evolution (n): (1) in biology, the change of a gene pool; the way a species adapts to selective pressure; (2) in categorization, a shift in selective emphasis shared by members of a population in response to change in the environment, usually or even always in response to increased novelty. The shift may raise analytical acuity, which, in turn, alters the size, shape, and number of categories—color categories among them—enabling people to communicate effectively with each other about their current view of their surrounds. The adaptation helps them to survive as a society (VT).

evolutionary sequence: See *universal evolutionary sequence of color naming*.

extended focus (n): a single focus that covers three or more adjacent color chips (CE). See *single focus*.

extended theory (n): general theory. See Preston (1993:216). See *theory*.

extension(s) (n): All possible referents of a word. "The Sun" from the common view has one extension. "Red" has as many extensions as there are *just noticeable differences* among red and reddish perceptions (L). See *range*.

family resemblances (n): similarities based on shared qualities; the qualities that bind entities or concepts into a category. Wittgenstein cited "game" as family resemblances that link activities as diverse as Russian roulette and hopscotch. Rosch recast this idea as *family resemblances to a prototype* so as to allow different *members* to belong to a *category* by sharing *attributes* with a *prototype* while not necessarily sharing any with each other (Ph, Psy, L).

feature (n): a component of a meaning, as [adult] [male] [human] are features of "man"; the core concept of *semantic feature theory* (L); a *marker*. See *markerese*.

feature (v): to pick out from alternatives and treat as prominent; for example, categories that *feature* hue, saturation, or brightness are thereby of the color domain.

figure-to-ground relation (n): A relation projected by a viewer from a position by which an object in attention is plotted in relation to, or contrasted against, another entity, especially one that is larger, more stable, or farther away from the viewer (Psy; see epigraph).

final division (n): the completed separation of parts of one category to produce different categories; establishing autonomous sets of coordinates from a set that previously included two arrangements (VT). See *division*.

fixed coordinate (n): a point of reference that is treated as a ground, regardless of what it is inherently (VT). See *inherently fixed coordinate*.

focal color (n): a tautology that confuses an individual's choice of a focus with a perceptually salient color, such as an elemental hue (CE); MCS and WCS foci disappoint this expectation. See *focus* and *elemental color*.

focus (n): one individual's choice of the best example(s) of a term or a category (VT); *foci* (pl).

focus (v): to choose the best example(s) of a term or category (CE). *Focus* contrasts with *attend to* and *concentrate*.

focus aggregate (n): the foci selected by two or more individuals for a category or term; a diagram of these (as dots or numbers) on a grid that represents stimuli (CE).

folk linguistics (n): nonlinguists' beliefs about language (Preston 1993:181); anyone's untested beliefs about language, including those of linguists and anthropologists (L). See *problem* (2).

form (n): (1) structure irrespective of dynamics; an external configuration apart from its origin or cause, for example, a *semantic range* or *extension*. See *continuum* and *relation;* (2) the phonology of a word apart from its meaning, as in *linguistic form;* synonym: *item* (L).

formalism (n): a stark expression of a dynamic, a relation, a model, or all of these. The expression breaks down its subject into its essentials and represents each with a symbol pertaining only to that element; formal (adj). See *mathematics*.

formula of stressing (n): symbolic representation of a category in terms of the way its stressed coordinates are arranged, placing its unstressed coordinate last in order (see Appendix VIII) (VT).

formula of zooming (n): symbolic representation of a category in terms of the order in which all of its coordinates are arranged, starting with its *primary fixed coordinate* (VT).

fovea centralis (n): the tiny pit in the retina where L cones and M cones (maximally sensitive to long and medium wavelength) concentrate most densely but no S cones or rods (short wavelength and luminance) occur; the spot on which a person confines an image to sharpen and clarify it (VR). See *macula lutea*.

frame (n): (1) a set of parameters that includes particular selections while precluding consideration of others (PhL; Goffman 1974). Forge (1970) provides this example of framing: ". . . among the Abelam of the Sepik District, New Guinea . . . in the context of the tambaran cult, boys and young men acquire a set of fixed expectations about what they will see in two dimensions . . . that polychrome two-dimensional paints become a closed system, unrelated to natural objects . . . or, indeed, to anything outside the paintings. These expectations act to prevent them 'seeing,' that is making sense of, anything in two dimensions that is not part of the closed system" (p. 269). "Even people . . . who . . . knew I had taken a photograph of a relative . . . were initially unable to see him at all, turning the photograph in all directions. Even when the figure dominated (in my eyes) the photograph I sometimes had to draw a thick line round it . . . I had the impression that they willed themselves to see it rather than actually saw it in the way we do" (p. 287). (2) one relation between two vantages; whereas inherently fixed coordinates set parameters, inherently mobile coordinates bind them into a closed system while establishing the degree to which the viewer will differentiate; while the viewer participates in this opposition of arrangements, balances of similarity and difference within other oppositions will not influence its dynamics; shifting the balance will require a transposition of viewpoint to another frame (VT); *to frame* (v.), *framing* (qv.). See *chain-relations, vantages, inherently fixed* and *inherently mobile coordinate, transposition, observer, dynamics, frame breaking,* and *frame shifting*.

frame breaking (n, ger): abruptly discarding established parameters to replace them with new ones, as the institution of the Anglo-Saxon *thegn* was replaced by that of the French *baron* (Dahlgren 1985). In color categorization, it might have happened in some Polynesian languages if they jumped from Stage II to Stage V (Snow 1971). See §9.3 and note 13 of §4.4 on dormant languages. Frame breaking violates the widely recurrent principle of continuity in change (VT). See *frame*.

frame shifting (n): gradually changing preference from an old frame to a new frame while they coexist, or even while they are *linked*. The old frame is used less and less until a new generation does not learn it, as will be the fate of the Mazatec *crossover category* or, to address this change at its root, the *crossover formula* that constitutes the frame (VT). See *frame* and *linked*.

function (n): the purpose of a behavior; for example, categorization reduces infinite stimuli to manageable groups (Psy).

function (v): achieving or serving to foster a purpose, as plastic categorization functions to help *Homo sapiens* to survive.

functionalism (n): the belief that models of cognition may be explanatory if they address its functions (Psy). See *primary motivations.*

fuzzy-set theory or fuzzy logic: See *logic* (2).

gloss (n): a definition of a term in a second language, shown in single quotes, as *verde* 'green' (L); any brief definition; *gloss* (v).

grid (n): See *array.*

ground (n): See *figure-to-ground.*

head lexeme (n): the word that is grammatically indispensable to the meaning of a clause, as is 'green' to 'dark green'; the word that is qualified or built upon by others in a clause; the clause nucleus (L). See *lexeme.*

hesitation (n): a pause before a reply during an interview, registering doubt or forethought (VT).

high: See *up.*

historical vantages (n): zooming in through time while leaving physical evidence of past levels of concentration that have disappeared from current cognition (general VT); a documented overview or long-term cognitive change by which successive generations have subtracted levels from the top of a zooming hierarchy while adding levels to its bottom, usually maintaining three levels at any period. See M. MacLaury (1989: figs. 16–19) for examples from urban planning and architecture.

hue (n): the horizontal circumference of the Munsell color solid and of the psychological color solid of reflective samples (Appendix III); the prismatic dimension of any system of color; a sensation produced by *reflexes* of opponent neural channels in the optical nerve (VR). See *saturation* and *brightness.*

hue-stressing category (n): a category that people construct by placing strongest attention on its hues as its inherently fixed coordinates and slightly less attention on the relations between hues as its inherently mobile coordinates; a cool category that consistently skews toward one elemental hue and undergoes transference if not originally skewed toward green, obstructed, or discouraged (VT). See *crossover category.*

hue-stressing formula (n): $H + S^2 - D$, which expresses the emphasis that defines *hue-stressing category;* the *transference formula* (VT). See *crossover formula.*

hyponymy (n): See *inclusion, subordinate, superordinate;* hyponymous (adj). The antonyms *nonhyponomy* and *nonhyponymous* mean not included in a more general semantic range, only in complementation (L).

hypothesis (n): (1) *null hypothesis:* a prediction that a coincidence of data is insignificant, that is, not a pattern and, thus, insusceptible to explanation; (2) *research hypothesis:* an effort to explain a pattern; the account requires further prediction and testing against independent patterns. See *theory.*

inactive parallel (n): (general VT). See Preston (1993:218).

inclusion (n): (1) by conventional wisdom, a relation between semantic ranges in which one engulfs the breadth and extent of the other while covering substantial additional stimuli; a relation of embedding one range inside another (PhL); (2) a relation among vantages that includes among shared coordinates very strong attention to distinctiveness; the ranges pull away from each other with the smaller range leading the separation while each pertains to stimuli the other precludes (VT); (3) in Mesoamerican folk terminology, a relation of dominance and dependence, as "red rules pink" or "pink depends on red." Synonym: *hyponymy*.

inherently fixed coordinate (n): a unique point of reference that exists by itself as a salient apex or bounded perception; a point that is independent of an axis (VT). See *coordinate, fixed coordinate, mobile coordinate, inherently mobile coordinate*, and *axis*.

inherently mobile coordinate (n): a point of reference selected from an axis (VT). See *inherently fixed coordinate* and *axis*.

instantiate (v): to constitute a concrete example of a schema, part of a schema, a class, a type, a principle, or other abstraction; *instantiation* (n) (CogL, PhL).

intention (n): the abstract definition of a word apart from what it may refer to; a named concept that generates the *extensions* of the name, for example, a *vantage* as opposed to a *range* (L).

introduce (v): to recognize a coordinate by including it on the *bottom* level of concentration of an arrangement (VT). See *recognition* and *ascend*.

invariant (adj): unchanging, immutable; for example, *invariant perception* is a sense unedited by cognitive selection, an unlikely event in human experience (VT).

invert (v): to reverse the *order of preference* among a set of coordinates, for example, as a recessive range is derived from a dominant vantage within a domain, or as one meaning is derived from another meaning between domains (VT); *inversion* (n). (1) *full inversion:* inverting the inherently mobile coordinates of a three-coordinate arrangement $(X S^2\text{-}D > X D^2\text{-}S)$ or all coordinates in an arrangement of more than three (figs. 6.8 and 6.10), which derives a relation of near synonymy, coextension, or inclusion; (2) *partial inversion:* inverting only the inherently fixed coordinates, which changes the emphasis of a category (as from brightness to hue) or which derives a close relation between meaning across separate semantic domains, as between "amber" the fossil resin and "amber" the color. See *promote, polysemy, closely related*.

item (n): See form (2).

just noticeable difference or *JND* (n): a unit and measure of perceived difference between colors; the minimal increment of difference perceivable between two almost identical colors, one that is "confused 50 percent of the time" (Halsey and Chapanis 1951:1057). A few JNDs make a "small color difference" while many make a "large color difference," as between elemental green and blue. The larger the difference, the less reliable are JNDs as a metric (VR).

laterally polarized (adj): (1) placed wide to the right or left of the two unique hues of a cool category, usually said of a focus (CE, VT); (2) in the warm category, outside the diagonal axis between elemental yellow and red; the axis is four chips wide in rows D–F, two chips wide in rows C and G (MacLaury MS-1: fig. 22). See *vertically polarized*.

level of concentration or *level* (n): two coordinates within an *arrangement* or zooming
     hierarchy that are held in greater awareness than other coordinate pairs. In van-
     tage theory, a person can concentrate on only one *figure-to-ground relation* at a
     time, even though a *category* by definition is more complex (having at minimum
     three coordinates: X, S, D); complexity is managed by storing other coordinates
     in memory as presuppositions. See *concentrate* (VT).

lexeme (n): a word plus the inventory of its inflectives; one form of a word when used
     to represent all of its forms, as "red" represents 'reddish', 'redness', 'redder', and
     'redden'. Some linguists depict lexemes in capitals, as RED, to stress that it is an
     abstraction, although others do not follow this practice (L).

light (adj): Munsell values 6/ through 10/ for reflective samples (Appendix III); imbued
     with light, illuminated; emanating light. Reflective lightness may combine with
     desaturation to produce paleness, especially among very light samples of the
     color solid where maximum and minimum saturations converge (VR). See *dark*.

lightness (n): See *brightness* and *light* (adj).

link (n): (1) either of two frames in a chain relation; (2) the vantage that is shared by
     the frames (VT). See *frame, linked,* and *chain relation.*

linked (adj): to be coupled as are two frames when the recessive vantage of one provides
     the dominant vantage of the other (VT). See *frame, link,* and *chain relation.*

logic (n): a system of making sense based on a *metaphysic* and an *epistemology.* The
     metaphysic specifies what the world is like while the epistemology determines
     how we know this world; (1) *classical logic* specifies that the world is observer-
     independent while an observer may know it by successfully applying to it logical
     operations, such as identity, intersection, inclusion, and union; (2) *fuzzy logic*
     assumes the same metaphysic but adds that the world is naturally graded, which
     allows people to apply the same operations with relative success on the basis of a
     decimal calculus; (3) *prototype theory* also assumes the graded metaphysic,
     called *correlational structure,* but substitutes an epistemology of *family resem-
     blances to a prototype;* (4) vantage theory adopts an observer-dependent meta-
     physic: although observers are hard-wired to sense the world in a species-specific
     manner, they edit the senses by selective recognition and emphases; then they
     organize selections into an arrangement or point of view. Observers know the
     world through such vantages, which they adjust to new information by introduc-
     ing additional selections, demoting old ones, and shifting emphases. Instead of
     performing operations, observers either relate vantages or separate them; they
     construct chains of relations and frame each link.

low: See *up.*

luminous (n): emitting light, as does fire or a glowworm (VR); *luminance* (n); syn-
     onym *luminant.* Light emission from a source other than heat is called *lumines-
     cence,* as in bioluminescence or chemiluminescence. See *reflective.*

macula lutea (n): the area of the retina surrounding the fovea centralis to 10% in any
     direction where cones concentrate to a density seconded only in the fovea; the

most sensitive part of the retina outside the fovea where most central but uncon-
centrated vision initiates (VR). See *fovea centralis*.

map (v): to select stimuli as extensions of a term, as when placing rice grains on the
Munsell array (CE). See *mapping*.

mapping (n): a selection that blankets stimuli to identify them as members of a category or as within the range of a term. In ethnoscience, mapping was called
"classification" and opposed to *naming* or "identification" as the essential procedures for eliciting categories (CE). See *naming* and *focus*. See *semasiological*.

mapping step (n): a pass at mapping followed by a pause, which may be followed by
another mapping step or an assertion that the mapping is complete; steps are a subject's approach to mapping, not its objective. Mapping steps are valuable data (CE).

markerese (n): the theory that lexical meanings are composed of semantic *features*
or *markers* comprising the minimum number required to contrast each sense
against others, as "man" [adult, male, human] versus "woman" [adult, female,
human], that each meaning is such a *contrastive set;* synonym: *theory of distinctive features* (L).

mathematics (n): a rigorous system of expressing relations that symbolizes concepts
according to complementary rules. For example, in vantage theory, the order
of symbols represents the relative importance of concepts to an observer, as in
the *transference formula* versus the *crossover formula*.

member (n): (1) a stimulus within a category (Psy, L, CE); (2) a denizen of a community (A, L, CE).

membership (n): the status of being a member (Psy, L, A, CE).

membership value (n): (1) the extent to which a stimulus is a member of a category
(Psy, L, CE); (2) the extent to which a stimulus is within the reaches of a vantage
(VT), that is, its *proximity* to the vantage point. Note: vantage theory adopts
membership value from fuzzy-set theory to avoid overwhelming use of new
terms; yet, *proximity* is more consistent with vantage theory and, in time, might
replace *membership value*.

mental image (n): a schematic remembrance preserving selected parts and relations of
the remembered entity or event (Psy, CogL); a broad genre of cognition covering
the results of any mental process (VT).

Mesoamerican sample (n): results of color interviews collected in southern Arizona,
Mexico, Guatemala, and Honduras between 1978 and 1981 by the MCS and
WCS, those listed in Appendix I. See *world sample*.

metaphor (n): an equation between selected parts of a source domain and a target
domain that lends coherence to thought (PhL, CogL, A), as the Aztec metaphor
"people are plants" enables pervasive conception of human actions, processes,
and creations as though they were flowers, leaves, stems, roots, sprouting,
growth, blooming, ripening, wilting, and much more; for example, *in xochitl in
cuicatl* 'the flower, the song' equates the most beautiful achievement of people
with that of plants (Knab 1986; Hill 1992).

metaphysics: See *logic.*

metonym (n): an attribute-to-whole relation by which the attribute is treated as though it were the whole (PhL, CogL, A). For example, as motion has the attribute of notability, the foregrounded coordinate on any level within a vantage is regarded as one would a moving object that stands out against a stationary ground.

middle brightness or *middle value* (n): row F of the Munsell array, which is midway between the lightest and darkest of the eleven rows of the unabridged Munsell solid (compare figures III.1 and 1.1–2.); a bench mark for specifying other levels of brightness and for assessing *vertical polarization* (CE, VT).

middle column (n): Munsell column 23, which is equidistant from column 17 of unique green and column 29 of unique blue; a bench mark for statistical analysis (CE).

migration (n): gradual movement of a focus as an apparent *reflex* of cognitive change, for example, the focus of Tarahumara speaker 1 in different years, figure 8.24. Foci only migrate short distances, never across a category, as from blue to green. See *transference* (CE).

"mistake" or *informant error* (n): (1) among builders of mechanical models, an amateurish dismissal of data that belong in *residue;* synonyms: "confusion," "influence of the colonial language," "the result of rapid culture change" (A, L); (2) among statisticians, an acceptable *term* meaning deviation, outlier, or "noise." See *residue* and *cancel.*

mobile coordinate (n): a point of reference that is treated as the figure in a figure/ground relation, regardless of what it is inherently. It is, thus, highlighted as would be a moving object when viewed in contrast to a stationary background; it acquires metonymic properties of motion by virtue of the attention it receives (VT). See *inherently mobile coordinate, fixed coordinate, coordinate, virtual motion,* and *metonym.*

mode (n): See Preston (1993:216).

model (n): an ideational representation of how something operates that is set up to enable testing and revision of this explanatory scheme.

model (v): to devise and to revise a model.

monochromat (n): one who lacks two of the three photopigments and therefore discriminates visually on the basis of only light and dark (VR).

motion (n): any velocity between a dead standstill and the speed of light, limited in its upper range to fast-moving objects in the knowledge of the unschooled observer (see epigraph); part of the *source domain* of the analogy by which a categorical vantage is created (VT). See *time* and *space.*

motivation (n): the rate of change and amount of information proffered by a sociophysical environment so as to impinge on the individual who is under study; the amount of novelty that the individual is capable of discerning and the amount that he or she allows to impinge, not the amount detectable by a dispassionate index or the amount channeled though routes that affect people other than the subject of study. Further, motivation is individual cognizance of the rate at which exposure to information accelerates. These forces motivate an individual or successive gen-

erations of individuals to shift their emphases away from similarity and toward
distinctiveness as a means of coping. All cases observed have been *progressive,*
that is, increasingly favoring attention to distinctiveness (VT). See *evolution* and
progressive versus *regressive evolution.*

Munsell array: See *array.*

mutually polarized (adj): of data rendered in apparent opposition to each other so that
both occur wide of their usual dispositions, for example, foci that are placed
beyond opposite margins of their naming ranges (VT).

naive (adj): unreflective, unaware of alternatives; taking a subjective or submerged
perspective; *naivety* (n) (A, L, VT) See *subjective, submerged, reflective.*

naive realism (n): the doctrine that people perceive and act upon the world straightway
without cognitive editing, as with Rosch's idea that categories reflect "the correlational structure of the environment" (Ph). Synonym: objectivism (Ph); antonyms:
nonobjectivism (Ph), construal (CogL), experientialism (VR, CogL) (Hering
1920; Lakoff 1987).

name (v): to designate a stimulus or concept; *name* (n)(L). See *term.*

naming (n): the stimuli designated by a *term;* a *semantic range* or *naming range* volunteered in response to loose Munsell chips; the interview procedure by which stimuli
are identified with terms. See *mapping* and *focus* (CE). See *onomasiological.*

near synonymy (n): a relation of two semantic ranges that cover almost the same referents and whose best examples are almost identical (L); a relation between vantages in which attention to similarity is very strongly emphasized (VT). See
synonymy, semantic ranges, vantages, continuum, coextension, inclusion, and
complementation.

neural opponency: See *opponent process model.*

nonbasic (adj): not fitting Berlin and Kay's four criteria of a *basic color term* (CE)
or its definition of $X\ S^2$-D (VT); *secondary* (CE); *recessive* or $X\ D^2$-S (VT).
See *nullify.*

nonhyponymous: See *hyponymy.*

nullify (v): to attend so strongly to the coordinate of distinctiveness within a basic
color category that one applies the category to a narrow range of stimuli or, in
theory, to no stimuli; in real cases, subjects name a red or a yellow category on
only a chip or two of the Munsell array, even though the category is basic ($X\ S^2$-
D). Corbett and Morgan (1988:44) note as an oddity the reduced use of the basic
"yellow" term in Russian and ten other major languages. *Nullification* is common
in basic categories of yellow (fig IV.4*b;* MacLaury 1992*a:* fig. 5 French, 1986*a*
Appendix I: figs. 3*c* and 4*a*) or red (figs. VI.1*a,* 2*b,* 5*a;* Hoogshagen and Hoogshagen 1993:422, fig. C; MacLaury, Almási, and Kövecses in press; MacLaury
1986*a* Appendix I: figs. 1*a,* 2*a,* 3*e,* 4*a,* 8*a*). In basic green and blue categories,
darkening counteracts nullification (VT).

null response (n): a nonsubstantive reply to a query, such as "I don't know." Synonym:
zero response (VT).

objective (adj): detached from one's own point of view, as when simultaneously occupying it and an overview of it (Psy, PhL, CogL, VT). See *subjective, decontextualized,* and *abstract.*

objectification (n): disengaging one's point of view from a partiality toward a particular coordinate; leaping to the second point of view or, at least, *recognizing* it and occupying it at increasingly longer intervals while maintaining oversight of the first perspective (CogL, VT). See *objective* and *recognize.*

objectivity (n): the state of occupying an overview (Psy, PhL, CogL, VT). See *objective.*

observer (n): one who constructs cognition from senses; one who categorizes; one who selects coordinates, assigns them emphases, and arranges them from a particular standpoint; one who occupies a vantage point while creating and modifying a category as a means of assimilating information and adjusting to change (VT). Synonyms: *conceptualizer* (PhL), *speaker* (L), *subject* (Psy), *categorizer, viewer,* and *agent* (VT).

onomasiological (adj): of one referent named by more than one term that each has a different meaning; identifies a type of lexical variation in which a category may be named by terms of distinct semantic or conceptual bent, as some people name with *burgundy* and *maroon* a single dark red category to emphasize either its purplish or its brownish half, that is, as they name the category coextensively; designates the analytical perspective on language that separates this kind of variation from other types that may impinge simultaneously on one usage or domain (L, CogL); *onomasiology* (n) is used less than *onomasiological variation.* See *semasiological.* (John Taylor contrasts *onomasiological* and *semasiological* in his Foreword with regard to ways that analysts have interpreted data pertaining to coextensive color names; in using the terms as analytical instruments, he highlights how they denote views on data rather than objectively exclusive events. He adopts this nomenclature from Geeraerts, Grondelaers, and Bakema [1994:3–4], who combine these terms with two others to partition a system of concepts by which they analyze variation in meaning. The authors [pp. 14–15] compare their system with the approach taken in this volume to Mesoamerican color terminology.)

opponent process model (n): a scheme stipulating that two neural channels between the retina and visual cortex each process two firing rates, one fast and the other slow, that result in antagonistic sensations of unique hue, red versus green via one channel and yellow versus blue via the other. Since each channel can only fire at one rate at any time, the opponent hues cannot be sensed simultaneously in one place; each is seen as unique when the opposite channel fires at a basal rate that processes no information; interactions of channel outputs produce blended or nonunique sensations. *Opponent processes* or *opponency* (n): the activity of these channels.

order of preference (n): the ranking of coordinate pairs within a vantage by an observer who would prefer to concentrate on some pairs more than on others (VT). See *arrangement* and *invert.*

orientation (n): the direction taken by a vantage among other possibilities due to selection of certain coordinates rather than others; for example, with a green-

with-yellow category instead of a green-with-blue (cool) category, the orientation
is established by choosing yellow instead of blue (VT).

outlook (n): a predisposition toward either emphasizing similarity or emphasizing difference, used mainly in the latter sense of "an analytical outlook" (VT).

panning (n, ger): "movement back and forth between dominant and recessive" vantages (Preston 1993:216); *switching.*

paragon (n): a *quintessential prototype,* as the eagle is the paragon of birds, as
opposed to, say, the starling, sparrow, or other *representative prototype* (L). See
prototype.

pattern (n): a meaningful or orderly recurrence of data, one whose regularities are statistically significant.

perception (n): (1) to psychologists, *cognition;* (2) to linguists and anthropologists,
sensation, as used in vantage theory. See *cognition* and *sensation.*

phase (n): the composition of a category at a particular point in its development,
including any composition constituted by two or more vantages; the relation
between vantages at a particular point in its development (VT). Whereas *phase*
refers to segments of a sequence within a category, *stage* denotes relations
between categories within a domain as it evolves. See *stage* and *domain.*

photopigment (n): any of three substances in the retinal cones that absorbs short,
medium, or long wavelengths at maximum efficiency to initiate the process of
color perception (VR).

polar (adj): placed in opposition to a central point or to another vantage; a choice
approximate to a margin, usually said of a focus or other performance that is
more marginal than another (VT). See *central, polarized,* and *mutually polarized.*

polarize (v) and *polarized* (adj) (n): See *polar* and *central.*

polarized inclusion (n): (1) a relation between dominant and recessive ranges in which
the recessive range is focused outside of the dominant range that, in turn, over-
arches much of the recessive range; (2) two ranges that remain mutually polarized in spite of their covering different stimuli; two vantages that remain related
as inverse arrangements of the same coordinates in spite of the separated appearance of specific surface data, as with ranges that hardly overlap (VT); synonym
of (2): *apparent complementation.*

polysemy (n): of more than one related meaning, for example, Mamean *č'el* names a
green parrot-species or chartreuse color or the cool category, including blue; *poly-
semic, polysemous, polysemantic* (adj); in vantage theory, a *polysemous* relation
between meanings is produced by *partially inverting* coordinates to create categories of separate domains, as of bird versus color among the meanings of *raven.*
Homonymy refers to two unrelated meanings under one lexical form, such as
'pale' and 'pail'; *homonymous* (adj). Polysemy and homonymy can resist distinction; for example, Does Mixe *tsoxc* 'green, unripe' bear two related meanings
or two that are cognitively separate? Mixe speakers do not know the *etymologies*
of their words. A *dominant-recessive relation* is produced by *fully inverting*
coordinates without creating a category of an extraneous domain and, therefore,

within one category (L, VT). See *closely related, dominant-recessive, family resemblances, domain, invert.*

precondition (n): a prerequisite; a situation or state that must exist before others can develop; the others depend upon these earlier states. For example, people must have been able to construct categories of considerable plasticity before they evolved linguistic syntax; mutable categorization is *preconditional* to syntax.

prediction (n): a pattern that would emerge in data if a hypothesis were correct; *predict* (v). See *hypothesis* and *pattern.*

predominate (v int): to be assigned more emphasis than something else; for example, in the *transference formula* hue predominates but in the *crossover formula* relations predominate; *predominance* (n) (VT).

preference of concentration (n): the level in an arrangement on which the viewer wishes to concentrate (VT).

preferred fixed coordinate (n): the *inherently fixed coordinate* on the highest or *preferred level of concentration* within an *arrangement* (VT).

preferred level of concentration (n): the coordinate pair within an *arrangement* that people most comfortably keep in awareness under *default* conditions; in a *formalism*, it is represented as topmost (VT). See *arrangement, zooming hierarchy, default, formalism.*

prerequisite: See *precondition.*

presupposition (n): an antecedent condition inescapably implied by present conditions; any condition that must be inferred from the current state of affairs; the *coordinates* on *levels of concentration* not immediately activated, for example, emphasis on distinctiveness is *presupposed* when one emphasizes similarity (PhL). See *entailment.*

primary color category (n): In fuzzy-set theory, the result of the operation of identity on one unique hue or on black or white; in vantage theory, the equivalent is *elemental color category.* "Primary" is awkward because it calls to mind the paint mixing triad of red, yellow, and blue, which is unrelated to cognitive theory (CE). See *elemental color category, derived* and *binary color category, composite color category, desaturation category,* and *brightness category.*

primary motivation (n): the reason that people engage in a behavior, irrespective of *function;* for example, the function of dating is reproduction, although a couple on a date may have a social motivation. Primary motivation is an object of modeling apart from function, even though the two complement each other in adaptive behavior. In vantage theory, people categorize to establish a view on the world, although a category also manages information. In prototype theory, people categorize to manage information, and, hence, categories fit *correlational structure.* See *function.*

priority (n): a ranking of preference; see *predominance* and *preferred level of concentration.*

privative (adj): of a word or affix that denotes a reduction or deprivation of a normal, positive state, as in 'off-white', 'reddish', 'pale yellow', and 'dull green', or as with 'bland' or 'bleak'; an affix that converts a positive meaning to its negative opposite, as in nonbasic, desaturated, atypical, unclear, or colorless.

problem (n): (1) *real problem:* an enigma or paradox among data that flags the inadequacy of current models; an opportunity to formulate and test hypotheses and, ultimately, to improve theory, for example, the problem of explaining the dominant-recessive pattern of coextension; (2) *pseudoproblem:* a figment rooted in scientists' unrecognized folk beliefs about how data ought to behave, an obstacle to effective modeling; for example, the image of the category as a bounded container led to models that first took boundaries for granted and later were obsessed with marginal vagueness. See *logic* (1–2), *hypothesis, theory,* and *folk linguistics.*

progressive evolution (n): derivation of many narrow categories from few broad categories on the *basic level,* as in the 1975 Berlin-and-Kay hue sequence; strengthening emphasis on distinctiveness (CE). See *regressive evolution, evolution,* and *motivation.*

promote (v): to move an inherently fixed coordinate "upward" through an arrangement so that it occupies a "higher" level of concentration; to assimilate a coordinate more thoroughly into a category or to give it more prominence; the only means by which to intensify emphasis on an inherently fixed coordinate; *promotion* (n). For example, hue coordinates are promoted and brightness coordinates demoted as a brightness category changes to a hue category (VT). See *demote, inherently fixed coordinate, arrangement,* and *level of concentration.*

protanope (n): one who lacks the long-wave photopigment, which produces a red-green blindness (VR); *protanopic* (adj). See *dichromat.*

protoform (n): a reconstructed form hypothesized to be ancestral to later forms or *reflexes;* for an example, see *cognate* (L); the form can be the phonology of a word, its gloss, a category, or other cognition or practice (VT). See *form, etymology, protolanguage,* and *historical vantage.*

protolanguage (n): a hypothesis and reconstruction of a language ancestral to others; an argument that the others are related (L).

prototype (n): (1) a mental image of the most representative member or quintessential member of a category; the mental image to which members bear a family resemblance and, thereby, pertain to the category to some degree (Psy, Rosch); (2) a tautology by which a category is formed or defined in reference to a typical member or ideal image while this member or image derives its typicality by incorporating more attributes of the category than any other member or image (VT); *prototypical* (adj). See *category* (3), *mental image, paragon, stereotype,* and *family resemblance.*

prototype effects (n): the uneven *membership values* within a category (L); *typicality effects* (Psy).

prototype theory: See *logic* (3).

prototypicality (n): the state of being prototypical or the status of such (Rosch); arcane synonym: *prototypy.*

purview (n): the area of a terrain or a domain that a person beholds from an *oriented* vantage point (VT); a *scope.* See *vantage.*

qualifier (n): an adjective or adverb, a lexical modifier (L).

range (n): The extensions of a word; the stimuli that the word may designate (L); the color chips named or mapped by a *color term* (CE). *Range* is atheoretical and *descriptive;* unlike *vantage,* it imparts nothing of *intention.*

rank (n): (1) the position of a coordinate or a level of concentration within the hierarchical arrangement of a vantage (VT); (2) a level in a taxonomy (A). See *level of concentration, arrangement,* and *taxonomy.*

recessive (adj): to be derived from and linked to a *dominant vantage* per full inversion of coordinates (VT); *dependent.* See *recessive vantage, recessive range, dominant, vantage, dependent,* and *invert* (1).

recessive formula: See *recessive vantage.*

recessive range (n): a range that covers many of the same stimuli as does another but that is the smaller and more skewed of the two (VT).

recessive vantage (n): an arrangement of coordinates derived by inverting a dominant arrangement so as to move attention to distinctiveness from the bottom level of concentration to the preferred level of concentration, producing the recessive formula, D^2-S. The formula endows the recessive vantage with stronger differentiation and faster retraction than obtains within the dominant vantage (VT). See *zooming hierarchy, level of concentration,* and *preferred level of concentration.*

recognition (n): positive emphasis beyond a threshold of zero; admitting a sensation into awareness sufficiently to incorporate it into some kind of cognitive organization, such as a *category* (VT); *recognize* (v). See *suppression, selective emphasis, cognition,* and *axis.*

reconfigure (v): to alter extensions of a range without merely expanding or shrinking it, as when changing emphasis from brightness to hue (VT).

reflective (adj): (1) maintaining awareness of one's own thought or behavior from an outsider's point of view (A, PhL, Psy); *reflectivity* (n); (2) of a surface that reflects wavelength that reaches it from an extraneous source, said of "reflective samples" such as Munsell chips (VR). See *luminant.*

reflex (n): a linguistic form that has descended from an earlier form, expressible as "Y is a reflex of *X" (L); *reflect* (v). For examples, see *cognates.* See *protoform.*

regressive evolution (n): a shift from narrowly categorizing to broadly categorizing on the basic level; increasing the emphasis on similarity while de-emphasizing difference; reformulating a current system into an ancestral system; a return to the past; synonym *devolution* (n), *devolve* (v). For example, Kristol (1980*b*) asks if latter-day Italian peasants who name green and blue *verde* did not regressively evolve from the epoch of Classical Latin, when scribes, he suspects, applied ancestral *viridis* only to green objects. But did the peasants descend from the scribes? How did the scribes *think?* No evidence stronger than this supports color-category devolution (CE). See *progressive evolution* and *basic level.*

relation (n): (1) a juxtaposition of forms in space, such as mappings on the Munsell array; (2) a dynamic of countervailing forces, as the balance of attention to similarity and difference within a vantage. Synonym: *relationship;* (3) *positive relation:* the process of sharing particular points of reference, as coordinates are shared between a dominant and a recessive vantage or as coordinates are shared across domains, as between *amber* the fossil resin and *amber* the fossil-resin yellow-brown; (4) *negative relation:* the state of sharing no coordinates while, nevertheless, occupying the same domain, as *red* and *green* or *green* and *blue;* (5) *nonrelation:* the state of sharing nothing and of pertaining to disparate domains, as *green* and *large.* See *continuum* and *form.* See *coordinates, domain, dominant-recessive, near synonymy, coextension, inclusion, complementation, close relation, polysemy.*

reportative (n): a voice in discourse with which speakers distance themselves from their topic by attributing agency to others, for example, "people call that color chartreuse" or "Grannie used to say 'vermilion'"; not attributing agency, as "it is called red."

residue (n): data that do not fit current hypotheses; a problem to think about (L). See *problem* and *"mistake."*

row (n): a horizontal level of value or "brightness" of one chip in width on the Munsell array (CE); chips identified by the same letter on the array (VT). See *column.*

saltant (adj): of change that surges ahead by skipping one or a few steps or stages that others will take; for example, Snow (1971) argues that Samoan skipped from Berlin and Kay's evolutionary Stage II to Stage V (A, CE); *punctuated* (adj), *disjunctive leap* (n), *frame breaking.*

saturation (n): the vividness of a hue in terms of its distance from white-grey-black (VR). See *hue, brightness, desaturation,* and *just noticeable differences.*

scope: See *purview.*

secondary (adj): nonbasic (CE).

secondary category (n): a logician's term for an *included range,* assuming that categories can be related as are boxes within boxes; a *nonbasic* color category (CE). Vantage theory calls an included range a *dependent range* (after indigenous Mesoamerican folk terminology) or a *recessive vantage,* treating cases of multiple inclusion as framed links of chain.

secondary color term (n): the name of a nonbasic color category (CE); the name of a recessive vantage (VT), such as Russian *goluboj.* See *basic color term.*

selection (n): a choice among various senses by which some are recognized while others are suppressed (Psy, VT). See *recognition* and *suppression.*

selective emphasis (n): the degree of awareness devoted to a sensation; some awarenesses can occur in pairs whose degrees are reciprocal in strength, as of similarity and distinctiveness. No sensation can obtain by itself without some degree of emphasis, even if it is the negative emphasis of *suppression* (Psy, VT). See *cognition.*

semantic (adj): anything observed of the application of a *term* to stimuli, such as a pattern; of any stipulation about the extensions or intention of a term. Models of its intention are also semantic; they may incorporate social forces, cognition, or both (L). See *cognitive.*

semantic primitive (n): an irreducible component of the sensory world, such as [ani-

mal] or [eat] or [red], that contributes over and again to meanings; a elemental
building block of conception (CogL).

semantic range: See *semantic* and *range.*

semantic type (n): an ideal configuration of semantic ranges clearly showing *near
synonymy, coextension, inclusion,* or *complementation;* a real configuration of
ranges showing any possibility between the ideals or showing true complementation (VT). See *continuum* and *form.*

semasiological (adj): of different referents named by one term when each referent
constitutes a separate meaning; identifies a type of lexical variation in which one
word refers to distinct categories, as *burgundy* refers to both a wine and a color,
that is, application of one term to more than one domain; designates the analytical perspective on language that separates this kind of variation from other types
that may impinge simultaneously on one usage or domain (cf. Espejo Muriel
1990; Herne 1954; Rečeva 1984; Wood 1902) (L, CogL); *semasiology* (n) is used
less than *semasiological variation.* See *onomasiological,* which includes further
information on both terms.

sensation (n): receipt in the cortex of proximal stimuli transmitted by sense organs
from distal stimuli; for example, receipt of neural signals originally transformed
from wavelength by the retina, reorganized by ganglia, and transmitted to the
visual cortex via the optical nerve (Psy). See *perception, cognition, selection,* and
suppression.

sequence: See *universal evolutionary sequence of color naming.*

shine (v), *shiny* (adj), and *shininess* (n): See *surface effects.*

similarity (n): (1) an assessment of affinity based on common qualities and on emphasizing relations over particulars. Psychologists Rosch et al. (1976), Tversky (1977),
Tversky and Gati (1988), and Medin, Goldstone, and Gentner (1990, 1993) have
identified aspects of similarity judgments; (2) an emphasis on unity rather than
on its polar opposite of disparity (VT). See *distinctiveness* and *category.*

single focus (n): one selection of a best example of a range or category, chiefly on the
Munsell array (CE). See *dual* and *triple foci, ambivalent focus, alternative foci,*
and *canceled focus.*

singularity (n): a unit without differentiated parts, a point; a vantage whose viewpoint
and coordinates are coterminous, which occurs only in the first person; its symbol is VP-1 (VT). See *semantic primitive.*

skewing (n, ger): sustaining or increasing the importance of one part of a vantage
while reducing the importance of other parts that are, nevertheless, of comparable perceptual salience (VT); a process of category division (CE); always
assigning the same fixed coordinate to the preferred level of concentration in a
vantage, even though there are options (VT).

source domain (n): the domain that a metaphor or analogy is based upon, which is
more tangible than the *target domain,* that to which the metaphor or analogy is
applied (PhL, CogL). In vantage theory, an analogy pertains between the source
domain of spatiotemporal coordinates and the target domain of categorization.

The two domains of some metaphors may be equally concrete from VP-4, as is the Aztec "childbirth is like battle" (Hill and MacLaury 1995:322, note 18), although unequal from deictic views, VP-2, such as andro- and estrocentric standpoints that assign concreteness to opposite sides of the equation. See MacLaury (1995a:fig. 10) for dominant and recessive metaphors, the latter of which are constructed in reverse direction: from a remote source to an accessible target.

space (n): (1) territory that takes time to traverse and that is gauged in reference to landmarks and known velocities, as in Q: "How far to Palenque"? A: "One day" (see epigraph); (2) part of the *source domain* for the analogy by which a categorical vantage is created (VT). See *time* and *motion.*

stage (n): a configuration of relations between categories during the development of a domain (VT), for example, hue Stages I, II, etc., in Berlin and Kay's 1969 and 1975 order of basic color-term evolution. See *phase, domain,* and *step.*

step (n): a mapping or partial mapping of a category that an interviewee executes in response to a request to map and before pausing as if finished (CE). See *stage.*

stereotype (n): a prototype that represents a category by preconception of a typical member; a representative prototype based on under-representative information (Psy, L). See *prototype* and *paragon.*

stimulus (n): (1) *proximal stimulus:* any sensory response in the cortex that warrants cognitive treatment; (2) *distal stimulus:* an event in the world outside the body, such as wavelength reflected by a color chip. (1) and (2) are connected by *intermediate stimuli,* as wavelength excites a photochemical retinal response that, in turn, transforms into the neural transmission that provides the proximal stimulus; (3) *physical stimulus:* the object that reflects or emits wavelength, such as a color chip (VR).

stress (v): to emphasize hues more than their relations or to emphasize relations between hues more than the hues as individuated stimuli; to be closer to or partial toward either fixed or mobile coordinates from the engaged deictic standpoint, VP-2; *stress* (n). The two *stresses* are expressed as the *hue-stressing formula* or *transference formula* versus the *relation-stressing formula* or *crossover formula* (VT). In vantage theory, *stress* is reserved for these uses and opposed to *concentrate, attend,* and *focus,* which are restricted to other parts of the theory. See *emphasize.*

structure (n): the organization of a category; a term mainly used by Rosch and others who did not integrate theory with category dynamics and process; *structure* has a static, descriptive connotation (Psy). Structural terms are *form, semantic, range, relation* (1), *family resemblances,* and *prototype.* Processual terms are *vantage, arrangement,* and *continuum.*

stylistic synonym (n): an ordinary and/or defective word substituted for a technical *term* to avoid using the latter with numbing repetition.

subject (n): one whose responses are observed in a psychological experiment (Psy). A *consultant, helper, assistant, native collaborator,* or *resource person* is one whom an anthropologist or linguist interviews or learns from or works with (A, L). *Informant,* now a stigmatized term, names the forerunner of this expanded role.

subjectification (n): collapsing a viewpoint with its coordinates or increasing partiality toward one of them (CogL). See *subjective.*

subjective (adj): involved in a point of view to an extent that alternatives remain out of scope, especially a viewpoint that is coterminous with one of its own coordinates (CogL, VT). See *objective, contextualized,* and *concrete.*

subjectivity (n): involvement in one viewpoint. See *subjective.*

submersion (n): engagement in a point of view to any extent but especially the extent to which it is impossible to conceive of alternative perspectives; the subjective end of a scale between *immersion* and *objectivity* (Psy, L, A, VT). See *detachment.*

subordinate (adj): (1) in classical theory, *hyponymous,* having a range that is included within a broader range; (2) In vantage theory, *recessive.* See *recessive* and *super-ordinate.*

subroutine (n): a prescribed procedure for performing a task or solving a problem, for example, deciding that the "face" of a featureless object is the part closest to the viewer (as opposed to alternatives). Speakers of distinct languages decide this and countless other matters according to different prescriptions (VT).

superordinate (adj): (1) in classical theory, *nonhyponymous,* having a range that includes another plus additional extensions (L); (2) in vantage theory, *dominant.* See *dominant* and *subordinate.*

suppression (n): to devote zero attention to a sense, which is accomplished at the negative end of a scale that ranges from nil attention to the maximum possible; for example, some hue categories entirely preclude attention to brightness (Psy, VT); *suppress* (v). See *recognition, cognition,* and *axis.*

surface-effect category (n): (1) a category, such as *shininess,* that pertains only to a surface effect, not to color (CE); (2) an *arrangement* of coordinates that includes coordinates of *color* and of *surface effect* and that features the latter on the *preferred level of concentration* and over the former (VT). See *surface effects* and *color category* (2).

surface effects (n): qualities of texture that modify reflected wavelength and thereby add to color the appearance of being shiny, dull, glossy, matte, frosty, iridescent, phosphorescent, or metallic (VR). See *color category* (2).

suspended figures: See Preston (1993:220).

synonymy (n): a relation of substitutability between two *terms* that each name the same intention or the same vantage (L), a theoretical possibility never confirmed empirically among color terms. See *near synonymy.*

systemic corollary (n): a condition that will transpire in a system because of the way the system is composed; for example, skewing entails that the original cool term name only the hue favored by the skewing if the cool category divides or—because of the cardinal opposition of red and green—skewing will favor green if nothing exists within the system that may divert this corollary, such as crossover or a yellow-with-green category (VT). Although systemic corollaries are entailments, vantage theory confines *entailment* to synchronic accompaniments of the way particular vantages are composed.

target domain: See *source domain.*

taxonomy (n): (1) categories related hierarchically, often in tiers of *superordinate,*
   basic, and *subordinate* ranks (Psy), although ranks may number up to six and are
   named differently in anthropological folk systematics (Berlin 1992); (2) a *chain*
   relation (VT); (3) any system of relations among categories (L, PhL). See
   MacLaury (1995b).

term (n): a word, phrase, or clause that designates a referent within a domain, as a
   color term names a category within the color domain, for example, "green" or
   "kelly green," or as a technical term names a concept within a domain of expertise. See *name.*

test bed (n): an exceptionally measurable and common domain with unusually few
   variables in which the hypotheses of a *special theory* can be efficiently tested.
   See *hypothesis* and *theory.*

theory (n): a system of explanation; a statement of relation between hypotheses that is
   capable of incorporating further hypotheses and of generating new ones as it
   accommodates additional observations that previously appeared disparate;
   (1) *special theory:* a theory pertaining to a delimited realm, such as to the color
   domain or to straight-line velocity; (2) *general theory:* a theory pertaining to
   phenomena at large, such as to categorization, to cognitive organization, or to
   velocities that move through any trajectory. A special theory may precede a
   general theory by revealing principles under tightly controlled conditions. A
   general theory may build on a special theory by extending principles, modifying
   them, and adding new ones.

time (n): a function of motion gauged by comparing simultaneous versus sequential
   events (see epigraph); an essential within the source domain of the analogy by
   which a categorical vantage is created (VT). See *space* and *motion.*

top: See *up.*

transfer (v): to switch a *focus* within the cool category from blue to green; to *recog-*
   nize the cardinal contrast between green and red as attention to distinctiveness
   strengthens, and accordingly to adjust the *arrangement* of the cool category so
   that its prominent identity is green (CE, VT).

transference (n): see *transfer.*

transform (v): to change a fixed coordinate to a mobile coordinate or vice versa (VT).
   This term is little used. See *zooming.*

transformation: see *transform.*

transposition (n): a shift of view from one *frame* to another within a *chain of relations*
   linking three vantages; the shift is instigated by the *observer* who wishes to place
   more emphasis on similarity or difference; it allows a broader girth of emphases
   than pertain within one relation between two vantages (VT); *transpose* (v). See
   panning, triple coextension.

trichromat (n): one who possesses the three *photopigments* needed for normal color
   vision or *trichromatic* vision (VR). See *dichromat.*

triple coextension (n): a chain relation between a dominant, recessive, and ultra-recessive coextensive range (VT). See *chain relation* and *coextensive.*

tritanope (n): one who lacks the short-wave photopigment and thereby suffers a blue-green blindness (VR); *tritanopic* (adj). See *dichromat.*

type (n): a particular relation that is distinguished vis à vis other kinds, as between vantages related by coextension opposed to vantages related by inclusion (VT). Whereas *type* designates a class within a *typology, phase* and *stage* properly denote a point within a sequential development. But *stage* is used in the sense of *type* to classify segments of basic color-term evolution (CE), and *phase* is used almost synonymously with *type* of semantic relation or type of relation between vantages (VT). See *phase* and *stage.*

typicality effects (n): See *prototype effects.*

typology (n): a classification of the relations that may occur between the same entities (L), as between the vantages of a category or the categories within a domain (VT).

ultra-recessive vantage (n): the last vantage in a chain relation of three, in which the middle vantage is recessive in relation to the first vantage but dominant in relation to this last one, which, in turn, is even more recessive; as each link between vantages is a frame, the last vantage is in the second frame where it is bestowed with stronger emphasis on distinctiveness than that which prevails across the first link and within the first frame (VT). See *chain-relation* and *frame.*

unique hue (n): an irreducible sensation of red, yellow, green, or blue through all levels of brightness above zero saturation; a result of neurochemical response to wavelength shared with little variation among *Homo sapiens* with normal color vision. People with anomalous vision and other species perceive different unique hues than do the majority of humans. See *elemental hue* and *elemental color* (VR, VT).

universal evolutionary sequence of color naming (n): (1) 1969: Berlin and Kay stipulate that basic *color terms* name eleven focal colors in predictable order (CE); (2) 1975: Berlin and Berlin and, separately, Kay revise their sequence to one in which basic color terms partition the spectrum in a predictable order of configurations whose boundaries mold themselves around the locations of the focal colors; basic color terms name all colors at any stage (CE); (3) 1991: Kay, Berlin, and Merrifield attempt to accommodate categories of hue and of brightness to one series of stages, making the sequence multilineal (CE); (4) 1992: MacLaury proposes that brightness categories merge with the 1975 hue sequence from origins outside of it, but hue categories never convert to brightness; binary and desaturated basic color categories emerge at any point from hue Stages IIIa–b onward; a yellow-with-green hue category may develop directly from yellow-green-blue brightness apart from the 1975 sequence (VT).

up: a heuristic for describing diagrams that represent an arrangement or zooming hierarchy; in cognition there may be no *up, down, high, low, top,* or *bottom* (VT).

vantage (n): (1) a point of view constructed in reference to coordinates. In *vantage theory,* it is either the point of view or this position plus the view that it commands. The latter may be distinguished as *purview* or *scope,* apart from the *standpoint;* (2) one arrangement of the coordinates by which a category is constructed; it may be the only arrangement, one among two, or rarely one among more. *Vantage* derives from medieval French, in which it referred to an advantageous military position, as on high ground. Stylistic synonyms: *point of view, viewpoint, standpoint, angle, angle of viewing, view, slant, perspective,* or *position* (see epigraph).

vantage algebra (n): a system of principles for using symbols to represent any category according to a *formula of zooming* or a *formula of stressing,* as shown in Appendix VIII.

vantage theory, the general (n): the hypothesis that people make sense in the abstract by analogy to the fixed and mobile coordinates by which they make sense of their positions in space and time.

vantage theory of categorization, the specific (n): as people make sense by analogy to fixed and mobile coordinates, they categorize by including attention to similarity (S) and distinctiveness (D) among the mobile coordinates; the balance of strength between S and D consolidates the category at a specific shape and width while it affords flexibility for change; the arrangement of coordinates binds the categorizer and the category into a relation that constitutes a point of view; a category may be composed by more than one such arrangement, and each such vantage will be uniquely shaped and may be separately named. This specific theory has been developed and tested almost entirely within the domain of color categorization, which has produced an even more specific theory of that domain alone. See *logic* (4).

variability (n): the capacity of an individual to behave or to use language differently when adopting distinct views on selfhood and surrounds in reference to social context (VT).

variable rule (n): a statistical description of variability between two ways of speaking by the same individual(s); a coextensive pattern that may be modeled in terms of dominant and recessive vantages on self and society; modeling variability as such, and for an individual, links cognitive and social approaches to language (general VT). See *variability.*

variation (n): differences between individuals, usually but not necessarily in a community. In color categorization, individuals vary immensely, but not totally; most who name a color category coextensively show the dominant-recessive pattern (VT); most who name hue exhibit a stage of the 1975 sequence (A, L, CE). Variation does not pertain equally to all aspects of cognition; *vary* (v). Synonym: *variability.*

vertically polarized (adj): (1) of a cool-category focus placed in rows H–J or C–A on chips that are at least two rows darker or three rows lighter than *middle brightness;* the asymmetry is imposed because statistics suggest that it is harder to discriminate between dark chips than light chips (MacLaury MS-1); (2) of a warm-category focus placed in row B or rows H or I, lighter than elemental yellow or darker than elemental red (VT). See *laterally polarized.*

virtual motion (n): emphasis on a figure vis-à-vis a ground that makes the figure stand out to the viewer as notably as though the figure were moving; the metonymic property that warrants calling a figure "the mobile coordinate" regardless of whether it is actually in motion (VT). See *mobile coordinate* and *metonym*.

world sample (n): the results of color interviews collected under an NSF grant to Paul Kay, Brent Berlin, and William R. Merrifield in 22 countries of Asia, Africa, and the Americas; for purposes of regional analysis and comparison, these data minus those included in the *Mesoamerican sample* (CE).

worldview (n): all cognitive constructions of an individual, related to each other or not. These do not constitute a hodgepodge, as a particular balance of emphasis on similarity and distinctiveness crosscuts all, giving worldview a particular predisposition toward discrimination and analytical thought. Further, members of a society may share a degree of submersion or detachment of viewpoint. Color categories comprise a small but readily measurable part of worldview (A). See *similarity, distinctiveness, submersion,* and *detachment*.

zooming (n, ger): changing *levels of concentration* within a vantage, as from broad to refined or the reverse. To *zoom in* is to fix a formerly *mobile coordinate* while relating another mobile coordinate to it, as a figure to a ground. To *zoom out* means to ascribe mobile status to a previously *fixed coordinate* while relating it to another fixed coordinate, again as *figure to ground*. Zooming in or out may require repetition of this process if coordinates number more than three (VT). See *zooming hierarchy*.

zooming hierarchy (n): an arrangement of three or more coordinates into two or more pairs that are ranked according to which pair among them an individual will prefer to concentrate upon when calling to mind a category (VT). *Zooming* occurs when the individual shifts concentration through the ranking from one pair to another. See *arrangement, preferred fixed coordinate, preferred level of concentration, preference of concentration, level of concentration, vantage*.

BIBLIOGRAPHY

Abbreviations

AA	*American Anthropologist*
AAA	American Anthropological Association
AE	*American Ethnologist*
AGI	*Archivo Glottologico Italiano*
AJPA	*American Journal of Physical Anthropology*
AJP	*American Journal of Psychology*
AL	*Anthropological Linguistics*
ARP	*Annual Review of Psychology*
ARSI	*Annual Report of the Board of Regents of the Smithsonian Institution*
BBS	*Behavioral and Brain Sciences*
BJP	*British Journal of Psychology*
BJPS	*British Journal for the Philosophy of Science*
BLS	*Proceedings of the Annual Meeting of the Berkeley Linguistics Society*
CA	*Current Anthropology*
CLS	*Papers from the Annual Regional Meeting of the Chicago Linguistic Society*
CRA	*Color Research and Application*
CW	*The Classical Weekly*
EY	*Eranos Yearbook*
IJAL	*International Journal of American Linguistics*
IJSLP	*International Journal of Slavic Linguistics and Poetics*
JA	*Journal Asiatique*
JAFL	*Journal of American Folk-Lore*
JAI	*Journal of the Anthropological Institute of Great Britain and Ireland*
JAR	*Journal of Anthropological Research*
JASP	*Journal of Abnormal and Social Psychology*
JCCP	*Journal of Cross-Cultural Psychology*
JCL	*Journal of Child Language*
JCLTA	*Journal of the Chinese Language Teachers Association*
JEP	*Journal of Experimental Psychology*

JFC   The Jacobs Fund Collection, Univ. of Washington Library Archives
JL   *Journal of Linguistics*
JLA   *Journal of Linguistic Anthropology*
JLS   *Journal of Language in Society*
JOSA   *Journal of the Optical Society of America*
JSA   *Southwestern Journal of Anthropology*
JSP   *Journal of Social Psychology*
LS   *Language and Speech*
MCS   Mesoamerican Color Survey
PAPS   *Proceedings of the American Philosophical Society*
PB   *Psychological Bulletin*
PICA   *Proceedings of the International Congress of Americanists*
PMLAA   *Publications of the Modern Language Association of America*
PMS   *Perceptual and Motor Skills*
PRs   *Psychological Research*
PRv   *Psychological Review*
PSCL   *Papers and Studies in Contrastive Linguistics*
REG   *Revue des études grecques*
SA   *Scientific American*
SAJL   *South African Journal of Linguistics*
SELAF   Société pour l'Étude des Langues Africaines
THSC   *Transactions of the Honourable Society of Cymmrodorion*
TNC   *The Nineteenth Century*
TPNZI   *Transactions and Proceedings of the New Zealand Institute*
UCPL   University of California Publications in Linguistics
UMI   University Microfilms International
VR   *Vision Research*
WCS   World Color Survey
ZE   *Zeitschrift für Ethnologie*

Abramov, I. 1968. "Further Analysis of the Responses of LGN Cells." *JOSA* 58:
    574–579.
Adam, A., E. Mwesigye, and E. Tabani. 1970. "Ugandan Color Blinds Revisited."
    AJPA 32:59–64.
Adams, Francis M., and Charles E. Osgood. 1973. "A Cross-Cultural Study of the
    Affective Meanings of Color." *JCCP* 4:134–155.
Ademollo Gagliano, Maria Teresa. 1985. "La terminologia dei colori in prussiano
    antico." *AGI* 70:1–17.
Agoston, G. A. 1987. *Color Theory and Its Application in Art and Design.* Rev. ed.
    Springer Series in Optical Sciences 19. New York: Springer-Verlag.
Albright, Thomas D. 1991. "Color and the Integration of Motion Signals." *Trends in
    Neuroscience* 14:266–269.
al-Jehani, Nasir M. 1990. "Color Terms in Mecca: A Sociolinguistic Perspective." *AL*
    32 (1–2):163–174.

Allen, Grant. 1878. "Development of the Sense of Color." *Mind* 3:129–132.

———. 1879. *The Color-Sense, Its Origins and Development.* Boston: Houghton Mifflin Company.

Allott, R. M. 1974. "Some Apparent Uniformities Between Languages in Colour-Naming." *Language and Speech* 17:377–402.

Almqvist, Ernst B. 1882. "Studier öfver tschuktschernas färgsinne." In *Vega-Expeditionens Vetenskapliga iakttagelser,* vol. I, Nils A. E. Nordenskiöld, ed., 185–194. Stockholm: F. & G. Beijer.

———. 1883. "Studien über den Farbensinn der Tschuktschen." In *Die wissenschaftlichen Ergebnisse der Vega-Expedition,* vol. I., A. E. Freiherrn von Nordenskiöld, ed., 42–49. Leipzig: Brockhaus (translation of Almqvist 1882).

Anawalt, Patricia R. 1992. "Nahuatl Clothing Terms Correlated with Aztec Textile Motifs." Paper presented at the 91st Annual Meeting of the AAA, San Francisco.

Andersen, Johannes. 1942. *Maori Place-Names, Also Personal Names and Names of Colours, Weapons, and Natural Objects.* Wellington: Memoir 2 of the *Journal of the Polynesian Society of New Zealand.*

Anderson, John M. 1973. "Maximi Planudis in Memoriam." In *Generative Grammar in Europe,* F. Kiefer and N. Ruwet, eds., 20–47. Dordrecht: Reidel.

André, Jacques. 1949. *Étude sur les termes de couleur dans la langue latine.* Paris: C. Klincksieck.

———. 1957. "Source et évolution du vocabulaire des couleurs en latin." In Meyerson, ed., 327–337.

Andree, Richard. 1878. "Über den Farbensinn der Naturvölker." *ZE* 10:323–334.

Anglicus, Bartholomaeus. 1582 [1250]. "De coloribus." Numbered lvs. 387–396 (first part of Book 19). In *Batman vppon Bartholome, his booke, De Proprietatibus Rerum.* London: Thomas East (1398 John de Trevisa English translation, enlarged and amended by Stephan Batman).

Anonymous. 1858. "Azur und purpur." *Aus der Natur: Die neuesten Entdeckungen aus dem Gebiete der Naturwissenschaften* 11:1–46. Leipzig: Abel.

Anonymous. 1864. "Purple Dyeing, Ancient and Modern." *ARSI* 1863:385–401. Washington, D.C.: Government Printing Office (translation of Anonymous 1858).

Aoyagi, Munekazu H. 1995. "Selection of Japanese Categories during Social Interaction." In Taylor and MacLaury, eds., 331–363.

Arias Abellán, Carmen. 1994. *Estructura semántica de los adjetivos de color en los Tratadistas Latinos . . .* Cadiz: Univ. of Seville.

Armstrong, M. E. 1917. "The Significance of Certain Colors in Roman Ritual." Diss., Johns Hopkins Univ.

Arnold, Dean E. 1967. "*Sak luʔum* in Mayan Culture and Its Possible Relation to Mayan Blue." *University of Illinois Department of Anthropology Research Report* 2. Urbana: Univ. of Illinois.

Aschmann, Herman. 1946. "Totonac Categories of Smell." *Tlalocan* 2:187–189.

Babcock, Barbara A., ed. 1978. *The Reversible World: Symbolic Inversion in Art and Society.* Ithaca, N.Y.: Cornell Univ. Press.

Bacmeister, Adolf. 1874. *Keltische Briefe.* Strassburg: Karl Trübner.

Baines, John. 1986. "Color Terminology and Color Classification: Ancient Egyptian Color Terminology and Polychromy." *AA* 87:282–297.

Barley, Nigel F. 1974. "Old English Colour Classification: Where Do Matters Stand?" *Anglo-Saxon England* 3:15–28.

Barsalou, Lawrence W., and Daniel R. Sewell. 1984. *Constructing Representations of Categories from Different Points of View.* Emory Cognition Project, Report 2. MS in possession of primary author, Department of Psychology, Univ. of Chicago.

Bartlett, Elsa Jaffe. 1976. "The Acquisition of the Meaning of Colour Terms: A Study of Lexical Development." In *Recent Advances in the Psychology of Language,* Vol. 4a: *Language Development and Mother-Child Interaction,* Robin N. Campbell and Philip T. Smith, eds., 89–108. New York: Plenum Press.

Bartlett, Harley Harris. 1928. "Color Nomenclature in Batak and Malay." *Papers of the Michigan Academy of Sciences, Arts, and Letters* 10:1–52.

Basset, R. 1895. "Les noms de métaux et de couleurs en berére." *Mémoires de la Société de l'Anthropologie* 9:58–92.

Basso, Keith, ed. 1971. *Western Apache Raiding and Warfare—from the Notes of Grenville Goodwin.* Tucson: Univ. of Arizona Press.

Bastian, H. 1869. "In seinen Ausführungen über den Farbensinn der Urzeit . . .". *ZE* 1:89–90.

Batchelor, John. 1926. *An Ainu-English-Japanese Dictionary.* Tokyo: Kyobunkan.

Battig, W. F., and W. E. Montague. 1969. "Category Norms for Verbal Items in 56 Categories: A Replication and Extension of the Connecticut Category Norms." *JEP* (Monograph) 80 (3, part 2):1–46.

Baxter, William H. 1983. "A Look at the History of Chinese Color Terminology." *JCLTA* 19 (2):1–25.

Beaglehole, Ernest. 1939. "Tongan Color-Vision." *Man* 39:170–172.

Beaglehole, Ernest, and Pearl Beaglehole. 1938. *Ethnology of Pukapuka.* Bernice P. Bishop Museum Bulletin 150. Honolulu: Bishop Museum.

Bechtel, Fritz. 1879. "Ueber die Bezeichnungen der sinnlichen Wahrnehmungen in den indogermanischen Sprachen." *Ein Beitrag zur Bedeutungsgeschichte.* Weimar: Hermann Böhlau.

Beek, W. E. A. van. 1977. "Color Terms in Kapsiki." In *Papers in Chadic Linguistics,* P. Newman and R. M. Newman, eds., 3–20. Leiden: Afrika Studiecentrum.

Beffa, Marie-Lise. 1978. "Référence directe et connotation: Remarques linguistiques sur les noms de couleurs en turc et en chinois." In Tornay, ed., 249–257.

Bénaky de Smyrne, N.-P. 1897. "Du sens chromatique dans l'antiquité. Sur la base des dernières découvertes de la préhistoire, de l'étude des monuments écrits des anciens et des données de la glossologie." Paris: Maloine.

———. 1915. "Des termes qui désignent le violet dans l'antiquité et de la signification des épithètes composées de ἴον 'violette.'" *REG* 28:16–38.

Bender, M. Lionel. 1983. "Color Term Encoding in a Special Lexical Domain: Sudanese Arabic Skin Color." *AL* 25:19–27.

Benhar, Efraim, and Heinrich Zollinger. 1974. "Color Me Palm (Green)." *Rehovot* 7:19–21.

Bennett, T. J. A. 1988. *Aspects of English Colour Collocations and Idioms.* Heidelberg: Carl Winter.

Berlin, Brent. 1968. "Covert Categories and Folk Taxonomies." *AA* 70:290–299.

———. 1970. "A Universalist-Evolutionary Approach in Ethnographic Semantics." In *Current Directions in Anthropology,* Ann Fisher, ed. Bulletin of the American Anthropological Association 3 (2):3–18. Washington, D.C.: American Anthropological Association.

———. 1992. *Ethnobiological Classification: Principles of Categorization of Plants and Animals in Traditional Societies.* Princeton, N.J.: Princeton Univ. Press.

———. MS-1. *Tzeltal Color Terminology.* (Forty data sets in Munsell format. Referenced in Berlin and Kay 1969.) Original in possession of author.

———. MS-2. "Initial Classification of Color Lexicons Found in the C. Hart Merriam Vocabularies." MS in possession of author.

Berlin, Brent, and Elois Ann Berlin. 1975. "Aguaruna Color Categories." *AE* 2:61–87.

Berlin, Brent, and Paul Kay. 1969. *Basic Color Terms: Their Universality and Evolution.* Berkeley: Univ. of California Press (2d ed. 1991).

Berlin, Brent, Paul Kay, and William R. Merrifield. 1985. "Color Term Evolution: Recent Evidence." Paper presented at the 84th AAA Meeting, Washington, D. C.

Berlin, Heinrich, and David H. Kelley. 1961. "The 819-Day Count and Color-Direction Symbolism among the Classic Maya." *Tulane University Middle American Research Institute* 26:9–20.

Berman, Howard. 1979. "Central Sierra Miwok Color Terms." *IJAL* 45:352–353.

Bernardo, A. G. 1967. "Matigsalug Color Categories." *U.P. Anthropology Bulletin* 3 (1967–1968):11–13 (University of the Philippines).

Bernstein, Basil B. 1971. *Class, Codes and Control,* vol. I: *Theoretical Studies Towards a Sociology of Language.* London: Routledge and Kegan Paul.

Bertoni, Giulio. 1925. "I Nomí spagnuoli dei colori del cavallo nel manoscritto di Leida CLXX (231 Scal.)." In *Homenaje ofrecido a Menéndez Pidal: Miscelánea de estudios lingüísticos, literarios e históricos,* vol. I., 151–154. Madrid: Librería y Casa Editorial Hernando, S. A.

Best, Elsdon. 1905. "Notes on the Colour-Sense of the Maori." *The New Zealand Official Year-Book,* 1905, E. J. von Dadelszen, ed., 637–642. Wellington, N.Z.: John MacKay, Government Printer; London: Eyre and Spottiswoode.

Beyer, H. 1921. "El color negro en el simbolismo de los antiguos mexicanos." *Revista de Revistas* (July 10) 583.

Bickerton, Derek. 1990. *Language & Species.* Chicago: Univ. of Chicago Press.

Biggam, Carole P. 1993. "A Lexical Semantic Study of Blue and Grey in Old English: A Pilot Study in Interdisciplinary Semantics." 2 vols. Diss., Univ. of Strathclyde, U.K.

———. 1995. "Sociolinguistic Aspects of Old English Colour Lexemes." *Anglo-Saxon England* 24:51–65.

Birren, Farber. 1979. "Color Identification and Nomenclature: A History." *CRA* 4:14–18.

———, ed. 1969. *A Grammar of Color: A Basic Treatise of the Color System of Albert H. Munsell.* New York: Van Nostrand Reinhold.

Black, Mary B. 1969. "Eliciting Folk Taxonomy in Ojibwa." In Stephen A. Tyler, ed., 165–189.

Blommaert, Jan M. E. 1985. "The Semantics of Bantu Color Terms." *Grazer Linguistische Studien* 24:63–76.

Bloomfield, Leonard. 1933. *Language.* New York: Holt, Rinehart and Winston.

Blümner, Hugo. 1889a. "Die rote Farbe im Lateinischen." *Archiv für Lateinische Lexicographie und Grammatik* 6:399–417.

———. 1889b. "Ueber die Farbenbezeichnungen bei den römischen Dichtern." *Philologus* 48:142–167, 706–722.

———. 1892. "Die Farbenbezeichnungen bei den Römischen Dichtern." *Berliner Studien für klassische Philologie* (monograph series) 13 (3).

———. 1912. *Technologie und Terminologie der Gewerbe und Künste bei Griechen und Römern,* vol. I. 2d ed. Leipzig: B. G. Teubner. Reprinted 1979, New York: Arno.

Boas, Franz. 1896. "The Limitations of the Comparative Method of Anthropology." *Science* 4:901–908.

———. 1911a. "Introduction." In *Handbook of American Indian Languages,* Part 1, Franz Boas, ed., 1–83. Smithsonian Institution: Bureau of American Ethnology Bulletin 40. Washington, D.C.: Government Printing Office.

———. 1911b. *The Mind of Primitive Man.* New York: Macmillan.

———. 1920. "The Methods of Ethnology." *AA* 22:311–321.

Boehmer, Ed. 1872. "De colorum nominibus equinorum." *Romanische Studien* 1 (2):231–294.

Boggess, Julian E. 1981. *Perspectives and Color Terminology: The Effects of Looking at the Subject of Colors and Color Names from Different Perspectives.* Diss., Univ. of Illinois at Urbana-Champaign.

Bolinger, Dwight. 1961. "Generality, Gradience, and the All-or-None." *Juana Linguarum* NR 14. The Hague: Mouton.

Bolton, Ralph. 1978a. "Black, White, and Red All Over: The Riddle of Color Term Salience." *Ethnology* 17:287–311.

———. 1978b. "Salience of Color Terms in Dreams of Peruvian Mestizos and Qolla Indians." *JSP* 105:299–300.

Bolton, Ralph, and D. Crisp. 1979. "Color Terms in Folktales: A Cross-Cultural Study." *Behavior Science Research* 14:231–253.

Bolton, Ralph, A. T. Curtis, and L. L. Thomas. 1980. "Nepali Color Terms: Salience on a Listing Task." *Journal of the Steward Anthropological Society* 12:309–322.

Bonser, W. 1925. "The Significance of Colour in Ancient and Mediaeval Magic: With Some Modern Comparisons." *Man* 25:194–198.

Borg, Alexander, ed. In press. *Language of Colour in the Mediterranean.* Wiesbaden: Otto Harrassowitz.

Bornstein, Marc H. 1973a. "Color Vision and Color Naming: A Psychophysiological Hypothesis of Cultural Difference." *PB* 80:257–285.

———. 1973b. "The Psychophysical Component of Cultural Difference in Color Naming and Illusion Susceptibility." *Behavior Science Notes* 1:41–101.

———. 1975a. "The Influence of Visual Perception on Culture." *AA* 77:774–798.

———. 1975*b*. "Qualities of Color Vision in Infancy." *JEP* 19:401–419.

———. 1985*a*. "Colour-Name Versus Shape-Name Learning in Young Children." *JCL* 12:387–393.

———. 1985*b*. "On the Development of Color Naming in Young Children." *Brain and Language* 26:72–93.

———. 1987. "Perceptual Categories in Vision and Audition." In S. Harnad, ed., 287–300.

Bornstein, Marc H., W. Kessen, and S. Weiskopf. 1976. "The Categories of Hue in Infancy." *Science* 191:201–202.

Bornstein, Marc H., and Lawrence Marks. 1982. "Color Revisionism." *Psychology Today* 15 (1):64–73

Bortleson, C. J. 1972. " 'Color': A Nominal Definition." *Journal of Color and Appearance* 1:31–45.

Boster, James S. 1986. "Can Individuals Recapitulate the Evolutionary Development of Color Lexicons?" *Ethnology* 25:61–74.

Bouma, P. J. 1946. *Kleuren en kleurindrukken.* Amsterdam: Meulenhoff.

Bousfield, J. 1979. "The World as Seen as a Color Chart." In *Classifications in Their Social Context,* R. F. Ellen and D. Reason, eds., 195–220. New York: Academic Press.

Boynton, Robert M. 1979. *Human Color Vision.* New York: Holt, Rinehart and Winston.

———. 1988. "Color Vision." *ARP* 39:69–100.

Boynton, Robert M., and James Gordon. 1965. "Bezold-Brücke Hue Shift Measured by Color-Naming Technique." *JOSA* 55:78–86.

Boynton, Robert M., Robert E. MacLaury, and Keiji Uchikawa. 1989. "Centroids of Color Categories Compared by Two Methods." *CRA* 14:6–15.

Boynton, Robert M., and Conrad X. Olson. 1987. "Locating Basic Colors in the OSA Space." *CRA* 12:94–105.

———. 1990. "Salience of Chromatic Basic Color Terms Confirmed by Three Measures." *VR* 30:1311–1317.

Bragg, Lois. 1982. "Color Words in Beowulf." Paper presented at annual Patristic, Mediaeval and Renaissance Conference, Villanova Univ., Villanova, Penn. *Proceedings of the PMR Conference* 7:47–55.

Branstetter, Katherine B. 1977. "A Reconstruction of Proto-Polynesian Color Terminology." *AL* 19:1–27.

Brenner, Athalya. 1982. *Color Terms in the Old Testament.* Sheffield, England: Sheffield Academic Press.

Bright, William. 1952. "Linguistic Innovations in Karok." *IJAL* Native Text Series 18:53–62.

———. 1957. *The Karok Language.* UCPL 13. Berkeley: Univ. of California Press.

Broch, Harald B. 1974. "A Note on the Hare Indian Color Terms." *AL* 16:192–196.

Bromley, M. 1967. "The Linguistic Relationships of Grand Valley Dani: A Lexico-Statistical Classification." *Oceania* 37:286–308.

Brown, Cecil H. 1983. "Cool Hue Categories in Taracahitic Languages." *AE* 10:605–606.

Brown, Roger. 1976. "Reference: In Memorial Tribute to Eric Lenneberg." *Cognition* 4:125–153.

———. 1978. "A New Paradigm of Reference." In *Psychology and Biology of Language and Thought: Essays in Honor of Eric Lenneberg,* George A. Miller and Elizabeth Lenneberg, eds., 151–166. New York: Academic Press.

Brown, Roger, and Eric H. Lenneberg. 1954. "A Study in Language and Cognition." *JASP* 49:454–462.

Bruce, R. E. 1937. "Colour and Its Symbolism." *Occult Review* 64:30–38.

Bruce, Robert D. 1975, 1979. *Lacandon Dream Symbolism: Dream Symbolism and Interpretation among the Lacandon Mayas of Chiapas, Mexico.* Vol. I: *Dream Symbolism and Interpretation;* Vol. II: *Dictionary, Index and Classifications of Dream Symbols.* Mexico City: Ediciones Euroamericanas Klaus Thiele.

Brückner, A. 1957. *Słownik Etymologiczny Jezyka Polskiego.* Warsaw: Wiedza Powszechna.

Brugman, Claudia M. 1989. *The Story of Over: Polysemy, Semantics, and the Structure of the Lexicon.* New York: Garland.

Brumbough, R. S. 1951. "Colours of the Hemispheres in Plato's Myth of Er (*Republic* 616E)." *Classical Philology* 41:173–176.

Brumeister, August. 1859. "Homerisches glossarium von Ludwig Doederlein." *Neue Jahrbücher für Philologie, und Pädagogik* 79:160–171.

Bruner, Jerome S., O. R. Oliver, and P. M. Greenfield. 1967. *Studies in Cognitive Growth.* New York: John Wiley and Sons.

Brunner-Traut, Emma. 1977. "Farben." In *Lexikon der Ägyptologie,* vol. 2, W. Helck and W. Westendorf, eds., 117–128. Wiesbaden: Otto Harrassowitz.

Bruno, Vincent J. 1977. *Form and Color in Greek Painting.* New York: W. W. Norton and Company, 123.

Bryant, Alfred T. 1949. *The Zulu People: As They Were before the White Man Came.* Pietermaritzburg: Shuter and Shooter.

Buchholz, B. 1977. "Eine Magisterarbeit zu den Farbbezeichnungen im Finnishen und Deutschen." *Finnish-Ugrische Mitteilungen* 1:249–252.

Buck, C. D. 1949. *A Dictionary of Selected Synonyms in the Principal Indo-European Languages.* Chicago: Univ. of Chicago Press.

Bucke, Richard M., ed. 1947 [1901]. *Cosmic Consciousness: A Study in the Evolution of the Human Mind.* 13th ed. New York: E.P. Dutton (originally published by Innes and Sons, Philadelphia).

Bullough, E. 1907. "On the Apparent Heaviness of Colours: A Contribution to the Aesthetics of Colour." *BJP* 2 (2):111–123.

———. 1908. "The 'Perceptive Problem' in the Aesthetic Appreciation of Single Colours." *BJP* 2 (4):406–463.

Bulmer, R. H. N. 1968. "Karam Colour Categories." *Kivung* 1:120–133.

Burgess, Donald, Willett Kempton, and Robert E. MacLaury. 1983. "Tarahumara Color Modifiers: Category Structure Presaging Evolutionary Change." *AE* 10:133–149.

————. 1985. "Tarahumara Color Modifiers: Individual Variation and Evolutionary Change." In *Directions in Cognitive Anthropology*, J. Dougherty, ed., 49–72. Urbana: Univ. of Illinois Press.

Burling, Robbins. 1993. "Primate Calls, Human Language, and Nonverbal Communication." *CA* 34:25–53.

Burnley, J. D. 1976. "Middle English Colour Terminology and Lexical Structure." *Linguistische Berichte* 41:39–49.

Cairo, James Edward II. 1977. "The Neurophysiological Basis of Basic Color Terms." Diss., State Univ. of New York at Binghamton (UMI, 1981).

Callaghan, Catherine A. 1979. "Miwok Color Terms." *IJAL* 45:1–4.

Cameron, A. 1968. "The Old English Nouns of Colour; A Semantic Study." Baccalaureate thesis, Oxford Univ.

Campbell, Lyle. 1979. "Middle American Languages." In *Languages of Native America*, L. Campbell and M. Mithun, eds., 902–1000, Austin: Univ. of Texas Press.

Capelle, W. 1958. "Farbenbezeichnungen bei Theophrastus." *Rheinisches Museum* 101:1–41.

Caprile, Jean-Pierre. 1971. *La dénomination des couleurs chez les mbay de Moïssala: Une ethnie sara du sud du Tchad*. Bibliothèque de la Société pour l'Étude des Langues Africaines 26. Paris: SELAF (Klincksieck).

————. 1974. "La dénomination des 'couleurs': Méthode d'enquête avec application à une langue du Tchad, le mbay de Moïssala." In *Méthodes d'enquête et de description des langues sans tradition écrite*, 1–22. Nice: Colloques Internationaux des C.N.R.S. (Centre National de la Recherche Scientifique).

Carneiro, Robert L. 1970. "A Theory of the Origin of the State." *Science* 169 (3947): 733–738.

Carroll, John B., ed., 1956. *Language, Thought, and Reality*. Cambridge, Mass.: M.I.T. Press.

Casad, Eugene H. 1982. "Cora Locationals and Structured Imagery." Diss., Univ. of California, San Diego

Casad, Eugene H., and Ronald W. Langacker. 1985. "'Inside' and 'Outside' in Cora Grammar." *IJAL* 51:247–281.

Caskey-Sirmons, Leigh A. 1976. "An Analysis of Variation in Color Terminology among the Kashkuli Kuchek of Southern Iran." Thesis, Texas Tech Univ., Lubbock.

Caskey-Sirmons, Leigh A., and Nancy P. Hickerson. 1977. "Semantic Shift and Bilingualism: Variation in the Color Terms of Five Languages." *AL* 19:358–367.

Casson, Ronald W. 1994. "Russett, Rose, and Raspberry: The Development of English Secondary Color Terms." *JLA* 4:5–22.

Casson, Ronald W., and Peter M. Gardner. 1992. "On Brightness and Color Categories: Additional Data." *CA* 4:395–399.

Catlin, Jack, Carolyn Mervis, and Eleanor Rosch. 1975. "Development of the Structure of Color Categories." *Developmental Psychology* 11:54–60.

Centlivres-Demont, M., and P. Centlivres. 1978. "Dénomination de couleurs en milieu pluri-ethnique: l'exemple nord-afgan." In Tornay, ed., 259–284.

Cerbus, G., and R. Nichols. 1963. "Personality Variables and Response to Colour." *PB* 60:566–575.

Chandler, Albert R., and Edward N. Barnhart. 1938. *A Bibliography of Psychological and Experimental Aesthetics, 1864–1937.* Berkeley: Univ. of California Press. Reprinted 1979, New York: AMS Press.

Chang, J. J., and J. D. Carroll. 1980. "Three Are Not Enough: An INDSCAL Analysis Suggesting That Color Space Has Seven (± 1) Dimensions." *CRA* 5:193–206.

Chapanis, Alphonse. 1950. "Relationships between Age, Visual Acuity and Color Vision." *Human Biology* 22:1–33.

———. 1965. "Color Names for Color Space." *American Scientist* 53:327–346.

———. 1968. "Color Vision and Color Blindness." In *International Encyclopedia of the Social Sciences,* David L. Sills, ed., 16:329–336. New York: Macmillan and the Free Press.

Charencey, Charles Félix H. G. de. 1899. "Variété des noms de couleurs en basque." *Bulletin de la Société de linguistique de Paris* 11 (1898–1901), No. 1 (whole 47):53–55.

Chiri, M. 1953. *Bunrui Ainu-go jiten—Daiikkan shokubutsu-hen* (Dictionary of Ainu, vol. I: Plants). Tokyo: Nihon Jomin Bunka Kenkyūshō.

Chomsky, Noam. 1965. *Aspects of the Theory of Syntax.* Cambridge, Mass.: M.I.T. Press.

Christoffel, H. 1926. "Farbensymbolik." *Imago* 12:305–320.

Cian, V. 1894. "Del significato dei colori e dei fiori nel rinascimento italiano." *Gazzetta letteraria* 18:163–165.

Clark, Grahame. 1992. *Space, Time and Man: A Prehistorian's View.* Cambridge: Cambridge Univ. Press.

Clements, Forrest. 1930. "Racial Differences in Color-Blindness." *AJPA* 14:417–432.

Clerke, Agnes Mary. 1892. *Familiar Studies in Homer.* London: Longmans, Green, and Co.

Colby, B. N. 1966. "Ethnographic Semantics: A Preliminary Survey." *CA* 7:3–32.

Cole, R. A. 1952. "Adjectives of Light and Colour in Greek Lyric Poetry from Aleman to Bacchylides." Diss., Univ. of Dublin.

Coleman, Linda. 1975. "The Case of the Vanishing Presupposition." *BLS* 1:78–89.

Colenso, W. 1882. "On the Fine Perception of Colours Possessed by the Ancient Maoris." *TPNZI* 14:49–76.

Collier, George A. 1963. "Color Categories in Zinacantan." Honors thesis, Harvard Univ., Boston.

———. 1966. "Categorías de color en Zinacantan." In *Los Zinacantecos,* E. V. Vogt, ed., 414–432. Mexico City: Instituto nacional indigenista.

———. 1973. Review of Berlin and Kay (1969). *Language* 49:245–248.

Collier, George A., et al. 1976. "Further Evidence for Universal Color Categories." *Language* 52:884–890.

Color Group of Great Britain. 1972. "Color Bibliography." *Journal of Color and Appearance* 1:46–48.

Conklin, Harold C. 1955. "Hanunoó Color Categories." *SJA* 11:339–344.

———. 1972. *Folk Classification: A Topically Arranged Bibliography of Contemporary and Background References through 1971.* New Haven: Department of Anthropology, Yale Univ.

———. 1973. "Color Categorization" (Review of Berlin and Kay 1969). *AA* 75: 931–942.

Conley, K., and W. E. Cooper. 1981. "Conjoined Ordering of Color Terms by Children and Adults." *Studies in Language* 5:305–322.

Corbett, Greville, and Ian R. L. Davies. In press. "Linguistic and Behavioral Measures for Ranking Basic Colour Terms." In C. L. Hardin and L. Maffi, eds.

Corbett, Greville, and Gerry Morgan. 1988. "Colour Terms in Russian: Reflections of Typological Constraints in a Single Language." *JL* 24:31–64.

Córdova, Fray Juan de. 1942. *Vocabulario castellano-zapoteco.* Mexico City: Instituto nacional de antropología e historia, Secretaria de educación pública.

Cornsweet, Tom M. 1970. *Visual Perception.* New York: Academic Press.

Cotton, G. 1950. "Un équation sémantique: 'mouvement rapide' = lueur, éclat." *Les Études Classiques* 18:436–441.

Crawford, T. D. 1982. "Defining 'Basic Color Term'." *AL* 24 (3):338–343.

Cruse, D. A. 1977. "A Note on the Learning of Colour Names." *JCL* 4:305–311.

Cuervo Marquez, Carlos. 1924. "La percepción de los colores en algunas tribus indígenas de Colombia." *PICA* 20:49–51.

Cunliffe, Richard J. 1931. *A Lexicon of the Homeric Dialect.* London: Blackie and Sons.

Dahlgren, Kathleen. 1985. "Social Terms and Social Reality." *Folia Linguistica Historica* 6:107–125.

Dal, I. 1938. "German *brun* als epitheton von waffen." *Narsk Tidskrift for Sprogvidenskap* 9:219–230.

Dalton, John. 1798. "Extraordinary Facts Relating to the Vision of Colours with Observations." *Memoirs and Proceedings of the Literary and Philosophical Society of Manchester* 5:28–45.

Dana, Francis M. 1919. *The Ritual Significance of Yellow among the Romans.* Diss., Univ. of Pennsylvania.

D'Andrade, R., and M. Egan. 1974. "The Colors of Emotion." *AE* 1:49–63.

d'Ans, André-Marcel, and María Cortez Mondragón. 1973. "Términos de colores cashinahua (pano)." *Documento de Trabajo* 16 (April). Lima: Universidad Nacional Mayor de San Marcos, Centro de Investigación de Lingüística Aplicada.

Darwin, Charles. 1877. "Biographische Skizze eines kleinen Rindes." *Kosmos* 1 (1):367–376.

———. 1968 [1859]. *The Origin of Species by Means of Natural Selection.* Harmondsworth, U.K.: Penguin Books.

Davidoff, Jules. 1991. *Cognition through Color.* Cambridge, Mass.: M.I.T. Press.

Davies, I. R. L., G. G. Corbett, G. Laws, H. McGurk, A. E. St. G. Moss, and W. Smith. 1991. "Linguistic Basicness and Colour Information Processing." *International Journal of Psychology* 26:311–327.

Davies, I. R. L., C. MacDermid, G. G. Corbett, H. McGurk, D. Jerrett, T. Jerret, and P. Sowden. 1992. "Color Terms in Setswana: A Linguistic and Perceptual Approach." *Linguistics* 30:1065–1103.

Davies, J. Glyn. 1914. "The Welsh Bard and the Poetry of External Nature: From Llywarch Hen to Dafydd ab Gwilym." *THSC* Session 1912–1913:81–128.

d'Avino, R. 1958. "La visione del colore nella terminologia greca." *Ricerche linguistiche* 4:99–134.

Davis, M. Gerald. 1945. "Colour in Ronsard's Poetry." *The Modern Language Review* 40:95–103.

Davis, S. L. 1982. "Colour Classification and the Aboriginal Classroom." In *Application of Linguistics to Australian Aboriginal Contexts,* G. B. McKay and B. A. Sommers, eds., 68–77. Brisbane: ALAA.

Dawson, G. M. 1887. *Notes and Observations on the Kwakiool People of the Northern Part of Vancouver Island and Adjacent Coasts, Made During the Summer of 1885.* Fairfield, Wash.: Ye Galleon Press (1973).

Décsy, Gyula. 1981. "Alte und neue Farbennamen in Tamil." *Ural-Altaische Jahrbücher* 53:141–142.

Dedekind, Alexander. 1896. "Recherches sur la pourpre *oxybatta.*" *Archives de zoologie expérimentale* 4:481–516.

———. 1898. "Sur la fausse pourpre de anciens." *Archives de zoologie expérimentale* 6:70–78.

———, ed. 1898–1911. *Ein Beitrag zur Purpurkunde,* 4 vols. (1898, 1906, 1908, 1911). Berlin: Mayer und Müller.

Dehouve, Danièle. 1978. "Transformation de la dénomination des couleurs dans les langages dominées: Un cas mexicain." In Tornay, ed., 285–304.

Delitzsch, Franz J. 1878. "Der Talmud und die Farben," *Nord und Süd* 5:254–267.

———. 1888. *Iris. Farbenstudien und Blumenstücke.* Leipzig: Dorffling & Franke. Trans. 1889 by Alexander Cusin under the title *Iris: Studies in Color and Talks about Flowers.* Edinburgh: T. & T. Clark.

———. 1896. "Farben in der Bible." *Realencyklopädie für protestantische Theologie und Kirche* 5:755–762.

Deregowski, Jan B. 1967. "The Horizontal-Vertical Illusion and the Ecological Hypothesis." *International Journal of Psychology* 2:269–273.

———. 1989. "Real Space and Represented Space: Cross-Cultural Perspectives." *BBS* 12:51–119.

Derrig, Sandra. 1978. "Metaphor in the Color Lexicon." *CLS (Parasession on the Lexicon)* 14:85–96.

Derrington, A. M., J. Krauskopf, and P. Lennie. 1984. "Chromatic Mechanisms in Lateral Geniculate Nucleus of Macaque." *Journal of Physiology* 357:241–265.

Descoeudes, A. 1930. *Le développement de l'enfant de 2 à 7 ans.* Paris: Neuchâtel.

De Valois, Russell L. 1965. Analysis and Coding of Color Vision in the Primate Visual System. *Cold Spring Harbor Symposium on Quantitative Biology* 30:567–579.

————. 1971. "Contribution of Different Lateral Geniculate Cell Types to Visual Behavior." *VR* (supplement) 3:383–396.

————. 1973. "Central Mechanisms of Colour Vision." *Handbook of Sensory Physiology,* vol. VIII, part A. Berlin: Springer-Verlag.

De Valois, Russell L., and Israel Abramov. 1966. "Color Vision." *ARP* 17:337–362.

De Valois, Russell L., Israel Abramov, and Gerald H. Jacobs. 1966. "Analysis of Response Patterns of LGN Cells." *JOSA* 56:966–977.

De Valois, Russell L., and Karen K. De Valois. 1975. "Neural Coding of Color." *Handbook of Perception,* vol. V, *Seeing,* E. C. Carterette and M. P. Friedman, eds., 119–166. New York: Academic Press.

————. 1993. "A Multi-Stage Color Model." *VR* 33:153–165.

De Valois, Russell L., and G. H. Jacobs. 1968. "Primate Color Vision." *Science* 162:533–540.

De Valois, Russell L., and Richard T. Marrocco. 1973. "Single Cell Analysis of Saturation Discrimination in the Macaque." *VR* 13:701–711.

De Valois, Russell L., M. A. Webster, Karen K. De Valois, and B. Ingelbach. 1986. "Temporal Properties of Brightness and Color Induction." *VR* 26:887–897.

de Vries, Jan. 1965. "Rood—Wit—Zwart." In *Kleine Schriften* by J. de Vries, 351–359. Berlin: Walter de Gruyter.

Dimmick, Forrest L., and Margaret R. Hubbard. 1939. "The Spectral Location of Psychologically Unique Yellow, Green, and Blue." *AJP* 52:242–254.

Disselhoff, Hans-Dietrich. 1931. *Die Landschaft in der Mexikanischen Lyrik: Mit einer Einführung in die Eigenart mexikanischen Schrifttums. (Beiträge zur hispanoamerikanischen Literaturgeschichte).* Studien über Amerika und Spanien, Philologisch-literarische Reihe 3. Halle (Saale): Max Niemeyer (Diss., Würzburg).

Dixon, R. M. W. 1982. *Where Have All the Adjectives Gone?: And other Essays in Semantics and Syntax.* Berlin: Walter de Gruyter.

Dixon, Roland B. 1899. "The Color-Symbolism of the Cardinal Points." *JAFL* 12:10–16.

Dornes, Jacques. 1978. "Les races de couleurs: une optique jörai (Viet-Nam)." In Tornay, ed., 369–399.

Dougherty, Janet W. D. 1975. "A Universalist Analysis of Variation and Change in Color Semantics." Diss., Univ. of California, Berkeley.

————. 1977. "Color Categorization in West Futunese: Variability and Change." In *Sociocultural Dimensions of Language Change,* B.G. Blount and M. Sanches, eds., 103–118. New York: Academic Press.

————. 1978a. "Error Types and Their Significance in Children's Responses." In *New Approaches to Language Acquisition,* B. Kettemann and R. St. Clair, eds., 33–48. Tübingen: Günter Narr.

————. 1978b. "On the Significance of a Sequence in the Acquisition of Basic Color Terms." In *Advances in the Psychology of Language,* R. Campbell and P. Smith, eds., 133–148. New York: Plenum Press.

————. 1978c. "Salience and Relativity in Classification." *AE* 5:66–80.

Douglas, Mary. 1966. *Purity and Danger: An Analysis of Concepts of Pollution and Taboo.* London: Routledge and Kegan Paul; New York: Praeger.

Dourgnon, M. Boll-J. 1946. *Le secret des couleurs.* Paris: Presses Universitaires de France.

Dreher, B., Y. Fukada, and R. W. Rodiek. 1976. "Identification, Classification, and Anatomical Segregation of Cells with X-like and Y-like Properties in the Lateral Geniculate Nucleus of Old-World Primates." *Journal of Physiology* 38:467–474.

Dronke, Peter. 1974. "Tradition and Innovation in Medieval Western Colour-Imagery." *EY* (1972) 41:52–107.

Duby, Gertrude. 1961. *Chiapas Indígena.* Mexico City: Universidad Nacional Autónoma de México.

Ducatez, Guy, and Jacky Ducatez. 1980. "Formation des dénominations de couleur et de luminosité en arabe classique et pre-classique. Essai de périodisation selon une approche linguistique et anthropologique." *Peuples Méditerranéens* 10:139–172.

Duczmal, S. 1979. "A Contrastive Semantic Analysis of Colour Adjectives in Polish and English." *PSCL* 9:181–191.

Dumézil, Georges. 1958. *L'idéologie tripartie des Indo-Européens.* Collection Latomus 31. Brussels: Latomus (Revue d'Études Latines).

Duncan, R. M. 1975. "Color Words in Medieval Spanish." In *Studies in Honor of Lloyd A. Kasten,* T. S. Beardsley, et al., eds., 53–71. Madison, Wis.: Hispanic Seminary of Medieval Studies.

Dunn, John A. 1985. "Tsimshian Colourological Semiotics." Paper presented at the 20th Annual International Conference on Salish and Neighboring Languages, Vancouver. MS, Univ. of Oklahoma.

Durbin, Marshall. 1972. "Basic Terms—Off Color?" *Semiotica* 4:257–288.

Dyson-Hudson, Neville. 1965. *Karimojong Politics.* Oxford: Clarendon Press.

Eco, Humberto. 1985. "How Culture Conditions the Colours We See." In *On Signs,* Marshall Blonsky, ed., 157–175. Baltimore: Johns Hopkins Univ. Press.

Einstein, Albert. 1961 [1920]. *Relativity: The Special and the General Theory.* R. W. Lawson, trans. New York: Crown Publishers. This text, first published by Methuen [London, 1920] in English, was translated from a MS comprising two earlier published works, which apparently never appeared together in German.

Eisiminger, Sterling. 1979. "Colorful Language." *Verbatim* 5 (1):1–3.

Ekman, Gösta. 1954. "Dimensions of Color Vision." *Journal of Psychology* 38: 467–474.

Ellis, Havelock. 1896. "The Colour-Sense in Literature." *Contemporary Review* 69 (January–June):714–729.

————. 1900. "The Psychology of Red." *Popular Science Monthly* 62:365–375, 517–526.

Ember, Melvin. 1978. "Size of Color Lexicon: Interaction of Cultural and Biological Factors." *AA* 80:364–367.

England, Nora C. 1992. *Autonomía de los idiomas mayas: Historia e identidad.* Guatemala City: Editorial Cholsamaj.

Ervin, Susan M. 1961. "Semantic Shift in Bilingualism." *AJP* 74:233–241.

Espejo Muriel, María del Mar. 1990. *Los nombres de los colores en español: Estudio de lexicología estructural.* (Publicaciones de la Cátedra de Historia de la Lengua Española, Serie Lingüística). Granada: Universidad de Granada.

Essock, S. 1977. "Color Perception and Color Classification." In *Language Learning by a Chimpanzee,* Duane Rumbaugh, ed., 207–224. New York: Academic Press.

Euler, Karl. 1903. "Über die angebliche Farbenblindheit Homers." *Jahresbericht des Königlichen Gymnasiums zu Marburg für das Schuljahr 1902/1903* 70:1–21. Marburg: R. Friedrichs.

Evans-Pritchard, E. E. 1933–1935. "Imagery in Ngok Dinka Cattle Names." *Bulletin of the School of Oriental Studies* 7:623–628.

———. 1937. *Witchcraft, Oracles and Magic among the Azande.* Oxford: Clarendon Press.

———. 1969. *The Nuer: A Description of the Modes of Livelihood and Political Institutions of a Nilotic People.* Oxford: Clarendon Press.

Ewald, A. 1890. *Die Farbenbewegung kulturgeschichtliche Untersuchungen.* Berlin: Weidman.

Ewer, Mary Anita. 1933. *A Survey of Mystical Symbolism.* New York: Macmillan (Thesis, Columbia Univ.).

Eysenck, H. U. 1941. "A Critical and Experimental Study of Color Preferences." *AJP* 54:385–394.

Fäger, Bustao. 1877. "Einiges über Farben und Farbensinn." *Kosmos* 1 (1):486–495.

Falk, Dean. 1992. *Braindance.* New York: Henry Holt and Company.

Faris, James C. 1972. *Nuba Personal Art.* Toronto: Univ. of Toronto Press.

Faymonville, Karl. 1900. *Die Purpurfärberei der verschiedenen Kulturvölker des klassischen Altertums und der frühchristlichen Zeit.* Heidelberg: Wiese (Diss., Univ. of Heidelberg).

Fergenbaum, A. 1959. "Le terme 'glaucome', son histoire et son premier usage populaire connu dans l'antiquité pour désigner une certaine espèce de cécité." *Le Scalpel* 112:396–400.

Ferreira Brito, Lucinda, and Elizabeth Angélica S. Siqueira. 1989. "Termos básicos para cores em línguas dos sinais." In *Anais do IX–X Encontro nacional de lingüística,* 508–20. Rio de Janeiro: Pontíficia Universidade Católica.

Fijalkow, Jacques. 1974. "Ordre lexical et formation des concepts de couleur chez l'enfant." *Psychologie Française* 19:199–205.

Filliozat, J. 1957. "Classement des couleurs et des lumières en sanskrit." In Meyerson, 303–311.

Fillmore, Charles A. 1975. "An Alternative to Checklist Theories of Meaning." *BLS* 1:123–131.

———. 1982. "Frame Semantics." In *Linguistics in the Morning Calm,* The Linguistic Society of Korea, ed., 111–137. Seoul: Hanshin.

Filton Brown, A. D. 1962. "Black Wine." *Classical Review* 12:192–195.

Findeis, Richard. 1908. "Über das Alter und die Entstehung der indogermanischen

Farbennamen." *Jahresbericht des K. K. Staats-Gymnasiums in Triest über das Schuljahr 1907–1908* 58:1–27. Trieste: Buchbruderei des Österreichischen Lloyd.

Forbes, Isabel. 1979. "The Terms *Brun* and *Marron* in Modern Standard French." *JL* 15:295–305.

Forge, Anthony. 1970. "Learning to See in New Guinea." In *Socialization: The Approach from Social Anthropology,* Philip Mayer, ed., 269–291. Association of Social Anthropologists Monograph 8. London: Tavistock.

Franciscan Fathers, The. 1910. *An Ethnographic Dictionary on the Navaho Language.* Arizona: Saint Michaels.

Franklin, Christine L. 1901. "Color Introspection on the Part of the Eskimo." *PRv* 8:396–402.

French, Chris N. 1992. *The Computer Book of Color.* Manchester: UMIST Eye System, Optometry and Vision Sciences.

Friedl, Erika. 1979. "Colors and Culture Change in Southwestern Iran." *JLS* 8:51–68.

Friedrich, Johannes. 1946. *Hethitisches Elementarbuch.* Lesestücke in Transkription, part 2. Heidelberg: Carl Winter.

Frish, Jack A. 1972. "Mohawk Color Terms." *AL* 14:307–10.

Frontispiece. 1900. Professor R. S. Woodworth, President of the American Association for the Advancement of Science. *Popular Science Monthly* 57 (4):338.

Frumkina, Revekka M. 1984. *Tsvet, Smysl, Skhodstvo: Aspekty Psikholingvisticheskogo Analiza.* Moscow: Nauka.

Frumkina, Revekka M., and Aleksei V. Mikheev. 1983. "Vozmozhnosti sopostavitel'nogo izucheniia leksiki v èksperimente." *Sŭpostavitelno Ezikoznanie* 8 (2):51–63.

Fukui, Katsuyoshi. 1979. "Cattle Colour Symbolism and Inter-Tribal Homicide among the Bodi." In *Warfare among East African Herders: Papers presented at the First International Symposium, National Museum of Ethnology, Osaka, 1977.* K. Fukui and D. Turton, eds., Senri Ethnological Studies 3, 147–177. Osaka: National Museum of Ethnology.

Fuld, K., B. R. Wooten, and J. J. Whalen. 1981. "The Elemental Hues of Short-Wave and Extraspectral Lights." *Perceptual Psychophysics* 29:317–322.

Furrell, James W. 1885. "Light from the East on the Colour Question." *TNC* 17:321–330.

Gage, John. 1978. "Colour in History: Relative and Absolute." *Art History* 1:104–13 0.
———. 1995. "Colour and Culture." In T. Lamb and J. Bourriau, eds., 175–193.

Gallavotti, C. 1957. "Nomi di colori in Miceneo." *La parola del passato* 12:5–22.

Galloway, Brent D. 1993. *A Grammar of Upriver Halkomelem.* UCPL 96. Berkeley: Univ. of California Press.

Galton, Francis. 1885. "On the Anthropometric Laboratory at the Late International Health Exhibition." *JAI* 14:frontispiece, 205–221.

Gamst, Frederick. 1975. "Rethinking Leach's Structural Analysis of Color and Instructional Categories in Traffic Control Signals." *AE* 2:271–295.

Gardner, Peter M. 1966. "Ethnoscience and Universal Domains: A Culture without Color Categories." Referenced in Berlin and Kay 1969. MS in possession of author, Univ. of Missouri, Columbia.

———. 1972. "The Paliyans." In *Hunters and Gatherers Today,* M. G. Bicchieri, ed., 404–415. New York: Holt, Rinehart and Winston.

Garmadi Le Cloirec, Juliette. 1976. "La dénomination des couleurs en arabe tunisien et en français: Essai d'étude contrastive." *La Linguistique* 12:55–86.

Garro, Linda. 1986. "Language, Memory, and Focality: A Re-examination." *AA* 88: 128–136.

Gartell, Richard B. 1971. Review of Berlin and Kay 1969. *Journal of Communication* 21:190–191.

Gatschet, Albert S. 1879a. "Farbenbenennungen in nordamerikanischen Sprachen." *ZE* 11:293–302.

———. 1879b. "Adjectives of Color in Indian Languages." *American Naturalist* 13: 475–485.

Geddes, W. R. 1946. "The Color Sense of Fijian Natives." *BJP (General)* 37:30–36.

Geeraerts, Dirk, Stefan Grondelaers, and Peter Bakema. 1994. *The Structure of Lexical Variation: Meaning, Naming, and Context.* Berlin: Mouton de Gruyter.

Geertz, Clifford. 1973. *The Interpretation of Cultures.* New York: Basic Books.

Geiger, Lazarus. 1869. *Der Ursprung der Sprache.* Stuttgart: J. G. Cotta (2d ed. 1878).

———. 1871. *Zur Entwickelungsgeschichte der Menschheit,* Stuttgart: J. G. Cotta. Trans. 1880 by David Ascher under the title *Contributions to the History of the Development of the Human Race* (London: Trübner).

———. 1872. *Ursprung und Entwickelung der menschlichen Sprache und Vernunft.* 2 vols. Stuttgart: J.G. Cotta.

Geiger, Paul. 1916. "Die blaue Farbe bei den Totenbräuchen." In *Festschrift für Eduard Hoffmann-Krayer,* Hanns Bächtold, ed. *Schweizerisches Archiv für Volkskunde* 20:156–159.

Gellatly, Angus. 1995. "Colourful Whorfian Ideas: Linguistic and Cultural Influences on the Perception and Cognition of Colour, and on the Investigation of Them." *Mind and Language* 10:199–225.

Gernet, Jacques. 1957. "L'expression de la couleur en chinois." In Meyerson, ed., 295–301.

Gernet, Louis 1957. "Dénomination et perception des couleurs chez les grecs." In Meyerson ed., 313–326.

Gerschel, L. 1966. "Couleur et teinture chez divers peuples indo-européens." *Annales* 21:607–632.

Gesche, Irma. 1927. "The Color Preferences of One Thousand One Hundred and Fifty-two Mexican Children." *Journal of Comparative Psychology* 7:297–311.

Giacalone Ramat, Anna. 1978. "Strutturazione della terminologia dei colori nei dialetti sardi." *Italia Linguistica Nuova ed Antica* 2:163–181.

Gibson, K. S., and F. K. Harris. 1927. "The Lovibond Color System, I: A Spectrophotometric Analysis of the Lovibond Glasses." *Scientific Papers of the Bureau of Standards* 22:547 (whole):1–46. Washington, D.C.: Government Printing Office.

Gimple, Mark. 1979. "Notes on Basic Color Terms (BCT) in Uto-Aztecan Languages, and Speculation on the BCT System of Proto-Uto-Aztecan." MS in possession of author, Department of Linguistics, Univ. of California, Berkeley.

Gipper, H. 1964. "Purpur." *Glotta* 42:39–69.

Gladstone, William E. 1858. *Studies on Homer and the Homeric Age,* vol. III. London: Oxford Univ. Press.

———. 1877. "The Colour-Sense." *TNC* 2:366–388.

Gleason, H. A. 1961. *An Introduction to Descriptive Linguistics.* New York: Holt, Rinehart and Winston.

Göbel, A. 1855. "Das Meer in den homerischen Dichtungen." *Eine philologische Untersuchung. Zeitschrift für Gymnasialwesen* 9:513–545.

Godlove, I. H. 1956. *Bibliography on Color, 1936–54.* Cleveland: Inter-Society Color Council.

Goethe, Johann Wolfgang von. 1810. *Zur Farbenlehre.* 2 vols and atlas. Tübingen: J. G. Cotta. Trans. 1840 by Charles L. Eastlake under the title *Goethe's Theory of Colours* (London: J. Murray); trans. 1970 by D. B. Judd under the title *Theory of Colors* (Cambridge, Mass.: M.I.T. Press).

Goetz, K. E. 1905. "Weiss und Schwarz bei den Römern." *Festschrift 25 jährigen Stiftungsfest des Historische-Philologischen.* Munich: Verlag Universität München.

Goffman, Erving. 1974. *Frame Analysis.* New York: Harper and Row.

Gombert, Jean E. 1992. *Metalinguistic Development.* Chicago: Univ. of Chicago Press.

Gómez, P. Aniceto M. 1933. "Estudios de la lengua Cora." *Investigaciones lingüísticas* 1:110–111.

Goodman, J. S. 1963. "Malayalam Color Categories." *AL* 5:1–12.

Goodman, Nelson. 1972. "Seven Strictures on Similarity." In *Problems and Projects,* N. Goodman, ed., 437–447. New York: Bobbs-Merrill.

Goodwin, Charles. In press. "The Blackness of Black: Color Categories as Situated Practice." In *Discourse, Tools and Reasoning,* Lauren B. Resnick, Roger Saljo, and Clotilde Pontecorvo, eds. Berlin: Springer-Verlag.

Goody, Jack. 1977. *The Domestication of the Savage Mind.* Cambridge: Cambridge Univ. Press.

Gottschalk, H. B. 1964. "The De Coloribus and Its Author." *Hermes* 92:59–85.

Gould, James L., and Peter Marler. 1987. "Learning by Instinct." *SA* 255 (1):74–85.

Gouras, Peter, ed. 1991. *The Perception of Color.* Vision and Visual Dysfunction 6. Boca Raton: CRC Press.

Gouras, Peter, and H. Eggers. 1984. "Hering's Opponent Color Channels Do Not Exist in the Primate Retinogeniculate Pathway." *Ophthalmic Research* 16:31–35.

Gradwohl, Roland. 1963. *Die Farben im Alten Testament.* Berlin: Alfred Töpelmann.

Graham, Daryl A. 1994. *Sex Specific Differences in Describing Color.* Honours Thesis, Univ. of Regina, Saskatchewan, Canada.

Granville, Walter C., Dorothy Nickerson, and Carl E. Foss. 1943. "Trichromatic

Specifications for Intermediate and Special Colors of the Munsell System." *JOSA* 33:376–384.

Greenfeld, Philip J. 1977. "The Semantics and Syntax of White Mountain Apache Basic Color Terms." MS: San Diego State Univ., Department of Anthropology. Pp. 34.

———. 1980. "Evolutionary Change in the Athapaskan Color Term System." Paper presented at the Symposium on Athapaskan Comparative Linguistics and Language Planning, Linguistic Society of America, Univ. of New Mexico, July 1980. MS: San Diego State Univ. Pp. 20.

———. 1986. "What Is Grey, Brown, and Sometimes Purple: The Range of "Wild-Card" Color Terms." *AA* 88:908–916.

Greenfield, Patricia M. 1972. "Oral or Written Language: The Consequences for Cognitive Development in Africa, the United States and England." *Language and Speech* 15:169–178.

Grimes, Barbara F., ed. 1984. *Languages of the World: Ethnologue.* Tenth ed. Dallas, Texas: Wycliffe Bible Translators.

Grossmann, Maria. 1983. "Analisi semantica dei termini di colore nella Lingua Ungherese." In *Scritti Linguistici in onore di Giovan Battista Pellegrini,* vol. 2, 1331–1356. Pisa: Pacini.

———. 1988. *Colori e lessico: Studi sulla struttura semantica degli aggettivi di colores in catalano, castigliano, italiano, romeno, latino e ungherese.* Tübingen Beiträge zur Linguistik 310. Tübingen: Gunter Narr.

Guillaumont, A. 1957. "La désignation des couleurs en hébreu et en araméen." In Meyerson, ed., 339–348.

Gummere, Francis B. 1899. "On the Symbolic Use of the Colors Black and White in Germanic Tradition." *Haverford College Studies* 1:112–162 (Haverford, Penn.).

Gutia, I. 1952. "Senso del colore e sua expressione in Ungaretti." *Convivium* 20:641–652.

Haas, Mary. 1970. Letter to Paul Kay re Creek and Natchez color. WCS files.

Hacker, P. M. S. 1986. "Are Secondary Qualities Relative?" *Mind* 95 (whole 378): 180–197.

Haegerström-Portnoy, Gunilla. 1990. "Color Vision." In *Principles and Practice of Pediatric Optometry,* A. A. Rosenbloom and M. W. Morgan, eds., 449–466. Philadelphia: J. B. Lippincott Company.

Hage, Per, and Kristen Hawkes. 1975. "Binumarien Color Categories." *Ethnology* 24:287–300.

Hale, Ken, et al. 1992. "Endangered Languages." *Language* 68:1–42.

Halleux, Robert. 1969. "Lapis-lazuli, azurite ou pâte de verre? A propos de *kuwano* et *kuwanowoko* dans les tablettes mycéniennes." *Studi micenei ed egeo-analici* 9:47–66.

Hallpike, Christopher R. 1979. *Foundations of Primitive Thought.* Oxford: Clarendon Press.

Halsey, Rita M., and Alphonse Chapanis. 1951. "On the Number of Absolutely Identifiable Spectral Hues." *JOSA* 41:1057–1058.

Hamayon, R. 1978. "Des fards, des moeurs et des couleurs." In Tornay, ed., 207–247.

Hamp, Eric P. 1971. "Some Colour Words in -no-." *IJSLP* 14:1–4.

———. 1980*a*. On Participial **-do-* and Verbs and Adjectives and Colours." In *Wege zur universalien Forschung: Sprachwissenschaftliche Beiträge zum 60. Geburtstag von Hansjakob Seiler,* G. Brettschneider and C. Lehmann, eds., 268–273. Tübingen: Gunter Narr.

———. 1980*b*. "Notes on Proto-Polynesian Colours from K. B. Branstetter, *Anthropological Linguistics* 19: 1977." *AL* 22:390–391.

———. 1982 "On Some Color Terms in Baltic and Slavic." In *Slavic Linguistics and Poetics: Studies for Edward Stankiewicz on His 60th Birthday,* K. Naylor, H. I. Aronson, B. J. Darden, and A. M. Schenker, eds. *IJSLP* 25/26:187–192.

———. 1984. "Armenian *Dalar* 'Green', ϑαλερός 'Moist'." *Die Sprache: Zeitschrift für Sprachwissenschaft* 30:156–159.

Harbin, S. P., and J. E. Williams. 1966. "Conditioning of Color Connotations." *PMS* 22:217–218.

Hardin, Clyde L. 1988. *Color for Philosophers: Unweaving the Rainbow.* Indianapolis/Cambridge, Mass.: Hackett Publishing Co.

———. 1990. "Why Color?" In *Perceiving, Measuring, and Using Color: Proceedings, SPIE/International Society for Optical Engineers, 15–16 February, 1990, Santa Clara, Calif.,* vol. 1250, Michael H. Brill, ed., 293–300. Bellingham, Wash.: SPIE.

———. 1992. "The Virtues of Illusion." In Tolliver, ed., 371–382.

———. 1993. "Van Brakel and the Not-So-Naked Emperor." *BJPS* 44:137–50.

Hardin, Clyde L., and Luisa Maffi, eds. In press. *Color Categories in Thought and Language.* Cambridge: Cambridge Univ. Press.

Hardman, Martha J. 1981. "Jaqaru Color Terms." *IJAL* 47:66–68.

Hargrave, Susanne K. 1982. "A Report on Colour Term Research in Five Aboriginal Languages." *Work Papers of SIL-AAB,* Series B:8:201–226. Darwin: Summer Institute of Linguistics, Australian Aborigines Branch.

Harkness, Sara. 1973. "Universal Aspects of Learning Color Codes: A Study in Two Cultures." *Ethos* 1:175–200.

Harnad, Stevan, ed. 1987. *Categorical Perception.* Cambridge: Cambridge Univ. Press.

Harris, J. R. 1961. *Lexicographical Studies in Ancient Egyptian Minerals.* Publication 54, Deutsche Akademie der Wissenschaften, Institut für Orientforschung. Berlin: Akademie.

Harrison, Bernard. 1973. *Form and Content.* New York: Barnes and Noble.

Hattori, Shiroo. 1964. *Ainugo hoogen jiten* (Ainu Dialect Dictionary). Tokyo: Iwanami Shooten.

Hay, David R. 1846. *A Nomenclature of Colours Applicable to the Arts and Natural Sciences, to Manufactures, and Other Purposes of General Utility.* 2d ed. Edinburgh: W. Blackwood and Sons.

Hays, David G., et al. 1972. "Color Term Salience." *AA* 74:1107–1121.

Hazaël-Massieux, M.-C. 1973. "Note à propos du système des couleurs dans quelques langues de la République du Congo." Bulletin du Centre de Linguistique Appliquée et de Littérature Orale. *Dimi* 1:108–123.

Heider, Eleanor Rosch. 1971. "'Focal' Color Areas and the Development of Color Names." *Developmental Psychology* 4:447–455.

———. 1972*a*. "Probabilities, Sampling, and Ethnographic Method: The Case of Dani Colour Names." *Man* 7:448–466.

———. 1972*b*. "Universals of Color Naming and Memory." *JEP* 93:10–20.

Heider, Eleanor Rosch, and Donald C. Oliver. 1972. "The Structure of the Color Space in Naming and Memory for Two Languages." *Cognitive Psychology* 3:337–354.

Heider, Karl G. 1972. *The Dani of West Irian: An Ethnographic Companion to the Film* DEAD BIRDS. New York: Warner Modular Publications.

Heine, Bernd, Ulrike Claudi, and Friederike Hünnemeyer. 1991. *Grammaticalization: A Conceptual Framework.* Chicago: The Univ. of Chicago Press.

Heinrich, Albert C. 1972. "A Non-European System of Colour Classification." *AL* 14:220–227.

———. 1974. "Colour Classification of Some Central Canadian Eskimos." *Arctic Anthropology* 11:68–72.

———. 1977. "Some Notes on Central Eskimo Color Terminology." In *Language and Thought,* W. McCormack and S. Wurm, eds., 45–59. The Hague: Mouton.

———. 1978. "Changing Anthropological Perspectives on Color Naming Behavior." *Journal of Psychological Anthropology* 1:341–363.

Helmholtz, Hermann L. F. von. 1856–1866. *Handbuch der physiologischen Optik.* Hamburg: L. Voss. The publisher brought out a second edition in 17 parts (1886–1896, Arthur P. König, ed.) and a third (1909–1911, A. Gullstrand, J. von Kries, and W. Nagel, eds.,) in 3 volumes. The third edition was translated and edited by J. P. C. Southall in 1924 under the title *Helmholtz's Treatise on Physiological Optics* (Rochester, N.Y.: Optical Society of America).

Hering, Ewald. 1920 [1878]. *Grundzüge der Lehre vom Lichtsinn.* Berlin: Springer-Verlag. Edited and expanded posthumously in 1920 from the original 1878 *Zur Lehre vom Lichtsinne* (Vienna: Carl Gerold's Söhn). The 1920 edition was translated in 1964 by Leo M. Hurivich and Dorothea Jameson as *Outlines of a Theory of the Light Sense* (Cambridge, Mass.: Harvard Univ. Press).

Hermann, Alfred. 1969. "Farbe." In *Reallexicon für Antike und Christentum,* vol. VIII, T. Klauser et al., eds., 358–447. Stuttgart: Hiersemann.

Herne, Alf A. G. 1954. *Die slavischen Farbenbenennungen: Eine semasiologische etymologische Untersuchung.* Uppsala: Almqvist and Wiksells.

Hersh, H. M., and A. A. Caramazza. 1976. "A Fuzzy-Set Approach to Modifiers and Vagueness in Natural Languages." *JEP* 105:254–276.

Hess, J.-J. 1920. "Die Farbbezeichnungen bei innerarabischen Beduinenstämmen." *Der Islam* 10:74–86.

Hewes, Gordon W. 1992. Comment on MacLaury 1992*a*. *CA* 33:163.

Hickerson, Nancy. 1953. "Ethnolinguistic Notes from Lexicons of Lokono (Arawak)." *IJAL* 19:181–190.

———. 1971. Review of Berlin and Kay (1969). *IJAL* 37:257–270.

———. 1972. "Murray Island Color Terms: W. H. R. Rivers, 1901." In *From Sound to Discourse: Papers from the 1971 Mid-American Linguistics Conference,* Daniel G. Hays and Donald M. Lance, eds., 206–213. Columbia, Mo.: Linguistics Area Program, Univ. of Missouri.

———. 1975. "Two Studies of Color: Implications for Cross-Cultural Comparability of Semantic Categories." In *Linguistics and Anthropology: In Honor of Carl F. Voeglin,* M. D. Kinkade, K. L. Hale, and O. Werner, eds., 3–30. Lisse: Peter De Ridder Press.

———. 1980*a.* Review of Tornay, ed. (1978). *Language in Society* 9:255–267.

———. 1980*b.* "Naturalness vs. Arbitrariness in the Domain of Color." In *Semiotics 1980,* M. Herzfeld and M. D. Lenhart, eds., 217–226. New York: Plenum.

———. 1983. "Gladstone's Ethnolinguistics: The Language of Experience in the Nineteenth Century." *JAR* 39:26–41.

———. 1988. "A Reconstruction of Lokono Color Terms." Paper presented at 46th International Congress of Americanists, Amsterdam.

Hilbert, David R. 1987. *Color and Color Perception: A Study in Anthropocentric Realism.* Stanford: Center for the Study of Language and Information.

———. 1992. "What is Color Vision?" In Tolliver, ed., 351–370.

Hill, Clifford A. 1975. "Variation in the Use of 'Front' and 'Back' in Bilingual Speakers." *BLS* 1:196–206.

Hill, Jane H. 1992. "The Flower World of Old Uto-Aztecan." *JAR* 48:117–144.

Hill, Jane H., and Kenneth C. Hill. 1970. "Uto-Aztecan Color Terminology." *AL* 12:232–238.

Hill, Jane H., and Robert E. MacLaury. 1995. "The Terror of Montezuma: Aztec History, Vantage Theory, and the Category of 'Person'." In Taylor and MacLaury, eds., 277–329.

Hinds, John V. 1974. "Make Mine BURAKKU." *Language Research* 10:92–108.

Hjelmslev, Louis. 1953. *Prolegomena to a Theory of Language.* Univ. of Indiana Publications in Anthropology and Linguistics 7. Baltimore: Waverly Press.

Hoijer, Harry. 1958. "The Athapascan Languages." In *Studies in the Athapascan Languages,* H. Hoijer, ed., 1–29. UCPL 29. Berkeley: Univ. of California Press.

Hollander, Camilla. 1966. "Field-Work on Color Concepts." Fourth Conference of Nordic Anthropologists, Stockholm, 1965. Supplement to *Ethnos* 31:92–98.

Hollenbach, Barbara E. 1969. "A Note on Concepts of Political Geography." *IJAL* 35:263–264.

Hollingworth, H. L. 1913. "Judgments of Similarity and Difference." *PRv* 20:271.

Hollins, Mark, and Elizabeth K. Kelley. 1988. "Spatial Updating in Blind and Sighted People." *Perception and Psychophysics* 43:380–388.

Holmer, Nils M. 1956. "Amerindian Color Semantics." *International Anthropological and Linguistics Review* 2:158–166.

Holmgren, Alarik F. 1877. *Om Färbenblindheten i dess Förhållande till Jernvögstrafken och Sjöväsendet.* Uppsala: E. Berlings. Translated anonymously into French under the title *De la cécité des couleurs dans ses rapports avec les chemins de fer et la marine* (Stockholm: Imprimerie Central, 1877).

———. 1878. "Color-Blindness in Its Relation to Accidents by Rail and Sea." Trans.

from the French of Holmgren 1877 by M. L. Duncan. *ARSI for the Year 1877:* 131–195.

Hoogshagen, Searle, and Hilda Halloran de Hoogshagen. 1993. *Diccionario Mixe de Coatlán,* Apéndice E: "Los Colores," 421–427. Vocabularios Indígenas 32. Mariano Silva y Aceves Series. Tucson: Summer Institute of Linguistics.

Hopkins, E. W. 1883. "Words for Color in the Rig Veda." *American Journal of Philology* 4:166–191.

Houston, H. E., and W. W. Washburn. 1907. "On the Naming of Colors." *American Journal of Psychology* 18:519–523.

Hull, Elaine M. 1967. "Corticofugal Influence in the Macaque Lateral Geniculate Nucleus." Diss., Indiana Univ., Bloomington.

Hulstaert, G. 1969. "Les Couleurs chez les mongo." *Bulletin des Séances de l'Académie Royale des Sciences d'Outre-mer* (Classe des Sciences Morales et Politiques) 2:236–237.

Humboldt, Alexander T. von. 1814–1829. *Relation historique du voyage aux régiones équinoxiales du nouveau continent, fait en 1799, 1800, 1801, 1802, 1803, et 1804 par Al. de Humboldt et A. Bonpland.* Paris: N. Maze; J. Smith. English translation by Helen M. Williams published in 1971 under the title *Personal Narrative of Travels to the Equinoctial Regions of the New Continent During the Years 1799–1824 by Alexander von Humboldt and Aimé de Bonpland.* 9 vols. London: Longman, Hurst, Rees, Orme and Brown.

Hunt, R. W. G. 1977. "The Specification of Color Appearance, I, Concepts and Terms." *CRA* 2:55–68.

Hurvich, Leo M. 1981. *Color Vision.* Sunderland, Mass.: Sinauer Associates.

Hurvich, Leo M., and Dorothea Jameson. 1957. "An Opponent-Process Theory of Color Vision." *PRv* 64:384–404.

———. 1969. "Human Color Perception: An Essay Review." *American Scientist* 57:143–166.

Iijima, Toshiro, Wolfgang Wenning, and Heinrich Zollinger. 1982. "Cultural Factors of Color Naming in Japanese: Naming Tests with Japanese Children in Japan and Europe." *AL* 24:245–262.

Ikegami, Yoshiko. 1978. *Eigo kiso goi no kenkyū* (A Study of English Basic Vocabulary). Tokyo: Nippon Hoso Shuppan Kyokai.

Innes, D. C. 1972. "Sight and Sound in Bocchylides." *Classical Review,* n.s. 22:15–16.

Irwin, Eleanor. 1974. "Colour Terms in Greek Poetry." Toronto: A. M. Hakkert, Ltd.

Ishak, I. G. H. 1952. "The Photopic Luminosity Curve for a Group of Fifteen Egyptian Trichromats." *JOSA* 13:529–534.

Ishihara, Shinobu. 1971. *Tests for Colour Blindness.* Tokyo: Kanehara Suppan Company.

Istomina, Z. M. 1963. "Perception and Naming of Color in Early Childhood" (Izvestiia Akademii Pedagogicheskikh Nauk). *Soviet Psychology and Psychiatry* 1:37–45.

Izutsu, Toshihiko. 1974. "The Elimination of Color in Far Eastern Art and Philosophy." *EY* (1972) 41:429–464.

Jackson, K. 1935. *Studies in Early Celtic Nature Poetry.* Cambridge: Cambridge Univ. Press.

Jacobs, W., and V. Jacobs. 1958. "The Color Blue: Its Use as Metaphor and Symbol." *American Speech* 33:29–46.

Jacobsohn, Minna. 1915. *Die Farben in der mittelhochdeutschen Dichtung der Blütezeit.* Teutonia: Arbeiten zur germanischen Philologie 22. Leipzig: H. Haessel.

Jaffe, J., G. F. Pringle, and S. W. Anderson. 1985. "Speed of Color Naming and Intelligence: Association in Girls, Dissociation in Boys." *Journal of Communication Disorders* 18:63–66.

Janda, Laura A. 1986. *A Semantic Analysis of the Russian Verbal Prefixes za-, pere-, do-, and ot-.* Munich: Otto Sagner.

Jannsens, H. F. 1957. "Les couleurs dans la Bible hébraïque." *Annuaires de l'Institute de Philologie et d'Histoire Orientales et Slaves* 14 (1954–1957):145–171.

Jeoffroy, J. 1882. "La dénomination de couleurs dans l'antiquité." *Mémoires de la Société d'anthropologie,* 2d ser. 2.

Jernudd, Björn H., and Geoffrey M. White. 1983. "The Concept of Basic Color Terms: Variability in FOR and ARABIC." *AL* 25:61–81.

Jettmar, K. 1953. "Blonde und Blauäugige in Zentralasien." *Die Umschau: Halbmonatsschrift über die Fortschritte in Wissenschaft und Technik* 53 (17):519–521.

Jochelson, Waldemar. 1908. *The Koryak.* Publications of the Jesup North Pacific Expedition, Franz Boas, ed., Memoir of the American Museum of Natural History 6:2. Reprinted, New York: AMS Press, 1975.

Jodin, André. 1903. *Étude comparative sur les noms des couleurs.* Paris: Chevalier-Marescq.

Johansen, Cheney. 1992. "Quechua Categories of Blue." Paper presented at the 91st Annual Meeting of the AAA, San Francisco.

Johnson, Allen, Orna Johnson, and Michael Baksh. 1986. "The Colors of Emotions in Machiguenga." *AA* 88:674–681.

Johnson, E. G. 1977. "The Development of Color Knowledge in Preschool Children." *Child Development* 48:308–311.

———. 1986. "The Role of Bilingualism in Color Naming." *Psychologia* 29:156–164.

Johnson, Mark. 1987. *The Body in the Mind: The Bodily Basis of Reason and Imagination.* Chicago: Univ. of Chicago Press.

Johnson-Laird, P. N. 1983. *Mental Models: Towards a Cognitive Science of Language, Inference, and Consciousness.* Cambridge, Mass.: Harvard Univ. Press.

Johnston, Mark. 1992. "How to Speak of the Colors." In Tolliver, ed., 221–263.

Johnston, Mary. 1934. "Purpureis ales oloribus (Horace, *Carmina* 4.1.9–11)." *CW* 28 (3, whole 747):24.

Jones, Loyd A. 1943. "The Historical Background and Evolution of the Colorimetry Report." *JOSA* 33:534–543.

Jones, Loyd A., et al. (Committeee on Colorimetry). 1943. "The Concept of Color." *JOSA* 33:544–554.

Jones, Rhys, and Betty Meehan. 1978. "Anbarra Concept of Color." In *Australian Aboriginal Concepts,* L. R. Hiatt, ed., 20–39. New Jersey: Humanities Press.

Jordan, N. A. 1975. *Des couleurs et des signes. Essai sur la symbolique des couleurs chez quelques auteurs du Moyen-Age et de la Renaissance.* Diss., Univ. of California at Berkeley.

Judd, Deane B. 1940. "The Munsell Color System: Foreword." *JOSA* 30:574.

Juillerat, B. 1978. "Vie et mort dans de symbolisme iafar de couleurs (Nouvelle Guineé)." In Tornay, ed., 495–523.

Kallay, U. von. 1939. "Die zweierlei Farbenortungen einigen Indianerstämme Nordamerikas." *Mitteilungen der Anthropologischen Gesellschaft* 49:11–23.

Katz, Jerrold J., and Jerry A. Fodor. 1963. "The Structure of a Semantic Theory." *Language* 39:170–210.

Kaufman, Terrence. 1964. "Materiales lingüísticos para el estudio de las relaciones internas y externas de la familia de idiomas mayanos." In *Desarrollo cultural de los Mayas*, E. V. Vogt and Alberto Ruz Lhuillier, eds., 80–136. Mexico City: Universidad Nacional Autónoma de México, Facultad de Filosofía y Letras.

———. 1970. *Proyecto de alfabetos y ortografía para escribir las lenguas mayances.* Guatemala City: Talleres Offset de la Editorial José de Pineda Ibarra, Ministerio de Educación.

———. 1972. *El proto-Tzeltal-Tzotzil: Fonología comparada y diccionario reconstruido.* Centro de estudios mayas Cuaderno 5. Mexico City: Universidad Nacional Autónoma de México.

———. 1973. "Areal Linguistics in Middle America." *Current Trends in Linguistics* 11:459–483.

———. 1974. *Idiomas de Mesoamerica.* Guatemala City: Talleres Offset de la Editorial José de Pineda Ibarra, Ministerio de Educación.

———. 1976. "Middle American Languages." *Encyclopedia Britannica,* 1973 ed., 956–963.

———. 1982. Correspondence to MacLaury, re Proto-Mayan color terms. MCS files.

———. 1983. "New Perspectives on Comparative Otomanguean Phonology." MS in possession of author, Department of Anthropology, Univ. of Pittsburgh.

———. 1988. "Otomanguean Tense/Aspect/Mood, Voice, and Nominalization Markers." MS in possession of author, Department of Anthropology, Univ. of Pittsburgh.

Kay, Paul. 1966. Comment on Colby 1966. *CA* 7:20–23.

———. 1975. "Synchronic Variability and Diachronic Change in Basic Color Terms." *JLS* 4:257–270.

———. 1977. "Language Evolution and Speech Style." In *Variability and Change: Sociocultural Dimensions of Language Change,* B. G. Blount and M. Sanchez, eds., 21–33. New York: Academic Press.

Kay, Paul, Brent Berlin, Luisa Maffi, and William R. Merrifield. In press. "Color Naming across Languages." In C. L. Hardin and L. Maffi, eds.

Kay, Paul, Brent Berlin, and William R. Merrifield. 1991a. "Biocultural Implications of Systems of Color Naming." *JLA* 1:12–25. (Originally presented at the 88th Annual Meeting of the AAA, Washington, D.C., 1989.)

———. 1991b. *The World Color Survey.* Dallas: International Book Store. Microfiche.

———. In preparation. *The World Color Survey.* MS, Univ. of California at Berkeley.

Kay, Paul, and Willett Kempton. 1984. "What is the Sapir-Whorf Hypothesis?" *AA* 86:65–79.

Kay, Paul, and Chad K. McDaniel. 1975. "Color Categories as Fuzzy Sets." Language Behavior Research Laboratory Working Paper 44. Berkeley: Univ. of California.

———. 1978. "The Linguistic Significance of Basic Color Terms." *Language* 54: 610–646.

Kees, Hermann. 1943. "Farbensymbolik in ägyptischen religiösen Texten." *Nachrichten von der Akademie der Wissenschaften in Göttingen, Philologisch-Historische Klasse* 11:413–479.

Kelley, Kenneth L. 1949. "Color Designations for Lights." *Journal of Research of the National Bureau of Standards* 31:271.

Kelley, Kenneth L., and Kasson S. Gibson. 1943. "Tristimulus Specifications of the 'Munsell Book of Color' from Spectrophotometric Measurements." *JOSA* 33:355–376.

Kempton, Willett. 1978. "Category Grading and Taxonomic Relations: A Mug is a Sort of a Cup." *AE* 5:44–65.

———. 1981. *The Folk Classification of Ceramics: A Study of Cognitive Prototypes.* New York: Academic Press.

Kennedy, Donald G. 1931. *Field Notes on the Culture of Vaitupu, Ellice Islands.* Memoirs of the Polynesian Society 9. New Plymouth, N.Z.: Thomas Avery and Sons.

Kepner, William A. 1905. "Observations of Color Perception among the Bisayans of Leyte Island, P. I." *Science* 22 (599):680–683.

Kieffer, M. M. 1974. *Color and Emotion Synesthesia in Tzutujíl Mayan and Spanish.* Diss., Univ. of California at Irvine.

Kikuchi, Atsuko, and Frantisek Lichtenberk. 1983. "Semantic Extension in the Colour Lexicon." *Studies in Language* 7:25–64.

Kim, Andrew I. 1985. "Korean Color Terms: An Aspect of Semantic Fields and Related Phenomena." *AL* 27:425–436.

Kinkade, M. Dale. 1988. "Proto-Salishan Color." In *In Honor of Mary Haas,* W. Shipley, ed., 443–466. Berlin: Mouton de Gruyter.

Kinnear, Paul R., and J. B. Deregowski. 1992. Comment on MacLaury 1992*a.* *CA* 33:163–164.

Kirchhoff, Alfred. 1879. "Über Farbensinn und Farbenbezeichnung der Nubier." *ZE* 11:397–402.

Kirchhoff, Paul. 1943. "Mesoamérica: Sus límites geográficas, composición étnica y caracteres culturales." In *Acta Americana* 1:92–107. Article translated by Norman McQuown under the title "Mesoamerica: Its Geographical Limits, Ethnic Composition and Cultural Characteristics," in *Heritage and Conquest: The Ethnography of Middle America,* Sol Tax, ed., 17–30 (1952, Glencoe, Ill.: Free Press).

Kirk, Paul. 1966. "Proto-Mazatec Phonology." Diss., Univ. of Washington, Seattle.

Klineberg, Otto. 1935. *Race Differences.* New York: Harper.

Knab, Tim. 1977. "The Long and Short of Aztec Dialects." *BLS* 3:74–102.

———. 1980. "Talking, Speaking, and Chatting in Aztec." *BLS* 6:180–190.

————. 1986. "Metaphors, Concepts, and Coherence in Aztec." In *Symbol and Meaning beyond the Closed Community: Essays in Mesoamerican Ideas,* Gary H. Gossen, ed., 45–55. Studies on Culture and Society, vol. 1. Albany, N.Y.: Institute for Mesoamerican Studies.

Knab, Tim, and Liliane Hasson de Knab. 1979. "Language Death in the Valley of Puebla: A Socio-Geographic Approach." *BLS* 5:471–483.

Kobayashi, Shigenobu. 1974. *Nihonjin no Kokoro to Iro* (Color in the Japanese Heart). Tokyo: Koodan-sha.

Kober, Alice E. 1932. "The Use of Color Terms in the Greek Poets: Including all the Poets from Homer to 146 B.C. Except the Epigrammatists." Geneva, N.Y.: W. F. Humphrey.

————. 1934. "Some Remarks on Color in Greek Poetry." *CW* 27 (24, whole 741): 189–191.

Koch, Gerd. 1965. " 'Farbenindifferenz' bei pazifischen Völkern." In *Festschrift Alfred Bühler,* C. Schmitz and R. Wildhaber, eds., 235–242. Basler Beiträge zur Geographie und Ethnologie, Ethnologische Reihe 2. Basel: Pharos-Verlag Hansrudolf Schwabe AG.

König, Günter. 1957. "Die Bezeichnungen für Farbe, Glanz und Helligkeit im Altenglischen." Diss., Johann Gutenberg Univ. of Mainz.

König, J. 1927. "Die Bezeichnung der Farben. Umfang, Konsequenz und Übereinstimmung der Farbenbennung, philologisch-historisch Betrachtet, sowie experimentell-psychologisch Untersucht." *Archiv für die Gesellschaft für psychologische Forschung* 60:129–204.

Kopp, James, and Harlan Lane. 1968. "Hue Discrimination Related to Linguistic Habitats." *Psychonomic Science* 11:61–62.

Kranz, W. 1912. "Die ältesten Farbenlehren der Griechen." *Hermes* 47:126–140.

Krause, Ernst. 1877. "Die geschichtliche Entwicklung des Farbensinnes." *Kosmos* 1 (1):264–275.

————. 1880. "Zur historischen Entwicklung des Farbensinnes." *Kosmos* 7 (4): 393–398.

Krauskopf, John., D. R. Williams, and D. W. Heely. 1982. "Cardinal Directions of Color Space." *VR* 20:1123–1131.

Krauskopf, John., D. R. Williams, M. B. Mandler, and Angela M. Brown. 1986. "Higher Order Color Mechanisms." *VR* 26:23–32.

Krieg, Martha Fessler. 1979. "The Influence of French Color Vocabulary on Middle English." *Michigan Academician* 11:431–437.

Kristol, Andrés M. 1978. *Color: Les Langues romanes devant le phénomène de la couleur.* Romanica Helvetica 88. Bern: Francke (Diss., Univ. of Zurich, 1977).

————. 1980a. "Il colore azzurro nei dialette italiani." *Vox romanica* 38:85–99.

————. 1980b. "Color Systems in Southern Italy: A Case of Regression." *Language* 56:137–147.

Kucharski, P. 1954. "Sur la théorie des couleurs et des saveurs dans le 'De Sensu' aristotélicien." *REG* 67:355–390.

Kunihiro, Tetsuya. 1970. "A Contrastive Study of Vocabulary—with Reference to English and Japanese." In *Studies in General and Oriental Linguistics: Presented to Shirô Hattori on the Occasion of His Sixtieth Birthday,* R. Jakobson and S. Kawamoto, eds., 325–347. Tokyo: TEC Company.

Kuschel, Rolf, and Torben Monberg. 1974. "'We Don't Talk Much about Colour Here': A Study of Colour Semantics on Bellona Island." *Man* 9:213–242.

Kutzelnigg, A. 1965. "Die Herkunft des Wortes Farbe und einiger deutscher und fremdsprachinger Farbwörter." *Zeitschrift für Mundasforschung* 32:221–250.

Labov, William. 1973. "The Boundaries of Words and Their Meanings." In *New Ways of Analyzing Variation in English,* C.-J. Bailey and R. W. Shuy, eds., 340–373. Washington, D.C.: Georgetown Univ. Press.

Laceaze-Duthiers, H. 1859. "Mémoire sur pourpre." *Annales des sciences naturelles* 12:1–83.

La Farge, Oliver II, and Douglas Byers. 1931. "The Year Bearer's People." *Tulane University Middle American Research Series* 3:330–336.

Lakoff, George. 1973. "Hedges: A Study in Meaning Criteria and the Logic of Fuzzy Concepts." *Journal of Philosophical Logic* 2:458–508; originally 1972, *CLS* 8:183–228.

———. 1982. "Categories and Cognitive Models." Berkeley Cognitive Science Report 2. Berkeley: Cognitive Science Program, Institute of Human Learning, Univ. of California at Berkeley.

———. 1987. *Women, Fire, and Dangerous Things: What Categories Reveal About the Mind.* Chicago: Univ. of Chicago Press.

———. 1990. "The Invariance Hypothesis: Is Abstract Reason Based on Image-Schemas?" *Cognitive Linguistics* 1:39–74.

Lakoff, George, and Mark Johnson. 1980. *Metaphors We Live By.* Chicago: Univ. of Chicago Press.

Lamb, Trevor, and Janine Bourriau, eds. 1995. *Colour: Art & Science.* Cambridge: Cambridge Univ. Press.

Lander, H. J., S. M. Ervin, and A. E. Horowitz. 1960. "Navaho Color Categories." *Language* 36:368–382.

Landsberger, B. 1967. "Über Farben im Sumerisch-Akkadischen." *Journal of Cuneiform Studies* 21:139–173.

Langacker, Ronald W. 1985. "Observations and Speculations on Subjectivity." In *Iconicity in Syntax,* J. Haiman, ed., 109–150. Amsterdam: John Benjamins.

———. 1990a. "Subjectification." *Cognitive Linguistics* 1:5–38.

———. 1990b. *Concept, Image, and Symbol: The Cognitive Basis of Grammar.* Berlin: Mouton de Gruyter.

Lange Dzn, H. de. 1958. "Research into the Dynamic Nature of the Human Fovea → Cortex Systems with Intermittent and Modulated Light, II: Phase Shift in Brightness and Delay in Color Perception." *JOSA* 48:784–789.

Langham, Ian. 1981. *The Building of British Social Anthropology: W. H. R. Rivers and His Cambridge Disciples in the Development of Kinship Studies, 1898–1931.* Dordrecht: D. Reidel.

Lansing, Jeff. 1995. "Genus, Species, and Vantages." In J. R. Taylor and R. E. Mac-
Laury, eds., 365–375.

Lantz, D. L., and V. Stefflre. 1964. "Language and Cognition Restudied." *JASP*
69:472–481.

Laude-Cirtautas, Ilse. 1961. *Der Gebrauch der Farbbezeichnungen in den Turkdialek-
ten.* Wiesbaden: Harrassowitz.

Laudermilk, Jerry. 1949. "The Bug with a Crimson Past." *Natural History* 58
(3):114–118.

Laws, Glynis, and Ian R. L. Davies. In press. "A Stroop Investigation of Russian
Blues." *Journal of Psycholinguistic Research.*

Leach, Edmund. 1970. *Lévi-Strauss.* London: Fontana and Collins.

Lehmann, Winfred P. 1964. "On the Etymology of 'Black'." In *Taylor Starck
Festschrift,* Werner Betz, Evelyn S. Coleman, and Kenneth Northcott, eds.,
56–61. The Hague: Mouton.

Lenneberg, Eric H. 1953. "Cognition in Ethnolinguistics." *Language* 29:463–471.

———. 1957. "A Probabilistic Approach to Language Learning." *Behavioral Science*
2:1–12.

———. 1961. "Color Naming, Color Recognition, Color Discrimination: A
Re-Appraisal." *PMS* 12:375–382.

———. 1967. "Language and Cognition." In *Biological Foundations of Language* by
E. H. Lenneberg, 329–370. New York: John Wiley.

Lenneberg, Eric H., and John M. Roberts. 1956. "The Language of Experience: A
Study in Methodology." Memoir 13, supplement to *IJAL* 22 (2).

LePan, Don. 1989. *The Cognitive Revolution in Western Culture, Vol. 1: The Birth of
Expectation.* London: Macmillan.

Lerner, L. D. 1951. "Colour Words in Anglo-Saxon." *Modern Language Review*
46:246–249.

Levengood, S. L. 1927. *The Use of Color in the Verse of the Pleiade.* Paris: Presses
Universitaires de France (Diss., Princeton Univ.).

Lévi-Strauss, Claude. 1963. *Totemism.* Boston: Beacon Press.

Lévy-Bruhl, Lucien. 1923. *Primitive Mentality.* Boston: Beacon Press.

Lewis-Jones, W. 1893. "The Celt and the Poetry of Nature." *THSC* Session 1892–93:
46–70.

Lewitz, Saveros. 1974. "Recherches sur le vocabulaire cambodgien VIII: Du vieux
khmer au khmer moderne." *JA* 262:143–170.

Li, Fang-Kuei. 1930. *Mattole: An Athapascan Language.* Chicago: Univ. of Chicago
Press.

Lieberman, Philip. 1991. *Uniquely Human: The Evolution of Speech, Thought, and
Selfless Behavior.* Cambridge, Mass.: Harvard Univ. Press.

Lienhardt, Godfrey. 1961. *Divinity and Experience: The Religion of the Dinka.*
Oxford: Clarendon Press.

Linton, William James. 1852. *Ancient and Modern Colors from the Earliest Periods
to the Present Time: With Their Chemical and Artistical Properties.* London:
Longman, Brown, Green, and Longman.

Lionnet, Andrés. 1986. *Un idioma extinto de Sonora: El Eudeve.* Instituto de Investigaciones Antropológicas, Serie Antropológica 60. Mexico City: Universidad Nacional Autónoma de México.

Livingstone, Margaret S., and David H. Hubel. 1984. "Anatomy and Physiology of a Color System in the Primate Visual Cortex." *Journal of Neuroscience* 4:309–356.

———. 1988. "Segregation of Form, Color, Movement, and Depth: Anatomy, Physiology, and Perception." *Science* 240 (4853):740–749.

Loewenthal, Wilhelm M. 1901. *Die slavischen Farbenbezeichnungen.* Leipzig: A. Preis.

Loffler-Laurian, A. M. 1983. "Fonctionnement des lexies complexes: cas des lexies contenant des noms de couleur en finnois et en français." *Contrastes* 6:51–68.

Lombardo, Natal. 1702. *Arte de la lengua Teguima vulgarmente llamada Ópata.* Mexico City: Miguel de Ribera.

Lovejoy, T., and E. S. Foster. 1913. " 'De Coloribus.' " In *The Works of Aristotle,* vol. 6, W. D. Ross and J. A. Smith, eds. and trans., 791a–799b. Oxford: Clarendon Press.

Lovibond, Joseph W. 1887. "The Tintometer—a New Instrument for the Analysis, Synthesis, Matching, and Measurement of Color." *Journal of the Society of Dyers and Colorists* 3:186–193.

Lü, Ching-Fu. 1985. *A Primary Investigation and Research of Color Names.* National Science Council, Republic of China, final report No. NSC74-0301-H003-04. Department of Industrial Arts Education, National Taiwan Normal Univ.

Lubbock, Montagu. 1882. "The Development of the Colour-Sense." *Fortnightly Review* 31:518–529.

Lucas, Alfred, and J. R. Harris. 1962. *Ancient Egyptian Materials and Industries.* 4th ed. London: Edward Arnold.

Lucas, C. W. 1859. "Observationes philologicae de nigri coloris significatione singulari." *Neue Jahrbücher für Philologie und Pädagogik* 79:597–607.

Luckiesh, M. 1918. *The Language of Color.* New York: Dodd, Mead and Company. Second printing 1930.

Lucy, John A. 1985. "Whorf's View of the Linguistic Mediation of Thought." In *Semiotic Mediation: Sociocultural and Psychological Perspectives,* E. Merz and R. J. Parmentier, eds., 73–97. New York: Academic Press.

———. 1992. *Language Diversity and Thought: A Reformation of the Linguistic Relativity Hypothesis.* Cambridge: Cambridge Univ. Press.

Lucy, John A., and Richard A. Shweder. 1979. "Whorf and His Critics: Linguistic and Non-Linguistic Influences on Color Memory." *AA* 81:581–615.

———. 1988. "The Effect of Incidental Conversation on Memory for Focal Colors." *AA* 90:923–931.

Ludat, Herberto. 1953. "Farbenbezeichnungen in Völkernamen. Ein Beitrag zu asiatisch-osteuropäischen Kulturbezeichnungen." *Saeculum* 4:138–155.

Lumsden, Charles J. 1985. "Color Categorization: A Possible Concordance between Genes and Culture." *Proceedings of the National Academy of Science of the U.S.A.* 82:5805–5808.

Lumsden, Charles J., and E. O. Wilson. 1981. *Genes, Mind, and Culture: The Coevolutionary Process.* Cambridge, Mass.: Harvard Univ. Press.

Luria, A. R. 1976. *Cognitive Development: Its Cultural and Social Foundations.* M. Lopez-Morillas, L. Solotaroff, and M. Cole, trans. Cambridge, Mass.: Harvard Univ. Press.

Lyons, John. 1977. *Semantics.* 2 vols. Cambridge: Cambridge Univ. Press.

————. 1995. "Colour in Language." In T. Lamb and J. Bourriau, eds., 194–224.

————. In press. "The Vocabulary of Colour with Particular Reference to Ancient Greek and Classical Latin." In A. Borg, ed.

Maass, Alfred. 1912. "Anhang zu dem 'Beitrag zur Anthropologie der Minangkabaur' des Herrn Dr. Med. J. P. Kleiweg de Zwaan: Über das Farbenempfindungsvermögen bei den Minangkabauern." In *Durch Zentral-Sumatra,* vol.2, Alfred Maass, ed., pp. 134–152. Berlin: Wilhelm Süsserott. Translated by Maass from his original in Dutch, n.d., n.p. "363 Farbenuntersuchungen bei den malaien Zentral-Sumatras," a pamphlet of 22 pp. and 2 tables published as a companion to Johannes Pieter Kleiweg de Zwaan, 1908, *Bijdrage tot de Anthropologie der Menankabau-Maleiers.* Amsterdam: Meulenhoff.

McCrea, N. G. 1894. "Ovid's Use of Colour and of Colour-Terms." In *Classical Studies in Honour of Henry Drisler,* 180–194. New York: Macmillan and Co.

McDaniel, Chad K. 1972. "Hue Perception and Hue Naming." Honors thesis, Harvard College.

McDougall, William. 1908. "An Investigation of the Colour Sense of Two Infants." *BJP* 2:4:338–352.

McGuinn, M. 1991. "Wittgenstein's 'Remarks on Color'." *Philosophy* 66:435–453.

Machek, Václav. 1951. "Trois noms slaves de couleurs." *Lingua Posnaniensis* 3:96–111.

————. 1957. *Etymologichy Slovnik-Jazyka Cheského a Slovenského.* Prague: Nakladatelstivi.

Mackenzie, D. A. 1922. "Colour Symbolism." *Folk-lore* 33:136–169.

MacLaury, Maria I. 1989. "La Placita: Vantages of Urban Change in Historic Tucson." Thesis, Univ. of Arizona, Tucson (Ann Arbor: UMI 1339280).

MacLaury, Robert E. 1970. "Ayoquesco Zapotec: Ethnography, Phonology, and Lexicon." M.A. thesis, Univ. of the Americas, Mexico City (relocated at Cholula, Puebla).

————. 1975a. "Some Methods for Reconstructing the Temporal Order of the Encoding of Basic Color Categories within Particular Languages." Paper presented at the 17th Annual Kroeber Anthropological Society Meeting, Berkeley, Calif. MS, MCS and WCS files.

————. 1975b. "Reconstructions of the Evolution of Some (50) Basic Color Term Lexicons: A Step Toward Developing Diachronic Methods for Testing the Berlin-Kay Hypothesis." MS, Special Collection in Linguistics, the German Research Society.

————. 1982. "Prehistoric Mayan Color Categories." MS in possession of author.

————. 1986a. "Color in Mesoamerica, Vol. I: A Theory of Composite Categorization." Diss., Univ. of California, Berkeley (Ann Arbor: UMI 8718073).

————. 1986*b*. "Color Categorization in Shuswap, Chilcotin, Kwak'wala, and Makah: A Description." *Working Papers of the 21st Annual International Conference on Salish and Neighboring Languages,* MS Univ. of Washington Library, Seattle.

————. 1987*a*. "Color-Category Evolution and Shuswap Yellow-with-Green." *AA* 89:107–124.

————. 1987*b*. "Coextensive Semantic Ranges: Different Names for Distinct Vantages of One Category." *CLS* 23 (I):268–282.

————. 1987*c*. Letter to Robert M. Boynton describing the technique of laminating color chips in acetate. MCS and WCS files.

————. 1988*a*. "Proto-Otomanguean Color Categories." Paper presented at the 87th Annual Meeting of the AAA, Phoenix.

————. 1988*b*. "A Description of Lillooet Color Categories Based on Munsell Stimuli." MS, *JFC.*

————. 1989. "Zapotec Body-Part Locatives: Prototypes and Metaphoric Extensions." *IJAL* 55:119–154.

————. 1990. "A Description of Sechelt Color Categories Based on Munsell Stimuli." MS, *JFC.*

————. 1991*a*. "Social and Cognitive Motivations of Change: Measuring Variability in Color Semantics." *Language* 67:34–62.

————. 1991*b*. "Exotic Color Categories: Linguistic Relativity to What Extent?" *JLA* 1:26–51.

————. 1991*c*. "Prototypes Revisited." *Annual Review of Anthropology* 20:55–74.

————. 1992*a*. "From Brightness to Hue: An Explanatory Model of Color-Category Evolution." *CA* 33:137–186.

————. 1992*b*. "Karuk Color: The Blue-Green-Yellow Category of Northern California." Paper presented at the 91st Annual Meeting of the AAA, San Franciso. MS, JFC files and the Phillips Collection, American Philosphical Society Library, Philadelphia.

————. 1995*a*. "Vantage Theory." In Taylor and MacLaury, eds., 231–276.

————. 1995*b*. "Taxonomy." *Handbook of Pragmatics: Manual,* Jef Verschueren, Jan-Ola Östman, and Jan Blommaert, eds., 628–633. Amsterdam/Philadelphia: John Benjamins.

————. In press. "Basic Color Terms: Twenty-five Years After." In A. Berg, ed.

————. MS-1. "The Universal Pattern of Coextensive Color Naming: Categorizing by Analogy to Points of View in Space." Submitted to *Behavioral and Brain Sciences,* March 1996.

————. MS-2. "Zulu Color Categories." MS, MCS.

MacLaury, Robert E., Judit Almási, and Zoltán Kövecses. In press. "Hungarian *Piros* and *Vörös:* Color from Points of View." *Semiotica.* Paper presented at 93rd Annual Meeting of the AAA, Atlanta, 1994.

MacLaury, Robert E., and Brent D. Galloway. 1988. "Color Categories and Color Qualifiers in Halkomelem, Samish, Lushootseed, Nooksack, and Yakima." *Working Papers of the 23rd Annual Conference on Salish and Neighboring Languages,* Eugene, Ore. N.p.

MacLaury, Robert E., and Philip J. Greenfeld. 1986. "How to Say 'Blah' in Fifty Languages: Residual Color Categorization." MS in possession of authors.

MacLaury, Robert E., Margot McMillen, and Stanley McMillen. 1979. "Uspantec Color Categories: An Experiment with Field Methods." Paper presented at the 4th Annual Mayan Workshop, Palenque, Mexico.

MacLaury, Robert E., and Stephan O. Stewart. 1984. "Simultaneous Sequences of Basic Color-Category Evolution." Paper presented at the 83rd Annual AAA Meeting, Denver.

McManus, I. C. 1983. "Basic Color Terms in Literature." *Language and Speech* 26:247–252.

McNaught, Carmel. 1992. "Learning Science at the Interface Between Zulu and English: An Overview of Research Issues." *SAJL* 10:234–239.

McNeill, Daniel, and Paul Freiberger. 1993. *Fuzzy Logic: The Revolutionary Computer Technology That Is Changing the World.* New York: Simon & Schuster.

McNeill, Nobuko B. 1972. "Colour and Colour Terminology." *JL* 8:21–33.

Maerz, A., and M. Rea Paul. 1930. *A Dictionary of Color.* New York: McGraw-Hill.

Maffi, Luisa. 1984. "Somali Colour Terminology: An Outline." *Proceedings of the Second International Congress of Somali Studies, University of Hamburg, August 1–6, 1983,* vol. I: *Linguistics and Literature,* T. Labahn, ed., 299–312. Hamburg: Buske.

———. 1989. "Cognitive Anthropology and Human Categorization Research: The Case of Color." MS, WCS files.

———. 1990. "Somali Color Term Evolution: Grammatical and Semantic Evidence." *AL* 32:316–334.

———. 1991. "A Bibliography of Color Categorization Research, 1970–1990." In Berlin and Kay (1991) 173–189.

Magnus, Hugo. 1877a. *Die Geschichtliche Entwickelung des Farbensinnes.* Leipzig: Von Veit.

———. 1877b. Zur Entwickelung des Farbensinnes. *Kosmos* 1:423–433.

———. 1878. *Histoire de l'évolution du sens des couleurs.* Paris: C. Rheinwald.

———. 1879. *Die methodische Erziehung des Farbensinnes.* Breslau: Kern.

———. 1880. *Untersuchungen über den Farbensinn der Naturvölker.* Jena: G. Fisher.

———. 1883. *Über ethnologische Untersuchungen des Farbensinnes.* Berlin: Carl Habel.

Malkiel, Yakov. 1941. "The 'Amulatado' Type in Spanish." *The Romanic Review* 32:278–295.

———. 1953. "'Apretar', 'pr(i)eto', 'perto': Historia de un cruce hispanolatino." *Thesaurus: Boletín de Instituto Caro y Cuervo* 9:1–135.

———. 1954. "From 'Bay-Colored' to 'Spleen': The Romance Phase of Latin *Badius.*" *AGI* 39:166–187.

———. 1956. "Español 'negrestino' y 'blanquecino.'" *Quaderni Ibero-Americani* 18:89–92.

Maloney, Laurence T., and Brian A. Wandell. 1986. "Color Constancy: A Method for Recovering Surface Spectral Reflectrance." *JOSA-A* 3:29–33.

Mandelbaum, David G. 1980. "*The Todas* in Time Perspective." *Reviews in Anthropology* 9:279–302.

Mangio, C. 1961. "Cenni sulle teorie cromatiche dei greci e loro applicazione architettonica." *Studi classici e orientali* 10:214–223.

Mann, Ida, and Cecil Turner. 1956. "Color Vision in Native Races of Australia." *American Journal of Ophthalmology* 41:797–800.

Manniche, Lise. 1982. "The Body Colours of Gods and Men in Inlaid Jewellery and Related Objects from the Tomb of Tutankhamun." *Acta Orientalia* 43:5–12.

Manrique Castañeda, Leonardo. 1958. "Sobre la clasificación del Otomí-Pame." *PICA* 33:551–559.

Marcus, Joyce. 1973. "Territorial Organization of the Lowland Classic Maya." *Science* 180:911–916.

Marmor, Gloria Strause. 1978. "Age at Onset of Blindness and the Development of the Semantics of Color Names." *Journal of Experimental Child Psychology* 25:267–278.

Martí, Samuel. 1960. "Simbolismo de los colores, deidades, números y rumbos." *Estudios de cultura Nahuatl* 2:93–127.

Marty, Anton. 1879. *Die Frage nach der geschichtlichen Entwickelung des Farbensinnes.* Vienna: Carl Gerold.

Mátray, Ferenc. 1910. *A Magyar Színelnevezésekröl.* Kalocsa: Jurcsó Antal Könyvnyomda.

Matsuzawa, Tetsuro. 1985. "Colour Naming and Classification in a Chimpanzee." *Journal of Human Evolution* 14:282–291.

Matthew, Washington. 1907. "Color symbolism." In *Handbook of American Indians North of Mexico,* part i. Bureau of American Ethnology Bulletin 30. Frederick W. Hodge, ed., 325–326. Washington, D.C.: Smithsonian Institution.

Maxwell-Stuart, P. G. 1981. *Studies in Greek Colour Terminology.* 2 vols. Leiden: E. J. Brill.

Mayer, George. 1934. "Die Farbenbezeichnungen bei Ovid." Diss., Univ. of Erlangen.

Mayers, Marvin K. 1966. "Linguistic Comparisons." In *Languages of Guatemala,* M. Mayers, ed., 272–302. The Hague: Mouton.

Mead, W. E. 1899. "Color in Old English Poetry." *PMLAA* 14:169–206.

———. 1901. "Colour in the English and Scottish Ballads." In *An English Miscellany Presented to Dr. Furnivall in Honor of His Seventy-Fifth Birthday,* 321–334. Oxford: Clarendon Press.

Medin, Douglas L., Robert L. Goldstone, Dedre Gentner. 1990. "Similarity Involving Attributes and Relations: Judgments of Similarity and Difference Are Not Inverses." *Psychological Science* 1:64–67.

———. 1993. "Respects for Similarity." *PRv* 100:254–278.

Meetkerke, C. E. 1901. "Was Victor Hugo Color Blind?" *Gentleman's Magazine* 290:376–379.

Mehan, Hugh. 1990. "Oracular Reasoning in a Psychiatric Exam: The Resolution of Conflict in Language." *Conflict Talk: Sociolinguistic Investigations of Arguments in Conversations,* A. D. Grimshaw, ed., 160–177. Cambridge: Cambridge Univ. Press.

Meltzer, Francoise C. 1975. *The Painted Veil: Color and Cognition in Symbolist Verse.* Diss., Univ. of California at Berkeley.

Menges, Karl H. 1965. "Farbbezeichnungen in den Türkdialekten." *Anthropos* 60:825–832.

Mensching, G. 1957. "Die Lichtssymbolik in der Religionsgeschichte." *Studium Generalis* 10:422–433

Merker, G. S. 1967. "The Rainbow Mosaic at Pergamum and Aristotelian Colour Theory." *American Journal of Archaeology* 71:81–82.

Merrifield, William R. 1971. Review of Berlin and Kay (1969). *JL* 7:259–268.

———. 1992. Comment on MacLaury 1992a. *CA* 33:164–65.

Mervis, Carolyn B., Jack Catlan, and Eleanor Rosch. 1975. "Development of the Structure of Color Categories." *Developmental Psychology* 11:54–60.

Mervis, Carolyn B., and Eleanor Rosch. 1981. "Categorization of Natural Objects." *ARP* 32:89–115.

Mervis, Carolyn B., and E. M. Roth. 1981. "The Internal Structures of Basic and Non-Basic Color Categories." *Language* 57:384–405.

Meurnier, Annie. 1975. "Quelques remarques sur les adjectifs de couleur." *Annales de l'Université de Toulouse-Le Mirail,* n.s. 11 (5):37–61.

Meyer, K. 1927. *Die Bedeutung der weissen Farbe im Kultus der Griechen und Römer.* Freiburg im Breisgau: K. Henn.

Meyerson, Ignace, ed. 1957. *Problème de la couleur: Colloque du Centre de Recherche de Psychologie Comparative.* Paris: Bibliothèque Générale de l'École Pratique des Hautes Études.

Meylan-Faure, H. 1899. *Les epithètes dans Homère.* Lausanne: G. Bridel.

Michaels, David. 1978. "Linguistic Relativity and Color Terminology." In *Language, Culture and Ideology: Selected Proceedings of the 1977 Conference on Culture and Communication.* Temple Univ. Working Papers in Culture and Communication 2 (1):55–71.

Mignot, X. 1972. "Considérations sur l'étude sémantique des suffixes dans les langues anciennes." In *Mélanges de linguistique et de philologie grecques offerts à Pierre Chantraine,* A. Ernout, ed., 123–137. Paris: Klincksieck.

Miklosich, Franz. 1886. *Etymologisches Wörterbuch der slavischen Sprachen.* Vienna: Wilhelm Braumüller.

Miller, David L., and Billy R. Wooten. 1990. "The Elemental Hues of Spectral Lights, and the Occasionally Anomalous Nature of Green." *Investigative Ophthalmology and Visual Science* 31 (4):262.

Miller, George A. 1956. "The Magical Number Seven, Plus or Minus Two: Some Limits on our Capacity for Processing Information." *PRv* 63:81–93.

———. 1970. Review of Berlin and Kay 1969. *American Scientist* 58:565.

Miller, Wick R. 1967. *Uto-Aztecan Cognate Sets.* UCPL 48. Berkeley: Univ. of California Press.

Mills, Carl. 1976. "Universality and Variation in the Acquisition of Semantic Categories: English Color Terms." In *Language Use and the Uses of Language,* Roger W. Shuy and Anna Shnukal, eds., 197–204. Washington, D.C.: Georgetown Univ. Press.

———. 1984. "English Color Terms: Language, Culture and Psychology." *Semiotica* 52:95–109.

Mitsunobu, Meiyo. 1972. Review of Berlin and Kay 1969. *Studies in English Literature: A Journal Devoted to English and American Languages and Literature Published by the English Literary Society of Japan.* English, no. 1972:170–184. (Three issues/yr, one English and two Japanese.)

Molina, Alonso de. 1944 [1571]. *Vocabulario en lengua castellana y mexicana.* Colección de incunables americanos, siglo xvi, vol. 4. Madrid: Ediciones Cultura Hispánica.

Mollison, Th. M. 1913. "Eine neue Methode zur Prüfung des Farbensinnes und ihre Ergebnisse an Europäern und Somali." *Archive für Anthropologie* 12:26–43.

Mollon, John D. 1982. "Color Vision." *ARP* 33:41–85.

———. 1986. "Questions of Sex and Color." *Nature* 323:578–579.

———. 1990. "The Club-Sandwich Mystery." *Nature* 343:16–17.

Molrieu, P. 1957. "Développement de la perception des couleurs chez l'enfant." In I. Meyerson, ed., 115–130.

Monberg, Torben. 1971. "Tikopia Color Classification." *Ethnology* 10:349–358.

Mondry, Henrietta, and John R. Taylor. 1992. "The Russian Blues: *Sinij* and *Goluboy.*" Paper presented at the 91st Annual AAA Meeting, San Francisco.

Monro, S. R. 1983. "Color Metaphors and Cultural Confusion in Chinese and English." *JCLTA* 18:27–45.

Mooney, James. 1891. "The Sacred Formulas of the Cherokees." *Annual Report of the Bureau of American Ethnology* 7:307–395.

Moonwomon, Birch. 1983. "Color Term Theory and Ancient Greek." Thesis, Sonoma State Univ., Santa Rosa, Calif.

Moorhouse, A. C. 1954. "Ex- in Colour Adjectives." *Classical Quarterly,* n.s. 4:96.

Morelle, Jean. 1943. "Étude sur les adjectifs de couleur en grec ancien: Leur valeur évocatrice, leur emploi métaphorique." Diss., Univ. of Liège.

Morgan, G., and G. Corbett. 1989. "Russian Colour Term Salience." *Russian Linguistics* 13:125–141.

Morgan, G., and Anthony E. St. G. Moss. 1991. "The Two Blues of Russian: The Referents of *Sinij* and *Goluboj.*" *Die Farbe* 35/35 (part 2):353–357.

Moseley, Christopher, R. E. Asher, and Mary Tait, eds. 1994. *Atlas of the World's Languages.* London: Routledge Reference.

Moser, Mary B. 1964. "Seri Blue." *The Kiva* 30:27–32.

Moskovich, V. A. 1960. "Sistema tsvetooboznachenii v sovremennom angliiskom iazyke" (The system of words denoting color in modern English). *Voprosy Iazykoznaniia* 6 (1):83–87.

Moss, A. E. 1988. "Russian Blues and Purples: a Tentative Hypothesis." *Quinquereme* 11:164–177.

————. 1989*a*. "Basic Color Terms: Problems and Hypotheses." *Lingua* 78:313–320.

————. 1989*b*. "Does Russian Have a Basic Term for Purple?" *Linguistics* 27:145–155.

Moss, A. E., I. Davies, G. Corbett, and G. Laws. 1990. "Mapping Russian Basic Color Terms Using Behavioral Measures." *Lingua* 82:313–332.

Mugler, C. 1964. *Dictionnaire historique de la terminologie optique des grecs: Douze siècles de dialogues avec la lumière.* Paris: Klincksieck.

Müller-Boré, Kaete. 1922. *Stilistische Untersuchungen zum Farbwort und zur Verwendung der Farbe in der älteren griechischen Poesie.* Berlin: E. Ebering (Diss., Kiel Univ.).

Mulvany, E. M. 1901. "Colours in Greek." *Journal of Philology* 27:51–69.

Munsell, Albert H. 1905. *A Color Notation.* Boston: Ellis. 2d ed.: 1971, Baltimore: Munsell Color Company.

————. 1921. *A Grammar of Color.* Mittineaque, Mass.: Strathmore Paper Company.

Munsell Color Company. 1966. *Munsell Book of Color.* Glossy finish collection. Baltimore: MCC.

Musters, George C. 1897. *At Home with the Patagonians.* London: John Murray. Reprinted, New York: Greenwood, 1969.

Myers, Charles S. 1908. "Some Observations on the Development of the Colour Sense." *BJP* 2:353–363.

Nagasaki, Seiki. 1974. *Iro no Nihon-shi* (Color in Japanese history). Tokyo: Tankoo-sha.

Nagel, Wilibald A. 1900. "Contributions to the Diagnosis, Symptomatology, and Statistics of Congenital Color-Blindness." *Archives of Ophthalmology* 29:154–168.

Nathans, Jeremy. 1989. "The Genes for Color Vision." *SA* 258 (2):42–49.

Neitz, Maureen, and Jay Neitz. 1995. "Numbers and Ratios of Visual Pigment Genes for Normal Red-Green Color Vision." *Science* 267:1013–1016.

Neu, Erich. 1983. *Glossar zu den althethitischen Ritualtexten.* Wiesbaden: Otto Harrassowitz.

Newcomer, Peter, and James Faris. 1971. Review of Berlin and Kay (1969). *IJAL* 37:270–275.

Newhall, Sidney M. 1940. "Preliminary Report of the O.S.A. Subcommittee on the Spacing of the Munsell Colors." *JOSA* 30:617–645.

Newhall, Sidney M., Dorothy Nickerson, and Deane B. Judd. 1943. "Final Report of the O.S.A. Subcommittee on the Spacing of the Munsell Colors." *JOSA* 33:385–418.

Nichols, Michael J. P. 1974. "Northern Paiute Historical Grammar." Diss., Univ. of California, Berkeley.

————. 1980. "Renewal in Numic Color Systems." In *American Indian and Indo-European Studies: Papers in Honor of Madison S. Beeler,* K. Klar, M. Langdon, and S. Silver, eds., 159–167. The Hague: Mouton.

Nickerson, Dorothy. 1940. "History of the Munsell Color System and Its Scientific Application." *JOSA* 30:575–586.

————. 1981*a*. "History of the Munsell Color System." *Color Engineering* 7:42–51.

————. 1981*b*. "OSA Uniform Color Scale Samples: A Unique Set." *CRA* 6:7–9.

Nickerson, Dorothy, and Sidney Newhall. 1943. "A Psychological Color Solid." *JOSA* 33:419–422.

Nowaczyk, Ronald H. 1982. "Sex-Related Differences in the Color Lexicon." *LS* 25:257–265.

Nowotny, Karl A. 1969. "Beiträge zur Geschichte des Weltbildes, Farben und Waltrichtungen." *Veröffentlichungen des Instituts für Völkerkunde der Universität Wien.* Vienna: Ferdinand Berger und Söhne.

Ogle, M. B. 1929. "The Blonde Aeneas: Vergil, Aeneid 1.592." *CW* 23 (4, whole 615):28–30.

Ohman, Susanne. 1953. "Theories of the Linguistic Field." *Word* 9:123–134.

O'Neale, Lila M., and Juan Dolores. 1943. "Notes on Papago Color Designations." *AA* 45:387–397.

Opler, Morris. 1973. *Grenville Goodwin among the Western Apache: Letters from the Field.* Tucson: Univ. of Arizona Press.

Osborne, H. 1968. "Colour Concepts of the Ancient Greeks." *British Journal of Aesthetics* 8:269–83.

Osgood, Charles. 1975. *Atlas of Affective Meaning: Japanese.* Urbana: Univ. of Illinois Press.

Osgood, Charles, E. William May, and Murray Miron. 1975. *Cross-Cultural Universals of Affective Meaning.* Urbana: Univ. of Illinois Press.

Osgood, Charles, George Suci, and Percy Tannenbaum. 1957. *The Measurement of Meaning.* Urbana: Univ. of Illinois Press.

Ostheeren, K. 1971. "Toposforschung und Bedeutungslehre." *Anglia* 89:1–47.

Ott, André G. 1899. *Étude sur les couleurs en vieux français.* Paris: E. Bouillon (Diss., Univ. of Zurich).

Ottoson, D., and S. Zeki, eds. 1985. *Central and Peripheral Mechanism of Colour Vision.* London: Macmillan.

Padgham, C. A., and J. E. Saunders. 1975. *The Perception of Light and Colour.* New York: Academic Press.

Palmer, F. R. 1981. *Semantics.* 2d ed. London: Cambridge Univ. Press.

Panoff-Eliet, Françoise. 1971. Review of Berlin and Kay 1969. *L'Homme* 4:100–103.

Parsons, John Herbert. 1915. *An Introduction to the Study of Colour Vision.* Cambridge: Cambridge Univ. Press (2d ed. 1924).

Peeples, David R., and Davida Y. Teller. 1975. "Color Vision and Brightness Discrimination in Two-Month-Old Human Infants." *Science* 189:1102–1103.

Peirce, H. Wesley. 1964. "Seri Blue—An Explanation." *The Kiva* 30:30–39.

Peralta, Jesus T. 1980. "Perception and Color Categories: A View from the I'wak." *Philippine Sociological Review* 28 (1–4):51–59.

Perez, B. 1888. *La psychologie de l'enfant; Les trois premières années de l'enfant.* Paris: Alcan.

Pérez de Barradas, J. 1932–1933. "El color en la vida y en el arte de los pueblos." *Actas y memorias, Sociedad Española de Antropología, Etnografía y Prehistoria* 11:137–207, 12:3–88.

Petyt, K. M. 1980. *The Study of Dialect: An Introduction to Dialectology.* Boulder, Colo.: Westview Press.

Phillips, T. M. 1919. "Color in George Meredith and Other Modern English Poets." *Manchester Quarterly* 147:190–196.

Pickford, R. W. 1951. *Individual Differences in Colour Vision.* London: Routledge and Kegan Paul.

Pittman, Richard S., Barbara F. Grimes, and Joseph Evans. 1988. *Languages of the World: Ethnologue.* 11th ed. Dallas, Texas: Wycliffe Bible Translators.

Platnauer, Maurice. 1921. "Greek Colour-Perception." *Classical Quarterly* 15:153–162.

Ploss, E. 1956. "Die Färberei in der germanischen Handwirtschaft." *Zeitschrift für die Philologie* 75:1–21.

Pokorny, J. 1959. *Indogermanisches etymologisches Wörterbuch I.* Bern: Francke.

Pollnac, Richard B. 1972. "Variation in the Cognition of Luganda Color Terminology." Diss., Univ. of Missouri, Columbia.

———. 1975. "Intra-Cultural Variability in the Structure of the Subjective Color Lexicon in Buganda." *AE* 2:89–110.

Portal, Frederic. 1837. *Des couleurs symboliques dans l'antiquité, le moyen-age et les temps modernes.* Paris: Treuttel et Wurtz (Library of Congress Microfilm, 1964).

Post, Richard H. 1962. "Population Differences in Red and Green Color Vision Deficiency: A Review and a Query on Selection Relaxation." *Eugenics Quarterly* 9:131–146.

Pouchet, G. 1888. "La prétendue évolution du sense des couleurs." *Revue scientifique* 3:16:464–467.

Pratt, Alice Edwards. 1898. *The Use of Color in the Verse of the English Romantic Poets.* Chicago: Univ. of Chicago Press.

Preston, Dennis R. 1993. "The Uses of Folk Linguistics." *International Journal of Applied Linguistics* 3:181–259.

Preyer, W. 1887. *L'âme de l'enfant, observations sur le développement psychique des premières années.* Paris: Alcan.

Price, Thomas R. 1883. "The Color-System of Vergil." *The American Journal of Philology* 4:1–20.

Price-Williams, D. R. 1961. "A Study Concerning Concepts of Conservation of Quantities among Primitive Children." *Acta Psychologica* 18:297–305.

———. 1962. "Abstract and Concrete Modes of Classification in a Primitive Society." *British Journal of Educational Psychology* 32:50–61.

Priestly, Tom M. S. 1981. "On Basic Color Terms in Early Slavic and Ukrainian." *Studies in Ukrainian Linguistics in Honor of George Y. Shevelov,* Jacob P. Hursky, ed. *Annals of the Ukrainian Academy of Arts and Sciences in the U.S.* 15 (1981–1983/39–40):243–251.

Pritsak, Omeljan. 1954. "Orientierung und Farbsymbolik. Zu den Farbenbezeichnungen in den altaischen Völkernamen." *Saeculum* 5:376–383.

Proulx, P. 1988. "Algic Color Terms." *AL* 30:135–149.

Quinn, Paul C., B. R. Wooten, and Evette J. Ludman. 1985. "Achromatic Color Categories." *Perception and Psychophysics* 37:198–204.

Rabl-Rückhard, H. J. J. 1880. "Zur historischen Entwicklung des Farbensinnes." *ZE* 12:210–221.

Radke, G. 1936. "Die Bedeutung der weissen und der schwarzen Farbe im Kult und Brauch der Griechen und Römer." Jena: Gustav Neuenhahn.

Radloff, W. 1871. "Die Hausthiere der Kirgisen." *ZE* 3:285–313.

Raskin, L. A., S. Maital, and M. H. Bornstein. 1983. "Perceptual Categorization of Color: A Life-Span Study." *PRs* 45:135–45.

Ratliff, Floyd. 1976. "On the Psychophysical Bases of Universal Color Terms." *PAPS* 120:311–330.

Ratner, Carl. 1989. "A Sociohistorical Critique of Naturalistic Theories of Color Perception." *Journal of Mind and Behavior* 10:361–372.

Ray, Verne F. 1952. "Techniques and Problems in the Study of Human Color Perception." *SJA* 8:251–259.

———. 1953. "Human Color Perception and Behavioral Response." *New York Academy of Sciences,* ser. 2, 16:98–104.

Rečeva, M. 1984. "Zur semasiologisch-etymologischen Behandlung der slawischen Farbbezeichung **zelenъ*." *Zeitschrift für Slawistik* 29:748–753.

Reichard, Gladys A. 1983. *Navaho Religion: A Study of Symbolism.* Tucson: University of Arizona Press. Reproduced from the 1974 edition, Princeton: Princeton University Press.

Rensch, Calvin R. 1976. *Comparative Otomanguean Phonology.* Bloomington: Indiana Univ. Press.

———. 1977. "Classification of Otomanguean Languages and the Position of Tlapanec." In *Two Studies in Middle American Comparative Linguistics,* I. Davis and V. Poulter, eds., 53–108. Arlington, Tex.: Summer Institute of Linguistics and the Univ. of Texas.

Rich, Elaine. 1977. "Sex-Related Differences in Colour Vocabulary." *LS* 20:404–409.

Riley, Bridget. 1995. "Colour for the Painter." In T. Lamb and J. Bourriau, eds., 31–52.

Riley, Carroll L. 1963. "Color-Direction Symbolism: An Example of Mexican-Southwestern Contacts." *America Indígena* 23:49–58.

Riley, Charles A. 1995. *Color Codes: Modern Theories of Color in Philosophy, Painting and Architecture, Literature, Music, and Psychology.* Hanover, N.H.: University Press of New England.

Rips, Lance J. 1975. "Inductive Judgments about Natural Categories." *Verbal Behavior and Verbal Learning* 14:665–681.

Rivers, W. H. R. 1901a. *Reports of the Cambridge Anthropological Expedition to Torres Straits,* Vol. II, *Physiology and Psychology,* Part I, A. C. Haddon, ed., 1–132. Cambridge: Univ. of Cambridge Press.

———. 1901b. "The Colour Vision of the Natives of Upper Egypt." *JAI* 31 (July–December):229–247.

———. 1901c. "Primitive Color Vision." *Popular Science Monthly* 59:44–58.

―――. 1901*d.* "The Colour Vision of the Eskimo." *Proceedings of the Cambridge Philosophical Society* 11 (1900–1902, part 2): 143–149.

―――. 1903. "Observations on the Vision of the Uralis and Sholagas." *Bulletin of the Madras Government Museum* 5: 3–18.

―――. 1905*a.* "Observations on the Senses of the Todas." *BJP* 1: 321–396.

―――. 1905*b.* "Visual Acuity in Different Races of Man." *BJP* 1: 316.

―――. 1906. *The Todas.* London: Macmillan.

―――. 1911. "The British Association for the Advancement of Science: The Ethnological Analysis of Culture." *Science* 34 (874): 385–397.

Robson, J. A. 1983. "Morphology of Corticofugal Axons to the Dorsal Lateral Geniculate Nucleus in the Cat." *The Journal of Comparative Neurology* 216: 89–103.

Roesler, R. 1868. "Zur Etymologie der Farbenbezeichnungen auf dem romanischen Sprachgebiete." *Zeitschrift für Österreichisches Gymnasium* 19: 325–339.

Rosch, Eleanor Heider. 1973*a.* "On the Internal Structure of Perceptual and Semantic Categories." In *Cognitive Development and the Acquistion of Language,* T. E. Moore, ed., 111–144. New York: Academic Press.

―――. 1973*b.* "Natural Categories." *Cognitive Psychology* 4: 328–350.

―――. 1974. "Linguistic Relativity." In *Human Categorization: Theoretical Perspectives,* A. Silverstein, ed., 95–121. New York: Halsted Press.

―――. 1975*a.* "Cognitive Reference Points." *Cognitive Psychology* 7: 532–547.

―――. 1975*b.* "Cognitive Representations of Semantic Categories." *JEP (General)* 104: 192–233.

―――. 1975*c.* "Universals and Cultural Specifics in Human Categorization." In *Cross-Cultural Perspectives on Learning,* R. W. Brislin, S. Bochner, and W. J. Lonner, eds., 177–206. New York: Halsted Press.

―――. 1975*d.* "The Nature of Mental Codes for Color Categories." *JEP (Human Perception and Performance)* 1: 303–322.

―――. 1977. "Human Categorization." In *Studies in Cross-Cultural Psychology,* vol. I, N. Warren, ed., 177–206. London: Academic Press.

―――. 1978. "Principles of Categorization." In *Cognition and Categorization,* E. R. Rosch and B. B. Lloyd, eds., 28–48. Hillsdale, N.J.: Lawrence Erlbaum Associates.

―――. 1983. "Prototype Classification and Logical Classification: The Two Systems." In *New Trends in Conceptual Representation: Challenges to Piaget's Theory?,* Ellin K. Scholnick, ed., 73–86. Hillsdale, N.J.: Lawrence Erlbaum Associates

―――. 1988. "Coherences and Categorization: A Historical View." In *The Development of Language and Language Researchers: Essays in Honor of Roger Brown,* F. S. Kessel, ed., 373–392. Hillsdale, N.J.: Lawrence Erlbaum Associates.

Rosch, Eleanor Heider, and Carolyn B. Mervis. 1975. "Family Resemblances: Studies in the Internal Structure of Categories." *Cognitive Psychology* 7: 573–605.

Rosch, Eleanor Heider, Carolyn B. Mervis, Wayne D. Gray, David M. Johnson, and Penny Boyes-Braem. 1976. "Basic Objects in Natural Categories." *Cognitive Psychology* 8: 382–439.

Rosch, Eleanor Heider, Carol Simpson, and R. Scott Miller. 1975. "Structural Bases of Typicality Effects." *JEP (Human Perception and Performance)* 2:491–502.

Rowe, Christopher. 1974. "Conceptions of Colour and Colour Symbolism in the Ancient World." *EY* (1972) 41:327–364.

Royer, Francine. 1974. "La terminologie des couleurs en montagnais." *Recherches amérindiennes au Québec* 4:3–16.

Rudzka-Ostyn, Brygida. 1985. "Metaphoric Processes in Word Formation: The Case of Prefixed Verbs." In *The Ubiquity of Metaphor,* W. Paprotté and R. Dirven, eds., 209–241. Amsterdam: John Benjamins.

Ryalls, J. H. 1986. "Synesthesia: A Principle for the Relationship between the Primary Colors and the Cardinal Vowels." *Semiotica* 58:107–121.

Sahlins, Marshall. 1976. "Colors and Cultures." *Semiotica* 16:1–22.

Sapir, Edward. 1914. *Notes on Chasta Costa Phonology and Morphology.* Univ. Museum Anthropological Publications vol. 2, no. 2. Philadelphia: Univ. Museum.

———. 1958 [1944]. "Grading: A Study in Semantics." In *Selected Writings of Edward Sapir,* D. Mandelbaum, ed., 122–149. Berkeley: Univ. of California Press.

Saunders, Barbara A. C. 1992*a. The Invention of Basic Colour Terms.* Utrecht: ISOR (Interdisciplinary Social Science Research Institute).

———. 1992*b*. Comment on MacLaury 1992*a*. *CA* 33:165–167.

Saunders, Barbara A. C., and Jaap van Brakel. 1988*a*. "Re-Evaluating Basic Color Terms." *Cultural Dynamics* 1:359–378.

———. 1988*b*. "Are Colours Cultural Universals?" *Proceedings of the 12th International Wittgenstein Symposium,* P. Koller, A. Schram, and O. Weinberger, eds., 296–299. Vienna: Hoelder-Picheler-Tempsky.

———. 1989*a*. "On Cross-Cultural Colour Semantics." *International Journal of Moral and Social Studies* 4:173–180.

———. 1989*b*. "Is Colour an Inner Oracle?" *Proceedings of the American Philosophical Society* 62:646–647.

Savage-Rumbaugh, E. Sue, K. McDonald, R. A. Sevcik, W. D. Hopkins, and E. Rubert. 1986. "Spontaneous Symbol Acquisition and Communicative Use by Pygmy Chimpanzees *(Pan paniscus)*." *JEP (General)* 115:211–235.

Schaefer, Ronald P. 1983. "The Synchronic Behavior of Basic Color Terms in Twana and Its Diachronic Implications." *Studies in African Linguistics* 14:159–194.

Schefrin, B. E., and J. S. Werner. 1990. "Loci of Spectral Unique Hues throughout the Life Span." *JOSA-A:* 305–311.

Scheinert, Moritz F. 1905. *Die Adjectiva im Beowulfepos als Darstellungsmittel.* Halle: E. Karras (Diss., Univ. of Leipzig).

Schenkel, Wolfgang. 1963. "Die Farben in ägyptischer Kunst und Sprache." *Zeitschrift für ägyptische Sprache und Altertumskunde* 88:131–147.

Schmandt-Besserat, Denise. 1993. *Before Writing.* 2 vols. Austin: Univ. of Texas Press.

Schmitz, John R. 1983. "Color Words in English and Portuguese: A Contrastive Analysis." *PSCL* 17:37–49.

Schrödinger, Erwin. 1970. "Outline of a Theory of Color Measurement for Daylight Vision." In *Sources of Color Science,* D. L. MacAdam, ed., 134–182. Cambridge, Mass.: M.I.T. Press.

Schulbaum, S. 1930. "La symbolique de la lumière et des couleurs chez Virgile." *Eos* 33 (1930–1931):117–136.

Schultz, Wolfgang. 1904. *Das Farbenempfindungssystem der Hellenen.* Leipzig: J. A. Barth.

Schulze, Wilhelm. 1910. "Etymologisches." In *Sitzungsberichte der königliche preussische Akademie der Wissenschaften* (Berlin) 1910 (2):787–808.

Schumann, K. B. 1922. *Die Farben als Charakterisierungsmittel in den Dichtungen des Vergil und Horaz.* Erlangen: Univ. of Erlangen.

Schwentner, Ernst. 1915. *Eine sprachgeschichtliche Untersuchung über den Gebrauch und die Bedeutung der altgermanischen Farbenbezeichnungen.* Göttingen: Huth (Diss., Univ. of Münster).

———. 1925. "Eine altgermanische Farbenbezeichnung." *Beiträge zur Geschichte der deutschen Sprache und Literatur* 49:423–429.

Schwyzer, E. 1929. "Germanisches und ungedeutetes in byzantinischen Pferdenamen." *Zeitschrift für deutsches Altertum und deutsche Literatur* 66:93–99.

Segall, Marshall H. 1979. *Cross-Cultural Psychology: Human Behavior in Global Perspective.* Monterey, Calif.: Brooks/Cole.

Segall, Marshall H., D. T. Campbell, and M. J. Herskovits. 1966. *The Influence of Culture on Visual Perception.* Indianapolis: Bobbs-Merrill.

Selényi, Pál. 1946. "Piros és Veres." *Magyar Nyelvör* 70:12–14.

Seligman, Charles G. 1901. "The Vision of Natives of British New Guinea," appendix to W. H. R. Rivers 1901*a*, 133–140.

Senft, Günter. 1987. "Kilivila Color Terms." *Studies in Language* 11:313–346.

Shemiakin, F. N. 1959. "Kvoprosu ob istoricheskom razvitii nazvanii tsveta [On the Historical Development of Color Names]." *Voprosy Psikhologii* 5:16–29.

Sheppard, Joseph J., Jr. 1968. *Human Color Perception: A Critical Study of the Experimental Foundation.* New York: American Elsevier Publishing Co.

Shields, Kenneth. 1979. "Indo-European Basic Colour Terms." *The Canadian Journal of Linguistics* 24:142–146.

Shweder, Richard A., and Edmund J. Bourne. 1984. "Does the Concept of the Person Vary Crossculturally?" In *Culture Theory: Essays on Mind, Self, and Emotion,* R. A. Shweder and R. A. LeVine, eds., 158–199. Cambridge: Cambridge Univ. Press.

Simon, Herbert A. 1974. "How Big Is a Chunk?" *Science* 183:482–488.

Simon, Kurt. 1951. "Colour Vision of Buganda Africans." *The East African Medical Journal* 28 (1):75–79.

Simpson, Jean, and Arthur W. S. Tarrant. 1991. "Sex- and Age-Related Differences in Colour Vocabulary." *LS* 34:57–62.

Sivik, Lars. 1974. "Measuring the Meaning of Color: Problems in Semantic Bipolarity." *Göteborg Psychological Reports* 4:13.

Sivik, Lars, and Charles Taft. 1994. "Color Naming: A Mapping in the NCS of the Most Common Color Terms." *Scandinavian Journal of Psychology* 35:144–164.

Skard, S. 1946. "The Use of Color in Literature." *PAPS* 90:163–249.

Sloane, Patricia. 1989. *The Visual Nature of Color.* New York: Design Press.

Slobodin, Richard. 1978. *W. H. R. Rivers.* New York: Columbia Univ. Press.

Smallman, Harvey S., and Robert M. Boynton. 1990. "Segregation of Basic Colors in an Information Display." *JOSA* 7:1985–1994.

Smith, Buckingham, ed. and trans. 1861. *A Grammatical Sketch of the Heve Language.* New York: Cramoisy Press. Smith extracted this publication from the anonymous seventeenth-century *Arte y Vocabulario de la Lengua Dóhema, Héve o Eudeva* and deposited the manuscript in the library of the New York Historical Society.

Smith, Edward E., and Douglas L. Medin. 1981. *Categories and Concepts.* Cambridge, Mass.: Harvard Univ. Press.

Smith, Michael B. 1993. "Cases as Conceptual Categories: Evidence from German." In *Conceptualisations and Mental Processing in Language,* Richard A. Geiger and Brygida Rudzka-Ostyn, eds., 531–565. Berlin: Mouton de Gruyter.

Smith, N. S., T. W. A. Whitefield, and T. J. Wiltshire. 1990*a.* "Comparison of the Munsell, NCS, DIN, and Coloroid Colour Order Systems Using the OSA-UCS Model." *CRA* 15:327–337.

———. 1990*b.* "A Colour Notation Conversion Program." *CRA* 15:338–343.

Smyth, Herbert W. 1900. *The Greek Melic Poets.* London: Macmillan.

Snow, Charles T., and Craig A. Molgaard. 1978. "A Semantic Analysis of *Sélish* (Flathead) Color Terms." Paper presented at the 12th Annual International Conference of Salish and Neighboring Languages, Victoria.

Snow, David L. 1971. "Samoan Color Terminology: A Note on the Universality and Evolutionary Ordering of Color Terms." *AL* 13:385–390.

Solta, George R. 1966. "Lat. *viridis* und deutsch *grün* (Ein Beitrag zur Wortbildungslehre)." *Die Sprache* 12:26–47.

Sorabji, Richard. 1972. "Aristotle, Mathematics, and Colour." *Classical Quarterly,* n.s. 22:293–308.

Soustelle, Jacques. 1935. "Le totemisme des lacandons." *Mayan Research* 2:325–344.

Spencer, Baldwin, and F. J. Gillen. 1927. *The Arunta: A Study of a Stone Age People,* vol. II. London: Macmillan.

Spense, Nicol C. W. 1989. "The Linguistic Field of Colour Terms in French." *Zeitschrift für Romanische Philologie* 105 (5/6):472–497.

Sperber, D. 1980. "Remarks on the Lack of Positive Contributions from Anthropologists on the Problem of Innateness." In *Language and Learning: The Debate between Jean Piaget and Noam Chomsky,* M. Piatelli-Palmarini, ed., 244–249. Cambridge, Mass.: Harvard Univ. Press.

Spitzer, L. 1941. "Die Gelben, Les Jaunes." *Journal of English and German Philology* 40:530–537.

Squires, Bernard T. 1942. "Colour Vision and Colour Discrimination amongst the Bechuana." *Transactions of the Royal Society of South Africa* 29 (Pt. 2):29–34

Stack, James W. 1880. "On the Colour-Sense of the Maori." *TPNZI* 12 (1879): 153–158.

Staehelin, Elisabeth. 1977. "Hautfarbe." *Lexikon der Ägyptologie,* vol. II, W. Helck and W. Westendorf, eds., 1068–1072. Wiesbaden: Otto Harrassowitz.

Stanlaw, James M. 1987. "Color, Culture, and Contact: English Loanwords and Problems of Color Nomenclature in Modern Japanese." Diss., Univ. of Illinois, Urbana.

Staples, Ruth. 1932. "The Responses of Infants to Colour." *JEP* 15:119–141.

Stapleton, Walter H. 1903. *Comparative Handbook of the Congo Languages.* London: Baptist Missionary Society Press.

Steckler, Nicole, and William E. Cooper. 1980. "Sex Differences in Color Naming of Unisex Apparel." *AL* 22:373–381.

Steele, Susan M. 1979. "Uto-Aztecan: An Assessment for Historical Comparative Linguistics." In *The Languages of Native America: Historical Linguistics and Comparative Assessment,* L. Campbell and M. Mithun, eds., 444–544. Austin: Univ. of Texas Press.

Stefflre, Volney, Victor Castillo Valles, and Linda Morley. 1966. "Language and Cognition in Yucatan: A Cross-Cultural Replication." *Journal of Personality and Social Psychology* 4:112–115.

Stephenson, Peter H. 1973. *Color: Its Apprehension and Symbolic Use in Language and Culture.* Thesis, Univ. of Calgary.

———. 1979. "Color Salience and the Organization of the Tricolor Traffic Signal." *AA* 81:643–647.

Sternheim, Charles E., and Robert M. Boynton. 1966. "Uniqueness of Perceived Hues Investigated with a Continuous Judgmental Technique." *JEP* 72:770–776.

Sturtevant, Edgar H. 1936. *A Hittite Glossary: Words of Known or Conjectured Meaning with Sumerian and Akkadian Words Occurring in Hittite Texts.* 2d ed. William Dwight Whitney Linguistic Series. Philadelphia: Univ. of Pennsylvania Press (published for Yale Univ. by the Linguistic Society of America).

Sturtevant, Edgar H., and George Bechtel. 1935. *A Hittite Chrestomathy.* William Dwight Witney Linguistic Series. Philadelphia: Univ. of Pennsylvania Press (published for Yale Univ. by the Linguistic Society of America).

Suchman, Rossyn G. 1966. "Cultural Differences in Children's Color and Form Preferences." *JSP* 70:3–10.

Sun, Richard K. 1982. "Towards a Model for the Encoding Sequence of Basic Color Terms." Honors thesis, Northwestern Univ., Chicago.

———. 1983. "Perceptual Distances and the Basic Color Term Encoding Sequence." *AA* 85:387–391.

———. 1984. "Reply to Truex's Comment on 'Perceptual Distances and the Basic Color Term Encoding Sequence'." *AA* 86:695–699.

Swadesh, Morris. 1971. *The Origin and Diversification of Language.* Joel Sherzer, ed. (posthumous edition of 1966 manuscript). London: Routledge and Kegan Paul.

Swaringen, Sandra, Stephanie Layman, and Alan Wilson. 1978. "Sex Differences in Color Naming." *PMS* 47:440–442.

Sweetser, Eve E. 1984. "Semantic Structure and Semantic Change: A Cognitive Linguistic Study of Modality, Perception, Speech Acts, and Logical Relations." Diss., Univ. of California, Berkeley.

————. 1990. *From Etymology to Pragmatics: Metaphorical and Cultural Aspects of Semantic Structure.* Cambridge: Cambridge Univ. Press.

Szemerényi, O. 1972. "A New Leaf of the Gothic Bible." *Language* 48:1–10.

Taft, Charles, and Lars Sivik. 1994. "Do You Mean Blue When You Say Blå? Cross-National Comparisons of Color Naming in a Color Appearance Space." *Die Farbe* 40 (1–6):101–113.

Talmy, Leonard. 1985. "Force Dynamics in Language and Thought." *CLS* 2:293–337.

Tanaka, S. and H. Mizuno. 1983. "A Study on Basic Color Terms: Lexico-Semantic Development of Japanese-English Bilinguals in New York." *Psychologia* 26: 203–213.

Tarrant, D. 1960. "Greek Metaphors of Light." *Classical Quarterly,* n.s. 10:181–187.

Taylor, G. A. 1934. "Primitive Colour Vision." *Southern Rhodesian Native Affairs Department Annual* 12:64–67.

Taylor, John R. 1989. *Linguistic Categorization: Prototypes in Linguistic Theory.* Oxford: Clarendon Press.

————. 1992. "A Problem with Synonyms (and a Way to a Solution)." *SAJL* 10: 99–104.

Taylor, John R., and Robert E. MacLaury, eds. 1995. *Language and the Cognitive Construal of the World.* Berlin: Mouton de Gruyter.

Teller, Davida Y. 1991. "Simpler Arguments Might Work Better." *Philosophical Psychology* 4:51–64.

Teller, Davida Y., and M. H. Bornstein. 1987. "Infant Color Vision and Color Perception." In *Handbook of Infant Perception,* vol. 1, P. Salapatek and L. Cohen, eds., 185–236. New York: Academic Press.

Terusuke, T. 1984. "Shikimei no Gengo Jinruigaku [The anthropological linguistics of color naming]." *Gengo Seikatsu* 392:36–48.

Thomas, Elizabeth M. 1959. *The Harmless People.* New York: Alfred A. Knopf.

Thomas, L. L., A. T. Curtis, and R. Bolton. 1978. "Sex Differences in Elicited Color Lexicon Size." *PMS* 47:77–78.

Thompson, Evan. 1992. "Novel Colors." In Tolliver, ed., 321–349.

Thompson, Evan, Adrian Palacios, and Francisco J. Varela. 1992. "Ways of Coloring." *BBS* 15:1–73.

Thompson, J. Eric S. 1934. "Sky Bearers, Colors, and Directions in Maya and Mexican Religion." *Carnegie Institution of Washington, Contributions to American Archaeology,* Publication 436, 2 (10) 209–242.

Thongkum, Theraphan L. 1992. *Khamriak si nai phasa Yao (Mian)* [Color terms in Yao]. Bangkok: Rongphim, Chulalongkorn Univ.

Thorndike, Lynn. 1959. "Some Mediaeval Texts on Colours." *Ambix* 7:1–24.

Thurnwald, Richard. 1922. "Psychologie des primitiven Menschen." In *Handbuch der Vergleichenden Psychologie,* vol. 1(2), Gustav Kafka, ed., 147–169. Munich: Ernst Reinhardt.

Tiffou, Étienne, and Yves C. Morin. 1982. "Étude sur les couleurs en Bourouchaski." *JA* 270:363–383.

Titchener, E. B. 1916. "On Ethnological Tests of Sensation and Perception with Special Reference to Tests of Color Vision and Tactile Discrimination Described in the Reports of the Cambridge Anthropological Expedition to Torres Straits." *PAPS* 55 : 204–236.

Titiev, Mischa. 1972. *The Hopi Indians of Old Oraibi: Change and Continuity.* Ann Arbor: University of Michigan Press.

Tivoli, A. 1893. *I colori nelle locuzioni italiane.* Nel XXV anniversario delle nozze dei reali d'Italia: Omaggio della scuola superiore femminile Margherita di Savoia. Torino: n.p.

Tolliver, Joseph Thomas, ed. 1992. "Papers on Color." *Philosophical Studies* 68 (3).

Toren, Christina. 1992. Comment on MacLaury 1992*a. CA* 33 : 168–69.

Torgerson, Warren S. 1958. *Theory and Methods of Scaling.* New York: Wiley.

Tornay, Serge. 1973. "Langage et perception: La dénomination des couleurs chez les Nyangatom du Sud-Ouest éthiopien." *L'Homme* 4 : 66–94.

———, ed. 1978*a. Voir et nommer les couleurs.* Nanterre: Laboratoire d'ethnologie et de sociologie comparative.

———. 1978*b.* "Perception des couleurs et pensée symbolique." In Tornay, ed., 609–637.

Toynbee, Paget Jackson. 1902. "The Color Perse in Dante and Other Mediæval Writers." In *Dante Studies and Researches* by P. J. Toynbee, 207–314. Port Washington, N.Y.: Kennikat Press.

Tozzer, Alfred M. 1907. *A Comparative Study of the Mayas and the Lacandones.* New York: Macmillan.

———, ed. 1941. *Landa's "Relación de las cosas de Yucatán."* Papers of the Peabody Museum of Archaeology and Ethnology 18. Cambridge, Mass.: Harvard Univ.

Tsukada, Kan. 1978. *Shinrisai no Bigaku* [Aesthetics of Colors]. Tokyo: Kinokuniya Shoten.

Tsuruoka, Akio. 1984. "Kimagure Koogengaku #30: Sepia-iro [Whimsical speculative linguistics #30: The color sepia]." *Gengo Seikatsu* 389 : 82–83.

Turner, Victor W. 1966. "Color Classification in Ndembu Ritual." In *Anthropological Approaches to the Study of Religion,* M. Banton, ed., 47–84. London: Tavistock.

———. 1967. *The Forest of Symbols: Aspects of Ndembu Ritual.* Ithaca: Cornell Univ. Press.

———.1973. "Symbols in African Ritual." *Science* 179 : 100–105.

Turton, David. 1978. "La catégorisation de la couleur en Mursi." In Tornay, ed., 347–367.

———. 1980. "There's No Such Beast: Cattle and Colour Naming among the Mursi." *Man* 15 : 302–338.

Tversky, Amos. 1977. "Features of Similarity." *PRv* 84 : 327–352.

Tversky, Amos, and I. Gati. 1988. "Studies of Similarity." In *Cognition and Categorization,* E. Rosch and B. B. Lloyd, eds., 79–98. Hillsdale, N.J.: Lawrence Erlbaum Associates.

Tyler, Stephen A., ed. 1969. *Cognitive Anthropology.* New York: Holt, Rinehart, and Winston.

Tyson, Rodney E. 1994. "Korean Color Naming and Korean-English Language Contact: A Study in Linguistic Variation and Semantic Change." Diss., Univ. of Arizona at Tucson.

Uchikawa, Keiji, and Robert M. Boynton. 1987. "Categorical Color Perception of Japanese Observers: Comparison with That of Americans." *VR* 27:1825–1833.

Uchikawa, Keiji, and Robert E. MacLaury. 1986. "Results of Six Munsell Interviews of Japanese Speakers." MS in possession of authors.

Uchikawa, Keiji, Hiromi Uchikawa, and Robert M. Boynton. 1989. "Partial Color Constancy of Isolated Surface Colors Examined by a Color Naming Method." *Perception* 18:83–91.

Uemura, Rokuroo, and K. Yamazaki. 1950. *Nihon Shikimei Taikan* [A Survey of Japanese Color Terms]. Nara: Yootokusha.

Uhlenbeck, E. M. 1956. "De studie der zgn. exotische talen in verband met de algemene taalwetenschap." *Museum: Tijdschrift voor Filologie en Geschiedenis* (Review for Philology and History) 61 (2):65–80.

Urry, J. W. 1969. "Cherokee Colour Symbolism." *Man* 4:459.

Valentine, C. W. 1914. "The Colour Perception and Colour Preferences of an Infant During Its Fourth and Eighth Months." *BJP* 6:363–386.

Vallier, Dora. 1979. "Le problème de vert dans le système perceptif." *Semiotica* 26: 1–14.

Vamling, Karina 1986. "A Note on Russian Blues." *Slavica Lundensia* 10:225–233.

Van Brakel, Jaap. 1991. "Meaning, Prototypes, and the Future of Cognitive Science." *Minds and Machines* 1:233–257.

———. 1992. Comment on MacLaury 1992*a. CA* 33:169–72.

———. 1993 "The Plasticity of Categories: The Case of Color." *BJPS* 44:103–135.

Vandeloise, Claude. 1986. *L'espace en français.* Paris: Editions du Seuil (originally "Description of Space in French," Diss., Univ. of California at San Diego, 1984).

van der Hoogt, Becky. 1975. "The Semantics of the Color System with Examples from Peruvian Spanish and American English." *Lenguaje y Ciencias* 15 (1):1–16.

Van Wijk, H. A. C. W. 1959. "A Cross-Cultural Theory of Colour and Brightness Nomenclature." *Bijdragen Land-, Taal-, en Volkenkunde* 115:113–137.

Vasmer, Max. 1955. *Russisches etymologisches Wörterbuch,* vol. II. Heidelberg: Carl Winter Universitätsverlag.

Vasyutin, V. V., and A. A. Tishchenko. 1989. "Space Coloristics." *SA* 255 (7):84–90.

Veckenstedt, Edmund. 1888. *Geschichte der griechischen Farbenlehre: Das Farbenbezeichnungen der griechischen Epiker von Homer bis Quintus Smyrnäus.* Paderborn: F. Schöningh.

Vels Heijn, Nicolaas. 1951. *Kleurnamen en Kleurbegrippen bij de Romeinen.* Utrecht: Kemink en Zoon N.V.

Virchow, R. 1878. "In Berlin anwesenden Nubier." *Verhandlung der Berliner Gesell-*

schaft für Anthropologie, Ethnologie und Urgeschichte 1878: 333–356 (Supplement to ZE 10).

———. 1879. "Nubier." *Verhandlung der Berliner Gesellschaft für Anthropologie, Ethnologie und Urgeschichte* 1879: 449–456 (Supplement to ZE 11).

Voth, H. R. 1912. "The Summer Ceremony of the Blue Flute Society." In *Brief Miscellaneous Hopi Papers* by H. R. Voth, 135–136. Field Museum of Natural History, Publication 157, Anthropological Series 11 (2). Chicago.

Vygotsky, Lev S. 1962. *Thought and Language.* Cambridge, Mass.: M.I.T. Press.

Wackernagel, Jacob. 1923–1924. "Dies ater." *Archiv für Religionswissenschaft* 22:215–216.

Wade, T. L. B. 1985. "Colour Phraseology in Contemporary Russian." *Journal of Russian Studies* 49:48–59.

Wald, P. 1978. "Clôture semantique, universaux et terminologies de couleur." In Tornay, ed., 121–138.

Walde, A. E., and J. B. Hofmann. 1938. *Lateinisches etymologisches Wörterbuch.* Heidelberg: Carl Winter.

Wallace, A. F. C. 1961. "On Being Just Complicated Enough." *Proceedings of the National Academy of Sciences* 47:458–464.

Wallace, Florence E. 1927. *Color in Homer and in Ancient Art.* Smith College Classical Studies 9. Northampton, Mass.: Smith College.

Wallen, R. 1948. "The Nature of Color Shock." *JASP* 43:346–356.

Walraven, P. L. 1973. "Theoretical Models of the Colour Vision Network." In *Colour 73: Proceedings of the Second Congress of the International Colour Association.* London: Adam Hilger.

Ward, James. 1905. "Is 'Black' a Sensation?" *BJP* 1:4:407–427.

Wardhaugh, Ronald. 1992. *An Introduction to Sociolinguistics.* 2d ed. Oxford and Cambridge, Mass.: Blackwell.

Waterman, Thomas. 1908. "Diegueño Identification of Color with the Cardinal Points." *JAFL* 21:40–42.

Watkins, Calvert. 1969. "Indo-European and the Indo-Europeans." In *The American Heritage Dictionary of the English Language,* William Morris, ed., 1496–1550. Boston: Houghton Mifflin.

Wattenwyl, André von, and Heinrich Zollinger. 1978. "The Color Lexica of Two American Indian Languages, Quechi and Misquito: A Critical Contribution to Application of the Whorf Thesis to Color Naming." *IJAL* 44:56–68.

———. 1979. "Color-Term Salience and Neurophysiology of Color Vision." *AA* 81:279–288.

———. 1981. "Color Naming by Art Students and Science Students: A Comparative Study." *Semiotica* 35:303–315.

Weeks, Kent R. 1979. "Art, Word, and Egyptian World View." In *Egyptology and the Social Sciences,* K. R. Weeks, ed., 59–81. Cairo: American Univ. in Cairo Press.

Weise, O. 1878. "Die Farbenbezeichnungen der Indogermanen." *Beiträge zur Kunde der indogermanischen Sprachen,* vol. II, A. Bezzenberger, ed., 273–290. Gottingen: R. Peppmüller.

———. 1888. "Die Farbenbezeichnungen bei den Griechen und Römern." *Philologus* 46:593–605.

Welmers, W. E. 1973. *African Language Structures.* Berkeley: Univ. of California Press.

Welmers, W. E., and B. F. Welmers. 1969. "Noun modifiers in Igbo." *IJAL* 35:315–322.

Werblin, Frank S. 1973. "The Control of Sensitivity in the Retina: How Can the Eye Maintain Contrast in a Wide Range of Illumination?" *SA* 228 (1):70–79.

Werner, Abraham G. 1814. *Werner's Nomenclature of Colors.* Patrick Syme, ed. London: William Blackwell and T. Caddell.

Wescott, Roger W. 1970. "Bini Color Terms." *AL* 12:349–360.

———. 1975a. "Proto-Indo-Hittite Color Terms." *Linguistics and Anthropology (in Honor of C. F. Voegelin),* M. D. Kinkade, K. L. Hale, and O. Werner, eds., 691–699. Lisse: Peter De Ridder.

———. 1975b. "Tonal Iconicity in Bini Color Terms." *African Studies* 34:185–191.

———. 1983. "Color Metaphors in Three Language Phyla." In *The First Delaware Conference on Language Studies,* Robert Di Pieto, ed., 90–97. London: Associated Univ. Press.

———. 1992. Comment on MacLaury 1992a. *CA* 33:172–73.

Westphal, Jonathan. 1987. *Color: Some Philosophical Problems from Wittgenstein.* Aristotelian Society Series 7. London: Basil Blackwell. 2d ed. 1991 entitled *Colour: A Philosophical Introduction.*

White, Leslie A. 1943. "Keresan Indian Color Terms." *Papers of the Michigan Academy of Science, Arts, and Letters* 28:559–563.

Whitefield, T. W. A. 1979. "A Categorization Approach to Evaluative Aspects of Design, with Particular Reference to Colour." Diss., Univ. of Newcastle upon Tyne.

———. 1981. "Salient Features of the Color Space." *Perception and Psychophysics* 29:87–90.

Whitehead, Alfred N., and Bertrand A. W. Russell. 1910–1913. *Principia Mathematica.* Cambridge: Cambridge Univ. Press.

Whiteley, Wilfred H. 1973. "Colour-Words and Colour-Values: The Evidence from Gusii." In *Modes of Thought: Essays on Thinking in Western and Non-Western Societies,* R. Horton and R. Finnegan, eds., 145–161. London: Faber and Faber.

Whorf, Benjamin L. 1956a [1940]. "Gestalt Techniques of Stem Composition in Shawnee." In J. B. Carroll, ed., 160–172.

———. 1956b [1940]. "Science and Linguistics." In J. B. Carroll, ed., 207–219.

Wienrich, Uriel, William Labov, and Marvin I. Herzog. 1968. "Empirical Foundations for a Theory of Language Change." In *Directions for Historical Linguistics,* W. W. Lehman and Y. Malkiel, eds., 95–188. Austin: Univ. of Texas Press.

Wierzbicka, Anna. 1972. *Semantic Primitives.* Frankfurt: Athenäum.

———. 1990. "The Meaning of Color Terms: Semantics, Culture, and Cognition." *Cognitive Linguistics* 1:99–150.

―――. 1993. "Semantic Primitives and Semantic Fields." In *Frames, Fields, and Contrasts: New Essays in Semantic and Lexical Organization,* A. Lehrer and E. F. Kittay, eds., 209–227. Hillsdale, N.J.: Lawrence Erlbaum Associates.

Williams, John E. 1964. "Connotations of Color Names among Negroes and Caucasians." *PMS* 18:721–731.

―――. 1966. "Connotation of Racial Concepts and Color Names." *Journal of Personality and Social Psychology* 3:531–540.

Williams, John E., J. Kenneth Morland, and Walter L. Underwood. 1970. "Connotations of Color Names in the United States, Europe, and Asia." *JSP* 82:3–14.

Williams, Joseph M. 1976. "Synaesthetic Adjectives: A Possible Law of Semantic Change." *Language* 52:461–478.

Willms, Johannes E. 1902. *Eine Untersuchung über den Gebrauch der Farbenbezeichnungen in der Poesie Altenglands.* Münster: J. Krick (Diss., Univ. of Münster).

Willson, George. 1855. "Researches on Color-Blindness, with a Supplement on the Danger Attending the Present System of Railway and Marine Colored Signals." Edinburgh: Southerland and Knox.

Windmann, I. B. 1922. "Bedeutung und Verwendung des Wortes caerul(e)us. Ein Beitrag zum Verständnis antiker Farbenbezeichnungen." Diss., Univ. of Munich.

Winick, Charles. 1963. "Taboo and Disapproved Colors as Symbols in Various Foreign Countries." *JSP* 59:361–368.

Witkowski, Stanley R., and Cecil H. Brown. 1981. "Lexical Encoding Sequences and Language Change: Color Terminology Systems." *AA* 83:13–27.

Wittgenstein, Ludwig. 1953. *Philosophische Untersuchungen/Philosophical Investigations,* G. E. M. Anscombe, trans. Oxford: Basil Blackwell; New York: Macmillan (volume contains original and translation on facing pages).

―――. 1977. *Bemerkungen über die Farben/Remarks on Color,* G. E. M. Anscombe, ed.; Linda L. McAlister and Margarete Schättle, trans. Oxford: Basil Blackwell (volume contains original and translation on facing pages).

Wolf, Eric. 1959. *Sons of the Shaking Earth: The Peoples of Mexico and Guatemala—Their Land, History, and Culture.* Chicago: Univ. of Chicago Press.

Wood, Francis A. 1902. *Color-Names and Their Congeners: A Semasiological Investigation.* Halle: Max Niemeyer.

―――. 1905. "The Origin of Color-Names." *Modern Language Notes* 20:225–229.

Woodward, James. 1989. "Basic Color Term Lexicalization Across Sign Languages." In *Sign and Culture: A Reader for Students of American Sign Language,* W. C. Stokoe, ed., 145–151. Silver Spring, Md.: Linstok Press.

Woodworth, Robert S. 1906. "Color Sense in Different Races of Mankind." *Proceedings of the Society for Experimental Biology and Medicine* 3 (1905–1906): 24–26.

―――. 1910a. "Racial Differences in Mental Traits." *Science* 31:171–186.

―――. 1910b. "The Puzzle of Color Vocabularies." *PB* 7 (10):325–328.

Wright, B., and L. Rainwater. 1962. "The Meanings of Colour." *Journal of General Psychology* 67:89–99.

Wright, W. D. 1928. "A Re-Determination of the Trichromatic Coefficients of the Spectral Colours." *Transactions of the Optical Society* (London) 30 (1928–1929):14–64.

Wunderlich, Eva. 1925. "Die Bedeutung der roten Farbe im Kultus der Griechen und Römer: Erläutert mit Berücksichtigung entsprechender Bräuche bei anderen Völkern." *Religionsgeschichtliche Versuche und Vorarbeiten* 20 (1). Giessen: Alfred Töpelmann (Diss., Halle, 1923).

Wundt, Wilhelm. 1900. *Völkerpsychologie,* vol. 1*a, Die Sprach.* Leipzig: W. Engelmann.

Wyler, Siegfried. 1984. "Old English Colour Terms and Berlin and Kay's Theory of Basic Colour Terms." In *Modes of Interpretation: Essays Presented to Ernst Leisi on the Occasion of His 65th Birthday,* Richard J. Watts and Urs Weidmann, eds. 41–57. Tübingen: Gunter Narr.

———. 1992. *Colour and Language: Colour Terms in English.* Tübingen: Gunter Narr.

Wyszecki, Günter. 1963. "Proposal for a New Color-Difference Formula." *JOSA* 53:13–18.

Wyszecki, Günter, and W. S. Stiles. 1967. *Color Science, Concepts and Methods, Quantitative Data and Formulas.* New York: Wiley.

Young, D. 1964. "The Greeks' Colour Sense." *Review of the Society for Hellenic Travel* 4:42–46.

Young, David. 1971. "Color Preferences, Self-Concept, and Role Expectations." *Western Canadian Journal of Anthropology* 2:44–72.

Young, Richard A. 1986. "Principal-Component Analysis of Macaque Lateral Geniculate Nucleus Chromatic Data." *JOSA-A* 3:1735–1742.

Young, Thomas. 1802. "On the Theory of Light and Colors." *Philosophical Transactions of the Royal Society of London* 90:20–71.

Zadeh, Lofti A. 1965. "Fuzzy Sets." *Information and Control* 8:338–353.

Zahan, Dominique. 1951. "Les couleurs chez les bambara du Soudan Français." *Notes africaines* 50:53–56.

———. 1974. "White, Red and Black: Colour Symbolism in Black Africa." *Eranos Yearbook* (1972) 41:365–396.

Zaręba, L. 1981. "Les noms de couleurs dans les expressions idiomatiques françaises et polonaises." *Języki Obce W Szkole* 25:303–307.

Zarruk, Rabi'u Mohammed. 1978. "The Study of Colour Terms in the Hausa Language." *Harsunan Nijeriya* 8:51–78.

Zeki, S. 1984. "The Construction of Colours by the Cerebral Cortex." *Proceedings of the Royal Institute of Great Britain* 56:231–257.

Zimmer, Alf C. 1982. "What Really Is Turquoise? A Note on the Evolution of Color Terms." *PRs* 44:213–230.

———. 1984. "There Is More Than One Level in Color Naming—A Reply to Zollinger (1984)." *PRs* 46:411–416.

Zollinger, Heinrich. 1972. "Human Color Vision as an Interdisciplinary Research Problem." *Palette* 40:1–7.

———. 1973. "Zusammenhänge zwischen Farbbenennung und Biologie des Farbensehens beim Menschen." *Vierteljahresschrift der Naturforschenden Gesellschaft in Zürich* 118:227–255.

———. 1976. "A Linguistic Approach to the Cognition of Color Vision in Man." *Folia Linguistica* 9:265–293.

———. 1979. "Correlations Between the Neurobiology of Colour Vision and the Psycholinguistics of Colour Naming." *Experientia* 35:1–8.

———. 1984. "Why Just Turquoise? Remark on the Evolution of Color Terms." *PRs* 46:403–409.

———. 1988a. Biological Aspects of Color Naming. In *Beauty and the Brain: Biological Aspects of Aesthetics,* I. Rentschler, B. Herzberger, and D. Epstein, eds., 149–164. Basel and Boston: Birkhäuser.

———. 1988b. "Categorical Color Perception: Influence of Cultural Factors on the Differentiation of Primary and Derived Basic Color Terms in Color Naming by Japanese Children." *VR* 28:1379–1382.

———. 1989. "Welche Farbe hat der antike Purpur?" *Textilveredlung* 24 (6):207–212.

NAME INDEX

LANGUAGE INDEX

SUBJECT INDEX

Boldface page numbers indicate references to figures and/or tables.

abstract(ion), 10, 37–38, 138, 179–180
acquisition of color terms, first language, 426, 469n16
acuity: cognitive, 44, 246, 264, 481–482n10; acuity tests, 17; diffuse vs. bounded naming ranges, 100–101, 104–105, 384, 451; visual, 137. *See also* analytical view or outlook; contextualization
agency/agent of categorization, xv, xvii, 36, 138, 180–182, 193, 393
aggregate, 221; aggregated foci, 32–**34**, **178**, **234–239**, 249, **250–251**, 252–253, 256, 260, **273**, **278**, 286, **304**, 314–**315**, 323–**324**, **334–335**, 347, 387, 454–455, 481n6
analogy, 9, 138, 180, 188; categorization as a space-time analogy, xviii, 8, 39, 109, 111, 130, 137–153, 179–180, 183, 188–193, 221, 262–263, 380, 385, 392, 419; equation of similarity or difference with distance, xv, 188, 190–191; force dynamics, 9, 180; Mesoamerican understanding of categorization by geopolitical analogy, 454, 490–492n4
analytical view or outlook, 187, 271, 273, 278, 286, 290, 317, 356, 359, 379, 450, 479n5; analysis vs. synthesis, 290–291, 389, 428, 496–497n11
apparent complementation. *See* inclusion: polarized
arrangement of coordinates, 8, 109, 144, 146, **148**, 168, 192, 211, 292, 301, 303–304, 331, 381, 385–386, 389–390, 419; re-arrangement, 147–148, 150, 152–153, 180–181, 188, 210, 218
asymmetry judgment, 6, 110, 188–**189**,

191–193, 393; from dominant and recessive vantages, 190; imperfection of opposites, 188, 190; perspectival differences, 149; psychological distance, 144–145, 188–189
attention (or selective emphasis), 8, 19, 33–**34**, 87, 140, 143, 181, 192, 211, 381; relation to dual foci, 272–273, 383; shift of, 44–45, 109, 149, **150–152**, 384
—differential attention to/emphasis on/judgments of: distinctiveness, 44, 94, 115, 123, 134, 137, 145, 152, 157, 160, 164–166, 170, 173–174, 194, 207–208, 218, 222, 230, 237, 248–249, 252–253, 263, 265–266, 270–273, 278, 286, 290, 307, 311, 342, 356, 358, 379, 382, 386–387, 390, 428, 431, 451–452; similarity, 188, 193, 389, 391–392; similarity and distinctiveness, xiv–xv, 7–8, 39, 86, 93, 96, 104–106, 110, 112, 122, 127–129, 131, 143–148, 164, 168–169, 178–181, 183, 187–192, 210, 219, 222–223, 243, 263, 292–293, 301, 331, 381–386, 393, 426, 481n9
attribute, 5, 37, 131, 188
attribute category or domain, 113. *See also* color domain
axiom, 86–87, 93, 96–97, 104–107, 112, 128–130, 143, 193, 223, 381, 385, 414
axis, general, 134, 144, 149, 168, 185, 192, 385

basic color category, 20, 30, 38, 47, 54, **80**, 94, 97, 99, 104–107, 112, 129, 152, 240–241, 382, 419–420, 452. *See also* formula
basic color term, 4, **12**, 20–26, 30, 37–38, 81, 96, 101; criteria of, 20–21, 105–107, 184, 419–420, 428–429; basic vs. secondary, 30, 62, 184, 234–236, 242, 419, 421,

CPSIA information can be obtained at www.ICGtesting.com
Printed in the USA
LVOW10s0913151115

462644LV00002B/273/P